For J.T.
Teacher, friend,
who knows that beauty
is timeless,
with fond admiration,

Dec 2004

Participant
Observer

Books by Robin Fox

The Keresan Bridge: A Problem in Pueblo Ethnology

Kinship and Marriage: An Anthropological Perspective

The Imperial Animal (with Lionel Tiger) *

Encounter with Anthropology *

Biosocial Anthropology (editor and contributor)

The Tory Islanders: A People of the Celtic Fringe

The Red Lamp of Incest:
An Inquiry into the Origins of Mind and Society

Neonate Cognition: Beyond the Blooming Buzzing Confusion
(editor with Jacques Mehler)

The Violent Imagination

The Search for Society:
Quest for a Biosocial Science and Morality

Reproduction and Succession:
Studies in Anthropology, Law and Society *

The Challenge of Anthropology:
Old Encounters and New Excursions *

Conjectures and Confrontations:
Evolution, Science, Social Concern *

The Passionate Mind: Origins of Destruction and Creativity *

* Available from Transaction Publishers: www.transactionpub.com
www.robinfoxbooks.com

Participant Observer

Memoir of a Transatlantic Life

ROBIN FOX

Transaction Publishers
New Brunswick (U.S.A.) and London (U.K.)

Copyright © 2004 by Transaction Publishers, New Brunswick, New Jersey.
www.transactionpub.com

This book is printed on acid-free paper that meets the American National Standard for Permanence of Paper for Printed Library Materials.

Library of Congress Catalog Number: 2004047953
ISBN: 0-7658-0238-4
Printed in the United States of America

Library of Congress Cataloging-in-Publication Data

Fox, Robin, 1934-
    Participant observer : memoir of a transatlantic life / Robin Fox.

      p. cm.

    ISBN 0-7658-0238-4 (alk. paper)
    1. Fox, Robin, 1934- 2. Anthropologists—England—Biography.
    3. Anthropologists—United States—Biography. I. Title.

GN21.F6A3 2004
301'.092—dc22   2004047953
[B]

This book is dedicated to everyone who appears in it,
even the apparently undeserving.
Thank you all for an interesting life.

Contents

Acknowledgements

The debts incurred over half a lifetime are implicitly acknowledged in the text itself. Those incurred later, especially to Lin, await another volume, and so may never be adequately recognized. I'm sorry. Several people were especially encouraging about this particular project: Bruce Nichols, Don Lamm, Adam Bellow. Others offered helpful corrections: Barnaby Conrad (on bullfighting terms), Richard de Mille, Desmond Morris, Trevor (Lord) Smith. My deepest thanks to Irving Louis Horowitz, prince of publishers, and Mary Curtis and the staff of Transaction, especially Laurence Mintz (prince of editors) and Karen Ornstein; to Chelsea Booth for reading the proofs, and Abigail Wright for the music. Also thanks to Laura Nader, Burton Benedict, and the anthropologists at Berkeley, who gave an oral version of chapter eight such a heartwarming reception, and to the Sandpipers of Sanibel Island, Florida, who were enduring friends during some lonely and painful times of writing.

I was gently dissuaded from adding to my dedication (without explanation) the remarkable Huguenot adventurer and poet, Agrippa d'Aubigné (1552-1630). As well as being the grandfather of Mme. de Maintenon, Agrippa was, along with Monluc and Montaigne, the inventor of the autobiographical style of the Roi-Sujet: a style now completely taken for granted. But unlike his contemporaries, Agrippa, in *Sa vie à ses enfants*, used the "il" and not the "je" — so part of my debt is obvious. (Thanks to Robert Muchambled for the introduction.)

R.F.
Princeton, NJ
June 2004

Introit

In his *Robert Browning: Essays and Thoughts* (1890) John T. Nettleship describes the poet's intention in writing his great epic *Sordello* (1840) to have been to show "step by step the development of a soul from infancy onwards." Sordello, the man, is a footnote in history, only remembered as a guide to Dante and Virgil, introduced in Book VI of the *Purgatorio*. He was a poet condemned to obscurity since, unlike Dante, he chose to write in Provençal rather than Tuscan, and thus wrote himself out of history. Dante, though, held him in high regard: *anima lombarda, come ti stavi altera e distegnosa*—a Lombard soul who bore himself with lofty disdain; *dolce duca*, gentle leader. But, as a poet who judged the work of princes, Sordello stood at a confluence of forces and ideas that influenced the course of European, and hence world, events. For a moment, as conceived by Browning, he held the balance of ideas and the potential for humanitarian action. He never in fact *did* anything—it was not in his peculiar nature to act, until it was too late—but he was a prism that refracted a hundred strands of light. The particularities of that prism —the development of that lonely soul thrust prematurely into the violent events of thirteenth-century Lombardy—were Browning's subject matter. Thus some of us stumble accidentally onto the stage of big ideas and their related events, even the biggest idea of the age. We are not important in ourselves. We shall, like Sordello, end up as footnotes. But insofar as we become a focus in the struggle of ideas, and insofar as our souls become their prisms where the refraction bends the light one way or another, then it is perhaps of some slight consequence to know how the soul developed. At the very least it might be entertaining, at the most instructive, and never less than curious.

"Who will, may hear Sordello's story told..."

Part 1

Stages in a Life

1

The Child:
Dancing for the Woolworth Ladies

He never knew how it started, the dancing business. But then, like so many supposed childhood memories, it only seems half real at a distance. How many were really his own memories and how many were things she had told him so often that he thought he remembered them? But this must be a real one in some way because he could see the dance itself, and she had never told him about that, just that he danced for the ladies. It was a strange little affair: hop skips in a circle, arms outstretched like an ungainly bird trying to take off; then hands above the head, palms together, and twirl and twirl and twirl until dizzy; then a dreamy swinging lurch in a circle in the other direction. A bizarre kind of bird dance to be sure. Perhaps he had been inspired by watching the plovers on the moors, with their pathetic attempts to feign wing injury, to lead him away from their nests. But surely that came later, when he was older? Dancing for the biscuit-counter ladies started when he was about two years old. But he would have already been to the moors by then. Not alone. They would have been with him. Alone came later. But wherever it came from, the dance was a hit. The Woolworth Ladies applauded and cooed, and gave him gingersnaps and biscuits with cream-filled centers: little luxuries that were way beyond the penny bag of broken arrowroots they came to get. He always saved the luxuries and gave them to her after they left Woolworth's, and then they shared them. At least that's what she told him. He was such a thoughtful toddler. Again in retrospect he wondered. A normal toddler would surely have scoffed the lot at the first chance. Two-year-olds are not known for delayed gratification on this scale. But then, was he a normal toddler?

For a start he should never have been born. He doesn't of course remember his birth except through her stories. But there again in dreams he finds himself in a giant water sack suddenly exposed to the light and loud sounds. He kicks to get free and can't and chokes and wakes up screaming. If this is a real memory, did they hear that fetal scream? Did they see him thrashing like a captured fish in a plastic bag, his gills working overtime, until he was pushed back into the dark and the quiet? Evidently it's written up in the medical journals of the time. But then there was no television and it didn't make the headlines. The doctors had told her that if the appendix was to be success-fully removed, the baby should really be removed first. They could try to move the womb out, take out the appendix, and then put the womb back, but the chances of normal birth after that were slim, and there would be no more children. The doctors discussed this with her, and with the father; together they decided to try to keep the baby. The doctors were against it, but it looked like a last chance anyway and the fateful decision was taken. He was hauled out thrust back and sown up like the contents of a haggis. During all this time she had barely eaten and couldn't eat much afterwards. He was probably only saved because when born he was so tiny (less than three pounds) that he came out easily. And after all, he'd had a kind of practice. Talk about the twice born. What do they know?

But he shouldn't really have been born nor should he have survived the double pneumonia of his first year. Tiny baby with the tiny bones: they bathed him in a salad bowl; he slept in a padded shoebox. Some lady doctor with sound common sense told her not to wean him at the fashionably early time but keep him on the breast. There he huddled, shivered and survived. Early on he beat the odds. The rest was all borrowed time. And he was the precious child, the only child, literally the unique one. The burden was to be all on him. But whatever the fright of the double birth might have done, he was henceforward held tight in a cocoon of love that had him live and dance and roam and never forget that he was a miracle. It's hard being a miracle; but he seemed to be succeeding with the Woolworth ladies at least. He had the gingersnaps to prove it.

A penny bag of broken arrowroot biscuits. Yes. That's a memory. Biscuits were sold loose then, and if you went at the end of the day they'd sell off the broken ones for next to nothing. It was part of the survival thing which at the time he never noticed but parts of which were graphic enough in memory. He had one absolutely genuine memory; all his own. He knew which these were because they were things the adults didn't know about and so they must be his and not just memories created by the praise poems she sang about him to the relatives and neighbors and friends and anyone who would listen. Here is the memory as he told it to them:

He was on a broad pavement with big stone squares. He was watching other small children play marbles or hop scotch. In the background was a large redbrick building with long grimy windows, and lined against the wall were men, lots of men, in cloth caps and waistcoats, smoking and talking. The men were laughing and occasionally pointing at the children. The men seemed so big and the voices so deep, and they seemed far away although they were really only a few steps. And for the first time he had the feeling: they knew something he didn't know. The grownups knew something and that thing made them different, like things from another world. Once he was a grownup he would know what that was and he would have that confident laugh, that authority with the world he never felt. No longer would he have to please the Woolworth ladies, to please her, because he would know the secret and he would have the power. He didn't tell them about this feeling. They wouldn't have understood and he couldn't have articulated it. But he was sure this was the first time. But where was he?

It was settled. There was only one place he could be said his father. On Saturday mornings when the men went to the labor exchange to collect the dole, they often took the children with them to play together on the wide pavement before they went in. The mothers liked this arrangement because it meant the men would come back home with the children and the dole intact and not take it off to the pub or the dog track or wherever. Not that his father would ever have done that she hastened to interject always, but some would and we knew who they were. It was bad enough only having eighteen shillings a week of which nine went on rent. How could they think to go off drinking and gambling? Man may not live by bread alone, but he'd better start with it or he'd not be around to do any of the other things. He heard and was proud of his father who was not like other men. But it was a genuine memory, and his own, and his earliest, and he must have been almost three—about the time of the Woolworth ballet.

Of course he didn't dance *for* the biscuits. They were buying the arrowroots anyway, and the other luxuries were only a tiny treat; they were not needed. He danced to please her because she was proud of anything he did, and she was anxious to have her pride confirmed. The child rescued from death was precocious, she knew that. But she was not well educated, having spent most of her young years in a TB sanitarium where they saw she had the basic three Rs and drawing, and where she became an avid reader. But her knowledge of the world was limited and she needed this outside confirmation. The Woolworth ladies were a small part of this, but their applause and cries of amazement were a contribution richly rewarding to her. He didn't usually sing for them, but he sang for the uncles. Again the uncles are a dim memory if a memory at all—and the hordes of cousins long forgotten. He never bothered much with the cousins. He was always looking to the adults. Always looking for the secret. The uncles knew hundreds of songs, as his father did, many of them World War I songs. He could do a fair version of *Roses of Picardy* before he had any idea what the words meant—except that they were sad.

> The roses will fade with the summertime
> And although we are far far apart
> There is one rose that blooms still in Picardy
> It's the rose that I keep in my heart

He knew to throw out his hand at the end and hold the last note because that is what uncle George did and it always got lots of applause. Nothing of course compared with the applause he got: he'd be another John McCormack, they said. But wasn't that the point. The uncles are a blur of jolly red faces with their perpetual waistcoats and watch chains and the smell of snuff, tobacco, and wet wool that always hung around them. They all worked in the wool mills and the smell clung. His father had no work at the time, hence the dole queue. He smelled of country things: wet grass, wood smoke, cheap cigarette tobacco (Woodbines in packs of five), chickens, and manure. They lived not in the town, but in the nearby country villages, where they tapped into the rural economy and the bounty of nature: rabbits and pigeons and the produce of the hedgerows. Now he did remember the big woven baskets and collecting berries and how the thorns and spines hurt his fingers. There were the wonderful smells afterwards in the kitchen—smells of blueberry and elderberry and raspberry and wild strawberry, and bilberry picked from the heather, all being made into jams and preserves. There was the wild thyme and mint and watercress and acres of free rhubarb which grew like a weed, and even the tender shoots of nettles boiled or made into delicious drinks with dandelion leaves—the smells of sugar and yeast and fermentation. It would always pain him to have to pay for any of these things. God intended them as free: you just reached out and took them. You didn't need to dance for these. Rabbit and pigeon made delicious pies, the hens gave eggs, and once they were old they gave themselves to be simmered for hours, with vegetables from the allotment, to get them tender.

He remembered sitting with Grandpa (an honorary title—both his real grandfathers were dead from the aftereffects of battlefield gas), cutting up old cabbages to throw to the hens. He remembered the disputes this caused: the first time he heard them quarreling. She said grandpa overstuffed the hens, sitting there day in and day out cutting up food and throwing it to them, and they couldn't lay properly. The father said it was all the old man had to do and they shouldn't spoil his pleasure. She said he didn't have to feed the family or he would care more. The father, as usual, went silent, never having many words except when singing, or occasionally telling his old army stories. She didn't care for these, but the boy was fascinated. It was another world—of desert and dry hills and scorching suns and wild men in turbans charging with swords, and heroic deeds of attack and retreat, and long days of boredom when the main activity was going out on the veranda to kick the punka wallah who had fallen asleep and let the fans slow to a halt. Then those terrible sad days on some burnt hillside at sunset where they stood to attention round a grave and the bugler played the last post, which his father imitated, making the unbearable weeping bugle notes. And days of languid sunny pleasure to see the Taj Mahal and the Vale of Kashmir.

He didn't realize at the time how desperate the father was for this life which was all the quiet man cared about; how restricted and imprisoned the man felt in this little Pennine village hanging on to the edge of the cliff above the town. How his head swarmed with raging Pathans and laughing pals and foolish officers and funny servants and cricket on the local maharaja's personal cricket field. But together they poured over the albums of tiny box brownie prints brought back and already fading: the rambling Red Fort at Agra, the unreal beauty of the Taj Mahal, the mythical Vale of Kashmir, the sinister Khyber Pass; groups of soldiers, grinning servants in dhotis, brilliant Sikh horsemen, and gallant little Gurkhas with their heavy knives. Even the King of Afghanistan escaping by plane from his fractious country stirred into rebellion by Russian villainy: Amantullah fleeing Nadir Khan on the first occasion in military history when troops were airlifted. These were vast lives the adults lead. The quiet man had helped to rescue a King.

It was all given up to come back and marry her. They argued about that too. He should have stayed in the army, she said; it was security, a house in the married quarters, status even. But she didn't realize that the army as such was not the thing: it was the army in India. Away from that he didn't seem to care what he did, and was as happy doing nothing as working. She had lied to her employer—a professor of Economics at Leeds University, for whose children (Bunty and Tony—both girls) she was the nanny. The professor and his lady, who had her absolute devotion, asked if her young man had a job. They were kind people and concerned for her, so she said he had; but he was to be more than two years without one. They had a shilling less a week than Frank McCourt's parents, and paid three shillings more in rent. But there was no sense of blinding poverty even though they were unquestionably poor. For a start, the father did not spend the pitiful few shillings on drink. And they were in the country with the vegetables and the chickens. They gathered those free goods of nature that stayed so vividly in the nasal memory. They cheated, as did every one on the dole who could get away with it. If you revealed any casual income the "means test" would make you sell "unnecessary furniture." The father worked a few hours a week for the farmer where she worked part-time as a cook—and the farmer threw in some meals, butter and vegetables, and all the rabbits and pigeons he could take on the farm lands. Someone ratted on them however. And for the first time he saw her anger—as much with the father for being so stoical about it as with the perpetrator. We were bound to get caught sooner or later, he said. But for her it was the unmitigated evil of the snake who told the authorities. He was frightened at the expression of her hate; he went outside and stayed there a long time with Grandpa and the chickens.

People often didn't like her. She had airs and pretensions above her station. She, unlike them, had worked in middle-class houses and absorbed middle-class values. (But what does a professor *do*, mummy? Very clever

Relief from Kabul. King of Afghanistan.

things. Oh.) She also had plenty of middle-class relatives and they remained her model of correct and decent behavior, not the feckless working class among whom she was unhappily trapped, and who could have been avoided if only the father had stayed in the army instead of just the reserves. But the reserve money—thirteen pounds and thirteen shillings a year, paid quarterly—made all the difference. It was the slight edge that gave them a holiday at Blackpool or Morcambe or Scarborough when the others, with their overlarge families—another subject of indignant scorn—couldn't afford it. But she never compromised. They had high tea and read *Winnie the Pooh* and listened to suitable programs on Children's Hour and saw Shirley Temple movies. They went to church on Sunday mornings with all new clothes for Easter Sunday and always said please and thank you (it would never have occurred to him to do otherwise.) He wore the fashionable little Teddy Bear coats and hats, even if they were either home made from patterns or bought at the cut-price store. He didn't get to play with the grubby children who didn't do these things—even the cousins who fell below par. So she was not liked, but she didn't care. She knew what the nice people did and she emulated it as best she could, especially after the father found work—in the wool mill of course. To work at all in those days was status.

She was uneasy about the father's passion for Rugby League, but sensible enough to know that it was a cheap and harmless pleasure—not like the pub or the dog track, and also could be made a family "outing" with sandwiches and thermos flasks of hot dark tea. Cricket especially was positively encouraged for these reasons. So every Saturday was a sports expedition. How could they have known that it was to lead to the little miracle's first public triumph—a triumph so great that any subsequent successes were always measured against it. "Why, it's just like Wembley all over again." And he would agree, but again without knowing if it was his memory or theirs. Of course, they would say, you must, absolutely must remember it. But he had heard the story and looked at the photographs so many times, that how much of it was really his he did not know. The band part he thought he remembered. That much was his. But he had really no idea what was happening, the little two-year old miracle. A lot of noise, a lot of people, an inordinate amount of attention, more than usual, and him performing at the top of his lungs and marching form, and the applause. Yes, perhaps he remembered.

For a start the team managed its own miracle. The Cinderella of the league, given no chance at all, produced a back called Joey after whom his budgerigar was named. "Joey, Joey, poor Joey!" it repeated in endless imbecility. And Joey on the field repeated feats of derring-do which landed the team—otherwise rank outsiders—in the league cup final. This was always played in London at Wembley Stadium even though the game was confined to the northern counties. The excuse was to publicize the professional game in the south (where the amateur Rugby Union held snobbish sway) but the real reason was to give twenty thousand northerners a chance for a cheap trip to the capital. The processions of coaches started south at ungodly hours of the morning and the barbarian hordes poured in. (They were good-natured and nonviolent hordes though in those days—the midst of a depression. Something frightening has happened since then.) For the occasion she had knitted (she knitted practically everything he wore) a blue and white stocking cap, a blue and white scarf, and blue and white mittens. They had blue and white scarves too, but he was the centerpiece with his long blue and white trumpet. The team, being cheered as it boarded the train for the momentous journey south several days earlier, spotted him in the crowd of supporters, adopted him as the team mascot, had their photo taken with him by the local press. The next day it happened. He was on the front page: "Keighley's Youngest Supporter Ready For Wembley." Sitting on his father's arm tooting the trumpet boldly at the crowd. The photo was mounted on a card and all the team signed it. She still has it.

That would have been enough, God knows, but once on the scene they had seats at the front and he went out on the field and marched up and down on the sideline blowing his trumpet for the crowd. The marching band was passing. Breathless hush. The bandmaster comes over and asks if he can borrow "the little fellow." The father wants to protest, goes red in the face with embarrassment; this is "making a fuss" it is "calling attention to yourself"—the greatest sin of all. But protesting would call even more attention, so it is dropped. Hand in hand the little trumpeter goes fearlessly (what should he fear, he is the miracle boy) to the head of the band, and marches, trumpet a-tooting all around the huge field to the wild applause of a hundred thousand people. Again, it should have been enough, but back home, at the next Shirley Temple film, on came the Movietone News (or was it Pathé?) and there it was. She leapt to her feet in real astonishment and pointed and all the cinema saw. Movietone had chosen to feature this event as much as the game itself. There he was, marching on the newsreel for all the world to see. The team lost the game, of course. But it was a miracle they were even at it. Miracles seek each other out it seems. The rest of his life could only be an anticlimax. But more for them than him. For it was their event really. If he doesn't really remember it at all, in what sense is it his? The trumpet he had for years. It disappeared somewhere in the wartime travels. It was taken out like a Plains Indian sacred pipe and the great deeds were recited. He thought about that trumpet a lot and about what you got for blowing away at it and pleasing the adults even if you didn't know what their secret was and what they really wanted. Keep blowing, keep marching, keep you chin up and smile and do the things for the adults that get you chocolate biscuits and two minutes on Movietone; you will find that secret out.

London had been decorated for the coronation of the new King. The previous one was not mentioned, banished from conversation for reasons that were part of that great adult secret. All the father would say was that the 'abdicated'

King was a bloody fool, and for once she didn't contradict him. The local street boys sang a version of the carol:

> Hark the herald angels sing,
> Mrs. Simpson's got our King.

But he didn't know what that meant, or who Mrs. Simpson was, or why she would want the King anyway. What would she do with him? Never mind. Street parties were held and he got a mug with the new King and Queen on it. Father had a job and mother a new polished gate-legged table for high tea and whist games with the uncles, when the other tables were brought out and winners moved on from table to table 'til the finalists ended up at the same table. The games went on late but he got to stay up so he could ring the little bell at the end of each round, and join in the break for refreshments when the uncles sang and recited. ("The Green Eye of the Little Yellow God," "Gunga Din," "The Charge of the Light Brigade," "They're Hanging Danny Deever in the Morning.") He got to do his turn of course, "The Teddy Bears' Picnic" or "Little Boy Kneels at the Foot of His Bed." This was a great favorite with its central character of Christopher Robin saying his prayers. He always ended it by laying his head on his praying hands and reducing volume to a whisper: "Hush, hush, whisper who dares, Christopher Robin is saying his prayers." The uncles and guests all agreed he was bound for the stage. She was delighted.

He remembers one night when he was sitting under one of the tables with his bell and the voices were droning and laughing and gradually getting further and further away, and he fell asleep. They discovered him several rounds later with much laughter and petting and putting to bed. He remembers the moments before falling asleep when a little panic set in. He was drifting away from the adults, losing them; he would never find out what their secret was; what they were laughing at; like Peter Pan he would never grow up. But that was not what he wanted. He wanted to join that world, and it was drifting inexorably away and he couldn't stay awake. After this he remembers the choking drowning dream and the fear of water. And he never has learned to swim. He just can't do it. The moment the water goes over his head his body starts to thrash voluntarily, and then it goes rigid.

But there were idyllic days at the seaside in the sand, paddling in the soft warm water, eating candy floss and big soft yellow pears, and staying up late to hear music and see the dancing on the pier. Warm summer days on the moors when he walked with them over to the village where it all started (it was called Haworth, they said, because it was high up above the river Worth.) His mother told him about the three little girls who once lived in the parsonage there; how they grew up to write wonderful books and become famous in London. He would do that too someday he decided, once he had figured out what it was the adults were doing, what they wanted, what their secret was. The three famous sisters had a brother, it seemed, and he never found that secret out either and went the way of the pub and disgrace and an early grave. Despite this the brother was somehow important, because their earliest house as a family had been just a few houses down from the inn at the crossroads (the Crossroads Inn, no less) where the brother used to walk in the rain with his writings rolled up inside his top hat. He went to read them to his friends in the room over the bar, and the friends said later that one of the sisters had stolen his story about ghosts on the moor, but no one believed them.

The poor brother wasn't much talked about. Instead she talked about the three girls with the funny name, (she wrote it for him: Brontë—Why were there those funny dots? So you knew to say the "e"—it wasn't just Bront.) and about their success, and how their father, like her father, was from Ireland, where his name had been plain old Brunty. (Why did he change it? Goodness knows; people do strange things.) So was the husband of the eldest girl from Ireland. He was a curate in the father's church at the top of the steep hill, past the dangerous pub, past the house where some of the cousins lived. And how they were church and respectable people like her own people (who, strangely, had the same surname as his father, causing much hilarity and innuendo and stories he didn't understand). The unrespectable Irish lived in their own part of town, where the police went always in twos. These were the "bog Irish" and they had built the canals across the Pennines, and so were "navvies"—for "navigators" she explained. The navvies stayed on after the canals were finished (seven locks, some of them had), and they had lots of children and got drunk and started fights on Saturday night when the paddy wagon came to get them. Then they "went to confession" and were forgiven, and then stared all over again. You must never get into a "paddy"—that was very bad; you had to keep your temper always. And you must never follow their bad example in other ways. There was a match seller known only as Emily Matchbox—a wizened old woman. She lived with two men, one of whom was her husband. They slept together in a small bed, the story went, but Emily said she knew which was which, because: "Ah allus meks me 'ubby keep 'is socks on." The adults thought this was hilariously funny; he thought Emily was just being sensible.

He didn't often see the uncles on her side, but they were different enough to cause wonderment. His uncle Jim was in the Lancers (17th/21st—the "Death or Glory Boys") and so a romantic figure out of Light Brigade legend. This uncle knew the family lore and told him of the Irish origins. The grandfather (his great-grandfather) was a Dubliner, called Augustin, who kept a bicycle shop. The family was Protestant (that was like Church of England) but he had married a girl from a Catholic family (they didn't like Protestants–it wasn't clear why.) The Catholic "priest" (they didn't have vicars) used to come round every Friday to collect his two shillings from the great-grandmother.

He would come up the steep back steps (the shop was on a slope) to the kitchen. He wouldn't come through the shop at the front because he was afraid of the grandfather who didn't like priests. One Friday he caught her frying bacon for Augustin's dinner, and this was very bad because the Catholics didn't eat bacon on Fridays. (Why? Because they're superstitious. What's that? Never mind.) The priest began raging at her and telling her she was wicked and would go to hell and she cried into her apron. Augustin came in and he said: "Neither priest nor Pope nor God almighty shall insult me own wife in me own kitchen!" He took the wee priesteen by the collar and threw him down the steps and broke his collarbone. The Catholic mob stoned his shop, so he took his family and moved to England, away from the "superstitious priest-ridden island."

The story was always told in the same way, by the maternal relatives, with exactly the same words from the great-grandfather, recited like a ritual. They were the creation myth that justified the migration to a strange land. And the family's success in that land added to the justification, for they all had respectable jobs—from health inspectors to headmasters to chief inspectors of police. And those who had been in the army had been in "good regiments" like the Lancers and the Coldstream Guards. One uncle (Jack) had been a pallbearer at Queen Alexandra's funeral. But his own grandfather (called Augustus) was a "black sheep." He had been gassed in World War I and hated work almost as much as he hated religion and his relatives, in that order. He wouldn't get a regular job and worked on and off in the pit, much to the horror of the respectable relatives. The mother didn't like to talk about him much, except to mention that he played the tin flute and had music in a cigar box, and that he would go out and argue with the Salvation Army when they were trying to play their hymns in the street. Sometimes, when the boy was particularly inquisitive and argumentative she would look sadly and say he was just like his grandfather. But he never met the fabled flute player and atheist. All these relatives were distant and tantalizingly out of reach.

His paternal uncles, who were nearby, did not have such dramatic stories, but they were still interesting. They had come originally from farms in the East Riding of Yorkshire, where they were not allowed to have bonfires on November 5th because they had been, long ago, related to the traitor Guy Fawkes who was burned in effigy every year on that day. This had caused Guy's understandably nervous relatives to change their name to the nearest phonetic English equivalent. (But wasn't he a Catholic? Yes. But we are Protestants? Yes. Why? Never mind.) Their ancestors had been people of substance, including maternal great-uncle Lyon, after whom he was, like his father, officially named, and who claimed to be related to the new queen—it was the same name. But they fell on hard times. While the old queen was still alive there had been a "great agricultural depression" in which they all lost their farms. The father told of how, as a young lad, he had been taken to the hiring fairs where, dressed in a smock and a straw hat, he had been taken on, given a bottle of water and some bread and cheese, and sent with a rattle to scare crows from the corn prior to harvest. The uncles came to the West Riding to find work in the wool towns. So: one clan moved from west to east and the other from east to west. They had the same name, they met in the middle, and here he was. It sounded awfully like "fate": something that had to happen. He would have liked to visit these far-off places of origin, but that wasn't possible then. There was no reason for regret, though; there was plenty to occupy him close to home.

There were the bright winter days when there was always eye-blistering snow on the moors above the sooty town, when he and his father took his sled to pull coal sacks up the steep hill because the horse-drawn coal wagons couldn't make it. Or they went out wrapped in sacking up to their waists to help the farmers dig out sheep. You could always tell where the sheep were because their breath melted the snow and you saw the holes with steam coming out. The dogs—black-and-white border collies—always found them and set up a barking and a scratching. The dogs were wonderful he thought; uncanny in the way they responded only to whistles and always knew exactly where to be. But they were a bit frightening too. For pets he stayed with his budgie, until it died from the pneumonia from which he had earlier escaped through love and mother's milk. Poor Joey had neither. He was surprised that he didn't cry, but he really didn't feel anything for Joey. He tried to appear sad because she seemed to require it, but he didn't feel anything really for the bundle of colored feathers in its cage. She was the one who cried. But he told everyone about it, and he got a lot of sympathy and chocolate biscuits.

Winter also meant Xmas, traditional and plum-puddingy and he knew all the carols of course and got to sing the page in Good King Wenceslas with an uncle doing the king. The street boys sang naughty carols, which she hoped he didn't hear:

> Hark the herald angels sing,
> Beecham's pills are just the thing.
> Move you gentle, move you mild,
> Two for adult, one for child...

Church was nice at Xmas too with the carol services, but it was cold. He liked Easter better because of the new clothes, but Easter was sadder because, on Good Friday, Jesus was killed by the wicked Jews and Romans. (So why did they call it Good Friday? Never mind, wash your face, it's time for church.) Again he found it hard to feel as sorry as he knew he should, and was glad for Easter Sunday when he could join in "Christ the Lord is Risen Today, Ha-a-a-a-a-lle-e-lu-u-jah!" and not have to pretend to be sad any more. In any case, their religion was conventional and social. Tip your hat to the vicar, always be super polite to his lady. After all, this vicar had been privileged to christen the miracle child and enroll him in the Little White Ribboners—an Anglican temperance society. He didn't find this out until later—much later. But she set great store by it like some magical enactment that would protect him against falling back into the abyss of the pub and the dog track and all they stood for.

The christening was marred only by the vicar's insistence that he be christened with the names on his birth certificate, which were his father's (and great-uncle Lyon's.) When she registered the birth some petty official insisted on entering Christian names even though none had been chosen. She put his father's. Later they decided on something else, but the vicar insisted on sticking with the original. So he was forever lumbered with names that were never used. This was another thing he only discovered years later. He vacillated after that according to which persona he was trying on in the attempts to please the adults. Sometimes his father's seemed more dignified, and he got to add "Jr." which seemed somehow distinctive. Sometimes he wanted to forget these connections and be "himself." Mostly he would just say that his name was a diminutive of his father's—which was true. It was all part of the dance.

Winter and Christmas meant the pantomime, the truly big ceremonial event of the season. The panto was the super-treat. Everyone went—more regularly than to church. It was a peculiarly British mish-mash of messy slapstick, archetypes and cross-dressing. The panto "Dame" was always an aging male comedian in well-stuffed drag (Widow Twankey, Mother Hubbard), while the "Principle Boy" was a leggy soprano in tights, high heels and a male jerkin (Dick Whittington, Robin Hood). The whole thing was spiced with popular songs and old favorites in which the audience joined. He had heard most of them from his father and enthusiastically joined in from the seats high up in the balcony. At the end of "When the Poppies Bloom Again" the Principle Boy took it faster than he was used to, and in the brief silence between end-of-song and applause his piping little "I'll remember yooooooo…" rang out like something from the chorus of boys high up in the dome in Parsifal. The startled soprano was a good sport; she doffed her feathered hat in his direction. (There was always a lot of audience participation in the panto—interactive theater before its time.) The spotlight swung on them, while the whole theater burst into applause for the "bold little chap" as the soprano called him. The father was again embarrassed and furious. You were being "made a spectacle of" once more. Attention was being called. Attention must *not* be paid. But the bold little chap was beginning to take it as his due.

It could have gone on forever. But the war put an end to it all, and of course was a new beginning. Between the Woolworth ladies and the war he had discovered roaming. Although he was, naturally, carefully watched over as the miracle child had to be, he found plenty of time to roam around the edges of the moors. This became easier once he started at the village school for those few months before the war. He doesn't remember the school much except that they were very keen on milk which he threw up and naps which he never took but only pretended to be asleep and thought his own thoughts. But he remembers that the back wall of the tiny playground gave directly onto the moor and that after school he would climb it and always go home the "long way round." This was forbidden because it went past dangerous places like the old quarry, but he had already decided that his agenda was different from theirs, and dangers were things to be courted. The old quarry, long disused, was filled with water, and despite his fear, or because of it, he used to wade out into the water in his Wellington boots (a la Christopher Robin) to see how far he could go.

Once he got stuck in the mud and had difficulty getting back to the shore and was full of excitement at the danger until he realized the water had come over the boots and they were full of dank slimy pond stuff. He emptied them out, but the socks (knitted) were soaked and there was no way to dry the socks or clean the boots. He delayed and delayed but in the end he had to go home and confess. To bed with no tea was the punishment. But worse was her anger, now turned on him not on the feckless neighbors. He was surprised however that it did not have much effect on his behavior except to make him more cautious in his roaming. For the pleasure of these solo wanderings was so great it was heady. He had no idea why, but it was better than applause and creamy biscuits even. Better than praise. Better than her approval, which he had in any case come to take for granted. For many years to come he was happiest when alone and wandering into unfamiliar territory.

The war "broke out" (like a rash?) and the quiet soldier, being a reservist, was "called up" and left amid tears and applause from the village along with the other reservists. He was supposed to be sad but he was more excited than anything else. The rough khaki uniform, the ammunition pouches (no ammunition for them), and above all the rifle with the shiny bolt that clicked and smashed into place. The warrior all complete again, smiling as he rarely smiled, hugging and smiling and saying it would all be over soon to comfort the crying women. War was then "declared (he didn't know what that meant—but evidently it made it official) just after his fifth birthday. He was waiting there on his birthday with the cake and the party favors, and no one came. They thought it would be called off because of the war and his father leaving. How could they imagine that she would not celebrate the birthday of the miracle boy? They both ran around the village and knocked on the doors to tell the children to come. The birthday was late and hurried but it happened. He got a flying suit, with a helmet with earflaps and even a pistol, just like the RAF: an odd present for the son of a soldier. But he didn't take it off for days. He even took it roaming and shot imaginary Germans at the old quarry. Then the call came.

He had often heard the father say that if the bullet had your name on it there was nothing you could do. Now he heard her saying the same thing about bombs. Evidently if the Germans put your name on a bomb (how did they know about you?) it would get you wherever you were. So she talked herself into joining the warrior at what was then the only battle front available to the beleaguered island: the blitzed ports of the northeast where his father's regiment was stationed to oppose the suspected invasion. He learned only later of the mixture of heroism and farce this entailed, for they had nothing to oppose it with. When the bullets for the guns came, each man had a miserable five rounds, but of course there was the bayonet and "you can always take one with you." He heard all this but it meant nothing from his small perspective compared with the marvelous new settings for roaming and the new opportunities to please new adults.

They followed the blitzes down the coast, since his father's task was to guard the anti-aircraft guns, and these moved as the bombing moved, from Whitby and Scarborough down to Hull. The Huns were softening up the port towns and doing a pretty good job of it. The London blitz got all the attention. People seemed to forget the battering these northern towns took. But he had no wide perspective on strategy, only an endless excitement at the bustle and tension and fear and noise and the nightly sound and light show that was the air raid. It was reduced to a ritual exercise. They always were staying in "digs" in the houses of usually old people; old people had spare rooms which they told you had once belonged to Jimmy or Sarah and then they often cried a bit.

You lay on top of the bed in your clothes until the siren sounded, as it always did sometime after sunset. Then you got up, put on your overcoat, little tin hat (just like a soldier's), put your gas mask over your shoulder, picked up the teddies and prepared to leave for the shelter. She had the bag with the thermos and the sandwiches and the few precious things that had to be saved from a possible direct hit—like the Wembley photo. Then off through the dark to the shelter, built by some genius under the arch of a railway bridge at the same time slated for demolition in case of invasion. The civilians and demolition crew sat side by side and swapped tea and stories and jokes. "When do you blow it?" "When we get the order Missus." "And what about us?" "We 'aven't got any orders about you, Missus." And everyone would laugh. He would play ludo or snakes and ladders with other children or the adults, and perhaps even sleep on the hard bench with his head on the hard tin helmet as the adult voices droned off into the distance, taking their secret with them. All this to the accompaniment of ear-cracking thuds and poundings and sirens and rat-a-tats from the outside.

What they all did through the long night he doesn't know, asleep as he was. What he remembers best is the morning walk back home, after the "all-clear" had sounded, with the constant anxiety that the house would not be there. They would walk round huge craters, and take long detours because of the fires, and the nervous troops on the street corners demanding identity cards (there was a spy scare.) This roused her indignation at the humiliation, and his fascination with the guns, always asking to stroke the barrels of the machine guns poking through the sandbags, and being pulled roughly away. Finally they would get to the house, and be relieved it was still standing even though half the street was gone and all its windows were out and there were firemen and wardens and rescue crews everywhere shouting and digging, always digging. For some people, particularly the old ones, wouldn't go to the shelters. Every night we "lost a few." He remembers bodies being pulled from the rubble—again, no horror or remorse, just intense curiosity. So that was a "dead" person. Just like Joey had been "dead"—whatever that was. Another of those adult secrets. He peered closely at the bodies. Apart from their battered and sometimes crushed appearance, when they were laid out in rows they just looked to be asleep. It was a relief to her to be able to explain it this way. Death was when you went to sleep and didn't wake up.

It was not a happy explanation. From that time on he was frightened of sleep. He didn't want not to wake up. He was not terrified, because he always did wake up and he came to expect that, but he was uneasy about going to sleep and risking that non-waking death. Every night he would keep himself awake, making up long elaborate stories with himself as the hero, based on things he had read. He was a merman, a wizard, a Roman soldier, a Red Indian, anything to keep the story going. He made up tunes and hummed them softly to himself under the covers. It was later he learned to read there with a flash-light. This exhausting game of postponing sleep became such an entrenched habit as the neural pathways hardened, that it led to a life-long misery of chronic insomnia. He could be very sleepy and wishing for sleep (once he knew for certain that sleep was not death) but as soon as his head hit the pillow the brain took over and started the churning thoughts. But for now they made their way home through the brutal destruction, the rubble, the stink of brick dust and cordite and gas, the rivers of filthy water. Home and sleep in his tiny attic room with an old coat hanging where the glass had been in the window.

> *... mere decay*
> *Produces richer life; and day by day*
> *New pollen on the lily petal grows,*
> *And still more labyrinthine buds the rose.*

There was never any school. The rule was that if the bombing went on after midnight—as it always did, there was no school the next day. In any case most of the schools had been taken for hospitals and refugee centers and the like. Occasionally he turned up only to be sent home again. One day when there should have been school it was closed anyway and they all went into the town to be present at what was the most important moment of the war for the battered citizens: a visit by the King and Queen. Flags were waved and cheers cheered and he was surprised that the King, even in his uniform, was not a more imposing man. He seemed quite ordinary. The Queen stopped and talked to people, so close to them, and she patted the arm of an old lady who was crying and told her to "have courage, my dear." She seemed very nice, the Queen, and he had always been told of their special connection with her because she was the "Colonel-in-Chief" of his father's regiment (the grandly named King's Own Yorkshire Light Infantry) and she had pinned his North-west Frontier Medal on him on his return from India. So that was why she must have brought the King to see them, and to stop and talk. The King was so important. They listened to his broadcasts on Christmas Eve, and praised his braveness for trying so hard to overcome his stammer. "She helps him a lot," the mother stated firmly.

But it was the Churchill speeches that sustained them. Even the stoical father had to wipe his eyes, and she wept freely and held him tight. The words were so grand and made them feel so proud: "They must break us in this island, or lose the war." The breaking was going on all around them, and the grown-ups found it hard to bear sometimes, but Churchill's words seemed to cheer them up and make them decide to "grin and bear it" and not give in to the Huns. The people were determined to be cheerful. They laughed a lot at the things on the wireless that he didn't always understand. But sometimes they were less than amused at the attempts made to cheer them up. When the soldiers were all together eating in their canteen (and the little soldier among them of course) there would be broadcasts over the loudspeakers. "Workers' Playtime" was very popular, but then the announcer would say, "The forces' sweetheart, ladies and gentlemen, Vera Lynn!" The invisible Vera would start to sing "We'll meet again, don't know where, don't know when..." But the soldiers would boo and throw things at the loudspeakers and shout "Ger 'er off!! She's 'orrible!!"

As for school, mostly no one even bothered. She spent her afternoons training as an army-nursing auxiliary and the old people didn't think it was their business to babysit a "big" boy such as he was. So again he was free to roam, and roam he did through the rubble and dirt and smoke. "How on earth did you get so dirty?!" "It's dirty out there. I was playing." The first true, the latter a mild sort of lie since she would understand it as playing with other children from the street, which he was not doing at all. If he did contact other humans it was always adults since they had so much more information, and he might get closer to the secret. They were always willing to talk to the curious little boy with the earnest questions. He doesn't remember the questions or the answers; pretty much everything was grist for his curiosity mill.

His father spent as much time with them as he could—when he could get a "sleeping out pass"—and there were weekends of picnics on the cliffs, and trips into the countryside. But whenever the sirens went father had to go "back to barracks." They all three went to the pictures sometimes. Couldn't be choosy here since one had to take whatever films they were able to show.

The Marx Brothers, Fred Astaire, George Formby, Paul Robeson, and Nick and Nora and the dog Asta in *The Thin Man* he liked. There were always the cowboys: Tom Mix, Roy Rogers, Gene Autry. Above all Nelson Eddy and Jeannette MacDonald, and his great favorite *Maytime* with all its opera and its sad ending and her dazzling tinkly-bell soprano. Much wonderment was expressed at the high fantasy of the "musicals" with Ruby Keeler and Dick Powell. The name Busby Berkeley would not have meant anything to him then, but the great surrealist left his imaginative mark. He didn't pay much attention to the details of the films, although he liked the newsreels, *The March of Time*, and the documentaries and "short subjects" like *Unusual Occupations* and *Popular Science*—and particularly Robert Benchley on *How to Sleep*. He daydreamed through them, sitting holding the rifle (the warrior had to have it "at all times") between his knees, stroking the smooth stock and the shiny barrel and being told to shush when he clicked the bolt. Sometimes he fell asleep on the rough khaki arm, which cradled him and never moved however long he lay there. It was never usually very long since the siren would go and they would all have to leave and go their separate ways, to barracks and to shelter. Perhaps that's why he didn't take much interest in the feature film. You never got to see the whole of it anyway.

Was it not dangerous people asked him later? Were you not afraid? Yes, he supposed it was; no, he was not afraid. What was there to be afraid of? The Germans? They were only an idea. The bombs? They fell on other people, not on the miracle child. Even when they did their worst, when a whole high garden wall, shaken loose by the bombs, collapsed on him, he survived with only a broken leg and brick dust in his lungs that took weeks to cough up. He was dug out from under the bricks, but unlike the old people he was not dead; his name was not on the bomb; they were right about that it seemed. Perhaps the Germans were as confused about his name as the vicar had been. Perhaps they put the wrong name on the bomb. The miracle followed on another event of an even more spectacular nature. It was a family pastime to sit out at night on the wall at the end of the garden and watch the searchlights and the dogfights they lit up and the explosions and the fires. Particularly exciting was the fiery demise and plunge to earth of a huge, floundering, flaming barrage balloon.

Part of the game was to try to identify the planes by the typical sounds they made. One night, when he was standing on a dustbin to get a better view, they heard a particularly loud whining. "Daddy, that's a spitfire" he suggested. "Spitfire be buggered" the father yelled, "it's a bomb." He was grabbed and they all ran inside to the cupboard under the stairs. The noise was such as stunned the whole body into immobility. The low garden wall on which they had been sitting was demolished. The back door was blown right through the house and out into the front street. The dustbin on which he had been stand-ing was later found three streets away. It had traveled that far through the air.

It was this blast bomb that loosened up the high garden wall that then fell on him. But the blast bomb hadn't got him. It was not his time. However, it confirmed his status as the miracle boy. God, they said, had things planned for him. He was being saved for something. But what? First he had find out the secret—or rather the two secrets: what did the adults know, and what did the adults want?

She took him every week to the library, sometimes twice a week and sometimes he went on his own. The library was itself a miraculous building since it had escaped a hit in the midst of a devastated area, and its small gothic tower pointed a civilized defiance at the barbarian-controlled skies. He definitely remembers his awe on the first visit. How could there be so many books? If the necessary knowledge was here, how could he even get close to acquiring it? But no child knows how long a lifetime is, so he set out to try. She must have taught him to read very early since he could never remember not reading and there was always reading matter to hand. In some of the houses where they stayed, the old people had shelves of dusty heavy volumes, which he read even if he didn't understand. A six-year-old struggling with the novels of Sir Walter Scott (he started with *The Abbott*.) But he got the general idea.

In one house certainly they had, left over from the distant time of their own children's childhood, a full set of Arthur Mee's *Children's Encyclopaedia* which he burrowed into like an infant literary mole. For years they subscribed to Arthur Mee's *Children's Newspaper*: the organ of the middle-class child establishment. In one house there was a tattered copy of the one-volume *Pear's Cyclopaedia*. The old people gave it to him, pleased with his interest, and he lugged it around with him throughout the war along with the teddies and the tin helmet. It was his constant reading companion. But not alphabetically; he went for what was interesting, particularly anything to do with history or mythology. This was real escape. It was a kind of roaming, but a roaming for which one got praise and pats on the head, particularly if one remembered poems, and he easily remembered poems—mostly patriotic stuff about admirals and battles.

> Admirals all for England's sake,
> Honour be yours and fame,
> And honour as long as the waves shall break
> To Nelson's peerless name.

Then Arthur Mee or *Pear's* would tell him about Nelson—and about "Effingham, Grenville, Raleigh and Drake." He liked Raleigh the best: obviously a fellow rover.

But his memories on this are confused as all his chronological memories are confused. This could not have all have been when he was five or six. Some of it must have come later (although not much). But he does remember that first library visit. He had probably been in libraries earlier, but then he played while she got her books—she loved to read and read to him, and never censored his reading at all. He took out whatever he liked. That was the point of the visit he remembers—it must have been in Hull—for that was the first time he went for his books. The way to the secret was open, and it lay through books. He knew all the stories of the Wagner operas from a large illustrated volume he borrowed. He borrowed it for the illustrations, which seemed magical to him even though he had no idea who Wagner was or what an opera was. Odd to recollect in later years: as the German bombs smashed and blasted all around him he read obsessively of Siegfried and Sieglinde and Wotan and Loki and Gotterdamerung, oblivious to the irony. Since there was virtually no school he also listened to the school broadcasts on the BBC. This was also unselective listening—everything from Grimm's Fairy Tales to History for sixth forms. On the latter they had a time-jumping reporter who went into the past and gave "live" commentaries on events and times. He was absorbed by the one that reported on the Stone Age, on cave men in the Ice Age. The idea of such primitive beginnings, of such vast reaches of time, gave him goosebumps the way no film ever did (until *King Kong*). This was something new against which to measure things like the war and the strange world of the adults.

For brief intervals they lived in the country, in the little villages just inland from the battered coast, when the troops moved back there for whatever reason. Then they lived on farms little changed since the nineteenth century—or the eighteenth for that matter: lit entirely by oil lamps; water from a hand pump in the yard; outdoor latrines full of spiders and centipedes; cooking on wood stoves. But farms were great places for roaming, with hidden areas and silent places deep in woods. The son of the farm family in one village was a gardener at the Hall. He used to go there and roam the Hall gardens, and the estate—the broken down stables, the overgrown tennis courts. He wandered through the Hall itself (the family was away somewhere—to escape the war perhaps, or perhaps to fight it) and looked at his first private library. He was astounded at the idea that all those books could be owned by people rather than public libraries; that people could live on this scale. It was as strange as the Ice Age. There were adults here who knew and wanted something different from the adults he knew. It was bad enough to have to try to break the secret of the adults without these complications. Sometimes, in the long gallery, he would do his dance, to appease the spirits of the place, to try to please these strange adults with their books and their pictures and their obvious power.

But mostly he learned to be a country boy again. He made his first kill, at harvest time. As the harvester went round and round the field in diminishing circles the rabbits crowded to the center. The men, boys and dogs ringed the decreasing patch of hay in an ever-tightening circle until the rabbits burst out in all directions. They fell on them with an orgy of flailing sticks. Those that escaped were chased by the dogs or brought down with shotguns or air rifles. He got six rabbits his first time out and carried them home slung on his pole by the legs. The men taught him how to gut and skin, and then there was the feast of pies and stews and roasted rabbits. No meat ever tasted so good as that you killed yourself. He strangled his first chicken and helped to hold a squeaking pig while they killed it. All the other pigs, even though they couldn't see what was happening, squealed along with it as if they knew, and then went totally silent themselves once it was dead. These farm adults were easy to please, and what they knew seemed easy of access, except that they still laughed at things he didn't understand and that were nowhere to be found in the otherwise comprehensive Arthur Mee.

The sea was never far away, and in the process of roaming he found out that he could easily get to the cliffs with a stiff walk. Here some other and older children were involved—probably boys from the farm who were persuaded to come along. The cliffs were forbidden and covered with anti-tank stuff and barbed wire, and the phony anti-aircraft guns made out of telegraph poles and stuck in equally phony earth bunkers. The poles were painted black so they would shine in the sun and so fool the German reconnaissance planes. Many of the soldiers had no rifles—his father the reservist was privileged—so they whittled mock rifles out of wood and polished them with boot blacking to the same end. This was pretty much all that stood between us and conquest, his father said, but the Germans didn't know that and kept on with their stupid bombing. You could crawl under the barbed wire—at least that wasn't phony— and get to the beach. He had no great love of beaches, but there were things that washed up there, and these made it always an adventure.

Bodies washed up there sometimes, German bodies. If you were lucky they still had badges on and you could get these. The bodies were the tag end of a failed invasion plan (Sea Lion?) They were eventually found by the adults and buried. But in the meantime they were loot for the boys. He used to tell her that he had swapped marbles or something with the other boys for the badges. This was perhaps his first out-and-out lie, but it was a start, and he improved with practice until it was virtually a way of life. He liked lying. It was dangerous, but it called on a lot of skills not otherwise easily brought into play: a subtle combination of imagination and logic that was fascinating for its own sake as much as for the results. How much could one get away with? The adults, he discovered, were almost infinitely gullible. "A good liar must have a good memory," she would say. Sound advice; he qualified.

Sometimes he would go to the barracks. He liked being among the soldiers. They were warm and masculine and protective. They made a fuss of him, overfed him from their vast vats of food and made him sick and then laughed and cheered him up. The regimental tailor made him a miniature uniform complete with cap. It was like having hundreds of nice uncles. Was there ever a happier boy? He recited his patriotic poems and sang his WWI songs and got even more applause than from the Woolworth ladies. This was a good war. His lovely soldiers paraded for his inspection, and he saluted them like little John-John. They mounted guard over him with rifles and bayonets and he was grateful. He was Caligula among the troops: little boots, the favorite of the legions. Not perhaps an auspicious start, but he felt so safe, so secure with the khaki uncles. Never ever in his life could he feel anything but love and admiration for the soldiers. Would they not lay down their lives for us like Jesus did? They were the image of the perfect good, and the perfect warrior was the perfect man.

One day, in the local town, there was a military parade. In charge was a young officer of The Royal Horse Artillery. He wore the dress uniform of that regiment: bottle green and tight with silver epaulet (one shoulder only), and skin-tight trousers tucked into shiny black riding boots with bright metal spurs hitting the ground sharply as he walked. His cap had the kind of peak— a black shiny peak—that came down straight and almost covered the eyes. He walked with his head thrown back so he could see, and this gave a swagger and arrogance to his stride of the sort that confident young officers have. Above all there was, attached by special straps, strung low, almost trailing the ground, his long silver sword that danced and sparkled in the sunlight. His left hand touched it lightly to steady it, and with the other he beckoned imperiously for his horse—a dapple, light and springy with the heavy cavalry saddle. He mounted with unbelievable ease like a dancer, and with cheers from the pedestrian proles he pranced off. He was Arthur and Lancelot, he was the Black Prince, he was Rupert of the Rhine, he was Marlborough and Wellington, he was Alexander. A little bit of the little soldier's heart went with the perfect warrior, and there was a curious jolt to the body, as though he were floating on air for a moment, and a suffusion of pure joy shivered through him. The next time he felt this peculiar sensation he would call it "falling in love."

He didn't at this stage follow the war too closely, although there was a lot of crying after a big battle called Alamein, where two of his father's younger brothers had been killed. They were in the Royal Horse Artillery, like the perfect warrior, but mechanized and without horses. One of them had played the kettledrums in the mounted band in peacetime. He didn't know—or at least didn't remember—uncles Tommy and Billy, but this "sacrifice" (they called it) brought him closer to the war, even if he was still hazy about what was happening and where. But Monty was going to win the war, and they sang "Run, Rommel, run Rommel, run, run, run" to the tune of *Run, Rabbit*. Winnie's words rolled so impressively on: "It is not the end, it is not the beginning of the end, but it is perhaps the end of the beginning." Even in that funny squishy voice it made your skin prickle. How could anyone be so clever?!

Then suddenly (or so it seemed) they were ordered south—to prepare the way for "something big" that no one was supposed to know about. His father, whose skills as a signaler, hailing back to flags and heliographs, were out of date, had gone on a course with the Catering Corps to learn how to organize cooking for thousands of men. He was happier as a signaler, but wanted to feel more useful. The signaling skills he passed on to the boy. Father and son used to tap out Morse code messages to each other when she had to be by-passed. "Stop that infernal tapping!" They never told her, and he has never had the heart to tell her. A boy should not keep secrets from his mother, nor tell her lies; but once he does, a marvelous new world of possibilities opens up.

He was never sure where he was in the south. He was never much good with maps, and was less interested about where he was in space than he was about relative chronology. It must have been Hardy country—on the Somerset, Devon, and Dorset border; a place with the impossibly English name of Midsomer Norton near the Somerset market-town of Crewkerne, and on the road to Bath, although he never knew that, and they never went to that most perfect of cities. Again they lived on farms which had not changed much since Hardy wrote about them. But all he knew was that it was a real disloca-tion; it was his first culture shock.

The country was different: rolling hills with woods and copses; all so manicured and cultivated it was as if they had tried to reproduce a painting in reality. The people were a foreign race. He rarely understood a word spoken to him, but she says that he mimicked them and left a year later with a broad Somerset accent. How can you please the adults if you don't speak their language? In this Hardy country they still spoke Hardy English. An inquiry as to someone's whereabouts brought the response "'E be down-up-along, sunshine." They always said "be" instead of "is" and "bain't" instead of "isn't" and they always added "a-" to participles: "Now do be a-goin' 'ome-along, my child." He found bilberries on the heath, but they were "whortle-berries." He was never to be seen "mollyhorning" or to be "mandy," so he turned the wheel of the mangle-wurzle, even if his efforts were "scammish"—and he was truly a bit clumsy. They indulged him for his singing, even if it made him "playward." They said "'E bain't a zany" despite appearances, and despite his "skittering" manner. They saw to the essence.

But it was great roaming country. He found a copse with a fox's den in it. The farmers were offering a shilling a brush if you found fox cubs they could kill. But he liked to watch the cubs playing with the vixen, to watch them grow and frolic. So he didn't tell. There wasn't much to do with the shillings anyway. The hunt was mostly abandoned because of the war, which is why the foxes were flourishing. But occasionally one was held to keep up the local spirits. They gave him a pony to follow the hunt, which he did cautiously because he was no rider, but when he joined them at the kill, they insisted on

blooding him anyway, as they had done with a few grinning and self-conscious youngsters already.

As the warm blood from the brush trickled down from his forehead to his
mouth, he felt the same goosebumps as he did when he learned about the cave
men and the ice age. Somehow they were related, but he didn't know how, he
couldn't articulate the feeling again, and somehow he didn't think the adults
would understand, nor would they have an answer. He never told her about
the incident. Clearly there were things that even the adults—at least these
adults—didn't understand. Perhaps somewhere, perhaps the people in the
Hall with their huge library would know. Someday he'd find the grown-ups
who knew; for now there was only the feeling, warm and sticky and more real
than anything he'd known before. He was glad, even so, that it was not his
foxes the hounds had mangled in the copse. They had to be killed, one knew
that; but not yet, not his.

They were rudely moved again, to yet another planet. This one was flat
and the sky seemed unnaturally huge to one raised always among hills. And
it was not like the huge sky of the sea for here there was no sea, just endless
marshy land with endless canals and drainage ditches, dense meadows of
reeds, and funny birds with long spindly legs and long thin beaks. They told
him it was the Norfolk Broads. The little town was called Diss. Never having
seen it written, he heard it as "Dis" and his scattered gleaning in mythology
told him they must be going to hell. Far from it, but there was still the war and
the danger and the big guns. The guns this time were protecting the huge
encampments of American airmen. But again the people here were strange
people with a strange tongue and strange ways, including the few Americans
he met. There were still, however, roaming possibilities. And even better, they
stayed not with old people this time but with a family of the Salvation Army
persuasion, whose grown son drove a lorry delivering pop and fizzy drinks to
local groceries. He rode around all day in the lorry and had all the pop he
wanted (he was sick again). They went to distant towns with Cathedrals and
busy streets untouched by bombs, and to little villages with windmills and
canal boats with flapping sails of heavy rust-red canvass. It was all water, as if
the land was barely keeping its head above the marsh – as indeed it was, and
floods were a commonplace. But above all it was here he saw his first black
men and Germans.

Black men were otherwise, like Germans, an idea. But an idea exemplified
by one man in particular, Paul Robeson. He was never sure why but Robeson
was a hero to his parents, mostly because his songs since they knew nothing of his political opinions and would not have approved if they had. His
father knew all the songs—"spirituals" they were called, he didn't know why.
He didn't know why Robeson was black, but they explained about Africa and
slavery and all that. He remembered reading a boy's story about "How I escaped from Tipoo Tip" which was all about Arabs taking slaves in Africa and

how "we" tried to stop them: General Gordon died to free the slaves didn't he? But Robeson it was, and "Deep River" and "Swing Low Sweet Chariot."

They had a picture of him in his robes as Othello, which was an introduction to Shakespeare. The army tailor who made his uniform knew the plots of all the Shakespeare plays. The tailor was "Jewish" they said, but he was "a nice Jew." As opposed, presumably, to the ones who killed Jesus. But this was strange. How were they still around? And what were they doing in the army looking like everybody else? Never mind. The nice-Jewish-soldier-tailor told the Shakespeare stories to him, when he asked about Othello, and even gave him the Lambs' *Tales from Shakespeare,* which he got practically by heart. He couldn't understand why Othello had believed Iago, or what it was that Othello thought Desdemona had done that was so bad, and they were evasive in their replies. It was another adult mystery. "You'll understand when you are older," they said. And he expected the knowledge to appear suddenly, fully formed. In the meantime there was the reality of Robeson.

During his roaming he wandered onto a forbidden area near the base. Two apparitions came over to him and, with great kindness, took him home to explain to her that it was dangerous for him to go there. They were incredibly tall black men. He had never seen anyone so tall. They dwarfed the little Englishmen he had always thought of as big—like Joey the rugby player. And their uniforms were magnificent beyond belief, with white braid and pistol holsters and scarves at their necks, and those funny helmets with no rims to them the Americans wore. They must be generals at least, he was sure. And they were so unbelievably polite and called her "Ma'am." No one had ever called her that before. She quite forgot to upbraid him this time and offered them tea which they accepted. It dawned on him that they were black men from America. "Do you know Paul Robeson?" he asked them. "Sure son," they laughed, "we know him." He was in ecstasy for a week.

The Germans were a different matter, along with the Italians. They were prisoners who came to work on the farms, usually accompanied by a bored lance-corporal who sat around drinking tea while his charges mucked out stables and cleaned the yard. You weren't supposed to "fraternize" with them, but he didn't know what that meant, and the curiosity conquered again. Some spoke English and told him about their families, their homes, and sometimes wept when he asked questions about their children. They didn't seem like the monsters propaganda made them out to be. They seemed rather sad and quiet men, a long way from home, and nice enough to him and patient with his questions. Their languages fascinated him and he tried to get his tongue round some of the words. It was easier to sing them, and he learned a few songs, or snatches of songs. He was amazed to find that things he had known in English through his parents' love of operetta were in fact German or Italian. This had never occurred to him—everything was sung in translation in those days. But what a difference it made when "Here, in Vienna now" became

"Wien, Wien nur du allein!" and "One little tear, one secret tear" turned into *"Una furtiva lagrima."* He even learned the real German words to *Lily Marlene*; he had always thought it was an English song until then ("Underneath the lamplight/By the barrack gate…") It seemed somehow unfair that the English had stolen it.

Not only did the adults have the secret, but they had it in numerous foreign languages (he could count up to ten in Hindi.) Was it the same secret or different? This was hard to ascertain from the prisoners. But one thing was clear: they were just as easy to please as the English adults, and the Americans were the easiest to please of all. He probably didn't clearly distinguish the Americans from the prisoners. He understood them only slightly better. But again he knew their songs, in particular "Alexander's Ragtime Band," and he easily curried favor along with gum (which he hated) and "candies" which he sang for like a starved canary. They were better than English sweets; and the "cookies" were often better than biscuits, certainly than arrowroots. One night he was allowed an incredible privilege and went out to a huge crowded hangar, all decorated and with a big stage, where, he was told, a very, very famous American band was playing. It did play, loudly and with staggering gusto, and the troops danced with the few WAACs and WAAFs who were there (she didn't dance; she never danced) and cheered and shouted wildly. He went home asleep on his father's shoulder. He had probably, without knowing it, seen one of the last (if not the last) concerts Glenn Miller gave before disappearing over the English Channel.

There were strange mixed interludes when war and peace touched each other with an odd grace. He remembers sitting in an apple orchard with her having a picnic; it must have been springtime. Suddenly a flight of huge bombers came over very low and very loud. The earth shook, and the trees shook, and all the white apple blossom showered down on them like a snowfall until they and the picnic were covered. The bombers were gone in an instant, and once the shock was over they looked around and at each other, and burst out laughing and threw the apple blossom about like confetti.

There were expeditions to the local town to pick up parcels the kind Americans had sent through the Christian Science church. He knew the Americans had more stuff than they ever needed, and were always giving it away. But it was still touching that they would make up these elaborate parcels and send them all that way to people they didn't know at all. It was in character with the Americans he knew on the base, though. They seemed happiest when they were giving things away. His father was suspicious of them. It will be seen, he said, whether they will make good soldiers. They don't behave like good soldiers, but they have the stuff and we need them. They all agreed though that they were very generous and well disposed to us. If they were "overpaid and over here" they were almost eagerly willing to share their bounty. The parcels were wonderful, especially the Spam. There was little meat to be had—one got tired of whale steaks, so Spam and corned beef in cans were luxurious delicacies. Spam was fried with eggs, it was battered and deep-fried with veggies, it was cut into chunks and added to the veggie pot to make a tasty stew. At tea-time there were thin Spam sandwiches with watercress and apple chutney, or cucumber and mustard. Glorious Spam!

But the generosity was two edged, because there were the clothes. Lord knows they were welcome enough, but what on earth did American parents think of, sending such weird things for children to wear? There was in particular a strange pair of short pants in navy blue, which bagged out like jodhpurs then came in to hug the knee, where three cute little buttons, like buttons on a coat cuff, were dotted on each leg. There was no way under the sun he was going to wear such things out of doors. The local roughs would have stoned him. Before that he would have died of embarrassment. She tried cutting them to a decent length and hemming them up, losing the buttons. Better, but they still bagged out ridiculously. In the end he wore them, suitably disguised under a long jersey, as football shorts. The Americans may have been nice to him, but they must surely hate their own children.

Time was running on now. The war was winding up to its climax and his father would soon go to France; they would go back to the Pennines and a different problem, since he really had no idea what schools were about, so little time had he spent in them. Schools were obviously part of the vast scheme and of adult frustrating life. He would have to go to school and this would be a way of pleasing the adults, and he figured he had mastered that (how wrong he was.) The school could also be the route to finding out what it was the adults knew and what they were laughing at (wrong again). But this was still in the future. In the meantime his only experience of school was really Sunday school, for if the day schools were closed or irrelevant, Sunday school was always available on Sunday afternoon with some obliging curate or churchwarden ever ready to "give instruction." He knew the Book of Common Prayer with its Anglican orthodoxy almost by heart, and vast swatches of the King James Bible were his. After all, the more you memorized the more you pleased the adults (and she set great store by these particular adults) even if much of it was meaningless. There were prizes to be got (mostly rather boring devotional tracts—*How Little Tommy Came to Jesus*), and at the very least, praise.

Even if he was hazy as to the content (the God of the Old Testament was inextricably confused in his mind with Wotan) the language was always mesmerizing. It was still the language of religious mystery, not of colloquial understanding, and the incantations and cadences alternately lulled and thrilled. He used to like to go to funerals to hear the service. He would stand with the crying people in black by the graveside and listen, mesmerized: "Man that is born of woman hath but a short time to live and is full of misery. He cometh up, and is cut down, like a flower; he fleeth as it were a shadow, and never continueth in one stay. In the midst of life we are in death: of whom may we seek for succour, but of thee, O Lord, who for our sins art justly displeased." This gave him goosebumps. He worried a bit when it came to "Thou knowest, Lord, the secrets of our hearts…" Not only had he to please the adults but also this mysterious God/Jesus, and he was even less sure what He (they— or for that matter all three of them) wanted, except that we should not "sin"— which seemed to be almost anything worth doing.

But piety paid off nevertheless. At an evangelical meeting one Sunday a visiting curate asked passionately who in the audience believed in Jesus; who would "declare himself for Christ?" There was no hesitancy; the hand went up. It was the only hand. The rest of the audience was, British fashion, more or less embarrassed by this kind of thing. This was religion getting out of hand: overflowing its Sunday boundaries. But the delighted curate rushed over to praise him, praise his parents, and press sixpence on him over their protests. He was furious and cried in bed that night when they made him put the sixpence in the poor box. The next time he would go without them and keep the sixpence. When he got a small money prize for reciting three psalms, all the kings of Israel, the Ten Commandments, the books of the Bible, the Twelve Apostles, the plagues in Egypt, and various other assorted lists, he didn't tell them for fear the poor (whoever they were) would appropriate his well-earned rewards once more.

Still, he always liked best the end of Evensong, when the Collect for Aid Against All Perils was said: "Lighten our darkness, we beseech thee, O Lord; and by thy great mercy defend us from all the perils and dangers of this night; for the love of thy only son, our Saviour, Jesus Christ." Once he had responded with the always quiet "Amen", the night did seem secured against perils, which, Lord knows, were real enough for much of the time.

The next sharp disjunction in his life followed on D-Day. His father sailed for Normandy and the abortive rush to save the paratroopers at Arnheim. The division only got as far as Nijmhagen, then stuck there, while the Panzers flattened the little Dutch town and killed so many of the British and Polish paratroopers. He was glad his father was there, being brave, but so many people around were crying because they had "lost" fathers and brothers and sons that he felt, perhaps for the first time, nervous and a little afraid. His father's letters, once they came, spoke of the terrible suffering of the Dutch people, particularly the children. There was precious little to send them, but his mother suggested that he give up such sweets as there were (liquorice sticks, jelly beans, gobstoppers) for a while and send them to the Dutch, along with canned food (the precious Spam) and knitted things. His father wrote that a local family had invited the soldiers into their house to share the stove since it was so cold that winter. When the sweets and things were handed over to them, the parents had to leave, weeping uncontrollably at the sight of the children's happiness. "We might not have much," she told him, "but those poor things have nothing." She kept at the knitting, and insisted he take a pair of needles and learn. He managed—knit one pearl one—a number of long, gaudy scarves, made from odds and ends of wool that the shops would sell for a pittance—like the broken biscuits. These pied piper efforts were strangely comforting: like the spitfire drives, or the raffles to buy the Stalingrad sword, they made you feel you were doing something.

At very short notice he was removed back to the Pennine foothills. But not to the pleasant moors and little villages and one-mill towns and farms, but to the big city full of huge crowds, noise, dirt, massive mills and schools and children. They had to go where there was a "house to rent," and these were scarce in wartime. He would have liked to have gone back to the east coast or Somerset or Norfolk, but he discovered the adults had strong notions of "home"—of where they "belonged" and so forth. He didn't know where he "belonged." Until now he had been happy enough wherever he landed and had adapted to whatever the place had to offer, the way children do. (Do they really?) But he knew somewhere deep that he didn't "belong" in the nasty crowded city, and in particular he did not belong at school and with children.

It didn't help that she hated the town and its people. It meant little to him where he was; he heard the name Bradford, but that was just a name. He automatically reflected her indignations and never questioned their rightness. How could he? Most of the men in the town had been exempted from military service because they were in "essential industries" making munitions, uniforms and the like. She maintained they were making cigarette lighters and selling them on the black market. They were all overpaid lazy cowards who were shirking their duty to fight. This showed in their characters. When there was chocolate available they took time off work to queue for it, and they wouldn't let the women and little children go first. In fact they snarled at them and threatened them. She told them what they needed was a good bombing, and a big self-important policeman told her to "move on" and that she was "disturbing the peace." There was, she reminded him, a war on, in case they'd forgotten, and their particular brand of peace needed disturbing. These were the types who were "red hot Labour" she told him. He didn't know what that was but it was obviously pretty awful. They were lazy, greedy spendthrifts, who couldn't control themselves and so had large families beyond what they could keep and took honest ratepayers' money and spent it on drink and things they didn't need, and they bought bread instead of baking it. This latter was the gravest sin: decent people baked their bread; only the irresponsible and lazy bought the dreadful soggy white stuff with the money they somehow got from the ratepayers, whoever they were. The "bought-bread people" were the pit into which it was forbidden to descend now or evermore, Amen.

The injustices of the system infuriated her. When she applied for some "supplementary" money to help out the inadequate soldier's pay, the inspector told her she was not entitled because she didn't have any debts. The thing to do, he explained seriously, was to run up a lot of bills, not pay them, then apply. That way you could be sure to get supplementary. Her reaction was predictable. Well before her time she had assembled all the arguments against the welfare mentality. He was daily bombarded with examples of crassness and unfairness, and his system was infused with automatic reactions against any sign of injustice. He never lacked for a stimulus. As the uncles had told him, this was not a fair world. But they had added that you might as well get used to it. She would not be party to such stoicism: injustice must be fought, or at least exposed, or at worst raged against. The problem with the town was that the decent people were hopelessly outnumbered by the bought-bread people, who voted their cronies into office so they in turn could dole out the decent people's rate money to their mindless greedy supporters. Why was it so? It was democracy, she said, which we were supposed to be for, but she thought that Winston Churchill should be made dictator for a while and "knock some sense into them." It was his first lesson in politics.

To ease the transition to town, and to make sure he was in solid contact with the decent people, she wisely enrolled him at a Church of England (parochial) school: "It will be just like Sunday School" she said. Well it wasn't, even if he couldn't appreciate how more like it was than the city schools would have been. He had to walk several miles there and back in all weathers, but he was used to walking. It was a kind of roaming, although always too rushed on the way there. On the way home there were streets and alleys and town-like spaces to explore. The streets of gray stone houses curved up the steep hillsides of the valleys the town sat in. The mills were mostly at the bottom where they had been originally built to catch the waterpower from the down-rushing streams. Now they were driven by coal and steam and had huge central flywheels that drove all the machines by pistons and belts. He could watch these monster machines for hours; they were like creatures out of myth with vast powers and hidden effects: sinister industrial Fafners, guarding their caves of woolen treasure.

The houses of the workers crowded round the mills; everyone walked to work. But then, before the coming of trams and buses, so did the managers, and their houses were only a bit higher up the hill. The owners, who came in originally by carriage, lived on the north side near the top where the prevailing winds would keep them from the soot and smog. Everyone was kind of thrown together. The streets were all cobbled so that the horses could get up and down the slopes without slipping. Horses delivered everything: coal, milk, furniture, groceries, scrap iron, machinery. The railroad yard at the bottom of his hill had a vast stable area with hundreds of horses. He used to wander round it drinking in the power of the huge cart-pulling animals. Sometimes he would go out with a bucket and shovel and collect their droppings for garden manure. There never were such roses as grew from the dung of big working horses.

They lived about half way up one of the hills as befitted their ambiguous status in the world. In the winter the street was transformed into a toboggan run. Neither the horses, nor anything else could get up and down, so it became a children's bobsled paradise. He didn't have a sled the first winter, so he took the broad coal shovel and sat on that. Grasping the short handle in front of him, he careened down the glistening hillside like some crazed little herm skimming the icy cobblestones. The underside of the shovel became so shiny you could see your face in it. He didn't like the house although it was big enough, with big stone walls and a little garden with thin soil where not much would grow. It had an enormous cellar with its own fireplace and huge copper vat for boiling water for washing clothes and filling big tin baths, and a stone-flagged pantry which was always cold even in the hottest summer. But it just wasn't a farmhouse, and while the massive dray-horses were a reminder, they weren't friendly farm horses either. They were, like everything about the town, so grimly purposeful.

The town people were not like country people. They saw children as a potential enemy, always ready for "mischief." He didn't mix with them. He was always on the outside, slightly hostile. The men were small and pale and grimy. They wore big flat caps and never smiled. They avoided their women and congregated in seething groups around pubs, working men's clubs, and union halls. The hard little women were always scowling, grim and dowdy, peering suspiciously at boys whom they suspected of all kinds of evil intentions. They were fanatically concerned with appearing clean. They scrubbed and scoured their front steps endlessly, then screamed at you when you stood on their artwork. The town was physically interesting for roaming purposes, but he could not imagine what would please these adults, except to stay out of their way, which he did assiduously.

School at first wasn't too bad. It was after all a church school so they had their share of scripture lessons and he liked those, doing countless drawings and paintings of crucifixions and learning yet more psalms and hymns. But the rest soon became a torment. For a start they expected him to be able to do joined-up writing, and the rapid-fire printing that he practiced would not do. He didn't dare admit that he had never learned the joined-up style—he was too busy reading to bother much with writing, so he printed the letters of each word and then went back and roughly joined them up. The result was disgraceful as handwriting, but he was never caught, and eventually managed to join the printed letters as he went along. His handwriting remained ever after an embarrassment, leading to jokes about how he should be a doctor, where it wouldn't be noticed. Children in large numbers were strange to him. He had

spent his life with adults: indulgent, praising, sixpence-dispensing and bis-
cuit-offering adults. He had no idea what all these children wanted, or even
what they were doing most of the time. The boys were obsessed with playing
cricket and soccer in the schoolyard. But he couldn't play either and found
them faintly ridiculous. Why would you want to kick and hit these silly
balls? The adults weren't interested in what you did, so what was the point? It
was dancing to no purpose.

These "school" adults were not like his uncles, or the Woolworth ladies, or
the soldiers, farmers and prisoners, and least like the Americans. They didn't
seem to like children: "limbs of Satan" they called them, "spare the rod and
spoil the child" they said, and they announced that "the Devil finds work for
idle hands" and the like. He was being introduced to the unpleasant puritan
strain of low-church evangelical Christianity, and he was lost. He looked in
despair at the hatchet-faced old spinsters and knew that his dance wouldn't
work with them, nor would "Alexander's Ragtime Band." He would have
to start from scratch even to please these adults, never mind find out their
secret. And those silly, noisy, giggling, physical, punishing children were
constantly in the way. How could one plan adult-pleasing strategies with
such distractions?

There was no knowing how to please them. The vicar was the easiest.
Either he or the curate came to do Scripture lessons, and scripture was mother's
milk to the Sunday-school hero. The school, and church, were St. Paul's, and
he had read H. V. Morton's *In the Steps of St. Paul* when tracing all those
journeys. He knew just where Antioch and Ephesus and Corinth were, and on
just which journey Paul had visited them and who it was he went to see. You
can guess how pleased the vicar was. The crucifixion pictures were also much
admired, and when he asked a question about exactly what "the veil of the
temple" was—to put it in the picture—the vicar was delighted, although the
answer was surprisingly vague: "Sort of curtain, I suppose." Vicars and cu-
rates were obviously a pushover.

Not so old hatchet face with the bun and mustache and huge loose dress
like a downed parachute with flowers patterns. She smelled. Not the old
people smell he was well used to, but a smell of sweat and stale talcum powder
that made him retch. She taught everything from singing through arithmetic
to history. Singing should have been a lollydoddle for the little canary, but
they didn't sing his songs at all and weren't interested when he volunteered
When the Poppies Bloom Again. Hatchet face was obsessed with "tonic sol-
fah"—some too-ingenious Welsh invention in which one learned songs by
chanting the doh-re-mees; note values and rests were indicated by punctuation. It was meaningless to one nurtured on spirituals, operettas and war
songs. He hated the doh-re-mees; it was a kind of anti-music. He sulked, and
for the first time in his life was hit across the head for insolence. The shock
was dazzling. It was bad enough pursuing the adult secret when they were

basically on your side, but this? What were you to do when they were actually against you? Go into an even deeper sulk. Get more thwacks across the head.

As if the doh-re-mees weren't bad enough, hatchet invented her own mnemonic system for learning the great themes of the classics: you sang words to them. Beethoven's Fifth began with "fate knocking at the door" so you sang loudly: "Let me come IN! Let me come IN!" Mendelsohn's lilting Hebrides Overture was reduced to: "How lovely the sea is! How lovely the sea is!" And horror of double horrors, Mozart's delicious *Eine Kliene Nachtmusick* was either chanted in the dreadful tonic sol-fa ("doh, soh doh, soh doh soh doh mee SOH!") or sung to the name of the great one himself: "C, HU, RCHILL; C, HU, RCHILL; Churchill, it's Winston Chu-urchill, yes Winston Ch-urchill, great Winston Ch-urchill!" Schubert was mauled. It was a good thing he never finished that symphony; it would have given hatchet more tunes to ruin. As it was the disgusting sound of "This is, the symphony, that Schubert-wrote-and-never FIN-ished" became lodged in his pathetically complaining memory. There were more. To this day acres of music are still ruined for him since he can never ever shake off the memory of those appalling words.

There was worse to come. The most frightening time of the week was "mental arithmetic" class. Hatchet face would pad about in pumps (sneakers) so you couldn't hear where she was in the classroom. You had to sit with eyes down and put your hands flat on the sloping desk; she prowled with a malacca cane. She would appear silently and suddenly behind you, call your name and demand "thirteen times seven, quick!" At this point, his mind simply froze. Some kind of mental portcullis came down; even if he knew the answer, he couldn't give it. He simply tensed up, closed his eyes, and waited for the sharp crack of the cane across the back of his hands. To this day he can't do "mental arithmetic." When a sum has to be done in the head, his mind still freezes. He can never make change or calculate it. The damage proved to be permanent.

History was no better. In those days they had no hesitation about teaching "values" in school. "Who was the monarch we could have best done without?" old hatchet face demanded. "Henry VIII" he ventured. After all, the business of destroying the monasteries, chopping off his wives' heads, how bad could you get? This caught him another sharp crack around the head. It seems the correct answer was Bloody Mary, of course. (Next monarchs in line? Kings John and Stephen, evidently.) Good King Henry was the founder of the Church of England. Did he know nothing? It seemed not. His world collapsed. He was lost. From being the golden boy he became the class idiot. He didn't know the things they had all learned somewhere along the way, like how many pints there were in an ounce, or rods, poles, perches and furlongs, or the depressing "times tables."

The vicar came to the rescue. He really liked the vicar. The vicar was a Victorian (as was just about everybody in charge of things then): an im-

mensely tall man with a shiny bald pate but longish white locks like a picture of Dean Swift, with an imposing manner and full authoritative voice. He was, in other words, everything a vicar should be, except that he would insist on singing the tune of the hymns out loud in his own powerful but errant version which drowned out the choir and caused serious embarrassment to everyone but him. He was a moderate low-churchman, but well disposed towards the choral revival and vestments and the like, and had done mathematics at Cambridge (whatever that was—it said "B. A., Cantab." on the Church notice board.) The verger, who doubled as school caretaker, had told the vicar about the mathematics, and one day after Sunday School, a tearful boy told the vicar about the mental arithmetic torture. The vicar was horrified and evidently had a word with the headmaster who called in old hatchet face, and the torments with the cane ceased. It did nothing but increase her obvious hatred of him, but this didn't matter. He had had a revelation of true power.

> Whence an accident
> Which, breaking on Sordello's mixed content
> Opened, like any flash that cures the blind,
> The veritable business of mankind.

Clearly in the scheme of things vicars ranked up there close to God—which was as it should be, he supposed. But this gave a whole new slant on adult values. Equally clearly the thing to be was a vicar. If you wanted to be at the top of the pinnacle of adult knowledge and power, this was the place to be. He couldn't figure out whether the vicar knew what the other adults were laughing at. People were very careful around the vicar. But that was all right. The children—those nasty runny-nosed bullying noisy children—were afraid of the vicar; the adults were deeply respectful of the office. Vicars got to run the whole show on Sundays, and headmasters did what they said. Actually being a vicar was a little far from his ambitions at this point. He had no idea how you became one (apart from going to Cantab.); but one thing was clear: it paid to stick close to the vicar and please him. You were only one step away from God. Now God hadn't been to Cantab., nor was he a mathematician, but despite his lack of qualifications, it was clearly prudent to be in his good graces.

So the church, and particularly the church choir, became his home away from home. Almost all his time outside home and school were absorbed by the church. He was the prize pupil in Sunday School of course—still devoted to rote learning of incomprehensible texts. He added the Beatitudes, most of the Abominations of Leviticus, along with the General Confession and the Athanasian Creed. This garnered him more prizes (uplifting anthologies by Robert Bridges, patriotic anthologies by W. E. Henley) and praises. He soon became the model chorister. Church and its music were like a magical time out of time. You got to wear these lovely colored robes with a white surplice and ruffles at the neck, and sit in the special place next to the organ and the altar. It was like being a junior vicar. When you sang a solo the whole church listened and the rapt approval was physical and dense. His first solo was "Sheep May Safely Graze"—a pretty tune with a nice accompaniment, by someone called Bach, who was, they said, like Handel but not as good. The whole setting with its gothic pillars and carved pews and crosses and flowers, and the Anglican smells of oiled wood and old leather and crisp linen, was a transport from the mundane and dirty world of cobblestone streets and crowded stone houses and rattling tramcars and horse carts. And there was always the strange sense of power—supernatural power—that he felt about the whole performance. "For behold, I tell you a mystery..."

The choirmaster, an accomplished musician who had some local repute as a composer of marches and drawing-room ballads, was noted in amateur dramatic circles for his brilliant female impersonations. His seductive placing of a powder puff in the top of a gartered stocking while singing, "Falling in Love Again," was regarded by connoisseurs of that art as a performance of consummate genius. He was later arrested for adult homosexuality, but was no pederast and decent to the boys. His real weakness was a morbid keenness for musical festivals. He entered everyone in these dreary local competitions, which involved sitting for hours in church halls and draughty school classrooms while dozens of boys sang through the same piece which had already been rehearsed to death anyway. Handel was very popular because the songs were so singable, like "Oh had I Jubal's Lyre" or "Let the Bright Seraphim" or "Silent Worship." But Handel surely had never meant these lovely things to be squawked to death by a hundred boys at an amateur musical sing-fest. It was an awful torment to the otherwise keen little warbler.

This might appear surprising since he loved to perform. But he found he hated this business of performing in competition; of being marked and judged relative to others; of discovering that one was not the golden boy as in the church solos, but thirty-seventh out of eighty-three or something such. The mere thought of it made him sick to his stomach and caused him to tremble so that he couldn't take the proper breaths. Before each performance he would go to the lavatories and be sick, then kneel by the bowl and pray tearfully to God to stop the trembling. But God could scarcely be expected to take an interest in so pathetic a request, and of course it was a selfish prayer and he knew these didn't find favor (there'd been a sermon on that). He tried to argue that it was for the sake of the choirmaster, or his mother, but God was not to be mocked. When it came to "He shall feed his flock, like a shepherd" (*Messiah*, of course) he was trembling so badly he missed his entrance and only managed to stumble through. Despite all his pleadings the choirmaster insisted on keep entering him and told him it was just "stage fright" and would pass with experience. It didn't. This was the only suffering he ever associated with church and the choir, and it was enough. Otherwise, church and choir were sheer bliss.

He even began to pay attention to the meaning of the otherwise meaningless bits and pieces about kings and prophets and apostles and miracles and crucifixion and resurrection. He actually read the Gospels through and not just as passages for rote learning. He was puzzled about the basis of what he desperately wanted to believe but didn't really understand. The Jesus of the Gospels, as he read them, didn't seem to have much to do with the Jesus of church worship, and all that fighting and quarreling, smiting and complaining in the Old Testament even less. Then one Easter they were singing Stainer's *Crucifixion* (every Easter they sang Stainer's *Crucifixion* and every Xmas Handel's *Messiah*, filling in with Mendelssohn's *Elijah* in the off season.) He was suddenly struck by the words: "He has come from above/In his power and love/To die on this passion day." He was overwhelmed by an epiphany, a visitation of wordless understanding. He felt it like a good angel descending and smothering him with its wings. He understood the feeling that one might have to take away all the pain and suffering in the world, to bear it oneself and thus rid the world of its burdens. It was like saying "please drop the bombs on me, not on those other children." Now here was the great opportunity to do it offered to the Son of God himself, but only through cruel torture and death at the hands of those He was saving. No wonder it didn't work. Our sin was so great that we couldn't ever match up to this incredible sacrifice.

He was so overwhelmed by this insight—so crushed under the weight of the angel's wings that enfolded him—that he went dizzy and passed out in the choir stalls. They all fussed over him and put it down to something he ate, or the heat in the church, and he never knew how to tell them, even the vicar. But one thing was now clear to him: he had to be a vicar; there was no other sure way to heaven. Sin otherwise had you beaten before you started. But God would never refuse heaven to a vicar, surely: not one who had been to Cantab.

Of all the church things, Christmas was still the best. Dickens would still have recognized it. The best part for him was the Christmas Eve caroling. The whole choir went walking round the parish, all muffled up and gloved against the cold. They carried lanterns on poles that were brought out at Christmas only. They stopped outside their various venues and sang one carol by lantern light, then went inside: a small hospital for old people, a home for retired tradesmen, a big and bleak orphanage. They would sing more favorites and some for the people or children to join in, and the vicar would lead prayers. Then they handed over a "donation" from the church collection, and some of the people cried. The orphans didn't cry. They seemed so small, and had such big eyes, and just stared. They didn't join in much. They were so quiet. But the grown-ups said how wonderful this visit was and what "joy" it brought, and such things. At least it made the choir feel good.

The best part was the visits to the big houses. It was like something from a film. In the tall entrance halls with stained-glass windows—halls as big as small churches, the snowy choristers clustered, singing their hearts out. Men with movie-star mustaches, wearing black suits with shiny lapels and bow ties, and ladies in lovely long dresses, stood on the heavy oak staircases and applauded and said the boys looked "sweet." Then the choir got Christmas cake and buns and hot punch and mulled wine for the grown-ups, and one of the tall men in black gave a "donation" to the vicar this time. The vicar led a prayer of gratitude, and everyone clapped and the ladies fussed and fixed their scarves, and it was all cozy and warm and safe. The church was always full at Christmas, and when he sang the haunting Holst/Rossetti "In the Deep Midwinter" as a solo, he could genuinely feel part of something palpably, physically real and grand and encompassing. He almost couldn't sing the last verse since it made him want to cry:

> What shall I give him, poor as I am?
> If I were a shepherd, I would bring a lamb;
> If I were a wise man, I would do my part;
> Yet what I can I give him: give him my heart.

One of the strangest things he had to adjust to was the whole business of "friends." He had never really known any children of his own age at all well. Odd ones had drifted in and out of his transient life, but his attention was always on the adults. Children with their peculiar obsessive concerns were no help in dealing with big questions. He didn't want to collect rocks or stamps, and if he did want to go roaming it was on his own where he could live in his imaginary worlds, not theirs. But it was evidently required of one to have friends and if one didn't one was thought peculiar and that wouldn't do. So, since the adults seemed to put some store by this as well as the children, he tried. He went to birthday parties of the other choirboys ("nice families" she said, people one should know), and accepted invitations to tea and to play— board games and charades and other pointless activities. He bore it patiently and reciprocated with his own invitations. Sometimes the whole choir went off for a "trip" to some local beauty spot or the seaside even, and they had jolly romps all day, which exhausted him with the effort of trying to appear enthusiastic.

He was duly enrolled in the Wolf Cubs and had to wear an unbelievably silly uniform and go once a week to meetings that were mostly about knots and clean living. They did give out badges though, and this at least was garnering rewards from the adults, so he threw himself into it with an effort that surprised his elders who had him marked down as apathetic and moody. There was a Morse Code badge, for example, which he passed on the spot, of course—that was almost cheating, as was the signaler's badge, and first-aid badge. The several volumes of the Red Cross first-aid manual had been family reading since her days as an army nurse. But many of them simply required rote learning of one kind or another and he could rote learn with the best. He soon had an armful of badges and a lot of pleased adults, but he never liked the whole business with the uniforms and the noisy giggling boys and the parades in freezing weather with "totem poles" and drums and bugles.

At least you didn't have to be "friends" with the cubs. You just met them one night a week and that was it. But there was another institution that was more troublesome at first: that of "best friend." You were evidently supposed to have one boy you liked better than all the rest, and you chose to do things with him most of the time. This was particularly exasperating since very little adult-pleasing or investigating could be undertaken if one were constantly doing these ripping "boy" things like fishing for minnows in the local canal, collecting tadpoles and frog spawn in the local ponds, or taking long walks over the local moors (easily accessible by bus.) He did have a best friend for a while. Jeffrey was the least boring of all the boys at school and liked things like Romans and Ancient Britons and The Stone Age and good stuff like that, rather than football and cricket. But in an excess of enthusiasm they took some slates from the roof of an old building to make "stone axes" (by tying them onto sticks), and were hauled in by the vigilant local police for trespass, willful damage, theft etc. etc.

She was mortified by the potential shame of it all. When the police came to see her, they interrupted preparations for tea. Milk was always religiously poured into a creamer for serving, but when she went to the door she left the milk bottle on the dining table. When the police left she was in a terrible state. He told her it was all right; they had said charges would probably not be pressed. But she was inconsolable: "The milk bottle! The milk bottle was on the table! What will they think of us? What will they think we *are*?!" It was damning evidence of a low-life home environment. Despite the milk bottle the vicar and the headmaster saved the day with their character references, and no charges were brought in the end. But each mother began to wonder if the other's son was really "suitable"—so the best-friendship experiment fizzled out. Jeffrey went on to become an eminent wildlife zoologist. Must have been all those minnows, tadpoles and frog spawn.

At school one day they suspended normal classes and gave out books of questions to be answered. He liked the "comprehension" ones with passages of prose followed by questions; they were easy. The essay was no trouble, nor were the tricky questions about nothing in particular but obviously conundrums to be solved. ("If a train sets off from point A at thirty miles an hour and another from point B...") The arithmetic, however, even though not mental this time, always had the threat of the cane and portcullis and he didn't like that. But he struggled through it. Then it was that he had the second visitation, the great blow to the head that came from nowhere like a blow from the wings of one of the evil angels who rebelled with Satan.

He remembered little of what followed for several weeks. He was kept in bed with heavy things at his neck so he couldn't move his head. He drifted in and out of consciousness. They talked about taking him to hospital, but another doctor was called —a "specialist"—who said he shouldn't be moved. The doctor came every day and talked of "cerebro-spinal meningitis" which meant nothing to him except that it was obviously to do with the blow from the angel and the great pain in his neck and head. He tried to tell the doctor about the angel, but it was hard to talk much. "He's wandering a bit," he heard the doctor say to them. They crushed up tablets and gave them to him in milk, (he thought he heard "sulphur" which was ominous, but it must have been "sulfa") and she cried a lot, with tears so heart rending it was almost more painful than the thing in his head. He knew then how much she really did love him, and he felt unbearably sorry for his lies and his lack of real feelings.

The vicar came solemnly every day and they prayed together—or at least he moved his lips to the Lord's Prayer for the pain hurt his mouth and jaw. The vicar said the prayers from the Visitation of the Sick, but he only heard them very distantly. The vicar understood about the wicked angel, but he said that God would send a good angel to drive it away and watch over him. One day, when they were crying more than usual, he heard someone say, "I think he's gone" and he found himself looking down on the scene: the bowed heads, the vicar's shiny bald patch, the crying, the prayers, and feeling himself being pulled inexorably away from it all.

And then it was all over. He was back—eyes open and a weak smile. There were cries of joy and more tears, and joyful prayers of thanksgiving. The vicar called him "a child of God" for he had been brought back from the boundary and reunited with the living, and even the doctor said it was a miracle, and surely it was. For he, despite all adversity, had not ceased being the miracle child. ("And thou didst not leave his soul in hell; not didst thou suffer thy holy one to seek corruption.") Weak and wobbly, and given to odd epileptic-type seizures from time to time, he gradually rejoined the living. They told him that the examination that day in school was the "Scholarship Exam" – it came to be known as the "Eleven-plus"—and that he had passed it (despite the worst efforts of hatchet face and the wicked angel.) He would be going to the Grammar School and onwards and upwards. She was proud, and his father (back from the war) was quiet, but nodded a lot and shook hands with the vicar and the doctor. School friends and choir and church friends (the vicar had preached a sermon on him called "The Power of Prayer") came to visit and bring little gifts and he was whole and happy again. For a moment at least his quest for the secret of the adults was put to rest. He was going to the Grammar School that was out in the country at Thornton: the village in which the three famous sisters and their sad brother had been born. He was going to go to Cantab. and be a vicar. God had chosen him and had obviously been watching over him from the beginning. God had kept his name off the bombs and had revealed a great secret to him.

He would still have to dance of course; all his life he would have to dance. But the Woolworth ladies seemed far behind him. He was doing bigger and better dances for much more important people now, and perhaps he even knew something the adults didn't. That was why everyone was so careful around vicars, because of what they knew. And if you said you were going to be one, they were careful around you too, treating you with a kind of cautious wonder. Once he could walk again he had nothing to do but stride confidently into the future, with only the dreams of thrashing in the wet sack and the memory of the sudden blow from the evil angel's wing to darken the smiling pathway.

Even the dark angel had helped in a way. The violent dislocation of his life and removal from the world had been like another mystical experience and had taught him, while he looked from the greatest distance possible—from the edge of death—that they were all still dancing, all the adults, everybody. The dances were more complicated and would take some time to learn, but the principle was the same. The Woolworth ladies never really disappeared. In some guise or other they were always there and always watching, ready to give or withhold the precious biscuits. It was all a matter of figuring out the right dance and the gingersnaps would come pouring in. Most adults were not dancing very well it seemed—if there was an adult secret then not all of them knew it; but they didn't have the powerful allies and the secret knowledge the miracle boy had acquired on his lonely quest. Somehow or other he would see to it that his dance was always noticed, and that the Woolworth ladies, whatever form they took, would always smile and applaud and hand over the cream centers, especially if the dancer wore his little dark suit and clerical collar. No shop girl could resist a dancing curate.

2

The Boy:
Making It to the Next Foxhole

One of the older great-uncles who had been in both the "Great War" (not like this latest sissy affair) and the Boer War, used to describe his life as "dodging the bullets lad" or more often "making it to the next foxhole." Making it from one foxhole to the next (where, incidentally, there were no atheists) was about the sum of it. On Spion Kop where the Boer farmers had maneuvered the British regulars into an impossibly exposed position and were pouring murderous fire down on them, that was all you could expect; it was all you could think about—nothing further: dodge the bullets, make it to the next foxhole. You took life, such as it was, then, one bullet, one foxhole at a time. And always the soldier's fatalism: either the bullet had your name on it or not; thus was your fate determined. This must have been why spies were so feared: they gave away the names of the soldiers to the enemy who could then put them on the bullets. In the meantime you "kept your head down" and waited for the dreaded order to go "over the top"—to dash to the next fox-hole, the next trench. What about shooting the enemy? "Didn't get much chance to do that lad." It was a wonder we ever won these wars. How could you win if you didn't shoot the enemy? "The sergeants made us unload the rifles so we wouldn't be tempted to stop and shoot. Got to get the cold steel at the enemy's throat. We never did of course. The artillery got most of 'em lad." Good for the artillery. Thank God there was artillery. What if you didn't have artillery? "Keep your head down and pray" (No atheists, remember?) Prayer was important; it kept your mind off the machine guns, and the mustard gas, and the artillery, and their bayonets—especially their bayonets.

As the world passed from an exciting war to an austere and boring peace, life for the wonder boy was passing from a sublime peace to a kind of guerilla warfare in which new excitements and new pains became incompatible traveling companions. There was the excitement of the new school and the world it opened up, and the pains of a family wrecked by savage emotions only poorly understood; by that wretched adult world on which he couldn't get a handle. These adults were driven by such violent feelings over things he couldn't begin to comprehend. All he did know was that his little, comfortable, enclosed world had now become a battleground of hate, vengeance, recrimination, sullen withdrawal, and cruel, cruel words, many of which he had never heard before—but there was no mistaking their import; they were meant to wound and they did.

The worst thing was that he was expected to take sides. He became part of the machinery of attack and counter attack. In particular she used him to hammer the father. He was subjected to the constant battery of "you don't want to end up like your father"—"if you go on like this you'll end up like your father." And how was that? Unless they explained their terrifying emotions to him how could he know what to avoid? But they would never do that. "You'll understand when you're older; when you're grown up; later." But in the meantime he was supposed to take sides. How to choose? He didn't want to. He wanted it all to go back to how it was when he could easily please them with his winning little ways: when she was all love and pride and the father was the uniformed warrior hero, and life was pleasant and simple and easy if you danced and sang a little.

He liked his new school in the country village of Thornton. It was a bus ride along the road that led from the big town, over the moors, to the crossroads where he was born, thence to the valley town which he still thought of as home, if he thought of anywhere as home. And it was new: a spanking modern building. It had moved from the village and its rambling gothic original to the spacious playing fields just outside. But the old lintel had been transferred and built over the new assembly hall doorway: "Gymnasium Literarium 1673"—very imposing. Founded by a charter from Charles II, it was mandated to teach "the English and Latin tongues, Mathematics and Good Manners." Things hadn't changed much. The original funds came from four local worthies: Messrs. Drake, Ellis, Sunderland and Sagar, after whom the school Houses were named. There were still Drakes at the school. This sense of continuity thrilled him for reasons he didn't understand.

As a wanderer by default, he was always amazed by other people's sense of place and connection. Mr. Brontë, when the curate there, had preached in the now ruined Old Bell Chapel. The famous sisters had chosen the pen name "Bell" and Emily was even "Ellis Bell." This couldn't be coincidence. He would go stare at the tiny birth house—half of it now a butcher's shop—with the little commemorative plaque, and wonder, and dream of nothing too definite, but of things beyond here, beyond now, in that world still to be discovered where all would be revealed. In the meantime he was enveloped in the warm bath of tradition of one of the "Ancient Grammar Schools," where the teachers wore their black degree gowns, and on grand occasions their bright-colored hoods and mortar boards. School uniforms were worn, school songs were sung, school customs were observed, and school deeds recited. It was a miraculous change from the elementary school; it was, at least at first, a wonderland for the wonder boy. He was a fish in water.

The foregoing is still in the third person. How long must the reader be tormented with this fictional form for a real life? Until the writer is sure of his connection to the past being described, one supposes. Note that "one supposes": the writer still does wish to commit himself to the first person. Most autobiographies seem to present the life in question as a seamless continuity. The authors have no doubt who they were from the beginning, and the early stuff is seen, like the prophecies of the Messiah, as simply a necessary prelude to the inevitable glorious after. But we know the prophecies were picked out after the event, and so we suspect it is with the great white males who usually write the autobiographies. Or perhaps not. Perhaps other lives are really like that: smooth progressions with one phase building inevitably on the next. "My love of nature and my curiosity about the natural world were aroused during my long vacations in the Louisiana bayous where uncle Joe had a small shrimp-fishing business. Day after day I would accompany him on trips into the estuary..." And on and up until the Nobel Prize for biology (marine). Well, perhaps that's how it is for great white males, and perhaps why the feeling of becoming one is so peculiar: like an Ionesco character feeling that first stirring of rhinocerosness. "*Non!*" he shouts, "*je suis un homme!*" This *homme* has no such sense of continuity, which is perhaps why writers like Ionesco, Beckett, Hume, Kafka, and even Lewis Carroll and Vonnegut are so appealing. Life makes little sense; there is no continuity of a "person"; there are only sharp metamorphoses as drastic as man into beetle that mark the jerky passage.

Hume was right: the very idea of a "self" is a colossal act of faith: an imaginative imposition on the random passing of events. The past is indeed another country. An expedition there is almost ethnographic. A recording of its doings and customs would be fieldnotes from an alien tribe; it would be an attempt to penetrate an alien consciousness. We have met the Other, and He is Us. A good autobiographer is writing an ethnography of his own life, and he should treat his task with the proper detachment and regard for the facts. But like an ethnographer he must also weave this into a narrative to "make sense" of the facts which have no sense in their own right. He treads a fine line. Thank goodness this is not an autobiography then, not really even a memoir, but *memories*: literally, that which is remembered. If it isn't remembered, it doesn't go in. Memory doesn't respect chronology or topography, but it imposes its own unreliable order; we'll go with that.

The life of his imagination, a life that was almost more real than the heavily impinging real world, had to be fed. Its appetite was voracious. But it was the only safe place—safe from the adult rules—so it had to be fueled. Here is a felt continuity with the peculiar little boy. Head in a book. "He always has his head in book," they would say. And he would smile his winning little smile then slide further down in a chair with the book between him and them like a protective shield. The content was almost immaterial. "He'll read anything. At breakfast he reads all the details on the cornflakes boxes. We let him read over tea. It's easier than arguing with him." They had a vague feeling that reading was probably good for you, like porridge and cod liver oil, so it was alright—even if taken to excess. "Get your head out of that book and go for a walk or play outside." Too much reading could make you daft; they'd heard that somewhere. But she in particular was obviously not-too-secretively proud of his reading, of the piles of library books. She even knew he read under the bed covers by flashlight when he was supposed to be asleep—fending off sleep was still a desperate thing with him, but she never interfered. "Proper walking encyclopaedia" his father would say, half puzzled. Where did he get it from?

Together they read numerous popular periodicals: *Picture Post, Titbits, Young England, John O'London's Weekly.* He read the comics—*Wizard, Hotspur, Boy's Own,*: not comic books with cartoons, but weekly doses of dense but jaunty prose encompassing patriotism ("Our Finest Hours"), responsible imperialism ("My Life with the Faithful Gurkhas"), healthy sport ("The Amazing Wilson"), boarding-school soap-operas ("Smith of the Lower Third"), and one or another uplifting "adventures" ("With Burton and Speke to the Source of the Nile.") Father read Agatha Christie and Zane Grey, so he read those too. She read women's magazines and romantic novels, so Daphne du Maurier went into the hopper. For a while he thought *Frenchman's Creek* the greatest novel ever written, Scott not excepted. Zane Grey was his early introduction to the great American West. He drank in the descriptions even though he didn't know what half the words meant: mesa, sagebrush, canyon, dry gulch, wash, cottonwoods, arroyos, mescal, cedar forest, greasewood, juniper, pinyon, sand-devils… But the music of the words—from *Riders of the Purple Sage* or *Wildfire*—sang hauntingly in his ears, and they were stored for future reference.

Where this parallel life of the mind touched, in Descartian fashion, the "real" world of school, all was harmony, and the autonomous life and the demands of the school adults meshed happily and he was indeed again the wonder boy as he had been in Sunday school. In History and English, French and Latin (Greek was added later, then dropped), even Geography and Nature Study, and certainly Civics and Scripture, he excelled; they were pleased. He was praised, and it was as it should be. For what they offered was endless stores of fuel for the imagination; endless amounts of material for him to weave his own fantasies about how his life would have been in the ancient world, or in distant places, or might be in the future, as far as he could foresee it. And the thought of being a vicar, while not as strong, was still uppermost, largely because it still carried weight with the adults. A little piety could turn away much wrath. How could you be angry at a potential clerk-in-holy-orders? But it was becoming more of a game all the time. He saw the alternative possibilities vaguely and they were more and more exciting. "Explorer" was high on the list—although he was totally vague as to how you went about this. But "having adventures" in the modern world meant being an explorer, it seemed. The characters in H. Rider Haggard's novels—Alan Quatermain the exemplar—were his models. *She* (Who-Must-Be-Obeyed) and *King Solomon's Mines* remained the touchstones. Outer space was still to be discovered as a place for exploration until Edgar Rice Burroughs and the Martian novels smacked him between the eyes. But in the meantime he had the classic explorers and explorations; Geography and History fed him the details.

When subjects offered no such fuel, he was miserable, inattentive, bored, even hostile. Mathematics, physics, mechanics, "general science"—perhaps they should have sparked curiosity. They did in short bursts, like knowing about the solar system and Newton's laws for example. This was the stuff of imagination. But mostly they were dreary formulae to be learned by rote for mysterious purposes that were beyond him. Only geometry caught his imagination occasionally. He appreciated the ruthless logic of it. And you could see it. With algebra you couldn't see it. All this manipulation of abstract symbols; what was it for? No one ever explained. It was as if the adults had invented it especially for the torment of young boys, like some tribal initiation procedure: meaningless and painful but conducive to good order and discipline. And always in the background was the memory of the thwack! The malacca cane across the hands out-stretched on the sloping desk. Mathematics = Pain. This basic formula was never forgotten.

Even the languages, which he liked, were taught like this sometimes: monotonous chanting of declensions and conjugations. It wasn't hard for him since rote learning was by now a well-honed skill and he grimly committed the stuff to memory to survive. But it was not, at this stage, fun. It was only fun when it gave a glimpse into that sunny and beautiful marble world of Greece and Rome, or when it made some aspect of France—that tantalizingly near yet as-distant-as-another-planet country, come alive. Not much came alive in the pluperfect subjunctive of irregular verbs and all that. It was learned; it was not enjoyed. The initial pleasure of new knowledge wore off. Boredom made for distraction; distraction made for gaps in information; the total made for poor marks. It was essential to please the adults, yes, but sometimes the pain was too great. He was totally unused to pleasing the adults through suffering. It was manifestly unfair. But then, as he was rapidly learning (oh such an important lesson!), life was unfair. The example of Jesus in this case didn't help. Jesus pleased his particular adult by suffering, and in the process he saved the world. The wonder boy had no such ambitions. He just wanted to survive—to get to the next foxhole. The suffering was out of all proportion to the goal.

It was almost as bad in that other area of the "well-rounded" youngster, games, gymnastics, and woodwork. These were meant, it seemed, to develop the outer man as the classroom subjects the inner. This was still the world of the "all-rounder": the perfect amateur, good at a range of things. One could get praise and recognition for being good just at scholarship or just at games, certainly, but one only got fame and glory and immortality by excelling across the board. There was, ideally, no division between nerds and jocks, between aesthetes and hearties. The school heroes he was supposed to emulate were glorious all-rounders. Boys who got Cambridge scholarships and medals for Greek verse, were honored all right, but they only became school legends if they did this and also ran a record mile or captained their college at cricket as they had captained the school. And they had to do all this with a becoming and totally charming modesty: "nothing really"—lots of chaps could do the same"—and similar nonsense. Well, he figured, this would never be for him.

He was hopeless at cricket. Unlike the other boys he had never played it before and had no natural aptitude. Thus he was relegated to long hours fielding on the boundary, where he daydreamed until frantic yells woke him to the unwelcome fact that the nasty hard ball was travelling like a vengeful comet in his direction. Rugby, oddly, he quite took to. He liked the rough and tumble. Unlike cricket, enough gusto and enthusiasm could cover up a lot of ineptitude here. He was fearless tackler where other boys held back or groped and grabbed. He loved the dive at the legs and the feel of a large body slamming into the ground. His father taught him all the clichés. "He can't run without his legs." "The bigger they are the harder they fall." For once the clichés seemed like profound wisdom, for they worked.

Again, he had no real natural aptitude, and as was the custom of the day he was relegated to the forwards—to the scrums and the line-outs, to the dog work. The runners and catchers and natural ball-handlers had the interesting positions in the backfield. He toiled away though, and didn't feel too bad in his strange "sport" even if, like algebra, it didn't seem to serve any purpose and had little, except the distant promise of glory, to feed the imagination. By far the worst thing—even worse than the "gym" with its intolerable jumping and waving and rope-climbing burns—was "woodwork." (The rough equivalent of "shop" in an American high school.) He never progressed to the higher reaches of "metalwork" since his unfathomable clumsiness was evident from the start. He could see no virtue in all this hammering, sawing and chiseling. He produced a dreadful little bookcase of zero appeal that his mother still keeps to his embarrassment.

The height of his accomplishment was a "towel roller." You planed the cylinder from a four-by-four in the junior classes; you could not use the lathe. It took hours of miserable effort. After dismal marks and piles of sarcasm from the woodwork master the final blow came when he was caught using a rasp to repair a joint he had chiseled backwards. (Had he got the mortise where the tenon should be? Who knows?) The exasperated teacher drove him from the class, hurling pieces of wood and shouting that he should never, never come back. He was sent to the headmaster and sat and waited a long time. The headmaster, a bitterly sarcastic Scot given to elaborate verbal hammerings, returned quite shaken from his visit to the woodwork room, stared at the culprit and asked, "Wha' in God's name did ye do tae Mr. Smith, boy?" Reply: the absolutely standard "I don't know, sir." But there was no punishment. Somehow the headmaster saw that there was never going to be a marriage of true minds here, and assigned the offender to extra art classes. This was fine. Art was fun. An otherwise unfair world tilted slightly in his favor again. He had made it to the next foxhole.

Even the friend thing could work to your advantage in the dash across no-man's land. Among the tortures inflicted by the system was the appalling "cross-country run." Five-plus miles of exhausting slog and scramble, whatever the weather; a menace of mud, rocks, thorns, marsh and stones that was murderous to feet shod in flimsy sneakers. This, according to the sports master, was the real "test of character." He was a miserable failure. But ingenuity and deceit could always retrieve something from the worst situation. He befriended Leslie, a headmaster's son who was a studious math wizard, and who hated the miserable cross-country as much as he did. They would stuff their math homework books under their running togs (schoolboy slang from Latin "toga") and, as was expected, fall well behind the aptly named "pack." Once it was out of sight, and at a point where the outward and inward routes came close together, they would hide in a copse and sit and do the math homework. Well, to be honest, Les did the homework. By the time it was done and fair-copied, they could hear the baying of the returning pack. Once it had passed them, they up and followed close on the heels of the hard-pounding idiots. This way they not only avoided most of the torment, got the homework done thus freeing up the evening, but into the bargain got praise from the master for catching up. It showed, he said, that they were "doing their best" and they got the usual lecture about how it wasn't winning that counted but "making the right effort." That was the stuff of character. Yes sir, they said, thank you sir. He often thought of the real no-man's land in WWI: how all those young men put their character training on the cross-country run to perfect use as they went stumbling through the Flanders mud, in a close pack, towards the machine guns, ending up dead on the barbed wire. Yes sir, thank you sir.

Yet we must be fair to that old code: the playing fields of Eton and all that. It is easy to mock; it invites cynicism when its outcome is dumb conformity and death. But more than moral lectures and fuzzy religion it gave them some sense of decency and fairness that was not all bad. (For all its datedness, is there a better summary of human decency and integrity than Kipling's "If"?) "That's not cricket" pretty well sums up the young Englishman's simple but effective morality of those times. "Fair play" was indeed the root moral imperative. The cunning Gandhi understood this with his non-violent civil disobedience. Make them feel they're not playing fair and they'll waver, was his tactic; it worked. "Sportsmanship" meant not arguing with the umpire even when he was blatantly wrong, for rules must be obeyed if a game is to be played: they understood that. It also meant not hitting a man when he was down, not taking unfair advantage, and accepting defeat gracefully ("never apologize, never complain.") "The team is more important than the player" was a guide to selflessness, as was "keep your end up"—another cricketing commandment that meant you should not put your own glory in scoring before the needs of the team. You were to "play a straight bat"—not indulge in flashy slogging, but stay with the correct "strokes" which always paid in the long run. You must always give your opponent a fair chance, never, never cheat, and even be prepared to acknowledge the virtue of good play or a win against yourself. At the end of a Rugby game the home team, whatever the result, ran off the field first, lined up in two lines, and clapped the opponents into the pavilion. You always thanked them for a good game whatever the result. Sir Henry Newbolt, Rudyard Kipling, and William Ernest Henley—the poet laureates of "The Law"—were always there to remind them that it was not winning that counted, but how you played the game.

Of course you tried your best to win, and winning was wonderful. But the moral was there for the consolation of the losers, and a good thing too. For one lost often enough, and to know you had done your best and fought the good fight was something to take home. They were a small school, all the time facing bigger and better sides. But they had a great reputation for giving their all and making their opponents fight bitterly for that win, and sometimes pulling off the big upset that made the season. They kept their fixtures because it was no disgrace for the big schools to have played and beaten them. Now was this such a bad morality to learn? Not that they always slavishly followed its strictures, the bullies certainly didn't, but it was always there as a prick to the conscience: an aptly named Jiminny Cricket. At its worst it sent young men to their deaths in uncomplaining droves: at its best it ruled with relative fairness an Empire acquired in a fit of absent mindedness, then gave it up relatively gracefully. It left a legacy of decency that is sometimes all the new nations have to cling to in the midst of their brutal post-colonial chaos—along with the cricket they often love more than independence, and certainly more than the slovenly bullies who now rule and exploit them.

But, the reader is asking, where is all the conventional biographical material? Where are the character sketches? Where the descriptions of landscapes? Where is the catalogue of contemporary events? Where the sensitive and moving portraits of family life? Where, where, where...? Where are all those things the reviewers love to catalogue? But does it matter? Some of these things have arisen and will crop up with increasing frequency as we proceed. But this is a narcissistic exercise. We are dealing, as was Browning in *Sordello*, with the development of a soul. It is purely what impinged on that soul that matters to our purpose, and at this stage in its evolution, very little of outside consequence had impinged. It was a little world, and we shall deal with its salient characteristics in due time insofar as they obtruded. We have had a miraculous birth, movie stardom, a world war, an escape from live burial, a near death experience, and a religious revelation. That should be enough to hold us for a while; for the time it takes us to discover the underlying brushstrokes, the basic dispositions. Deviousness, curiosity, wariness towards the adults, discomfort with age-mates, a probably overdeveloped memory, a devotion to the life of the imagination always ready to substitute for reality, a clumsiness with practicalities, a taste for physical violence, a too-keen sense of injustice, and a passion for reading close to dementia. It is building; it is coming along.

The combination of curiosity and earnestness as positive motivations, with dissimulation and evasion as negative ones, was not a good foundation for "character" as it was still called in those simpler days. No combination seemed to please the increasingly exasperated adults. They tried him with piano lessons since he obviously had some musical ability, but he couldn't concentrate on the necessary exercises. So they sent him to more advanced teachers who tried to make him master Bach fugues and Scarlatti sonatas before he was ready for them. In any case he neglected to practice and then made up ever more ridiculous excuses. He tried the cello in the small school orchestra, but again he wasted practice time making up dreamy melodies of his own and got no further than mastering the bass clef. But he did manage the walking cello part to Bach's misnamed *Air on a G String* and even sawed away at the first movement of the *Eine Kleine Nachtsmusik*—something that seemed worthwhile pursuing and helped erase the memories of old hatchetface and her mad musical mnemonics.

But again he couldn't concentrate on the exercises. If it didn't come easily he easily lost interest. If he couldn't just do it, then clearly he couldn't do it, and he gave up. He read the music easily enough in his head, and could compose quite intricate pieces of his own, but he rapidly became bored with repetition and the cello went the way of the piano. It was endemic, this restlessness. Once he had mastered the principles of something such that he understood how it worked, he had no interest in the drudgery of technical exercises. It was the same with languages. He loved to read through grammars and find out how languages worked, but he had no interest in the business of practice, practice, practice. Once he knew the principles he wanted to move on to a new one. The curiosity was obsessive, but it was easily satisfied; it had no depth. Somehow he was in the grip of a mania: the more information you could gather the safer you were. It was a camouflage that would get you to the next foxhole. This worked well for some things. He was always winner of the "general knowledge quizzes" that were so popular. For subjects like History and English, wide reading was considered a plus. But cautious teachers, who were alarmed by his feeding-frenzy for facts, wrote troubled term-end reports.

Part of the problem was that his own musical or reading agenda was mostly off at a tangent from the school syllabus. He followed curiosity wherever it led, not where the textbook said it should go. This became so bad that school came to seem to him like an irritating interference with learning, so he took to playing truant regularly. Perhaps he was the only schoolboy ever to skip school in order to learn? He had a pattern of irregular attendance anyway, since he was often ill and had been ever since the meningitis. His mother was also ill as often as not, and he had to stay home to do shopping and chores. So no one much questioned when he was "ill" yet another time. He was supposed to go down into the town twice a week for "sunray" treatment. He stretched it into a half-day, sometimes more. He had favorite places to go: when the weather was fine, a golf course or a cemetery—quiet places to go where he wouldn't be bothered. In the winter or on rainy days he would go to the town, to the wonderful nineteenth-century covered market: one of those neo-gothic marvels in glass and iron that has no doubt been pulled down to make a parking lot or a mosque. It had many virtues for the fugitive boy: it had several stalls that sold cheap food (he remembers pork pies, and peas with vinegar, and mugs of strong tea.) It was next to the huge and apparently unlimited Reference Library, where they would let you sit and read whatever you wanted for as long as you wanted.

Above all it had the second-hand book, sheet music and record stall. This became a second home to him. He would stand there and read tattered old books and particularly those small editions of the classics they still produced then: the Everyman Library, the Home University Library, Morley's Universal Library, the Thinkers' Library, Bohn's Libraries, the Walter Scott Library, the Phoenix Library, the Mermaid Series, Sir John Lubbock's Hundred Books. Sometimes he would buy a cheap one—a Routledge's Excelsior Series perhaps—for sixpence or so, take it and read it over his pie-and-pea lunch, then take it back and resell it. They never objected. They even smiled when they saw him coming and pointed things out to him. Occasionally he bought one and kept it if he really wanted it, like Palgrave's *Golden Treasury of English Songs and Lyrics*, and had some spare pocket money from his shilling-a-week.

Sometimes he would forego the pie and just have peas and a slice of bread and beef dripping, so he could pay for the book. He never skipped the tea. He sipped it continuously while reading—a habit he kept all his life. They liked him at the pie and pea stand and would refill his mug for free. No one questioned whether he should be at school or not. It was a safe place to be. So he devoured the little books: those volumes aptly called "Libraries." People forget the little books—the small hardbacks that came before the paperback revolution. And they were small, and had tiny print that ruined the eyes, and they were cheap, cheap, cheap. At least second hand they were cheap, and returnable! He loved one of Morley's called *Ideal Commonwealths*. It contained More's *Utopia,* Bacon's *New Atlantis*, and Campanella's *City of the Sun.* He was enthralled by the old utopias, not because he believed in them, but simply because it was amazing that one could think that way: redesigning society from scratch as it were. There was also old sheet music—ballads and popular music-hall songs, and always some ragged scores of the popular oratorios: *Messiah* (of course), *The Crucifixion, The Dream of Gerontius, The Apostles, Elijah, The Creation.* He liked to read the scores to see how they did it—how they got the effects. It amazed him how the nuts and bolts of orchestration produced those magical sounds.

Music dominated his life along with reading. They were the great escapes before politics and rugby took over. Music came first from the Church, then from the school, then from the town's remarkable musical life, but perhaps most from the BBC. When he was ill and supposedly dying his parents had bought him a small plastic (Bakelite?) wireless—a good one for its day—so he could listen to the BBC, since he was too weak to sit up to read. In the war he had listened to the "schools" broadcasts but now he spent many hours in his half-awake state, drinking in music, week after week. It was the first time he had taken orchestral music seriously—as opposed to that which accompanied the oratorios. Another of those whole new worlds opened like casements on fairylands afar. Especially at the time it was the impressionists—his first taste of them. They astonished him. That music could even sound like that. Ravel's *Introduction and Allegro* seduced him. It was, he thought, how music must sound in heaven. Perhaps being dead wouldn't be so bad if there was music like that all the time.

And Delius—that other local wonder boy—with his *First Cuckoo in Spring* and *Walk to the Paradise Garden* and *La Calinda.* Debussy, Fauré, Chausson, Saint-Saëns—they floated through him like physical surges and eddies, taking over his pain-wracked body. Handel and Mendelssohn had thrilled and enchanted, but this! The BBC was naturally big on British composers, and Elgar was already a favorite (*Enigma Variations, Pomp and Circumstance*), but of them all Vaughan Williams was king: a revered national institution, his symphonies were often played by the BBC. At first it was the smaller pieces that enthralled. *Serenade to Music* almost supplanted *Introduction and Allegro* for a while, and *The Lark Ascending* overshadowed Delius. But the Fifth Symphony was the first modern symphony he drank in and learned by heart.

One Christmas the surprise "family" present was a radiogram. It was a vast improvement on the old wireless; it didn't need the horrible heavy acid batteries that had to be carried and re-charged every weekend, and the sound, even of the 78s, was not half bad through the big console speaker. And you didn't have to wind it up. This incredible luxury (they had saved for several years to get it, since they would never buy through hire-purchase—the "never-never" was debt) enabled him to buy all nine records that made up the Fifth Symphony—one at a time with saved-up pocket money. He played them over and over while his parents were out or on days stolen from school. The strange little five-note opening, and the incredible crescendo where every instrument mounted upwards finally leaving the violins to peak and shimmer and then drop in a golden cascade. Decades later he could still close his eyes and replay the entire first movement, note for note, in his head.

At church, in the choir, he tried his hand at putting together some psalm chants. The Anglican chant might seem boring to outsiders, but it was a great school of four-part harmony. He tried a few hymn tunes as well, "Now the Day is Over" and the Scottish metrical version of the twenty-first psalm.

His music master at school, the talented and eccentric Mr. Coghill, no mean composer himself, had always said, "Try to give each part an interesting tune. Learn from the madrigals." So he tried. His twenty-first psalm was a success, except for the tenors. Giving interesting tunes to the other three parts left the tenors with a dramatic but boring single note line. So he gave them a little flourish, descending from a showy high F sung pianissimo, that he borrowed from "All in the April Evening" to end their otherwise dull first line. It was much admired and the lay reader asked him if he was going to be a composer. "I've never really had any composition lessons." "Neither did Haydn," said the lay reader. So he hit the reference library again and found a book on the lives of the great composers. Sure enough, Haydn had been bamboozled into joining the choir at the Vienna cathedral to get a musical education, but complained that he never received one. He picked it up through doing it. If it worked for Haydn, it could work for him. Composition would come through osmosis, and there would be no need for all those boring exercises.

The school had a good choir, Mr. Coghill was a fine teacher, and he was a loyal and dedicated member. He sang treble until his voice began to break. But it didn't break quickly or totally. That is, he developed a nice baritone, but he could still sing a good treble if he wanted to, and often did. The "natural" thing to do would have been to develop a counter-tenor range. But no one was so sophisticated in those days. The only exception was Fatty—every class had a Fatty—whose odd dual allegiance to High-Anglicanism and Communism left everyone bewildered. Fatty sang "male-alto" in a high-church choir, but embarrassed everyone by refusing to say the prayer for the royal family. One avoided imitating Fatty, who's odd combination of radical-ism and snobbery had him eventually owning a private school for the children of the rich, while campaigning for left-wing candidates at elections. There were altos in the choirs, of course, but except at the heady level of cathedral or college choirs, these were usually trebles who sang "second soprano." Alfred Deller had not yet popularized the voice, so our budding baritone ended up mostly singing tenor, because they were always short of tenors.

His unusual vocal range (he greatly admired Yma Sumac) led to some odd escapades over the years. Around Christmas—starting as early as November—every church, every chapel and musical society (there were many) did its *Messiah*. The culmination was the Huddersfield Choral Society and the BBC Symphony Orchestra in its grand evening-dress-only extravaganza under the direction of the ever dapper and precise Sir Malcolm Sargent. It was a northern obsession, and particularly a Yorkshire one. The local societies were always short of singers, and welcomed volunteers. So he and some choir pals became *Messiah* groupies, going round offering their services to all takers. They knew it by heart—the Novello edition. He can therefore claim to have sung all the parts in *Messiah,* including the solos, and even to have done them in one season. The record was something like thirteen *Messiahs.* Guinness doesn't have it, but that's one of its many gaps. He often thought that if all musical scores were disastrously lost—perhaps through a book-banning tyranny as in Ray Bradbury's *Fahrenheit 451*—at least *Messiah* would be safe: he could recreate it entirely from memory.

The other musical sing-fest in which he wallowed deeply and happily was the ever-present operetta, and above all the cult following of Gilbert and Sullivan. This passion he derived from his parents who were in love with Lehar, Tauber, and Romberg, even Ivor Novello, Noel Coward, and Edward German: with *The Student Prince, The Chocolate Soldier, The Red Shadow, The Waltz Dream, Bittersweet, Merrie England*—the whole panoply of light opera. This was the heyday of the local "Amateur Operatic and Dramatic Society." There were hundreds of them; some were G & S specialists. He listened to them, sang in them, and memorized them. Once, later in life, he was able, for a bet, to sing the whole of *The Pirates of Penzance*—choruses and all.

But we leap ahead in this saga of the soul. We are, at the moment, fixing the almost hallucinatory importance of music and the written word in the growing, tumbling, confused mind of the post-eleven-plus and heading-for-puberty grammar-school boy who was, to escape the miseries of a home divided and a school too unresponsive and restrictive, heading for various foxholes wherein he could lay his head, cry a little, and lose the world for a while. He made attempts to accommodate. While mathematics simply frightened him, and was not helped by a sadistic Algebra teacher who picked him up by the hair and the ears when he couldn't give the right answer, thus conjuring up old hatchetface and the mental arithmetic horrors, Geometry fascinated him. It must have been the diagrams; these he could grasp. He bothered the teacher with his puzzlement about Pi. Obviously (to him) a circle had a fixed and definite area. But in the formula for its area, one multiplied the square of the radius by the constant Pi (diameter divided by circumference) which was by definition an infinite number. The area of the circle so calculated must always therefore be an approximation: up to infinite decimal places, but still an approximation. How could this be? Could we never in fact know what the *true* area of a circle was? Did the answer have to stretch into infinity? It seemed a fair question, but as usual he was told to shut up and do the calculation.

One term, in an unusual fit of rectitude, he actually took the set books of Euclid and learned them by heart (not hard for our little rote-learning machine of the bible-class success.) On the exam he scored 100 percent. The teacher was not pleased but horrified. Clearly he had cheated. Again he was marched to the headmaster, but this time he protested his innocence. How could he have cheated without having the Euclid out on the desk? He didn't know what theorems would be set as questions. Q.E.D. The headmaster was puzzled. So a compromise was reached. Another exam was set with different theorems and he took it in the headmaster's study under that grim Scotsman's baleful gaze. Again he scored perfectly. There was no other conclusion possible: he knew the Euclid. The teacher never apologized. If anything he was treated worse for having proved the teacher wrong. It all served to increase his disgust and his truancies. In later years he was to listen to a great deal of agonizing from educationalists about the problem of boosting the "self-esteem" of their pupils—almost to the exclusion anything else. Thinking back, he saw his own early education as little more than a vicious, calculated attack on his self-esteem, from opening prayers to closing bell.

He began to develop his paranoid streak as a result of such episodes. He saw himself as the constant victim of injustice. Her attitude to the world in general had fostered this, but the shock of finding himself no longer the wonder boy had exacerbated it for sure. He was constantly at the wrong end of arguments where he knew he was in the right, but was faced with incomprehensible refusal to acknowledge it on the part of others. This was not just about opinions, but about facts. Trivial example: passing through a very small country village on a school trip by bus, one of the class said it had a cinema that held a thousand people. He said this was obviously absurd and a row ensued. Later, some classmates accused *him* of saying the village had such a cinema, and this showed he was stupid. In vain he protested and called upon them to remember what in fact had transpired. They stuck to their story. It was his first lesson in the utter unreliability of eyewitnesses, for they obviously totally believed their version. He had the same problem with people who held patently ridiculous beliefs: that Americans didn't know any "classical" music is one he remembers (he'd heard a record of the Philadelphia Orchestra playing the *New World* symphony and *Sheherazade*.) These people—some of them amazingly were adults—appeared normal, spoke normally in normal sentences, seemed quietly sane, and yet held these astonishingly idiotic beliefs about facts that could not be in dispute.

When one moved to the area of opinion it was worse, since often facts could not be adduced in refutation. But even when they could, these normal-seeming people were not moved. In the face of facts they stuck to their ridiculous opinions. Because they seemed so normal he would assume that they could be argued with and persuaded of their errors. After all, he had often been persuaded of his and had changed opinions in the face of facts that contradicted his notions, so this must be true of others. Not so. He went to a conference on missionaries organized by some church association. A very firm and confident headmistress presided. She spoke of the great benefits Christianity brought to the heathen, and after hearing some accounts of their work from "field missionaries" asked for questions. He had heard a talk on the wireless by Arnold Toynbee on "India and the West" and he asked the headmistress about Toynbee's conclusion that India (and the East in general) was willing to accept the West's technology, but rejected their values and ideas, having a long and effective tradition of their own. The headmistress called on a little Indian lady on the panel. She said that she had seen Indians during the famine years turn to Christian missionaries whom they trusted. So, said the positive headmistress, that is clearly a very profound reply from an impeccable source, next question.

She was wrong, and what she said was rubbish; it was even stupid. It didn't even address the question. But she was a headmistress, with a degree; she was an adult in authority. She had the *manner* of an adult: that infuriating self-assurance combined with superior vocabulary. It suddenly struck him that he had stumbled on the adult secret: there were really no grown-ups; *adults did not exist*. All that happened was that one's vocabulary increased and one assumed an air of self-assurance. The content was immaterial—it could be the most egregious foolishness—what counted was simply *the air of authority* in which you cloaked the idiocy. To do this effectively it was better actually to believe sincerely in the silliness you were propounding. Most adults managed this quite easily. The ones who were genuinely puzzled and uncertain and plagued with questions, were called "immature." You evidently decided (or it was somehow decided for you) what you "believed" and then you assumed the air of calm authority and maturity, and smiled tolerantly at the questioners. Not all adults managed this gracefully—some did not manage it at all, but the ones he had been taught to admire, and expected to admire, were uniformly like this, like the firmly superior headmistress. It might not seem like a world-shattering revelation, but the sudden realization that the elusive maturity was solely a matter of form, and that substance was irrelevant, was both a cold shock and a wavering hope: he was an actor, he could do maturity with a little practice.

But despite his revelation he stubbornly persisted in his pathetic faith in adult rationality, and argued away to no avail. If only he could have learned just to avoid argument with the terminally wrong and get on with his own business he would have saved years of his life. But the dogged faith in reason, combined with the puritanical insistence that the unrighteous must acknowledge their sins and atone for them, kept him busily employed in futile attempts to convert and punish the obdurately ignorant.

> *No prophecy had come to pass: his youth*
>
> *In its prime now—and where was homage poured in truth*
>
> *Upon Sordello?—born to be adored*
>
> *And suddenly discovered weak, scarce made*
>
> *To cope with any, cast into the shade*
>
> *By this and this.*

How, you ask, was he coping with his fellow pupils? He was not a popular boy, not one of the gang. He was too odd, too opinionated, too talkative, too know-all, too inclined to argue for argument's sake. He had two problems: friends and bullies. He somehow managed both. He had various friends, usually very different from himself. He drew his friends from school and church, and they did the friend things: going for Sunday walks, going to the Boy Scouts, going to the pictures (*King Kong* shattered him—it stirred something unfathomable), bicycle rides into the country, singing round the piano, and going to each others' houses for tea and play—board games mostly. He even began to enjoy his friends, having given up more or less (but with some flickers of hope) on the adults. He always had one eye cocked for the chance to dance the adults into a charmed and giving state, but he had to make peace with his peers first of all.

The bullies were another matter. They were the chief horrors of no-man's land, waiting every time you tried to go over the top. Every school had them, and reading *Tom Brown's Schooldays* proved that boarding schools were even worse. At least at day schools you could get out at the evening and at weekends. There is always a small bunch of systematic sadists, and they always have their sycophants and lackeys. The prefects—the older boys who essentially ran the school—were supposed to intervene, but they turned a blind eye. Coping with bullies was assumed to be part of "character building." One tried to steer clear of them. He had never had to fight before this; it was totally foreign to his nature. But he was a chatterbox and a know-all and hence a prime target for the philistine bullies and their toadies. The school rule of *omerta* applied as strictly as with the mafia. Whatever they did, you never told. This was the greatest of all the great schoolboy sins: the ultimate breaking of the code. And what they did varied from straight beating up and extortion to ingenious homosexual humiliations. They would capture smaller (always) boys, pull down their pants, and according to whether they were or were not circumcised assign them as "Roundheads" or "Cavaliers." Even bullying, in those days, had a touch of literacy to it. The circumcised Roundheads, of whom he was one (circumcision was routine for babies when he was born) were selected out for genital and anal tortures of various refined kinds. Most of the little boys simply took it, cried a lot, and then crawled off, too humiliated to tell or share their shame. He wouldn't take it. He knew he was going to get beaten up. That was inevitable: they were roughly five to one and bigger and older. But he was resigned to that; he knew about pain, and he preferred the pain of beating to what they would otherwise do to him.

He discovered a strategy: by hook or by crook hurt at least one of them very, very badly before they got you down and beat hell out of you. A heel brought down savagely on an instep, a toecap (all boys wore heavy lace-up boots still) smashed into a knee, and, best of all, a swift sure kick in the testicles. You usually couldn't punch because they had your arms twisted, but they were usually too stupid to grab your legs. He suffered some heavy beatings, which he took stoically, but all had been preceded by a searing scream from the badly injured bully, for he did not hold back. This he found was the secret. In most boys' fighting, even bullying, one held back: no one tried to inflict serious, breaking, dangerous damage on the other; bruises were enough. He had no such compunction. Things cracked and splintered; the school nurse had to deal with the serious results of "falls" several times. In the end the bullies left him alone. The savagery unnerved them. They couldn't "tell" either. What could they have told?

It all made his friends more than a little nervous however, which made him grateful for the loyalty of the few, for the bullies were inclined to take it out on them, and there was no way he could protect them. But he and several others did join a local athletic club where they learned to box, wrestle and fence, and he became tolerably good at all three. Thin-boned and skinny as he was, he was tall for his age and had a long reach. Boxing then was of the "keep up the straight left" variety. Knockouts were unheard of; point-scoring was every-thing. He took punishment from bigger and stronger boxers, including a broken nose, which remained permanently bent. No one bothered with re-setting such things then. You bled until it stopped, and the cartilage re-formed itself at its leisure. He didn't mind all that much; he was used to punishment from the bullies, and at least in the ring you had a fair chance to give as good as you got. But the utterly useless fencing had his wide-eyed allegiance. The sheer archaism of it, the French terms, the elegance, the point-lessness. He recited Cyrano's fencing ballade to the astonished company as he lunged. He was a pubescent decadent without knowing it.

All these activities had the latent function of keeping him away from home. There was choir practice two nights a week, athletic club one night and Saturday mornings, Boy Scouts one night, pictures Friday night, church and Sunday school and friend stuff on Sundays. On Saturday afternoon they watched school or club rugby games, and Saturday night was sacred to motor-cycle speedway (dirt track) racing, then the most "in" sport in town. During the vacations, in the summer, there were languid games of cricket on those seemingly endless summer days, arranged between church choirs or scratch teams. There were long hours hiking across the moors—only a short bus ride away. He would drag his friends to the ruins of Top Withens, the supposed site of *Wuthering Heights*, close enough to his natal village, where he would commune like a brooding Heathcliff with the souls of the three sisters whom he now knew to be the famous Brontës. He only seriously read *Wuthering Heights*; the rest were seen as women's romance slush. He would lean on the broken windowsill at twilight, close his eyes, and imagine the ghost of Cathy crying out in the night. Sometimes he would just walk by himself to a place where he could see nothing in any direction but the moors themselves; noth-ing but heather and rocks stretching to a purple horizon. Perhaps nowhere else in England could you stand in the midst of such pure wilderness. At twilight again he could positively feel himself as the anguished Heathcliff howling for his lost love. In more healthy daylight moments they went cycling up the Dales to the Lake District, where they read Wordsworth while boating on Windermere. They stayed in rough but cheap youth hostels, and drank the still clear and clean river water, and used it to cook simple campfire stews of sausage and potato, flavored with wild thyme and mint.

The cinema ("pictures") became more and more important. Every Friday night, and at the Saturday morning cinema club, in the wonderfully lavish picture palaces (Odeon or Gaumont), the gang of schoolboy movie buffs lapped up whatever was going. They were omnivorous and took in everything pretty uncritically, but they were limited by the sensibilities of the British Board of Film Censors. There was a slew of nostalgic Empire movies of *The Four Feathers, Lives of a Bengal Lancer, Charge of the Light Brigade* style, including *Gunga Din*—the best movie ever, no question, no argument. There were the much-admired Olivier films of *Henry* V, *Hamlet,* and *Richard III,* that set off a passionate devotion to Shakespeare well before the Bard became required reading at school. The Orson Welles *Macbeth* was perhaps an even more shocking revelation of Shakespearean power. The Ealing comedies and Alastair Sim convulsed them all. David Lean was the great director, while Alec Guinness was accounted—rightly—a great genius.

Above all, he wanted to be (not be like, *be*) James Mason: that voice, that power. When Mason took the whip to Margaret Lockwood in *The Man in Gray* he aroused emotions impossible to assess but impossible to ignore: strange, spooky things. Light relief came from Chaplin and the Marx brothers. He was drawn to the oddity of Groucho, his outrageous puns and the odd little songs he sang: "show me a rose/Or leave me alone." He never got the supposed humor in the Three Stooges, but laughed politely to go along. The Tarzan films were popular with the boys, but he hated them. He had read the books, and even in these relatively uncritical years he could see how bad the movies were; they were wretched caricatures of the Tarzan stories he loved so much.

There were films that schoolboys were not supposed to see, including those of Esther Williams with all those ladies in bathing suits. He pretended to a drooling interest, but again he found them boring, and couldn't see the point of the fuss. Some of the gang dressed up in overalls to look like mill workers, hence over sixteen and qualified to see *The Outlaw* with the dangerous Miss Russell. He liked the story of Billy the Kid, but he had to pretend again that he understood the danger posed by Miss Russell's tight sweaters and uplift bra. These prohibitions continued to puzzle. The popular song "I'd like to get you on a slow boat to China/All to myself alone" was officially banned for its "suggestive content." Suggestive of what? he wondered. Unrelieved boredom most likely. Were there books on the boat? The BBC? Cinema? No matter: American films, largely Westerns and gangsters, and glorious film noir (Bogart and Mitchum as cynical tough-guys easily ousting the old-colonial chaps,) gave them a nicely skewed version of the USA, tempered only by the sanity of Alistair Cooke's weekly radio *Letter from America.*

For the BBC continued to be, in those pre-television days, the major source of information and daily pleasure. The families would sit watching the "wireless" as if it were a television. But the pictures were in their heads. The imagination was ruthlessly stimulated. There was the music, but also a smorgasbord of serials, comedies, documentaries, news programs, "talks" on all possible subjects, straight plays (especially Shakespeare and Shaw—and of course Sherlock Holmes), children's programs, the frightening "Man in Black" with his horror playlets, and serial book readings. He listened to all he could, especially "Book at Bedtime." Many books he knows quite well—most of the nineteenth-century novelists like Dickens, Trollope and Thackeray, for example—he in fact never read. He heard them on Book at Bedtime, unabridged, dramatically read, unforgettable. He particularly liked the "Brains Trust" and especially the crusty and eloquent Professor C. E. M. Joad, who actually sounded as if he wore pince nez and a goatee. It made him wonder what a "philosopher" really was; it was obviously something very important and got you on the BBC spouting about everything with eye-popping confidence. Most of the comedies (ITMA, Round the Horne, and the like) date horribly, but they culminated in the brilliantly funny Goon Show, the British Theatre of the Absurd, and the precursor of all that genre up to Monty Python. God bless Spike Milligan and Peter Sellers! Then came the astonishing Third Programme (was it in '49?), much the target of satire and scorn from the philistines, but altogether riveting for him with its concerts and lectures and solemn discussions. Above all the exponential increase in scrumptious, lovely music. God bless Auntie!

All was not hell at home. There were inexplicable truces. There were holidays together like before the war, at seaside towns. There was Blackpool with its Eiffel-like tower, its tooth-rotting "rock"—pure sugar, and its cheerful vulgarity. Scarborough, with its faded gentility, and its beautiful open-air theater where he saw an operatic version of *Hiawatha's Wedding Feast* by Coleridge-Taylor, with Indians in canoes on an artificial lake, at night, with torches. He swore to learn "Onaway, Awake Beloved" once his voice broke. There was a coach trip to north Wales where he heard Welsh spoken for the first time, in Harlech—it was a trip around famous castles. Back home he hit the bookstall and found an "imitated pronunciation" teach-yourself Welsh book, convinced he was going to return and speak this beautiful language for himself. He did learn a few Welsh songs (*Cwm Rhondda—Sospan Bach*) from old 78s, but that was as far as it went. She was devoted to stately homes so they did the local big houses (Harewood), and he liked the Abbeys (Fountains, Rivaulx), the Priories (Bolton), the Minsters (York), and Cathedrals

(Ripon, Durham.) If you have never heard sung Evensong in one of the spectacular English cathedrals, you have never understood what being English is all about (or at least used to be about.) In these peaceful family moments—even the Saturday evenings at the speedway, which he spent with his parents rather than his friends—his heart almost broke, for he knew they were only interludes. Once the cease-fire failed he was back to fleeing home again.

He only once spent any time in the mill where the happy warrior had become the resigned worker. It appalled him. He liked to see his father in charge of such immense power, knowing how everything about the huge wool-processing machines worked. He seemed larger and more important than he ever could be at home. The looming tweed-suited big-voiced owner, Sir Kenneth, straight out of *The Crowthers of Bankdam*, announced that they "didn't make men like your father any more." But how could anyone stand the unceasing screeching hammering racket? And the stench! Boiling wool had a smell that dwarfed the stink of rotting corpses and leaking gas mains. It was a vision of hell and he was glad to escape it. Now he thought he knew what she might mean, and that he should do anything to avoiding ending up there. But he went there to look, and then swore a silent oath that he would not, ever, have to work in such a place. They were doing "The Industrial Revolution" in History class, and the visit to the mill had been part of the class project. He wrote his report, which he called, predictably, "Dark Satanic Mills" and which turned into a hymn of praise for the bucolic paradise that had been usurped so that wealth could accumulate and men decay. He was still at heart the country boy, of the whispering moorlands, the dripping fens, the villaged woodlands; of the bird watching, the barge sailing, the fox hunting.

He often thought of running away, but he didn't know how or where. When the fair came each year to the local park he used to watch in fascination the Gypsy boys who ran the stalls and rides and lived in caravans and seemed so free and confident. He had read all the Tarzan books by now and had fantasies about living in the forest and leaping on—what? to rip out its throat and secure his food. Probably a badger. He read a critic of Burroughs who poured scorn on the author for making his apes carnivorous and predatory, when one knew them to be vegetarian. This bothered him; he didn't like his hero authors to be at fault. But he had seen the canines of chimps in zoos and was not convinced. What irony that one day he was to be involved in proving them to be flesh-eating hunters after all. Edgar Rice Burroughs vindicated! (But oh my how we jump ahead. Steady!)

There were other escapes that let his fevered mind spill over into fantasy while guiding it down useful culverts. There was the very fine museum (and art gallery) in the town's spacious park, where he spent many a Sunday afternoon after Sunday school. (His mother and father helped to run the café there at weekends for a while; they were locally famous for their homemade cakes and scones.) Here the assemblage of stone-, bronze-, and iron-age artifacts held him in trance-like fascination. They were collected from the moors where he had grown up, and this sense of familiarity with these ancient savage times, fueled by the BBC's reporter from the past and something indefinable from *King Kong*, sent him into transports. He was fascinated by the "ring stones"—boulders with hundreds of little circular indentations in them. No one knew what they were for: perhaps a counting device, or some kind of star map or calendar? The museum organized "field trips" to the actual sites out on the moors, and he went along to trudge in the field furrows that scored the hillsides with their unnatural regular lines, and which he now knew to be three-thousand years old, like the circles of stone that marked the walls of the pit houses. He imagined himself there, feet wrapped in animal skins, hoeing the furrow with a crude flint-edged stick. There were ring stones still in place and he would lie on them and put his fingers in the holes until all ten were accounted for. Somehow it seemed to give him some kind of direct contact with the old ones, and he shivered with the occult thrill of it.

In the little town up the valley where the miracle birth occurred, and which they visited often, there was a smaller park and museum. It had a magic addition: a conservatory of high-Victorian glass, whose dank, humid interior housed a miniature rain forest, incongruously planted in the midst of those cold, bleak, northern moorlands. To add to the realism, there were huge, brilliantly colored parrots, macaws, peacocks and other exotic jungle birds, sitting and strutting in the dark green ferns and palms and vines. For a brief time there he could be Tarzan, naked and wild, communing with the sinister, beautiful birds that stared at you with their intelligent, hard eyes. They appraised you, found you wanting, and ignored you. You were only passing through their world; you were not food, you were trivial to them. It was best to go there in the winter, so you could step from the frozen white outside and have the hot wet air and dank green finery and the colored denizens overwhelm you suddenly and make you almost pass out. It was a sensation like the ring stones. What things fill a boy's mind with wonder? Those things that are absolutely strange, yet which he knows were somehow always part of him.

Most of the time he had to make do with his usual foxholes, and he buried himself in books and music, boxing and fencing. He was of course at church a lot, but he couldn't be said to have buried himself in religion. It was the music he went for. The vicar thing had faded and he dropped it. He had no idea what he would do. His only interest was in escape. For one summer vacation he got a scholarship to a Royal School of Church Music summer session at Rossal School in Lancashire. The taste of boarding school living, straight out of Tom Brown, with the gothic (if Victorian mock gothic) houses, chapel, dining hall and classrooms and quadrangles, gave him a taste of this impossible refuge from home that was hard to give up. Once, his school's junior cricket team played a team from a "reform school." It was evidently doing them a great favor and was virtuous and charitable. The "reform boys" all had neat gray uniforms and seemed happy enough and talked about their dorms and comradeship. This seemed like a possible answer. But how did you get to a reform school, or "Borstal"? You had to do something very bad like stealing stuff from shops, he was told. He hung around shops and made tentative moves, but no one seemed to notice and he found he hadn't the nerve to steal the stuff anyway. This was no better than running away. But a change was to come.

He couldn't really date the change. It came partly with the impending terror of the School Certificate exams. These were taken at age fifteen—most people left at fifteen or sixteen; only the elite who did super well stayed on in the sixth form to become prefects, run the school and prepare for college or university. At the time he had no such ambitions and no one seemed to have them for him. His record was just too dismal even if his talent was recognized now and then. It must have been at age fourteen or so that some serious attention was paid to this ordeal by public examination, and you were turned over to the senior masters for preparation in the eight or nine subjects required. Quite suddenly things did change. Two masters in particular began to take his shallow but extensive knowledge seriously enough to engage him in his dance again, and two casual encounters were to fix his attention on journalism and politics as possibilities for entry to the elusive adult world.

At this point we might very well pause, because at this point the contact begins to feel a little stronger. Oh dear—another digression on the impossibility of autobiography? No, but when you are fifty-odd years from the events and have not visited the place except briefly in thirty years, you do only have the haziest notion of chronology and connections. Certain people and events come back vividly. Others that must have been critically important in their ways have sunk forever under the flood of subsequent trivialities. This business of dredging them up is painful: a pulling of psychic teeth that causes massive invasions from the subconscious in the form of exhausting nightmares. And what do we mostly remember and dream about? The great triumphs, the happiness, the good times, or even the major disasters and tragedies of death and loss? Not at all. It is *the social embarrassments* that overwhelm us, and stick in our underground memories. They surface again and again. We are such intensely social creatures that our social failures—our constant fear of ostracism, of solitary confinement, banishment or exile—are what sit heavily on our backs long after the world—even our little personal world—has forgotten them. Told of some of the most excruciating things later, friends, enemies and teachers, had all forgotten them, or denied they ever happened. What they tended to remember were things that seemed inconsequential or trivial: things that seemed to matter to them, or that they had, for God knows what reason, remembered.

But here we have it. Our miracle boy who had danced and suffered his way into the adult hearts, and thought himself set for a future as a golden favorite had, after an initial flourish, been rudely cast down—shattered even. His life had gone from a lyric roundelay to a cacophony of humiliation and misery. The dance had lost its magic. He had somehow to find his way again, find a new dance. He already knew that erudition dazzled them, and that it was the only soft-shoe shuffle he had left in his repertoire. He had to work on that. It wasn't hard: he was still reading like a junkie and was king of the general knowledge quiz circuit. He always knew what the Koran was, or where the Golden Horn was, or what tapioca was made from, or to whom Eleanor of Aquitaine was married, or what the original thirteen American colonies were, or who was the last of the Ptolomies, or who were the Boyars, or what a dirigible was… It was endless and easy. There were those rainy days when he was escaping algebra, and the reference library and the bookstall beckoned. There were those evenings when he retreated to his bedroom, turned up the music on the BBC—*Brigg Fair, The Wasps*—and read himself silly. Being "sickly" he was often in bed at home and reading and music were positively prescribed. That was when he got to spend days in his parents' bedroom because it had a fireplace and the sick boy had to be warm. Wrapped in a blanket before the mesmerizing fire, armed with a pile of books and fortified with lemon and barley water (homemade), he was ill but happy, and the thought of school again was unbearable.

Up to this point his considerable but haphazard erudition hadn't been much use with the adults, as we have seen, because it was his syllabus, not theirs. From their (not unreasonable) point of view, he was lazy and disobedient and failed at his appointed tasks. "Could do better if he would apply himself," read the inevitable comment on the school report, or with more of a flourish, "He wants the palm without the dust." And if we are looking for the development of the soul's dispositions, here is one: anything defined as compulsory work was to be avoided. It had to be defined as "fun"—as his own interest—to be acceptable. The only way he could get assignments done was to trick himself—to pretend that he wanted to do them for his own amusement. Robert Benchley confirmed that this kind of self-delusion was the only way to get things done. It didn't work with algebra.

But the change to the senior syllabus had two soul-forming effects. The senior English master was yet another Scot (why did they all come south?), gray and aged, with huge bristling white eyebrows. He was affectionately known as Basher Birrel for his readiness to clap the ears of those who couldn't construe a sentence quickly. But he never hit in anger, only for ignorance. Once, in a moment of confidence, Basher told of how as a boy in Scotland he was only ever beaten for ignorance. "What did they do when you were naughty?" "They rrreasoned with me." It was then that he realized that the Scots were truly different, and it scared him a little and made him more attentive. To understand the sea change about to be wrought you must understand the mores of such schools. There was a great taboo against "putting on side." Basically this was a taboo against boasting and pretension, and no bad thing in general. But it permeated the classroom: one should not be obviously outstanding and different and certainly not "better" than the others. One should not, for example, pronounce French with too correct an accent or intonation. This would be putting on side. Obviously some would do better than others, but they should be apologetic and reserved about it—attribute it to luck and so on. Thus, in the compulsory weekly English essay, one did a neat, preferably factual little thing of the "What I did on my vacation" genre. One did not show off with any kind of individual writing style. Teachers accepted this, expected it. The consensus took it for granted. Get the grammar right and that was enough; style was not considered: a boring formula, but a safe one.

He had read the great essayists in several of the little books, and collections of "Modern Masters of the English Essay" were assigned in class: G. K. Chesterton, V. S. Pritchett, George Orwell, and the local hero J. B. Priestley among others. He loved the broadcast essay of Alistair Cooke's "Letter from America"—along with the cinema it excited his interest in the USA. But no students thought to write like that. However, something happened in his new senior English class. One day, in fit of disgust, Basher threw their essays back at them. "You people are afrrraid tae wrrrrite!" he sneered. "Do me somethin' that disnae send me tae sleep!" It was an invitation of sorts, so he took it. The set essay topics were always trivial—this one was "pockets" or something such. Drawing on every trick from Addison and Steele through Lamb, Hazlitt, and de Quincey, to Alistair Cooke, he crafted an elegant and even funny piece, with cunning digressions that led back to the main subject, odd allusions, Latin puns, Shakespeare misquotes, and all. Basher read it out to the embarrassed class with obvious glee and announced "We have a borrrn wrrriter in this class!"

It was like a spiritual rebirth. Suddenly he could dance again. He could come out of the foxhole and hop and skip and cavort, even if only in the weekly essay. It was something. It made up for the pain. God knows he offended the cantankerous Scot in almost every other way, but the old fellow seemed willing to forgive him a lot for his limitless quotes and clever long sentences. He began to see how long he could make the sentences without losing the grammar or the sense. They got to paragraph length at times, and he got away with it. It was his first taste of the heady idea that you could actually do things with words and sentences—carve, create, manipulate. But not with his other new mentor in History. Mr. Whatmuff was down-to-earth and thorough: a devout Baptist and exemplar of the best of the Protestant ethic, but a wonderfully imaginative teacher who made history come to life. "Write short sentences," he said. "You otherwise tend to elevate style over substance. History is about substance." So he wrote short sentences and developed substance. Mr. Whatmuff did not mind, or at least never complained about, his incessant questions and observations. Mr. Whatmuff's patience was Jobian, and he would never have dreamed of hitting anyone. Between the encouragement of style in English, and substance in History, he was actually getting good marks for a change, and, more importantly, regaining a sense of what pleased the adults. He worked indifferently at languages and miserably at math and science—but he did well at art for that was pure enjoyment. But Mr. Birrel's challenge and Mr. Whatmuff's stimulation hauled him up from the slough of despond and set his pilgrim feet once again on the (albeit mist shrouded) mountain.

The two casual remarks? Buoyed by the success of his essays he began writing almost as much as reading. He imitated every poet he knew and covered all styles and genres, partly deliberately, partly because he didn't know what else to do. He had, as they say, no voice of his own. He wrote some things for the church Parish Magazine—just amusing snippets about choir outings and the like, and little satires for the School Magazine, and skits for the end-of-term festivities. The Boy Scouts and church together, to raise money, put on a "flower festival" selling flowers, bulbs and plants, and having an evening entertainment of "flower songs." He wrote some verses to introduce each of the songs ("The Floral Dance" "The Perfect English Rose," even, "I'm a Lonely Little Petunia in an Onion Patch"). It was easy enough. A church elder, Mr. Needham, a churchwarden and life-long bachelor (this is only mentioned because there still were such, known as such, and honorably so), had followed his pieces and one day casually remarked: "I suppose you're planning to use these writing talents? Perhaps you'll be a journalist?"

A journalist! *Journalist*! It was another of those epiphanies. Sure enough, newspapers were taken at home, one national daily (the *Daily Mail*) and the local evening paper (the *Telegraph and Argus*.) He devoured them as he devoured all print. But as with books, he took them entirely for granted. He had no idea, nor did he care, how they came to appear on the shelves or pop through the letterbox. "They" took care of that. It was a service the adults performed like so many others. But from that day on he began to read about newspapers—to find boy's stories about young men who made it in the newspaper world. It was blindingly clear. His shallow voracity for facts, his flashy but undoubtedly effective talent for assembling them into readable prose, these were the very things that "journalism" was about. It was the obvious outlet. It was a kind of salvation, at least for this world; by now the terrors of the next had taken second place. He discovered there were such things as "foreign correspondents" and even better "war correspondents" and these promised to add travel and adventure to the mix. It had everything. Then there were the essayists and "critics": you got to sound off your opinions in readable prose and people ("editors") actually paid you to do it. It seemed too good to be true.

Instead of solemnly announcing he was going to be a vicar (he'd actually given up on that since no one now believed him) he announced casually that he was thinking of journalism—"perhaps a foreign correspondent"—people were equally impressed. The adults nodded sagely, waved their pipes and talked of it as a "risky career" but one with "good prospects" for the right person. They professed to admire his courage in "striking out" in such a direction as opposed to the "safe alternatives" of teaching or banking. He was often told he would need shorthand and typing. The latter was impossible as yet, but he hit the bookstall again and there indeed was a second-hand Pitman's manual. He started on the squiggles, not with much enthusiasm, but with an initial seriousness of purpose. He didn't see himself as a "reporter," although he knew that was where he must start (a "cub" reporter), but as a "correspondent" or "critic"—one of the loftier rungs. Aim high, they always told him. So his days of dodging and hiding would have to end. He would now have to crawl out of the foxhole and go over the top.

Yes, it was perfect. Whatmuff and Birrel hammered at him however. Style was all very well, but substance, facts, they were the essence of journalism. He didn't find this a problem with Literature and History, for he enjoyed both, and he could still fairly easily commit facts to memory. Yes, they kept the reins on. "He too easily allows cleverness of writing to substitute for soundness of argument," wrote Mr. Whatmuff in the by-now familiar tone of the end-of-term report. "While breadth of reading is to be commended," wrote Mr. Birrel, "he must try to pay more attention to the set texts." The old problems wouldn't go away. Set texts were "work" and this must be avoided. This attitude spoiled his otherwise obvious talent for languages: in Latin, Greek, and French he mastered the grammar easily enough, but wouldn't work on the texts. But they were pounded away at in class where he couldn't avoid them, and he could memorize whole scads of them for regurgitation purposes in the exams. History was tougher, but again Mr. Whatmuff's well-organized classroom lessons, and devotion to the material and the students, were not only an object lesson in good teaching, but did half the work anyway. He fought down the revulsion to do "set" homework in these subjects at least.

As his school life—or some of it—got slowly back on track, as the new dance steps worked their new charm ("a natural essay writer"—"the makings of a good historian"), the second shoe dropped. Exactly how it happened he doesn't remember. Somehow through some contact at school or church, or through some friends of his parents, or through the tennis club, or something, it was suggested he join the Young Conservatives. He knew his parents were Conservatives; at least they voted that way, although they took no active part in politics. The papers they read were Conservative, and come election time the usual Conservative clichés were repeated, the votes cast, and that was that. These were the post-war years of the crusading but beleaguered Labour government. It was, in retrospect, one of the great reforming governments.

But its reforms were a mixture of the humane (National Health Service, Education Act) and the socialist doctrinaire (Nationalization). They were attempted in a devastated economy shattered by World War II and sabotaged by outdated management and rapacious labor unions; in 1947 potatoes, clothes, coal and bread were still rationed. Austerity had become something like a force of nature.

He wasn't clear in any fundamental way why they were Conservatives (Tories to the Labour enemy.) To his father it was something to do with old soldiery: The Empire, King, and Country. To his mother it was largely to do with respectability and the Church of England ("the Tory Party at prayer.") Most of his friends, like their parents, were Conservatives. It wasn't one of the things he'd given much thought to, unlike religion, although he had an inbuilt horror of the authoritarian and doctrinal tone of the Labour party. They sounded like those old Utopians in the little books: we-know-how-the-world-should-work-and-you-must-all-do-it-our-way-for-your-own-good. They sounded like a party of bullying schoolmasters. The Tories, on the other hand, seemed to figure that the world was better off muddling along as it always had, tinkering with this and that, but not changing any fundamentals. Nothing he read in history inclined him to doubt this. The major meddlers—even those with the very best intentions—were always major trouble: look at those Roundheads and Jacobins, obvious ancestors of the do-it-our-way-or-else socialists.

He didn't know what to make of the Soviet Union, to which the Left in those days was still inclined to prostrate itself like Muslims to Mecca. They had been our great and good allies in the war. Uncle Joe Stalin had beamed benignly from posters, and schoolchildren, him included, had contributed their pennies to buy the jewel-encrusted Stalingrad sword in genuine admiration for the courage of that splendid city. But now they were our enemies. It was an Orwellian switch that baffled him, but it did seem that they were another of those arrogant, assertive attempts to re-write the book of history, an attempt that had gone wrong. The book of history wrote itself. We read it, learned from it, and turned to the next page. If he had any political philosophy at all this was more or less it, and it was more or less conservative in a broad sense, and all a relatively indifferent fourteen-year-old could manage.

The local ward where his church was located was trying to organize a branch of the Young Conservatives. He was invited to go along. The meeting was to be at the Conservative Club, an unquestionably adult institution. This alone was enough temptation. He put on his new long trousers—another rite of passage into adulthood bought for Easter Sunday, and his weekend sports coat (shedding the tell-tale school blazer.) The crowd surprised him; he thought "young" meant at least under twenty-one, but evidently Young Conservatives went up to thirty. They were all much older than he, but seemed charmed that should be there. They appeared to like his chatter, and his ambition to be a "political journalist." He moved quickly on his feet when the dance called for it. When the time came for nominations for the shiny new offices, someone nominated him for treasurer. But the thunderbolt was not so much the nomination itself as the words: "I propose Mister ..."

MISTER. MIIIIISTER. Mr. The word rolled around his head like a pinball banging about, ringing bells and lighting lights. They had accepted him without question as one of them, as an adult. It had happened. He was no longer a despised and humiliated schoolboy, he was a Mister, an adult, a Treasurer, a "party official"—a thing of the adult world; he was a creature of the mystery he had so long sought to understand. In one flick of the comb, one straightening of the tie, he had made the leap. And the Young Conservatives had done it for him. They were to have his unreasoning loyalty for a long time in consequence.

Remember, in those late forties there were no "teenagers"; that was a later American invention. The word was unknown. You were simply a "schoolboy" or colloquially a "lad." Then you worked and while still an apprentice you were still a lad, or perhaps a "young man." If you went to college or university you became that half-real creature a "student." But otherwise you stayed juvenile until you joined fully the profession or the union or whatever, and these, like marriage, gave you adult status. But here, suddenly, he was Mr. Mister. The heart of the Mistery. He floated home and announced that his life forthwith would be devoted to the Young Conservatives, Winston Churchill, Anthony Eden, Rab Butler, Harold Macmillan, Quintin Hogg, and the defeat of the socialist takeover: Attlee, Bevan, Bevin, Cripps, Foot. All must go! Running for the foxholes was over. Life had a purpose. They were pleased.

Since we are recording a profound change in the development of the soul, we have to add one unlikely thing that served to buttress the change and intensify it: Rugby Football. Again, it is not our business to judge or weight these things; we can only pick up the things that vibrate with the most resonance for this soul: the things that made a difference in the short and the long run. Rugby was surely one. To persuade the little delinquent that it was worthwhile to toe the line and become a pillar of the community, something was needed as bait. Politics was indeed to play its part, but it was not enough that he had decided his future lay in Parliament ("Into Parliament, into Parliament, Parliament, Parliament he shall go.") This was only his personal ambition. It was necessary to have some real achievement in the real world—as it was locally defined. He had always liked Rugby, as we have seen, but he had been defined as one of the toilers in the field: OK to fill a place in the scrum (loose forward at the back) but not skillful enough with the ball to take one of the elevated positions among the backs. Then, in one of those sudden redefinitions of the situation that he was experiencing more and more, he one day picked up a loose ball in the backfield and wove and dodged and sped his way down three-quarters of the field to score a glorious solo try. The games

master was impressed; his peers were amazed. He could handle the ball and he was fast. Overnight his status changed. He was moved to the backfield. This was like singing solos in Messiah: glorious flights of invention and all attention on him: the nippy fly-half with the magic feet.

But this was just a beginning. He was still a raw talent fifth former and the School first and second fifteens were drawn largely from the sixth form. His newfound success was essentially in-house (literally—playing on the House team.) But there were outside outlets that had the advantage of being forbidden fruit, and so appealed to the delinquent in him. Reader, the subtlety of British class-sports distinctions is not really our business. They are part of the ingrained snobbery of British life that give it a lot of dramatic color, and a great deal of personal pain. But to follow you must know a minimum. There were two codes of Rugby Football. There was the original middle- and upper-class amateur version, founded at Dr. Arnold's great Rugby School, when the immortal William Ellis decided to pick up a soccer ball and run with it. This was known as Rugby Union, had fifteen players a side, and was played by schools and colleges and the gentlemanly sports clubs. Then there was the other, derivative, professional version, Rugby League, played with thirteen players and different rules (but basically the same game) and with a largely working class following in the northern industrial towns. (Soccer was a proletarian affair entirely, played only for amusement.) To complicate matters there were also amateur leagues, formed among chapels, boys clubs, and the like, that played according to the professional rules: amateur Rugby League. In his newfound passion for Rugby, in any of its forms, he turned to playing this amateur version of the pro game for a local club.

He was on dangerous ground. The dividing line between the codes was rigid. The great school hero, Jack Kitching, had switched codes and ended up playing center three-quarter for England in the professional game. The boys had to worship him in private, for the headmaster refused to allow his name to be spoken in the school. But the pull of Rugby was too great, and so it was to the junior team of a local club, coached by another great England player, prop-forward Frank Whitcombe, that he turned, and received a brutal schooling in the no-nonsense and very ungentlemanly bone-crushing amateur-pro game. These players were not nice middle-class boys; they were mill-hands and street toughs, chapel boys and cigarette smokers. They were old beyond their years and cynically unsentimental. They played as they lived—hard. And how they cursed. His vocabulary was bloated with novel obscenities; but with words and phrases useless except on the restricted field of play. The upshot was that he learned to play with a kind of ruthless ferocity that intimidated his school-fellows and shot him up to the School second then the first fifteen, and hence away from the necessity of clandestine Rugby League.

In one year he strode into the top ranks of school Rugby, and for the moment there was no higher he could go in this little world. He genuinely loved the game. He began to live for it. He couldn't get enough games. He played twice a week at school in inter-House and inter-school games, and often picked up club games (strictly Rugby Union) with adults twice his size and weight at weekends. He often played two games in one day, and one on a weeknight. He was ridiculously under weight—a mere 110 lbs.—and with his small and brittle bones was in constant danger of injury. But he made up for this lack with a nippiness and nimbleness—a kind of artful dodger syndrome. He developed his technique of tackling, avoiding the thighs, where you were taught to tackle, and going low for the ankles and the truly satisfying crash to earth of an opponent twice the weight. This carried the risk of being kicked in the face, which he was several times. He bore the resulting wounds proudly through his life like dueling scars, and entered them on his passport under "distinguishing marks." To add to his marketabilty he became a good place kicker, spending whole lunch hours in practice. His drop kick was thing of beauty.

The point of all this, patient reader, is that he was now the all-rounder (his cricket even improved a bit—some of the Rugby confidence spilled over) and could look to a different kind of place and future. He had made it to a significant foxhole. The sixth form, prefecture, university: these things no longer seemed like pointless ambitions reserved for the golden elite that he could never join. He could easily slip into the young-gentlemanly, sporty, eloquent, scholarly role that had seemed so elusive before. It was a different dance, to be sure, but the basics were the same.

There was a fascinating new world out there. The adults were still the key, but one could still impress them with the right steps, and they would smooth the way to Olympus. Rugby, politics and music—still music. A potent mix. A magical formula. Journalist and M.P. were still possibilities, but one could take the higher route to both. He began to pay more attention to the prefects. He began to imitate their lofty manners, to chatter less, to be less of a class clown, to affect a bored indifference to childish things. He was seen openly reading poetry and casting pensive glances at the landscape, talking more languidly and with less earnestness and more irony, cultivating a world weariness along with punctilious good manners, and above all being elegant and successful without appearing to try. One must never appear to be trying too hard. It should appear to come easily, whatever the secret sacrifice. He was, as we know, quick on his feet. The transformation from the awkward clog dance of the unhappy schoolboy to the graceful galliard of the young lordling, did not appear, at first, too troublesome.

3

The Youth:
Coming in on Roller Skates

Fred Astaire—the incomparable, the unique, the prince of elegance, the king of charm, who danced away our unhappiness through the Depression, the war, the austerity—wasn't much given to commentary on his films. He did, however, discuss *Shall We Dance* in an interview once, and made a telling observation. The film was not well crafted (how many were? Fred danced them out of trouble most of the time) and they reached a point where they had to go on filming but had no idea how to advance the plot. The compromise was to do an awkward and pointless dance on roller skates, to the tune of "Let's Call the Whole Thing Off." It was only saved by the inability of Astaire and Rogers to do anything wholly bad (even if no one had ever said "potahto.") Fred was of the opinion that whenever you saw the hero coming in on roller skates, you could be sure the director was completely at a loss. The roller skates were enough of a novel distraction that they kept the audience from realizing that the plot was going nowhere, and probably had nowhere to go.

Examinations were to dominate his life for the next decade. If the unexamined life is not worth living, then Socrates would surely have found his sixth-form life the most worthwhile of any, for he was dizzy with examination. As a child of the meritocracy, the Eleven-plus was obviously his baptism, even if he hadn't realized he was taking it. There were exams at the Grammar School all the time, but they were in-house affairs that determined one's ranking in the class—something that he didn't pay much attention to. She did, and it led to constant traumas— "I've come up from seventh to fifth"—"If you can be fifth, why can't you be fourth?" He felt it would be unkind ever to be first (not that there was any danger) since it would take away her best lines. He had dreams in which he became prime minister, and she demanded, "Why couldn't you have been king?"

It was all a spur to greater effort, he supposed. But the exams, which now dominated, were public exams and they ruthlessly determined one's fate. The

Eleven-plus weeded out some eighty percent of the age cohort. The School
Certificate weeded out three-quarters of those left. Then the Higher School
Certificate cut down the proportion of those going to university to about four
percent. Open Scholarship exams showed who of that tiny percentage were of
the élite—reducing it to less than one percent. Degree examinations equally
ruthlessly ranked the four-percent from the very few Firsts to the mere Passes.
American friends could not understand why higher degrees were not a necessity for academic appointments in Britain. He had to explain that if you had
an Open Scholarship and a First, you represented a tiny fraction of one percent of the age group. Further selection was pointless. Post-graduate degrees
were often a way those with second-class undergraduate degrees made up for
a bad start.

The system would let you climb to very top of the meritocratic ladder, but
the price was constant high performance in public examinations, set and
marked by impartial people you did not know, and who did not know or care
personally about you. They cared about "standards"—and God help you if
you fell below the highest. Most people quit along the way, opting for ap-
prenticeships, or professional courses, or night classes: all easier ways to a
decent living. There was no disgrace in this back then; it was a choice you
made. Not everyone wanted to go to university. To the vast majority it was not
even an appealing route to worldly success. To go often far away from home,
to live in dormitories, to struggle and survive in that competitive world, in
that medieval educational system—often in those days monastic in its sex-
segregation, was distinctly unappetizing.

It was accepted that only the "very academically gifted" went that probing
route. You could become a lawyer, an architect, a banker, a civil servant, an
engineer, a pharmacist, a nurse, even a dentist (but not a doctor) by the "professional qualifications" route, which had the advantage that you could earn
while you learned. "College" was for the gifted few, and there was no resentment of them. There was rather an admiration, as for outstanding athletes who
did expertly what you tried, but only did indifferently. It was recognized that
the examinations were tough, impartial, public and unforgiving. Pass or out:
no social promotion for the little meritocrats. Thus "students" (especially
medical students) were allowed some excessive high jinks, without much
sanction, as compensation for the arduous uncertainty of their constantly
examined lives, and their future usefulness to society.

We are setting the scene, since the newly emboldened and ambitious boy,
translated into a Mr., at least out of school, had decided that with a few
adjustments he could probably make it up the ladder of merit. He didn't mind
exams all that much, at least in the humanistic subjects he enjoyed, since it
was largely a matter of making the little you knew go a long way with the
appropriate window dressing. He could strap on the roller skates with the best
of them and wing his way through to the next scene. He had passed the School

Certificate; at least he had not actually failed anything. It was a close run thing though in some subjects, and he would have to "do much better" to make a university place. But the good news was that in the Sixth Form, in preparation for the newly minted "A Levels," you only took three subjects for two years, and these were obviously the things you were good at.

The nightmare of algebra was over. History and English (literature only now—no more language) were obvious; the third subject was a problem since he had not done that well in any of the others, except Art where he got a coveted "Distinction." He was competent, even imaginative at drawing and painting, the compulsory subjects, but in the optional papers he chose History of Architecture and Stage Design, both of which had some satisfying intellectual content. Bannister-Fletcher's heavy tome, *A History of Architecture on the Comparative Method* was his first introduction to a work of serious scholarship, and the example stayed with him. But art was not considered suitable, since universities would not rank it with the more scholarly subjects. He toyed with Latin, which he truly liked, but he had not done well in it because, surprise, he hadn't paid attention to the set books. He much preferred reading the love poems of Catullus to construing the windy sentences of that blowhard showoff Cicero. You had to do some Latin anyway since it was required on many scholarship exams. Geography was considered, but he foolishly despised it as pedestrian; it was one of those "safe" subjects the struggling students took. So he settled on French. There had been a school trip to Paris (usual sights) where they were allowed to taste wine and eat snails in restaurants, so he developed one of his unreasoning enthusiasms for all things French.

He had done pretty well in French, but more through cunning than a thorough knowledge of the language. They had had a talk by an examiner (of the Northern Universities Joint Board) about how the French essay was marked, and the essay counted for some twenty-five percent of the exam. Ace that, and you couldn't really fail. The examiner was clear enough: the method of marking was to take points off for each mistake. There was no nonsense about marks for style and originality. The grammar had to be perfect. So: at all costs avoid mistakes in grammar, however stupid and irrelevant was your subject matter, and however clumsy your style. If it was a narrative essay you could write it in the "past historic" tense: a simple little tense with not much room for mistakes anyway. So he contrived a list of all-purpose past-historic sentences that would fit just about any subject. The subject was always conveniently simple-minded: "Mes vacances comme enfant" or something equally challenging. It worked. But it disguised such faults as a complete lack of knowledge of the subjunctive (off ill? playing truant? mind elsewhere?) But most of his friends were taking it, so he opted, disastrously, for French.

Does it matter? It matters. We have to know what was impinging on the confused and tentative soul to know how it was developing. Up until now, apart from very recently in History and English, and always in Music, the school and its agenda had been more of a nuisance than an inspiration. Rote learning had helped him get doggedly through, but real stimulation was from elsewhere. From now on, though, ideas were to dominate and they were to come largely from the schoolwork. For by now he was passing the schoolboy stage and into the next stratum of "student." Residua of the schoolboy stuff remained in French, and were to give untold trouble. But in English and History, he was welcomed into a different world where you were allowed, nay expected, to think things out, to come up with original ideas, to criticize and analyze and generally use the pre-frontal cortex for something other than rote memorization. You were rewarded for having an opinion—suitably backed up with examples and argument of course. Until then you were supposed to have "opinions" but you essentially learned which were appropriate and regurgitated them when the time came. A truly original opinion—for exam purposes—was not expected or encouraged.

They were told to read Hamlet in the vacation in preparation for the compulsory Shakespeare exam. He had read, seen, heard, Hamlet, but he dutifully read it again. The first thing Basher Birrel asked the small lower-sixth English class, assembled round a table in the hallowed sixth-form study room, was, "Why did Hamlet nae go ahead and kill Claudius rrright after hearring frae the ghost?" Reader, you might think this an obvious, even routine, question, with hindsight, but what was startling was that they were expected to come up with their own answers. And, amazing, there was no right answer. There were good and bad answers, but you were expected to form a view and argue for it. Was Hamlet mad? No, he was, as he said, putting an antic disposition on. Was he a coward? No, he fought duels and pirates; he wasn't afraid to risk his life. Did he think the ghost was evil? No evidence of that. On the contrary, he was absolutely convinced by it. So why? The eager-to-be-original Student found his answer: Hamlet didn't kill Claudius right away because then he would have missed a terrific chance to torment his mother.

Hamlet is so important to young men because they know they are supposed to "identify" with the hero. But how do you identify with such a chronic procrastinator with his whining excuses for inaction? It's embarrassing. The whole business with the "delay" depends entirely on Hamlet's shallow, histrionic nature: he enjoys the whole fandango. He poses as one smitten by the *mal du siècle*, but in fact he has no real feelings, except for an enjoyment of playing at real feelings. Young actors feel bound to say they empathize with the tortured Hamlet and want to play him because he "expresses their feelings." But the prince's moody post-adolescent mutterings are all play-acting. (He was at least thirty, so what was he doing still at university anyway? One of those perpetual graduate students?) It is necessary to appreciate this to understand that Hamlet is a play about someone acting a part. This is what makes it interesting: it is a play about a play-actor who spins out the yarn for his own narcissistic fascination.

He does get carried away with his own performance, as in the nasty scene with his mother, where he is not so much over-reacting as plain over-acting. He stabs Polonius (through the arras) in a fit of overdone bravado, then does a great improvisation to cover it. This histrionic streak in him is what explains the otherwise puzzling interpolation of the players, and the plays within the play: it effectively and conclusively demonstrates this basic trait of Hamlet's character. He would rather mess about with the representation of the real thing than get on with the real thing itself. For him the play *is* the real thing (he says so) and he only kills the king more or less by accident. Young actors, however, can never say that they want to play Hamlet because they empathize with his narcissistic shallowness, lack of real feelings, and crude enjoyment of being the star in his very own B movie. But our post-adolescent, procrastinating, manipulative little Woolworth-dancer understood this very well, at some murky subconscious level, even if there was no way he could then articulate it into an exam answer, which was probably a good thing.

Details don't matter, except for their curiosity value. What matters was the sea change from passive, rote learning, to active, creative learning. Birrel gave him Wilson Knight's *The Wheel of Fire*: a whole book of luscious essays on Shakespeare's tragedies, with an answer to the Hamlet question that he stored away for future exam reference. Basher expected "a critique"—and then a comparison with A. C. Bradley and his tortured attempts to treat the Shakespearean characters as though they were real people with real motives, such that you could ask questions like "What happened before Macbeth began?"

Then in History the same. Whatmuff gave them the problem: "In what sense were the Whigs and Tories, in eighteenth-century England, political parties?" How would we answer that question? What evidence would we look for? The "Whig historians"—Lord Macaulay the chief culprit—said they were, and used this as a basis for attacking the still sane but "unconstitutional" George III and his Tory chums. But Whatmuff had studied under Namier at Manchester, and Sir Lewis thought they weren't, and made George guilty of nothing worse than bad judgment. That magnificent piece of empirical political history, *The Structure of Politics on the Accession of George III*, became a new testament, and an assertion of the need for a massive factual base before attempting generalizations, that remained somewhere in the intellectual subconscious ever after. But again, you were expected to make your own mind up in a serious way. These were not just things to be hoarded in the memory for exams, even if the habit was now ingrained: they were real, true issues and problems in the real world of history and literature. This wasn't "school" at all. Whatever it was, it was wonderful. Aladdin had rubbed some intellectual lamp by accident, and found a fabulous treasure cave where he could be eternally happy.

Good so far. The goal might still be politics and high-class journalism, but the route could now be through university, although the details of this were still a bit hazy to him. The only person in his far-flung, if largely unknown, extended family who had been to university was his mother's cousin Sydney. He had been to Liverpool, "reading" Classics, and surprisingly, Esperanto. This was still popular as part of a hope for a peaceful world and universal justice via a common language. Cousin Syd was teaching at a grammar school in a nearby town, and the school played them at Rugby. So after an away game (lost) he went and tapped on the older cousin's door. (Syd was a resident housemaster.) Syd and Mrs. Syd were truly hospitable if a little puzzled about the exact relationship (he was their father's brother's daughter's son—first cousin once removed.) They gave him tea, and thus encouraged, he asked the cousin about university. Syd talked of "freshmen" and "lectures" and "tutorials" and "dons" and "prelims" and "finals"—and our boy didn't like to admit he had no idea what these things were. But Syd's nice house on the school grounds, his pretty wife who smiled and fussed over his bruises and cuts from the game, the bookshelves and substantial desk, the papers scattered around like something from a stage set for *Goodbye Mr. Chips*: all this entranced him, gave him a sense of a way of life way beyond his present experience, but one that was gracious, safe and calm. He left reluctantly, but the next week he hit the second-hand stall and found a cheap Esperanto text. He was disappointed with this boringly regular romance-based ersatz mish-mash, but he even went to a few meetings of the local Esperanto Club, only to find it was locked in passionate war with the rival Golapük Society with its universal panacea based on Germanic models. So much for a universal language for universal peace. But the idea continued to enthrall and he even thought he might devote his life to a perfect language that was truly a mélange of all the best in all languages. Youth is wonderful at whatever age it kicks in.

Some things were not dealt with so happily. He still went to church, and in however loose a way, believed. Then it happened. As swift and unexpected as the visitation of the first angel came the second epiphany. He woke up one winter morning with the frost on the windows and the water frozen in the water jug on the dresser of his unheated bedroom (heat in bedrooms was deemed unhealthy.) As he stepped out into the cold room watching his breath freeze in the air in front of him, a thought crystallized at the same instant: it's all transparent, blatant nonsense! There was no lead-up of profound thinking and questioning, no agonies of indecision; it was sudden and complete and decisive. It was a complete de-conversion experience. God, if not dead, was at least badly mauled.

Everything they had told him, everything he had believed, was a bunch of rather silly fairy stories. If they had been the stories and beliefs of some exotic tribe they would have been dismissed as primitive nonsense. It was only their familiarity, their complete taken-for-grantedness that rendered them plausible. "Very God of very God, begotten not made, being of one substance with the Father by whom all things were made. Who for us men and for our salvation, came down from heaven." (Athanasius) "Born of the Virgin Mary, suffered under Pontius Pilate, crucified, dead, and buried. On the third day He rose again from the dead and ascended into heaven, and sitteth on the right hand of God the Father, from whence He shall come again in glory to judge both the quick and the dead, whose kingdom shall have no end." (Apostles) He had recited it all for so long it had taken on the aura of a truth as incontrovertible as "the sun rises each morning." His whole world assumed it. His nation assumed it. Western civilization assumed it. Who was he to question?

But the conviction for him was absolute. It was simply astonishing to him that he could ever have believed all those biblical fairy tales, that all the adults of his world could believe them. What was wrong with them? They were the adults; they knew everything. True, they could be unjust and even wicked and often wrong about this and that. But could they be wrong about this biggest thing of all? If the Garden of Eden and the Fall of Man were all the obvious fairy tales they seemed to be, then all that followed was equally nonsense. There was no need for salvation, and the odd little rabbi telling his odd morality tales in Roman-occupied Galilee was just that, and all the Son of God stuff was just propaganda added by his disappointed followers when he failed to come back in glory to judge... etc. But they obviously seemed to believe it; it wasn't just hypocrisy. What about his parents, the vicar and the church, the headmaster and the school, the Queen and the C. of E., and the whole history of Christianity?

It was too bewildering. But the revelation was absolute, obvious, complete: so clear and self-evident that he couldn't ever look on it all as he once had. The whole mythical house of cards came tumbling down. Was he insane? He remembered the psalms: "The fool hath said in his heart that there is no God." Well, maybe he was a fool, but at least this was an admission that it had been said before. Even in that God-besotted age of the hairy and holy Israelites, someone had doubted. But did he doubt God, or just the fairy tales peddled in his name? There must be a God or nothing made sense, but what if they had got it wrong? What if the God of the Old Testament Jews that we inherited was just a picture of an Israelite father and his unreliable offspring? What if God was not like that at all? Or not like anything we could even imagine? If he really was looking after the whole universe (which was infinite—something beyond comprehension) then did it make sense to think he cared at all about what we did with our neighbors' fences, or whether or not we gathered firewood on Saturdays, put pictures in churches, or cut the ends of our willies off?

Patient reader, we shall recite no more of this cascade of bewilderment. In an age of religious indifference it probably seems very tedious and obvious. But we are trying to see what it was that affected and afflicted our developing soul. We must follow where events lead. It was an overpowering blow to him, all the more amazing for its suddenness and absoluteness. All the questions and the arguing and the search for allies and the research into skepticism and agnosticism were to come later and to be important and formative. But this was all after the event. What we must grasp here is the importance to him of the event itself. It was a spiritual trauma of gigantic proportions for his little soul. It left him feeling physically different, "emptied out of all constituents," like Elgar's (or rather Cardinal Newman's) Gerontius on his way to heaven. (Old habits of thought died hard.) To follow out its implications unflinchingly would throw his world into convulsions. But it was to him like Joan's voices: too immediate and authoritative to be doubted or ignored. He didn't yet know about compromise, and the indignation took over as always: how dare they not recognize that their whole system of belief was ridiculous? How could they claim to be intelligent and educated and rational people and yet subscribe to the nonsense? How dare they inflict years of this rubbish on him and threaten him with hell if he didn't believe? He would have to put them right. But how do you put a whole civilization right? Even he quailed before what was required of him. He was reading the Shaw version of *St. Joan* as a set book now, and he had no wish to end up like that silly girl, going stubbornly to the stake. He would obviously have to tread carefully. He was in effect getting a quick lesson about compromise: a necessary lesson, but one not graciously accepted by the little absolutist.

This was of course part of the disease of adolescence, and we would not be true to our task if we ignored the obvious questions that go with that unhappy state: what about girls and sex? Well, there were girls; sex was something else. Something now has to be revealed that may be unbelievable: he attended an institution quite unusual in the Grammar School world of his day: a mixed school; girls had been there all along. So why haven't we heard about them? Remember that what matters is what impinged. Girls, while present, had just not impinged. This was a sex-segregated age. All Public (i.e., private) schools were single-sex institutions, as were most Grammar and High Schools. The Eleven-plus failures were dumped into custodial institutions that were also of the mixed-but-segregated variety. But they were to leave at fourteen to swell the workforce; they were not being trained to become Guardians of the perfect state (or wives of same.) Towns had their Boys and Girls Grammar Schools. But a few small towns or country districts, such as the one he was in, could not support two institutions and so had that anomaly, the mixed school.

Even here the segregation worked. There were separate entrances, separate cloakrooms, separate playgrounds, separate sports facilities. The girls, who were dressed to look as much like boys as possible with shapeless "gymslips" and collars and ties, sat on one side of the class, boys on the other, and fraternization was not allowed. Outside the classroom everything was separate. On top of this the informal code of the boys did not allow for fraterniza-

tion. Girls were an unhappy necessity. One supposed th[...]
it was obviously a handicap. If this were an all boys sc[...]
be many more recruits for the sports teams, and they [...]
Being friends with, even acknowledging, the girls, set [...]
boy" or a "mary jane" : the ultimate in derision and [...]
played sissy games like rounders (baseball), netball [...]
hockey; the boys engaged in manly sports such as Rugby, cricket and boxing.
Even in tennis, which both played, the games were divided by sex. If there
was interaction at all it was confined to teasing, often quite refined. Reducing
a girl to tears was considered the only suitable way to deal with one of these
peculiar, annoying creatures.

Such a strenuously structured world could not, however, ignore puberty
with all its grubby, hairy, odiferous reminders. It came with all its confusing
emotional baggage, not helped by the total lack of sexual information and
the full panoply of puritanical injunctions against "dirt." In the Boy Scout
Manual (or was it in Lord Baden-Powell's own *Scouting for Boys*?) there was
a long section he had not previously understood. It concerned "unrest." Animals, it said (drawing of noble stag), were fortunate since they only felt "unrest" once a year. Neither the purpose nor the mechanics of "unrest" were
revealed. We children of Adam, however, as part of our curse, felt "unrest" all
the time. The answer was not the obvious: so do what the stags do (whatever
that was) but do it all the time. The stern answer was to resist "unrest" with
every fiber of one's being. The means were pure thoughts, spiritual exercises,
cold baths, and manly sports. It was a kind of test, like the cross-country run,
of character. Not a good omen for the little cheater.

Nor was it helped by the smut passing for information that was traded in
the schoolyard. For several years, being true to the Scout promise to be "clean
in thought word and deed" he wouldn't even listen to the "dirty" things. He
was hideously embarrassed when they told their stories, which in any case he
didn't understand. He was also deeply guilty because he knew he got pleasure
from touching himself—a lot. He knew it was dirty and evil and God knew all
about it, but he couldn't stop. It was the perfect accompaniment to his nightly
fantasies. He became convinced that it was one of the things that would right
itself once he was an adult. He would be able to "put away childish things"
and it would stop. But it didn't. It became more alarming as the stickiness
ensued and greater precautions had to be taken to conceal it. But then, he
heard on the playground grapevine that doing it would make you go blind. If
so he should be in a darkness-at-noon as deep as Samson's. But he wasn't. And
if the other boys were doing it—and he gathered from the jokes and stories
that they were—why weren't they blind? Did divine retribution have a flawed
intelligence service? Was the troublesome wet willie another bomb that didn't
have his name on it?

Insofar as parental guidance was concerned, again embarrassment reigned. One would not be caught dead discussing such things with parents; they would be the very last people to talk to. Whatever they did about it, if anything, was a mystery and rigidly concealed. His father had told him when he was very young and didn't know better and persisted, that babies were made the way hens laid eggs and he should watch the hens. The result was that he thought for years that intercourse was anal and birth the same. He had no idea of the actual plumbing. He wasn't sure how the cock got its "seed" into the hen really, until such time as he had his first erection and divined for himself the purpose of it, particularly when he remembered that the bigger boys called their willies "cocks." But it still seemed strange to him that God would put all the business of baby making into the same places he had designed for excretion. Perhaps it was a sign of divine economy though: two jobs for the price of one.

But once in the sixth form, the girls could not be ignored. For a start, they did not have to wear gymslips—although ties were still required—and the blouses and skirts could not hide their budding and often quite ample breasts. Those who put their shoulders back, stuck their little breasts out, and walked gracefully, were even given "deportment badges." They all studied in close proximity in the seminars, even though there were separate boys' and girls' sixth-form rooms. But most of all there were the dances. House dances, Rugby Club dances, Prefects' dances, Parents' Association dances—any excuse for a dance to raise a bit of cash. Terrible four-piece bands (trumpet, sax, drums, bass) playing stolid old favorites, a few decorations, someone on the lights, a few floor prizes and some minor refreshments, and a dance was on. This meant learning ballroom dancing, and in one of the truly silly moves the school made in an attempt to be "progressive," dance lessons were instituted at lunchtimes, but segregated! The boys learned their steps and the girls theirs in different dance classes. Somehow it was hoped they would put them together when the time came. The results were clumsy, but that didn't matter. What mattered was that on the night you actually got to hold onto a girl.

You weren't supposed to have actual physical contact except for the hands; the crucial inch was to be observed at all times. But there was lot of accidental bumping given the dismally bad dancing that was going on. But that was it: if you could manage a quickstep, a foxtrot, and above all a slow waltz, together with the "old time selection," you got to hold onto a girl. (The "Latin" selection—rumba, samba, cha-cha, was for the show-offs, and the tango only for the very few true experts.) If you went to dances outside school it was even better, for in the various public ballrooms there were no one-inch rules. In fact, the private dance teachers to whom some of the boys went to improve their skills insisted on your using the body to "lead" and "guide" the partner: hips and hands were fair game. He had a buxom lady teacher who made him grab her tightly and move her around with his hips: "pivot! young man, pivot! pivot!" she would call out over the scratchy sound of "Walking My Baby Back Home," or "What'll I Do?," or "Red Roses for a Blue Lady."

The dancing was essential to his getting close to girls because he was crushingly shy about doing anything more private and personal. For a start he didn't know what to do. He had only ever teased girls, and clearly you couldn't tease these girls—these young women. You had to do something else, but what? The novels, stories, plays and poetry, and above all films, said you had to "fall in love" with them, but how did you do that? You had to have some sort of working relationship with them and the mechanics of this were beyond him. He was hopelessly romantic and believed in the purity of love (whatever that was), and the perfect object of love, as fervently as the most anguished troubadour poets. He just didn't know what the feeling of being in love was really supposed to be like. It was just supposed to happen when you looked at the beloved: "You'll know it when it happens. Hit you like a brick." But he only felt a mild terror when contemplating any sort of approach to the undeniably pretty girls around him.

He was also terrified of possible rejection. What if you asked her to "go for a walk" (one of things you evidently did) and she refused? This was unthinkable. How would you live with it? She might tell everyone, and you would look a fool. Better not to risk it. And then what did you do with them if the miracle of contact happened? The only real sexual fantasies he had were about breasts and the fondling and kissing of same. All he could imagine that came of any serious interaction with a girl was that he would get to stroke her breasts for hours and hours. (Something to do with his very late weaning?) Of course you would never do that with a "nice" girl, and nice girls were the only candidates. Many of the boys were of the opinion that only marriage would solve the problem. The whole point of marriage, they earnestly explained, was that with a wife you could do whatever you liked as much as you liked whenever you wanted. What a dismal surprise these little lechers were in for.

He had been in hospital for a near burst appendix, and took weeks to recover. He became fixated on the nurses who in those days still wore the starched, brilliant uniforms, with colors and designs according to rank, and with elaborate high caps and stiff white collars and cuffs. Unbearably cute little upside-down watches dangled over their starchy bosoms. These were still Florence Nightingale nurses, and they were all nice girls from good homes and excellent schools, and they were all beautiful in their starched white and colored finery. One day, two of the very prettiest had to lift him— he was too weak to get himself up from the bed—and they took him from both sides, enveloped him in their arms, and pulled him to a sitting position. For a moment there he was crushed between them, their breasts obvious even beneath the starch, and the smell of sheer young, scrubbed, female flesh and shampooed hair rose like steam into his nostrils. My God, he thought for a moment: this is what they are like! He passed out. They called the doctor who put it down to his weak condition and made them repeat the whole process to lie him down. He passed out again. He would have to stay at least another week to recover, said the worried young doctor, who couldn't know that he would never recover: he had the virus now for life.

Even so, the naiveté was almost unfathomable. But these were the days before sex education. Or rather there was Sex Ed. but it consisted of one word: don't! We have to do the first kiss, if only to reveal the worst. Her name was Pam, and she was lovely, with dark hair and a tiny mole on her cheek like a beauty spot. They were in the back of a car being driven home from a school dance. This was rare. Cars were rare, but a friend's parents were giving a lift. Usually you would be on a bus, and that was well-lit and very public. It was dark; her head was close to his shoulder; they had been dancing; there had been contact; they kissed. It amazed him: she was cooperative, not horrified or embarrassed. Could it be that they liked it? That they didn't just do it under protest? But he then had a sudden shock to the system as serious and heart pounding as any religious revelation: he had a simultaneous erection. He sat back in the dark, amazed and fighting for breath. How could the soft, perfect, romantic kiss be associated with the dirty thing? Why had it done that? Just as suddenly he knew. It was the cock and the hen; it was the stag's unrest; it was the thing you must never do, but which was now as urgent as music or playing Rugby. The pure romance and the dirty unrest were necessarily entwined. This was going to need some very special roller skates.

Meanwhile, back at the religious de-conversion. After the shock he had to manage the adults as best he could. The reaction was predictable. His mother cried and told him she had "felt something special" when he was confirmed and took his first communion. He didn't doubt it, but how could he tell her that such a genuine, loving, protective feeling didn't validate all the silly beliefs? The adults would often do this: state a very strong feeling about some belief and assume that the strength of the feeling made the belief correct. He hated these strong adult feelings, and the authority they were supposed to give to any and all crackpot notions. The vicar and the choirmaster and everyone just couldn't believe it. Had he been keeping bad company? It was a temptation by the devil, which he should resist and just persevere. But he couldn't. He tried for a little while but it was too much. He couldn't repeat all those things. He just stopped going. It was a wrench. All that was familiar and gracious about that church world, the safety and security it promised: the beauty of the music above all.

But he couldn't pretend. This was not something you could lie about. The headmaster was new, the first "doctor" (or Dr. as it was always printed) the school had had in a long time. He had done a doctorate in French Romanticism at London University, and was a reasonable man. He didn't wither you with sarcasm as the Scots had done, but he did reason with you. He was not a devout practitioner himself, but this was a religious school and they had at the very least to observe the forms. School prayers and services were a must, and he would have to take his turn at reading the lesson and the like. Don't take it so hard, the good doctor said: no one in their right minds would confuse the Church of England with religion, or even Christianity. It was a social thing and very good for keeping order and stability in society. We needed fairy tales for that? Well, yes, apparently we did, said the doctor, and he was probably right. It was a sad conclusion for our budding rationalist, but he decided that he could live with this thought as an interim compromise. If he wanted to be a prefect and go to university and all that, he had to play the ongoing game to some extent. Time enough for wholesale thought-reform when he was himself a bit better equipped to carry it out. Let the adults have their fairy tales if they needed them so badly.

While the compromise worked socially it left him in an even deeper quandary about the adults. He had premised so much of his life on their infallibility, on their possession of the ultimate knowledge that was the key to everything. "When you are older" had been the holding pattern. Well, he was older. He knew about the sex thing—not much but enough to know that the adults were as confused and emotional about it as most other things. The closer he got to them the more confused they seemed. He had some kind of ideal of a rational creature, not moved by sentiment and savage emotion, ruled only by logic and standing above the turbulence of the inner life, not needing the prop of pathetic beliefs to face life and death and uncertainty. They didn't exist around him, but they must exist somewhere. Socrates had been such a man. The Stoics had been such. Was it possible only in ancient Greece? Surely not. Surely it would be in the academy that he would find them, the rational ones, the logical ones, the ones who faced the world unflinchingly. At least this was something to keep him going through the *sturm und drang* of this unfolding *bildungsroman*.

He was obviously struggling badly with the defalcation of the adults (he got that word from Lamb—he liked it.) If they were so clever, how could they not see that what they believed was nonsense? And why did their intelligence not prevent them from being so often cruel and wicked? Another epiphany was granted: *intelligence is neutral regarding wisdom and virtue*. He probably didn't phrase it so neatly, but it came to him with the force of a totally apt aphorism, and this was the essence of it. It was hard at first to grasp, but once grasped it made everything clear. It was frightening since it meant that intelligence could be put easily into the service of fantasies and fiendishness. But in neither case need it be stupidity that was involved. Wrong belief was not a result of stupidity, necessarily, although surely it was in many cases. He had to account for the obvious examples of clever people who believed stupid things, and to ponder the strength of that belief. While his sudden insight explained a lot he found it hard to live with. He just couldn't accept, at some level of frustration, that if they were indeed intelligent they would see as clearly as he did that their beliefs were childish nonsense.

Since church had failed so badly, he turned even more hopefully to politics. Even here he had his doubts. The adults in politics he should admire—his Conservative heroes—were a mixed bunch. Churchill was unassailable of course, but there was uneasiness over the Gallipoli thing. Eden was his mother's hero (almost as adored as Ronald Coleman and Leslie Howard), but while he might have been right about Germany, he didn't seem very effective in the post-war peace. Then there were the "men of Munich" who had betrayed us, but who were also Conservatives. His mother felt sorry for Chamberlain: he had trusted Hitler's word as a gentleman. His father said Chamberlain was a bloody fool. Some of the ones he saw up close when canvassing and organizing for the party did not impress him as any more rational and wise than those at school or church. They got irrationally excited, they got drunk, they boasted about sex (horrible embarrassment), and generally had feet of clay. But if the adults were not all-knowing or all-wise, they were still all-powerful; if he no longer craved their secret, he still had to play their game since it was the only game in town.

Some of the old tweed-and-corduroy socialists he came across in the park, where they had a "speakers corner," seemed if anything more reasonable and informed. They almost approached the calm wisdom he was looking for. This was embarrassing because they were so obviously wrong. They had a stand next to the Catholic Truth Society spouting its fanatic brand of the worst of the fairy tales. Here again the contrast between the Pope-worshiping rigidity of the Catholics and the materialistic atheism of the socialists embarrassed him: his Tory friends were subscribing, if not particularly devout, Christians—largely Anglicans. The socialists ("The Fabian Society" they were called—he didn't know why) seemed even more rational by contrast. So where did this lead? He wilted under the scorn they poured on the intellectual capacities of Tories. "'Tory intellectual' is an obvious oxymoron," one had said, "like 'military intelligence.'" The sympathetic crowd of largely working men may not have really known what an oxymoron was, but they roared approval at this palpable hit. He was naked before such put-downs. They made him uncomfortable about his leaders who did indeed seem to suggest that "intellectual" was a dirty word only to be applied to socialists. Tories prided themselves on being the pragmatic opposite. This bothered him because he wasn't much interested in the pragmatics of politics but in the political ideas that Whatmuff (himself a non-conformist Labourite) was introducing him to in Burke, Hegel, Spencer, Mill and the like. The State as Metaphysical Absolute versus the State as the Greatest Good of the Greatest Number, was a lot more fun than the finer points of public housing policy and the devaluation of the pound.

The collapse of the idea of adult authority, which began with the religious thing, was constantly reinforced. He read Mark Twain on Shakespeare and a whole part of his world came tumbling down. If we couldn't be sure that Shakespeare wrote Shakespeare—and clearly the boring Stratford business-man Mr. Wm. Shaksper hadn't written those exquisite, aristocratic poems and plays—then of what could we be sure? Lytton Strachey then destroyed the Victorians for him—the Victorians who still ruled his world from Churchill and the vicar on down. Bernard Shaw mocked everything. The socialists hammered away about the "depression" and the collapse of the very capital-ism, which, as a Conservative, he was supposed to defend. But he had been born on the dole and his family was a victim of the hated "mean's test." Where should he stand on this? His parents explained either that the depression was the fault of the 1929 Labour government, or, contrariwise, that it was a world-wide depression and therefore not the Conservatives' fault. It was under a National government, they said, so Labour and the Liberals were just as much to blame. Somewhere there must be the truth to all this, but the adults were engaged in a bitter war of insults about it, and he was in truth bewildered, even if he couldn't admit it.

He couldn't admit it because, in yet another roller-skating episode, he had become the Conservative candidate in the school's mock election, shadow-ing the general election of 1950. He was still then only a fifth-former, a junior, and the other candidates—Labour, Liberal and "Democratic Communist"—were sixth-formers and prefects. But he was known to be active in the Young Conservatives, running debates (did you guess? he reveled in debates) and canvassing and doing exit polls on election day. So the Classics master, Mr. Evans, who had been seconded to advise the Conservative camp, strongly suggested him as candidate, and the caucus agreed. He could have declined. There were seniors with all that aplomb and savoir-faire who could probably have done better. But he evidently had some mysterious "experience with practical politics" that counted. He didn't refuse, setting a pattern that was to cost him dearly.

He borrowed ideas from party manifestoes and the works of the propagan-dist Colm Brogan (a favorite of the young Margaret Thatcher at much the same time.) He copied the speeches of the local parliamentary candidates, and patched together a winning campaign: not difficult since the vast major-ity of the school came from nice Conservative middle-class families, and the result was a foregone conclusion. He didn't do as well in debates as he thought he might, because he was always skating on the thin ice of superficial knowl-edge about things political. He even managed to invent something called "voluntary conscription" that he was in favor of, and which caused embar-rassing laughter. But he shrugged and continued and warned of the red men-ace and won.

The danger was that it was all too easy. It was seductively easy, this whole politics thing. It got you right there into the adult world on the most serious of levels; the rewards in terms of approval, perks, attention and advancement

were unbelievable. The same superficial qualities that attracted him to journalism were operative here: indeed the two went perfectly together. There
would be university, yes, but only as a way of establishing him more firmly in
these two flashy, wordy, quick on your feet, whirls around the roller-skating
rink. For those of his shallow but ambitious inclinations, these temptations
should not exist. They played to his worst characteristics. But the swirl of his
excitement and the heady thrill of winning and being thunderously applauded
and feeling at the absolute center of centers, swept him along. It made him
bury his doubts and embrace the noisy public world. Fame was indeed the
spur, at least for now.

If we are looking for those impingements, then this is the place to note how
the wider world rushed in on him. It was of course the wide world of a northern
provincial mill town, but it was no less exciting for that. For this was in its
way an interesting and democratic little world, with a lot to offer the tumbling, absorbent, growing mind. Bradford was an old town that had been
staunchly Parliamentarian in the civil war. But the modern town was an industrial city built on the wealth that wool had brought. There was a lot of
civic pride of the nineteenth-century kind that built museums, art galleries,
concert halls, Mechanics Institutes, Technical Colleges, theatres, sports sta-
diums and a superb gothic-revival Town Hall and perfect Ruskinesque Wool
Exchange—eventually saved from developmental vandalism by John
Betjeman and Niklaus Pevsner.

T. S. Eliot made the city famous, if for the wrong reasons, with his lines
from *The Waste Land* describing his seedy clerk as: "One of the low on whom
assurance sits/As a silk hat on a Bradford millionaire." But perhaps because
this was a world of self-made men whose lineages were as shallow as everyone
else's, there was a kind of rough democracy about the place in which ability
really did count for at least as much as wealth or birth. Once you made it, into
the magic circle of Grammar School, Young Conservatives, and particularly
Rugby and tennis clubs, there was no social exclusiveness; there was much
reward if you were a convincing performer. The silk hat—Fred's top hat—was
there for the taking, if, like Fred, you were skilful enough with the roller
skates (puttin' on my white tie, puttin' on my tails.)

There were citywide organizations among the schools for sixth formers:
the Junior Civic Society, the European Languages Society, the Debating Society, the Interschool Drama League. He was the school's representative to all
of them: they asked, he couldn't say no. He was the secretary or such of
several: he was asked and couldn't refuse. He took on too much and made a
mess of it, but nothing could cure him of his passion for joining. He took on
too many parts in too many plays, but he found a new roller-rink in which all
kinds of action could be advanced, in the theatre. He could learn parts quickly,
and since he had no inhibitions about speaking "proper" English—as opposed to the "refined Yorkshire" that most affected, he made a hit in the

favored classics—Sheridan, Goldsmith—and was in demand as the junior lead for Galsworthy, Wilde, Barrie, and Pinero. His languidly studied performance in *The Admirable Crichton,* despite being painfully overdone, actually got him his first friendly press-notice outside the parish magazine.

The wider world brought him into contact with the sixth-formers of the other schools, who struck him always as so much more sophisticated than he was. He was probably over impressed because of his sheer lack of knowledge of their world. But they seemed so at home in their light and easy use of knowledge. They spoke their foreign languages like natives, and even joked in them: something quite beyond his surface mastery. He tried hard to acquire the knack of bantering about serious things, but it came hard. Once he decided that something was serious, he felt he had to be serious about it. He had more sheer information about more things than any of them, but he couldn't maneuver among it with their ease and wit. He was fine in a debate because he could think it out ahead of time, but spontaneity was hard for him. He tended to pour it out in great gobbets, and while they showed polite amazement, they soon lost their interest. This needed work. But one thing struck home: the girls liked the talk. These were girls on their way to college, and they knew poetry and plays and languages, and they liked the powerful talk more than powerful muscles. If you were a local Rugby star it didn't harm though, and you could all meet on the tennis circuit. He still didn't know really how to tailor his encyclopaedic outpourings to meet the demands of petty courtship, but he was learning.

These were wonderful girls because they were, in their unfamiliarity, almost exotic—particularly the Catholic girls. The Catholics had their own Grammar Schools—separating boys and girls, naturally. He almost liked the Catholics despite their absurd superstitions, because they, unlike the Protestants, really believed in intellectual argument about these things as opposed to falling back on that irritating "faith" thing. Like him they despised that route and trotted out the logical-sounding arguments from Aristotle and Aquinas they brought from their classes in "doctrine." He agreed with them about the "first cause uncaused"—he was attracted to the Deism of the enlightenment he was learning from Hume and Voltaire—but he refused to follow this into the "logical" derivation of the fairy tales. This was deciding the answers in advance and making up the arguments to anticipate them. He couldn't phrase it very well, but it made him suspicious and unconvinced. All this pseudo-logic, nevertheless, made them worthy opponents. The girls too, although not inclined to argue like the boys, seemed attracted to the words. What is more they seemed to find him attractively dangerous in his agnosticism (he had learned the word and was reading T. H. Huxley.) Each was forbidden fruit to the other and excitingly sweet.

The Civic Society had debates about religion and he took the lonely anti stand. The Catholic girls were trooped out in force to "defend the faith" at these events, and he enjoyed shocking them en masse, and watching their open mouths and flushed, excited faces. Not until he discovered cosmopolitan Jewish girls was he to experience a thrill of xenophilia quite as intense as with the dark Catholic girls with their Irish names and shy yet interested glances. But a Catholic girl, with the enticing, forbidden whiff of incense in her hair, was still a girl, and a girl was still a problem creature.

The theatre scene was pretty lively. He was encouraged to look at live theater by the success of his school's most famous girl, Billie Whitelaw—a cousin in fact of his current friend Pete-the-Wog. (These were simpler days: small dark curly-haired boys were always Wog.) Billie had been several years ahead of him when she rocketed to fame as Bunkle on BBC Children's Hour. She left school because the dismal Scot disapproved of her time-off for radio theatrics. One could take courage from the fact that people who became famous had always seemed to incur the school's disapproval. But Billie was now touring with the great Donald Wolfitt (maybe the best Tamburlaine ever) and when his company came to town the gang turned up to cheer her performance. He thought she was the most beautiful thing he'd ever seen, and the best actress: an opinion later to be shared by Samuel Becket, who demanded her for all his plays. But Billie inspired his love of the stage.

There was a good local repertory company that put on a play a week in the season, varying from dialect comedy (*The Passing of the Third Floor Back*) to Tennessee Williams (*Streetcar Named Desire*) and the ever popular local-boy-made-good, J. B. Priestley (*An Inspector Calls.*) On Monday nights they sold two seats for the price of one, and since his mother loved the theater they used to go, and had been going for several years. Now he discovered that the local grand musical theatre had visiting opera companies, and he thrilled at Carmen and wept at Butterfly. They were great events to take the beloved ones to—he was to discover later. For the girls liked the operas in particular, and most boys didn't. He almost had an edge, but not one he knew how to exploit as yet.

The other discovery was the Civic Theatre, subsidized by the town and doubling as an acting school and foreign film theatre. It had a famous professional director (Esmé Percy), sophisticated students and high-class amateur devotees. (It figured prominently in the novel/film that faithfully showed the many sides of Bradford, John Braine's *Room at the Top.*) It became a second home, supplying some of the needs of the sorely missed church. The Theater was obviously the Church itself, the Green Room doubled for the Vestry, the Stage was the Sanctuary, the Play was the Ritual, the Director was a solid substitute for the Vicar, the Audience the Congregation. The bohemian theater crowd was irreligious and cynical and self-consciously witty, and discussed the "meanings" of the plays and films incessantly in a way that was new and mind-buzzing.

The women there were clearly not girls, and equally clearly way beyond his reach. They were like creatures out of the nineteen-twenties: they were older and "experienced" and wore long dresses and long flimsy scarves. They tended to extreme slimness and small breasts, but breasts he would willingly have kissed and stroked, and did in those muffled nightly fantasies. They gestured eloquently and intimidatingly with long cigarette holders. He really didn't like cigarettes (tasteless hot smoke) but he had to try them because, among the many forbidden things, they were the most accessible. She had realized this, in her strangely tolerant way over some things, and one day gave him a straight briar pipe, tobacco pouch with light Virginia tobacco— his father had advised against the strong stuff for a beginner—and a metal tool intended for scraping and tamping. "If you're going to smoke," she said, "then do it like a gentleman."

He began to train his personality around that pipe like a tentative vine, following the leads of Leslie Howard, Bing Crosby, and of course Basil Rathbone. The theater women were amused by him and his pipe, which he used strategically to emphasize points in his discourse, thus countering the intimidation of the cigarette holders. But he was still a boy to them, and they tolerated him because he amused them. It could have been crushing, but it rather excited him for reasons he didn't altogether fathom, but didn't dispute. These were Woolworth ladies for whom he was quite willing to dance, even if for the moment he was winging it on adolescent roller skates. And mixing his metaphors to boot.

He got his first taste of Cocteau, Clair, Giraudoux, Chekhov, Ibsen, Synge, and Pirandello. Shaw was performed rather than read as a text. He wondered at the verse plays of Christopher Fry, and T. S. Eliot. And then there was Sartre: the great revelation of something big out there called Existentialism that he knew had to be assimilated. He tried reading Camus and Sartre and de Beauvoir, but he couldn't make much of it. The plays and novels were good as litera-ture, (hell was definitely other people, he knew that, and existence was un-questionably absurd, and very probably contingent) but what exactly was the "philosophy"? It seemed to be a call to some kind of stubborn bloody-mindedness, but he couldn't fathom the basis of it. He did however figure out how to strike the right attitudes to pass as one of the Left Bank cognoscenti, and that had to do. One of them loaned him Kierkegaard's *Diary of a Seducer*, which to his amazement was not classed as Victorian pornography, but as serious philosophy. He struggled excitedly through it; he had no idea what was going on, and as far as he could see the seduction never occurred. He didn't complain; he was afraid he might have missed the point. He had. Oth-erwise he floundered about with bits if half-informed wisdom from the in-tense young acolytes like: "You are absolutely responsible for everything about yourself; even your wavy hair is your own responsibility." Some big, gloomy, truth was lurking there, but on the way to finding it the black sweaters, awful black coffee, black berets and cough inducing Gitanes (rapidly abandoned) were something to be going on with. And more fun too.

When they were not lapping up concerts by the Hallé Orchestra under the powerful Sir Thomas Beecham, they were very much into jazz and big bands. There was even a sort of jazz scene. Dixieland bands were in favor and a lot of refugees from the strict industrial Brass Band tradition found an outlet in these. The local brass bands—like the regimental bands on which they were modeled—were actually fine schools for musicians and a way into music for many who would otherwise never have encountered it. But some of the lads yearned for something other than the heavy repertoire replete with Sousa and Verdi. The outlet was in Big Band groups and White Jazz. To our little aesthete with a head still full of Debussy and Delius this was alarming new stuff. Glenn Miller he had heard when very young (we suppose), but Paul Whiteman and Benny Goodman were a revelation. Even more so he was staggered by the almost chamber music appeal of Dixieland: chamber music with a beat and an excitement and improvisational spontaneity.

Composers were not so important here; it was the tunes that mattered. As yet he knew little from mechanical sources, but he practiced "Muskrat Ramble" and "Careless Love" and "When the Saints go Marching In" on the piano (badly) and with friends in a comb-and-paper ensemble that made up in enthusiasm what it painfully lacked in skill. Somehow the blues ("Basin Street," "Trouble in Mind," "St Louis Blues") seemed made for his existential theatrics. Louis Armstrong—he heard some records at the theater—became a genius to add to his growing hagiography of heavenly talents—"Cornet Chop Suey" blew him away (as he learned to say.) New Orleans, Chicago and Paris (Django Rhinehart) were added to his multiplying list of musical Meccas. He toyed with a guitar, and thought about the banjo. But he couldn't afford such things for himself.

He stored the idea away, and rattled on with the insane buzz of the comb-and-paper band, which was deeply into "novelties." They did a not-bad version of Spike Jones and his City Slickers with "Tea for Two." They did an ambitious two-part "Saber Dance" and "Twelfth Street Rag" then, abandoning the combs, stretched a string across the piano wires to make them vibrate and produce a zither-like sound for the "Third Man Theme." The great Orson struck again, and he went several times to see what he thought to be the greatest movie since *King Kong*. He tried to marry Harry Lime's cynicism to Existentialist despair in a befuddled attempt at synthesis, truly beyond his scope. It collapsed, but not without a profound reinforcement from Peggy Lee. This was Peggy Lee before "Fever" or "Is That All There Is?" It was the Peggy of "I Ain't Got Nobody" and "I Got It Bad" (and that ain't good); but the voice somehow conveyed the despair of the blues, and he sang them to himself as he deployed his breast-stroking, hopelessly unfulfilled, fantasies. The gloom was mitigated when he learned a few chords on a borrowed guitar and did a passable "Cool Water" (after The Sons of the Pioneers), including the fancy falsetto repeats with the (as he later leaned to call it) post-vocalic retroflex apico-palatal trill: "WateR! WaterR!" He had to give the guitar back, but filed away the experience for future reference, while the asthmatic kazoo ensemble went back to its favorite: *Moma don't 'low no Jazz Band playin' here*!

School once more became a pale irritation. The theatre and jazz adults were simply in a different category from the teachers. He couldn't put his finger on it, but this was a world he felt at home with despite his naiveté and lack of much obviously necessary experience—particularly with the opposite sex. He began to try his hand at writing plays, some of them in verse and heavily influenced by Hugo, Strindberg, and Yeats. He wrote some music for some of the Shakespeare plays: *Twelfth Night, The Tempest.* It was well enough received that he began to dream of a bohemian life of writing, theatre and music, but had again no real idea how one got into or sustained such a life. It was universally condemned as "risky" by his adults, even those in the theatre world itself, who should know. There was nothing for it. He had to stick with the school thing to get to university to get into journalism to get into politics—perhaps as a "political agent" — for he had no other real plans. He was almost diverted.

One of the gang-about-town among his new friends was a real junior journalist—a cub reporter on the local evening paper. Beverly was a creature out of film noir, with his grubby trench coat with its belt casually tied, his permanent trilby hat, and equally permanent cigarette dangling from his almost feminine mouth. He was the acknowledged leader of the avant-garde group that met in a cozy bar under the grandly-gothic Wool Exchange. He had done things with girls, reported the gruesome details of domestic murders, and lived on his own! He spent his nights and weekends, when he wasn't with girls, telling his tales to the enthralled gang of underage would-be Bogarts knocking back Guard's Ale, Barley Wine and the occasional port, while listening in rapt devotion. Bev could "put in a word" for him. With his writing reputation he could probably get a cub reporter job on the local rag, and work his way up from there. Temptation, temptation! But he panicked. Again it was risky; it was not the approved way. It might please him, but the university plus journalism (or law—that was being touted, he might make a good "barrister" with his debating skills) was still the route into politics. So he danced, like the coward he was, down that straight and very narrow—adult delineated—path.

Exams left him little time to debate the higher issues. One Christmas he took more exams than he sang in Messiahs. He realized that the end must indeed be nigh as he turned down Rugby games to swat for the damned things. Something had to give. He was skating for his life. Many of them were "mock" exams. The notion was that the best way to prepare for exams was to do them: mock A-levels, mock State Scholarships, mock Oxbridge College entrance. The gang became punch-drunk with exams. If they had been set an exam in quantum physics they would have simply picked up the pens and plowed ahead. But they were well prepared, and when the question loomed they recognized it and wrote with speed and often with confidence and real flair. On the other hand they were often faced with unfamiliar questions and they faltered. This separated the men from the boys in the exam world: what to do with the unfamiliar question? Here our roller-skating con man was in his element. How to make something out of nothing was in fact the only real challenge.

Whatmuff had a bright idea. Some of the lower-sixth History class should take History A-levels after its first year. It was supposed to be a two-year course, but he reckoned that they knew enough after one year to find four questions from each of the papers (European history 1493-1815; English history 1714-1815. Outside these periods there was no history.) Even if they could only get two good answers, a weak third and a filler for fourth, he reasoned, they could still get a respectable mark. Colleges would be simply wildly impressed by this one-year feat, and the likely lads would have something to put on their applications other than hopes, expectations and hollow boasting. And of course it would be good practice. It was. Our hero and one other boy (Brian) tried it, and indeed got quite respectable marks. Precocious little buggers they were, and very pleased with themselves, but they did do it. It would have been impossible to do in English because the texts were distributed strictly over the two-year period and so they would only have done half of them. But they were still writing silly with the mocks.

All this kept him impressively busy and in a constant mental whirligig. The paperback revolution changed the face of reading and book ownership. Penguin Books had made their appearance and substituted henceforward for the little hardbacks. Was it E. V. Rieu's translation of the *Iliad* that came first? Whatever, he had the Penguin Poets and the Penguin Classics, the Penguin Modern Classics and the Penguin Philosophers, and the Penguin Histories and on and on. Endless Penguins. A Penguin education doubling with the Third Programme. After one of his showy debating performances on the future of everything, someone was reported as saying of him: "Chap must read a lot of Penguin books." Susceptible as he was to putdowns of this kind, he stubbornly stuck by the source of avian inspiration. One day, he thought, perhaps he would write a Penguin Book. But that was too dizzy a thought, and he tabled it for future consideration. He contented himself with using a kit to give all the copies hard backs and gilt lettering. One did that sort of thing then—or gave them brown paper covers. Books were still precious. Some day he would write one.

At the moment he was having a hard enough time with his disinclination to do the set books. It never bothered him in English since he read them along with everything else he was reading and in history there were no set books as such. But in French he bogged down in the Corneille, Racine, and Hugo. He liked them well enough, but he just wasn't good enough at the language to read them easily. One result of being in a mixed school was that some of the drudge work of language teaching was put off onto junior mistresses, leaving the senior masters free to do the lofty literary stuff. It was his misfortune to get a lady teacher for French language with whom, for whatever reason, it was hate at first sight. It could have been his insistence on making all his essays into political and anti-socialist diatribes. To do this was irritating enough, but to do it in bad French was unforgivable and she came down hard. Quite right. But our stubborn junior reactionary attributed it to her political prejudices and there was no room for constructive negotiation. C'est la guerre.

In a fit of misery at the Christmas of his second year, with his mother in hospital yet again with serious eye trouble, his ankle in plaster from a Rugby injury, his party having lost an important by-election—all the weight of the world on his soul, he declared that he would leave school and join Bev on the newspaper. She wept through her painful eyes, and he was flooded with guilt again. His father said, as usual, do what you want. The headmaster was just furious, which didn't help, but dear Whatmuff took him aside and pleaded, appealing to his vanity (smart move) and suggesting compromises. Drop French. But that didn't mean giving up everything as he had supposed. Two A-levels and the General Paper (of which more later) would still get him into many good universities, and he could always take a third year in the sixth form and try for the really good ones. People doing Oxbridge entrance did that anyway. He succumbed.

Once the hateful French language was gone it was like a boil had burst and he could actually begin to enjoy the business of acing the A-levels. He still liked Hugo, Voltaire, Montaigne, Verlaine, and Anatole France. He thought the latter's story about Pontius Pilate the cleverest thing he had read to date: Pilate retired in Rome recalls his life in Palestine in great and entertaining detail, until someone questions him about the trial of Jesus of Nazareth. "Jesus of Nazareth?" he replies, puzzled, "I don't recall anyone of that name." Bloody marvelous! He tried to read *La Nausée* in the original (further puzzlement—he bogged down on inkwells and chestnut trees.) With the awful language class behind him, paradoxically, he quite enjoyed some French reading. It had moved from chore to fun; it was thus permissible.

The details don't matter. What matters to our narrative of the soul is again the impingements and the room for impingements. What got into his head and his motives, how it got there, and why it stuck. He was indeed to get a third year, and it was to matter. It changed the whole course of the narrative, making for a richer and more complicated plot. At least we suppose. The cub reporter could have ended up somewhere interesting, but it would not have been where we see him and the story would have been very different. For a start he was rudely reminded that if he did leave school he would have to do his National Service, which meant the likelihood of serious stuff in Korea. His father of course thought that it would be the making of him, but it was too much to contemplate at the time; it was too violent a swing in another direction. He still had things to find out, and while he had no conscientious objection to military service—he would be back with his soldiers again after all—this didn't seem the time. So the rough and tumble of events and ideas continued apace.

The W. H. Rhodes Canada Educational Trust, founded by a Canadian businessman who settled in England and wanted to encourage interaction between his two countries, each year sent thirty or so fine examples of British young manhood (no girls) to Canada for a tour, receptions and a wilderness camp. All splendid Commonwealth stuff, and our hero was nominated by the Dr. and much to his genuine amazement was selected. He was still getting used to the idea that he was not a behavior problem and troublemaker. With his list of civic, political, musical, theatrical and (thanks to Whatmuff's tactic) academic accomplishments, he was beginning to look good on paper at least. But somehow he could not avoid feeling that the selectors had been drunk or something.

A summer in Canada with a group of splendid young English and Scottish sixth formers all bound for the academy, the civil service, the foreign office, the higher reaches of the army and church and the arts and sciences. Heady company. He made particular friends, on the boat, with a boy from Battersea, Keith, due to do English at Cambridge. Keith's knowledge of Eng. Lit. was staggering. He described how, when faced with doing an essay on Milton, he would take a suitcase to the school library and fill it with every book on Milton, then take them home and "make notes" on all of them. This was necessary if one were to make an impression in scholarship exams where they expected an undergraduate level of discussion at least. The idea was totally novel. At school you never tackled more than one book at a time. This raiding of the library shelves was a daunting new idea, but he took it to heart. He wasn't afraid of the reading, it was the method that amazed. But Keith was truly impressive, and his easy confident public school manner presaged well for his future as a C. of E. bishop. He wouldn't discuss religion. Like a good Anglican he took it more or less for granted, and enjoyed rather singing part songs and competing in verse recitations (from memory) to while away the boat trip (on one of the old Cunarders long ago scrapped.) Keith pitted his *Lady of Shalott* against our man's *Pied Piper of Hamelin* and the assembly declared the duel a draw.

By a strange attraction of opposites, his other friend was a Catholic Jesuit-to-be (Basil) who also ended up as a prince of the church. The future doctor of canon law (Gregorian University, Rome) reveled in the verbal battle with the junior agnostic, whom he described in his journal (shown around quite freely) as "the intense fellow with the nervous mouth." This led to long sessions in front of the mirror trying to pinpoint the twitch in question and bring it under conscious control. He vowed to let up on the intensity to the point where he was rebuked by one of the masters for his "unrelenting flippancy."

The ship was shared by a party of young Canadian university women who had been touring Europe. They were unbelievably attractive, but they were college women and by definition out of reach. They were so sophisticated and secure; so different from the girls at school or even from the theater crowd. They sounded like women from movies, and they looked and moved like them too. They drove cars, drank cocktails and smoked cigarettes. But, amazingly, they seemed to like the schoolboys, or at least those of the school-boys who were most grown-up themselves. They particularly liked the Scots in their kilts for formal dining, and he cursed that fact that the English had no national dress, unless sports coat and flannels counted. Especially they liked the tall, suave handsome lordling with the French name who was eventually to become the first male centerfold for Cosmopolitan.

He knew he couldn't compete. His winsome dances were just not enough to get the goodies these movie-style ladies commanded. But some of the quieter ones talked to him and seemed even to like his company, in the moonlight, on the deck. One even told him he was "good looking in an English sort of way." His heart raced and pounded, and he feared he was going to faint again, for he could smell perfume. There were possibilities here, to be sure, but he still didn't really know what they were. The remembrance of an accidental touch of the hand had to carry him through the night.

Canada itself was jaw-sagging wonderful beyond all reasonable belief. There was a sense of vastness, of sumptuousness, boundless energy and pos-sibilities. Everything was oversized: the distances, lakes, mountains, steaks, cities. Quebec, Montreal, and Toronto dazzled, and at Niagara Falls—defy-ing as it did all the superlatives—they let him put a foot in the United States just to say he'd been there. The whirl of receptions (photographed with Mounties) and dinners (such food! whole chickens, buffalo tongues, racks of this and that: food at one sitting that would have fed the family at home for a week) combined with jet lag, lack of sleep and exhaustion, rendered the whole thing in memory as a kind of hallucinatory dream. The comparison with his provincial, pinched, austere experience so far was almost painful.

The wilderness camp he did not like. He had expected Indians and there were no Indians. Since he couldn't swim he was not allowed on the canoe trips which took up most of the day. He spent the time trying to fish (boring, but giving an excuse for long private reflection) and thumbing through the little camp library. There he found strange authors who must have been North American: Fennimore Cooper, Jack London, Washington Irving, Nathaniel Hawthorne, Edgar Allen Poe, Herman Melville, Henry James even (*The Turn of the Screw*), and strange Walt Whitman whom he knew only from settings by Delius and Vaughan Williams, but who now rolled out in all his self-regarding glory. The only other ones he'd known were Twain and Longfellow, but there were new treasures even of these old favorites, and mischievously marvelous Twain on missionaries added to his rationalist arsenal.

So the wilderness camp (the wilderness bit was frankly horrific, full of itches and scratches, prickly heat and biting things, supposed to be part of the inevitable character-building program so beloved of the muscular-Christian thugs who ran these things) was not entirely a waste. He learned new songs at campfire sessions while systematically swatting mosquitoes (*The Ballad of Jesse James* and songs from a Québecois canoe-guide never contemplated in French class.) A new interest in this continent was kindled: a flame that would not easily die, fanned as it was by film-noir cops and killers, Fred Astaire, Western movies, Dixieland jazz, sophisticated ladies, cocktails before dinner, buffalo tongue, Hiawatha, big bands, baseball, Zane Grey, and A-level History.

For yes, he was back to that with the proverbial vengeance and a new goal: through university he would find a way to get back to that fabulous continent and explore it in detail. He brought home a blue baseball cap (obtained at a game in Toronto), that he insisted on wearing for cricket. They knew by now that it was no use arguing with him, and let these little breaches of the code pass, as the English are wont to do, as "harmless eccentricity"—which they unofficially really rather prized. The cap at least was blue, which was the school color. For the moment there was little he could do about it other than flourish the cap and practice his Amercan singing voice with the blues and imitations of Frankie Lane (brother of the old wild goose...) But fortuitously, in History, they were doing the eighteenth century; they lived and breathed the eighteenth century. History *was* the eighteenth century. He knew the eighteenth century better than his own, and often felt he'd have been more at home in it. Some knowledge of the previous centuries was allowed as background, but History ceased abruptly with the Battle of Waterloo (and in truth did not get beyond the French Revolution—causes of.)

In English the syllabus did extend further, but the Augustans dominated just the same. Within each syllabus there was room for some specialization, some special area to cultivate. So he happily plumped for the history of the American colonies, which given the kings-and-battles approach meant the Seven Years' War (French and Indian War to the Yanks) and the Revolution (causes of, course of, results of.) He brought in a (small) suitcase and tried his new role model's method, scavenging across a range of books, although he preferred to read them and not "take copious notes." While you are making notes on one book, he reckoned, you could have read two more. And he could trust his well-honed memory enough to make the drudgery unnecessary.

So the Americas it was, highly colored by superman Hawkeye, noble Uncas and the evil Magua. He had a permanent wall map in his bedroom with all the major battles of both conflicts marked in different colored crayons. How terrible it was he thought, even then, that the Englishmen who had stood together against the unspeakable French should have had to fight each other over what appeared to be a bunch of minor quibbles about tea and taxes. But his conservative hero Edmund Burke, and his putative relative Charles James Fox, had stood out against fighting the Americans, and he could take pleasure from that. "Ignore all those supposed causes," Whatmuff told him, "remember that the revolution began the day the Mayflower left Plymouth."

It was however the new General Paper that was to jolt in him in yet another direction. It was a bold and brave attempt to bridge (Lord) Snow's notorious Two Cultures—for despite a lot of criticism Snow was right: the distinction between Arts and Science was quite rigid by the sixth form, and even before. This new exam subject became a pet project of the enlightened Dr. It involved some English and History (not set books but "trends and topics"), a bit of General Science, some basic Psychology, Civics, International Affairs and Economics. All pretty rudimentary, but it opened up new casements on curious new landscapes. For the English they had a new energetic young lady teacher, Miss Pegg. She was keen on modern drama and the like, and had them do studies of great directors. He plumped for Orson Welles, and for the first time, in dissecting *Citizen Kane*, understood what great directing really meant. He went on to Harley Granville-Barker and the play as a thing purely for the stage, not a literary text. His almost unthinking belief in the value of the death penalty as a deterrent was shattered when Whatmuff made them read the crime statistics and discover that there was no relationship between murder rates and the use of the extreme sanction. They ploughed on with the difference between instinct and habit, the "g" factor in intelligence (and the taking of the tests—he was a not a genius, but delighted with "superior adult"), the life and work of Galileo, the problems with European union, patterns of history, the trouble with the gold standard. This was all grand stuff for the walking encyclopaedia. He could eat and drink it for breakfast.

In particular he relished the Economics, and went far beyond the narrow syllabus in his interest in marginal productivity and unusual demand curves. Economics promised ways of dealing with questions about society that could be solved definitively with formulae and diagrams: geometric diagrams—he could handle that. The "trends in history" questions had him debating Fisher (whose *History of Europe* was their bible on that subject) and his "no patterns in history," versus Toynbee (*A Study of History*—abridged edition) and his roiling periodicities. Dimly he saw the emergence of big issues about man and society that went way beyond his narrow experience. He fumbled with Philosophy but, having little guidance, couldn't fathom just what it was. He read his Penguins and ploughed through Professor Joad (of BBC fame) and his jaunty introductions.

He stumbled on the Rationalist Press Association via some tattered journals on the second-hand bookstall: a whole organization for people who doubted religious truths! He spent some birthday money on a subscription. His greatest and most beloved discovery, while searching for support in his religious revolt, was the grand Bertrand Russell. *Why I am not a Christian* and particularly the essay (in *Sceptical Essays*) "A Free Man's Worship" were triumphs that sustained him and comforted his sometimes shaken confidence. So was the other discovery of Albert Schweitzer on the historical, apocalyptic Jesus, the *interimsethic*, the decay and restoration of civilization, the reverence for life. The greatest philosophers in the world seemed to be on his side! It didn't get better than that.

We must pause to look at where the progress of the developing soul stood. University was still in, but he didn't want to spend a third year at school, Oxbridge or no Oxbridge. He was anxious to be up, up and away, but not too far away. His music and theater, his Rugby and local politics (where he was now a big junior wheel in the party organization, speaking on the same platforms as Macmillan and Butler), his continuing interest in journalism and his connections with the local papers, all led him to want to stay around. He put in applications to various universities, including Manchester, Birmingham and Liverpool (in deference to cousin Syd), but his attraction was to local Leeds. It was near enough that he could keep in touch with everything, but far enough away that he would have to live there and do the full-fledged student thing. The good Dr. knew the Dean of the Arts Faculty there. This Dean and the head of the Economics department (an applied economist called Brown— successor to the professor for whom his mother once worked) invited him to visit, and they put a proposition to him.

They were instituting a new General Degree—you took three subjects rather than the usual one—which, unlike in the past when it was just pass-fail, was to be awarded with honors, and the chance of the coveted First. They were looking for good students who would take adventurous combinations of subjects—not just the usual what-I-was-best-at-in-school. How would he like to do something like political science, history, and economics, for example? Since he had given up the idea of English or History at Oxbridge, and the necessary extra year, he thought this a splendid idea, and the matter was settled with a metaphorical spit and handshake. It now only remained to ace the A-levels, and the accompanying S-levels (S for "scholarship") which might—a very outside chance—draw the rare State Scholarship: the highest of high achievements in this world: the entrance card for everywhere.

Well wasn't that all splendid? And didn't it all come tumbling down. Oh yes, he aced the exams, with marks that had never been seen on the history of the examinations. The State Scholarship even would have been his. But the bureaucracy struck in one of those iron-headed blasts of injustice that had her nearly apoplectic. He was caught between the old School Certificate system and the new General Certificate system, with its O- and A-levels. The details are too tedious, but it transpired that a higher standard in the old School

Certificate was being demanded of the transitional students, and his Mathematics mark was not good enough. The goalposts had been shifted; it was blatantly unfair. But the powers were unmoved. Exceptions could not be made. The Dr. and the Dean protested to no avail. And that was that. It really was. A third year anyway. He was stoical. He got to go on playing Rugby and doing all his familiar musical, political and theatrical things. He would even be made head boy (school captain), about which he was ambivalent, but his vanity was touched. And he could now do the Oxbridge thing at his leisure, if that's what was in the cards.

The disaster was, serendipitously, to bias his life along the trajectory that, in retrospect acquires a kind of inevitability. He could regroup, reconsider and think of a future that was not just patched together out of ongoing concerns. Practicalities: to matriculate he otherwise needed three A-levels at one sitting. (The General Paper, it turned out, did not, contrary to what the teachers had assumed, count as an A-level.) Here he took a momentous decision in his little life, for he had learned through Professor Brown at Leeds that there existed an A-level paper in Economics. Very few people took it, since this was not a subject taught in schools, and most of the takers were doing business courses at technical colleges. He could not, the headmaster said, do a two-year course in one year. Why not; had he not done it in History? There was a syllabus, recommended textbooks, and previous exam papers as a guide. He didn't need a distinction, just a respectable pass. But, they insisted, you have no teacher. Unhappily, Whatmuff left to be a headmaster somewhere else. It was a depressing blow, but the marvelous man had done his job so superbly that History was now engraved in his synapses—he could do those papers in his sleep. The new master was a Cambridge man who had done economic history there, and he offered to give a weekly tutorial in economics and supervise a weekly essay. It turned out that what he did was take an old textbook, copy out the chapters, and read them out one week at a time: in return for getting to call himself Senior Economics Master, draw extra pay, and buck for promotion. No matter. Economics got learned somehow, there being much time for it, since, apart from the new set books in English for that year, there was not much new he needed to learn for the strict purposes of passing exams.

Economics was exciting, no question. It was so very definitive, not like History or Philosophy. He read somewhere the aphorism: "If you have price, you have everything." Another of those revelations. Supply and demand was all. Wages were the price of labor and determined by supply and demand for same: and woe betide any government or union that interfered with this law of nature. Rent was the price of land, ditto. Interest was the price of money, same. He even managed Keynes on liquidity preference and the multiplier effect once he realized that real math was not involved—just logical formulae that were easy to follow. He tried to plough through two volumes of George

Stigler on *The Theory of Price* (the school library actually had them) but had to confess most of it beyond him.

He did see though that politics was going to be different for him. Not many of his political acquaintances knew much about economics; they were mostly lawyers. The Tory businessmen knew about business, but this was not the same thing as knowing about the gross national product and national income theory. But even more so, it was the sense of having some definite truths about human behavior and the strange business of how society "worked" at all. This also gave him respectable arguments against state socialism. Nothing else came close. Whatmuff (still then a Labour supporter) had introduced him to these issues. He had read Herbert Spencer's criticism of Carlyle's "Great Man Theory" of history, and knew there were forces at work over which individuals had little control. Marshall, Keynes, Adam Smith—here surely was at least some of the answer. It lay in "the hidden hand." Even the little he knew of Marx, was nervously explored. The Communists, Whatmuff assured him, had distorted and betrayed Marx. Much as the Christians had done with Christ. Food for more thought. So he was launched—more-or-less self launched—on a journey of the mind that radically altered the development of the soul in question.

There was still the ongoing stuff of exam preparation to attend to, although it always took second place. Again, though, he had a stroke of luck. Once more an examiner—a lofty figure from one of the universities—gave a talk on how to survive exams. One thing stood out. Most exam answers, he said, when they were not plain bad were still predictable. One went though marking them half-asleep as the same old examples and clichés were repeated. People passed, but it was not very interesting. What was certain to garner high marks, he said, was the occasional answer that jerked the reader awake: some new idea, some odd notion, some curious argument, some set of facts not on the "required" list. He didn't give examples, but the idea stuck in the imagination and gimmicks were thought about. Thus, there was always a question about the "enlightened despots"—either collectively or at least one of them. You were supposed to swot up on the enlightened despots.

By chance, he had picked up an odd, very slim, volume at the market stall: *The Education of the Enlightened Despots,* by the unlikely Prince Chula Chakrabongse of Siam. Something the little prince had done at Cambridge, and was no doubt published more because of the exotic author than the subject matter. But it was a nice little survey of despotic childhood and youth: Louis XV, Frederick II, Joseph II, and, of course, Catherine. Frederick fascinated him the most, with his frightening brute of a father and his near escape from execution. Following Keith's example, he looked for other biographies, and found Lavesse's wonderful *Youth of Frederick the Great.* It was as if providence (he could not say God) had rewarded his for once conscientious, if perhaps a little cunning, efforts, when the exam produced "What right has Frederick II to the title of The Great?" Oh boy, now to wake that examiner up with juicy details that were not in the standard textbooks: like Frederick's penning of a treatise in his teens (when under house arrest by his father) on the economy of Silesia and its importance to Prussia. And we all know what happened to Silesia. Stir in some (brief) quotes of his (youthful) French verses, a few lines of his (youthful) flute music, his later patronage of Bach and Voltaire, his numerous writings on all subjects (list remembered) and you could forget all those battles and treaties with dates and details too tedious to remember. The examiner was good and awake, and the silver roller skates were skimming round the golden rink. Saved again!

English rolled on. This third year was ecstatic. So much time, so many books. Birrel had them trying to translate Milton into Latin so they understood his sentences better. Not popular; but Birrel was a product of the Scottish university system (Glasgow) with its broad education in the humanities, and had been a Classics master before being converted to English in an emergency. Otherwise they construed scads of Shakespeare. "Knowing the text thoroughly" was the order of the day, and Basher was the man to make sure they did. No harm. When stuck for some intelligent noises to make about a play, one could at least give a decent synopsis of the plot with illustrative quotes. Just enough so that the examiner didn't nod off.

Specialization allowed him to concentrate on the poets, dramatists and essayists. He was relieved not to have to do the novels. Richardson, Fielding, Austen, Thackeray, Trollope, Dickens, Elliott, Hardy—these were all too heavy going. He'd heard many of them on "Book at Bedtime" and he reckoned that would serve. He read one of each for the record and rushed back to the fun stuff. Chaucer, Spenser, Marlowe, More, Bacon, Milton, Dryden, Vanbrugh, Swift, (Donne was not included and was discovered later through Eliot) Addison, Johnson, all of Pope, Cowper, Sheridan, Goldsmith, Gray, some Byron, some Blake, much Wordsworth. The essayists: Walpole, Hazlitt, Lamb, de Quincy, Peacock, and Coleridge, and then, oh blessed relief, skip over the moonstruck Romantics (Basher didn't like them) and on to jangly, tangly contorted and complex Browning: Robert, not the wife. *Men and Women* became the new poetic bible to be much imitated—endless dramatic monologues in the manner of "An Epistle of Karshish the Physician." And further afield there was the whole glorious corpus of Browningism to explore, and never enough time because of the onrush of the later Victorians. Tennyson was nice, Arnold intrigued, but only Swinburne thrilled, and the choruses from *Atalanta in Calydon* chanted out loud and often in tears, were his lonely pagan substitute for the Apostles' Creed. "All we, all we are against thee, O God most high!" But, via the Penguin Poets and the *Faber Book of Modern Verse* there arose the T. S. Eliot problem, and the skittish roller skates were seriously derailed by what promised to be a truly serious issue.

Consider that at this time "modern verse"—more or less anything after Robert Bridges—was simply off limits as far as school was concerned. Birrel once read W. H. Auden's heartbreaking elegy "Stop all the clocks, shut off the telephone…" only as an example of how poetry should *not* sound. What he would have done if he'd realized it was a homosexual love poem doesn't bear thinking about. But at least Auden operated more or less within accepted prosodic parameters. "Free verse" was simple not poetry, which should preferably "Rrrhyme, scan and mak' immediate sense tae any educated perrrson." Not bad advice as it happens, but not something welcome to the truculent literary rebel who had absorbed avant-garde prejudices from the bohemian existentialists in the smart bar at the local railway hotel. He knew that *The Waste Land* was the key philosophical poem of the age. Everyone must come to terms with it. He struggled, entirely on his own time since this was surely not in the syllabus, with this overtly strange mini-epic. He actually did fill a small notebook (brown paper backing) with garnered comments and interpretations. He memorized it. He searched out explanations of Eliot's own gnomic "explanatory" footnotes.

One in particular struck him: the one about using the two volumes *Adonis, Attis, Osiris* from Sir James Frazer's *The Golden Bough*, "a work of anthropology," Eliot said, "which has influenced our generation profoundly." It evidently explained the business of "vegetation ceremonies." He didn't know what these were. There was Harvest Festival at church, which was a ceremony and about vegetation. But for Eliot is was something to do with corpses and regeneration. Resurrection? Myths of the dying God? This seemed promising. Jesse L. Weston's *From Ritual to Romance* was also praised, and the school library had that fine study of the Grail Legend—devoured at once with wonder that such questions could even be asked.

Frazer they did not have (some lesser translations—*Pausanias*, but not the magnum opus), so he hit the faithful reference library and there it was, all thirteen shiny volumes with the two in question practically untouched by human hands. But it was golden in truth. It was a voyage in a sea of wonderful information from classical literature and this marvelous new thing called "anthropology" which dealt with ancient and primitive people and European peasants, their strange customs, beliefs and legends. And there it all was indeed. The corpse you planted in your garden last year did spring to life only to be killed and buried in a thousand disguises and to rise again on cue. The vegetation God was thus exposed for what he was, despite C. S. Lewis's casual dismissal (he now knew what Lewis was so afraid of.) Keats looking into Chapman's Homer could not have been half so smitten as was our lad by the realms of gold in the Virgilian bough.

By coincidence they were doing *Aeniad VI* in the "keep up your Latin" class, and this is the book where Virgil invokes the fabulous Golden Bough which is the source of Frazer's subject and his title. So another brown-paper-backed notebook was filled with passages of Virgil and Frazer's translations of same. But there was a fundamental grave doubt running through all this excitement. Frazer was revealing the naked truth of religion as simply vegetation myths. The dying and rising God with the Holy Mother, virgin birth, miraculous youth, etc. was thus explained away. But Eliot was a known card-carrying Anglican convert who wrote (unfortunately) beautiful devotional poems ("The dove descending breaks the air/ With flame of incandescent terror...") and thought we ought to strive for *The Idea of a Christian Society*. Not good. How could the great poet hold two contradictory ideas at the same time?

Digression—but one ultimately relevant. The mother of a friend who took an interest in his fumbling poetic efforts, offering sound criticism which he wouldn't accept, was a member of the Unitarian Church. He was mildly attracted to this form of the Arian heresy, since it denied the divinity of Christ while keeping many of the forms of Anglican worship which still tugged at his heart. A happy compromise. So he was persuaded to go to some services at the local church. The attraction of these was not the service per se, a pretty dismal affair with a poor choir, but the remarkable preacher. Mr. Bullock's sermons were not really that at all. He was a polymath who used the pulpit to talk about whatever took his fancy: history, literature, politics, theology, philosophy. His son, Allan, was, our boy thought, the luckiest youngster alive. And said youngster indeed went on to become a famous historian, master of an Oxford college, and peer of the realm. Mr. Bullock's sermons were pure magic. And he often talked of literature, and yes, of Eliot, whose poems he read in his rich Yorkshire nonconformist preacher-voice, sounding like a Pennine version of Richard Burton. He was approachable, so he was approached, and the question re. Eliot's apparent contradiction posed. Mr. Bullock's eloquent reply sticks unforgettably in the memory and was written down in the empty pages at the end of the Virgil/Frazer notebook:

"Why do you think I celebrate a form of Holy Communion? Not because I believe in the real presence or even because of the explicit Christian symbolism. Or why do we (Unitarians) celebrate Easter or even Harvest Festival? All these key ceremonies go back to something older and more profound. They have been borrowed and adapted by our religious tradition, but their origins, and therefore their meanings, are derived from the things Frazer displays for us. Eliot understands that."

How to describe how thrilling this kind of thinking was? It went beyond Economics. It was a delving into the great mysteries that was not religious belief but rational insight and analysis. He couldn't place it exactly but it had something to do with the "anthropology" that Eliot had recognized and Frazer practiced. Mr. Bullock advised getting the abridged edition of Frazer: easier to handle, and he could get the whole argument.

He had just won the school prize for English, and had to choose a "suitable book" to be embossed. He chose the Frazer, the abridged 1922 edition, with the green binding and the golden misletoe, and then the school crest in gold with the three thorn trees and the grim motto: Stulti Doctrinam Spernunt. There was some doubt as to whether this was a suitable book. There was a new headmaster—the Dr. had gone on to better things—and he clucked a little, but a previous art prize had yielded Byron, and the history prize the collected essays of Namier. So he claimed that dues to suitability had been paid and got his Frazer, which he kept lovingly for life. She, knowing how he liked H. G. Wells, had bought him *The Outline of History* for a birthday, and he marveled at a history so ambitious, that started with the origins of life on earth. He had read T. H. Huxley for Darwinian ammunition in the cause of agnosticism. He now went back and read him for pure and simple evolutionism, and he was back again with the BBC reporter from the past, and felt his mental fingers groping into holes more ancient than even those in the stone-age boulders on the pre-historic moors.

The year passed. His party had won its election, but nothing radical seemed to follow. It was almost as if everyone had glumly accepted that the central-ized state system had come to stay and that politics in future was going to descend into eternal quibbles about who could build the most council houses. He had dreams in which Harold Macmillan was his father. The Korean War depressed everyone and mostly they put it out of mind. McCarthyism both frightened—because one didn't want the Yanks to lose their grip again—and amused, but again seemed so distant. They did year-end skits including one of a "senator McRory" who was terrified of the word red. A new Queen had been crowned. The Festival of Britain had been visited (was it that year? It all blurs in memory.) He was hit by Rugby injuries: dislocated shoulder (twice), ligaments in both feet (very slow to heal), and finally a devastating crack to his left knee cartilage that put him in miserable plaster for many weeks. It reduced his leg to skin and bone, and finished the idyllic days of mud and frost and the crash of bodies and the rush of speed and contact. It was over. A little tennis was all that was left to him, and the odd, languid cricket game.

How these things seem like the end of the world, and how at the time they were. But he had then even more time for the lunatic reading (Aldous Huxley, D. H. Lawrence—he could read the Lovers bit but found the Sons too pain-fully close to home—Greene, Waugh, Graves, Hemingway, Dennis Wheatley.) Above all there was Orwell. He didn't know why, but somehow he found Orwell's unadorned, blunt but witty English style, the one he wanted to emulate. He didn't try consciously to imitate anyone, but he began to sound more and more like Orwell, and he didn't fight it. There was more time even for girls, since without Rugby he had weekend time on his hands, and could still dance. Kissing (in the dark of the cinema) was cultivated to an art: a prodigious advance to be sure, but nothing beyond that. These were nice girls, some of them the exotic

Catholics—the dark Rosaleens, the Moiras, and Eileens—and that was as far it could conceivably go in those days of frugal lust and fumbling ignorance. During the last slow waltz, in the darkened ballroom, he often wondered if they felt the urgent pressure against their thighs. If they did, they didn't recoil; they kept their heads pressed into his shoulder and responded warmly to the last kiss before the lights and the applause. Sometimes he thought they blushed a little, but no one said anything, ever. You just didn't.

At home the truce continued. His father was promoted, and came to be much valued as the new immigrants from India (or rather Pakistan) hit the northern industrial cities. The father "knew how to deal" with these new workers; he even spoke a bit of their language. He did sensible things. They wanted to eat their own food, not the eternal fish and chips from the canteen, so they used to cook in the toilets. Banned, naturally. So the old Indian army man took charge, divided the canteen down the middle, put up trestle tables at one end with primus stoves for them to cook their curry on (ate it himself) and kept them all satisfied. He educated them on not trying to bribe everyone in sight, and his "chop-chop" briskness, far from being resented, seemed to remind them of home and familiar things. It was a way of managing the world our budding economist could almost admire, but could never hope or wish to emulate. She did well in her "institutional catering" career, ending by running the surgeons' dining room at the local Royal Infirmary. Her continuing illnesses and hospitalizations quieted down the arguments and hostilities; the father had fallen into a kind of silent resignation. They were somehow receding from him. He loved them and recognized their love for him, but they seemed to inhabit a different world that barely overlapped with his except for the maintenance functions and the animal affection of parents and only child.

The year passed, and decisions had to be taken. He enjoyed being head boy/school captain more than he might have imagined (he got to drop the now hated school uniform which so glaringly announced schoolboy status) for although he was still a bit awkward, he was no longer the loner and the outcast. He had passed imperceptibly into the thing he once saw as a distant dream: he was part of the school establishment, in fact head of it, since the prefects ran the school as far as discipline outside the classroom was concerned. Only major punishments like expulsion were reserved for the headmaster. He continued to buck custom though, and abolished caning, knowing from long experience that it was a useless deterrent to hardened cases. He also abolished the hated writing of "lines" during after-school detention ("I must not talk in assembly"—one hundred times), and substituted doing math problems, which he thought was more constructive.

This enlightened innovation fell apart when the senior Mathematics master objected to the subject being used as punishment. His school status led to a greater acceptance in the wider society of the town, and he felt more confidence with the cosmopolitan ones. He began to appreciate his classmates more, and see their virtues. One was to solve some intractable mathematical theorem and become the youngest ever professor of mathematics, with a special chair created for him at Sheffield University. Another went to Edinburgh, and ended up as head of surgery at the local Royal Infirmary. Another became head of the Geography department at Bradford Grammar School. He felt more at ease now with these his peers. He needed the roller skates less, but he was glad they were somewhere easy to find.

He still wrote masses of music and won the new headmaster's pet prize for the best vacation project with a submission of songs, which were performed at the next speech-day concert. To hear his own music; how much better it actually sounded than it looked on paper. It worked. It was melodious ("She Walks in Beauty"); it was harmonic ("The Stolen Child"); it was dramatic ("When the Hounds of Spring"). It was applauded. His poetry began to be less derivative; a voice was emerging. He tried to emulate some of the poets in the Faber book with their "free verse" but he couldn't do it. It was like a game where everyone made up his own rules as he went along (viz Frost's comment that it was "like playing tennis without a net.") Without the rules how could you measure what you were doing? How did you know if it was any good? Variations within the rules were infinitely possible, but the complete abandonment didn't make sense.

He discovered a knack for translation: Catullus, Verlaine—for keeping the translation close but making the result still decent poetry. But there was now no question of his allegiance to Economics as the new intellectual hunting ground. He rejected the pressure to do the Oxbridge scholarships because all they appeared to offer was a future of English or History. Wrong, of course. No matter what subject he got the scholarship in, he could have majored in some other. The great PPE (Politics, Philosophy, Economics) at Oxford would have been perfect, but he didn't know that; he was poorly informed generally, and not inclined to listen to advice if it didn't suit his mood. And his mood was insistent: Get to London!

Several things conspired to draw him to London. There were the romantic impressions left by various visits, as well as the sheer centrality of the capital in all things: politics, theater, literature, music, art, journalism, even jazz. This was, like France, a one-city country: aut Londinium aut nihil. His new Catholic friend, Mike, who was aiming to be a doctor, was bound for one of the great London teaching hospitals. Where else would you go but Guy's or Bart's or, in Mike's case, University College. What were Oxford and Cambridge?—for all their mediaeval glamour, just small provincial towns (one industrial, one market). He had done that.

The late Dr. had talked much of the greatness of London University, and before he left had given out some literature on the various London colleges. Several of the sixth form—girls and boys—had set their hearts on Kings, Imperial, Bedford, or University. This was a departure, since no one previously had ever gone to London. For our budding universal problem solver there was one obvious choice: The London School of Economics and Political Science. Didn't that title say it all? Despite its Fabian foundations, its whiff of Shaw and the bossy Webbs, and its left-wing reputation in politics, the standing of the LSE as a training ground of economists and politicians generally, was unchallenged. It was as hard to get into as Oxbridge, but less socially exclusive. It even favored older students—those who had done national service—and particularly foreign students. It was a genuine international meritocratic academy. It was waiting. It called.

His classmate Brian, who doubled as a math wizard and clarinet virtuoso, was determined to try for it. The two cultures had forced Brian to choose the Arts stream, but when he saw the possibility, his strength in math had led him to want to take the high road to Economics as well. They took the London scholarship papers together. The Scholarship questions were always lofty and general. In English they asked for a "compare and contrast" between one modern play or long poem and one from a past century. Aiming to keep the examiner wide awake, he chose *The Waste Land* and Pope's *Essay On Man*. The answer wrote itself. In History it was the same: "In the longer view the individual is of no account. Discuss"—or something such. They went for interviews (the school paid.) They wandered up and down Fleet Street and the Strand and round Covent Garden and Soho, staying overnight at the YMCA in Tottenham Court Road and eating in a Lyons Corner House on Oxford Street. They took the underground to South Kensington and got cheap seats for an Albert Hall concert. Way up near the roof the Beethoven and Carl Maria von Weber, and, heaven of heavens, *Fantasia on a Theme of Thomas Tallis* drifted up to them like melodious incense.

They went refreshed to the interviews. The board was enchanted with Brian's math ability. They were just as impressed with self-taught Economics and not at all put out by the Young Conservatism, especially when he invoked Edmund Burke. On the contrary, they seemed to think any interest in politics a good predictor of success at the School. (The chairman of the board was a Professor Oakeshott; he couldn't know the significance at the time.) His mere mention of an interest in anthropology via Frazer brought smiles of almost avuncular pleasure. He knew R. H. Tawney had taught at the School (the good Dr. told him), so he worked in *Religion and the Rise of Capitalism*, which Whatmuff (who else?) had made him read. You should think of Sociology for your Part II (major), they said. Magic, magic. These were workable adults. Not to be there would be intolerable. But for once the gods dealt a royal flush. The scholarships were obtained, the A-levels aced again, including a more than respectable mark in Economics; even the coveted State Scholarship was in hand.

So why did he have the feeling he was still on roller skates, skating for his life in fact? The results were genuine, but he still felt as he were swimming just to keep afloat. He was still dancing like an injury-faking bird, still not sure who he was or what he was doing, or why. (And still mixing his metaphors.) He still could not assume the air of confidence that seemed mysteriously to inhere in those born to rule. He was not born to rule; he was a information-gathering gypsy loose in a settled society that wanted him to be respectable and sedentary. How could he assume that air of confidence when he automatically assumed that any criticism made of him must be justified, and that he should go right on the defensive and try to explain himself, usually at ridiculous length? Never complain, never apologize, never explain. The awkwardly growing skater worked on the opposite principles to the Secret Service motto. He complained pathetically, apologized excessively, and explained at boring length.

A lot of the time he curbed this and people thought of him as he would like to have been thought of: the young milord, one of the natural guardians, the skeptical—slightly foppish even—creature of ready wit and easy achievement. But the mouth was still nervous. He developed the habit of mentally rehearsing beforehand even the slightest conversation, and then rehashing it afterwards; the lips would often betray this internal dialogue. He was still terrified of rejection and, while being accounted a rebel, was infused with her fear of what they might think, of making a terrible gaffe. It shouldn't matter; it didn't matter to others, but it mattered to him. He wanted not to be like this, but that was when he discovered that we are not captains of our souls; our souls rattle on regardless of us, and have their own obsessive ways that we can regret, but cannot alter. He was puzzled by his apparent lack of real emotions other than a shallow sentimentality, plentiful self-pity, and, of course, indignation. It's the still waters that run deep; he was a shallow babbling rivulet.

The only real thing about him, he thought, was the true driving and driven curiosity about anything and everything. That drove him to want even more information. But he still felt he didn't really know what he was doing, and most of the time felt that nothing was worth doing; so how was he to put that to any purpose greater than making it through the next exams with the latest in flashy roller skates? Even so, he went off that summer—high enough on success to put off the pain—for a few weeks of Shakespeare at Stratford with Mike. They wallowed in the exuberance of the bard, unfettered by exam worries, and declaimed the sonnets to a polite youth hostel gathering. There he met a pretty girl from a south-London suburb who spontaneously slipped her arm around him while in the standing-room-only for *Measure for Measure*, and he was hit for the second time with that sense of total emotional jolt that could only be, he figured, falling in love. He was off and away now, and perhaps he wouldn't need the roller skates—not as much anyway. But it was nice having them to hand, in case the plot faltered.

4

The Student: Putting on the Masks

Mrs. Gaskell, in *The Life of Charlotte Brontë,* first told the world the story of the Rev. Mr. Brontë and the business of the mask. The eccentric clergyman has had a poor press, but here he stands out as a decent father and a wise psychologist. The villagers in that hard, cliff-hanging village, straggling stubbornly up the hillside, knew all about this anyway, although some of the rougher of them had never read the good biographer. Even so, they were quick to denounce her known defamations. The story they told, handed down over a hundred years, was this: Mr. Brontë was a strict, but conscientious and concerned, Victorian father. He knew that if the children wanted to speak to him of personal matters they would find it hard to do so directly. But he had "a mask"—he doesn't say (in his letter to Mrs. Gaskell) what kind of mask. He would line them up—Maria, Elizabeth (the forgotten one), Patrick Branwell, Charlotte, Emily, and Anne—and have them speak from behind the mask. This was evidently successful, even if the questions and answers he recalled gained eloquence with hindsight.

Revisionist biographers have declared him to be not nearly the monster of Gaskellian legend, but in fact a kind and intelligent, if stern, paterfamilias, whose devotion to the wayward Branwell bordered on the heroic. If he did discharge his brace of pistols out of the window every night, well, these were troubled Luddite times when all gentlemen carried pistols, and undischarged powder deteriorated and caused accidents. There was method in most of his seeming madness, not least with the mask, for this would have seemed decidedly peculiar at the time to the no-nonsense West Riding hill-folk so well (if sensationally) described by the good lady and friend of Charlotte. Things had not changed all that much between the 1860s and the 1930s. There were very old people who as children had known the aging, virtually blind, clergyman, and his sad, bereaved, son-in-law, with their Irish accents, and their lonely life at the parsonage. And the principle of the mask was unchanged: the voice behind the mask was still the safe voice, the one that did not expose you, that let you weigh your answer according to the circumstances. The old vicar had been so very right: when dealing with the adults, reach for the mask.

The compulsive wanderer had new vistas and opportunities. Unlike school where every minute was accounted for, university had a few classes and lectures each week and lots of free time. None of the lectures was even compulsory. Much was left to the student's initiative. You were to prepare for the almighty final exams in three years time; what you did to ensure you were prepared was largely up to you. The joke was that you could disappear to China for three years then come back and take the exams and succeed. It wasn't quite like that, but the story had a point. Apart from your weekly tutorial session there were no real formal demands, only a set of recommended lectures, and some more or less required seminars. If you missed too many of these someone might raise an eyebrow, but on the whole no one fussed over you; you were on your own. And on his own, when initial interactions with people were difficult, and he felt wholly unsure of himself in this strange environment, he could always wander.

The LSE, a hodge-podge of buildings on the east side of Aldwych, was breathtakingly central. When Americans would ask him: "What was your campus like?" he always replied: "London was my campus." He wandered north past the Old Curiosity Shop out into Kingsway and up to the graceful squares of Bloomsbury, in particular Red Lion Square with the headquarters of the Ethical Culture Society and the house where William Morris had lived; to the art deco, sky scraping, federal buildings of London University in Russell Square; thence to the classical columns of the British Museum and University College, passing RADA on the way, down Gower Street where Rossetti had lived. He might come back via High Holborn and Grays Inn Road through Lincoln's Inn with its Oxbridge-like dining halls and chapel and Georgian quadrangles. He wandered south across Aldwych, past the Royal Courts of Justice and India House where the students flocked to eat cheap curries in the staff cafeteria, and were tolerated; past the grand façade of King's College/ Somerset House (where his birth certificate with the wrong names was kept); down through the Georgian elegance of The Temple, past the Templar church with the barristers swaying about grandly in their gowns and wigs; down to the Embankment and the Thames and Waterloo Bridge.

East he would go along Fleet Street past St. Clement Dane's ("oranges and lemons say the bells of St. Clement's) and Temple Bar and the offices of the great daily newspapers (*Mail, Express, Telegraph*), past the Cheshire Cheese Tavern (shade of Dr. Johnson), up Ludgate Hill to St. Paul's Cathedral, the City of London and the exquisite Wren churches. West he went along the Strand and its theaters, past the Savoy and its theatre (joy for the young Savoyard) to Trafalgar Square; then either further west down Whitehall to the Houses of Parliament, or, more exciting, turn north past the National Gallery and Leicester Square, up Tottenham Court Road with its bookstores and snuff shops and music stores culminating in the heaven-on-earth of Foyle's with its deep canyons of books, and eventually the turbulence of Oxford Street. Back through Covent Garden with its colorful vegetable-and-fruit clutter, past the Opera House and then through exciting, foreign Soho with the clubs and restaurants and Mediterranean smells, and little window advertisements for the enigmatic "lessons" in various subjects and languages ("young lady gives lessons" being perhaps the most brutally frank.) He found the headquarters of the precious Rationalist Press Association. All along these routes there were little cafés and coffeehouses where he would sip the compulsive tea, read the brand new textbooks, and listen to the odd nasal chirping of the London natives.

Do not be alarmed; our boy was not neglecting things of the mind. He was just a bit puzzled about what he was at and who he was supposed to be: the usual problems. The change in environment was a shock. He had come from the very top of one hierarchy to be plunged into anonymity at the bottom of a bigger one. No one knew about his record marks, about his State Scholarship, and what is more they didn't care! He didn't know how to use his time. He had perhaps thought that university was like school only you worked harder—or something. Not so. It was not even remotely like school, and whether you worked or not was largely up to you. This gave a dangerous latitude to those whose main joy in life was either ongoing argument or gambling. And there were plenty of both. The bar, the coffee shop, the lounge (a scruffy affair of broken down sofas and pulverized armchairs) were always full of students arguing or playing poker or bridge. Since he didn't have the skills or the money to gamble he fell in—oh how naturally—with the arguing fraternity. Here was a chance to try out at least one mask. But it was not so easy. The arguments were heavy duty, and these people were not schoolboys or easily impressed adults. They were mostly older students who had seen something of the world, or colonial students, or foreign students—a lot from America and India. They were not interested in being impressed. They were actually interested in the ideas. And they demanded more than eloquence: they knew so much about so much and were serious about the outcome. Argument was the local sport. But it was a sport in deadly earnest; not really a game, since the outcome was the perfect society and how to run it, and these people might very well end up running it. The thought both amazed and appalled.

It amazed because he knew he was among those whose opinions were actually going to matter; it appalled because they were mostly socialists. Of course he had known of the reputation of the LSE as the cradle of Fabiansim—founded in fact by the Fabians. The shades of Sidney and Beatrice Webb hung over the place: those élite, well-lettered know-alls who knew what was best for the workers and would lick them into shape in the manner of their admired Stalin. The hall of residence was named after them—Passfield Hall, since, as was true of their kind, having opposed the principle of aristocracy all their socialist lives, in the end they accepted a peerage (Lord and Lady

Passfield) as their due—as superior people. Gatherings took place in the pleasant Shaw Library—named naturally for that other guru of the Left, and the large portrait of Lord and Lady P. dominated the wall over the fireplace there. R. H. Tawney, Graham Wallas and Harold Laski, resident intellectuals of the left, had not been long gone. There were more Labour MPs who were alumni of the LSE than any other college in the country. It was a natural magnet for the left-wing student. The ethos of the place was one of determined, earnest, Fabian socialism: the gathering of facts about society and the economy to be used in forcing governments to redress social wrongs. This was the essence of Fabiansim: a gradualist rather than a revolutionary approach to eventual true socialism. But there was also the big attraction of theory, of ideas about the good society. These were what were argued daily in the shabby atmosphere of low living and high thinking.

He knew this, but he also knew the other side of the LSE, the one that belied the popular myth. The majority of students may have been mildly left in their thinking, but it was not the virulent argumentative left of the coffee room theorists. The LSE was also a factory for mandarins: it produced the civil servants who, along with their Oxbridge counterparts, really ran the country, as well as the great international organizations. It had its big departments of Finance, Money, Banking, Accountancy, Law and Social Administration. The colonials who came were usually lefties, but the Americans (like Moynihan, Rockefeller and the Kennedys) were not. They came, like so many others, to learn the skills of economics and political science that were necessary for government service or the political life. And if there was a big socialist presence there was also a big representation of Liberals (the most famous Director of the school had been the almost revered Liberal architect of the welfare state, Lord Beveridge) and, yes, Conservatives. Even on the faculty there were great figures of the intellectual right: von Hayek (to become Mrs. Thatcher's guru), Karl Popper, and the Professor Oakeshott, Laski's successor in political science, who had interviewed him and seemed so unfazed by his Young Conservatism. He naturally joined the Conservative Society (Con. Soc.) first thing, and found it surprisingly large. It was in fact the biggest university Conservative club in the country. The truth was that the LSE, while definitely predominantly left in its sympathies, was simply the most politically alive and active of all the colleges—across the whole spectrum of beliefs.

He enjoyed being one of the school's Conservatives. It appealed to the antinomianism that he had eventually adopted during the religious revolt. There was something basically thrilling about being different. Whatever the majority was, be something else. He began to realize how much he liked this underdog position. It so annoyed the majority, and majorities were always so damned cocksure that it was a pleasure to puncture their sanctimony. The socialists were so self-righteous, just like the religionists; they couldn't bear that anyone should doubt—and particularly doubt in a measured and well-argued way—their oh so obvious truths. So it became both a necessity for intellectual survival, and a lot of fun, to challenge their self-evident convictions at any opportunity. But he had to be careful, because, to their credit they were, like the Catholic apologists, clever and well prepared. And they really believed, sincerely and even desperately, in their authoritarian formulations.

In particular the Marxists had a system as well constructed and formidable as that of Aquinas (there were a lot of similarities, he thought, in manner and method if not in substance.) The Marxists were dogmatic and arrogant, but there was nothing personal about it. They fully understood that the dialectic of history required there to be two sides to the class struggle; someone had to be, of necessity, on the wrong side. He formed an almost perverse friendship with the most orthodox of the Stalinists, Marshall-the-Marxist. He liked Marshall because he looked the part of the classical anarchist: wooly hair, Zapata moustache, soulful eyes, dirty duffle coat, scraggy long wool scarf and generally suspicious demeanor that suggested he really did have a bomb in his pocket. Marshall sadly dismissed him as a dupe of the capitalists who sought to emasculate the proletariat by recruiting its most able members into its bourgeois establishment. It at first astonished him that this should be thought a fault. Surely becoming part of the bourgeois establishment was what life was all about? Was it not the reward for all that effort? Otherwise, what was it all for? He got used to Marshall and the Marxists, but they were ruthless. If you didn't know Marx as well as they did, you were simply despised. They even despised the moderate socialists, Fabians and anarchists—more than they despised the Tories. They were particularly adept at despising.

To keep in the game at first he needed some fancy footwork. It was no good going head on with the Marxists. He tried some bobbing and weaving. Your arguments may be good he told them, but your premises are weak. This always gave him a few minutes breathing space while they blustered. Then: I never really did understand the labor theory of value; it seems so self-evidently wrong. Some of the most valuable things in the world took very little labor to produce. That put them on the defensive, always a good position to put them in. They would hit him with his "bourgeois individualism" but he was prepared: on the contrary, it was the acceptance of the Burkean premise that society was an organism that caused him to reject Marxism; they weren't the only collectivists in town. Nifty, but he knew he would have to do the Marx thing, and he didn't mind. This was what he was here for. But Con. Soc. was delighted and offered him a place on its committee and debating team there and then. Of course he accepted; he never learned.

He still had the joining mania. When in doubt join; when asked to serve agree. It was a true addiction; he could not resist an invitation. As well as the Conservative Society he joined the Music Society (secretary of the choir? of course), the University choir, the India Society, the debating society, the drama club (committee? Certainly), the jazz club, the newspaper—*Beaver* (assistant editor? naturally), the college review (for the end-of-term performance), and the bar committee (of the student bar, *The Three Tuns*—he would stay on this for his whole tenure.) He went to London University choir practices one evening a week at the Senate House, and to the LSE Union meeting one other evening, and to one of his other club functions or rehearsals on at least one of the others, and usually to a hop at the weekend. So what? you might ask. But his silliness over the pretty girl met at Stratford led him to take digs out near where she lived in Sydenham, way off in south London, a miserable commute away involving long walks, slow trains and then busses once in town. In the inevitably bad weather it was quite awful despite the addition to his wardrobe of the necessary ex-Navy duffle coat (from the surplus store) rolled umbrella and leather briefcase (from the railway lost-property store) and the official sign of student status, the long, gaudy School scarf. The girl was nice enough, but, compared with the girls he was now meeting, uninteresting. They played some tennis and went to some films, but it was not enough to make up for the terrible journey. You were supposed to have your evening meals in the digs, and his mothering and possessive landlady insisted, so on nights when he stayed up in town he had to come home late to a warmed-up meal in the oven. One night he missed the last train and had to stay in a cheap hotel near London Bridge station. It might have been cheap to them, but it took an unacceptable bite out of the one hundred twenty pounds a year his precious scholarship afforded.

Something had to give. He persuaded an unhappy landlady to let him go "bed and breakfast" so he had his evenings free, but there was still the dreadful commute. Then he found a focus that really demanded change in many directions. The Jazz Club functioned fitfully according to the whims of whoever was taking responsibility, and the jazz crowd was not big on responsibility. But one evening they went to hear, and dance to, Humphrey Lyttleton's band at 100 Oxford Street, and the world changed again. Humph himself (brother of a Tory minister) on the horn, with Wally Fawkes (a distant relative perhaps, but certainly a cartoonist on the Tory *Daily Mail*) on the clarinet, and Lonnie Donegan on the banjo. Donegan and Fawkes together (they had made records) were just a delight. It was a new and perfect world. The amateur jazz he had heard to date was nothing. This was real white jazz, the best Dixieland available in Europe outside Paris. Ken Colyer's band ranked second to Humph: home grown talent but pure New Orleans sound. The Marxists despised it as a symptom of nihilistic bourgeois decadence, which was the best possible recommendation. He could re-adapt his Existentialist manners—put that mask back on—and sink into the pure pleasure of smoke-filled, noisy, swinging and swaying, jazz-basement happiness.

He gave up the choir, and began to miss his various meetings. He still went to the Union meetings especially the debates, since this was still the focus of all the School activities, as well as big fun and excitement. The debates drew famous figures mostly from the political world. He was still nervous of the big time, but at least in the prepared debates you could make a good case without interruption (except heckling of course, that was standard.) His baptism was a debate on "equality and freedom" or something such in which he took the Tory side (freedom was more important than equality?) along with a then little-known MP, Enoch Powell. He was truly impressed, over conversation in the bar afterwards, with Powell's intelligence and power of personality. A strange man, not even really like a politician, more of an academic—which evidently he had been in Australia: a professor of Greek. He was a passionate believer in the claims of the Earl of Oxford to have written "Shakespeare." This gave them something in common because our skeptic had never recovered from Twain's debunking of the Stratford businessman. In some ways Powell was perhaps too intelligent, too academic, to be a successful politician. When he finally fell from grace it was really because he was too honest: he said what many of his party thought but could not say out of political necessity: another hard lesson in political reality.

But all this activity plus the commute (oh how we whine) was too much. The pretty girl notwithstanding, he knew he would have to move. He had a friend on the bar committee, Ken, who had a primitive garret in Highbury—a slum in fact, but only a brief tube ride away from the school. Ken had glamour because he had worked on the *Daily Mirror*—in the circulation department it was true, but a job on a paper nevertheless. All he had to offer was an army cot in the corner, or in the adjoining small kitchen if you wanted privacy. There were no bathrooms in the slum house, and one toilet down the stairs. Ken took showers in the school gym changing rooms, and explained that it was all right to piss in the sink if you ran the water afterwards. Ken, a big man who had been a boxer in the army, was a pretty no-nonsense character, and a panjandrum in the Labour Society. But they got on well. It was difficult because he was not supposed to be there, and the landlord, a pale, unhappy man, who lived like a troglodyte below stairs, had made it a life-project to catch them. It never happened, and the game became a kind of end in itself. No matter. It was heaven on earth for the little existentialist Tory jazz fiend. They lived on shellfish—cockles, mussels, winkles—from local street vendors, which, along with faggots, jellied eels and fish and chips, were swigged down with cheap "Bordeaux-type" wine. *La vie* so very *bohème!*

All this was consolidated by his purchase of a guitar—steel-stringed, danceband, cello-style. It was second hand and hard to play because it needed a repair to the neck. But he had worked over Christmas at the Bradford postoffice (everyone worked in vacations, although the rules of grants and scholarships actually prohibited working: you were supposed to be studying) and, with the help of a Christmas gift of five pounds from his ever-indulgent parents, saved enough to buy it. Django was his inspiration. Despite only three fingers on his left hand Django outplayed the world's guitarists. No emulating this, but our lad bought the inevitable instruction book with the chords and began plonking away. Another friend from the jazz club had become quite expert at chords in the army, and helped him mightily. Remember, this was well before the days when everyone and his grandmother had guitars. This was the early fifties; *no one* had guitars. It was a decidedly strange thing to be doing outside the ranks of professional musicians. But oh my, did it promise popularity. Take your guitar to a party, and no matter how fumbling you knew you were, a few chords could go a long way. The twelve-bar blues, that epitome of existentialist music, took only a few chords, but with the right accent and feeling could sound really quite impressive. He revived old favorites: "St. Louis Blues," "Trouble in Mind," "Alcoholic Blues," and even "Stormy Weather." His best was "Round the Clock Blues" with its rich innuendo—so removed from his real experience, still stalled at kissing. Bill Hailey was to convert this into "Rock Around the Clock" and, by hitting hard on the off-beat, start his own revolution; but that was still to come. In the meantime, a little could be made to go a long way. It was perfect for the young-man-in-a-hurry, whose ambition outran his skill.

He might have been tempted to keep it there but for another accidental encounter. In one of his walks up Tottenham Court Road, on his way to Foyles, he passed a small entrance way with an insignificant sign "Spanish Guitar Centre." He didn't know anything about Spanish guitars except what he had seen in Gypsy movies, but they advertised "free demonstrations" and that was simply too much to resist. The demonstrator was the owner, Mr. Leonard Williams, and he did indeed demonstrate, playing delicately on the nylon strings a piece called "Lagrima" with a sound that was once more like something new in the world; a sound of such purity it was surely what music was like in Eden. Mr. Williams was scornful of experience with the jazz guitar: a percussion instrument, he sneered, might as well bash a cymbal. Django and his three-fingered brilliance? Didn't know him. Didn't care to. Nor Wes Montgomery nor Herb Ellis. He put on a record: listen to Segovia. Who? The greatest classical guitarist in the world. Bach. Beautiful, divine, astonishing; the adjectives fail.

Then Mr. Williams calls into the next room of the little crowded warren of rooms, and his son John comes out: a small slightly tubby boy, only just peering over the big guitar he carried. He had just come back from studying with Segovia; he played. It was more wonderful than his father. His little fingers danced over the frets in a cascade of stomach-lurching sound—something by a Brazilian, Villa something. I can never do that. Of course you can. You read music, you know the tuning of the guitar, you know the fingering of the basic chords, you are at a positive advantage. John had none of this and now Segovia says he will become the best guitarist in the world. John blushed and excused himself, but what was our boy to do? This was fated. (No, no, no!

That can't be right. John would only have been about five at the time. This was a decade later, back in London, on a visit to his old teachers. Yes. Then he had heard John-the-Prodigy play Villa-Lobos. The gentle étude in e-minor. The one he would record a few years later. But the memory wants this to have been at the beginning. That is the way with myth. Never trust the myth-making memory with chronology.) At the time everything else faded. He had to do it. He could buy a guitar they made at the Centre from materials brought from Spain, and pay for it in installments. Some work in the summer vacation and it could be managed. He would not abandon jazz—no question, but he would enter this new world of musical magic that was literally within his grasp.

Leonard Williams would cross his path again much later. The guitar mentor kept a monkey colony in the West Country and wrote an excellent layman's book on monkey behavior called *Simba and the Monkey Mind*. The dominant male, the Simba of the title, bit his owner badly in the left hand, leaving it crippled. Unlike Django he could never play again, but he refused to feel anger with Simba: the dominant male was simply protecting his band. Williams had intruded and paid the penalty. Son John however more than made up for it. Segovia's prediction was spot on. But our little seeker of attention had now another weapon. To be fair he did work fanatically hard at his lessons and drew praise from serious teachers, but he cut corners in order to increase his party repertoire.

This was the time of the "folk song revival" and Burl Ives and Pete Seeger were teaching a whole new way of singing and appreciating "folk song." This had been the preserve of more or less academic musicologists and nationalist composers. His much-revered Vaughan Williams was a patron of the English Folk Song and Folk Dance Society, and visits were paid to Cecil Sharpe House to hear talks and demonstrations. But this was mostly chase-me-round-the-maypole stuff, while Ives and Seeger brought home a treasure house of earthy, funny songs, singable with guitar accompaniment. Guitar accompaniments were published and books of songs with chord arrangements were available. He wallowed. Starting with "Jimmy Crack Corn" and "Goober Peas" and the Guthrie and Leadbelly favorites ("John Henry") he worked up to "Leather-Winged Bat" and "Fox Went Out on a Chilly Night." As the chords and finger skills grew he went further afield including Elizabethan lutenist songs (especially Dowland—"Flow My Tears") and his own arrangement of "Greensleeves" based on the Vaughan Williams setting, and an easy tango version of "La Paloma." It was a good time for the happy little troubadour.

A good time all round, for this was what Lord Dahrendorf in his magnificent history of the LSE was to call "A Golden Age for Students." Every student thinks his college time was the golden age, of course, and that things have gone to the dogs since. But there seems to be a general consensus among commentators that this time was somehow special. The School was smaller and more exclusive then. But it had a very special character that is hard to put into words. Its very cosmopolitanism was part of it; the whole world came there. But they came with a self-confident purpose to re-mould the world for the better. It was a time when intellectuals still felt at the center of things, and the students reflected this confidence. Socialism had a lot to do with it, but by no means everything. There was a general feeling that the old pre-war order was inadequate to the new circumstances, and that some form of statism was the answer. Even the Tories did not really quarrel with this, only on how the state should manage things. A young Margaret Thatcher was simmering in the wings, but otherwise no one was seriously challenging the welfare state. Why should they? They were all the beneficiaries of it.

The students were the future managers of this utopia; the young mandarins who stood on the verge of power. Even so, they were a strangely passive lot. They were clever and cynical, but not rebellious as younger generations are supposed to be. But then how could they be? The generation of their fathers had just made such huge sacrifices to win the battle for their freedom and prosperity. How could they ever match that? How could they really challenge that generation? At best they could offer to help it run efficiently the new world order it had fought and died for. At worst they could stay out of its way. Kenneth Tynan described them (incongruously in a book on bullfighting) as being unerringly able to spot phoniness, and irritatingly unwilling to do anything about it. Well didn't that just sum up our strumming, plucking and folk singing Tory cynic. Was he finding a mask that would let him get on with his studies behind its charming if whimsical protective smile? Cultivate the enigmatic. Make them guess.

So much student time was spent on fun and games it was a wonder they ever did get any work done. Somehow they did: play hard, work hard. But in the process of amusing themselves they raised hell with the hard-working public that was paying their way. Things that were dismissed as "pranks" when done by students would have landed East End street lads with jail time and nasty fines along with stern moral lectures from the beak. All the magistrates had been students themselves, and if you ever did appear in Bow Street magistrates' court, the police read a more-or-less ritual charge sheet, the beak pronounced "ten shillings" and you were out of there. On Boat Race night (and forget not that only Oxford and Cambridge were allowed to monopolize the Thames, as if they owned the damn river) it was considered good form to steal public property like street signs, and private property like pub signs or Oxbridge college scarves. These were really prized, and a lot of the class war was waged in those London streets as students from Magdalen ("Maudlin") or Brasenose or Jesus or Sydney Sussex and other such ridiculously named institutions were relieved of their bright neckware. The Marxists, announcing "all property is theft" as their justification, actually seemed to get some pleasure from this banditry, which was nice for them, for they didn't find very much amusing. The scarves, along with policemen's helmets—the other coveted trophy—were displayed in the bar the next day. One sign, pinched from a pub, was the hit of the season when placed over a bed. It said:

This Game is for Amusement Only
No Gambling or Betting Allowed.

Every year all the London colleges had a Rag Day, in which students dressed up in costumes, had a parade of floats, and collected substantial sums for charity. One year an overzealous Commissioner of Police banned the Rag on some grounds of public security. It was explained that the Commissioner had come up from the ranks; he was not a college man and did not understand. Ken and our man convened the curiously named Pickwick Club: an ad-hoc inter-collegiate committee that existed for such emergencies. (Ken had a curious medallion of Mr. Pickwick that he wore, on a ribbon round his neck, for meetings.) Since the Chief Plod had invoked "danger to public order" as his reason for the ban, it was decided to give him just that. The engineers, mostly from King's College, knew how to fix traffic lights at red and so gum up the streets, starting with Piccadilly Circus. The chemists, from Imperial College, made colored soap flakes which everyone helped to dump in the fountains in Trafalgar Square, covering everything in colored foam to a depth of about three feet, and solving the pigeon problem temporarily. The LSE led a phony demonstration in Fleet Street to draw Old Bill away from all this. Meanwhile, the medical students tied firecrackers to the tails of police horses and threw barrels of marbles in the streets on which the poor animals skidded about in fright. Something was done to stop the tube trains (jamming the doors?) and of course numerous fire engines and food deliveries ended up at the miserable Commissioner's doorstep. None of this was done for any other reason than that the imperial students had been crossed in their desire to have a little lawful mayhem according to tradition. They took their fun much more seriously in those days.

But he did have to get on with his studies, and he was, despite the distractions, doing so, if jerkily. It seemed to be everything he had longed for. Here was the rational discussion of the big issues, the questions about society and history, that he had known must exist somewhere. Here were adults of dazzling erudition who had no trouble with the big questions, and no nonsense about religion either. It was not so much actively despised (except by the Marxists) as simply not noticed, except as a "sociological phenomenon" along with all the others. Apart from the inevitable few Catholics no one was much interested. This was no problem for the hardened agnostic however, since the Marxists and doctrinaire socialists served as adequate substitutes. Pricking their intellectual bubbles was almost as satisfying; he liked to hear the mental bones of the intellectual bullies go crack. He had to stop mixing his metaphors.

Yet he could not help liking and admiring the moderate socialists like his friend Ken, and their friend Frank (as another socialist Lord , to become head of Oxfam) who had their hearts in the right place. They were not particularly indoctrinated with anything other than a wish to see a fairer society. Who could quarrel with that? They were of that non-Marxist, basically non-conformist, rugged working-class socialism that went back to the Cromwellian Levellers and up through the earliest trade unions to the Cooperative movement and the original Independent Labour Party. They were as English as the Tories, and in many ways more sympathetic. He couldn't feel truly hostile to them, even if he thought them naïve in their belief that a huge centralized bureaucracy running nationalized industries, along with invidiously punitive taxation, was the way to utopia. In fact his interest in politics was ceasing to be much other than formal. He stuck with the Conservatives more-or-less out of dumb loyalty, for he was just not interested in the meat and potatoes issues of politics they debated. He weighed in on the abstract issues, the theory, the philosophy; he left the municipal housing issues to others.

By the same token he was becoming disillusioned with economics. For a start he had done most of the first-year syllabus for A-levels. They only got junior lecturers who were stiff and nervous and unimaginative. The great George Stigler (of price theory and a Nobel Prize to come) had left, Harry Johnson had yet to arrive. He wasn't much interested in the heavy doses of economic history either, although he enjoyed Lionel Robbins on the history of economic thought. He only really liked the logic and scientific method, which introduced him to formal logic (Imre Lakatos), and to questions of how to know anything about anything that he remembered from Russell, and that were clearly fundamental. He mentioned to his then tutor—an older economist whose name didn't stick—that he might like to do sociology for Part II (the second two years.) He was hazy about what exactly it was, but they had recommended it at his interview, and it seemed it might be closer to his broad interests than the narrowness of economics allowed. The tutor, sensitive to his restlessness, told him that there was a relatively new B.Sc. degree in sociology and he might be better suited to it; it was not too late to change.

He went to see T. H. Marshall (still there before his departure for UNESCO) who welcomed him and said yes, they were looking for students, since as yet the degree was not known about in schools, so they depended a lot on "transfers." Look what you can do said Marshall: social psychology, demography, criminology, social theory, social institutions, social philosophy, ethics, and statistics. And not to worry; the latter was dealt with very systematically from basics, and advanced math was not necessary. There were two papers in economics to be taken at the end of the second year, everyone at the School took these whatever his major was, but he had covered most of that syllabus already. O.K. But then there was the question of the "special subject": the major or concentration that would be three papers in the final exam. Most students took "modern Britain," and "Greek and Roman society" was on the books. He would have leaped at that, and the saga might have been completely different, but there was no one to teach it until Keith Hopkins came a decade later, so it was not available. However, there was also "social anthropology." Frazer, exotic peoples, strange customs, fun stuff. He could take up where he left off with *The Golden Bough*. He was hooked.

Marshall sent him off to see Maurice Freedman on the fourth floor of the Old Building, down the hall from the Colonial Studies Room, on the way to the Shaw Library. Freedman was agreeable but wanted to know if he'd read anything in Social Anthropology. Oh yes, *The Golden Bough*, abridged edition. Freedman had the grace to be a bit amazed, but a few questions showed it to be fact. "Well," he said, in the brusque manner that was to become so very familiar, "you won't be doing much of that sort of thing here." Frazer, it appeared, was a "classic" but like most classics was out of date; he was revered but not read. A copy of Radcliffe-Brown's *Structure and Function in Primitive Society* was produced. "You must get this by heart," said Freedman. He was to join the first-year class already in session, and there was a lot of ground to be made up. Freedman said he was still deciding whether or not to "double up" the first-year class, which they usually did because they found once a week didn't suffice. These people clearly meant business. "Read the book and come back next week with an essay on the difference between patrilineal and matrilineal succession," he added. "You've a lot to do." He would eventually have to pick a "special ethnographic area" as one paper in the finals. Was he interested in any particular primitive peoples? North American Indians perhaps (memories of Fennimore Cooper?) Freedman sniffed at the idea that "reservation Indians" were a fit subject, and for them he would have to go to Professor Forde at University College; Africa and Polynesia, or with Freedman himself, China and Southeast Asia, were more convenient, but it was up to him. Well. He was in, Frazer was out; incomprehensible things were being demanded of him at short notice. This was the LSE.

So we recognize a major junction in the saga of the soul, do we not? Onwards and upwards into anthropology? Just as we might have thought. Not so fast. It was not nearly so simple. Indeed it ought not to have happened. Anthropology (social) was indeed exotic and enticing and fascinating and great fun. He enjoyed being part of its world (representative on the School Interdepartmental Committee? Assuredly): visits to the Royal Anthropological Institute in its marvelously book-stuffed house in Bedford Square, and receiving his monthly copy of *Man* with its lurid yellow cover and the photos of naked dark-skinned people that shocked those in the tube who peeked anyway. He liked using the Colonial Studies Room library, and talking to the actual and potential district officers and colonial civil servants doing their compulsory course there. He remembered *Sanders of the River*, and was entranced.

These were truly more innocent days, and Anthropology's affiliation with the Colonial Office was not only not questioned, it was regarded as an unqualified good; it paid for most of the research. The doctrine (invented by Lord Lugard) of "indirect rule" meant that we had to know what "customary law" was if we were to rule the natives through their own legal concepts. So there was a big call for research into systems of customary law, and hence a deep pocket for anthropological field research. This could been seen as benevolent and enlightened, or at least done with the best intentions. The Marxists, however, despised the subject as a running dog of bourgeois colonialist imperialism, which made it even better.

He certainly took to the subject matter. He wrote essays and class papers on Ruth Benedict's *Patterns of Culture* (falling in love with the Zuni Indians in the process.) He wrestled with the peculiarities of matrilineal and patrilineal succession, with Malinowski on culture, and Evans-Pritchard on witchcraft and magic. He read Firth on Maori economics and Tikopia kinship, Schapera on Bantu polygamy, and the difficult introduction to *African Systems of Kinship and Marriage.* He worked on the French: Mauss on *The Gift*— the Potlach and the Kula Ring, and Durkheim on religion. He even snuck in Frazer here and there despite clucks of disapproval. Yes, he was enjoying his Anthropology, but it didn't have his main loyalty or interest, and he did not for a moment think of ever being an anthropologist. He was finished with the Boy Scouts, and two years in the distant bush or jungle did not attract the would-be urban intellectual.

The guiding spirits of Sociology were Morris Ginsberg and David Glass. They represented two opposing poles of the very eclectic subject. {This eclecticism was, though, what made it so varied and so interesting.) Glass was the statistician, the quantitative demographer, the man on the population problem, the empiricist. The elderly Ginsberg inherited the mantle of Hobhouse and Westermarck, who both, like Spencer and even Darwin, saw themselves as heirs to the philosophical tradition of the study of morality: Ethics. What the Sociologists and Anthropologists added was the study of, to quote Hobhouse's best known work, *Morals in Evolution*, or as with Westermarck, *The Origin and Development of the Moral Idea.* Even if the evolutionary idea was now out of fashion, the comparative sociology of morals was still in, and Ginsberg was its prophet. Thus it was that the core of the curriculum was moral and social philosophy, and a background in general philosophy, anchored on the British empiricists—Hobbes, Locke, Berkeley, and Hume, was deemed necessary.

Students tended to like this even less than they liked statistics. They could see the use of statistics (they had to know about social surveys and such), and it could be mastered with diligent application, but they suffered from the formal arguments and arcane discussions of ethics, and never felt they could master the "philosophical" way of thinking and writing. The impossibly erudite Donald MacRae (yes, another Highlander come south to plague the Sassenachs) lectured without notes and without missing a step on every social and moral philosopher known to man, starting with Buddha and Confucius and ending with Russell and Wittgenstein. This added to the terror and helplessness felt by the intellectually timid students. Many of them really wanted to be social workers (something that was a problem for sociology in its expanding years), and they just didn't want this stuff on Plato and Spinoza, Leibnitz and Kant, the moral sense, utilitarianism and the freedom of the will. But guess, reader, who was just enthralled and delighted? Right! Little mister argument-for-its-own-sake was as happy as a bear in a honey barrel.

Professor Joad and Lord Russell were hauled out of the trunk, and even Sartre and Co. could be drummed into service. On the social philosophy circuit, Toynbee and Eliot, Burke, Spencer and Schweitzer, and even what little he remembered of Hegel and Mill, could be recruited to serve. And unlike his classmates he found the philosophical mode of argument just peaches and cream. It was like something that had been waiting for him; it was a destiny demanding to be served. Philosophical questions could always be dealt with initially by using Professor Joad's formula of "It depends what you mean by..." That was good for at least three paragraphs. Question: Was to say that something was "desirable" to say that it was "desired?" Mill's answer was that it was not; the two were distinct: desire was an emotion, desirable an evaluation. But you got to disagree: it depends what you mean by... He argued that to say that Jane Russell was desirable implied that someone desired her; the opposite defied the common sense meaning of the words, Mill notwithstanding. This got him pats on the head. No one cared if you were right or not; what mattered was that you knew how to make a philosophical argument, and that you were willing to challenge the big boys. He knew; he challenged.

Right there at the School there were evidently some leading philosophers who could be heard in the flesh: Popper and Oakeshott, for example. And they were not only not socialists, they were anti-socialist! MacRae said, go hear Popper, and pay attention to what he says about "refutation" or "falsifiability." Popper held a "revision class" in the basement of the Old Building. Speaking to an overcrowded room of obvious devotees (the Marxists despised him and didn't attend) he was knocking down all doctrines and systems, and in particular, on this occasion, the "Conspiracy Theory of History." The problem, he explained, was not that of "verification"—as the Vienna School would have it (the who?), but of "refutation": such a theory could never be refuted. If no conspiracy were to be found, the proponents would simply claim this as evidence of the cunning nature of the conspiracy. The theory was thus "invulnerable." It was "metaphysical" not "scientific" and we could safely disregard it.

Science meant the possibility of refutation; hypotheses must be falsifiable. It was simple, it was brilliant, it was not even difficult to understand. Popper was God. *The Poverty of Historicism* and *The Open Society and Its Enemies* were found in second-hand copies in the Economists Bookstore, and the world changed again, and decidedly in his favor. Away with grand predictions and schemes for social perfection: the only possible (not sensible but *possible*) course was Popper's "piecemeal social engineering" —a possibility friendly to Tory interventionism, but not to Fabianism which, for all its gradualism, was working towards the impossible utopia of socialism. Our new convert was ecstatic: he saw more clearly than ever the possibilities of playing "the philosopher." He could adopt the skeptical, critical, slightly-amused-at-the-confusion-of-the-world mask that went with exotic guitar music, jazz, a pipe, moderate conservatism and a growing appreciation of dry sherry. Oh joy, oh rapture!

These things were earnestly discussed over beer and chicory sandwiches in *The Three Tuns*: the student bar and club which was his second home. The beer was subsidized; they were not required to make a profit, just enough to cover the expenses. He and his fellow committee members (including Ken) got an insight into the profits to be made in the drinks trade when they saw how cheaply they could get booze wholesale and what an unbelievable mark-up the publicans added. They countered by buying cases of wine cheaply and having a "wine night" each week at which they sold the bottles of fairly good plonk at cost. A shilling a bottle for Sauternes and Burgundy was not uncommon. The Director (the admirable old-world expert on the population problem, Sir Alexander Carr-Saunders) politely asked them to go easy on the cheap hooch since he was worried about the "student drinking problem" that was getting some bad press. They liked and respected the old boy, and when, after one boisterous wine night, some lads dismantled an MG and reassembled it in an inaccessible alley, they cut out the special nights and sold the wine regularly at reasonable prices.

Above the Three Tuns were two more quintessential LSE institutions: Mrs. Popper's Tea Shop, and the offices of the newspaper, *Beaver*. Mrs. Popper was no relation to the great philosopher, but the coincidence was too good to overlook. A notice on the door read:

> Mrs. Popper's
> Society
> Always Open

Naturally the Poppereans favored it, and debated methodology over dark tea and hard scones. The Marxists despised it as an example of bourgeois laissez-faire exploitation of the oppressed students, and demanded a teashop run by the Union—as a collective of course. They lost on this one. The students may have been left, but they weren't crazy. *Beaver*, on the cramped floor above, was a poor affair compared to U.S. college dailies. It was only a single-fold broadsheet that came out once a week. But it was nevertheless the parish magazine and they worked hard to make it lively. Journalism was still the only contemplated employment possibility, so practice was sensible.

He wrote a column on the local pub and coffeehouse scene: "Through a Glass Darkly." He contributed book reviews (Colin Wilson, *The Outsider*), theater reviews (*Little Lord Fauntleroy*—revival at the *Savoy*), and poems: some of suitable existential gloom like *Inauthentic Lives*:

> I think that hell will be
> a suburbia of well-cut lawns
> stretching to a green eternity...

His miserable Sydenham experience showing through, and leading to:

> But how could we be sure
> we who were no more
> than echoes of forgotten aspirations
> patchworks of unrealized desires...

Thus character calcifies around old emotional wounds.

But more often he was comic and satirical as in "Neatly Rolled Umbrellas." These were still the days when ideological differences were sartorially expressed. The Marxists despised ties and shined shoes and all the appurtenances of bourgeois respectability. They affected facial hair, polo-neck sweaters, worn corduroys, duffle coats and crepe-soled "brothel creepers." The respectable left had modest ties, jackets with genuine patches to cover up genuine wear on the elbows, khaki shirts and gray flannels. The right had the smart blazers, the Windsor-knotted school ties on impeccable white shirts, cavalry twill trousers and shined or suede shoes, and of course, the Neatly Rolled Umbrellas. His poem concluded:

> They'll turn us into commies here, at least that what we're told,
> And when the workers run the country, as we did in days of old,
> We'll support the revolution, as discreetly as we can,
> If the Neatly Rolled Umbrellas are within the Five Year Plan.

So-called "free verse" continued to irritate him. He spent a ridiculous amount of time improving it into regular meter and rhyme:

> April is the cruellest month; it breeds
> Lilacs from the dead land, where desire
> And memory mix. Dull roots and rain conspire
> To rouse small life in tubers. Winter feeds
> Their drought with its forgetful snow...

Beaver was a good place to learn how not to overdo it; how to cultivate understatement, that most British of British attributes. The best example of it came while he was away from the School, in the early sixties. There was always a column on the back page, one that he edited as one of his first learning jobs, which carried "News of Former Students." In the week of the U.S. presidential elections in 1960, after the usual listing of appointments, marriages, births and deaths, in the same small print, at the bottom of the page, it read:

> J. F. Kennedy (General Course '35) has been elected
> President of the United States of America.

Of course, J. F. Kennedy had come over from Harvard, enrolled, then fallen ill and returned home. But he had enrolled, and his brother Joe had completed the General Course (a non-degree graduate course in Economics and Politics) a few years earlier. So they could be claimed as loyal sons, and everyone could celebrate, genuinely, the election that promised a new age of government by our philosopher kings. Almost everyone: the Marxists were scornful of an election bought for a privileged son by his capitalist gangster father, etc. etc.

His pieces on the coffeehouses and the jazz scene were a genuine reflection of where he spent his spare time (and a lot of his not-so-spare time.) The coffeehouses were part of a general "revival of normal life" that Mrs. Thatcher noticed in the middle fifties. The Festival of Britain had left its legacy of the Festival Hall on the South Bank, only a walk away, with its almost embarrassment of musical riches at reasonable prices, and the place where they held the School's annual ball. The coronation of the young and lovely Queen had raised people's spirits. (Her husband was a cousin of an LSE Anthropology graduate student: Peter, Prince of Greece and Denmark. He was writing a thesis on polyandry, when he wasn't badgering the family for more money.) The New Elizabethan Age was trumpeted, and whether it was real or not, there was a general sense of relative prosperity and optimism that had been sadly absent in the years of austerity and recovery.

The coffeehouses that sprang up everywhere were part of this revival, but, as he pointed out in his column, they were a revival of a venerable London tradition. From the seventeenth century on they had been at the center of literary and political life (White's), and even the foundation of international insurance (Lloyd's.) At present, though, they were very much the magnets of the bohemian crowd: artists, students, theater and music people, and the hangers-on at the fringes from the now more affluent young white-collar workers. Tony Hancock, that comic poet of upwardly mobile pretentiousness, in one of his films walks into one of them to try out his social skills. Presented with a bowl of brown sugar (then absolutely standard for devotees of the good stuff), he complained bitterly that someone had spilled coffee in the sugar, and demanded a fresh bowl. Free of such gaffes, our troubadour would earn coffee and sandwiches for an evening by entertaining with his growing repertoire of songs and simple pieces ("Nature Boy," "Kisses Sweeter than Wine," "The Foggy Foggy Dew," "Taboo," "Malaguena.") In between they would argue the issues of the day, largely artistic and musical, but some politics and residual Existentialism. His "philosophical" mask worked nicely, even if the Marxists despised it as petty-bourgeois linguistic nihilism.

> ... *abiding free meanwhile, uncramped*
> *By any partial organ, never stamped*
> *Strong, and to strength turning all energies –*
> *Wise, and restricted to becoming wise—*
> *That is, he loves not, nor possesses One*
> *Idea that, star-like over, lures him on*
> *To its exclusive purpose.*

The years merge in recollection. He was never good with chronology, never sure what year things happened in; he never kept a diary or journal, and could never understand the self-regarding motives of those who did. While you were writing your precious journal, you could read a book. He remembered events clearly enough, but it was hard to place them in time unless there was some obvious landmark. But this is not a chronological account: this saga of the development of the soul is concerned with the thoughts and events and circumstances that impinged to produce that eventual prism of ideas. There is at least one event and its dates that impinged and will be noted, but otherwise there is just a happy blur of activity interrupted by vacations at home, in which unpleasant menial work had to be done to pay for, at least, some travel or other. He knew now he hated such work, and whatever the cost he had to escape to a world where they would pay you for creative effort, not just for your time.

Going home in vacations was much less painful now. They had scraped up the down payment on a pleasant house on a pleasant edge of the town: the hills above the smog. The parental truce was holding: she was doing well, between illnesses, in the catering thing, and his father had received another promotion, although it was something accepted most unwillingly; it meant responsibility, as in hiring and firing, and called attention to oneself. But the quiet man was the booming Sir Kenneth's favorite still—"Broke the mould with your father!"—and was even persuaded to be chairman of the ward Conservative Association, but this brought too much attention and didn't last. She continued to be surprising in her stubborn way. She ran for the board of the local Co-operative Society over some issue or other (they were not going to pay a dividend?) The Co-op was a completely Labour organization—its political wing ran candidates jointly with Labour for the longest time ("Labour and Co-op Elected" ran the gloomy election-night slogan on the BBC.) She became the first Conservative to sit on its board. That didn't last either, but it was extraordinary that it was done at all.

He worked every Christmas at the Post Office; on the railway as a porter during the summer rush; in a bakery as a greaser of loaf pans; in a shoe factory as a packer of shoeboxes; and in a geriatric hospital as an orderly on a ward of dying male patients. He liked the railway porters in a way, for their cheerfulness and friendliness, but was horrified at their persistent cheating of what was—since they were loudly and proudly pro-Labour—supposed to be *their* railway, after nationalization. They had him putting "reserved" tickets on unreserved seats, which they then sold to passengers with families desperate for a place on the overcrowded seaside holiday trains. They stole coal so regularly it was not looked on as stealing—more like a bonus. They spent most of what they gained on drink and horse races. They didn't appear to like their children or their wives much, and were of the opinion that "a good shit was better than a good shag any day." Even if they were chronically constipated—and they were, this still seemed a bit extreme.

The work in the shoe factory—putting shoes into boxes then tying them with string—was screamingly boring and tore up his hands. The workers would often down tools and have elastic band fights until the foreman caught them and imposed sanctions. But he understood the impulse, and even thought he now understood strikes. It wasn't the overt issues (wages, hours, benefits) that were in fact the cause, but boredom. It was much more fun to picket and have meetings and marches than to do this debasing work. The bakery heat nearly killed him and he quit, but the geriatric ward was worse. Attending to these twisted, diseased, decaying old men—cheerful and stoic as they often were—convinced him that euthanasia was not the unnatural ending of life, but the termination of the unnatural avoidance of death.

Above all, his close encounters with the workers made him laugh aloud at those young socialists who still, in those days, maintained that only the proletariat could save us, and only they led authentic lives. Some of these deluded youngsters—always from comfortable middle-class homes—actually went off, in an orgy of privileged guilt, to live—Orwell-like—among the natives and imitate them in order to become authentic individuals, and thus able to save society. Apart from becoming painfully constipated, and mastering the daily form sheet, it wasn't at all clear what they learned. But the earnest little buggers persevered. Amazing.

Reading Ortega y Gasset (*The Revolt of the Masses*), as well as Orwell (*The Road to Wigan Pier*) bolstered his own observations of the hopelessness of the proles as a source of salvation. But they were both a bit unfair. There was, in the self-educated, striving, sober, hard-working proletariat a kind of integrity and decency (Orwell's favorite word) that was very English and very endearing. And it wasn't that he thought all that much of bourgeois society either, at least in its nouveau-riche money-worshipping tough-businessman version. Secretly he shared the Marxists' detestation of the worst of their vulgarity, and particularly their philistinism. But he saw in the university community the seeds of that rationality, impartiality and erudition, which he thought should be the hallmark of the rational-ethical guardian class. In this community it didn't matter where you originated: only your performance mattered, as long as it was outstanding. He was becoming an intellectual élitist. It felt good. The philosophers in particular seemed, at the time, to be the epitome of the rational guardian mentality, so he was drawn deeper into the web, with regular visits to hear the great ones at the meetings of the Aristotelian Society, held at the rooms of the British Academy. It was the sunlit rationalism of fifth-century Athens relived in rainy, grimy London.

The language philosophers came down from Oxbridge: R. M. Hare on the language of morals, Nowell-Smith on obligation, and R. B. Braithwaite with the "theory of games" solutions to ethical dilemmas, originated "around the poker tables at Princeton." His Penguin Philosophers— Karl Britton, Stuart Hampshire, Duncan Jones, D. J. O'Connor and T. D. Wheldon, kept him informed. Also come down from Oxford (this must have been in his second year) specifically to teach Ethics, was Ernest Gellner. He was known to be an iconoclast and critic of genteel north-Oxford philosophy, so even the Marxists were willing to give him a hearing. It didn't last. There was a big crowd at the first lecture, and what a disappointment. Gellner had a curved briar-pipe (a Peterson?) stuck firmly and permanently in his mouth. He mumbled in unintelligible English through a faintly discernable foreign (Czech?) accent, and, worst, mostly stood facing the blackboard with his face an inch from it while he wrote in tiny, indecipherable script. He might be brilliant, but this way no one was going to benefit from his brilliance.

Within two weeks, the audience was down to a half dozen desperate ones. But these dogged few knew that there were riches to be mined if they could just get him to overcome his chronic shyness and speak to them. So they approached him before the next lecture and put it to him bluntly: he must have noticed that he had lost ninety percent of his audience. He had. Then, to their astonishment, he appealed to them: "What should I do about it?" So they told him: let's turn this into a seminar; we'll sit in a circle, you'll leave the pipe out of your mouth when you talk directly to us. We'll do assignments and you'll comment on them: you may smoke while we present the papers. He agreed; it worked; the rest of the term was golden. They read Butler's *Sermons*, Hume's *Treatise*, Kant's *Critique*, Mill's *Utilitarianism*, Ryle's *Concept of Mind*, and Moore's *Principia Ethica*, on which our ever cocky young friend wrote an essay, roundly condemning it as a superficial piece of bad logic and blatant special pleading. Gellner liked it, with reservations, and gave it a B++. What's a B++? the puzzled boy asked. It's an A-minus, said Gellner, without a smile. Welcome to philosophy.

In those days of wonder, the famous A. J. Ayer was preaching "Logical Positivism" up the road at·University College. The hard core of the Gellner coterie went along. Ayer immediately banished Existentialism with the stunning put down that it was all "an egregious misuse of the verb 'to be.'" So all that agonizing about existence and essence could be safely abandoned. This rudely ripped off one carefully cultivated mask; he felt like the exposed phantom of the opera. But if nothing else, it meant a great saving of time. Otherwise the hard core had to admit they didn't understand Ayer. They needed to see the words on paper where they stood still, and so could be taken in slowly and savored. Gellner told them to read *Language, Truth and Logic*, although it was a not a requirement. It was a little book, and used copies were cheap. Like old times.

Written when Ayer was still in his twenties, this was the bible in English for the followers of the powerful Vienna School (which is what Popper had been referring to.) It had him seized in jaw-dropping astonishment for its one hundred fifty brief pages. The youthful Ayer had taken on the whole of philosophy and found the criterion—verification—by which it could mostly be dismissed. He left it only the more or less therapeutic "clarification of the language of science" as a goal. Religion and metaphysics were rudely chucked out, and ethics was reduced to emotive noises. It was the book every young man wanted to write, but rarely did. He swore that before he was thirty he would do the same, but in the meantime, this Logical Positivism had to be the new standard by which everything was judged. For if it were true, then what were all those philosophers, including Ayer, still doing? Well, yes, they were still clarifying things (in principle—they were in practice often unintelligible) and their philosophy was in this sense avowedly "linguistic." They were not doing metaphysics, for sure. Science was all. Russell was right.

But the Popperians were not all that enamored of Logical Positivism. It was, after all, the Master who had declared the "verification principle" inadequate (you could, in principle, verify anything), and substituted the necessity for "propositions" (the subject matter of the new philosophy) to be subject to "refutation." Also, with all the work he had put into ethical theory, our boy was not about to give it all to "emotive statements"—the "hurrah-boo" theory as it was tagged. All ethical propositions, he argued, could not be simply emotive, since it made sense to say, "I think that (whatever) is good, but I hate it." Equally we could like, often a lot, things we admitted were "bad." Thus "good/bad" must mean something other than "like/dislike." He came up with his own formula for "good" which would avoid this dilemma (the technicalities don't matter here), and Gellner thought it "ingenious" and gave him an A-minus. "Is this is a B++?" he asked. "No," said the wise man, again without a smile, "it's an A-minus."

It was probably in that same second year that the Conservatives almost lost the general election and a visibly weakening Churchill left, to be prime minister no more. Despite his waning enthusiasm, he had campaigned with his fellow club members, and there were some consolations. A young and keen Margaret Thatcher—another child of scholarships and the puritan work ethic—was elected. She lived, and believed in, that work ethic though, while our little meritocrat was more than ever determined not to join the world of workaday drudgery, although the alternatives were not clear. He did not yet think in terms of university teaching: it seemed so distant, and the erudition needed beyond even his absorbent energies. He thought a bit more about law. He had a friend in the law department, and they went over to Lincoln's Inn to play tennis and see young barristers "in chambers." They argued cases and laughed at A. P. Herbert's wacky examples of legal whimsy: The Thames is in flood and overflows the Embankment. A yacht then runs into a bus. The bus company sues the yacht which counter-sues. Who was at fault? It was the bus: the Thames, said the judge, was still a river wherever it happened to be flowing; hence motor should have given way to sail.

They went with the young lawyers between sessions to have lunches of bangers and mash in the numerous pubs round the Law Courts off Fleet Street. He was much taken with the barristers in their wigs, bands and gowns, and their easy manners and technical chatter about the case in question. The Marxists had only the harshest words for these mercenary lackeys of exploitative capitalism, but he liked them. They seemed to spend a lot of time *defending* those careless members of the proletariat who had fallen foul of the oppressive bourgeois legal system. They explained that it was a perfect profession to combine with politics, since you could take on cases to fit around parliamentary duties. But attractive as it was, it meant doing a law degree and then "reading for the bar" and he wasn't sure he wanted to do all that. "Freelance journalism" was more attractive, but perhaps less secure. There was in any case no hurry.

Some slight revenge for the poor showing at the general election came in the Union elections. The Cons and Libs, played on student resentment at the Labour club's assumption that it owned the Union and could simply nominate its officers (friend Frank was vice-president, Ken was a council member), with all the perks that accrued. They ran a successful campaign for the Honorary Presidency, for long a fief of the left and reserved for their various unsavory heroes. The only duty of the Hon. Pres. was to deliver a lecture, and the students were tired of being preached at. They wanted humor. So that year they elected Bernard Braden, then the popular host of the BBC humor show "Breakfast with Braden" (or was it "Bedtime with Braden"?) Everyone knew his laugh lines from the "Encyclopaedia Bradenica"—the source of all useful knowledge. "Q: In a strange house, where do you wash your hands? A: Start at the wrists and work down?" These *were* more innocent days. Braden gave a laugh-inducing lecture on "Fennimore Cooper's Literary Perversions" and an even greater party afterwards at the Savoy for his backers.

The next year they promoted, and won the election for, Malcolm Muggeridge, curmudgeonly conservative editor of *Punch*, the doyen of satirical magazines. He likewise entertained with a talk on how impossible it was to satirize some institutions since, like the BBC weekly guide, the *Radio Times*: they were satires of themselves. He read an actual page aloud and had the audience in fits. "'The Sex Life of the Newt'—a talk by the Rev. Evelyn Macgillycuddy, M.A., illustrated with his own recordings." (Near enough.) But they really slugged it to the Labour club, when, again, riding a wave of student resentment at the complacency of its leadership, they ran for Union President the editor of *Beaver*, a Tory who was slightly to the right of Bismarck. He used to boast about using prostitutes (he had his own income): "Get in, pay for it, get out, no problems, no consequences." He actually made a pretty good president, concentrating on efficiency rather than ideology. There is no moral to this story.

He and Ken, discovering that official college clubs received subventions for necessary expenses, revived the defunct Rationalist Society and had Popper give a talk on "Moral Progress: Confessions of an Optimist." Something he later published. They made him honorary president that year and used the funds for a grand party in *The Three Tuns* for the Poppereans and assorted optimists from the other camps. Disputes dissolved in the free wine and beer, and they decamped (without Popper) for Yates's Wine Lodge in High Holborn to drink port from the barrel and exhaust the funds entirely. They sank their differences in a convivial singsong celebrating, to the tune of *The Red Flag*, the inherent weakness of class-consciousness:

> The worker's flag
> Is palest pink;
> It's not so red
> As you might think.
> The working class
> Can kiss my arse
> I've got the foreman's
> Job at last

And yet more subtle analysis of the character of the notoriously belligerent secretary of the British Communist Party.

> Harry Pollit was a Communist, and one of Lenin's Lads
> 'Til he was foully murdered by reactionary cads.
> By reactionary cads! By reactionary cads!
> 'Til he was foully murdered by reactionary cads!
>
> Harry stood at heaven's gate, all quaking at the knees,
> "Oh could I speak to comrade God, it's Harry Pollitt please?"
> St. Peter said to Harry, "Are you humble and contrite?"
> "I'm a friend of Lady Astor." Said St. Peter, "that's all right."

The uniqueness of the event in the history of ideas was not appreciated by the bouncers, and our lads were thrown out.

The next year they had a quieter time with Bertrand, Earl Russell ("call me Bertie") and a session in a local pub after. He was entranced with Bertie's prototype noble head (and manner), but noticed at the same time that Bertie's pullover had moth-holes in it. Bertie had been for dropping an atom bomb on the Russians before they dropped one on us. He was also for putting the heads of the Western nations on trial for something or other. But he was firm in his rationalism and pronounced the eventual death of superstition: "It has to happen." A good technical philosopher, the Earl—you couldn't top *Principia Mathematica*, let's face it, and a great historian of philosophy; but our man was left wondering exactly how that helped when it came to judgments about the real world. But he could forgive the author of *A Free Man's Worship* an awful lot. Nothing could ever shake the gratitude he felt for the vote of confidence in his Rationalism that Bertie had bestowed. He didn't tell him; it seemed a bit foolish. But sometimes he wished he had.

Meanwhile he tore on. He and Ken had decided they had outgrown the garret, and moved to share a house in Holland Park (the quite tony Ladbrooke Grove) with a suicidal Pakistani air pilot. A lot of time was spent talking Khasi in off ledges. It didn't affect them all that much, but one had to be a bit concerned for the passengers. He learned much from the worldly Ken. Sent to get spaghetti from the pantry for an evening meal, he returned complaining that there was no spaghetti, only a packet of drinking straws. It may not seem much of a lesson, but to find out that spaghetti came other than in cans, and to whip up a reasonable Bolognese sauce from cheap minced beef and tomato paste (plus onions), was a valuable step on the road to cosmopolitan eating. Add learning the names of wines to ask for—Valpolicella, Chianti, Sancerre— and the route was open. But all was not at such a level of smooth sophistication. He and Ken were anchor members of the LSE beer-drinking relay team, otherwise staffed by the Rugby club. Their come-from-behind wins over the much-fancied Engineering and Medical School teams were the stuff of legend, or the ultimate in boorishness, depending on your sensitivities. The bar paid for the competition pints.

At a party nearby (there was always a party nearby) he played and sang, and talked to a tall wavy-haired fellow with big ears and very blue eyes who was at RADA. They sang together—some Percy French numbers—and the acting student, who said his name was O'Toole (he didn't sound Irish), told him to come along to the RADA theater to see the student play he was in (*Trelawney of the Wells*?) They would have some drinks and songs after with the cast. For some reason he didn't go; another road not traveled. But he saw Shakespeare at The Old Vic, and *Iolanthe* at Sadler's Wells (there were always cheap seats in the gods for students.)

Cinema in the fifties and sixties was more or less a blank for him (he remembers *La Strada* with a brooding Quinn, and *Julius Ceasar* with an amazing Brando) except for foreign films and classics at the Hampstead Everyman Cinema. But there was a wealth of musical theater: they saw (only ever a brief walk away from the School) first runs of *Kismet* (he rather liked the songs borrowed from Borodin), *Salad Days*—definitive musical of the college years, and *Paint Your Wagon* ("I Talk to the Trees" and "Maria" were the big numbers then; "Wandering Star" only came to fame through Lee Marvin's gravelly movie version.) For theater there was, above all, John Osborne's *Look Back in Anger*, which ripped up the script on the conventional stage marriage and ushered in the kitchen-sink school. More gently there was *I Am a Camera, Teahouse of the August Moon, Hippo Dancing,* and above all *Waiting for Godot.* Beckett was all the rage (although he hadn't discovered Billie Whitelaw yet), but no one could fathom the "meaning" of the play. It was like an active inkblot, and the Freudians had a field day, while the Marxists…

He wrote music and songs for an original verse play about Peter Abelard and the troubadours by Raymond Chapman, the School's only lecturer in English (*Songs of Spring.*) This was part of a self-conscious attempt to start a "verse drama revival" by one E. Martin Browne (leading with Fry's *The Lady's Not For Burning.*) Browne read his poetry and virtually demanded a "verse drama" for the revival. But he was not at all sure about drama. He didn't have the easy wit of Fry, and anyway he didn't feel comfortable with the free verse then de rigeur in drama (Eliot and all.) Browne was adamant that blank verse would just not do: "Not the rhythm of the modern age." To bad for the modern age; he let it slide. He was altogether unsure about all this "modern" stuff in art, music or poetry. His compatriots were always unsure and defensive about it, because they feared they might not be smart enough to understand what was going on, so they put on a mask of knowing enthusiasm as a cover. He hated poets like Pound, and took refuge in more measured contemporaries like Graves, Auden, MacNeice, Day Lewis and even the delightfully nutty Edith Sitwell. In music Vaughan Williams' *Job* was about as modern as he liked to get. He actually developed a sneaking admiration for Bartok and some other modern music (Prokofiev, Stravinsky), but he was less happy about art. He knew plenty of art people from the coffeehouses, and a friend was a friend of Lucian Freud whom he met. Bacon was even thrilling, but Moore seemed phony. He actually liked and tried to imitate John Bratby. The art and music people were OK as a diversion, but they didn't *know* anything, so couldn't keep his interest.

He ploughed on: music for more Shakespeare plays there including *Merchant of Venice* which they took on tour to France and Germany in the summer; music for the University drama club (*The Tempest*) where he collaborated with school-friend Brian in clarinet and guitar pieces. It was at this latter that he met a truly pretty girl playing Ariel. She was a dead ringer for Jean Simmons.

People stopped her in the street for autographs. His declared passion, in poems and music, won her over. (He stole her from the chairman of the Liberal Society.) It slightly amazed him, but she was not protective of her virtue like the others he had fondled and fumbled and given up on; she seemed actually quite eager. And so in a dark room at a small north-London ladies' college, after a cast party, and with her roommate in a bed across the room (politely feigning sleep), he finally, not so much lost his prolonged virginity, as gained everlasting sex. You want details? No details. This is not kiss and tell. Enough that it happened, and there was no looking back. Even if for the next years the sex was passionately and obsessively confined to Ariel, it was there and life was again different. It was jazz, impressionist music, *The Golden Bough,* the Spanish guitar, *Language Truth and Logic*, all rolled into one experience. It was life, where before there had only been a wordy fantasy of life. Even the Marxists didn't despise this.

You will see that there is a happy conjunction of work and play here. This was part of the "LSE Experience." Work and play intermingled almost inseparably most of the time. But sometimes work just had to take over, and to be honest at this point he was only doing the minimum to get by, except in philosophy and anthropology where he enjoyed it enough to make an effort. He coasted through social psychology on his knowing of behaviorism culled from reading a lot of Russell in school, and a no doubt irritating tendency to start methodological (Popperean or Positivist) quarrels with its fairly dubious assumptions. Freud fascinated, but to a good Popperean it was really all metaphysics and off the chart. The Behaviorists countered Psychoanalysis with H. J. Eysenck, who's "factor analysis" managed also to infuriate the Marxists with the psychological proof that they and the Fascists had identical personalities. Empiricist though he was, Eysenck garnered ideas ("tough-minded vs. tender-minded") from William James. Our man was thus led to the great American, whose brother he had first encountered in a bunk, in a log cabin, in the Canadian wilderness.

He liked William James, and *The Varieties of Religious Experience* in particular, but this wasn't on the syllabus. He also read with fascination Konrad Lorenz's *King Solomon's Ring.* The communicative world of animals seemed to say something profound about the pre-cultural conditions for social behavior, but he couldn't place it in the scheme of "roles and expectations" that seemed to concern the teachers. (He hadn't read any Darwin yet.) Otherwise the psychologists seemed obsessed with prejudice and particularly anti-Semitism. He got into trouble for suggesting that characteristics attributed to races or nations or any groups should be investigated as facts before they could be dismissed as prejudices. Didn't he realize that by definition *any* generalizations about groups were non-factual and the product of serious pathologies in the accusers? Well, he did now. Julius Gould, whose whole being drooped like his walrus moustache, lectured mournfully, an academic

Eeyore, on Theories of Society: all dismally pessimistic. The Venerable Ginsberg—who held the apostolic succession from the giants of the nineteenth century, lectured on the legendary Westermarck and Hobhouse and comparative morals. Tom Bottomore—who really looked like Orwell, was translating the collected works of Marx. He used to bring in his latest translation and discuss Marx's meanings with them; doesn't get more basic than that. Ernst Grebenik and demographers from the Registrar General's Office taught formal demography (life tables, population pyramids) but it was boring and he lost interest. He liked the stuff on world population trends and problems from Glass. It was the only set of social science facts that actually scared him a little.

The sociologists were fixated on "social class" and its accompanying "social mobility." Everything under the sun was correlated with social class. It was a very English preoccupation. He supposed German sociologists would be taken with power, French with food, and Italian (if there were any) with sex. But here it was class. Class differences existed, he didn't doubt that; he just didn't see why it should be examined to death and to the exclusion of almost all other institutions. He was happier with Gould who was into broad issues of the Indian Caste System versus European and Japanese Feudalism, and such more encompassing questions. He supposed he was, by their definition, "socially mobile," but he didn't see it as a "class" thing. It was obvious that other people had more money (most of them), spoke differently, had different manners, airs and attitudes. For some this went along with an assumption of "natural superiority"; he didn't accept that. He too was a snob, but, as we have seen, an intellectual snob. There was no greater claim to superiority than superiority of knowledge, and no one was born with information (although he was convinced from his IQ studies that people were different in ability from birth.) The sociologists recognized "achieved" versus "ascribed" status, and he happily endorsed the former. He felt he was in a class outside "class"—the class of *individual achievers* who might come from any of the Registrar General's fine social gradations: but *they knew each other*. He gently satirized the RG's categories (and the current song-writing scene) in a *Popular Song* (with redeeming social content):

> Two different wo-orlds,
> That's what they a-are;
> Two worlds so ne-ear,
> And yet so fa-ar.
> There's no way of solving this status riddle,
> "cos I'm lower-lower and you're upper-middle,
> O yeah, yeah, yeah!
> Two differ-e-ent worlds

Two different wo-orlds,
Such an aby-yss;
But we will bridge it
With a ki-iss.
Your Ma will agree and your Pa say OK,
When I get you in the family way,
O yeah, yeah, yeah!
Two differ-e-ent worlds.

The lectures on statistics, which he should have attended for he sorely needed this instruction, were early in the morning, and he just couldn't make the classroom at that hour. He got a textbook and a book on "statistical calculations" which took you through the basic formulae, and with help from Ken (a mathematical economist) managed to keep more or less abreast. He had another epiphany when the basic functions of the normal curve dawned on him. It was price all over again. Once you grasped the properties of the normal curve, everything else fell into place. When you understood the difference between the means of two related populations (male and female, for example) in terms of two overlapping curves, even more made sense. Never again need the argument that there was an exception ("But I know a woman who...") to the mean value have any weight: the exceptions were at the extremes of the curves, and the curves overlapped. But (Sir) Claus Moser, who taught the class, had noticed his absence, for Moser taught with an unusual combination of lectures and homework, thought necessary in the particular case of statistics. A note from the great teacher (and expert concert pianist of course) brought him in for an interview. He explained what he was doing, and showed the book in which he was working through examples. Moser said OK; it was up to him. The class had evidently asked if there was any correlation between attendance and exam success. Yes, Moser had told them, a negative correlation (some got the joke.) He was touched by the lofty one's concern, and immensely admired his playing of Mozart. For a few weeks he made an effort to get in to the lectures. But it couldn't last in the face of late nights and hangovers.

With Anthropology he did make an effort. Isaac Schapera had given the lectures on primitive political and legal systems (basically the Bantu), Raymond Firth the lectures on economics (Maori and Malaysia), and Freedman those on religion and magic (a lot on Chinese ancestor worship.) John Barnes was their tutor that year, making them read about central and east Africa, and giving the lectures on kinship and marriage. Kinship had elements of logic to it; it could be reduced to formal systems, and a geometrical facility with thinking in diagrams was helpful. So he took to kinship. "Lineage theory" was all the rage after the work of Evans-Pritchard and Fortes on Africa had made everyone lineage conscious. He heard visiting lectures from Nadel, Lienhardt, Gluckman, Goody, and Meyer Fortes who talked interestingly about Freud: unusual for an anthropologist in those days. Everyone was in awe of Edmund Leach's complex diagram-dotted prize-winning essay on *The Structural Implications of Matrilateral Cross-Cousin Marriage*. It was a great thing to wave at those in the other disciplines skeptical of the "scientific status" of Social Anthropology—particularly the Poppereans. It didn't impress the Marxists: they had Engels and Morgan and the dialectic of history, and didn't fall for this bourgeois neo-colonialist ideological super-structure...

But they were not the only ones who had doubts. He was willing to defend Anthropology as science to the outsiders, but he was at the same time disappointed with it. He hankered after Frazer. The grand old man had asked these sweeping questions about where religion had come from, why we had it at all, how it had changed through the ages. The social anthropologists dismissed all this as "old stuff" that one shouldn't waste time on. The new dispensation was the work of the School's own Bronislaw Malinowski, and the perpatetic Radcliffe-Brown, who started at Cambridge—as an admirer of his childhood neighbor Kropotkin and hence known as "Anarchy Brown" —toured the world, and ended at Oxford. This "school" (actually a couple of people reacting against the previous generation, as seemed standard) was called Functionalism—quite self-consciously. The term was invented by Malinowski to mark off his approach from the Evolutionism of people like Frazer. It was made to sound like a real theoretical idea, but it was a theory born of strange necessity.

The extrovert Pole had actually come into anthropology by reading Frazer, but during World War I had been in Australia, and as a technical enemy alien (Austrian) had been threatened with internment. He persuaded them to let him sit out the war in the Trobriand Islands, off the southeastern coast of New Guinea. He came away with a massive store of notes, which he wove into a series of massive books, and a feeling that everyone who claimed to know about primitive society should spend as much time as he had in studying one, albeit by default. This "fieldwork experience" would teach anthropologists to see customs and behavior "in context" in terms of their "functions" rather than, as Frazer and his like had done, to tear them out of context for the purpose of creating artificial evolutionary sequences: the dreadful legacy of Herbert Spencer and L. H. Morgan. The Evolutionists depended on material gathered by missionaries, colonial officers, explorers and the like. (Not reliable: one district officer responding to a Frazer questionnaire on native "manners and customs" replied: "Manner none, customs beastly.") The new Functionalists would go out and do their own data gathering, first hand, in the native language, over a decent period of time. Thus was modern Social Anthropology created, by the Polish émigré who, according to his student Firth's story, used to lie down between the seats at Covent Garden to listen to Wagner, because he couldn't stand watching fat Rhine Maidens. It paid to be a bit eccentric to make your mark.

This was all very well for the professionals, but our little man, being into big think, wanted some answers to those old questions, which, he reckoned, were still valid even if the Frazerian method had faults. Everyone was harsh with Frazer. He was, they said, guilty of simply "instantiating" rather than testing hypotheses. It was true that he would state a "proposition" and then look for as many examples as he could get to illustrate it, but he was (our man thought) simply saying "look how ubiquitous this association is." He wasn't trying to test hypotheses. But, they argued, he then ignores the "negative instances"—those cases that do not fit his proposed association (say, between pastoralism and dairy-food taboos: "Thou shalt not seethe a kid in its mother's milk." *Exodus*: 34:26.) But he had been doing his Statistics homework, and knew that a correlation did not have to be one hundred percent: this was the whole point of it. There would always be negative instances, but enough positive ones in the right direction would still yield a correlation between any two variables. Barnes, while not being sympathetic to Frazer, was a good teacher (he had early suggested a dose of Popper) and turned his attention to G. P. Murdock and the "Cross Cultural Method" then in vogue in America. This took lots of cases culled worldwide, and then ran correlations to test hypotheses, and even test hypotheses about successive "stages" of social change: it was even a conscious attempt to revive these despised social evolutionary concerns. So the American anthropologists were still interested in these things? It was something to be pondered.

But not pondered too much or too long: the exams would be in Functionalist theory and based on Functionalist assumptions. Back to the ethnographic texts. At least with Malinowski sex was out in the open as a legitimate subject. This was emancipating. Copies of *The Sexual Life of Savages* were obtainable in every rubber shop in London, although the lengthy discussions of matrilineal kinship must have been a disappointment to all those furtive men in dirty raincoats who slithered in to buy it. The alliterative *Sex and Repression in Savage Society* provided good material to hammer the Freudians—no Oedipus complex in the Trobriands. As for the big questions, the only person who entertained them was MacRae, a sociologist whose erudition both excited and terrified, because it was so obviously unachievable. If you spent the rest of your life reading five books a day you'd still never catch up. But MacRae thought burrowing in "the old stuff" was the sign of a budding scholar and encouraged it. Essays were set on Spencer and Morgan, Maine and McLennan, and even the reading of Darwin was encouraged (at least *The Descent of Man.*) The Soc. Anth. dogma of the time allowed for no such flirting with biology, even though Malinowski himself based his Theory of Culture firmly on biological needs.

There was a second-hand law bookshop in Gray's Inn Road where nicely bound copies of Spencer and Darwin were available cheap. They had been produced in quantity in the nineteenth century and plenty were still in circulation. For a shilling a volume he got the whole of Spencer's *Principles of Sociology* and other works of the master, and MacRae went through them with him, urging caution in the face of his over-enthusiastic embrace of Spencer's evolutionism. It was like that then: teachers really taught if you made the effort to learn. Is it still like that? Was it ever?

One summer (between the second and third years?) he went to a conference of the Rationalist Press Association, of which he was still a member. He had entered their student essay competition ("Can Society Exist Without Religion") and MacRae had vetted it for him. The prize was a trip to the conference, where MacRae (also a member) was a speaker. People didn't like MacRae (as they didn't like Freedman), but he was even quite friendly and they went punting: a mystery our lad never mastered. While expertly handling the punt pole, MacRae told him he was too influenced by the British Empricists and the Ayer-Popper connection. Social science would have been better to have paid heed to the Idealists. Go off, said MacRae, and read F. H. Bradley's *Ethical Studies* and see what kind of a social science was implicit in it. He did, and found in Bradley (brother of the Shakespearean critic) at least one philosopher who seemed to have understood Darwin's relevance to social theory in some way other than the crude "survival of the fittest" metaphor (Spencer's, not Darwin's.)

The conference was a mess, largely because the young Turks wanted discussion of something other than the old-fashioned religion bashing, and the old Turks seemed determined to adopt left-wing foreign policies as the official program of the Association, because one of their members was a Labour spokesman on foreign policy. He was talking to this member about hypocrisy in politics. "You know," he said, groping for an example, "like Labour MPs who send their children to private schools." The member went bright red and hurried away. The man's dirty little secret was uncovered. The unmasker should have felt pleased; so why did he feel guilty? He was asked to address the meeting, and took the opportunity to offer them a vote of gratitude for the comfort their existence and publications had given to a lonely agnostic youngster. The old fellows were obviously touched. A nice moment.

One day Freedman, when they were doing the standard stuff on the incest taboo—about how marriage to strangers protected the family from sexual conflict and all that, flung out the question: "Why can't we have a sexual free-for-all in the family and *then* marry out of it?" Some questions just stay with you. He became obsessed with the incest question, particularly the Freud versus Westermarck debate (primary incestuous sex choices versus natural aversion to sex with familiars.) Westermarck was more or less universally dismissed (except by Ginsberg), so naturally our man latched on with enthusiasm; anyone who was universally said to be "self-evidently wrong" could count on his support. He was certainly dismissive himself of the accepted solutions to the problem of the incest taboo. These were all of the "pick your favorite disaster" type: you "explained" the taboo by pointing out the disasters that would ensue if it *didn't* exist. It took only a few Popperean minutes to dump the lot. But that left the question still open, and he pondered it for future reference. It certainly seemed to him much more "self-evident" that Westermarck was right, but it would have to wait.

We are well into year three now, and the boys have moved again, to north London this time. Much time is spent playing bar billiards and, on the sunny days, lounging around Hampstead Heath (Keats country—the Vale of Health) reading contemporary philosophers, and such enthusiasms as Nietzsche and Spengler, the Metaphysical Poets and the Pre-Raphaelites, John Ruskin, and Pitirim Sorokin. Sorokin, a contemporary Harvard sociologist, was the latest of the Grand Theory of History genre, who outdid Toynbee by insisting on quantifying everything, thus marrying the quantomania of the social sciences to the social philosophers' great movements of civilization. It went a bit far when, in order to quantify the relative importance of philosophers in history, he took as his measure the geometric average of the number of lines devoted to each of them in the *Encyclopedia Britannica*. But, as MacRae would insist, at least he tried for some objective measure; it was in the right spirit. To our man, however, Sorokin was further proof that the Yanks had a corner on the really interesting stuff and were not afraid of the tough questions. He even read—if not all, a good deal of—the supposed leading U.S. sociologist of the day (again Harvard's) Talcott Parsons. He really admired Parsons' attempt to put all the great ones—Freud, Weber, Durkheim, and Alfred Marshall—together (*The Structure of Social Action*), and show how they were all saying the same thing. But when it came to Parsons' own effort at synthesis (*The Social System*) it was written in an English that was a kind of pidgin German—truly unintelligible. It was the moderns all over again: the more obscure and jargon-ridden you were, the more profound you were supposed to be. He suspended judgment.

Relief from the mind-buzzing effort came in the form of parties. And of these the best were those given by the well-off Jewish students, usually in Hampstead or Golders Green. There was always the biggest range of drinks, and somehow they always had a cornucopia of exotic food. He was as fascinated by the Jews as he had been by the Catholics. He had figured out by now who they were and what they doing still around (unlike the Hittites who, at the time, must have seemed better candidates.) But he had never known they had such numbers and influence. Many of his friends at the School, and a majority of his teachers, were Jews. They were there in numbers disproportionate to their presence in the population. These were not religious Jews but the secular, bright, intellectual set. Their fathers were academics or publishers, or in the arts or music, and classier businesses (art book sellers or international financiers for example.) They were the smartest people he knew, and the most worldly and confident. In his world, they were the aristocrats: they had the lineage, they had the wealth, they had the manner. Despite his admiration for Disraeli, he always felt a bit on the outside with them. He was tolerated, but never felt entirely at home. They carried an ancient secret that was impenetrable by mere Anglo-Saxons. He toyed with the mask of (Jewish) urban sophisticate, but it was not one he could wear with any conviction; he was just not to the manner born, racially or socially. He was stuck with the mask of "provincial lad makes good," but this was such a pathetic cliché, and so lacking in distinctiveness, he dropped it as quickly and donned "philosophical skeptic" again.

The Jewish girls—his Catholic-girl substitutes—were dark-eyed, sallow skinned, zaftig and sensuous. They were like a miniaturized Sophia Loren or Gina Lollobrigida, these Hannahs, Rachels, and Rebeccas. He remembered Lamb's remark about Jael having those same dark eyes and tried to remember what she had done (chopped someone's head off? No, that was Judith: ran in the family?) He would have risked it, but in truth he was afraid of their Mediterranean glamour. Even so, he was a hungry student struggling to make ends meet on an inadequate grant. His passion for books led to a constant battle between this food for the mind and that for the body. A paperback was OK, but hardback books at between a pound and thirty shillings dug deep into the week's food money. By the end of term he was reduced to chicory sandwiches in the bar and bacon-and-egg pie (Yorkshire quiche) sent by a long-suffering mother wrapped up in his washing, which he sent home by parcel post since this was cheaper than a laundry. Given these depressingly mean circumstances, there was no question that the Jewish parties should always be chosen over their competition since one could stock up on smoked fish and meats, chicken and meatballs, several different breads and fine sticky desserts. Mothers and maids were always ready to replenish the greedily emptied platters. He wisely stayed at a polite distance from the sinuous girls, and was content to accept their generous food and drink, and their endearing love of talk, and music.

If he couldn't be an intellectual Jew, he was becoming adept at being the schoolyard cynic. Working doctor Roger Bannister, on his rainy day off, took a lonely bus ride from his London Hospital to Oxford, and, watched by a handful of people and paced by Chris Chataway, ran the first sub-four-minute mile. (Oh my God, they *were* simpler days!) When the news hit the School, students danced and cheered and jumped about in jubilation: not nationalistic jubilation, just sheer joy that it should have been done and that they were there when it happened. With lofty detachment our man puffed a few delicate puffs on the philosophical pipe and declared that this was indeed an achievement symbolical of the twentieth century: we were now running round in circles faster than ever before. It was the nearest he ever came to a Socratic end, for the rejoicing ones near lynched him. Yes, we are amused; we see how all his fatally weak traits are now dangerously exposed. But for how much longer must we persist with this third-person charade? Until, gentle ones, we no longer want to grab his shoulders, shake the little brat, slap him around and yell: "Shut up! Stop it! Shape up! Get a life!" Since this was still true yesterday, we must be patient with the trope.

The big thing of the year was the Review. This annual show of skits, musical numbers, comedy and odds and ends was much anticipated, although not always very good. But of recent years its standards had been raised through the roof by the twin talents of Ron Moody and Fenella Fielding (Feldman as she was then) who both went on to stardom, she on television (*That Was the Week That Was*) he in movies (*Oliver, The Twelve Chairs.*) People wanted more of their comic brilliance; it was a hard act to follow. But with the help of the musical genius (word not lightly used) of Political Science student Jeffrey (Jewish of course), they pulled it off. There was also a rare talent from the Anthropology class, Nadia from British Honduras, who sang a West Indian kind of song—a "Calypso." The guitar came in handy here, and they performed two of her own pieces: "Yellow Bird" (sit on a banana tree) and "Long Time Boy I Never See You" (come let me hold your hand.) You still hear them on muzak in elevators.

Our warbler had a couple of amusing solo songs by Jeffrey. ("When I was a kid about seventeen/ I fell in love with a beauty queen/ But I didn't love her, I didn't try/ And here's the reason why…") But the *coup de théatre* came in an inspired spoof of the guardian spirits, Sidney and Beatrice Webb. Their large portrait dominated the Shaw library; everyone knew it by heart. So a clever stage designer mocked up the exact background from the painting, with fireplace and brickwork. A stuffed small pooch was found matching the one Beatrice was patting as she sat by the fire. Lancastrian talent Peggy was dressed in the Beatrice costume, and guess who donned a goatee and pince nez, sported the exact cravat and hair parted in the middle, and, holding papers in his left hand, joined in as the exact replica of Sidney. When the curtain went up nothing could go forward for a full five minutes as the audience whooped and hollered and clapped in instant recognition. Then, to the tune of "Two Sleepy People" he and Peggy launched into the words they had worked on together:

> Here we are, we've sorted out the bills,
> Now we sit and wonder, does life hold other thrills?
> Two intellectuals, alone by the fire,
> We both missed the streetcar named desire.

Pandemonium. He sang in a high, cracked, wavering, wheezy voice such as he had been told was the very sound of Sidney, while Peggy hit the right tremulous contralto. We don't need all of it, but here's some of the verse:

> Sidney: Do you remember, my darling,
>   On the night that we were wed,
>   We forgot to go up to bed?

Beatrice: We just wrote a paper
           On the lower income groups,
Together: And who would have believed
           That is how it was conceived?

(Chorus)

Sidney: Here we are, a husband and his neighbor,

Beatrice: Call me socialist or Fabian
           For I'll never be in (L)labour.

Together: Two intellectuals, by dawn's early light,
           But please tell us what to do at night.

The pun on the Labour Party and parturition is hard to render in print, but in song it rocked the house. There was more, and they added more for the other nights of the run:

Sidney: Do you remember the night
           The Fabians held their annual ball?
           Beatrice didn't like it at all.

Beatrice: Bernard kept having unpolitical ideas
           And though he asked me quite politely
           I said "not Pygmalion likely!"
Together: Here we are, condemning all the Tories,
           But we had to wait for Bernard to tell us what a whore is.
           Two intellectuals, put on another log,
           And leave reproduction to the dog.

But nothing could beat that sensational opening night; it was the talk of the town for weeks. Were they a new Ron and Fenella? Maybe not, but there was a heady time when producers and impresarios pursued them and talked about West End runs and tours and the like. But Jeffrey wanted to be a serious composer and a lecturer, Peggy went to America and married an architect and had lots of children, Nadia went back to the Caribbean, and the others had their own agendas. He was dazzled momentarily, and he still had no good ideas for the future, but it slipped by. Some characters from Oxford (or was it Cambridge?) who stole some of the Review's better ideas like spoofing the national anthem at the beginning, went on to international fame and even considerable fortune. The mask was worn and then dropped. Masks were for temporary use.

It was all moot because the final exams loomed. Perhaps it has changed, but then everything turned on these finals. No matter how many B-plusses or A-minuses you had garnered in seminars, classes and tutorials, nothing in the end counted except your performance on the finals. The rest was all preparation; this was the real thing. The final term was frantic as June and the appointment with destiny crowded in. Then came the almost predestined blow. He was living now with friend Mike-the-Catholic, who, being younger, had just come up to medical school. He and Ken had decided that sharing a room with each other was OK, but with girls in the picture it didn't work. He'd lived alone in a well-appointed but cruelly cold garret in West Hampstead (handy for the Heath) for a while, but it was too expensive; sharing with Mike cut the costs. But Mike was a handful. He had no idea about looking after himself. He spent fifty pounds of his tiny allowance on an overcoat, took an illegal job and got caught, was arrested for trying to cheat on a subway fare, and had to go home and start again. It was a terrible failure. This was his younger brother, his charge; he had let him down somehow.

Mike was not untypical of medical students, who were almost expected to be irresponsible and madcap. Some miracle happened between graduation and their becoming practitioners, for they all ended up as sober, respectable, and usually very good physicians. He was nevertheless horrified listening to Mike and the others revising for exams, when they ditched whole areas of life-threatening common ailments (TB, diphtheria, streptococcus...) in favor of obscure stuff known to be the favorite of the examiner (tropical enteritis...) Mike eventually became an army doctor, a major in the medical corp. But he had the good sense to send for the civilian doctor when one day our desperately cramming boy, after several painful sleepless nights, keeled over and hit the floor. They whisked him off to hospital and pronounced him very ill with infective hepatitis. He had gone quite yellow, spectrally thin, and decidedly wobbly on his pins. When slightly recovered a few weeks later, a distraught mother took him home and nursed him to eventual health. But that was the end of year three. It was the sixth-form experience all over again: there were no "make-up" exams; the year would have to be repeated. Freedman—whose stern reputation was belied by his many kindnesses—came to see him while he was in hospital. "Don't worry," he said cheerfully, "you can have a good time with your jazz and your girl friend, and perhaps sort out what you want to do with your life." Perhaps.

He spent part of the summer in Ireland, recuperating and enjoying the contact with ancestral Irishness. From Galway to Dublin town (and a brief excursion to sinister Belfast) he drank it in. He went to Sligo where there was a Yeats festival in progress (it was in fact the local industry) and made his homage at the grave under Ben Bulben's Head in the shadow of Maeve's cairn. ("Cast a cold eye on life, on death/Horseman, pass by.") Sligo was full of "cousins" of the bard who, for a pint, would regale tourists with recollections. One of them was, at least, a Pollexfen, and so plausible, but his recollections seemed too pat. The tourists drank it up, the cousins drank their pints, and all was dishonestly cheerful. Singing and drinking in Dublin, he felt he should have always been there, and wondered about trying to find some place in this daffy but delightful society. Except that there was always an uneasy hint of violence and cruelty just beneath the charm and humor of the surface.

Sinister also was the superstition of the place. People knelt in the dirt of the Dublin streets to be blessed by passing bishops, there were shrines with votive candles at every crossroads, and in all the squalid, poor villages, (Bally-this and Bally-that) there was a massive, expensive Catholic church. The people, even the supposed intellectuals, were piously subservient to this harsh, Augustinian, sin-obsessed ecclesia. He remembered his grandfather and shuddered. The pilgrimage was made to the Post Office where he put his fingers in the bullet holes, and recalled *Easter 1916* by the statue of Cuchullain. A terrible beauty may well have been born, but it didn't look that way to those hard-faced, incomprehensible men he had met in even-more-puritan Belfast, surrounded by large policemen with guns.

Still, he played with the punning obscurity of *Finnegans Wake* and wrote about "Miss tickle cymbals of whirled weiry soles." He saw Synge's *Playboy of the Western World* at the Abbey, with the ghosts of Yeats and Lady Gregory in attendance. He worshipped at the statue of Burke outside Trinity College (now there was a place to be and be happy.) He listened to passionate stories of the assassination of Michael Collins and the treachery of de Valera (or vice-versa in another pub on another night.) He met several enthusiasts for the everlasting Gaelic revival, and compared his residual Welsh to their Irish. Of course, a basic Irish grammar by the industrious Christian Brothers was purchased and read on the boat back, to be stored for future reference. He admired the sense of purpose of the revivalists, and was fascinated by the songs in Gaelic that they sang. Once back in busy and always-purposeful London, he had to try to renew his own sense of purpose, which was hard in this unreal extra time.

He had to keep up the stuff he already knew, but not lose the edge. He had been bored with demography, so he switched to criminology, which would give him something new to tackle. Marshall-the-Marxist despised criminology since it blindly failed to acknowledge that the legal system was simply an instrument of class oppression bent on incarcerating members of the proletariat enterprising enough to mount an assault on the capitalist property system. Be that as it may, he enjoyed delving into crime, its causes and cure, but was a bit wary of a subject who's subject matter was solely defined by legislation, so that whole swatches of it —homosexuality for instance—could be defined out of existence overnight. It was also subject to the bullying tendencies of the Left: potential "juvenile delinquents" were to be identified by "prediction studies" and properly dealt with before they actually committed any crimes. He wrote an essay blasting such a blatant abuse of the judicial system. Professor Manheim dismissed it as nonsense, but a young lecturer, Terrence Morris, took him aside and told him it was in fact very good, but not to write such stuff in the exam. Damn nice of Morris, but a sad lesson in its way.

The extra time he had let him read even more in ethnography and philosophy, and more and more of the old stuff, including some Frazer he had never read before, and recommended to him by Schapera (*Folklore in the Old Testament, Totemism and Exogamy*.) He toyed with doing American Indians and went to a few lectures by Daryll Forde at University College. He was intrigued by the prevalence of moiety systems (the tribe divided into two intermarrying halves) since this was the basis of Australian kinship/social systems also. Forde had worked in the Pueblos in the desert southwest of America, and so could be questioned about the Zuni and Hopi tribes which, as descendants of the ancient Cliff Dwellers, had lived in his imagination from the old encyclopedias and been revived when reading D. H. Lawrence. But he couldn't keep it up and went back to Schapera and his well-organized lectures on the Bantu, Hottentots and Bushmen of South Africa. He was fascinated by the Lovedu, since, with their "white" queen they had been the inspiration for *She (who must be obeyed)*. The Zulu and Swazi warriors and armies held him, but Schap told him to get off warfare and do more on law and economics, which he did, reluctantly. It was hard to shake off Shaka, whose vicious but brutally effective *impis* threw themselves on their spears when ordered to, on the death of the tyrant's mother. There probably is a moral to that story.

Freedman had him read the latest *wunderbuch* by the French anthropologist Claude Lévi-Strauss: *Les structures élémentaire de la parenté* (The Elementary Structures of Kinship.) He ordered a copy from Hachette in Regent Street, where the French clerk haughtily corrected his, admittedly bad, pronunciation. He found his School Certificate French more or less adequate to the task, but the book daunting in its challenge. At least he was able to point out to Freedman the passage where *le maître* credited Frazer with a basic breakthrough in the understanding of kinship. Freedman was less than impressed and told him not to wander too far from the syllabus. But he did say that he liked the effort, and that perhaps a career in Anthropology was not unthinkable. This was high praise from a demanding teacher who was not given to pampering students or praising lightly. But while it gave him a momentary light-headedness, it fell on stony ground. It may seem strange in retrospect, but he had never really even vaguely contemplated a life in the academy. University was like school: you passed through, gleaning useful information, then passed on into the supposedly "real" world. It was not somewhere you stayed forever. But such was his aversion to "real" work by now that he did begin to wonder about a life where you actually got paid to do things like read, write and chat to people about what interested you. He thought about it.

But not all the time. On the jazz front much was stirring. He had a friend from home of Irish extraction, Harry, who had been through a religious revolt against his Catholic heritage, and was now into Yeats, Schoenberg, Salvador Dali and jazz. He played a mean trumpet (learned in one of those northern brass bands) and, after attending teacher college, was an English master in a London school. After the Mike fiasco, and again to save on rent, they moved in with another teacher to a flat more spacious than any so far. Together they read many plays, for this was Harry's thing (O'Casey, O'Neill) and Irish writers (O'Flaherty, O'Faolain) but mostly Yeats. They chanted together, drunk on the beauty of it:

> Had I the heavens' embroidered cloths,
> Woven of the golden and the silver light…

This was a busy period of setting Yeats to music. He had already done "The Stolen Child" (the style a bit of a rip-off from Rutland Boughton, with the tenors and altos bleating away at "lah-la, lah-la, lah-la, lah-la…") He now tried *The Lake Isle of Innisfree* with accompaniment for Spanish guitar, clarinet (intended for Brian who had, however, now graduated and gone), and strings (two violins and cello—he never could figure out what to do with the viola.) It was modishly modal to get the folk-song feeling, with overtones of "Down by the Sally Gardens." The accompaniment had the guitar making like a Celtic harp, the clarinet weaving about in the manner of wind instruments in Canteloube (*Songs of the Auvergne*) and the strings shimmering away as in Vaughan Williams's *On Wenlock Edge*. Is this sounding all a bit derivative? So it was; that's how we learn. The little modal tune, to be fair, has its own haunting quality, and only remains in oral memory:

But mostly they played jazz. He had the joy of doing his favorite Armstrong, "Cornet Chop Suey" as a trumpet, guitar, and double-bass trio. Harry helped form an LSE jazz band—previous efforts had been sporadic and not impressive—with a full complement of trumpet, clarinet, trombone, guitar/banjo, bass and drums. The banjo player was his ex jazz-guitar helper, who really didn't play the banjo but tuned four strings to the top four of the guitar, and played guitar chords. Ingenious and effective. (John Lennon had done the same thing in reverse, using, initially only five strings of the guitar in banjo fashion.) He even found a use for his primeval "Alexander's Ragtime Band." It became a kind of signature tune, but not one the uncles would have recognized. The band was good—or seems so in fond recollection. Again they had offers to turn professional, which they were too uncertain to accept. But they had a standing room only audience every Saturday in *The Three Tuns*, and gigs around town for pocket money.

They still spent many nights at 100 Oxford Street listening and learning from Lyttleton and the best band in Europe (don't say that in Paris.) Purists were complaining that Humph was deserting true Dixieland for "cool" jazz of a modernist turn. The boys understood, though. On their gigs they had to go beyond the limits themselves, and actually enjoyed playing be-bop versions of "Cherry Pink and Apple Blossom White" or "Hot Toddy" which couldn't be converted to Dixie-language. Their attempts to imitate Charlie Parker and Dizzy Gillespie were pretty fumbling affairs. Parker and Monk fascinated them: musical mystics communing with their strange personal gods. The musicians expected them to smoke hemp, but he hated cigarettes. He put some in his pipe tobacco, but it burned hot and acrid and gave him a foul headache. He decided to stick with beer and Brubeck.

Despite these flirtations with heresy they were always welcomed back to 100 Oxford Street, and in the breaks were accepted into jam sessions with whoever felt like playing along. This was mostly Lonnie Donegan, who would announce "It's skiffle time!" and launch into one of his frighteningly large repertoire of songs. "The Rock Island Line" was head of the list, "Take This Hammer" and "Jump Down Turn Around Pick a Bale o' Cotton" came a close second. "The Battle of New Orleans" was less popular but turned out eventually to be the greatest recording success (at least in the USA). Skiffle was an offshoot of the old American South jug bands, and was derived from the one-string bass, guitar, fiddle, harmonica and washboard ensembles of Appalachia and Louisiana. Lonnie was to make it a national craze, but at the time was a banjo player and had not much facility with the guitar. He was so skilled with his fingers that he was a rapid learner, and our boys were eager helpers. The audience was surprised when he did appear confidently with his guitar and gave a good driving accompaniment to some of his favorites (even if, when recording, he brought in practiced session men to do the fancy stuff.)

Once recorded, these songs were taken up by skiffle groups around the country. The equipment was cheap or hand made, and the noise was cheerful. A little enthusiasm could make up for a serious lack of skill. In Liverpool, it is said, the street gangs gave up competing by fighting, and fought to have the best skiffle bands in their basement headquarters. Four young lads of Irish extraction, who had done their learning on the skiffle circuit, formed a group they called "The Quarrymen" in about 1957. In 1960, equipped with electric guitars and a decent drum set, they were sent by a canny manager to Hamburg, given cute haircuts and suits, and told to "mach show!" They did, and something magically new came into the world. But it was born from Lonnie, skiffle, 100 Oxford Street, and even, let's face it, our boy's bit of enthusiastic input. Once Lonnie was rich from recordings and driving his Rolls Royce up for Saturday nights, he forgot his old compadres; but they have the memories. They never knew the boys from Liverpool.

Back on the political circuit the song and dance was continuing, but he was almost tired of that mask. Not only was Anthony Eden a disappointment as PM, but the whole idea of a political life was fast fading. There was a move by a Con.-Lib. alliance at the School to run him for vice-president of the Union. They had a meeting in the gilded smoking room of the National Liberal Club—of which he became quite fond, and there was much pressure. His rival in romance, the very decent chairman of the Libs, actually masterminded this move. He was flattered, but rather to his own amazement, he turned them down. It even made him a bit uneasy: what had happened to the chronic accepter; where was the eternal yea-sayer? But there it was. Something had happened. Not only the working world, but the world of law and politics and even journalism was beginning to look less than enticing. He still hankered after the literary, poetic, dramatic, musical life, but had no confidence in his abilities or any idea how to enter it. He was, technically, a rank amateur in all these things, and while it was true that many of the great ones had started as amateurs in this sense, they always seemed to have fifty pounds in their pockets (from an uncle) to get started. He had nothing.

He tried writing a play—about the state of the world surrounding a young soldier killed in Cyprus, his cynical professorial father, his repressed homosexual friend, and his nymphomaniac sister—for the *Observer* playwriting competition. It was partly in verse in deference to the supposed verse-drama revival. It was returned without comment, and a play by a West Indian, in dialect, about a Jamaican boy who wanted to be a fast bowler, won. The judges said we needed more of this "indigenous sympathy," so that let him out. Also, he was now feeling that what he wanted to do was not be involved in the world, but to stand aside and examine the world, or the social world: to see how it worked and why it worked that way. He wanted to be a philosopher in the large sense: one who asked the big questions, not one who studied those who asked or, more likely, criticized them for asking.

He was alternately attracted and repelled by the culture of contradiction that dominated the academy. There were, he decided, two kinds of thinkers: the creators and the critics. Creators (always few in number) were happiest when proposing new, speculative, often daring, ideas. They mostly seemed to come from outside the academy. Critics are only happy when pouncing on the problematic aspects of ideas, especially new ones. Philosophers are almost entirely critics; most academics certainly are. It is a knee-jerk reaction on their part to utter the standard academic response: "On the other hand..." It took him a while to figure out that these were complementary positions and he did not have to choose. For while the critics' stance was safer, there had to be creators to keep the critics employed (see Toynbee and the historians.) His head was with the critics, but his heart was weaving systems and schemes that were certainly full enough of holes to invite the critics' gleeful cruelty.

The pressure was building, not only towards the exams, but assuming he didn't keel over again, to what he might do after. It was urgent because the whole question of National Service had to be dealt with. He was not a conscientious objector—in 1939 he would have been among the first to join up—but he was disgusted with the current "national interest" scene which was obsessed with pathetic remains of empire like Cyprus and Suez. We would have to give these places up eventually (pretty soon in fact) so where was the point dying to try to retain them? This was not defending Western civilization; it was bordering on the obscenely uncivilized. He wanted no part of it. He was fairly confident that with his health history he would be turned down anyway, but his medical resulted in a classification of A1: he was fit for the commandos! He appealed, and armed with a letter from his friendly doctor to the effect that he was on a diet, with suspected stomach ulceration, and taking Nulacin tablets (all true), he was demoted to something like A5. This meant he could not be posted abroad or sent on active duty, but he still would have to serve. He desperately inquired about getting into the intelligence or education corps, and this was possible; but even if not dangerous, it was a two-year waste of time. The only out was deferment for advanced education. So, *faut de mieux*, he had to work on this one. Otherwise, the best he could hope for was two years teaching illiterate and belligerent squaddies to read and write.

Given the state of things with his extra year, he had started to write a "thesis" without knowing really what that was, but having picked up the idea from graduate students in Philosophy. It was to be a revamping of Ginsberg's idea of a "Rational Ethic" but not arrived at through the Comparative Sociology of Moral Systems, but rather by the examination of human needs and the conditions for their realization. He was drawing on Malinowski's "Theory of Needs"—pretty much ignored by the kinship-bedeviled anthropologists, and on an imperfect understanding of Darwin, particularly in *The Descent of Man*. (He found Darwin in general pretty exciting, but he didn't feel he knew enough biology and genetics to know what to do with him. In any case, at this point, he thought Spencer the greater thinker by far!) But before he could even get to the substance he felt he had to clear up the question of the Freedom of the Will. If we were to have ethical systems at all, we had to have an idea of what "responsibility" meant, for there could be no possibility of meaningful ethical action if we were not "free" to make rational choices. Of the abused words in Philosophy—"good," "cause" and "real" among them, "free" and "freedom" ranked pretty high. Some argued that free must mean "uncaused." But that didn't make sense since everything had a cause: how otherwise could it exist? And it couldn't mean "random" for the same reason: random was not the same as free. The negative was better: to be free was not to be coerced. But didn't any "cause" in effect coerce its effect? Some language clarification was called for here, and he set about it, as usual, with more gusto than finesse.

He also wrestled with the old chestnut of the "naturalistic fallacy." This was a dead cert. for an exam question, but more than that it stood in the way of any ethic based on needs. Supposedly Hume had said you couldn't move from "is" statements to "ought" statements: statements about how the world is to those about how it ought to be. He found that Hume had actually only said that he noticed how easily people did in fact move from is to ought *without justification*. So were there legitimate statements of value derivable from statements of fact? The consensus was no; but he found an argument in Darwin of all people to the contrary: if you are speaking of *function* said Darwin, then it does make sense. His example was a pointer (dog that is—D. had been a passionate hunter in his youth): what a pointer did (its function) was point; it therefore made sense to say that a pointer *ought* to point. If it did not point it was not being a pointer. Thus a parent ought to care for its children; it was part of the definition of being a parent, and so on. He of course claimed Darwin as a great linguistic philosopher, which rather startled his teachers, but they were used to this sort of thing by then.

In those days you got merit marks for original effort, and Gellner, MacRae, and the newly arrived Watkins, were patient and interested. He didn't dare approach Popper, or Oakeshott. The latter should have been an ally, given his conservative organicism. But he proved to be a disappointment. The almost rigid rejection of any rational approach to society or behavior, while nice when directed against the doctrinaire socialists, left our man uneasy about his claims for a rational ethic. He meant it to be in the best critical tradition, but he did hope for a usable outcome, and that was going to be anathema to Oakeshott, as indeed it was to the anthropological doctrine of "cultural relativism" which denied any universal standards for behavior. This was more or less just assumed at the School (except by Ginsberg and Gellner—for different reasons), but was actively preached in America, as in Herskovits' *Man and His Works*. Your dances couldn't please everyone all of the time; some of the people some of the time would have to do. They would just have to be the right people.

In one of those chance encounters that have accounted for so much so far, like random events in a Hardy novel (the crucial note from Tess to Angel goes under the doormat), he was explaining his dilemmas (he did a lot of that) to Norman Birnbaum. Birnbaum was an American sociologist from Harvard who was teaching theory (mostly Max Weber.) Birnbaum said, get a scholarship to an American University, preferably Harvard, and hightail it over there for a few years to do a Ph.D., thus getting a chance to be the philosophical observer, and being at a healthy distance from the draft board. Was this possible? Sure, there was the Social Relations Department at Harvard, and they were doing a "Values Study" there. Wasn't that what he was into? Not sure, but worth a look. Birnbaum would write to the "Dean of Admissions" and get the forms. Go see Firth, he said, he has friends at Harvard like Clyde Kluckhohn (he knew him from the Navaho—courtesy of Daryll Forde) and George Homans; see what he says.

Raymond Firth, a New Zealander and the head of Social Anthropology, had always seemed rather distant, but proved to be concerned and interested. He called in Freedman, who confirmed that he thought there was a future for the lad, and Firth dragged out some formidable volumes of the "Values Study." Well, it wasn't the philosophical study of the rational ethic, but it wasn't totally unrelated either. Firth would write to Harvard. But Firth warned him: Anthropology could be a difficult discipline to sustain if you didn't have an independent income. It had always appealed to the upper classes as an off-shoot of empire, and because they had the money to travel. Our boy, on the verge of rescue from the terrors of boot camp, didn't want to stress too hard that he really didn't want to be a "fieldwork anthropologist" at all, and was ready to desert to Philosophy at the first opportunity. One thing at a time.

He was in a whirl. It was all a bit too much. From being concerned to save his miserable skin from EOKA or the fellahiin, he was in danger of actually getting on a positive track to an academic career: something he never really contemplated. You must get a First or an Upper Two at least, Firth said. A good chance, said Freedman. But was there? There was much he hadn't done, and only he knew how much. He had messed about in this free year, and was in some ways less well prepared for some papers than in the year before. But he was bewildered by the confidence these kind people showed in him. What if they were right? He confided in Gellner that he really wanted to do Philosophy, not this empirical study of values. If you're going to the USA, said Gellner, why not apply to a good Philosophy department? Nothing to lose. Like where? Cornell. What's that? It has the best Philosophy department in the States: remember Max Black and Norman Malcolm? He did. He had read quite a bit of their stuff. Why not? He got the address, and wrote them a joint letter: could he come and do a thesis on the Freedom of the Will at Cornell? He looked it up on the map: in the middle of nowhere. But it was America. All the accumulated sensations of Canada, the movies, the books, the jazz, swam through him like a flood tide.

In the event both Harvard and Cornell responded positively. Harvard offered some high-sounding "fellowships"—he guessed they were the same as scholarships, and Cornell a "teaching assistantship" which was a mystery, but according to Birnbaum meant he would have to teach for his living, assisting the "professors" with undergraduates. It didn't sound too bad either way, but his preference was for Cornell, since Malcolm wrote him a nice letter that was quite encouraging about the Freedom of the Will. How was he to get there? No problem. Birnbaum directed him to the American embassy and the Fulbright Commission. Yes: get accepted by an American institution and they would pay his boat fare and "local transportation" as well as medical insurance, which was evidently a big deal (no National Health Service there.) It all turned on his class of degree, but it was all so easy so far that he was convinced there was some huge snag he couldn't see. He hit the books with redoubled effort, dropped the thesis, went easy on the jazz, but still tried to fit in a hour of classical guitar practice a day. There were some absolute priorities.

The world was, as always, too much with us: Wordsworth had it right. He felt like a juggler with too many clubs in the air: if he stopped to pay attention to any one the others would all fall. So events crashed around his ears and what residual confidence he had in the adults of the government and his party crashed with it. First, there was the frustrating suppression of Hungary, with our total inability to do more than make noises in the UN. The Marxists despised the insurgents as neo-Fascist reactionaries flaunting their Horthy uniforms (no evidence for that), and for the first time he almost came to blows with them. Some of the students in the uprising escaped to England, and to the disgust of the Marxists, he served on a committee to help relocate them in the UK. One of the most endearing was a young man who had been at some Marx-Lenin Institute or other. What was he studying? "Proletarian Philosophy." What did he now want to do? "Go to Oxford University." To study what? "Bourgeois Philosophy." He was going to be fine.

At more or less the same time the idiotic Suez venture was undertaken by Eden in collusion (at first indignantly denied) with France and the Israelis. Eden was in thrall, like so many ego-drenched politicians, to his "legacy"— especially when compared to mentor Churchill. He too wanted to cry "no appeasement" and stand up to a "dictator"—a "bully" naturally. Well Nasser was undoubtedly both, and for many Tories it was enough to yell "dictator" to justify an appallingly misjudged attack on Egypt, fraught with lies and hypocrisies. The Egyptians crumbled before the Israelis. The Yanks, who, in the person of Dulles, were furious, vetoed the whole thing. Gellner made the choice witticism of the season by saying that this was the first time since 1870 that the French had actually *wanted* to fight someone. Eden and British pretensions collapsed together. The hypocritical Labour Party at first supported the venture then, when it saw public outrage growing, switched and opposed it. Our miserable ex-Tory joined Ken in reconvening the Pickwick Club and mobilizing the student hordes. Pushed by an urgent need, very new to him, to *do* something, he took to the streets with the protestors, chanting "No war in Egypt! Eden must go!"

He was horrified at his own behavior; this was not the mask of the detached observer who expected little of his fellow men. He was in the streets with the socialists for God's sake, chanting "Well done Nutting!" in praise of the only Tory cabinet member to come out against the nonsense (Edward Boyle soon joined him.) He spoke against the affair in the Union and got friendly applause from the Marxists. It was unbearable. Worse, during a demonstration, he was clubbed and kicked by the police in Parliament Square, and dragged, by the socialists, into the lobby of the House of Commons. There his new friends called out one of the Labour MPs for Bradford, who returned to the floor of the House, covered his head, and asked an angry question about the police tactics. How would he ever explain this to his parents?

They were actually very decent about it on the phone. His mother was more worried about how he was physically. Had a police horse kicked him? His father had never been one of the Edenistic persuasion. He thought the matinee-idol had turned out to be a bloody fool. His question: "Why hadn't the police arrested you?" No idea. Perhaps because they knew they had no case against him particularly—he was just one other demonstrator who got underfoot, so they were content to put the boot in and leave it at that. They were pretty frustrated themselves, and they hated, not without good reason, the privileged students who caused them such grief.

There were Parliamentary protests and "inquiries" resulting in the usual bureaucratic stalling. He was a momentary celebrity, but for the wrong reasons; he was heart-weary and disillusioned in his very bones. This disillusion was no mask. He wanted just to get away from all this messy, emotional, degrading stuff that stuck to his psyche like slime on a garden slug. In America he would be a stranger; he would have no stake in the society, no feeling of responsibility to it; there would be no urge to put it right; he could concentrate on his big questions in these distant places and let his heart heal. He was tired of what he was doing: was he really finding answers or just piling up questions? Was that all one ever did, really? Given the zeitgeist of Philosophy, you did not even get to ask the questions, just elegantly criticize them. Was he gaining depth and "maturing" or just acquiring a larger portfolio of masks? Was he truly finding a focus, or just accumulating ever more information about anything and everything? And did any of it matter? That thing again: those empty feelings of ultimate pointlessness, that William James had called "vastations."

He shook himself free from this long enough to take his exams. There was almost a disaster when his bus route, on the way to the University Examination Halls in South Kensington, was held up for an hour by a rehearsal for the Queen's birthday. It seemed to tell him something, but he was too panicked to figure out what. He had to do in two hours what should have taken three, and this was the Social Philosophy paper. He didn't have time to plan or even think. He let the paper write itself. It turned out to be his best. There was a heat wave—it was in the nineties outside, and higher in. He was in the front row of desks in the vast cavern of a hall, and at intervals he heard gasps and then crashes as people toppled from heat exhaustion, followed by the sound of them being dragged out. He didn't look back, especially during the Statistics exam (no notes or texts, only log tables and a slide rule—he had one; you had to memorize all formulae then.) Sweat dripped down onto his exam book, smudging the writing. He had to sit back from the desk and tie his handkerchief round his brow to avoid this. He had a bottle of glucose (Lucozade?) his mother made him take, and it saved him. She came down for the week of the exams, leaving his father, who hated it, to take care of himself. She wanted to free him from the daily chores of living so he could concentrate on the exams. Their gesture was so pure in its love and care he cried himself to sleep; the sleep was good and necessary.

He got his First. It was one of only two that year. They gave him the Hobhouse Memorial Prize for Outstanding Merit in Sociology: fifty pounds worth of lovely books. Gellner said his papers on philosophy were the best he had ever seen. Gellner was trying to convert to Anthropology and had started fieldwork on Morocco, so our grateful junior philosopher found a copy of Westermarck's classic *Marriage Ceremonies in Morocco* in a Charing Cross Road bookshop and inscribed it to him. Freedman said all his papers in Anthropology were Firsts. He joined his classmates in buying this good teacher a nice Japanese lacquer wastebasket. They attached a note to the effect that when he used it he would always be reminded of them. It was like that then. He even managed a decent performance in Statistics, despite the awful heat, with a saving essay on the properties of the normal curve, and a Chi-square test (positive and significant) on the relation between cigarette smoking and cancer.

In sociology proper he did well with key essays on Herbert Spencer, the decline of aristocracy, Parsons and subjectivism, and the impossibility of defining social class. He would have given a present to MacRae, but the learned and eloquent Scot told him not to waste his meager funds on such crudely sentimental gestures; thanks would come from his continued application and success. He was still in awe of the Scots; this was rectitude well beyond his effete English grasp. His Psychology was so-so (Julius Gould, who had gone over all the results, dejectedly told him), and the only paper he did badly on was criminology. He had forgotten Morris's advice and slashed away at "prediction studies." He said goodbye to the Marxists (Marshall had left the previous year.) They despised his passion for America, the ultimate bad example of decadent and doomed monopoly capitalism, but they couldn't overcome their basic English decency and offered him a hearty bon voyage. He would miss the Marxists.

He married Ariel. The feelings were there, if you count limp sentimentality, self-pitying dependency, retrospective jealousy and glum possessiveness, but it was more a case of not knowing what else to do. She knew if he went alone to America, that would be the end. He was no match for a determined woman's persistence. They had all the tickets marked for Ithaca, New York, and at the last minute, when they were about to leave for the Queen Elizabeth II, a letter came from Cornell: he was certainly admitted to the Philosophy Ph.D. program, but they had run out of funds for teaching assistants. Sorry. So the tickets were changed to Cambridge, Massachusetts, and off he went to the Promised Land, full of hope but dangerously low on accurate information about what would be required of him. As the giant ship pulled away from the Southampton docks, he was irresistibly reminded of the world's largest man-made metaphor, and shuddered at the thought of the icebergs out there in the big uncharted waters of his murky future. But the die was cast now, and he was either beyond masks or needing a mask so effective that even the formidable Mr. Brontë would have been impressed. Young Branwell had failed so badly in London. Our would-be philosopher king had, on paper, succeeded there, but in the Brave New World they would put him back to the bottom of another precipitous hierarchy. Pray God (in whom he did not believe) that he would not have to crawl back to those unforgiving moorlands in disgrace.

5

The Novice: Mixing with the Yeast Enzymes

Kurt Vonnegut, the most whimsically effective of the anthropological novelists (a student of Redfield at Chicago), describes a conversation between two yeast enzymes. They are drinking grape juice and excreting sugar, which gradually turns into alcohol. All the while they are debating whether life has any meaning. As they slowly drown in their own excreta, they continue the discussion, never knowing that they are making champagne.

As he looked at the cold Atlantic from the deck—for the second time in his life—he thought of Schopenhauer's image of consciousness as a cork bobbing on a vast ocean of emotion. The cork thinks that because it is floating it is superior to—even in charge of—the ocean that supports it. Consciousness was, for our favorite pessimist, a helpless observer, verbalizing, rationalizing, justifying, puzzling, expostulating, but never controlling or determining. It was like a swimmer with his head above water taking in the scene, but with no idea what was below the waves, and certainly not what was in the deep ocean currents and the fathomless vortex of the sea. The water supported him as long as he kept moving, but if he ever stopped to contemplate the secrets of the deep, he would be sucked down into those green-black depths and disappear.

The landing was an experience of light and wonder. It was dawn, and as the boat moved slowly into New York Harbor, the formless shadows looming in the darkness began to take shape, a few lights at a time. Like a mountain of stars they made the outlines and then filled in the mass of buildings, showing a fairyland of brilliant towers and dark canyons moving up and up into the now faintly gleaming sky. It was like something out of Wells' *Shape of Things to Come,* except that it was there: the future present and alive and huge and unbelievable, but there. And he thought as he fought for breath while the ship docked, its immensity dwarfed by the castles of light: "Men made this! Men did it!" It was a miraculous, unnatural wonder: the work of men. How could you ever look at mankind in the same way again?

The America he landed in was the almost forgotten America of the fifties. Popular culture goes through fits of nostalgia for various periods, and while the forties had their turn, and the twenties and thirties were all the rage, and even the sixties and seventies have had their due, the fifties are still something of a blur. The returned GI generation, to which he still felt the unpayable debt of gratitude, had settled down to its version of "normalcy" (Warren Harding?) This included college on the GI Bill, marriage and 2.3 children, wife as homemaker, house in Levittown, job in gray flannel suit, small black-and-white TV, Chevy in the garage. They had Billy Graham as Pope, Cronkite as chronicler, Murrow as conscience, Winchell as gossip, conformity as the watchword, and everything in the hands of Papa Eisenhower, guaranteed not to rock any boats. Sinatra sang the songs, Lucy led the laughter, and Elvis was the sorry excuse for a real rebel—as opposed to the Brando and Dean movie versions. Labor unions were strong, but socialists were as rare as mosquitoes on an iceberg. This America, while it was there and impinging, did not have a lot of direct effect on the would-be elitist headed for the most elite institution of them all.

It was, as we have seen, entirely Plan B, but he was intrigued at the prospect nevertheless. For a start, it had a magical effect on people in this democratic land of equality: mention Harvard and there was almost deference. He had known it was a leading university: it was a cliché with the English that Harvard and Yale were to America what Oxford and Cambridge were to England. (Where did that put the LSE? Perhaps a kind of MIT, but of the social sciences?) Many of the people he read were at Harvard, or had been: Parsons, Kluckhohn, Skinner, Sorokin, Allport, James, Royce, Pierce, Longfellow, Santayana, and Adams (Henry—education of.) But he knew nothing of its dominance in society or the American psyche, or of its actual physical or organizational setup. A brief stay in New York (by daylight—free from the magic) was bustling and confusing. The city was scruffier then; the overwhelming impression was of street-level dirt. The old Pennsylvania Station was there, and should have been magnificent. But it was so dirty that its grandeur was disguised, and only a few seemed sad when it was finally dismantled. It was, though, the gateway to the north: to Boston, to Cambridge, to Harvard. "But that's our very best school!" No harm in that. If you're traveling on the Titanic, you might as well go first class. (Not original: a hippie said it to Ashley Montagu... later, later.)

So he was there: in Boston itself since there were no available apartments (flats) in Cambridge, and the University regarded these problems as entirely the responsibility of the student. But a big, if dirty, apartment on Massachusetts Avenue (with fireplace) was at least a home base. Forays could be made into the surrounding country. The metaphor of living off the land was very much with him. His misery over the state of affairs in the English body politic had soured him on social practicalities. He had no wish to set anything straight;

that was something for the ever-corrupt and always vote-soliciting politicians to attend to—and the do-gooders, never in short supply. He was moving to the margins; he was the eternal observer, the escaped prisoner, the outlaw, the foreign correspondent. He wanted to know why it was all thus, and perhaps at Harvard they could tell him, or at least offer some help in finding out.

But that was it. The life of science and reason was all; the objective pursuit of information was all. He must get away from the tyranny of the emotions, of oppressive sentimentality, of all that *stuff* which ruined the life of the adults; those disappointing adults who were unable to sustain the rational attitude. In a fit of revulsion against the life of the emotions, and a gesture to the life of the mind, he had burned all his poetry, drama and music before leaving England. Yet he couldn't face the paradox that this very act, done in the name of reason, was itself impulsive, emotional and irrational. Auden had burned all his poems once and dedicated himself to science; Hopkins had done the same when pledging himself to God; Rossetti had buried his poems with Lizzie Siddall. Renunciation—of something—was perhaps a necessary rite of passage.

In the meantime he had to adjust to Harvard and the very different atmosphere of an American "campus" university. It was indeed very grand with its spacious "Yard" and its Georgian-style buildings with gold cupolas and white Wren-like spires. It was incongruously set in a slum (so was Yale, so was Chicago, so was Columbia, he discovered: being built in the old parts of old cities, they were collegiate oases in the midst of urban wasteland, created by the flight to the suburbs.) There was no easygoing democracy of all students as at the LSE where all students attended the lectures by the great ones and shared equally in student life. He had helped elect an American postgraduate student as president of the student union. Not so here where a rigorous demarcation existed between "graduate students" (i.e., postgraduates) who had their own bureaucracy, and totally separate "courses" and seminars, and the undergraduates. The latter were almost entirely socially privileged and white, and, of course, all males (females went to attached Radcliffe College.) It was more like an English boarding school in some ways, than college as he knew it.

Graduate students were treated much as English aristocrats had treated those "in trade." They were apprentice professionals, not "young gentlemen." The self-consciously superior young gentlemen had their Houses (colleges), their clubs, their student publications (the *Crimson*) and societies, including the intriguingly named Hasty Pudding Club, given to female impersonations. All were closed to the tradesmen in the Graduate School. And the tradesmen didn't seem to notice, didn't seem to care. They were all grateful to be there, obsessively concerned with their professional futures, and grindingly attentive to their "requirements," "courses," and "course work." His impressions of them were mixed. He had known a few American postgraduate students at the LSE, and they differed a lot, some being very easy and likeable, others being the too-obvious product of some local or class culture and unable to overcome their parochialism, but all being very clever. The Harvard ones were also clearly very smart indeed, but many of them were truly peculiar. Being so smart seemed to have made them odd-men-out in a society where being too obviously superior was a major offense (except in sports.)

He wanted to talk to those who would be his supervisors so that he could work out how to reconcile his thesis ideas with what they were doing by way of "values" research. But he could get no farther than the dragon of a departmental secretary in Emerson Hall, home of the Social Relations Department (and, ironically, Philosophy.) She told him loftily that such things were for the distant future. For two years at least he would find it all he could do to meet the "course requirements" and prepare for his "comprehensives." He had, in the first year, to take mostly compulsory courses in sociology, social psychology, clinical psychology, statistics, social anthropology, and linguistics. There might be one "elective"—evidently a free choice of subject. "But when do I get to work on my thesis?" he wailed. "When you have proved yourself worthy to work on it," said the dragon lady without a flicker. Horrible flashes of hatchet-face and the malacca cane surged through him as he protested that he *had* proved himself: he had a first class honors degree from the University of London! "Everyone here has a first-class degree," she replied, "or they wouldn't be here."

Somewhere along the line he should have thought to find out just what "graduate school" was all about in these United States. The English had no such formal organization. If you wanted to do a Ph.D. in a subject, you applied to that department, and if accepted, you wrote your thesis. You would usually only be accepted if you had a first-class (loose sense) degree in the subject to start with. (Those who didn't could do a "diploma"—one year of undergraduate courses to bring them up to scratch.) Once in, you were more or less on your own to do research. The old joke was that a really good post-graduate student appeared before his advisor twice: first with his thesis proposal, then three or more years later when it was written. In anthropology, you actually disappeared to some remote part of the globe for a couple of years, before re-emerging and "writing up" your fieldwork. But not so here in the land of the free. It was back to "school"—as they called it quite openly, with a vengeance. He remembered in *The Magnificent Ambersons* where a gilded youth rebukes a girl who asks him if he going to "school." "College" he replies quite firmly. So the distinction used to be important. Perhaps like everything else it had been subject to democratization? What bit of de Tocqueville he had read took on new significance.

Life now would be spent in the classroom eternally preparing for tests and exams (at the end of every course) and the writing of "term papers." The dragon lady presented him with a "reading list" of some three-hundred items, for which he would be "responsible" in his "generals" (or "comprehensives") after two years, in addition to his "course work" and his presentation of his own two "bibliographies" for his "specials" on an "area" and a "topic"— there was more but he turned off. The powers obviously had some notion that there existed a mountain of sheer facts that you had to know, rather than being examined for your ability to handle *any* facts in your subject, and then let loose on a particular set of them. Well, there was, as he had learned to say in Ireland, no help for it. He could still rote-learn if he had to; he was there, he was stuck, there was no alternative, so he might as well look on the bright side and reckon that he would soak up information like the sponge he was, and be the wiser for it. Suck in the grape juice of information and who knows what delicious stuff one might excrete into that portfolio of term papers, etc. First, stop mixing the metaphors, then find the other yeast enzymes.

The first thing he was actually asked to do was to volunteer to interview people in the street about Sputnik, whose launching had sent a thrill of terror up the collective U.S. spine. The Reds were ahead; it was unthinkable. Thus began a wave of spending on science education that was to shape a lot of futures, including his own. But Margaret Mead, from her base in New York City (American Museum of Natural History), wanted to poll public opinion on its reaction. He was unsure about Mead. She was evidently something of a popular celebrity at a time when pop-academics were a rarity. The Harvardians were given to wry smiles at her popular efforts, and he had always been taught that she was only one step above a novelist and not to be taken seriously. *Coming of Age in Samoa* was used as an example of how *not* to do Anthropology: subjective, based on too little fieldwork, value-loaded, superficial, anecdotal, etc. He actually admired her work on Manus kinship—and it was allowed that this was her only serious contribution, but shared the general low opinion he had learned.

Here, however, she was a "big name" and evidently wielded power and patronage that could not be ignored. Being a "celebrity" and having a public following, obviously counted for a lot when it came to academic influence. Her Samoan stuff was regarded, by this public, with the awe usually devoted to religious revelations, presumably because it was critical in a liberalizing way of the puritanical repressions of American adolescence. For all their patriotism and conformity, people were nervously obsessed with "what was wrong?" There was skin-deep confidence and subcutaneous angst. An industry grew up of "what's wrong with America" books like *Generation of Vipers* with its attacks on "momism" and *The Man in the Gray Flannel Suit,* with its attack on conformity. *Peyton Place*, tame as it seems in retrospect, was supposed to have exposed the sexual hypocrisies of respectable small-town prudes. Samoa, at least in Mead's version, was some kind of utopia that touched a cultural nerve. Still, he declined the job, even though it was well paid, since he felt he couldn't be distracted from the dragon-lady's requirements.

There was no opportunity for wandering, although he would have liked to see more of Boston than the walk down Commonwealth Avenue to the Cambridge bus and the dreary journey though a blitzed-looking area past MIT. He grabbed a glimpse of the Old North Church, start of Revere's abortive ride, Boston Common (end of the road), Fanuiel Hall, the Harbor (tea party), and the graceful Beacon Hill, where the Brahmins dwelled. On New Year's Eve they set out their silver in the bright-lighted front rooms for the plebs to walk by and gawk at. He took in Bunker's Hill (minus the apostrophe now), and felt bound to point out to the paean-singing guide that the Americans actually lost that one. OK. It was a moral victory. But he enjoyed this sense of being in the footsteps of the history that otherwise he knew only from books. His mother-in-law was a Christian Scientist—not exactly a comfortable point of contact, but the connection had them meeting some of the journalists of their odd daily magazine—scarcely a newspaper, but with terrific world coverage.

He even went, out of politeness, to the Mother Church of Christ Scientist and, with almost superhuman tact, discussed Mrs. Eddy with a straight face. His mention of Mark Twain's book on the "horse-traders daughter" brought looks that suggested he had uttered a vile obscenity by an unfortunate slip of the tongue. He hurriedly passed on. They suggested he submit some poetry, as long as it was "positive and not satirical." It was as well that it was all reduced to ashes in the self-righteous holocaust. These were nice people, if in a total state of denial (the local Freudians had taught him that one.) But their delusional projective system (guess whom?) was no worse than that of any other religion; they were truly generous, and very benign in their attitude to the world. You couldn't imagine the Christian Scientists burning anyone at the stake.

Meanwhile it was back to the grind of daily coursework. He was for moment distracted on a weekend when they were invited to go see the changing Fall (Autumn) leaves and the coastline in Maine. It was before the "peak" for the leaves (still a glorious riot of almost Wagnerian beauty-in-death), but there had been rumors of really cheap lobsters available, and one should take advantage. The students believed in "socializing" out of class, and two in particular struck him. There was Roy, from New Jersey, who was ultimately of Portuguese descent (via the British West Indies.) He had been to Rutgers, the college where Paul Robeson went, and then the University of Connecticut. He knew Freud backwards, and was sage and shrewd and impressively intelligent. Laura (Lebanese ancestry) was darkly beautiful, like the Jewish girls. She had come (to Radcliffe, since Harvard was then officially still all-male) for the positive reason that Parsons favored "generalizations at the system level." This was very impressive to one who had no good positive reason to be there. Her brother was later to become a famous consumer advocate and run for president. For the moment he liked her for her beauty and brains and for, like Roy, having a car. They would have to get a car; you could live without one, but the restriction was annoying when the leaves were turning and the two-pound lobsters ("do you want a cock or a hen?") were a dollar, all steamed and served with drawn butter, French (?) fries, and cold lager. This was bearable.

Culture shock there was, to be sure, made worse by the complication of supposedly speaking the same language. Trying to make oneself understood to ostensible speakers of English was never less than embarrassing, especially when they were southerners, who seemed to have abandoned consonants altogether. They stayed initially with a Christian Science family in Brookline. The father took him on one side and explained that they would have to share the third floor with "the colored girl" and did they mind? They had separate rooms, of course, but some people would object even so, since it meant sharing a bathroom. He was speechless (for once.) Fortunately he simply stammered that no, they didn't mind, and left it at that. This was going to be hard. But harder still was trying to understand this maid. The almost complete muting of consonants made her speech unintelligible. While serving an ample and tasty breakfast, (with "biscuits" that were in fact little scones) she demanded: "Yoehdonuffyoosuh?" The intonation suggested a question, and it seemed to be about doughnuts. After several tries the hosts cut the misery short and explained that she wanted to know if the egg was done enough.

Even so, his anthropological self was always telling him that he had not to be fooled by the supposedly common language: this was a different tribe, a different culture, and one must not judge it, one must understand it on its own terms etc., etc. His moral sense was nevertheless bristling all the time at one thing or another, only tempered by his constant remembrance that things were not so hunky-dory in dear old England either; that injustice was everywhere, differing only in its cultural guise. One must sort out the sense of strangeness—of difference, from the sense of wrongness. On the whole he mostly liked what he found; the good outweighed the bad, and his new friends found the same things offensive that he did. Above all there was the pervading sense of "fix it." Things that were wrong did not have to borne; you could, with enough effort and education, put them right. There were no Marxists here with their ruthless solutions (nor, at Harvard, any Jews either), but there was this constant optimism that things could be fixed; an optimism that he could wed to his Popperean doctrine of "piecemeal social engineering" and so relax the moral muscles. Was he not, in any case, the outside observer, the foreign correspondent, the permanent houseguest, the visitor from another planet, the liver-off-the-land, maybe even the anthropologist? Sort of.

He did get a supervisor. Evon Vogt was an "associate professor." What was that? Was it a professor to be called "Professor," or what it said: an associate of a professor, to be called what? There were also "assistant professors" who ranked somewhere lower; were they assistants to the associates? Everyone was democratically a professor, but then carefully graded into sub-categories.

Bottom of the heap were the pariah "Instructors"—new PhDs doing their stint of what was charmingly called "up or out." This was a very ruthless system. Oh well. The salutation problem was solved because everyone was called "doctor" anyway. Dr. Vogt was an amiable man, with that very American insistence on friendliness and first names (or diminutives) that amounted to a formality. But at first it was hard to pay attention to his words because his appearance dazzled. For a start he wore a "bolo tie" (he explained): a shoestring threaded through a kind of ornamental buckle. This was an assertion of his "southwestern" (New Mexico) origins and character, which he wore like a self-conscious assertion. The professor as cowboy? This was a new one. But then attention was riveted on his head, for he had a "crew cut." Why is this so strange? It was just that our lad had never seen one so close. Didn't the American soldiers have them? Not that he remembered; they had nice hair combed and parted like everyone else. Vogtie's hair was cut off absolutely flat and close to the head. It wasn't that it was short, it was the manner of the shortness: the dead-level flatness of the cropping, as though it had been measured with a spirit level; the way it met the shaven sides at right angles, and this on a professor, associate or otherwise.

Vogtie was telling him things, but he was only half listening. Hypnotized by string tie and crew cut he vaguely heard that the Social Relations Department (Soc. Rel.) was Parsons' brain child, and involved the amalgamation of the four subjects that comprised the building blocks of his Theory of Action: Sociology, Social Psychology, Clinical Psychology and Social Anthropology. Hence the compulsory courses in these four. But in addition it was considered necessary to have a sound basis in Statistics, and for the Soc. Anth. specialists, Linguistics. So two more mandated courses. It got worse. The problem with Soc. Rel., said Vogtie, was that it was peculiar to Harvard. There were no other such departments. So the eventual doctors would have to get jobs in standard departments, which would expect them to be able to do the teaching that people with real degrees in the subjects could do. They would get the jobs because they were from Harvard, but the demands of teaching meant that our super-stars must also do courses in Physical Anthropology and Archaeology. They could "audit" these—which meant you took the course but not the exams, or you took the exams but didn't get an official "grade" or you just sat in on the lectures, or... He had to shake himself free from the observation that the sunlight was now reflecting off the top of Vogtie's head, which was visible through the sparse hair like hard earth through a closely mown lawn.

Dr. Kluckhohn would like to see him, he heard, because of the Values thing, because Firth had written. How was Raymond? Who? Oh, Professor Firth. OK, he supposed. Vogtie told him of the Values Project in the Southwest and how he (Vogtie) had studied the values of Zuni veterans, with "projective tests" among other things, and the "rugged individualism" of "Anglo" homesteaders in New Mexico. Now he was working on "dowsing" or water divining. But attention had wandered again. He was drifting into a consideration of American values, including the very low value placed on body hair, and the absurdly high value placed on perfect teeth. Part of the compulsory friendliness thing—"What will your friends think of you if you have too much hair on your head and face and if your teeth aren't absolutely straight?" Hideous devices were attached to children's teeth to ensure their perfection, and body hair was painfully removed every day by women. He had normal enough hair by European standards, but children in Boston called after him in the streets: "Tarzan! Tarzan!" Long(ish) hair cast doubts on your masculinity (they were very uneasy about that), and facial hair suggested un-American politics. He had shaved off his (rather dashing, he thought) student beard before coming. Just as well.

So the whirligig of enzyme feeding began and gathered pace. Some of what he heard in the sociology and social anthropology courses was familiar, but a lot was not. Robert Bales taught Sociology and was much given to his own "small group dynamics" stuff—all unfamiliar. He found that when small groups were given tasks to do, those with a hierarchical structure did best. No surprise there, but the finding obviously worried the egalitarians, Bales not the least. Robert Bellah seemed to be in a recognizable tradition and his *Tokugawa Religion* echoed Max Weber's thesis on the Protestant Ethic: the ethic of the Tokugawas predisposed them to excel at modern capitalism. The Japanese may have been down and out, but Bellah could see that they had all the right (Protestant) stuff to recover and overtake. Prescient. In Social Anthropology, William "Bill" Caudill taught much about Values—the going thing—and "Culture and Personality." Bill had studied a mental hospital by passing as an inmate. It was easy to get "diagnosed" by exaggerating some personality trait only slightly, he explained. It figured: everyone was, let's face it, neurotic; you only had to be a bit more neurotic than the average to warrant incarceration, classification among the mildly distressed, and appropriate "therapy."

Ruth Benedict and Margaret Mead loomed large, and this was irksome to one reared to regard this sort of thing as ruled out by Durkheim's fiat against psychological reductionism. It was then he learned that he was supposed to be a representative and spokesman for something called "British Social Anthropology" (they always said British even when they meant English.) He was constantly under attack for views he was assumed to hold, many of which were news to him. He explained (at length as usual) that he was a really a language philosopher, only doing anthropology under protest, but no one took him seriously. They assumed, again, that this was "irony"—something that the "British" were noted for evidently. Actually, Freedman had warned him that the Yanks confused irony and sarcasm; it was best not to try to be ironic. Certainly they confused solemnity with seriousness. (Russell Baker was later to make a big thing out of this same observation.) This was a constant problem for the would-be wit: wit was un-solemn and therefore presumed to be un-serious. These were minefields, with the Freudians as major minelayers. His easy wit, they told him, was repressed material returning from the unconscious (or was it subconscious?) Either way, it was nothing more than emotional vomit.

It was the clinical and social psychology that were the worst trouble. He was familiar with Allport's stuff on prejudice and attitudes, but not prepared to have to buy both heavy volumes of the *Handbook of Social Psychology* and commit them to memory. The big thing was "cognitive dissonance" and the book about a cult of alien worshippers whose expectations of transportation to another planet were disappointed, was the text. *When Prophecy Fails* was based on the premise that people could not hold two contradictory ideas without mental pain, and so resolved them by proselytizing. He wondered why no one mentioned Orwell's "doublethink"—but contented himself with reminding the class that Fitzgerald had said that the sign of a great mind was the ability to hold two contradictory ideas and still function. Fitzgerald was not a clinical psychologist, they reminded him (how true), what is more he went to Princeton, which rendered him unserious (evidently.) The Freudians added that Fitz was a victim of both infantile narcissism and emotional regression, and hence not to be trusted (probably so.) So he didn't bother to add that anyone who had spent even a short time with the Irish knew you could hold a dozen contradictory ideas in your head and function quite cheerfully. They had a pretty dismal view of the Irish, whose literature clearly showed them to be suffering from unresolved Oedipal conflicts (oh yes!)

He examined his own behavior—not something he was otherwise prone to do—and decided that his proselytizing was based, not so much on cognitive dissonance, as on feelings of insecurity: these could only be assuaged if everyone came to the same conclusions as he did. This insight made him pay a little more attention to Clinical Psychology. The Clin. Psych. faction was dominated by Freudian thinking. It is hard in the era of post-Freudianism to appreciate just how dominant this was. Students were desperate to "get into analysis" and there was a faction that insisted that, in order to be qualified for fieldwork in an alien culture, all anthropologists should be psychoanalyzed (or marry a Russian, suggested Bales. He decided he liked Bales.) "Personality" was the big thing; even the non-Freudians were obsessed with it, and the core idea of "motivation." They were ruthlessly assiduous motive hunters. What makes people different from each other? "Socialization" was the big answer: as the twig is bent, so grows the tree (his father would have said.) Hence the fascination with early childhood and Freud's theories of same, and with the Skinnerian processes of "secondary reinforcement" that did the job. Skinner's sordid utopian tract *Walden II*, was the favorite fiction of the Clin. Psych. crowd, and the fascistic Skinner-box actually had its devotees among those who thought children should be reared without the messy intervention of parental emotions. He knew he should be revolted by the inhumanity of it, but the idea did have its obvious fascination.

They were immersed in what was fondly known as "the meaning of weaning" school of personality formation –alternatively "tots and pots" since toilet training and its rigors lurked behind most dirty deeds in adulthood. By and large it was safe, when looking at adult "personality malfunctions" to blame the parents. He could relate to that. But his suggestion that in large part people were the way they were because they were born that way, was greeted with indulgent but patronizing laughter. He thought of IQ, but kept quiet. He was going to have to get through this minefield, and not by stomping on the mines.

In his intellectual world so far, it had been assumed that people were, of course, different: this was how you told them apart. But unless the differences were either evil or saintly, not much interest was shown in why there were differences—at least not to this obsessive extent. It might be intrinsically interesting (he doubted this) or of great value to novelists, but it was not useful for social science. All societies had a range of "personalities" but these washed out when one was dealing with social institutions. Personality differences did not explain the difference between patrilineal and matrilineal descent. This was to miss the point, said the Motivation Mafia. "Typical personalities" were the machinery of "culture traits" whose "ethos" in turn was the source of the socialization practices that molded the basic personalities, and so on in a viciously closed circle. "Culture and Personality" (C & P) was the accepted approach—indeed to the believers the only approach—and was what justified the inclusion of Anthropology (cultural) in the Parsonian synthesis. Along with a dose of Freud, it showed how, to paraphrase the poetry of Parsons, "the objective value orientations of society become the internalized need-dispositions of the individual actor." Like the language of the Old Testament, you could pretty easily manufacture it once you had the hang.

So the surging Id and the selfish Ego were restrained by the socially intrusive Super-ego, carrying the society's (or culture's) mandate, via Socialization and the mechanisms of reinforcement. What a neat scheme! But did it pass the Popper test? It sounded decidedly metaphysical. But his attempts to turn it into testable hypotheses were scorned by the hard-liners (although the Skinnerians were sympathetic). It was the conspiracy theory all over again: if you sought to find counter evidence, you were "in denial" and suffering from a "reaction formation." His excited reaction in itself, followed usually by a profound sulk when disagreed with, were, they patiently explained, evidence of his "manic-depressive type personality." No doubt about that. But, as Roy said, and he a believer, Psychoanalysis was the new secular religion in which salvation was achieved through full-time couch sessions (confessionals?) over three years. This was very expensive, our suspicious lad ventured, and so available only to the rich. Unfortunate, they said, but the high payments were necessary because they ensured "a commitment to the therapy." When it came to parting anxious sinners from their money, the older religions had nothing to teach the talking cure.

He actually liked the few things of Freud's that he now read seriously for the first time; mostly the works of grand synthesis, and the iconoclastic *Future of an Illusion*. You didn't have to agree with the conclusions to see that a vigorous and original mind (as they say in the reviews) was at work here. But, strangely, the devotees tended to downplay *Civilization and its Discontents*, and especially *Totem and Taboo*; they were interested in the strictly clinical stuff, not these "philosophical speculations." He had heard the same disdain from the non-Freudians at the LSE, and again his contrarianism leaped up like a punch-drunk boxer at the sound of a bell. Almost as an exercise he wrote a defense of *Totem and Taboo* in a term paper for Bales: on the explanation of incest taboos, where he tried his first reconciliation between Freud and Westermarck. But this only annoyed the Freudians further. He warmed even more to Freud when he discovered that the old guy was a passionate devotee of the case for the Earl of Oxford as the author of "Shakespeare." (How unfortunate, though, that the originator of the case was the oddly named "J. Thomas Looney": an old Manx name, and pronounced "Loney"—but no one knew that, and it didn't help the cause.) In the end our boy's knight-errantry on behalf of the wise old-one, was patently a neurotic mechanism of ego defense, clucked the orthodox.

He was undeterred: "Where Id was, there shall Ego be!" He quoted Freud right back. Great words, he said, that should be set to music. Oh yes, that regurgitation of repressed anger through wit. You couldn't win. "How do you test your hypotheses?" he would challenge. They were baffled. No one in this state of methodological innocence thought about testing anything. You simply tried your best to prove it with piles of evidence, and denigrated counter examples. And invoking Popper was no way out, because, they kindly pointed out (they were never, never angry) he had definitely incorporated Popper, a surrogate father figure, into his super-ego, evidenced by his affectionate reference to him as "Pop." Well, Pop probably did end up in the old conscience (as it used to be called) along with the now sinister parents, the vicar, the King, policemen, Mr. Whatmuff, and Harold Macmillan. It was pretty crowded in there.

Life became a grim round of classes and work, tests and exams, quizzes and papers, and the presentation of "reading notes." This was relieved by student gatherings—to call them parties suggests a gaiety that was lacking. Much beer was drunk, or rather the kind of weak, over-carbonated, refrigerated lager that passed as beer, along with an insistence that "the British" preferred their beer warm: one of those pervading transatlantic myths, like the British one that all Americans chewed gum. Everyone talked earnest shop, hunted motives, and gossiped obsessively about the lords of creation who held their futures in thrall. For humor they read Peanuts and Pogo and told "Mommy! Mommy!" jokes. ("Mommy! Mommy! Why am walking round and round in circles?" "Shut up or I'll nail your other foot to the floor.") Next favorite was knock-knock jokes. He added his own, with its acquired Texan flavor: "Knock, knock!" "Who's there?" "Armageddon." "Armageddon who?" "Armageddon tired of these-here damn knock-knock jokes." (One has observed that these were, they really were, simpler times.) He liked best the small group that, as the weather grew colder, clustered around Roy-the-Magnet over hot rum toddies (with butter and cloves) at the Wursthouse in Harvard Square. This was where the real learning took place, as usual in the interstices of the system. He became installed as one of the local characters when he persuaded the barman to keep a case of Guinness out of the fridge. He explained that cooling it killed the yeast enzymes and turned it to vinegar. The yeast enzymes had to be kept warm and active. So a case was kept out if he guaranteed to drink it. Done. The enzymes were saved; discussion flourished; meaning remained elusive.

If there are not many details of local life and times here it is because there was not much happening outside the intense class-and-homework round, except for occasional visits to the Brattle Street Cinema which showed the classics. He caught up on the rest of Bogie, Kurosawa, and Hitchcock. Things were happening in the world. *The Organization Man* was the most discussed book, although the grad students didn't seem to think it applied to them. The civil rights movement was underway, thanks to Rosa Parks, and so integration was an issue. Grad students more-or-less subscribed to the standard "liberal" attitudes (they were all Democrats.) There were many poor black people in the streets; the poverty of the old ones was obvious, and many of the homeless wandered about mumbling to themselves.

For all their liberal poses, the students were mostly apathetic about it. While they were adamant about not being prejudiced, they didn't see much changing, nor did they have any idea how to change it. You could change the laws, of course, and you should, but they were pessimistic about changing attitudes. The fix-it approach was noticeable here by its absence. There were no black people at Harvard, or Jews for that matter. (It was impolite to use the noun; you had always to use the adjectival Jew-*ish*—as though they were not quite the real thing.) There was a murder down at Boston Harbor: a black man (it was actually still polite to say Negro then) who had been living with a white woman, was stabbed to death. The grad students shook their heads: it was terrible of course, but "they knew the rules." The rules of the Boston Irish Catholics, presumably. He wrote a song about it to the tune of *St. James' Infirmary*:

> A white woman bending over him,
> Her eyes were dim, and she bowed her head,

Then she turned her face towards me
And this is what she said.

"He loved me like a proper man,
I loved him back like a woman should,
But now he lies on the sidewalk dead
And his blood is as red as a white man's blood."

The students liked this sentimental stuff, but when it went on:

As I came away from the harbor,
The blood wet under my feet,
I knew only cold black violence
Could clean that bloody street.

I went down to Boston Harbor,
Was the hottest time of the year,
A nation lay on the sidewalk there,
It smelled of blood and it smelled of fear.

they didn't like it at all. It was political, it was dangerous, it was above all
impolite. It was best not to express such uncomfortable sentiments. Certainly
guests should not behave so in their host country. He half agreed: no-involve-
ment, remember? No one called too much attention to it, but the shadow of
McCarthy hung heavy, and while the liberals deplored the vulgar senatorial
inquisitor, they avoided any too obvious "revolutionary" statements. They
didn't want to lose the jobs they were working so frantically to get. One even
said: "That's a bit radical." "So was the Declaration of Independence," he
countered. That incorrigible wit. How useful that it didn't have to be taken
seriously. Poetry and music were, the Freudians loftily pointed out, only a
sublimation of repressed libidinal urges anyway.

Food was a decided plus on most fronts. The delicatessen sandwich was, to
a meat-starved child of austerity, a colored fairy-food from wonderland. Lay-
ers of pastrami, corned beef, baked ham and pressed tongue, on speckled
brown rye bread, with green lettuce, red to*may*to, bright yellow mustard and
pink Russian dressing, accompanied by thin French fries, sweet cole slaw,
sour dill pickles and weak black coffee. And they always gave you a glass of
ice water without being asked. He gorged and dribbled and laughed. But his
favorite was the "student's friend"—the Howard Johnson's 99-cent lunch
special (anything over a dollar was subject to Massachusetts Old Age Tax).
This was a fried clam sandwich—a heap of crunchy clams served in a hot dog
roll, with tartar sauce, the inevitable French fries (with free tomato ketchup,
the queen of sauces,) lettuce and tomato, refillable coffee and a scoop of ice
cream (he always and only had vanilla) for desert. If anyone could think up a
better value meal, he would be as rich as the Johnsons. The Harvard undergrads
liked the HoJo on Mass Ave. in Cambridge. Once a year one of the patrician

student clubs would take it over, lay white linen tablecloths on the tables, set them with silver and glass ware, finger bowls and candelabra, order up the 99-cent special, and dine elegantly by candlelight. But you only got to watch this. He wished he could get into that unsolemn world, just a little, just once.

He could only be a spectator: literally at a "football" game. Derived as it was from Rugby, he thought "football" should be interesting—Robeson had been a star at Rutgers, and it was. It comprised brief episodes of violent activity interrupted by what looked like prayer meetings. It nicely reversed the rules: things that were penalties in Rugby, like forward passing and obstruction (blocking), became the essence of the game. Once you got used to the stop-and-go rhythm of the thing it was quite exciting. The huge stadium and the big enthusiastic crowd were not something he associated with amateur sports, but he liked it. In Britain everybody played and scarcely anybody watched; again they reversed it here. And there was something very American about the precision assigned to each assembly-line player, and the specialization of offense and defense, with as many as ninety players on the "squad." Harvard was playing an old rival, a lesser-rank college from the sub-Ivy League, and was losing badly. Once the result was beyond doubt, the Harvard fans, far from sulking, pulled out their white handkerchiefs, waved in unison, and chanted: "That's all right/That's O.K./You'll be working/For us someday!" Probably true, but a revelation of rank snobbery that was breathtaking in its brutal honesty. This was some country, where this sort of thing went hand in hand with an almost fanatical lip service to equality. Everyone was accounted as good as everyone else, just not as rich. Fair enough. The only Freudian present (what was he doing there anyway?) spoiled the fun by pointing to the quarterback groping the genitals of the center in order to take the snap, and insisting the whole game was nothing more than a thinly disguised homosexual ritual.

They drank a lot, but he was well practiced in that area. The ID problem was new to him: no one would believe he was over twenty-one. He took to carrying his birth certificate as undeniable proof, to say nothing of a great talking point as it was unrolled like a papyrus by the dazzled waitress. The food front was not all glory. They bought what was advertised, as bacon only to find it was "streaky" carefully layered in the packet to look as if it were lean instead of ninety-percent fat. He took it back and complained. Back home the butcher gave away streaky for larding lean joints or putting on the breasts of roasting fowl; here it was all the "bacon" there was, except for something called curiously "Canadian bacon" which was little rounds of inferior ham. They were told to try "bagels" and did. Again they took them back, complaining that the bread was hard and dry and obviously a week old. No. These were "bagels" and they were like that. Culture shock doesn't hit harder than in the level of the stomach. But there were delicious compensations. Bourbon was discovered and even preferred to Scotch for a while; the fresh juices were nectar; but so-called "dry martinis"—the focus of so much ritual—were just an excuse to drink gin.

Food and drink were important, because apart from work there was very little else. Ariel was employed as an editor on the Harvard Library Bulletin, a job she excelled at. The Bulletin was housed in the Houghton Rare Books Library where he knew they had the copy of Rossetti's poems that had been dug up from Lizzie's grave. Under very controlled conditions he got to see them, the pages obscenely stained and marked by her decaying body's juices: the stuff of Gothic. Materially, life was good. They would never live as well again, even when on supposed full salaries. What was Auden's paean? "God bless the USA! So large, so friendly, and so rich!" The choice of everything was amazing, and everything was relatively cheap—except for services, since American workers expected to be paid at the rate of European higher professionals, and to live as well. Did they realize there was a wide world of very poor people out there willing to do these things at a hundredth the cost? But those wretched of the earth weren't here, so you paid up for plumbers, electricians, mechanics and window washers. It was a wasteful society. The heat in the apartment was fierce to the point of punishment; the only way to control it (no thermostat) was to shut off radiators. Doing this caused panic, since it evidently stopped the flow of hot water throughout the building. They were forced to turn them on again, and the "super" told them to leave the windows open instead. A small fortune in heat floated out into the frigid Boston night.

He looked in vain for some jazz as he knew it, but the Gillespie revolution had become institutionalized, and be-bop was king. Dixieland-Chicago was something for tourists in New Orleans; real aficionados went downtown Boston to hear Oscar Peterson's trio (Ray Brown, bass, Herb Ellis, guitar), and he went willingly, and to hear Hank Jones and Ella Fitzgerald, and Coleman Hawkins with whomever he was playing. But no one wanted to play themselves. There was no Harvard Jazz Club, and his attempts to start one bombed for lack of players and interest, as well as an obvious feeling that graduate students shouldn't be doing this kind of thing. It was all professional, like sports. The professionals played, and the mass of spectators paid to listen. But the professionals were very, very good, and the attitude was: why do badly yourself what you can pay to hear done well by experts? There was no sympathy for the amateur ethic here (golf and tennis were exceptions for the wealthy.) You did one thing well, got well paid for it, and used it to buy your pleasures from the pros. So his guitar (he had brought only the jazz guitar) regressed to its role as party entertainment, where his unnerving knowledge of classic blues and American folksong was pronounced "cute." And so it was. He learned fun new songs—*The Titanic* (It was sad when that great ship went down) and *Charlie on the MTA* (He may ride forever/'neath the streets of Boston/He's the man who never returned)—which he sang delightedly. A Freudian did say he was over-identifying with the aggressor, but here he really took exception, since this bountiful and generous country had been nothing but nice to him. Aggression didn't have to be physical to be real, said the disciple. He was tempted to hit him with the guitar. Try that for reality testing.

But the Freudian had a point. Was he over-identifying? The system was brilliant at terrorizing you and using the terror to get you to conform—as willingly as Winston Smith conformed to Big Brother's insistence that two-plus-two equaled five. Sartre had taught him to fear the inauthentic life of the role-playing automaton. But his cheerful notion that the academic life was of its nature proof against in-authenticity was taking some blows. The academic mask was just another mask. But surely the anthropologist, the eternal observer, the professional outsider, was...Alas. It was becoming obvious that this profession, despite the superficially exotic nature of its impedimenta, was just another academic profession. It practitioners were as ruthlessly professional as surgeons or stockbrokers. No. A mask was a mask. The secret of the authentic life was to wear the mask for its purpose, but *not to get trapped in the mask.* The professions were masks that had blended into the face. Resist! But it was not that easy. The whole point of the initiatory process was to make sure that the mask stuck, and what's more that the initiand, in the end, welcomed the fatal facial. The paradox was that in avoiding the skin-meld by constantly changing masks, he was in fact blending with the mask of *dilettante.* The philosophers had a name for this paradox, but it was a measure of his confused state that he couldn't remember it.

Meanwhile, back in the classroom, they continued to pile it on. The system required the memorization of many details, and their regurgitation at frequent intervals. He kept his head down and slogged away, since there was really no alternative. But the grape juice was threatening to overwhelm the little enzyme. The sugary excretions in papers and quizzes and tests and exams seemed to be producing, if not Veuve Cliquot, at least a plonk agreeable to the chief tasters. He had been introduced to the idea of the "culture carrier"—the anthropological version of a human being, into whom culture was poured (through socialization) and from whom appropriate behavior dutifully emerged (unless something went wrong.) He imagined the culture carrier as a cartoon character in the shape of an empty tin-can with little arms and legs into which ideas, values, norms, rules, customs, and above all words, were raining down, their accumulated pressure forcing the pathetic little creature into jerky motion. All the little culture carriers then joined hands in a dance, producing culture traits and culture patterns (overt and covert.) He used to doodle the carrier on his notebook in bored moments and add items to the input and output as they were suggested in the classes. But the page got too crowded as the oppressed little culture-carrier creature drowned in the torrential fizz of symbolic champagne.

Parsons was on leave that year, but George Homans (himself a Boston Brahmin—"We have the money" he explained) was a visiting lecturer in one class. An embarrassed lad was singled out as "a special student from the LSE" and asked to construe the difference between patrilineal and matrilineal succession with regard to "the locus of jural authority." It was a freshman (as he learned to say) exercise for him, but the assembly regarded it as advanced technical wizardry, and he dimly saw a strength he could play on here. Homans used it as a demonstration of "where they had to get to." His status took a jump like the Dow in a bull rally. This was reinforced when Robert Bales asked the class for a definition of a "social institution" and they variously mumbled some Parsonian jargon that no one truly understood. He volunteered "a regular way of doing things" and Bales was delighted. That wonderful British understatement, but it "hit the nail on the head." More brownie points (he was really learning the language.)

But he didn't shine in the Psychology division. He could not but laugh at Rorschach Tests, the symmetrical inkblots that were evidently being thrust at puzzled savages throughout the third world. These same savages lived, one psychiatrist told them, "under the shadow of castration anxiety." Pretty grim stuff, as was the nervous obsession with penis envy (why didn't the women object?), anal-retentive neuroses, pre-genital primary-object fixations, and projections of infantile hostility. They were into something called "direct analysis"—considered dangerous and daring, where the psychoanalyst treated the truly mentally ill by entering into—playing a part in—the patient's fantasies. "Ok, I'm your father, go ahead and kill me then you can have mommy all to yourself! Go on! Go ahead, kill me, kill me!!" Then what? Delayed remorse, renunciation of related women, then totems with food taboos, he suggested. The class watched a film of Bushmen hunting a giraffe, and slowly killing it over several days with poisoned arrows, and what looked like maximum inefficiency. The shocked class, asked to "interpret," insisted it was all about "aggression"—the giraffe was a subject for displacement of aggression against the father etc. He insisted it was about hunting a very big animal with inadequate weaponry. His naïveté appalled them. It was attributed, like so much else, to his being British. What could one expect? What indeed?

David McClelland taught "Personality Psychology" and Gardner and Lindzey *Theories of Personality* was the text, along with McClelland's own book on the subject, and *The Abnormal Personality* by White (who was chairman of Soc. Rel. that year.) Hence they got a another heavy dose of motive hunting, with teacher's favorites n-Ach and f-Fail way up front. They loved these technical-sounding acronyms (for "need for achievement" and "fear of failure") and tended to let them run riot as explanations for everything, including the whole of Western civilization. But he rather liked McClelland's bold attempt to take over the Protestant Ethic from the sociologists, and reduce it to the Puritan/Calvinist institution of "independence training." This included the crucial early weaning and toilet training: kid was shoved out to fend for himself—result: a crushing need to *achieve* translated into *capitalist activity*, (hard work, reinvestment, accumulation.) This in turn was spurred by a terror of failing, understood as eternal damnation. It wasn't clear whether the theology or the socialization gave this sequence the push, but once institutionalized, it rolled along automatically. There was much interest in the Protestant work ethic. It was a defining feature of the civilization and pervaded even the ivory tower, as he was discovering to his distress. "Why are we driven to work so hard," they asked. If they stopped, it was not a pleasurable release, but an occasion for painful anxiety. "The neurotic," said Freud, "knows no satisfaction without pain."

He went to lunch at the Faculty Club with Kluckhohn, who didn't insist on being called Clyde (or Kluckie), which was nice. He had done a paper on Kluckhohn for Vogtie's Social Anthropology class. He read the works, and concluded that here was a considerable intelligence, but one without a theoretical focus, unless a nagging concern with "culture" was to be counted. But culture for K. was like the Holy Grail for Lancelot: religiously sought after, sometimes glimpsed, but never found. Along with A. L. Kroeber, and with the help of slave labor from a graduate assistant, he had surveyed hundreds of definitions, found them wanting, and then come up with one of his own (big emphasis on guess what: Values) that was more obscure than those they had dismissed. What kind of subject was this that couldn't figure out what its subject matter was? But they insisted they were doing Cultural Anthropology (as opposed to the "social" of the British), and culture was everything.

The class read Leslie White on *The Evolution of Culture*, Julian Steward's *Theory of Culture Change*, and Robert Redfield's *The Folk Culture of Yucatan*. While he liked these reversions to nineteenth-century evolutionary big-think, he was alarmed at the ferocity of the cultural determinism involved. It was partly a turf war: the anthropologists wanted some bit of reality that was theirs alone, and so campaigned for culture just as Durkheim had campaigned for "society" on behalf of Sociology. White, to his eternal credit saw that these were the same thing, but still saw them as some metaphysical force that moved everything. His protest, in a class paper, that these were categories of interpretation, not aspects of reality, thus in reifying Culture they were making a "category mistake" (Ryle), was not appreciated. Somehow, perhaps out of German nationalistic romanticism with its *Kultur* of the *Volk*, Culture, whatever that was, became everything. They then assigned to Culture powers that an ambitious theologian would have been embarrassed to attribute to God.

But he enjoyed talking of these things with Kluckhohn, a smallish man whose body seemed to be in constant slight motion, and who did not have Vogt's steady high-noon gaze, even though he was from the Southwest, ranch and all. But K. didn't stint on the hospitality—several pre-prandial whisky sours for the lad—and spoke learnedly and interestingly about Franz Boas and Marcel Mauss (whom Lowie had completely misunderstood) and how the anthropologists in Soc. Rel. were disturbed by Parsons' reduction of culture to mere values and ideology. The reluctant British ambassador expressed some of his own doubts, rather nervously since so much seemed to be at stake, but K. told him that his doubts were in good order, since at Harvard they liked students who "bucked theory." The rodeo reference had to be explained, and led to a disquisition on the Southwest and its Indians. K. was looking for "good students" who would take the Indians seriously. There was a danger, he said, of the Navaho, Apache, Zuni, Hopi, and the others being relegated to second-class anthropological status—only used for student training, while the ambitious students went off to study "real" natives in Africa or the Pacific.

Someone should do for kinship in the Eastern Pueblos (those along the Rio Grande) what Eggan had done for the Western (the Hopi of northern Arizona and the Zuni of western New Mexico.) Would he be interested? He munched his enormous whale steak (with French fries and creamed butternut squash), enjoyed his third glass of excellent California chardonnay (there was a discovery and a half—like a good white burgundy.) He tried to clear his head, and to think clearly and quickly whether he should, there and then, confess that he was a thinly disguised philosophical stowaway waiting for the first chance to jump ship. Or not. He decided not, since in truth he hadn't thought much about philosophy in the face of the onslaught of coursework. They seemed to like him, opportunities were being offered, and he had no other plans. Best look interested, accept the large slice of Boston cream pie, the offer of a brandy, and agree to K's suggestion that he take a "reading course" on the Southwestern Indians, their physical anthropology, languages, archaeology and, of course, their culture.

K. bounced him back to Vogtie (who, it transpired, was K's son-in-law—leading to much clucking on the gossip circuit, as did wife Florence K's appointment at Radcliffe, and son Richard's admission to the graduate school.) Vogtie had already raised the issue of the nine-month's fieldwork (minimum) requirement for the PhD, and the first question was one of finance. But V. was a great wheeler and dealer; he had fingers in many grant-giving pies. The result was always good for his lucky students: he had foreseen the problem and persuaded the SSRC to institute training grants for graduate students to cover summer fieldwork. Fix on a project, and an application would be forwarded. But what project? First he would have to "read everything on the Southwest"—something the course with K. would fix. He used to whine to Vogtie about the insane piling up of requirements, leaving no time to think. Vogtie was not sympathetic: you had to do all this, he said, because otherwise there were "too many gaps in your information." What you had done as an undergraduate was not reliable; undergraduate degrees were very variable.

The British system, or lack of system, was all very well, said Vogt. It produced people who could write well and were very smart at "handling theory" but who "didn't know anything." By this he meant extensive comparative ethnographic knowledge, he explained. He cited Jack Goody as an example: he had been through Harvard recently, giving his incest paper, which was very clever, but when questioned about details in Titiev's *Old Oraibi*, or Opler's *An Apache Life Way*, he had, embarrassingly, never heard of them. "We're sure not gonna have this happen with one of our guys!" Vogt (the Vogtie thing gets cloying after a while) was notorious for asking highly specific questions on the generals (or was it the specials?) like "How do the Blackfeet break their horses?" (They ride them into swamps, apparently.) So he shut up and listened while Vogt explained that he had to have a "topic area"—a special subject from one of the subdisciplines, which would be half of those dreaded oral exams. And here we must make the most important digression yet, for another of those great epiphanies had occurred, as major as the religious de-conversion or the Ayer-Popper revelations: he had discovered Linguistics.

Paul Friedrich was a young Instructor in Anthropological Linguistics; a recent PhD from Yale, back from studying the Tarascan Indians in Mexico. He was their age, tall and gawky, shy and awkward, but certainly handsome; his jacket had knife-like creases in the sleeves that threatened to distract attention. But he was a passionate and deeply conscientious teacher, who loved his subject and was determined that his first class in anthropological linguistics should be a success. The new teachers usually piled it on thick in their determination to do everything at once and display all their talents. But if they could spark off a like enthusiasm in the students, the result could be golden, and was so in this lucky case. The class was compulsory, so Roy was there and several other students who went on to be first-class linguists in their own right. It was tough but wonderful. The text was dense (Gleason, *An Introduction to Descriptive Linguistics*) with an accompanying "workbook" of homework exercises, and numerous "pop quizzes" and tests. But he didn't resent it because he realized that when teaching something as difficult as Linguistics to neophytes, in a hurry, it was necessary. Starving in the midst of intellectual plenty, he gulped down Linguistics in gobbets, and found his mental digestion up to the task. Champagne appeared more and more likely, although the Freudians dismissed his new enthusiasm as a pre-genital oral fixation, probably resulting from late weaning. Very probably.

It was not just the technicalities of phonetics, phonemics and semantics that dazzled, but the whole of language theory: Jespersen, Saussure, Bloomfield, Sapir, Jakobson, Whorf, Pike, Swadesh, and the great Zelig Harris with the bible: *Methods in Structural Linguistics*. It wasn't language philosophy, but it was the next best thing. The "Sapir-Whorf hypothesis" had everyone's attention: the grammar of a language actually determined the speakers' view of reality. As Whorf explained in *Language Thought and Reality*, The Standard Average European languages (SAE) had an "actor-action" construction (speaker, verb, object) that led to a thinking in terms of cause and effect, which in turn led to metaphysics, science and social activism. Hopi, on the other hand, saw things in terms of events and their modalities—rather than as objects in linear time, so the Hopi did not see nature as something to be manipulated, but only responded to through ritual. SAE said "the lightening strikes"—which led to metaphysical queries about what it was doing when it wasn't striking, and hence about essences and the like. This was foreign to Hopi (or Navaho), which simply stated the equivalent of "lightening occurring" and the manner of its occurrence (currently, continuously, on-and-off, etc.) He was reminded of Russell's similar point about European language, and his wish to develop a mathematical language for science that was an "event language"—a language which would abolish the need for metaphysics. Friedrich told him the linguistic world hadn't appreciated the parallel and he should "work this up" for a paper. He was back home. He returned in a daze to the overheated Boston apartment, where he lay on the couch (sofa), clutched Otto Jespersen's *Philosophy of Grammar* to his chest, and smiled and laughed until he was in tears of joy and relief.

From then on he neglected everything for Linguistics. Friedrich used the class as a language laboratory for phonetics: Spanish, French, Chinese. Our boy happily contributed some remembered Welsh, especially the rare unvoiced labio-apical lateral aspirated stop as in Llewellyn or Llandudno—a stop that marvelously reappeared in Navaho! They brought in "native speakers" for other languages—Arabic, Hindi, Japanese, and even Irish Gaelic by a student from Comparative Philology. He was pleasantly reminded of his Irish episode and pulled out the almost forgotten grammar (traveling by ship he had been able to bring all his books) for revision. But they had to choose a language to analyze for the term paper, which Friedrich insisted was to amount to "the equivalent of a master's thesis." The emphasis was agreeably on analysis; no one was expected to learn the language, to actually speak it. Learning to speak the languages was in fact frowned on: this was not Berlitz, not a conversation class. Languages were subjects for analysis (except those necessary for fieldwork of course, which were both.)

He should, given the expectations, have chosen a Southwestern language—Roy picked Navaho, but he panicked at its difficulty and plumped for Swahili, since he knew some basic Bantu from Schapera and Barnes, and this was a particularly easy little language. Swadesh had just come out with his monument to structural linguistic analysis, *The Phonemes of Swahili*, and it was a juicy place to start. He worked with a speaker from East Africa, and came up with a phonemic-semantic sketch that dotted an I and crossed the odd T, and satisfied Friedrich's strict demands for scholarship. The lonely, intense hours he had spent in the carrel in the Widener Library paid off with the teacher's note on the paper in his tiny handwriting: "All sources consulted." Friedrich had checked—for each and every paper. Do they still do that? Did they ever?

The survey of world language families was breathtaking. They veered from Slavic (Russian was Friedrich's other specialty—he was working on Sanskrit) with its emphasis on moods rather than tenses, to agglutinative Turkic, to monosyllabic Mongoloid, to Hindi and Semitic, Malayo-Polynesian and Bantu, and the economically named Amerindian. He did a paper on orthographies—especially Sanskrit, and learned to avoid "orthographic dazzle"—the tendency, when doing phonetic transcriptions, to confuse orthography and pronunciation. Thus in English there is a tendency to transcribe the word "what" with an initial "w"—it is in fact "hwat" phonetically. Anglo-Saxon was closer in its orthography to its pronunciation. The many accretions of modern English made it drift far away, and caused Shaw to leave his fortune to a fund for reforming English spelling. What happened?

The other big thing was "lexico-statistical dating" which aimed at finding the precise degree of relationship between languages within a family, by finding similarities and differences in "basic vocabulary": those items that changed the least, in effect—body parts, numbers, family terms, pronouns, verbs of motion. This promised to add a historical dimension to supplement archaeological dating, and at the time created an excitement comparable to the one the discovery of the "genetic clock" would do thirty years later. "Collect vocabularies in the Southwest and revamp the dates for the Pueblos," suggested Friedrich. Possibilities were springing up like fungi after summer rain.

Phonemic analysis was the big thing. It was fast becoming a paradigm (as they said) for all cultural analysis. A phoneme, he learned, was a "minimal unit of meaning." It was not a sound as such; it could be composed of many sounds. Thus a consonant could be voiced or unvoiced ("d" versus "t"), aspirated or unaspirated, palatalized, glottalized, retroflexed etc. But what mattered was which of these were the "discrimating features" that produced meaning. In English the only one that counts is voicing: "d" versus "t" as in "cad" versus "cat." In Hindi it is aspiration and retroflexion, which gives the "funny" sound so beloved of Peter Sellers ("goodness gracious me!") "Foreign accents" are the result of our trying to force other languages into our own phonemic patterns, a result of what Sapir called "the psychological reality of the phoneme." He noticed that stress, or emphasis, so important as a phoneme in the oddly named "British English" (which he evidently spoke) had disappeared from the American version: "PERmit" (the noun) versus "perMIT" (the verb), "FREquent" (the adjective) versus "freQUENT" (the verb)—for example. The peculiar (to Anglophone ears) chopped-up monotonic sound of English spoken by American Indians was due to their imposition of glottalization, a major feature of their languages not much present in English except in some dialects (Scottish "wa'er" for "water"—for example.)

Enough. We do not want a lesson in phonemics here, just enough to convey the excitement that all this technically precise analysis roused in our renegade philosopher, lost in the sticky marshes of Freudianism, the barren assertions of the Skinnerians, the confusions of culture theory, and not convinced that analysis of variance was the royal road to knowledge. Perhaps all "culture"—of which language was the most important part—could be analyzed in terms of discriminating features, to find the social and behavioral equivalents of phonemes? Kenneth Pike had already put forward a formidable effort in this direction and coined the the terms "emic" and "etic" derived, of course from "phonemic" and "phonetic." Kluckhohn had tried to apply the idea to, yes, Values, and down the road at MIT, a young lecturer called Noam Chomsky was talking exciting things about "transformational grammar"—although the suggestion that the capacity for this must be inborn was greeted with patronizing astonishment and dismissed. It ran in the face of all the behavioristic assertions that the Bloomfieldians had established as unquestioned truths. Language was "the noises you made with your face"— nothing more. Skinner was writing a definitive book on verbal behavior, and Skinner was God. But, said Roy, we should listen to this Chomsky: his little book *Syntactic Structures* was beginning to circulate, and there was much buzz about the impossibility of finite state grammars and the like. The idea that a language was "generated" from a few rules of application, and that this might lead us to find to the ultimate rules of all grammar—the Ur-language of mankind, was wickedly exciting.

The distant Lévi-Strauss, about whom they knew not (and those who claimed to, like Homans and Schneider, clearly misunderstood—Schneider didn't even read French) was equally toying with a linguistic model from Saussure (who originated the discriminating feature) and calling it Structuralism. *Anthropologie Structurale,* was obtained from Schoenhof's Foreign Books Inc., of Massachusetts Avenue, but he couldn't interest anyone in it, particularly in the "atom of kinship" which was to replace the weary concept of the "nuclear family." Take away the nuclear family and the whole Freudian C & P enterprise was shipwrecked. Even so, something new was in the air, and he felt he was part of it. He sucked merrily on the grape juice, and drowned happily in the bubbling intellectual excreta.

Pause. Where are we? He was surviving, even doing well. The end-of-term exams were passed (even the psychology) with "straight A's"—still a big deal in those days before grade inflation, when students were glad to get a B and stay in the game. The exams were odd affairs to someone reared on the expectation of four well-considered, well-written essays in a three-hour exam. They were often just lists of things to be "identified" in one sentence. The notorious generals/comprehensives had, in the written portion, the agonizing "Atlaltl to Zulu" list: twenty-four items, or tribes to be so identified. B is for Berdache, H is for Hottentot, K is for Kava, P is for Potlach, X is for Xhosa... Vogtie's favorite was M for Mano y Metate—a stone corn-grinding system used by Mexican Indians. Answers to essay-like—but often long and complicated— questions, were again only required to be a paragraph. Some sections were simply "true/false" or "multiple choice" and required you to tick the correct answer out of several suggestions. Vogtie explained that "writing" as such was done in term papers: the exams were "to make sure you knew all the facts." Friedrich's exam was similar, but for Linguistics it kind of worked; on technical papers essays were out of place: it was more like statistics.

Friedrich did not tell him directly (F. was typically shy about these things), but had told Roy and some of the others, that his linguistics papers were the best in the class, including those people who had done first degrees in the subject and were specializing in it. He was concerned about statistics, his usual bugbear. For some hidden reason the classes were again held early in the morning. What was it about mathematics that required it to be taught at dawn? He had to take a bus into Cambridge, and turning out so early was simply not in his behavioral vocabulary, so he missed his fair share of classes. (He decided that for him, getting out of bed after a deep sleep was a recapitulation of the birth trauma. He was learning the language.) Roy became his Ken, and kindly shared his notes and considerable math expertise. But although he had the basics, these non-parametric statistics were a far cry from the social survey stuff he was used to. They were really for experimental work, and the all-powerful analysis of variance, and he chaffed at the added burden. But you could take up to two years to pass the requirement, so he didn't panic—yet. About such things he was the arch-procrastinator: never do today what you can possibly put off forever.

The brutal winter did not help. He had never known such knife-edged cold. Snow was cleared from the streets and landed on the parked cars, which then froze solid under the snow piles, and had to be left until the thaw or burned out with torches. His duffle coat, by now worn thin, was no match for the cold. She had sacrificed her only fur coat ever (rabbit—and she said it was worn out, which it wasn't) by cutting out the sleeves, turning it inside out, and having him wear it as a lining during the London winters. It was useless against this kind of bone-numbing freeze, but he stubbornly stuck to it for its sense of parental warmth. "No boy who was his mother's favorite," said Freud, "need ever fear failure." He had no competition, but he knew it was both a wonderful and a terrible thing to be a parent's only hope in life, and he did fear failure. Given the Freudian prognosis it may not have been a reasonable fear, but it was always there, if for no other reason that, unlike the others, he was in no way committed to this Ph.D. thing. Most of what he did was half-hearted, and he only worked at the things that interested him. Even so he knew he was too obsessed by it all, neglecting all his former enjoyments, and his marriage to boot. He enjoyed being married—it meant you were not alone to face strange things, but he found it hard to shake off the feeling that rather than a support it was a burden that, at this point, he could do without. Then he was overwhelmed with guilt, and the vastations crept in like incubi in the night to terrorize him.

More troubling in some ways were the feelings less terrible than hopelessness, but more like a total disassociation from reality. He stood outside himself and his life—almost as in his one out-of-body experience, but not looking down: more looking in. It was as though he was somewhere outside, and reality was on a screen. He looked at the screen with disbelief and incomprehension. What was happening? What on earth was he doing? He was the Platonic prisoner in the cave, he was the alien invader from some indefinable outer space of the soul, and he was bewildered by what he saw his simulacrum doing. The moments passed. It was lack of proper sleep, he thought; sleep was a useless period that interfered with information gathering. The moments were something to be ignored; some leftover of the terrors of childhood. Nothing much in the Psychology he had learned was of any help. The answer was to work even harder. He threw himself into the work whether he cared for it or not, and so far he did OK at the exams and papers. The lords of creation seemed to like him. The Freudians said this was a clear case of severe counter transference, but the Freudians troubled him less than the uncompromising cold.

> *Come home Sordello! Soon*
> *Was he low muttering, beneath the moon,*
> *Of sorrow saved, of quiet evermore,—*
> *Since from the purpose, he maintained before,*
> *Only resulted wailing and hot tears.*

This was a land of extremes on all fronts, including the weather: the summers were tropically hot and humid; the fall was an aesthetic delight; the winters were an icy horror. But the brief spring was gentle, the crews came out on the unfrozen Charles River and scudded along under the numerous bridges in the shadow of the cherry-pink- and apple-blossom-white tree-lined banks. They traveled over to Brandeis, where the Jews (sorry, Jewish people) were. He saw his dark-eyed girls again, and they made him just as uneasy, but the trip was to hear Francis Fergusson the famous writer on theater, whom Roy and his wife had admired at the inevitable Rutgers. (The place seemed to be dogging him; could it be an omen?) Fergusson talked about *Othello* as "Shakespeare's first modern tragedy" and they went off and read his book on *The Idea of a Theater*, which started, not with Gamma Gurkin's Needle or even Thespis, but with Pueblo Indian ceremonials.

Vogt had recommended he read a book on New Mexico by one Erna Fergusson: it turned out she was Francis's sister, and there was the connection. He wandered about from concerts in Memorial Hall, to luxurious exhibits at the Fogg Museum, to the crescendo of classes and lectures and the year passed, and he could contemplate his lot as not a bad one, considering. He had not intended any of this, but he was gathering knowledge unto himself in ever-greater globs like some intellectual Quatermass monster, and this was intrinsically enjoyable. Above all there was the insistent truth that he had no other plans; like Mr. Micawber, he assumed that something would turn up.

Vogtie (habit again) was calling in markers. He had a colleague called Chuck (for Charles) Lange at Southern Illinois University. The grad students said it was a "cow college" and regarded it as little more than a trade school, but he had learned to take such evaluations with the proverbial pinch of sodium. Lange had been for some years working on a definitive account of the archaeology, history and ethnography of the Pueblo of Cochiti (pro-nounced—and properly written—with an accent on the final vowel—CochiTEE) in New Mexico—near the Rio Grande, some forty-plus miles across the desert, southwest of Santa Fé. But Chuck, who was basically an archaeologist, was not too confident about kinship, or language; he would welcome, or at least couldn't refuse, the help of someone willing to address these areas. In pursuit of his full and long list of necessary qualifications our boy could spend some time in the U. of S. I. "field school" and earn some "credits" towards the archaeology requirements. Sounded painless enough, so there it was. At least it wasn't Values. He drew the line there: no Rorshach tests, attitude questionnaires, or personality inventories. Roy was going to do those things in a little Spanish town in northern New Mexico: they could drive out together in Roy's car. It was to be Lawrence country: the land of cliff-dwellers, classic Indians, matrilineal clans, moieties, elaborate rituals still in place and enacted in colorful dances. He was already captured by the Hopi Snake dance and the Zuni masked Kachina dancers. The Freudians told him it would be a good opportunity to study a projective delusional system, with obsessive-compulsive rituals based on infantile dependency neuroses, first hand. So it would.

He hit the Peabody Museum library (where the real anthropologists doing real degrees in the subject were housed) and gorged in his usual speed-read-ing fashion. "Papa" Boas, while founding academic American Anthropology at Columbia (ousting the evolutionist L. H. Morgan, who had the good sense not to be an academic) had taken his various pretty female graduate students to the Southwest and planted them in various Pueblos for a summer or two. Cochiti had seen two: Ruth Benedict (*Cochiti Tales*) and Esther Goldfrank (*Social and Ceremonial Organization of Cochiti*). Mead, the not-so-pretty student, had been packed off to the South Seas. Boas himself had done Cochiti and produced his *Keresan Texts*, the only thing near to a grammar (more of a grammatical sketch) of the language. He had to admire Boas's facility with Amerindian languages and sheer fact gathering; the man was unbelievable. He could knock off a basic grammar before breakfast, and have the details of every ceremonial costume by lunchtime. But there was little "analysis" of the kind he had been taught to aim for by the anthropologists at the LSE. This was provided by Fred Eggan, who, they said at Harvard, was a British Social Anthropologist anyway. He had been Radcliffe-Brown's prize student at Chicago, and went on to become head of the department and carry on the R-B tradition. R-B's classic stuff on kinship systems had drawn on Amerindian examples gleaned at Chicago. So Eggan's *Social Organization of the Western Pueblos* became the new linchpin text. Was he not to do for the Eastern Pueblos what Eggan had done for the West?

Maybe. But Eggan again was prone to attribute any variation he couldn't explain to the panacea of acculturation. If it didn't fit it was "acculturated to Spanish and Anglo models"—even when these models were nothing like the Indian culture traits being explained. By accounting for everything, it accounted for nothing. It was a kind of theory of the Golden Age: there was a "pure" culture that was hit from the outside, and the purity was gradually eroded and replaced piecemeal by bits of the intruder culture. This theory was also espoused by Leslie White, who had done the definitive monographs on the other Keresan-speaking Pueblos—evidently by taking informants to a Santa Fé hotel room and pumping them for information. This was fine if you thought "culture" was something in the heads of the natives; the anthropologist's job then was just to pry it out somehow, and where and how didn't much matter. His "British Social Anthropology" bias couldn't accept that: you had to be a "participant observer" to get at the "social structure." But he suppressed his doubts. The thing was to find out as much as possible and get out there. His brief was to learn the language, produce his own grammar on modern principles of structural linguistics, and use this to examine changes in kinship terms. Benedict and Goldfrank had used interpreters: Boas had learned the language in his usual top-speed fashion, but hadn't used it to do fieldwork. There was room for maneuver here; there was a niche to occupy; there were metaphors to be mixed.

They went as group to Albany for meetings of the American Ethnological Society. He rode in Vogtie's car since he didn't have one. Part of the point was that some Indianists like Sol Tax from Chicago (another of the R-B disciples), and Esther Goldfrank herself, would be there. Goldfrank had married Karl Wittfogel, whose *Oriental Despotism* MacRae had had him read. Its "hydraulic hypothesis"—that centralized Oriental societies had become that way because of the need for a central control of water resources—had been applied by the new husband and wife team to the Eastern Pueblos. They were "irrigation societies" and needed the same sort of central control, not needed in the dry-farming Pueblos of the Hopi. It made sense. Wittfogel was busy hammering Tax on "penny capitalism." The manner was typical of a certain kind of central European intellectual: he would have called it simply arrogant, but Roy said it was in fact a good example of the "hard ego." He realized that this described the people he liked least in the world: the people who never apologized or explained because whatever they were doing, was by definition right; if you disagreed the onus of explanation was on you.

Goldfrank was a contrast—a sweet and friendly lady who modestly dismissed her own fine monograph by saying she was "wet behind the ears" when Boas took her out there, and he should start from scratch. She had practical advice. Her major informant had been one Caroline Trujillo, a formidable and independent Cochiti lady, but one who antagonized the people by her over-friendliness to whites. They had accused her of witchcraft—a terrible thing in that society—and it would be well not to be too friendly with her, although she had weathered all storms and was still, nearly thirty year's later, a force in the Pueblo. Her brother Joe was another matter: he was a moderate who stood between the extreme traditionalists and the pro-white progressives. He had been Governor of the Pueblo; the people respected him; cultivate him. The brother and sister were members of the Fox clan, which augured well: Indians, like Gypsies, didn't believe in coincidences. This was to be the best advice he received, and was confirmed by Lange, who had sent the manuscript of his forthcoming book on Cochiti. It was a marvelous compendium of all that was known, updated by Lange. Good. He would not have to do all that ethnographic stuff; he could absorb Lange and then get down to language and kinship, where Lange indeed was weakest. This was a great arrangement. The Freudians had nothing to say; he was for them a lost cause by now.

They had tried to persuade him to examine the source of matrilineal kinship in "maternal overprotection" and a weak male superego. He suggested it was the other way round: these were *a result* of matrilineal kinship, not a cause, which was probably more to do with subsistence. But he was getting to enjoy the Freudians; they had a twist to everything. He liked their solemn assurance that things as different as the cruciform shape of churches (whose west door could only be opened when struck by the bishop's staff—"it's a crozier," "same thing"), the layout of golf courses (where the man had to hit a ball with his club into a hole in the shaven green of mother earth), to the shape of women's evening gowns (slim, long and shiny with lots of frothy stuff at the end)—that all these were "body imagery", and sexual imagery to boot. Roy, who was now in a "training analysis" and working on salvation, reported some of these things to him. But Roy was a bit of a trickster, and you never knew, believer that he was, if he took it seriously. There was no question the Freudians did though; even humor wasn't funny to them.

The latest thing in kinship analysis, initiated by the linguistic model, was "componential analysis of kinship terms." This was very technical and still in its developmental stage, but was regarded by the avant garde as the next big thing. Duane Metzger, whom he had already met at Leverett House, was a Junior Fellow. This really was a big thing at Harvard, since it selected the best and the brightest, paid for everything, and let them do what they wanted. The idea was to let really brilliant students by-pass the Ph.D. Homans had been a Junior Fellow, and had stuck to the spirit of the thing, and was very proud of having nothing beyond his A.B. This didn't stop everyone calling him Dr. Homans. Indeed the whole system collapsed since no one took it seriously outside Harvard itself, and no one would appoint anyone without the sacred doctorate, and Harvard couldn't just hire all its Junior Fellows. So the superstars ended up doing Ph.D.s anyway: a typical Harvard well-meaning fiasco. They did so want to show that they were different and better, and that the rules for ordinary mortals did not apply to them.

He would have loved to be a junior fellow; it would have solved his problems nicely; but they hadn't offered. Duane was unquestionably very smart in a mathematical way. He gave the centerpiece graduate seminar in Anthropology that year: only the most advanced students got to do this, in this status-obsessed society. He gave a paper on the componential analysis of Zuni kin terms. Kluckhohn, as chairman, pronounced it the second most brilliant paper of the thirty- (or was it forty?) year series. Everything had to be ranked, but no one was ever ranked first, he suspected. No one understood this particular paper, and there was an uncomfortable silence when questions were called for. Vogtie tried to save the day by asking if it would work for Zuni veterans. Duane said yes. Silence. Kluckhohn, in obvious desperation, did the embarrassing thing, and called upon our supposed "kinship expert from the LSE." "Do you have a comment?" he asked. Our boy, who had been sitting on the floor of the overcrowded hall, scrambled clumsily to his feet and said awkwardly, "No. I didn't understand a word of it." There was a silence, a collective gasp, then a spontaneous burst of laughter and a round of applause. No one, they told him afterwards, had ever, in the thirty-plus-year series, made such an admission, even if it was the true feeling of everyone present. You *never* said you didn't understand: this was status death. Somehow, by hook or by crook, you thought up a question that suggested you did understand. They professed to admire his honesty, while saying among themselves (Roy reported) that they didn't believe him; he was doing the hypocritical and annoying "British understatement" thing again. They were wrong, but every culture needs its sustaining myths.

Just to be sure he checked with Freedman and Firth about Cochiti, and the Pueblos. He remembered Firth using the Goldfrank material in a lecture on matrilineal kinship, and Freedman had said that the only thing worth reading on Indians was the Pueblo stuff. They were positively enthusiastic, writing that this was a "great opportunity" and one to be seized. The Pueblos were a "classic culture" in Anthropology, and he would certainly not hurt his career by studying them (the career he still wasn't at all sure he wanted.) Like it or not he now had an "area" (geographic) and even a "people"—for anthropologists still grandly referred to "my people" in those days. The standard response to any generalization was to object that "among my people..." Freedman had called this "amongitis" and it was endemic. But there it was: he was set to go.

He dispatched the second term's exams and mourned the fall of the French Fourth Republic and the pathetic, but predictable, reassertion of the *Fuhrerprinzip* that plagued these uncertain democrats. He suffered a week in hospital after a near-fatal reaction to a tetanus shot the cautious Lange insisted he get (along with one for Rocky Mountain Spotted Fever.) He was in a bed next to an undergraduate with a wound from a fencing accident: a foil had snapped and pierced his right lung causing it to collapse. What an odd pair they were, but they got on, and Bill-the–Fencer, a Harvard child of privilege with the insouciant charm they wore like a skin, was to prove an interesting entrée to undergraduate life in the second year. The Laboratory of Social Relations (Vogtie) found him a tape recorder—heavy reel-to-reel thing in those days. He was off to his fieldwork novitiate, as naïve as a virgin nun and probably a lot less sure of his vocation than she. But if it was not exactly a calling, it sure as hell was exciting: there was no other way to go now; it was New Mexico or bust; champagne or vinegar. And it was entirely up to him.

6

The Initiate: Journeying through Wonderland

The great realist novelists of our age are Lewis Carroll and Franz Kafka, just as the great realist artists are Picasso and Dali. If *Guernica* and *The Persistence of Memory* expose a reality more real than that reproduced by the slavish camera, so do *Wonderland/Looking Glass* and *Trial/Castle* lay out for us the dilemmas of the unwittingly sane individual in a collectively bizarre world more surely than *Bovary* or *Karenina.* (And if we must do the playwrights then it is of course Ionesco and Beckett.) But the individuals differ interestingly in their response to the mad, mad world.

Disney never understood Alice. His wide-eyed, wondering, yoo-hoo-ing, oh-my-ing, precious little pre-teen, is as far removed from Alice as is King Kong. Alice was a no-nonsense, don't let's be ridiculous, stop-this-at-once, prim, sensible English girl, of sound upbringing and firm principles. What happened to her was not wonderful, it was nonsense, and she said so in plain terms. What kept her going through the indignities and absurdities that Wonderland inflicted on her, was this insistence that the world was not this way, and that sanity must reassert itself. It is part of the fun of Alice. It is what happens to us in lucid dreaming: we know it is a dream and we insist on waking, even if we can't immediately.

Kafka's anti-heroes, on the other hand, are faced with a less obvious absurdity. They know it is absurd, but they are basically either afraid or resigned. Can we imagine what Alice would have said to K.'s judges? We know what she said to judges, even royal ones. But the Kafka man is always uncertain, even to the point of half-believing his accusers, despite not knowing of what he is accused. Novelists get their effects by going to extremes with their protagonists, and the alarming worlds they live in. Real anti-heroes are more of a boring mixture: wonder, fear, skepticism, churlishness, puzzlement, resignation... Their worlds are more deceptively sane; their adventures are less a progress to an end, more a series of accidentally creative blunders. Somewhere between Wonderland and the Castle lies the Continental United States of America, from Harvard Yard to the Land of Enchantment.

He was to join Roy at his home in Metuchen, New Jersey, where a car would be purchased. You could get a good second-hand car for under a hundred dollars, and a splendid one for two hundred. There was a "gas war" on and petrol was as low as 17¢ a gallon; sharing the expenses and camping out they could make a cheap crossing of the country. He went down by train to New York and straight on to the Trenton local. He was still baffled by the accents, and missed Metuchen in the dark because he thought they were calling out "Jerusalem!"—which, given the cosmopolitan naming system for towns was not unreasonable; he had seen a train bound for Bethlehem, one for Lebanon, and one for Palmyra. He discovered the mistake and got off at the next stop, in his panic failing to find out where he was. He called Roy's number from a phone outside the station, but didn't know where to tell him to come. He opened the booth door and yelled to passers-by to tell him where he was, what the name of the town was. They backed away wide-eyed, or fled in terror of an obviously crazed drunk. Roy figured out he must be in New Brunswick, and Roy's brother would come and pick him up, since he was leaving work nearby and could collect him on the way. The cavalry came as he sat like a refugee on his cases and the unwieldy tape recorder.

The brother showed him, as they passed, the buildings of Rutgers College, where Robeson and Roy had gone, and where Waxman, as he knew, had got the Nobel Prize for developing streptomycin, which scoured the horror of diphtheria from the record. The light was too dim to make much out. He asked about the name: it had been Queen's College until the Revolution when these royal names went out of favor (King's College in New York became Columbia.) Colonel Rutgers was a hero of the Revolution who gave some money to the college, which was then renamed after him. In origin it was an institution of the Dutch Reformed Church; the seminary was still there. Now it was also the State University of New Jersey, since, the brother explained, the state was too cheap to build a new one.

They had not intended to take wives on the trip; they were to come later. But Roy's wife changed her mind. This was not good, since she was a tight little person who thought him a bad influence on Roy; that is, an influence other than her own. But there it was and it had to be borne. He had taken some driving lessons, but his newness scared her to death and so she and Roy had to do the driving. He had to admit though that he learned a lot from her, for she knew American literature and introduced him to authors he might otherwise have gone straight by in his hurry to assimilate what she would call, librarian fashion, "non-fiction." He discovered Wharton, Dickinson (oh lovely, lovely), Miller and Mailer, Williams (William Carlos), Stevens, dos Passos, Steinbeck, Faulkner (oh dear), MacLeish, Wolfe (Thomas—and no, you can't), Trilling and Hellman (the little foxes, who eat the fruit of their own vines...)

Roy was immensely patient with them both, although he did complain mildly about the "planting of little bits if England" all over the Blue Ridge

Mountains, so our excited lad stopped exclaiming, "Oh look, that's just like..."
at every change of scenery. He began to take in the immensity of these United
States, and to realize how narrow was a view of them based on Boston, or even
New England. They had told him that Harvard wasn't America, since it was
"just like England." Woefully wrong, but it sure as hell wasn't like the American South they were now driving through: Kentucky, Tennessee, Arkansas. It
was a string of small county towns, all very much alike, and all boasting two
large buildings: a High School and a Court House. He thought of the contrast
with Europe where similar towns had a Castle (at least the ruin of one) and a
Cathedral. It told you something. If Kafka's hero could never get into the
Castle, so here, they said, you couldn't fight City Hall.

As they stopped to eat friendly southern food (fried chicken, hominy grits,
catfish, hush puppies...) served by always-friendly southern people, they passed
old men on benches in the town square, whittling, smoking and discussing
law cases. One concerned a man arrested for "carrying a concealed weapon."
The old men were outraged: the judge should understand this was a professional gambling man; he had to have a gun. Would it have been legal if the
weapon had not been concealed, he wondered? Worn at the hip in a holster?
He didn't see any. Disappointing.

They passed through several language belts, where first the "h" went missing, and yumans had yuge appetites and a sense of yumor. "Youse guys" gave
way to "you all"—or more properly "yorl" as they crossed the line drawn by
the Englishmen Mason and Dixon. Adjectives and adverbs, as well as tenses,
became confused ("we done real good"), and the distinction between "lay"
and "lie" (transitive vs. intransitive?) began to operate on quite different
principles. The Southern politicians they listened to in turn abandoned a lot
of "d" and "t" and terminal "g" so that a song was "senimenal" and a proposition became "ineressin." The president became the "preznun." In fact, the
"preznunyoonighstaysmerka": for many of the cartilaginous vowels dropped
out too, and the consonants ground together like arthritic vertebrae. He annoyed his fellow passengers with his attempts to reproduce the speech styles,
including the ubiquitous politicians' greeting to the "Merkins" as in "Mahfluh
Merkins" along with the complaints about the "Comnis" who hid behind the
"Fithmemnun." This with universal praise for "PreznEyeznah." He remembered the old Boston cleaning lady who thought that Eisenhower was a great
president and a fine man, but was doing a lousy job. Did that say something
profound about the weaknesses of the presidential system of government?
When they reached Texas they would find the preznun was a "fah-ee-un may-
un"—on the principle that all vowels should be made tripthongs whenever
possible. Anything less was a crah-ee-um.

They stopped in Little Rock, which was still full of heavily armed troops
after the school desegregation troubles. You could get postcards with pictures of parachutists in the streets and "Greetings from occupied Arkansas!"

The people were pretty good-humored about it by now, but he could never take seriously a constitutional crisis in which the major villains were Orval Faubus and Virgil Blossom. He did enjoy the beloved Louis Armstrong becoming, somewhat surprisingly, a major progressive hero: a man of true principle and integrity when the chips were down. Robeson had always put himself and his career on the line, of course, naturally, but one didn't expect it of Satchmo, somehow. He could have just blown his heavenly horn, clowned for the white folks, and raked in the doubloons. They didn't see many black people, except when driving in or out of towns, on the shabby, furtive outskirts. "Downtown" the shops and diners were all white. Whenever they left a restaurant the people always said, "Yahll come back now!" Roy had to explain it was simply a custom and so prevent our too-literal traveler from telling them that, thank you very much, but in fact they were just driving across country and were unlikely to be back this way... You had to say "sure will!" or something like that. Knowing the customs of the Merkins was everything.

As they moved from Howard Johnson Territory to Dairy Queen country the airwaves were monopolized by religious stations interspersing fervent prayer (usually for material success) with even more fervent requests for money to keep the station going. "Make yoahr meal a *holy* meal! Sen' for ah Lahs' Supper table cloth in genu-wine pure co'on fahbric, with the reel lahkeness of ah Savior an' the dee-sciples. Only fahve-niney-fahve includn' shippn"! For only another two dollars we'll sen' you ah lahfe-size, lahght up, plahstic Jesus statue, foh yoahr fron' porch! Make yoahr gree'in' a *holy* gree'in'!" Somewhere along the line, salvation and selling had become interchangeable. Roy shrugged and smiled: it was the Bible Belt; it was what you'd expect. Just don't talk to anyone about evolution.

Moving away from Boston was like moving back in time. The music on the radio was "country"—ballads of miserable circumstances and dysfunctional families, but recognizably in the Irish and English folk ballad tradition, locally adapted. The beer brands changed, and the popular commercial was a phony, Longfellowesque Indian chant, with tom-tom:

> From the land of sky blue wa-aters
> Dah-di-da-di-da-di-da-di-da
> Comes the beer refreshing
> Hamms the beer refreshing.

The country became more rugged, the people more strange in speech: more and more consonants disappeared and "a-" was prefixed to all present participles, just as it had been in Somerset: "Ah'm a-fixin' to lay down..." Dress and manner changed more subtly to "Western"—high-heeled boots, bigger hats, laconic, deliberate—while the food became a lot simpler and cheaper. Beef, in every known cut, became less and less expensive the further west you traveled. By Texas they were practically giving it away. The son of austerity ate himself silly on cheap steaks with very little by way of vegetables except corn on the cob, sweet from the fields and dripping with butter, and the ubiquitous red beans. They had steak for every meal: with eggs at breakfast, as sandwiches for lunch, barbecued in the campground at night.

The campgrounds (in national or state parks) were cheap to stay in (dollar a car) and provided drinking water, electricity, showers and "rest rooms" which were lavatories, and were called "Johns" for reasons no one could explain. It was a while before he realized that "jahrn" was in fact "John." This was still a pretty prudish society: in *Oklahoma* there was a line "you can go to the privy in the rain and never wet your feet" which was regularly changed by local groups to something like "you can shop for groceries in the rain..." It suddenly made sense of the change in the funny lyric by Lorenz Hart:

> I'll cling to him
> Each spring to him
> And worship the trousers that cling to him

That last line was far too suggestive, and became: "And long for the day when I'll cling to him." Did it also explain why Congreve's line was regularly misquoted as: "Music hath charms to soothe the savage beast"? Were they unconsciously avoiding "breast"? Enough: leave that to the Freudians. (But for the insistent record, let us note that Congreve said "has" not "hath" and "a" not "the." There, the record is satisfied; move on.)

They slept in the open in sleeping bags, but he usually spent an hour or so in the car with a flashlight reading through another chapter of *Spanish Made Simple*. He resorted to this during the day when he got bored with the monotonously flat scenery. If you knew French and Latin, Spanish was not difficult, but it was interesting in its overuse of the subjunctive. He remembered Herbert Spencer's anticipation of the Sapir-Whorf hypothesis, in his insistence that the English use of the indicative mood showed their straightforward, open nature, while the subjunctive-obsessed Spaniards were obviously secretive and devious.

The most vivid memory of the Texas panhandle was the bugs. There was no air conditioning in cars then—at least not in a hundred-dollar car, so they drove at night to avoid the unbearable heat, sleeping in a campground in the day, in the shade. It was perhaps a cicada season—every seven or thirteen years they came out to breed; this was the unlucky one. Or perhaps they were "June bugs"—but it was still May. The gas stations were pools of bright light along the lonely unlit roads that led indefinitely west. The bugs came to them in their millions, hit the lights and fell to the ground in a thick carpet. As you left the car to find the John or the blessed cold can of Coke/Squirt/Dr. Pepper, you crunched your way over the carpet of squirming, two-legged, breed-for-a-day insects, leaving squelching footprints inches deep as you passed, beating them off from your face as you fled. Cars had to have plastic bug deflector shields on the hood, but even so you had to stop every so often and scrape off the bodies that clogged the windshield. Nature was intruding into culture with a suicidal ferocity. This was tough country.

Then, part way into New Mexico, there were the Rockies. You went along eye-tiring distances in the sun and dust, thinking how discouraging it must have been to the pioneers on foot with their slow ox-wagons, and how desperate must have been the sudden sight of this sheer wall of rock stretching vertically into the clouds. (See it in *Shane*: the implacable silent partner in every scene and dialogue.) The wall God put round Eden, with the burning swords of the Seraphim brandished to keep out the first parents, could not have been more daunting than these precipices were to the pioneers. He understood now why they needed their crude religion to sustain them, for these things were beyond the resources of the human spirit to conquer unaided. He also understood the incessant petitions to The Lord (or to Our-Lord-and-Savior-Jesus-Christ) for material success in this world. In the pioneer culture there was no other real measure of salvation, or the promise of salvation, than simple survival first, and beyond that, prosperity. It was the Protestant Ethic applied to the frontier struggle for existence. It was Vogt's homesteader value of "rugged individualism." They must have had very early weaning, severe toilet discipline, and strict independence training. No question: these people were very different.

Precipice, cliff, escarpment: he ran through all the descriptions, but "wall" was best, for these Rocky Mountains were somehow an unnatural barrier. Men had not made them as they had New York, but they seemed to have been put there by some power, deliberately to remind puny men that they were not in control. He felt like the suddenly shrunken Alice, in a universe that no longer made sense, where everything was ludicrously large. It was a great wall stretching up beyond the clouds, made all the more frightening by its suddenness. You were innocently crossing the dusty, infinite flatness, when it was just there: joltingly, immediately, seriously there, slap in your face: a great, sheer, God-made wall across your already weary path. The adjectives fail; you had to be there. You had to sense the lack of control one felt. The Indians accepted it; they never tried to control the place; they appeased it and cooperated. But the Puritans, however they might have been shocked by it, recovered and tried to take it over, as they had tried to break and tame the Plains with the plough. And God bless them they made a good stab at it, and now there were level roads reaching up into those mountains, and our latter-day pioneers were taking them, with suitable adjustments to the car engine for the increasing altitude. Eldorado was in sight.

They dropped him off in Santa Fé. This was still what is now designated the "Old Town"—one road led in from Albuquerque in the south, and another out to Taos in the north. Some of the hotels still had hitching rails and made special provision for cowboys coming to town. But the chic crowd was very much in evidence with its galleries and boutiques, and the tourists clogged the center of town in the season. The most impressive thing was the uniform "adobe" style of construction: everything from houses to hotels and gas stations was in this local style, and this gave a wonderful look to the place: unchanged from Spanish colonial times. Even the Woolworth's was in this style, with the name in discreet gold lettering. He checked it out, but there was no loose-biscuit counter, and the only dances were being done by Indians for the tourists. These Indians were, he was told, from Santa Clara, a Pueblo to the north, and they were colorful enough in their eagle costumes: men into birds, bobbing and sweeping in step with the relentless drum.

He asked about Cochiti Indians and was directed to the Palace of the Governors (now a museum), where many groups of women gathered under the long portico of the oldest public building in America to sell pottery and jewelry. They were small, squat, dark women, with black hair cut in severe fringes and done up in queues behind. They wore long colored dresses, hung about with turquoise beads and silver jewelry. They were friendly and smiled, talking in the clipped monotone that marked their English, and chatted among themselves in the glottalized local languages. His studies of Keres had been purely literary, and he didn't recognize anything, and was too shy to ask any questions. He was content to look and smile back and wonder at these people who were still so, well, Indian.

He stayed at the De Vargas hotel—a whole lot cheaper than the fashionable La Fonda, but right in town. He shared the bar with a bunch of telephone linemen in from Texas, and had a friendly rapport with these rough but agreeable characters. He liked the way people in The West more nearly approached the ideals of equality than those in Boston. Here you were very much judged by how you stood on your own feet, not by your background or qualifications. That he was from England and Harvard were interesting facts, but it was clear he would be judged by how he performed, not by these or any other attributes. He bought a pair of Western boots and a big hat, and went with his new friends to a local rodeo. They knew the performers and borrowed horses for an afternoon. He hadn't ridden since the pony of his secret hunting days in the war, but Western riding was strictly sit-full-legged-in-the-saddle stuff, without the silly posting that the English style required. He hung on and barrel raced (the horses knew what to do) and even tried roping, without much success. The Texans liked the effort though, and bought him much beer and steaks and took him to a tavern that catered to the cowboy crowd and played Western music for the jerky little two-step dancing they liked so much. He waited for the waltzes and danced with the tall, strong, rangy girls in jeans and Stetsons, who spurned his fancy dance steps while they loved his accent. But these confident amazons, who gripped him so firmly and looked right at him, scared him to death. So despite the amused encouragement of his new mates, it stopped there, and they helped him cheerfully back to the cheap room and a beer-induced long sleep.

The Hispanic family that owned the hotel was called Vigil (which he learned to pronounce "Veeheel") and befriended him also. They were warm and welcoming and saw him as a lonely *niño* far from his family and home. He didn't tell them he was delighted to be far from both and happy where he was; they wouldn't have understood. He tried out some halting Spanish, and amused them because his "book" Spanish was often different from theirs, which was full of American loanwords. They laughed over "el flashlight" and "el refrigerator" (ray-free-her-a-TOR.) There was a Spanish village close to Cochiti (Peña Blanca), and some Spanish people had lived in a "quarter" in the Pueblo, which was one reason it was considered more open and progressive (and consequently more acculturated) than the others, to the extent of allowing anthropologists to stay overnight. So he was glad to learn a little about these descendants of the first Europeans, even if government legislation had now turned them out of the Indian town. They were a local factor; he was learning something; it was fun too.

He was reveling in the new, and at that time very un-American, food. There were *huevos rancheros*—any kind of eggs with hot sauce or pickle. There were chili peppers in any and all varieties, raw green and sun-ripened red (strings of them hanging like bright flames outside the little mud-brick farm houses.) He particularly liked the green ones stuffed and deep-fried as *rellenos*, and the scandalously hot ripe-red ones, ground up with meat then served with red beans as *chile con carne*. The inevitable chicken, best as *pollo con mole* with bitter chocolate sauce, teamed up with all the variations on meat-stuffed *tortillas*: *burritos*, *tamales*, *quesadillas*, *enchiladas*, and the inevitable *refritos*—refried beans. The most famous local Pueblo ruins, which the Cochiti clamed as their ancestral home, were in *Rito de los Frijoles*: Bean Creek.

Chuck Lange with family and students came to get him, and took him to The Pink Adobe, the best Mexican restaurant in town. It was the day when a bookstore was having a book signing, and he was excited because Erna Fergusson was there and inscribed a copy of her *New Mexico* for him. They had a chat about brother Francis, and about the history of Indian-White relations. Did he know about the Pueblo rebellion? Not much—put it on the list. He did know about Billy the Kid, but only the legend; she gave him pointers to the real story—Pat Garret was not Billy's best friend, etc. She wished him luck. Lange was a pleasant Midwesterner with the measured style of his kind. The excited Harvard Englishman sometimes felt like an insect buzzing around these heavy people, who moved and spoke, and seemed to think, in slow motion. He had to tell himself to calm down, slow down, curb his impatience and stop finishing their sentences for them. But they were tolerant of him; to them he was exotic. This never ceased to amaze him: how could he be exotic? He could accept eccentric, but it was the Indians and the Texans, the Midwesterners and the Bostonians, who were exotic.

He learned to live with it, and happily found Lange to be a tolerant, serious and kind man, who seemed genuinely to welcome his "cooperation" on Cochiti. A large man with a big head and receding chin, he could have played a good Mr. Chasuble (Myles Malleson style) in an American *Importance of Being Earnest*. Primarily an archaeologist, he had nevertheless over many years compiled his encyclopedia of information on the Pueblo, and he shared it with an easy generosity. The students were another matter. The dig they were on was a "field school" and they were here to work and be examined and graded in the accepted fashion. He was only, technically, a first-year graduate student—some of them were much closer to their doctorates, but the Harvard thing kicked in. He was again a "special student" and was regarded more as a colleague of Lange's than one of them. But they too had their regional generosity of spirit, and it went well with them.

They went by pick-up truck down the Albuquerque road, turning off to Santo Domingo, the largest and most conservative of the Keresan Pueblos, beyond which, across the desert, was Cochiti. The desert road was washboard dirt, crossing many arroyos (memories of Zane Grey) where it was washed out in flash floods. A poor wooden bridge took them across the Rio Grande, into the land of yucca and cactus, cottonwoods and rattlesnakes, small fields of corn and chili peppers. Some Spanish villagers with donkeys and goats looked up as they passed, but didn't acknowledge them. On some of the low hills there were large wooden crosses at the summit. Lange explained they were for the *penitente* cult of the Spanish villages: these were *flagellantes* who ritually flogged themselves, and crucified a volunteer on Good Friday. It was illegal, but there was not much law out here, and what there was turned a blind eye to what it regarded as a deeply religious event, and so beyond the law of man—much like *sutee* for pious Hindus. The students had a puritan horror of this mediaevalism, but he saw it as part of the logical progression back in time that going west involved. You traveled beyond the primitive Protestant Puritanism of the Bible belt, to the sado-masochism of Catholic Spain: the Spain of the hooded processions, the *auto-da-fé*, and the self-torture of a tortured people. No wonder there was an implacable barrier between them and the neolithic Indians, even further back in time, who worshipped female deities (Spider Woman, Deer Maiden, Corn Mother), and called the pointed little mountain to the north, in Spanish, *la tetilla*, the teat.

He only caught an initial brief glance of Cochiti, on a small rise to the west of the river, since they were going first to the field school up in the hills. Low mud-brick brown houses with small windows and ladders, and outside each one an *estufa*—the hive-shaped oven where most of the cooking was done. But this was all. He was to stay in Joe Trujillo's house at the eastern edge of the village—Joe and his wife lived in a house by their fields in the summer, only a walk from the village. Joe had asked, however, that he stay with the Lange's for the first week or so, since this was the time of ritual preparation for the summer ceremonials. Joe didn't want to risk any trouble from the conservative elements in the village; they didn't like strangers there at this sensitive time. It was a useful introduction to Pueblo attitudes (Values?) All Pueblos, Lange explained, were split in this way: progressives wanted to adopt the better things of Anglo life and were open to outsiders; conservatives wanted to keep to the old ways and exclude outsiders, especially where ritual was concerned. Progressives were more often devoutly Catholic; conservatives favored the native religion. But they mostly compromised. Everyone in fact went to church, but the native "medicine societies" pretty much controlled it, and appointed its lay officers. Everyone equally attended the Kachina ceremonies—the masked dances—which were held, by common agreement, in secret, and in which only initiated men could take part. But some progressives had told Lange and previous investigators (Father Demarest) the details of the masks and their legends. Joe, unlike his sister Caroline, was wise about this: you could have your anthropologist, but you mustn't flaunt him. But this at least gave the anthropologist in the Pueblos some kind of rarity value, unlike the Navaho with their standard family of husband, wife, mother-in-law, five children and an anthropologist. The lesson was well learned. His shyness and foreignness would even be something of a protection.

There were some Cochiti young men helping on the dig. Archaeology was safe; it didn't uncover ritual secrets. They helped put up the camp, and they did a lot of the heavy digging, while the students sifted and sifted with almost idiotic patience. The theoretical issues of archaeology interested him—where had the various tribes come from and when?—but this ditch-digging in dust-choked heat that hit 120° and burned his unprotected northern skin horribly, was not for him. He had to help a bit to earn his keep, but he used the time to ask the Cochiti for words, which they seemed delighted to give him. They also sang him little songs, which he recorded and then transcribed at night.

The words were nonsense syllables (tra-la-la—hey-nonny-nonny), but he was getting the sounds, and learned the simple but pleasing modal tunes and reproduced them in the same falsetto the men used when singing quietly. They were amazed: no one had done this before to their knowledge. Anglos often didn't get there was really a melody; they called it "chanting." At the end of the week he had filled out his hundred basic words list, and had some sentences with the verbs of motion, and three songs. He also found that they used the same name for coyote and fox; a fox was, strictly speaking, a "blue coyote." A good start.

The night before he was to be abandoned in the village, he went out to the nearby water tank with its artesian well turned by a metal windmill that clanked regularly through he night. He had been overcome by panic and needed to get away. It was not really panic over the new start as such, he was quite looking forward to that. It was the old panic: what was he doing there, why was he doing it, why was he doing anything, what sense did it all make? He sat with his back against the big, cool tank, and watched the nearby moon with the rabbit along the side that the Indians saw—why did anyone ever see a man? The stars were brighter and more numerous than he had ever seen them; the mountains were sharp silhouettes in the moonlight; you could smell burning *piñon* in the distance. He was unable to get the little tune out of his head, which was good because it helped to push aside the panic, the feeling that there was a big void he was going to fall into; that he had to keep moving or he would drown. A coyote howled. He remembered that one of the young men—José Dolores—had told him it was indeed good that he was of "the Fox people." It couldn't be a coincidence; this was a powerful clan. "You will," Dolores said, "have many, many mothers. No one can have too many mothers." The Coyote howled again.

Joe Trujillo's house stood alone on the edge of the village, by the road. It was a good place to be to watch comings and goings. But it was unusual in that it was not attached to any other houses. The typical Pueblo (which after all just meant "town") consisted of houses joined together, sometimes on several levels, around plazas or squares. The ceremonials took place in the largest and most central of these. The groups of connected houses—more like connected rooms, held extended families based on the mother-daughter tie, the literature told him. The women owned the houses (room complexes), and men left their natal homes on marriage and moved into the wife's family complex. In many villages, including Cochiti, people had begun building their separate houses outside the dense-packed plazas, and Joe's was one of these. It looked out to the nearest of the two kivas, the Turquoise Kiva. The other kiva (*chitya* in Keres) was Pumpkin, at the other side of the village. The kivas were large, circular, windowless, and semi-underground ceremonial buildings, entered only through the roof by a ladder which could seen sticking up into the air. Here was the famous moiety principle made vividly visible: everyone in the village was either Turquoise or Pumpkin. You were a member of the moiety of your father, but women, on marriage (which was monogamous) joined that of the husband if it was different from their own. Unlike most such systems, there did not seem to be a rule of marriage out of the moiety, which made it unlike the matrilineal clan, which was, the literature said, strictly "exogamous"—you had to marry out of it.

So. You got your clan —there were ten (down form thirteen): Fox (Coyote), Water, Ivy, Cottonwood, Bear, etc.— from your mother, and your moiety from your father. Supposedly, residence at marriage was "matrilocal"—men moved in with wives (primly he corrected this to "uxorilocal"—more exact, certainly.) Families were, "maternal extended"—daughters stayed with their mothers and the men moved between these maternal groups. It was an elaborate social choreography; mothers were the pivot. He had been drilled at the LSE not to confuse "matrilineal" (relationship through females) with "matriarchal"—rule by females. This seemed true here since governance was by men, in the Pueblo Council and its officers, and in the so-called Medicine Societies (Giant, Fire, Flint…). But he had also learned from Firth that the rules of social structure were always compromised by the strategies of "social organization"—so he didn't pre-judge the role of women. Part of his job was to find out how closely the Cochiti followed the theoretical model the rules suggested. But first to the language.

He looked out on his first day, from the roof of "his" house—there was the inevitable ladder sticking up against the side and several feet beyond, and tried to take it in. He had been whisked in a time machine (or down a rabbit hole—that of the rabbit-in-the-moon?) from the industrial, "civilized" east coast; whisked back to this little neolithic farming village, with its customs and rituals not so different in principle, if very different in style, from untouched Melanesia or New Guinea. There were a few pick-up trucks, and a precarious electric line had been run in which meant he could have a small fridge and a fan, and run his tape recorder without batteries. But even so, the overwhelming sense was of the primitiveness of the place. It was impossible to believe one was still in the USA. It was necessary to keep remembering that the U.S. was not a nation but a continent, as vast as Asia or Europe. The differences within it were as great as those between, say, England and Bulgaria. This had to be grasped. But this desert, mountain and forest area was somewhere that the boisterous, European civilization had touched least. It wasn't all that long ago, that they still mounted "expeditions" to get to Zuni and Hopi country, several hundred miles to the west. There were roads and cars now, but this country was so vast it seemed to swallow them up. It was more desolate and lonely in its interior than his Yorkshire moors, and its arid wasteland was more frightening: it was cactus versus heather, and the cactus won. It was a tabula rasa on which men had only, so far, scribbled faintly. It was cleansing.

Nature's strict embrace
Putting aside the past, shall soon efface
Its print as well—factitious humours grown
Over the true—loves, hatreds not his own—
And turn him pure as some forgotten vest
Woven of painted byssus, silkiest
Tufting the Tyrrhene whelk's pearl-sheeted lip...

A village like this could go undisturbed by outsiders for most of the year. It was surrounded by its "reservation" land, which was a big buffer. The land was the same as that the Spanish conquistadores had allotted them, with a charter from the king: a grant that was confirmed and unchanged by the Americans after 1849 (Treaty of Guadaloupe Hidalgo.) The Church had a mission here—a lovely building at the far end of town, and they were all nominally Catholics. But the Medicine Societies controlled all the Church offices, and the traditional religion went on as before, even if the most important part—the masked dances of the gods—went underground. Public ceremonies, like the Green Corn Dance they were preparing for, stayed public and appeased the Church by having a bower for the patron saint (Bonaventura) and giving him a nod as the dance proceeded. These people seemed to be very in charge of themselves, acculturated or not.

He thought about this while he looked across the village, taking in the pervasive naturalness of the place. The shapes were cultural, human inventions, these cubes and squares and straight ladders, piled together like children's building blocks; there were no such shapes in nature. But they did not look at all unnatural they way the Anglo cities did. They were of the color of the earth—they were made from it—and seemed to grow out of it like trees and rocks grew out of it. It was as if this were a town sculpted by natural forces. The cliff dwellings—the homes of their ancestors to the far north in the San Juan valley—had been the same. They were intrusive, technically, but they looked as if they ought to be there. If nature had decided to fill those caves with something constructed, this is what she would have made. The city fathers in Santa Fé understood this very well, and made their architectural ordinances accordingly. This Pueblo (*kutyiti* in Keres, the young men taught him) on its little elevation, disturbed nothing; it settled comfortably into the dusty earth like a bird onto its eggs. (This metaphor was unmixed; he was improving.) But what about the language? He had to have "informants" although it sounded uncomfortably like "informers" and he must tread carefully, he knew that: no questions about rituals—even the public ones; Lange and Vogt had insisted. That was the way to get evicted. Lange was not even sure you could ask too much about clans over and above who was in which, since they were involved in ceremonies too—largely curing. Well, he'd survived the Anglicans, the Marxists and the Freudians, he'd even survived Harvard, so far. How hard could the Indians be?

He hated thus objectifying them as things to be studied. They were people, not specimens. But this was something he sensed was unresolved by anthropologists generally. You had to be a "participant observer" but how could you participate if you couldn't sleep with the women or take part in the rituals or interfere in any way with the culture? Could you stand by and watch a human sacrifice? Yes, Freedman had said, you watched and took notes. Freedman was a tough character. He remembered Max Gluckman in a lecture saying how he had to watch a man whipped almost to death, as a punishment, in Swaziland. It was a legal punishment said the equally tough Max; one couldn't interfere.

It wasn't the extremes though, he didn't think he'd have to face those here; it was just the general sense that he had to make these "subjects" exceptions to the human race for study purposes. As a still-convinced rationalist he should find their superstitions, colorful and graceful and staggering as he was to find them, as objectionable as he found the fairy stories of Christianity. But he knew he wanted them to be left untouched, pristine, so that he could study them in all their native purity. He didn't want these people to be enlightened and subscribe to the Ayer-Popper ban on metaphysics; he wanted their metaphysics to flourish. A mental slap-in-the-face brought him out of it; at least with language these unsolvable problems didn't arise. He could even been seen as doing a service in recording and analyzing it accurately for them. If he could complete a grammar! This was champagne where the meaning of life was simple and clear. Informants would be his new enzymes. It was his way into the Castle.

It was not a good time to be there. Joe Trujillo came by: a wonderful, dignified, older man, the epitome of what the romantic in him wanted in the Indian. Joe was quiet and humorous, and full of good advice. He brought some lime to put in the latrine: one great point about his isolated house was that it had one. He remembered Esther Goldfrank and made interesting comments about her monograph, of which he largely approved. But they agreed she hadn't known the language and this was a handicap. He told Joe about his interest in kinship terms. Yes, Joe said, it was hard to translate, they were not the same, and it was hard to explain using the English words. It was best to listen to people when they were talking about relatives. First learn to listen, learn to understand. It wasn't a difficult language, said Joe, even the Indians could speak it, although—he went on with a straight face—they didn't speak it any more. What?! Yes, said Joe, it was all Spanish now, look at the words: *chi'ri* was *chili*, *kawa'hyo* was *caballo*—horse, *pa'ni* was *pan* –bread, *k'anastya* was *canasta*—basket, and so on through a list of Spanish loanwords. Once over the shock, he laughed a lot and thought Joe would be good company.

But Joe had to get back to his fields; it was summer and everyone was working. Better to come in the winter when there was plenty of time. But Joe knew it didn't work that way with anthropologists; they were summer people. He had a suggestion: go to the village store which was run by a Spanish family (they were the only non-Indians allowed to live there permanently) and talk to the boys there; they spoke Keres like everyone else, and they didn't have a lot to do in the summer. He went, was welcomed (as was his trade—cans of everything) and the boys helped him fill out some more of his word lists. It was a start.

Then came an odd intervention. Joe's grandson, Andy, was on a visit. He didn't live there, and had been to college at New Mexico Highlands University as well as in the army for a while, and painted in the Disneyesque style then popular with Indian painters. Andy was chatty, and explained that he felt alienated from his Indian heritage (he said this), and was himself trying to get back in touch. He had renounced Catholicism, and had been taking lessons on the Native religion from the Cacique, the "chief priest" of the tribe, who was the only person exempted from work. Andy was going to start practicing it again, once he "knew enough." He changed his name officially from Trujillo to Ahsona—his grandfather's Indian name. This made Joe angry: he felt Andy was overdoing it; this wasn't the Indian way. "I'm a good Catholic and a good Indian," said Joe, "let me be both." But Andy ploughed ahead and insisted on finding a "real" linguistic informant, not those boys who spoke with a Spanish accent and didn't understand the customs. (One of them was training to be a Catholic priest.) Get one of the older men who is not working; they know the language best anyway.

So Joe arranged a visit to see an old blind relative called Epifanio Pecos, who had been a War Captain of the Pueblo—a kind of chief of police. He was named after the war god, *Masewi*, the elder of the hero twins (the assistant War Captain was *Oyoyewi*, after the younger brother.) With his long gray hair tied back in a short pigtail, his bead-decorated headband, his pierced ears with turquoise earrings, he was even more the epitome of the Indian than Joe. His English was good, his Spanish better, and his family of related females (must get the exact relationships) seemed happy with the idea of a dollar a session. Each day the pupil must come over and lead Epifanio to Joe's house, because they were busy with cooking, dressmaking and, most of all, pottery and neck- laces which they sold in Santa Fe. So it began.

He prepared his notebook by putting at the head of each page a word in both English and Spanish, then some sample short sentences using the word. "Child," *niño/niña*, "My child eats your food." "Your father eats with his child." And so on. He didn't rush it with kinship terms, except for the primary terms, since he didn't want to prejudge anything—just feel his was into the language gradually, so that he could listen. Epifanio was unhappy with the tape recorder, and he abandoned it after a few sessions. Joe didn't mind it, so he used to get Joe to repeat some of the sentences into the recorder on his frequent visits. Joe's brother Paul, who was head of the powerful Kwirena society, came round a few times and added to the recordings. But Epifanio was wonderful: he had no hesitations, knew exactly what was wanted, and carefully corrected pronunciation. He was a true teacher, and when the language was again taught in the school (at Santo Domingo) it was he who was asked to be the instructor. They worked on pronunciation first, although grammar accumulated through the examples; sense followed sound. His hopes were fulfilled: here were two enzymes who knew just what they were doing and what the end product should be. This was a welcome twist to the fermentalogical metaphor.

We can skip a phonetics lesson, but we are concerned with what our somewhat overwhelmed learner was stuffing his head and imagination with, and this was challenging. A lot of transcription was misleading: true to phonemic form, Anglos heard their own distinctive sounds, and repeatedly recorded voiced consonants when there were none. Thus they gave the common greeting word as *gowatzena*, when it was *kowatsina*, the voicing that was heard was just the unaspirated as opposed to the aspirated consonant: the same distinction as in Hindi! Sometimes they mistook the glottalized consonant for voicing: *k'atsenyi* becoming *gatzenyi*. Boas had not made that mistake, but being a little deaf he had occasionally missed the "whispering" phenomenon: suffixes in particular often contained unvoiced vowels, something unheard of in SAE, and hard to convey except to say the syllables were "whispered." So you might get something like *kushunyi^{sitiku}*—where the whispered syllables were conventionally written in superscript. You could get these voiceless vowels at any point in a long word, which would then be alternately voiced and whispered. It was the hardest thing to catch phonetically.

All there was to go on for grammar was the brief sketch that Boas had attached to his texts. Respect for Boas grew between the collaborators: once basic pronunciation was mastered, he would read out some of Boas's verb paradigms, and Epifanio would laugh, shake his head, and whistle in appreciation. "That old guy sure got it right," he would say admiringly. This was especially so with the complicated pronominal prefixes and suffixes which were the main characteristic of the language. In SAE we say them as subject and object: "he hits him," "I hit you," "we hit them," "je vous batte" etc. In Keres, each possible combination is contained in its own affix: "(I-him)-hit," or "(we-them)-hit." Keres, like Greek, had a dual number to complicate matters: "(we-two-that-one)-hit" or "(we-many-those-two)-hit." Running round all the combinations was dizzying.

Also, quick to note was the fact that all "nouns" could be inflected as verbs: in fact the distinction didn't exist. In English we can make nouns into verbs by adding "to" and then treating it as a verb. Thus "mother" becomes "to mother" and we can say "she mothered him," "she would have been mothered by him." Primary kin terms can be used this way, but we don't have verbs "to uncle" or "to cousin" or "to relative-by-marriage." In Keres all such nouns are inflected if they are nouns of reference: terms of address are not so construed. Thus "mother"—*naya,* has a present tense, *sanaya,* a dubitative or subjunctive—*atanaya*, a future—*nanayasi*. It is hard to give them meaningful SAE equivalents. The "dubitative" was interesting: Whorfian instincts sensed that this was a world divided into things that were known by immediate experience and those that were only known by hearsay, or guessed at, or hypothetical. Also, there was no present tense as such. There was a past/present, and a marked future. One indicated past or present time by attaching time designations like, "right now" or "yesterday" or "a long time ago." He puzzled about tenses: Flo Kluckhohn used to use them as keys to whether a culture was "past, present or future oriented" in its Values (yes). He dimly remembered that the Pueblos were supposed to be "present oriented"—but this one had no present tense, and its marked tense was future! English, on the other hand, unlike French and Spanish, had no marked future tense, but only a set of statements or questions of intention: "I shall eat soon," "I am going to eat tonight," "Shall you be there?" They were different, but they all got the same job done: that was the thing about language. Epifanio could move easily between the three languages, moods and tenses notwithstanding.

His notebook filled, the tape got used up, with some songs as well—the best way into a language, and he even got some "women's words" from Joe's wife, Old Juana, and her daughter, Juanita. They were Oak clan, and traditionalists. Juanita confided that she didn't believe "that Christian stuff." She thought it barbaric that any supposedly loving God would require the cruel torture and death of his only son in order to redeem people from "sin," which was just how people were. She thought torturing your children was the worst sin of all. The idea of hell repelled her; she didn't believe it. On death you joined the *shiwana* (the collective ancestor spirits) in the clouds and danced forever and brought rain to the people when they danced. There was no hell. Even witches would go to the clouds; yes, even the two-hearts, because they could not help what they were; they were born with two hearts, those that were human.

Juanita preferred the Indian gods, she said, like the Sun Father, the Hero Twins, and especially Spider Woman. This supreme goddess sat in a secret cave in the Grand Canyon, spinning a web from her body: a web that was human thought. All thoughts came from the body of Spider Woman: she was consciousness, and consciousness was a female principle. (She was also one aspect of Graves' Triple Goddess: she was, as Spider Old Woman, The Crone; as the parent of the Hero Twins she was the mature woman—The Mother; as the Deer Maiden she was just that—The Maiden.) Joe had, in defiance of tradition, built his own house away from the clusters round the plaza, but there was no question about who ran it and made decisions about it; that was not alterable the way adobe and plaster were.

It became clear that while the paraphernalia of government and ceremony was in the hands of the men, and the women appeared to play only a supportive role, the men constantly deferred to their women on many matters, if not all. Nothing to do with the houses, the land or the children, could be done without the consent of the women. The Clan Mother—usually the oldest woman of the clan (Juana was the Oak Clan Mother) was the authority on the children of the clan. Decisions would be carried out by her brothers, as the senior men, but they would never dream of going against the Mother. Even in public matters, Joe, an ex-Governor, said that the council must always look over its shoulder at "the old ladies." Only in strictly ceremonial matters, to do with the Kivas, the Medicine Societies, or the Kachina Cult, did the men operate with relative autonomy. Women would not presume to interfere on matters of ritual performance or the ceremonial calendar. The Cacique, who in his house kept the last remaining scalps still used in War/Hunt Society rituals, determined the calendar from observations of the sun, moon and constellations. But the polite term of address for him, particularly when he was fasting on behalf of the Pueblo, was *yaya*, mother.

The male-female, Clan-Kiva, division of labor and authority, became clear in many ways. When a house had to be plastered, it was the women of the house and their husbands who did the work. When a marriage had to be arranged, it was the mother and her sisters, and their brothers and maternal uncles, who initiated it, bringing in the other clan members for the actual ceremonies. When dances had to be taught to the children, it was brothers and their children, with their father and often the paternal grandfather, who had the responsibility as members of the same moiety. In the general melee it was impossible to sort out the relevant people until you knew who they were and what they did, since everyone would participate. It was seeing and hearing who made the speeches, who made the arrangements, that mattered. Only participant observation could do this, and he was on the way.

The major event of the summer—at the solstice—was the Rain or Green Corn Dance. These public dances, involving the whole Pueblo, attracted many visitors to the Rio Grande towns. Among others things he saw his first Navahos: tall silent men with tall black hats. People from all the Pueblos were there: Santo Domingo, the largest and most conservative of the Keresans; Tewas from San Juan and Tesuque to the north; relatives by marriage from Santa Ana and even from the most distant Hopi colony of Moenkopi; anthropology students from Albuquerque who explained things to visitors—"A moiety is any division of a tribe into two complementary halves…" Right. It was part religious event, part local fair and market. The conservatives were always trying to cut down on the latter, the progressives were for expanding it: it was good for the pottery and jewelry business. The governor this year was a jeweler, so things were pretty open. Some traditionalists were agitating for the return of "the old dances." He was puzzled until it was explained that

in the past, once the day's native ceremonies were over, the Spanish people had a dance with a *mariarchi* band. The reactionaries wanted this back. The night before the dance, he had been alone in Joe's house, unable to sleep for the drums, like some Noel Coward character in the Far East. ("The drums! The drums! My God! Why don't they stop?!") A Kwirena in full regalia and face paint, carrying his staff with the eagle feathers at the top, came in suddenly, out of the dark.

There were two powerful societies, wrongly called Clown Societies by Anglos, which managed the ceremonies. The Koshare (*kusha'ri*) were the First Men in legend, the oldest of the ancestors, and their earthly representatives painted their bodies in black and white stripes, put dead corn husks in their hair, and did clown about. But their clowning was often deadly satire against those who offended Pueblo customs (just like the "skimmity-riding" in Somerset), and they were much feared for their "power." The Kwirena, who alternated annually with the Koshare, were a more dignified society, but both were in charge of the public rituals. This impressive, even spooky, Kwirena had come, with a pinch of cornmeal he left on the little shelf by the door, next to the holy water. When he saw the white man there, he spoke first in ritual Keres—a stilted, formal speech delivered, as it were, to the house: then he gave an informal message in Spanish. It had been a ritual summons to Joe who must serve as a singer, and to Andy and the ladies as dancers, for the Turquoise Kiva: the kivas danced alternate dances on the day.

The excitement and tension in the days before the event were palpable. There had been a dispute in which the crew cut had reared its, literal, ugly head. Several of the young men and boys who worked off the reservation had had crew cuts—to fit in with their off-reservation friends. The conservatives maintained that only those with the traditional long hair could dance—for only in the long hair could they tie the macaw feathers brought from Mexico. The long hair was the rain, as the gourd rattles were the sound of the rain, and the *tablitas*—crenellated headdresses worn by the ladies and girls, were the clouds. The *shiwana* would be offended by the crew cuts. (Why did he feel so at home with these people who should have been alien to him? It put Vogtie's crew cut in a new perspective.) But compromise was the order of the day: harmony must be preserved; the dance must go on.

It was spectacular. The men wore Hopi dance kilts with a whole fox fur dangling from the belt behind, and sleigh-bells and shell rattles at their ankles, evergreen twigs stuck into armbands.. They carried gourd rattles in the right hand and tiny bows and arrows in the left. The women wore black mantas, one shoulder bare, the high *tablitas* on their heads, and wands of yucca in their hands. Each kiva was painted with its own body and face designs, and the dancers included teenagers and youngsters down to children who could barely walk. The big drum with its zinging two tones was wielded by the younger, stronger men, and everyone waited to see them switch from the low-toned to the high-toned end without missing a beat; they always did it perfectly. They danced in two rows, sometimes moving forward, sometimes in facing lines, and the women danced behind the men, their shuffling stay-in-contact-with-the-earth steps contrasting with the high-stepping pounding of their partners. Lawrence's x-ray vision had been turned onto this difference, and drawn the inevitable Lawrentian conclusions about the sexes and their contact with the dark forces.

The older men, dressed in Mexican-cotton, loose clothes, and hung about with turquoise and silver jewelry and "medicine bags," were the chorus, as in a Greek tragedy, keeping close together and singing a commentary on the drama enacted by the dancers, drummers, and "clowns." (Francis Fergusson had noted this; Lawrence had totally misunderstood it.) Paul Trujillo, Joe's younger brother, who was the Kwirena Nawa—head of the Kwirena Society, led his members in their supervisory function. They were always moving in rhythm, bending and swaying (unlike the rigidly upright dancers) as they kept people in line, escorted weary little ones to the sidelines, picked up fallen paraphernalia. At the head of it all a young man carried the pole, a long flagstaff topped with feathers and hung with a fox fur. The significance of this pole was a secret. Diffusionists thought it came from Mexican—even Aztec—rituals, suggesting human sacrifice, as the macaw feathers came from southern Mexico, and the abalone shells from California and the Gulf. In pre-Columbian days the Cochiti made long journeys south and west to trade for these ritual items.

He knew he should be noting who did what with whom, when, and how, and he did. But mostly he was swept up in the relentless power of the drum, the thud-thud of the dancers' moccasins on the well-beaten earth of the plaza, the force of the singers pointing always to the clouds, the ancestors, the *shiwana*, who that morning had risen from the beautiful lake *wenyima* to prepare their visit. With the song they pulled them overhead, invoking the four cardinal points and their associated colors and animals; with eloquent hand gestures they eviscerated them to bring down the seed-generating rain. There was nothing wild or plaintive about this Pueblo religion, no mutilation and self-torture and pleas for pity as with the Plains (or the Penitentes for that matter.) These people knew the rules that governed human-divine relationships; they knew that if they carried out the ritual correctly, intently and with a "good heart," then the response would follow as night followed day. Faulty ritual, bad intentions, and the machinations of witches, could sabotage this otherwise inevitable sequence.

In the old days, the War Captains, after a trial by the Society heads, would have shot an arrow into the heart (into the two hearts) of anyone condemned for witchcraft. Some said it had happened secretly even within living memory. He looked at Epifanio, out there with his thin white hair over his shoulders (his granddaughters had spent the morning combing and brushing it), in best blue shirt and long earrings, singing earnestly in his blindness the song he had helped to compose. Could he imagine this gentle, wise, kindly man executing anyone? But he hesitated. There was a tough center to the sweet old fellow; he was adorable, but you wouldn't want to cross him. Epifanio, they said, and they were very quiet when they said it, had handled the scalp ceremony in those old days. He asked the blind teacher who said yes, this was true, and added seriously, "the scalps were fresher then."

The great dance over, the captains and the kings departed, he became involved in the ceremonies surrounding a "clan cure" for one of Epifanio's granddaughters. This involved adoption into clans other than her own, thus giving her the "many many mothers" José Dolores prophesied, that would ensure her health and well being. Finding her a house was part of the problem, and again, it was the lineage of matrilineal kin—her mother, mother's mother, mother's sisters and their daughters, and the brothers of these women (not their husbands), who had to make the arrangements. Other kin would help, willingly—Epifanio as her paternal grandfather for example, but the lines of ultimate responsibility were clear. And this was a society that had been declared hopelessly acculturated to "Anglo and Spanish patterns." The clan was "in decline" if not defunct, since it no longer had an economic function: it used to help members with harvesting, but now the Pueblo as a whole handled this as a collective enterprise, with the communally owned combine harvester. But he began to suspect that this "decline and fall of the clan" theory assumed certain things must be necessary to the clan that might well have been accidental functions. The clan was about marriage and children primarily, not economics. But he was so indoctrinated with the prevailing wisdom, that he still assumed he was dealing with dying institutions. Why else was he there except to study the end results of acculturation?

"Let the flow of fieldwork carry you along," Firth had said. Don't analyze as you go along; just get the facts. He was drowning in facts, but the language lessons kept him too busy to overanalyze anything but the grammar. It was coming, though, and he was able to recognize verb paradigms and predict forms: given the first-person singular non-future of a word, he could, having recognized its type, tell Epifanio the dual-to-plural future, for example. This was something the teacher never ceased to marvel at; he understood the principle, but there was an air of magic about it that he couldn't shake. How could you know a word that you had never heard before? Just pull it out of the air like that? But he was pleased. Along with the dollar would go a few cans of corned-beef hash, or a watermelon bought from a Spanish vendor. In return would come visits with families deep in the alleys of the village to which he was introduced, and which he would never have overcome his shyness enough to visit independently. There were no invitations: you just took along a few cans, and joined in the evening meal. This was inevitably a thin green-chili stew, usually with mutton: the ubiquitous meal of the native Southwest. He got addicted to the taste and for a while could not eat meat without the green chili. To wean the infants (very late by Anglo standards) the mothers rubbed chili peppers on their nipples.

There was a plague of grasshoppers that year and most other vegetables failed. When they had little else, families would just roast some peppers on a grill and put them in tortillas as sandwiches. His cans of spam were welcomed on these austere occasions; dear, wonderful, life-saving Spam. Once, they had a couple of rabbits the young boys caught in snares. He offered to gut and skin these large but rather stringy bunnies, calling on almost forgotten childhood skills. The families were suitably impressed. He would have liked to cook *lapin rôti, sauce moutarde,* but the unhappy animals were unceremoniously dumped into the green-chili pot, and it was spicy stew and fresh-made *tortillas* again. But so very, very good.

Despite it all there were moments of great loneliness. He wished his wife were there to share all this. She would come in a few weeks: she had to work to earn the air fare and the job only allowed a three-week holiday (she had negotiated for four.) The sheer bombardment of alienness (is that a word?) could sometimes overwhelm; but overwhelm with intellectual and emotional exhaustion; there were no vastations; there was no time for those emotional luxuries now. Yet despite these occasional feelings he couldn't help also thinking that in some curious way he was more familiar and at home with this culture than with the culture of Harvard/Boston, or the South he had passed through. It might keep hitting the senses like an alien Wonderland, and sometimes seem as mysterious and impenetrable as the Castle, but was Cochiti, despite the obvious cultural strangeness, all that different from an English village?

There were no matrilineal clans in Midsomer Norton, or Haworth, Diss or Thwaites Brow, but there were tight-knit long-established families that functioned similarly. If not clans they were definitely clannish. There were no moieties as such, but the division between Church and Chapel had the same effect. The calendar was still basically ecclesiastical whichever side you belonged to, with the great seasonal festivals being shared, and the spring maypole dances, and the village cricket games bringing everyone together. Harvest Festival was still the greatest event of the year in an agricultural society; a ritual going deep into the past, as Mr. Bullock and Sir James Frazer had educated him to understand. The Pueblo First-fruits Dance was the counterpoint of harvest Lammastide. Midsummer was enshrined in the English village's name, and it was at the summer solstice that Cochiti held its absolutely central Green Corn Dance. The Morris Dancers wore deer-head masks, and Jack-in-the-Green wore a body mask of greenery. The Mummers at Christmas with their fancy costumes, masks, and stilted performances in rhyme, could have been mistaken for a "ceremonial society." The Medicine Societies were as much men's clubs as religious organizations; again the village had those, as with the various pubs with their "regulars" and darts teams, the British Legion (Warrior Society) the Men's Choral Society—all with their Ladies' Auxilliaries, Pueblo style, down to the almighty Mothers' Union. Even the belief in witches was not altogether dead in wartime Somerset, and disliked old women still had the evil eye and turned cows barren and milk sour. The factions were almost exactly mirrored in the Farmworkers' Union (Labour) and the Conservative Club. The Cacique was the vicar, that was easy, but there was no real equivalent to the Squire: Pueblo leaders were elected or appointed by the Societies; there were no classes; all clans were created equal. But the parallels were striking.

Above all the great Hunt Society bound both of them as a people. The English villagers symbolically tamed nature (the horse), and triumphed over it (the fox.) There was less hunting in the Pueblo now than had once been common, but the Warrior/Hunt society still had pride of ritual place, and rabbits, deer, and turkey were still hunted with appropriate rituals. The young people in both places wanted more modern dances, resisted adult authority in a desultory way, and drifted about in unisex gangs, until puberty had them giggling and pairing: the milk-and-white, rosy-complexioned, fair-haired English wild-rose country girls; the sallow, black-haired, dark-eyed Deer Maidens of the desert Southwest. These young girls were beautiful in the Pueblo; it could look like an Italian film set between takes. Then, like their delicate English cousins, they married, had children, blimped out and went dumpy, but kept the friendly, open smiles. No. It wasn't all that different under the cultural skin. Why should it be? Redfield had said that a folk society was a folk society wherever it was found. Vonnegut, his pupil and disciple, preached the same doctrine, and even invented kinship-based societies for his utopias of the future. You could take it a degree further, for such correspondences—although more subtly disguised perhaps—existed between all small natural communities even in urban society: the working class ghettos in northern England for example, or the small towns in Ireland. These were people first, culture carriers second. The French perhaps had it right: existence did precede essence.

Kluckhohn unexpectedly turned up: he got a message from Santa Fe to come up there and hitched a ride with a family going in to sell things at the Palace of the Governors. Kluckhohn was on his way to his farm at Ramah near Zuni, and offered to take him through Navaho country. It was an offer impossible to refuse: like Firth offering a visit to Tikopia. They dined at Cerillos with a local celebrity, Fra Angelico Chavez: a Franciscan who was also a poet and writer; a youngish man, very bright and witty. Good company for a priest. He explained the Church's position on native rituals: they were "natural religion"—untutored men approaching God in an untutored but essentially innocent way. Their dances were not heretical, they were the way divinity was experienced in the world before the gospel news arrived; they were even pleasing to God so long as they were not obscene. Wasn't obscenity natural? No, said the wise friar, sex was natural; obscenity was the mocking of sex. Perhaps it was only making fun of sex? There could be enjoyment in sex, said the celibate, even fun, but this was a by-product of its procreative functions, and these should not be mocked, for they were sacred. He thought the intelligent Fra Angelico had his tongue just a bit in his cheek, but he saw how, with such a very Franciscan attitude, an accommodation was possible between the faiths.

The Navaho world was another thing. Its very vastness was a rebuke to human intrusion. It stretched over northern Arizona and New Mexico, and parts of Colorado and Utah: the Four Corners country where, at one spot holy to tourism, you could stand in four states with one foot. A Wonderland mixture of fantastic canyons, mesas and weird rock formations, overgrazed desert scrub and bare rock, it was never less than totally overwhelming. The very scattering of the Navaho across the land in search of scant pasture for their sheep reduced their impact, and they were aesthetically appropriate to their surroundings. They were tall people, with unsmiling faces and slow gestures. They couldn't have been more different from the Pueblos who were short, heavy-set people, and trod mother earth solidly with both feet, as though not wanting to lose contact. The Navaho were horse people and nomads at heart; they would have preferred to be hunters and raiders, but their very ferocity had been their downfall. As with the Plains Indians, the Anglos (and Spanish before them) needed to tame and domesticate the Navaho and their Apachean relatives (as in Cochise, Geronimo.) The Pueblos, carefully tending crops in their settled towns, were less of threat and could be left to their own devices. They rebelled only once (1680), and then hunkered down to the accomodation that Brother Chavez tacitly recognized, and that guaranteed their relatively undisturbed existence.

But the Navaho's were tough; they were there; they were the fastest-growing tribe in the U.S., with the biggest territory. The Cochiti were respectful of Navahos—even a bit afraid of them, but they basically found them strange and didn't trust them. Bad memories died hard, and intermarriage was unheard of. He thought it was a similar attitude to that of the English villagers towards Gypsies. Now he could judge for himself, superficially. For a start the Navaho were very dispersed; there were no villages. They were herders of sheep, and planted a little corn and chili. They had been the scourge of the settled Indian peoples who were not unhappy when Kit Carson rounded them up and subdued them. There was no pan-Indian feeling in those days.

He had the most expert guide, of course, who knew to wait a long time outside a *hogan*—the eight-sided hut facing always east towards the rising sun, before approaching. You must never do anything sudden. And you had to be careful not to upset the most basic taboo (after clan incest) and cause a man to see his mother-in-law. A man would risk death rather than break this taboo, even though marriage was matrilocal and men moved in with the wife's family, as in Cochiti tradition. Kluckhohn told of a Navaho man who drove his jeep off the road and crashed it as he covered his eyes at the sight of his wife's mother. Our impressionable ethnographer was once again amazed to find that an item from undergraduate "theory" classes—the correlation between matrilocal marriage and mother-in-law avoidance—was very real and taken for granted by very real people. But the scattering of people trying to raise sheep in this scrub-land was the difference. They too had matrilineal clans, but these were dispersed along with the *hogans*. When they had ceremonials—always healing rituals incorporating the famous sand paintings, which were a borrowing from the Pueblos, they had to bring people together from hundreds of miles around. But they did; the advent of the pick-up truck had actually increased their ceremonial activity: acculturation supporting the indigenous culture!

Their clans were deeply meaningful to them, Kluckhohn said, and they would never dream of marrying within the clan; same as Cochiti. They added the father's clan: you were "born to" your mother's clan, but also "born for" your father's, and marriage, or even flirting or dancing with its members was absolutely taboo. The misunderstanding of this was one of the worst pains suffered in the Indian schools. Navahos were reserved, intense, perhaps suspicious; perhaps they had reason to be. The women and children were not the open friendly Pueblo type, they were shy; the children particularly would never look you in the eye. They clung to their mothers' long skirts and only peeped out. The women sat outside, mostly weaving colorful rugs with traditional patterns that were becoming popular with collectors. The silver jewelry the men made was already famous. The babies were wrapped tightly and tied in cradleboards propped by the looms, where they spent most of their childhood. The Freudians had had a lot to say about that.

When K, asked a man the distance to the next outfit, he held up two fingers close together. Distance was indicated this way, one finger near, four fingers far away. K. explained that it meant that if you held the fingers before your eyes, you could see more with only one, less if you held up the whole hand: it was a kind of distance by perspective. K.'s fluent command of the excruciatingly difficult (for Anglos) language was impressive and depressing. Would he ever be thus with Keres? Not without a lifetime at it, and he only had a couple of summers in prospect at best.

There was other coming and going: to Taos and Picuris to see Roy. Picuris was a near dead Pueblo, and had its resident anthropologist ("Bernie" Segal from Stanford) so Roy was concentrating on child rearing in the Spanish village of Peñasco. Diane didn't like it there; she was tighter than ever. It surely wasn't New Jersey. He went back via San Juan to see a Comanche dance: stealing the enemy magic. Quickly to Jemez in the mountains—the most remote of the Pueblos. Lawrence based his Indians on Taos, but when the Woman Who Rode Away made for the remote town in the mountains, it could have been Jemez he had in mind. This all cut into his time in Cochiti, but K. had insisted he visit widely to get the impression of the whole area: he was in for the long haul, said K.; this would be a good investment of time. Was he? Would it? It looked like the drift was taking him that way. It wasn't what he had meant to do when he thought about the future; but then he never did think about the future. He thought only about how to get to the next foxhole, how to make the next spin on the roller skates, and this (to continue the mixed metaphor) was an intrinsically interesting *entrepôt* on the way to...?

Wife came, and the women took to her, and this helped enormously. As he followed her progress round the various female households, it became clear that even if the mother-daughter extended household was less in evidence now, the maternal extended family was still an intact unit. Since everyone lived within two minutes of everyone else, it scarcely mattered, except for sleeping, where exactly you were located in space. Just before they left, the ladies came up with a gesture that stunned him. Juanita and Old Juana said they wanted to adopt them into the Oak clan. (Could married people be members of the same clan? Yes, in the case of adoption, where you acquired "little clans" and the rules were different.) This meant a ceremony, like the healing ceremony, in which they had heads washed in yucca suds, were fed along with the other clan members, and were given new names. So far he had just been *shrutsuna,* Fox, so now they asked José Dolores to pick a new one. It was to be *kutstiwa*, Antelope Man (with that strange "u" sound made by keeping the lips straight rather than rounded.). In contrast to the heavy tread of Pueblo man, said Dolores, this man walked with a light, springy step, like the antelope. The children imitated him behind his back, they said, and laughed. Ariel was re-christened Mist Girl, *heyashitsa*, to suggest her ethereal nature, they said (in so many words.) Then they gave him a drum that Joe had made and it was given to him as a present from the Fox Clan, now officially his "father's clan." He had so admired the drums that the Cochiti were famous for making. He played it gently and sang one of the songs he knew:

> amu amu hawerena maatsi
> yuni yusi tyinyi nuka 'ri kachanoma
>
> peace, peace, all growing things,
> from over yonder to nearby the little rains are falling

So heads were washed, prayers were intoned, speeches were made by the clan elders, bowls of corn, beans, and chili were eaten. The men smoked cigarettes of native tobacco and a green weed, rolled in dry corn husks, and the smoke was blown in the seven directions—including up, down, and cen-

ter. He became light-headed and dizzy, and it all seemed unreal and to be
drifting away into a hollow distance. For a moment he was back again under
the whist table listening to the laughter of the uncles as they too began to
disappear. Then he heard, through that smoky distance, the clan children sing
a song they had made up:

> kowatsina kowatsina sow'kyenyi shrutsuna
> kowatsina kowatsina, sa'tyumshe kutstiwa
>
> hello, hello, my friend the fox,
> hello, hello, my brother antelope man

thus celebrating the transformation. Then everyone sang a goodbye song:

> kutstiwa hati kaku
> kutstiwa hati kaku
> in England, in England,
> ya hati kaku he-ne-yo
> ya-he-ne-yo ya-he-ne-yo
>
> Oh where is antelope man?
> Oh where is antelope man?
> In England, in England.
> Oh where is he? Tra-la-la.

The second verse was about his friend Joe:

> ahsona hati kaku
> ahsona hati kaku
> i kutyiti i kutyiti
> ya hati kaku he-ne-yo
>
> Oh where is Joe?
> Oh where is Joe?
> In Cochiti, in Cochiti.
> Oh where is he? Tra-la-la.

Through the six-eight beat—DUM-di DUM-di DUM-di, and the fog of
smoke, he tried to remember exactly who was there with whom, who had said
what, so he could note it later. He tried to remember how correct they had been
in their use of kin terms, calling all the members of the Fox clan "father" as
was proper for the father's clan. What had they called the women? He struggled.
It simply didn't matter right then; something had to give; he gave up and
laughed and sniffled and wallowed in the warmth. Juanita said, "you are my
son now, don't forget that." "You can never have too many mothers," he said.

The journey back is a bit of a fog itself. Big drum took up too much room
in the car, annoying Diane. Sunburn and mosquito bites terrorized him. He

rigged up a mosquito net for sleeping with some cheap gauze curtain material and a few whittled sticks, which caused some hilarity in the Colorado mountain campsites. They went through southern Illinois to see Chuck Lange. It was a crazy drive along roads that kept veering off at right angles. They had to be built that way, along the edges of the fields, because the ruggedly individualist farmers wouldn't let them cross the fields. Chicago, briefly, with a quick look into the Field Museum. In the large entry hall they had an ingenious device, thirty feet high, that was a row of transparent tubes with ping-pong balls dropping towards them from a chute. The balls fell randomly into the tubes, but the distribution, after they all fell, was a normal curve! He often thought that this marvelous machine should be placed at the center of every university campus—in every city for that matter. The properties of the normal curve were the secret of nature: one thing he had learned and retained.

After Chicago, Michigan to some relatives of Roy's living in a suburban community of friendly people who, like the Langes, overprotected their children and were proud of their community; but the women wanted to know what was wrong. The men had sharp-edged personalities and soundproof imaginations. They were only interested in money and golf and not rocking the boat, which, they figured, "academics" were all too apt to do. They reminded him of the "hard men" back in Yorkshire, whom he despised as philistines, but rather feared. They took no prisoners. The women were bland and monotonic and smiled all the time. His face ached with smiling back, but if you didn't smile they got anxious.

There was a dispute in the schools, where some zealots had decided that books about Robin Hood (pronounced "robinhood") should be banned because said Hood was a Communist. Was he really a Communist? He was a thief who supposedly gave away his loot. Not the same thing? Not really. Swell. And the Indians, were they communists? Should he praise them so to our vulnerable children? The Indians, he assured them, were simply cooperative amongst themselves—good neighbors; they were not disciples of Karl Marx. The ladies were reassured and pressed macaroni-cheese and meatballs on him. Passing from Michigan into Canada, seeing the still-flying Union Jack, he proudly announced that they were now under Commonwealth protection and would be OK with him. But the unsmiling border officials let the Yanks through with a nod, while they detained the British passport holders for an hour, to complete the immigration formalities.

The car broke down somewhere in western Massachusetts, and they took a bus to Cambridge. It actually felt good to be back: it would soon be fall with the fire-bright leaves, cool weather, football tailgating and term papers. They had a new apartment in Cambridge proper, near the Fogg Museum and only a walk from everything. It made life much easier; he even went to the Statistics lectures in the morning. Vogt handed him over to a new Instructor for "hands-on purposes." This was truly fortuitous, since it was the young Dell Hymes,

Amerindian linguist and headed to become the doyen of socio-linguistic studies, and a nice guy. He poured over the Keres notebooks and pronounced them "a very good start." He set the happy lad to comparing Keres with Hokan, Lakota, and Iroquois, since Sapir had said it was in that phylum. Most people could find no related language, so this was a big issue, as was the question of relationships among the various dialects of Keres, where again there was dispute. Excellent topic for a thesis said Dell: lexico-statistical comparisons as opposed to grammatical: which method worked better; were they compatible? To work! But wait: a major impingement looms; an impingement so major it is like a prideful monument in his memory, with the inscription:

Research Associate with Professor JOHN W. M. WHITING
in the Laboratory of Human Development, Graduate School of
Education, Palfrey House, Harvard University, 1958-9.

On the pedestal would stand, a bit shamefacedly, a short but muscular man (an ex-varsity wrestler), bald and white-haired, with a constant merry grin, like an oversized leprechaun. Johnnie (in whose case the diminutive was cheerfully appropriate) came from Yale and the Miller and Dollard school of social learning: the C & P attempt to take Freudian hypotheses, link them to methods of learning from stimulus-response theory, and test them with the cross-cultural method. The latter involved using material from a large sample of societies to look for statistical correlations between child-rearing practices (age of weaning, severity of toilet training, maternal overprotection...) and adult customs (severity of initiation, theories of disease, belief in witches...) The method had surprisingly been invented by the English (British) anthropologist Sir Edward Burnett Tylor in 1889. He called it the method of "adhesions"—correlations between customs like matrilocal residence and mother-in-law avoidance (positive), which he used to determine the possible evolution of customs. The beauty of the method was that it allowed for exceptions, which otherwise could always be used by the congenitally skeptical to scupper interesting generalizations. What mattered was the preponderance of cases, and the probability of even a low correlation being significant. It was what John Barnes had presented to him as a solution to the Frazer problem: it was a way of testing hypotheses; it was Popperean; it should be tried.

Why was the apprentice linguistic anthropologist involved in this tot-and-pots enterprise, that a year earlier he scoffed at, even ridiculed? For a start his scholarships were only for one year. After that, Vogt pronounced, you had to work for living in case you got lazy. True to his protective role, Evon Z. had found him half of what he needed as a Tutor in Social Relations at Leverett House. This did many things, including making him technically a member of the Harvard faculty. He could count it as his first appointment. These Tutor-ships were much coveted; they avoided the drudgery that went with being a Teaching Assistant, which involved a lot of work on courses with large numbers of students. He only had to meet once a week with the undergrads doing Soc. Rel. in the House, and to "be available" with regular "office hours" during the week. For this they gave him a nice set of rooms—had he been single he could have lived there, and expected him to dine in the House several times a week, and attend its functions. One of his potential charges was the young Aga Khan (Karim—call me Kim), who was a soccer star when he was not dodging the young women in white plastic raincoats from *Vogue* and *Cosmopolitan* who were always trying to bag him for an exclusive. But Kim was doing not Soc. Rel., but the fashionable, and for him more relevant perhaps, Oriental History.

The students in Soc. Rel. tended to be, not the young gentlemen from the prep schools (who did Literature and History) but rather the scholarship boys from middle-income suburban families, most of whom wanted the answers to hard social questions. "My best friend became a delinquent and is still in jail. I want to know why some people become delinquents." They don't, necessarily; they break the law, maybe only once, and do time. "Delinquent" is an act, not a personality type. But don't tell that to the criminologists, as he knew so painfully. But they were bright, earnest boys (or they wouldn't have been there, as the Dragon reminded him) and he enjoyed this mentorship. It brought him into contact with more undergrads and their affairs, like operas and plays. Ariel got to act in *The Three Sisters* and was the only player to get a good review. They helped with a production of Handel's *Acis and Galatea* after he had given a spontaneous counter-tenor rendering of *Ombra Mai Fiù* when asked if he knew the aria. Handel! Did he know?! (He also knew it came from *Serse*.)

Leverett House was a marvelous sandbox for intellectual grown-ups to play in. The Honorary Associates (as they called Fellows) were Cabots (Henry B.) and Rockefellers (David), but they never seemed to turn up. President Pusey gave a talk at the annual House dinner on the subject of President Conant. Conant had started an unheralded revolution when he single handedly began to turn Harvard from a gentlemen's college into a meritocratic university. The revolution was far from complete, but as Pusey extolled his predecessor's virtues, our own little meritocrat looked over his Soc. Rel. boys, so eager, so "socially mobile" (did Conant invent that term?—he certainly used it) and saw—what? He saw himself, and he saw that despite the Presidential platitudes this was nothing to do with equality: it was a way of forming an elite of talent, just as the welfare state was doing back home. Michael Young had pointed out how incompatible it was with equality in *The Rise of the Meritocracy*. What was a fault to Young, was a welcome environment to our aspiring philosopher king.

He had lunch with the other tutors every Wednesday, and talked to an arrogant and unpleasant biologist named James D. Watson. No one liked him, but "Jim" was onto the very basis of the chemistry of life itself—the interior of the gene, and he had amusingly sarcastic anecdotes about Cambridge (U.K.) Receptions had our busy boy meeting Associates Oscar Handlin, Perry Miller, and Eric Havelock, perhaps the best commentator on Homer ever. He found himself cornered with famous poet Archibald MacLeish, (Professor of Rhetoric and Poetry) arguing, not about poetry but about the rules of war and the meaning of *War and Peace*. He was with Prince Andrei: abolish the rules, stop taking prisoners, and the true horror of war would be accepted; its abolition would surely follow. MacLeish, and John Conway, the Master (Mrs. Conway was to become the first woman president of Smith College) firmly disagreed. MacLeish pointed to the genocide of the American Indian: an example of what happened without rules of war. Conway demurred, and said with the Indians it was "a case of us or them"; their vile customs, such as torture, had to be stamped out.

A real row was brewing, when they were distracted by the arrival of a commanding, handsome young man, who became the center of a circle of attention and handshakes. It was another Associate of Leverett, a Massachusetts senator, whom, they said, was certainly going to run for President. They were disappointed that his beautiful wife was not there; she was his greatest asset, they said. A nod and a smile was all our exiled ex-politician got. Could he remember feeling he was face-to-face with destiny? He could not honestly say so, but he did remember the young senator's compelling, firm, slightly quizzical gaze (his eyes were too close together), and he really did think: "This one could be President." The handsome politician may have been Boston Irish Catholic in origins, but he was (a) very rich and (b) a Harvard man. How could he lose?

Tom Lehrer was denied promotion by the Math. Dept. and staged a farewell concert in Memorial Hall, which overflowed into the Yard, and a near riot of protest. Math. was adamant, and the rebels had to be content with the loud singing of *Poisoning Pigeons in the Park* (It just takes a smidgen/ to poison a pigeon...) and *The Wild West is Where I Wanna Be* (Mid the cactus and the thistles/ I'll watch the guided missles (sic)/ While the old FBI watches me...) Fidel Castro (the Bearded One—yes, this is reportage, not an invention) came to celebrate the triumph of democracy over tyranny, and filled the football stadium with the enthusiastic and the curious, who smoked large Havanas in sympathy. The Freudians had their predictable things to say about the BIG CI-GAR thing (and the Cochiti ceremonial pole for that matter.) The political scientists were predicting a wonderful democratic future for Cuba. The Great Leap Forward was ruining China, but the fanatical Chinese still took time to ravage and suppress Tibet. Cyprus, under the flamboyant Archbishop Makarios, became independent. Imagine if he had done his national service there and been killed like the hero of his abortive play; he was suffused with another attack of total, black, bottomless futility. There was another emergency in Nyasaland.

Such digressions, such distractions, only born to bloom and drop. Browning (Robert, not the wife) won't help us here. While still drowning under the input and outflow of the first year of fermentation, the bemused culture carrier had gone, at Roy's urging, to a seminar (in the evening) on "Complex Mechanisms in Human Social Learning" held by Whiting, and "Dick" Solomon in the basement of that same Mem. Hall. Solomon was a Skinnerian psychologist, and "secondary reinforcement" was the order of the day. He and Roy had been to some of Skinner's lectures, but he tired of pigeon learning-schedules and heretically dreamed of Lehrer's solution—it just takes a smidgen... This Behaviorism seemed only to say that with enough bribes or tortures you could get organisms to do anything. They knew that in the Middle Ages. He had learned it from early Bertie. The question for him was not that bribery and torture could get results, but whether this was the model for how people really learned things that mattered. Language for example: the young man at MIT—Chomsky?—didn't think so. But Whiting and Solomon were impressive in their insistence on strict experimental and statistical methods. They really put conjectures to the test, and their hypotheses were really falsifiable—part of the fun was seeing where there was no correlation, and going over the "wrong" cases to see what might have been missed.

Murdock's creation, at Yale, of the Human Relations Area Files (HRAF) had made cross-cultural comparison easier. There were problems he could see with the "cross-cultural" method: Were cultures (plural) really things you could isolate, count and add up? How did you decide if, say among the Apache, you had one culture or six? There was a relativity problem: you couldn't put in the balance "Yankee culture" (data from the *Yankee City* series) with, say, the tiny island of Yap. Or could you? But these things were in principle solvable, and one was undeniably doing science. He didn't much like Solomon, who used curare to paralyze dogs, then gave them electric shocks, for some good Pavlovian reason, but Johnnie Whiting was a joy. The merry mentor infused even the most abstruse statistical episode with laughter and bawdy irreverence, and he was oh so very bright. Not since Popper-Ayer (and Bertie of course) had he felt he was really in the presence of genius: a genial, bubbling, trickster of a genius. They made the "auditors" take the course and do papers, even though there was no grade at the end for them. They didn't want passengers. So he went back to incest and began to look for examples in the animal behavior literature—male and female puppies and rats reared together were very reluctant to mate at maturity—and to string together a theory that suggested a "proximal motivation" for incest avoidance, and variation in sanctions.

Johnnie liked it, and Roy's paper, and invited them to be Research Associates at Palfrey House (NIMH grant.) Part of the work was to be the reading of old "ethnographies" (*Behind Mud Walls...*) and coding their reporting of child-rearing practices. You could look for incest examples, said Johnnie. Otherwise, come for lunch each day. The Palfrey House seminar was held over lunch, and one of the resident psychologists or anthropologists, or a visitor, led a discussion over hot dogs and hamburgers, cooked on the spot. Johnnie was a firm believer in this commensal pedagogy: it was hard to get too rigid or defensive when you were wiping ketchup off your chin, he figured. It almost always worked.

The Palfrey House Paradigm was strictly behavioristic: as the twig is bent. They had a student from the Oxford Psychology department, who quoted people like Tinbergen (his teacher), Lorenz and von Frith. He was universally dismissed as "one of those neo-instinctivists from Oxford." Our eager Res. Assoc. who was busy learning the ropes of this new paradigm to survive, was not about to raise doubts over things like IQ. While he retained a lingering belief in the power of the genes, he got on with the totally interesting job of heavy reading—something he was best at, after all. He was not so hot on the potty and weaning stuff—he missed things for lack of interest, so they put him on reading about initiation procedures: degrees of severity in the rites-de-passage of young adolescent males. He didn't care much about looking for the childhood antecedents—nasty stuff done to boys in cultures where they had grown up with the women and had a "maternal identification" problem. But he liked spelling out the details of sub-incision—slitting the urethra—to the Freudians. Castration anxiety? We think so.

He was, however, interested in initiation for its own sake, and this was a way to get a soaking of information about it. They were, he told the lunch-munching afficionados, going through a typical initiation process themselves, in which all kinds of pain was inflicted, but which had the predictable effect of having the candidates identify with their tormentors, and, what is more, willingly inflict the same pain on the next generation. It didn't matter much what the content of the initiation was—it could be genital mutilation or construing dead languages; what mattered was that the pain was inflicted and that the boys understood who was boss. The slicing of the genitals made its own pretty direct point: "negative reinforcement" was, as Solomon and Skinner had taught, a powerful tool of learning—and remembering. He only lost them when he revealed that he took Freud's theories in *Totem and Taboo* seriously. Even the Freudians didn't want that ugly-monster to rise from the intellectual swamp. He would bide his time.

The second year was not so oppressive, given that his work for Johnnie supplied the equivalent of two courses each term (semester.) He had to take the "Fieldwork Seminar" in common with the other second- and third-year students. This was Douglas Oliver's province—no one called him "Duggie" or even "Doug." Dr. Oliver was a formal man with a pipe, mustache, tweed jacket, and Anglophile manner. His book *A Solomon Island Society*, was a great favorite locally, because, they said openly, it disproved the assertion (who made it?) that only the British could write ethnographies. It was a fine example of the genre, but he still thought the superiority of British accounts lay in the theory behind them, not in the writing style. Meyer Fortes wrote the best ethnography by far, but the English of it was awful. No matter. He gave his paper on the Cochiti and the state of clans and kinship etc. He had been in limbo since his early pats on the head, and his fellows suspended judgment until he had "demonstrated his fieldwork skills." Oliver said in class, and wrote on his paper, "Very impressive in both observation and analysis." Stock rising again? Absolutely.

But Oliver didn't like "the stuff about kinship terms" so he went back to Hymes and Friedrich for help and consolation. Dell said he must go back to the Southwest and would work on securing a grant. The Laboratory of Social Relations (Vogtie) had a slush fund for students who didn't have outside sources. Dell would have to be the "principal investigator"—a device to allow the money officially to go to the advisor who would then employ the indentured initiand. Fine. Whatever it took. But he blew the Oliver course: they had to do a "theory" paper as well as the fieldwork presentation, and he rushed through a brief, almost insulting, paper, since he wasn't interested enough to work on it—nor did he have much time. He was genuinely shocked when he got his only, but well-deserved, B+ (not even a B++.) It was a lesson, but he was not sure at this point that he was sufficiently under control to learn lessons.

He was falling apart a bit. While Johnnie's courses grouped some effort, and he was almost entirely at Palfrey House (Divinity Avenue, past the Peabody Museum, whose library they raided daily for the old stuff,) physical exhaustion, extremes of climate, lack of sleep, too much alcohol, serious eye-strain—all took their emotional toll. He needed to stop and recoup, but you didn't get to stop, even pause. Relaxation was still the same grad. student drinking and whining sessions. Someone actually cracked completely and beat Kluckhohn over the head with a rolled-up newspaper. The natives were definitely restless. K's son Richard (Dick) was a Palfrey House student, and had had his own problems: shooting someone when selling bibles in the South—details differed with the teller. He was a Freudian fundamentalist and destined for fieldwork in Ethiopia. He did not appreciate jokes about "Haile Selasie Come Home" and the like, but he did accept the parting gift of a Calypso:

> You're goin' away, but not for ever.
> Dickie you're goin' to Ethiopia,
> Nevertheless your friends all hope ya
> Will come back again, tell us all about it.

But fun and games apart, he was wilting and doubting. Of course, go back to the Southwest, to his Cochiti: anything for that, so keep working, keep surviving. He worked too hard on his weekly tutorials. The boys had been to Vogtie's lectures on kinship, which left them baffled and nervous. What did all the hand-out diagrams on Hopi and Zuni kinship mean? What the hell was it all about? Vogtie just gave the abstract stuff about matrilineal kinship: there was no sense of where such an institution came from or why it should be that way. To be fair, no one anywhere did much better. Kinship systems apparently fell from the sky onto societies, and you just had to learn them like electrical wiring systems. They were the way they were because that's the way they were. Even the mathematical Roy confessed himself baffled. The British Social Anthropologist manqué insisted it was only because kinship was poorly explained. "Then how would you do it?" Roy asked.

So he tried to start from simple ecological premises and examples: the patrilineal kinship of Australian hunters, versus the logic of going matrilineal among the planters of the Southwest. In each case he got them first to understand the local grouping: paternal extended families versus maternal, and why the latter were hard to operate in a nomadic hunting setting (although the Apache managed it.) He went to the Utes and Shoshone (Julian Steward) for an example of sister exchange leading to cross-cousin marriage, and showed how both patrilineal and matrilineal kinship were implicit in the resulting system: which way it ultimately went was probably linked to those crucial ecological factors. It made sense to the desperate Leverett House boys, and they begged him to type some of the basics out and have them duplicated and circulated, like the French *polycopie* system. He couldn't disappoint these boys, who were his friends as much as his students, so he complied, but it took a lot of time, typing (he was a bad two-finger typist) on those masters for the ink-messy ditto machine. Once that was done they appealed again: we just can't get this statistical stuff right, we don't understand the lectures, the book isn't helpful, would you...? He did. When asked, say yes. Dance boy, dance!

One half-term break took him to Plymouth, Mass., to see the famous rock. It had either been moved or wasn't the actual rock, or something, but it was there as a revered totem object. Obeisance was duly paid, both to the rock and the Puritan tradition which still dominated to the point where even leisure and enjoyment had to be worked at and justified. He liked Mencken's definition of Puritanism: the haunting fear that someone, somewhere, might be happy. It seemed to be changing, but he had the feeling that the newly emerging "counter culture" (still at the Beatnik stage) would be driven to work with Puritan seriousness at its fun and games. But he took heart from Cole Porter: if the current Puritans tried to stem change, "Instead of landing on Plymouth Rock/Plymouth Rock would land on them." But anything did not go. Unable to sleep, he left the motel during the night to walk along the road by the sea. Screeching brakes, flashing lights and sirens announced the arrival of at least three police cars. Guns were leveled, incomprehensible orders were barked (hit the ground with what? assume what position?), and his bafflement was taken as "resisting an officer…" He was roughly searched and even more roughly handcuffed. He thought of demanding to see the British Consul, but it seemed out of place, and he continued his "must be some mistake" mantra until, finally, at the police station, they accepted who he was and what he was doing. There had been a prowler about who might have been responsible for burglaries and attacks. "No one walks about at night," they told him, when he insisted he was just "out for breath of fresh air." But his innocence must have shone through, and his accent as usual did the trick; they drove him back, gently deposited him, and told him to stay indoors. They didn't apologize; he didn't insist.

The only other real break was a visit to Wheaton College to do a staged reading of *Under Milk Wood*. This was organized by Bill-the-Fencer and his undergraduate friends. The Wheaton girls "needed men" they explained, laughing, and added the Harvard adage: "sleep Wheaton, marry Radcliffe." He was recruited because he could do the Welsh accents. The others could only manage a kind of Brooklyn-accented Cockney, which they seemed to think was a universal British working-class speech. Non-academic Americans would often, when they heard he was "British," brightly announce something like "Pip pip and toodle-oo!" or "Jolly good show, ta-ta, and 'ow are yer mate?" Sort of mixture of Colonel Blimp and Stanley Holloway. Then they would smile an expectant smile and look intently for a response. He never knew what to do or say. "Thank you very much"? "That was very nice, do it again"? What? The Wheaton girls, all healthy, well-groomed WASPS from well-heeled backgrounds, didn't do this. They were smilingly polite (oh how they smiled), loved his accent (of course), and went into rhapsodies over his Dylan-Welsh. He read (from ingeniously arranged and lighted windows in an otherwise dark stage) several of the parts. He sang the appropriate songs, ("When I was a lad and in my prime/I worked as a chimney sweep…") and rolled out the innuendoes about Organ Morgan ("organ, organ, all the time with 'im.")

The girls applauded and they all dined in the splendor of colonial architecture and old-money charm. The place reeked of wealth, from the fine wood floors and the reflective table silver, to the ancestral portraits and lavish upholstery. They had some male teachers and were looking to expand in Anthropology, because, said the Katherine Hepburn-style president, of its "horizon-expanding vision." Well, he could do vision if he had too. But the girls were almost upsetting in their air of female luxury, with their perfect figures, lightly perfumed hair, and soothing manners. They gave two of these discreetly scented creatures a ride to Boston. The car was dark and overheated and he sat crushed in the back seat. She put her hand under his coat and whispered alarming things in his ear while she licked it. Her over-washed hair—roses and lilacs?—brushed his face, and he was mesmerized with the words. These nice, well-brought-up girls, said those things, thought those things, did those things? "But I'm married," was all he could manage. "All the more attractive. It's a challenge. Why don't we...?' This was not something that should happen to a British Social Anthropologist of visitor status and professional purpose. But it opened up thoughts of possibilities he had to suppress—and probably sublimate pronto. He had been reading Jack Kerouac (*On The Road*), Nabokov (*Lolita*), and even Truman Capote (*Breakfast at Tiffany's*), and he had an uneasy feeling that something was going on in America that he was failing to appreciate. Things were coming apart at the seams; the whole world was unstable, and the newly proven theory of continental drift was more than a metaphor. Was there a social tectonic shift in the offing? Was the Wheaton girl a freak encounter with New England's only collegiate nymphomaniac? Or was the "sexual culture" undergoing a frightening change while he wrestled earnestly with Keresan phonemes and Apache kinship terms?

But wrestle he did. They were interested in a lot of things at Palfrey house, the enduring tyranny of the super-ego among them. "Guilt versus Shame" was a big issue. It was all to do, of course, with socialization, and perhaps above all with the presence or absence of a father figure to do the appropriate rewarding and punishing in the right balance to produce that still small voice. Kids raised without fathers were more likely to cheat on tests; societies where boys were raised with mothers were more likely to have fierce male-initiation ceremonies. The implications of this for black Americans were not really appreciated at the time. Members of the local black community were simply seen as "subjects" for such experiments, since (a) they were available and needed the money, little as it was, and (b) they were then more varied on the "absent father" issue than whites and so provided control and experimental groups. To be fair, it worked with both white and black subjects, except there was an observer effect: white boys cheated less readily if the experimenter was a white male.

This interested him as a diversion from his frantic and massive reading and coding, since it went to the heart of his problem about incest: it was not so much prevented as *avoided*. Like the impulse to cheat: some people had it and couldn't resist it; others had it but could resist it; yet others didn't seem to have it—at least not strongly. Thus incest could be punished (or "subjected to negative sanctions" as they said) for all kinds of reasons, but most of the time most people did not do it, not because of sanctions, but from either internal controls (the "impulse control" that was the basis of guilt—and shame for that matter) or from genuine repugnance: they didn't want to do it. He began to reformulate his theory, such as it was, as a theory of the mechanisms of avoidance and their provenance, rather than the old chestnut of "incest taboos." There was a possible connection: where people were strong on avoidance, were the taboos less strict? Cross-cultural coding and testing might help. He was in the right place.

He was up against the problem as posed by Frazer and Freud: if people naturally avoided incest, as Westermarck said, then why were there fierce sanctions against it? Well, first of all there weren't always fierce sanctions, and second, sanctions were ambiguous regarding people's motives. Most people did not want to commit murder, but as long as a few did, we had to have serious sanctions against it. Westermarck had said this in effect, but he was ignored, and the Frazer-Freud position was established as an orthodoxy, accepted by Lévi-Strauss among others vocal on the subject. Our intellectual knight-errant was going up against a big-time establishment in taking up the gauntlet for Westermarck, based largely on Johnnie's observation that young brothers and sisters often engaged in near erotic play which, since it could not be consummated, ended up in frustration, anger and tears. Enough of this, and negative reinforcement would do its inevitable work. Wonderful! In any case he reckoned he could reconcile the two sides, but this was to involve a neat paradox, a kind of parody of human good intentions: the harder you tried to prevent incest from happening, the more likely you were to provoke a desire for it.

Johnnie suggested he transfer his registration from Soc. Rel. to Education. He could actually transfer most of his Soc. Rel. credits, and there was no fieldwork or statistics requirement. Take the minimum required courses in History, Theory, Psychology and Philosophy of Education, write up the incest stuff as a thesis, defend it in an oral exam, and he could have an Ed.D. (Doctor of Education) in another semester. Free and clear by Christmas. But he couldn't. To get this in he would probably have to give up a return to Cochiti, and that he couldn't countenance. Johnnie's point was that he could get out from under all the Soc. Rel. stuff, get a job, and then pursue his Linguistics or whatever he wanted. But yet again, he simply couldn't face Vogtie and Kluckhohn with such a proposition. They had got him there, supported him, been so damn nice to him. He couldn't do it. Better no degree than that. Roy discouraged him too. An Ed.D., while a genuine doctorate, was not well regarded by the profession. It would not even be a degree in anthropology, and a job might be that much harder to find. He was in a whirl. He would have liked to get out, to have more autonomy, not to have a face a barrage of stuff he didn't want to do. But he had obligations to fulfill, and what real alternative did he have but to plug ahead? His Micawber-like confidence in something turning up was beginning to fail him, when…

Letters out of the blue: the one from the Dean at Leeds suggesting he might like to do Economics; the one from Cornell that had him here in the first place; now this one from his former Criminology teacher. Terrence Morris, he of the friendly advice and interest, was still a lecturer at the LSE, and had heard of what he thought was a perfect job prospect. The University of

Exeter (in Devon—not far from Midsomer Norton) wanted to find someone to teach Sociology "with special reference to Social Anthropology"—preferably someone with "some experience of fieldwork." Further, Sociology at Exeter (old as a college, new as a full university) was within the Department of Philosophy, and the head, Dan O'Connor, was one of the Penguin philosophers: the heroes of his agnostic youth. O'Connor believed that linguistic philosophers should actually know some linguistics, and would welcome an anthropologist with these interests. His way back into Philosophy? The dream was not dead? Was there really a God? Was the non-existent deity stretching out a hand and arranging these things? He replied to Morris by return, but felt bound to add that he would have to clear this with his supervisors and didn't know if he could make it for the Michaelmas (Fall) term. Reply: Fall term or forget it: they needed to fill the post.

Decisions again. Vogtie was appalled. You have done so much, now to leave without a degree—and how could they offer you a job when you didn't have a degree? Vogtie did not understand the English system. I have a degree, he sputtered, a First Class Degree: I was first in the class, and I was a State Scholar. My two years at Harvard and the eight months in the field, are extra experience, but Assistant Lecturers were appointed without PhDs—some never got them. Vogtie couldn't understand; that's how it is with cultural differences. No wonder the British didn't know anything, he muttered, and got by on native intelligence and good writing. The anxious philosopher-anthropologist-sociologist lecturer wannabee tried to placate. He would still do all that was required for the MA (or AM) which was all the requirements for the PhD except the thesis and its defense. No way, said Vogtie. These were still the days of the "terminal" MA. There was no separate MA course as such. They gave you the MA when you had satisfied all those requirements, but you got it along with the PhD. If you passed, but not high enough to be allowed to go on, then they gave you an MA and threw you out. Thus an MA on its own was always "terminal"—a mark of Cain, a brand of failure. No way was Vogtie going to allow that. The initiate was stubborn: if I pass the requirements I can claim it, he insisted. Do that and you'll never work in the US, said the Sheriff. But I've told them I'll have an MA, he wailed. Untell them, said the Marshall. It was a high-noon standoff; he lost to the incumbent.

Why was he always in these frustrating, convoluted situations? Why did he create his own rabbit hole into his own absurd Wonderland? Why could he not just do the straightforward thing: take the damned exams, get the damned degree or whatever, press on? Why was he always trying to get around The Castle rather than just straight into it? Why did he never seem to understand what the grim judges wanted of him? This was not the fault of any inquisitors; he brought it on himself. So Roy reminded him of Freud: "The unconscious is diabolical."

Thus he railed against his submarine self, but he knew the old guy was right: he had decided his course of action at some level of consciousness some time ago. If not, Morris decided it for him. The argument: you could stay there another two or more years and get the doctorate, but then you would still need a job offer; you can't stay in the U.S. (student visa didn't allow it) and you are not likely to get an offer in England as good as this again for a while. Duncan Mitchell, the head of Sociology at Exeter, impressed by his fieldwork and two impending publications (more later) clinched it by offering a full Lecturer position: skip the assistant grade—it was the U.S. "tenure." They wanted him; they really wanted him! Done. He would do the return to Cochiti anyway. Vogt said: keep your options open, you can always come back and complete "the degree." Sure, Marshall, of course. But he knew he was handing in his badge and gun. Again Morris had the answer: register for a London University external PhD; as a first-class honors graduate you do not need to be in residence, you just need to submit a thesis. You can write up the Indian stuff for that, said his wise friend, and not lose time, money or status. Something had turned up. And he remembered that H. G. Wells, late in his famous life, but anxious for academic recognition, had taken advantage of the same clause and submitted a thesis as "H. George Wells" to try for anonymity. He got his degree; it augured well.

The great thing now was that he could relax, enjoy his teaching, work on his linguistics, and do a decent job for Johnnie. Publications? Hymes had put him in touch with the editor of the *Journal of American Folklore*, who wanted something on "contemporary folklore" in the Pueblos. He had an idea, but it would need the return trip to flesh it out. The New Mexico Pueblos had a well-kept anthropological secret: a baseball league. The game had been played since the 1920s, but it spoiled the "primitive" image, and no one had published about it. Lange, serious ethnographer that he was, had included photos and some details of the teams in his ms. But Cochiti went further: it had two teams, and they competed with each other in the league. This was so contrary to the accepted view of the "non-competitive" Pueblo "ethos"—promulgated by Ruth Benedict, that something needed to be said. The Cochiti had asked him, when he came back, to be an umpire for "friendly" games, since he would be impartial. He knew nothing of baseball (clearly a version of English rounders—although you couldn't say that) so he went to a few House games, and even saw Ted Williams, in his prime, play at Fenway Park. He wore his Canadian baseball cap, to the amusement of the Boston Red Sox crowd, which shouted "aboot! aboot!" at him; he didn't know why. Distinguish between a ball and a strike? Yell "Yer Out!!" and make the appropriate violent arm gesture? He could do that. And he would get the essential "publication." This, plus Lange wanted "A Note on Cochiti Linguistics" as an appendix to his book; length was no object. Here was the chance to do his linguistic thing handed on a platter. Things turned up. Friedrich and Hymes were pestered and patient. Lay it out, then go back and check it all, several times, they told him. He would, he would.

Vogtie was calling in the markers; he was doing to the impatient ethnographer what he had done to Chuck Lange. V. had a favorite undergraduate— "brightest kid I've ever taught"—who wanted to go West to do his honors thesis. Take him to Cochiti. No can do; it would ruin everything. Take him anyway, no refusal, no way out. He would meet the boy there. But he would have to live in Peña Blanca and come as a visitor to the Pueblo. The boy spoke Spanish well, was a Catholic and could serve as an altar boy, so why could he not make a survey of the Spanish village? It had such close ties to Cochiti that one should look for reciprocal influences. The boy was actually pleased with this scheme, and a reluctant Vogt accepted the alternative. The reluctant mentor actually liked the kid, who was not one of the gilded youths, but another Soc. Rel. scholarship boy who was not very tall, and who was bothered by this in what he called "this culture that overvalues height." The kid had learned the language at least.

Vance Packard wrote *The Hidden Persuaders,* but the grad students said they weren't ever fooled by advertising. He was enormously impressed by a book that never seemed to get great attention, *On Shame and the Search for Identity.* Helen Merrell Lynd (wife of Robert, both of *Middletown* fame) seemed to have tapped some essences, and anticipated the "self-esteem" movement's excesses. But these United States were not ready for this, and preferred *Goldfinger* and *Naked Lunch.* David Reisman had come to Harvard over the bitter objections of many of the sociologists, who thought *The Lonely Crowd* a piece of impressionistic pop-science. But it was famous, and, complained the purists, Harvard was indecently obsessed with fame. They had a car by now, a 1949 Ford with a sun-visor and a new plastic seat covers from Sears. Selling up their belongings, including a new-fangled VHF radio, they dumped their books and clothes at Roy's apartment and set of for New Mexico accompanied by mother-in-law.

Most of what happened on the journey is mercifully blocked from memory. Ma-in-law was actually pretty game for a timid and genteel English widow, but he hated backseat driving, and two thousand miles of it was a nightmare. She was endlessly curious but her questions were deeply trivial: "Why do they have such thick cups?" "Why are the baths so small?" "Why do they eat their food like four-year olds?" "Why don't they say please?" When deputized to ask for gas, she would go into a kind of Miss Marple fugue: "I say my good man, if it's not too much trouble, I wonder if you could possibly give us…?" His interruption: "Fill 'er up with reg'lar"—painfully learned, was painful to the old lady in its seeming rudeness. But they had to get the gas, and get on to the Grand Canyon via Colorado this time, from Silver City to Cripple Creek through Phantom Canyon. She wanted to see the Canyon, and what harm? See where Spider Woman lived. It defied all the adjectives, so we'll skip them. You know them by heart. They saw Indians, mostly Navaho, whom she equated with Gypsies, and couldn't otherwise figure out what they were.

She was to fly back, so for a few days they lodged her with the Jays in Peña Blanca. The Jays were Santa Fe socialites from back east who had a farm outside the village. Nelson was a Harvard graduate, N. C. was from Princeton (town not college) and her odd name, which was just the initials, nothing else, came from her father who had flown the first two-man flight across the Atlantic in the N.C. (Naval Craft) something or other. (It's in the National Aeronautical Museum.) Some Cochiti worked for them, hence the contact. The farm was a haven, but one that made him guilty. He should not flee from his people to the wonder of this fantasy hacienda with its lawns, fountains, peacocks, gourmet food, fine wine and records of everything by Bach. To be fair he tried to limit the visits, but the Jays liked the company. Their adopted daughter had come from Ireland via the Leslie family, and there were hints about her connection to the daughter of a famous Prime Minister. Their big house in Santa Fe—where the annual horse show was held on the rolling lawns—had a hotel-sized pool with a trapeze over it. N. C.'s father had made her suitors swing from the trapeze and drop into the deep end. Those who didn't were not, like the princes in *Turandot*, executed, but they could forget about N. C. It was the stuff of wonderland, but his Puritan soul wouldn't allow itself to be distracted, and having got serious sunburn on his unprotected skin at the famous poolside, he stuck to his anthropological last like the good little cobbler he was.

Baseball went well enough. He bluffed at his umpire thing, but the tension between the two sides (Redskins and Braves) erupted in witchcraft accusations, and it became very unpleasant. He got a taste of this dark side of Pueblo life. They didn't kill witches anymore, but they clearly would have liked to. These were scarcely the serene Apollonian Indians of Benedict's fantasy. In theory witches were born that way: they had two hearts. In practice accusations were made against those one disliked, but they were not made lightly, and mostly not openly. There was only muttering and suggestion, because today there could be no trials, with evidence of owl feathers, the witches' favorite weapon. The modern Catholic Church, while perhaps not disbelieving in witchcraft, had in practice abandoned its own campaign; it frowned on the whole business. And the Indians knew that they should not openly give Anglos the chance to accuse them of "savage" practices. They still performed medicine society cures, where the theory of disease said that it was caused by witches stealing the patient's heart. The doctors would rush out in the night, fight with the witch, capture it, bring it back screaming into the house, lit only by firelight, shoot it with magic arrows, restore the heart, and so heal the patient. All great psychodrama, and very effective, he thought, for psychosomatic illnesses at least.

Involvement in the baseball games, however, exposed the fault-lines in the social geology. It showed, to his amazement rather, that the classic analyses of his anthropology classroom were spot on: accusations revealed the basic tensions in the social structure. He looked carefully at the kin connections of the two teams, and found two constellations of clan and kiva membership to be the basis of the feud. They had led to the formation of the teams in the first place. The annual games (double header) had been banned by the council for some years, because of "trouble." They put them on again this year. He didn't umpire because these were official league games. It was a near fiasco. "Cheating" had become an understood synonym for witchcraft, and in the face of an unexpected upset by the underdogs, the supposed partiality of the umpire, and natural disaster (dry wind and sandstorm), the game was barely finished without a fistfight. But he got his article. The Governor said the games must be banned again, but no one believed it. "Governor" was an office invented so that the foreigners would have someone to deal with— they expected a "chief" but the Cacique could not taint his ritual purity with such matters. A Governor was elected annually by the council, and on his installation he had to make a show of resistance and be installed kicking and screaming. How well the Cochiti understood the basic flaw of elective politics: those who actively seek office are the last people who should be entrusted with it. One Governor, having been dilatory in his duties, was made to repeat his year in office as a punishment.

Although he could not attend the secret Kachina dances, he found some of the men were not averse to discussing them. They had described the details of the masks to Chuck Lange. They reasoned that the knowledge should be preserved rather than dying with them, and any case, Father Demarest had published most of the details anyway. After a visit to Zuni he drew some Mudhead figures in the dust, and this provoked long discussions of the meaning of the Mudheads and their relation to the Koshare. Both dated from the beginnings of time and were representative of the first Pueblo Indians. Both were satirists of human life and savage critics of human folly. He could not but ask if they really believed their ancestors came up through a reed from an underworld, spilling out the Koshare into this middle earth, the origin place now represented by the earth-navel (*sipapu*) in the kivas. Your people believe they were made from dust in a magic garden, they replied. Scientists don't believe that. What do they believe? That we were originally a kind of ape, and that we changed slowly into human beings over millions of years. That, they said, is a good legend. The ape was like cheetah in the Tarzan movies? Yes, a chimpanzee. Cheetah is very like a man in some ways, one said, but he gibbers like a witch; perhaps witches are a kind of reversion to the animal ancestor? No, said another, remember the Mudheads only hoot and gibber. Perhaps the first people were apes and did not have proper speech, just as the scientists say. No one says the legends are the whole story; perhaps there is this missing piece of the puzzle. It was agreed.

He was driven constantly back to his Frazerian questions: the ones that would not go away. He could see why these little communities, when isolated and alone in their pre-Columbian innocence, would have needed religion to help get them through the day—or the year, or eternity. Rain was the life-blood, but it was uncertain. Every corn plant had to be hand tended and watered. The irrigation ditches bringing water from the Rio Grande had to be constantly maintained. Drought could savage and destroy everything, forc-ing the abandonment of towns and people to move hundreds of miles in search of water. Anything you could do to turn the odds in your favor would stick and survive and be elaborated. Would you not look longingly to the clouds and wish they really were your kind, dead parents and ancestors, who could be cajoled and sung to and beseeched? And would you not need some explanation of the inevitable evil, and would not witchcraft supply it?

Clouds in the desert sky were scarce; they were little wisps and clusters most of the time, only gathering together in majesty and force when, as the mystical Eagle, the thunderbird trailing its tail, they formed a massive thun-dercloud. If the prayer and fasting, and the songs and dances, even *mostly* ended in some rain clouds forming, then at least you could feel in some kind of control over a world otherwise unacceptably uncontrollable. They needed their religion; it pulled together everything in their lives and made sense of it. We, of course—we of Western science and rationality—no longer needed it. Frazer had made the call: science would replace religion, as religion had replaced magic. We didn't need it, but many of us seemed to need the elusive something that science could not provide: to give us reassurance in the face of the many perils and dangers of this night…

This was a one hundred percent vegetation religion, and its ceremonies were vegetation ceremonies (the hunt ceremonies being there only as memo-ries.) Every detail of the agricultural cycle was writ large in ritual (Meyer Fortes' phrase.) And these were a religious, not a magical people. That Frazerian distinction came alive. There was nothing like the African or Polynesian intense working of spells, oracles, and mumbo-jumbo. The devotion to prayer sticks was positively Buddhist; but the magic was absorbed into religion, and the doctors in the kivas performed tricks with wands and forced-growth plants to mimic effects in the world—like the Gardens of Adonis. The witches were a supernatural conspiracy, but with human allies. These allies were not sorcer-ers, though. They were born that way; it was predestination (in theory: in practice they were people you didn't like.) Appeal to the gods and the cloud ancestors was at the heart of it. Witchcraft helped to understand why it often failed and the rains did not come. It was poetic, melodic, physically beautiful, and appealing in an aesthetic way. It was their theater, opera, art, and enter-tainment. And it was like a window into the Neolithic age: the first planting, pottery, weaving, irrigation communities, some of which, like Çatal Hüyük, in Turkey, actually looked like a Pueblo village. You weren't supposed to think this way, but he couldn't help it.

He also couldn't help thinking about the proposal to build a big dam on the Rio Grande just above the village. It would create a long lake which would attract tourists, and since it was on the reservation, the tribe would have all the concessions and make untold amounts of money. The progressives were happy, but the traditionalists knew this would push them all over the edge into the Anglo world. Why dance, sing, fast and pray for rain when millions of gallons of water sat there for the taking. They would continue some of their public dances, probably (the tourists liked these), but the heart would be gone out of it. They would not be rituals any more, just empty ceremonials. This is what Joe and Epiphanio feared, but they also knew that progress was inevitable, and that this intense, beautiful little world of theirs might not last.

Since the first visit someone had brought a little black-and-white television, which had become the favorite novelty. They used it to watch baseball games, and movies. Most of the other shows were unintelligible, and the movies were treated as miracle tales. Apart from Tarzan, who fascinated them, they particularly liked Westerns, which they thought were great fun, especially when Apaches were shown wearing war bonnets. The boys would pull him in to watch as some pseudo-Sioux, with blankets thrown over saddles to mimic bareback riding, yodeled and hollered insanely while attacking a wagon train. "Look, look!" they cried, "real Indians! real Indians!" He had found a copy of Adolf Bandalier's *The Delight Makers*, (a name for the Koshare.) It was an inspired novel about ancient Pueblo life, set in Frijoles Canyon, with a great plot including war with the Tewa, and details taken from Cochiti life as Bandalier had seen it in the twenties. They had taken him to *tyu'onyi* to plant prayer sticks in the cliff-house Kiva there, in the shadow of Los Alamos. He read parts of the book to them, and some of the literate ones read it themselves. Why couldn't Hollywood make a film of this? "Because we're not real Indians," they told him.

Vogties's protégé was going great guns in Peña Blanca, where the Jays looked out for him, and where he had done a complete survey of households, and ingratiated himself with the priests as a good son of the Church. The good fathers opened up the records of birth, marriage, death and baptism for the Pueblo, and there was a treasure-trove of information on kinship that would have taken months of work to elicit otherwise. The priests tried to prevent marriage within the "forbidden degrees" as "contrary to the law of nature as well as the law of God," one told him. It didn't work since the Indians who insisted on marrying cousins were traditionalists, and ignored the Church in these matters. They would go to Santa Fé and have a civil ceremony, so the children would be legitimate for Anglo purposes. The native notion of marriage was looser in any case, and in the old days would have simply involved the man moving in with his wife's family. The men spent their time in the kivas, the society houses, and their clan houses where the fetishes were kept.

If the couple didn't get along, the wife put the man's belongings outside the door, and he picked them up and went home, literally, to mother. It was his true home anyway, the house of his clansmen. The Church and Anglo civil authorities demanded more secure arrangements, and this had its effect. But the old values died hard. The data gathering came to an abrupt end when the protégé heard he had failed an exam and had to go back for a "summer session" to make it up. He thought he would gloat when writing Vogtie about this, but he was in fact sad to see the little guy leave, to go back and face the vertical values of the Anglos in The Castle in Cambridge, Mass.

If the bond of marriage was loose—far less strong than the bonds of mother-daughter and brother-sister, as befits a matrilineal society—making the right marriage was very important, since it decided which clan was the "father's clan" for the children, and determined the all-important kiva membership. This was ritually and in other ways central. He missed it at the time, but a careful look at what were considered the "best" matches would have shown that marriage into the father's father's clan was preferred. So a father had to be established, even if fathers did not last long as husbands. Since he and wife were now officially clan members, even if only honorary ones, they got to attend an "asking" ceremony. Cochiti was a society, let us remember, where acculturation supposedly had killed the clan as an institution, and replaced it with Anglo and Spanish customs, norms, and labels.

They should have told that to the clans that were gathered for the asking, where, formally, as clans, they exchanged speeches about the duties of the prospective couple. They concentrated especially on their duties as clan members to their sister's children, and then the groom's clan asked the bride's clan for her hand in marriage. With Epifanio's help he recorded the gist of the speeches, for they were in a very rhetorical form of Keres, purged of loan-words and rapid in its delivery. What he did note at the time was the use of kin terms; again they conformed to the classic matrilineal usage, even small children of the father's clan being addressed as "father and mother" and older people as "child" where appropriate. He carefully addressed all Fox clan males, including the teenagers, as "father" and they gravely responded with "child" or "son." His Oak clan males were *nawa*, and responded in kind, it being a reciprocal term. These were wise children, and knew who their clan fathers were, Anglo and Spanish customs notwithstanding. But Lange had told him he was lucky: the people he knew best were traditionalists, but they were enlightened traditionalists who recognized that recording their culture was important. He might not find such punctilious clan behavior among the progressives, or such cooperation. And the true conservatives were equally unhelpful. He might have a skewed sample, but it represented the most thoughtful and reflective of the traditionalists. He could live with that.

They did less scooting around the Southwest this time, and spent masses of time checking and rechecking words and sentences for the article, which was taking solid shape. (Part III: One Type of Transitive Inflection.) His precious Olivetti portable—a present from his parents on graduation, was pounded silly with draft after draft. Then he was hit with a volcanic bout of dysentery. No amount of pink stuff could control it. Juana was disturbed; she sang to him the *Ouwe* song that was one of the few that men and women sang together in the Kiva. It was intended to be soothing in its waltz-time rhythm:

> Shetye owameta, shalakwa owameta
> Yokeha hawemane yehe
> Ouwe ouwe ouwe ouwe

He never knew the meaning; the words were probably Zuni; there was no "l" in Keres, was there, only a retroflexed flapped apico-palatal "r" that people mistook for an "l"? He was in a fever and rambling. Juana sent corn meal to a Flint Society *chaiyanyi*, doctor, who boiled some of the dry green leaves and gave the bitter liquid to the patient to drink, in a native bowl with the signature gap in the painted rim, to let witchcraft out. A spirit snake had poisoned his bowels, the doctor said, a witch had put it there. They would have to drive it out. The doctor sang, but in a whisper, and shook the gourd rattle in rhythm. It was not so much that the cramps and spasms and fever receded when the drink began to attack the bowel-snake, as that after a while he didn't care. He had gone down the rabbit hole into the sacred underworld where he was greeted by a solemn rattlesnake shaking its tail and swaying, singing *heya heya heya ha, wa'na heya heya ha…* and moving, oddly, on two legs. The snakehead was a Kachina mask, the rattle was a miniature gourd: then it was all snakes again, with tiny deer heads and rattles going in rhythm, One-two One-two One-two One-two… Through the smoke of corn-husk cigarettes he thought he saw a witch in the form of a Koshare: ghostly black-ringed eyes and dead cornhusks for hair, snake rattles shivering at the ankles. If only the doctor would kill the witch it would stop the pain and the *shiwana* would ride over in the clouds and all would be peace: *amu amu hawerena maasi…*peace, peace little suffering things…

The cloud people were there, the great ladies of the pantheon were there: *Iatiku*, the Corn Mother, represented by a perfect ear of corn called *shka'anaya*—our mother; Spider Woman, spinning her thought-web, dark and smiling enigmatically; and the Deer Maiden, young and solemn and intolerably lovely. They breathed on him and their breath was *'ianyi*: the Holy Spirit, power, *mana*, *wakan*, grace. Holy Mothers, pray for us sinners now and in… They indicated to him a choice of Kachina masks, all colors and feathers and spruce-bough collars, standing in rows on the shelves in the

Shikame house, like a department-store display. And the masks were singing and hooting, and he had to choose which piece of divinity to wear, which god: *Hanyisatyame, Kashko, Heruta*, and he could not choose, for he was only one of the raw people—the *crudos,* the *sirshti*—not cooked liked the medicine men.

In this underground of the soul all were welcome. Dante and Vergil were there on their way to Purgatory, in the beautiful valley where Sordello showed them the ghosts of the noble and virtuous dead. Dante declaimed to the patient in perfect Tuscan:

> … Sordello a sé il trase
> dicendo: "Vedi là 'l nostro avversaro!"

And indeed there was the adversary: the witch-Koshare. It was shouting, in English: "I am your father! Kill me! Then you can have all the *yaya* to your-self!" And the perfect corn ear was calling: "Eat me! Eat me!" And the gra-cious, smiling ladies were holding their gifts: there were no ginger snaps, but there were the crisp, bright-colored Hopi *piti* wafers, and the colored Kachina dolls—if only he could pick the right mask. Then, for a moment, he hovered above them all, dancing with the cloud people. All local noise was suspended, and Debussy's *Nuages* filled the sound-gap. He was leaning forward with the heavy one-two step, looking down through his heavy mask (which one?) on the scene in the firelight…

Wife, Alice-like, had had enough of this nonsense. She was away through most of it desperately, practically, trying to commandeer a pick-up truck for the ride to town, fifty desert miles away. He bounced and shook on the sack-covered truck bed, still demanding the death of the witch, and was finally, in an appalling state, delivered to the rational center of civilization, a hygienic well-organized hospital. He was cleaned up by the horrified nurses, and put on IV and given pills by the young white-coated Anglo   shamans, but they were too late. The Cochiti shaman-cure had worked, and he had no further symptoms. They insisted, as they do, that he stay in "for observation and tests." When he wanted to go, they wouldn't give him his clothes until the unsmiling bureaucrat visited his bedside to discuss "method of payment."

The Flint Society accepted flour, some cans of meat, and a watermelon. The stony bureaucrat (who would have been welcomed at The Castle) wanted large sums of good US dollars, for the unnecessary attention of the doctors, and above all for all those tests. (It can't have been for the food; he touched not a morsel.) The patient displayed his instructions from the Fulbright Com-mission: do not pay hospital bills; give the hospital this information and it will bill the insurance company direct. Well, said the bureaucrat, in his steely, tough bureaucrat voice, that isn't our policy; we need payment "up front." But, said the now reasonable patient, back on his own rational, civilized turf, it may not be your policy, but it is the policy of your government. No it isn't said the bureaucrat, steadily, evenly; that may be Washington policy, it is not ours. Are we not, asked the baffled but still rational patient, still within the jurisdiction of the United States of America? We are in the jurisdiction of the State of New Mexico, said the steely one, and we will call the Sheriff if you refuse to pay your bill. I'm not refusing to pay the bill, I am adhering to my instructions from the Federal Government regarding method of payment, said the increasing irritated—and now somewhat alarmed—patient. I am a visitor here, and I cannot disobey your government's instructions. The Sheriff, and moreover "civil action" was again threatened and a telephone produced. Go ahead, said the now angry visitor, you call the state authorities and I'll call the FBI—I know they have an office here; we'll see whose writ runs west of the Pecos, pilgrim! For the first time the bureaucrat blinked, and suggested compromise. He generously agreed to accept an "out of town check" as a kind of surety; they would not cash it for a week while the suspicious patient made his phone calls and fixed up payment. He agreed just to get his clothes and get out of this increasingly unreal trial scene. The great Cacique in the city of the Great White Father, *yaya* Fulbright, would fix it.

Coincidentaly both Fred Eggan and Douglas Oliver were in town and lunched and consoled him. They tried to explain the Federal System, but he was too exasperated to listen to reason. Calmer, he told Eggan of his doubts about acculturation. Perhaps Cochiti and its Keres neighbors were not a rundown version of the Hopi and Zuni, but a type of their own that we had just not identified properly? Eggan thought not, but said "Do a great job in Cochiti" as he left. Oliver drove them back to the Pueblo, was taken round, and said extravagant things about it being like going round Kiriwina with Malinowski. He was a nice guy, and it was good to be reminded of the fine things of Harvard, out here in the sand, and the desert stillness. But Oliver was shocked to see some Pueblo boys, with improvised bats and wickets, playing a game of cricket—or at least a stripped-down, utilitarian version. You were not supposed to interfere in this way with "native culture." The boys had been curious, he had explained it to them, they wanted to try it. What harm? They had baseball. Still, Oliver tut-tutted a lot and suggested he wean the lads of it quickly, or future ethnographers might be seriously misled. Simple diffusion of culture, thought the ethnographer, but he agreed. It was obviously time to leave Wonderland and get on with the optimistically named real life.

The leave-taking was as sad as the first time. Juana told "her son" fiercely to return and gave him a St. Christopher medal and a prayer-stick. Epifanio sang a prayer over their notebooks, with the usual sprinkle of cornmeal and puffs of smoke. He was just beginning to feel that he had a grip on the language; that he could really soar now; that a grammar and dictionary were not far away. But a linguist from UNM was doing this (based on Santo Domingo Pueblo?) and was more advanced than he was. His work would have to be relegated to a personal "learning experience"—and he still was unsure what might come out of that small mountain of notebooks on kinship terms. It would all have to wait.

The journey back was no fun; it had to be hurried to save on expense. They were both tired and on edge. The boat trip from Montreal would be a rest. Roy and Diane worked overtime to get their things together—dozens of bales, and send them off to the ship. A man who wanted to go to Montreal also wanted to buy their car, and offered to buy it there if they gave him the ride up. Couldn't be better. Sad goodbyes to Roy, but many promises of paths crossing in the future somehow. Montreal gained; a strange immersion in temporary nasal French. The ship was at a pier called after Pius the Ninth (*Pie Neuf*). It was a journey full of young people going to, and returning to, Europe. They were full of the constant chatter that whites needed to fill the unacceptable silences in their nervous lives. It was thousands of physical and mental miles away from the still people of the land of enchantment, from the shamans and the mothers, from the great spiritual quiet of the desert.

7

The Apprentice: Letting the Soul Catch Up

In his film of hopeless liaisons, *Beyond the Clouds*, Michelangelo Antonioni has one of his heroines, in a Paris café, approach a strange man and tell him a story. She read in a magazine, she says, about some explorers in Mexico who hired native Indian porters to help them find an Inca city in the hills. (It can't have been an Inca city—or the story was set in Peru, not Mexico.) After a long march the porters insisted on stopping. It was not that they were tired, they explained, but that they had gone too fast and had left their souls behind. They had to pause and wait for the souls to catch up.

For the apprentice academic there was to be no pause. He had time to breathe briefly on the ship, but his soul was still in New Mexico, and he didn't use the respite well. While he still cultivated the fantasy that he was going to re-enter the world of Philosophy, it was more likely that to keep afloat he would have to push ahead with his thesis on Cochiti, and so dig himself deeper into Anthropology. His teaching was to be in this and Sociology, so Philosophy was still only a distant dream. Perhaps he could push into the "language and culture" area: but how? To be plausible you had to be dealing with languages different from English—even from SAE. He would have either to get back to Cochiti (and visa requirements would make this legally a two-year wait—practically much longer) or find another fieldwork venue. He abandoned all speculation and figured he had enough to do to survive in the situation as it was. He would have to launch into lectures and classes with nothing prepared. He would be only a week ahead of the students. He had a couple of ideas about short articles: you needed publications to establish a career, they had all emphasized. But where was he otherwise? In those two years of frenetic learning and examinations, and in the nearly eight months in the Southwest, what had he learned really? Was he any further towards mastering the big questions? Or had he just added incrementally to the mishmash of facts and theories he started with? It did not matter: the city has to be found, but there is a lot of climbing to do in the meantime, and the soul may never catch up.

He knew also that the pair of them were drifting apart, despite the bond that goes with shared intense experience. He had somehow to pry his mind away from all this exotic stuff and concentrate on a normal life as it was defined in his own tribe. Perhaps Exeter would help. It was a quiet cathedral town, dating from Roman times, in the lush West Country. Hooker, who wrote *Ecclesiastical Polity*, the definitive text on the Anglican Church-State, was born there and his statue stood outside the Cathedral. The town had been smashed in one of Hitler's hate raids (the cathedral only had slight damage) and was about half rebuilt with mediocre forties austerity buildings. But the old part, mediaeval and eighteenth-century, still had an air of Jane Austen about it. The university was small and not very distinguished. It had started as The Royal Albert Memorial College, in memory of the Prince Consort and with funds left over from his Great Exhibition. The original building was a charming Ruskinesque red-sandstone pile in the old part of Exeter. As The University College of the Southwest, it had moved out to an arboretum on a hill to the west of the city: the estate of Lord Northcote (he of the Northcote-Trevelyan Report, which revolutionized the Civil Service into an exam-based meritocracy.) It had worked on the London External system—the granting of degrees examined and bestowed by London University, which was the foundation of many of the new English and Commonwealth universities. As a newly created university, it now offered degrees in its own right, and was obviously anxious to rise in the world. Its campus, with a mix of old stately homes and uninspired but not hideous new buildings, amidst every known tree that could grow in the British Isles, was popular with students. It was a new star on the academic horizon. Good. Hitch the wagon and away.

He found it hard to shake off the hypnotic mantle of America. He had been to another planet, liked it, adapted to it. His return to England was like Gulliver landing in Lilliput. Everything seemed miniaturized. The houses were small, the cars were small, the people were small, and, above all, the portions of food were unacceptably small. Where were the many-layered and many-flavored club sandwiches when he needed them? He had brought back some chili sauces and salsas, and he emptied them over his bland food in desperation until they were used up. England was the green and pleasant land he remembered, but the pleasantness came at a price. "We don't do that" or more depressingly "That's not done" were the governing rules. Coming from the land of "Can do" it was frustrating. He had to go through a cultural decompression chamber, gradually shedding his new-world attitudes and idioms and taking on the motley of John Bull. He wore his bolo ties less and less, and even gave up arguing with restaurants about whether they were ties at all. He wore his large Zuni ring that had been a gift from his friends, with its silver, turquoise and jet; he sported Western shirts and boots. But no one understood, and he tired of explaining. Vogtie would have been proud of him though.

This was the England of the late fifties, a negative age in which the forties had not died, and the sixties had yet to be born. The Southwest—Dorset, Somerset, Devon and Cornwall—were perhaps as near as anywhere in the country to the idealized rural idyll of eighteenth-century bucolic society so beloved of foreign tourists and romantics of all stripes. Dominantly agricultural, some of its villages and small towns would have been recognized by characters from *Tess* or *Sir Roger de Coverly* or even *Lorna Doone*. One of the best ethnographies of this now lost society is Laurie Lee's *Cider with Rosie*, which captures life before the intrusion of mechanized farming. Cider, or Scrumpy, was the local drink rather than beer. Thatched cottages were still standard housing in the interior, and most towns except Exeter had not been touched by bombing, although most of the area had gone through the trauma of pre-D Day preparations. The coast was "The English Riviera" courtesy of the Gulf Stream; palm trees grew on the front at Torquay. Little Celtic fishing villages (Mousehole, Marazion), where Cornish was still spoken as late as the 1770s, were filling up with English artists in search of the simpler (and cheaper) life. The inland varied from the deep green gorges (including the one that produced Cheddar cheese) and wooded valleys of Doone country, to the rolling hills and copses of his Somerset childhood's happy hunting grounds. The high moorlands of Dartmoor and Bodmin—*Hound of the Baskervilles* scenario, which recollected his own moorlands in the cold stern north, fell away to the seaports and towns of the Bristol Channel, including the charming Porlock, the person from which had interrupted Coleridge's composition of "Kubla Khan," denying us the rest of the Unitarian preacher's opium-drenched vision. It was England's southwest corner and, like California in the USA, all the kooky stuff seemed to slide down there. It was the home of the minor dissenting sects with their odd theological obsessions. It was where the Pilgrims gathered to sail to America and a life which, while free of the old restrictions, would leave them at liberty to impose their own: kookiness unrestrained, the consequences of which had bemused and entranced him for much of the last two years.

He struggled with frustrations, as when, passing from London (in an ancient Ford bought for five pounds) to Southampton, to pick up the bales and baggage so carefully husbanded by Roy, he discovered that some minor officer of the shipping company had dispatched them back to Montreal. Why? No one knew. His wordy upset was obviously regarded as behavior in the worst taste. He had forgotten about English stoicism, about good form, about putting up with things, about muddling through, and, above all, about *not making a fuss*. He would have to wait for all his books, all his notes, all the clothes and household goods, his drum, his bottles of tequila. But Exeter was full of charm and a furnished flat was soon found. They could not afford very much on the laughable salary of some four hundred and fifty pounds a year—much less in purchasing power than his graduate-school scholarships. He had not even thought about salary; it had not even been relevant: they had to come back anyway. But the frustration of always too little money was to haunt him for the next eight years. At the time it did not seem to matter: wife would find a job, and the place was decidedly agreeable. Mitchell and O'Connor turned out to be friendly and welcoming. His office was in a new building at the top of the arboretum hill. He was surrounded by Japanese cherry, Norwegian pine, Asian willow, Floridian palmetto, Greek cypress, Chilean monkey-puzzle; by cedar, eucalyptus, hydrangea and cabbage palm. The air felt good and fresh, the trees were beautiful. The Faculty Club, which served a perfect steak and kidney pudding, had a large regulation croquet lawn, and the university librarian, John Lloyd, recruited him to the staff (faculty) cricket team. He was back.

He should have caught his breath and reflected on his good fortune. True, he had not planned any of this, but then what had he planned? He tumbled into it, and it was, like Harvard, not a half-bad tumble. Occasionally he woke in the night in panic and wondered where he was going. For better or for worse he was in deep now, and had no option, once again, but to press ahead with his "social science" career. Lecturer in Sociology with Special Reference to Social Anthropology. That was what he was and that was what he would have to be for the time being. Something would turn up. In the meantime he had to face teaching and the terror of facing an audience of eager undergraduates with his hastily written lectures. All his performance fears welled up to confront him, in reality not nightmares. His outgoing and confident pose was just that. He knew he was right about the air of confidence he had noted in his elders. You had to learn to cultivate that. Not only in performance but in writing was the air of confidence essential. You had to get out of feeling like the perpetual student trying to please the unsmiling teachers. You had to stop dancing, let your soul catch up, and put on the calm and assured mask. He had done it with his opening of the *Pueblo Baseball* article: "Ruth Benedict's confusion of institutions with personality traits…" Oh *that* was a good one.

This was a small department and you had to be jack of all the social science trades. Mitchell, whose subject was rural depopulation, was big on comparing industrial society with "the simple society" so the seasoned ethnographer was set to lecture on "The Social Institutions of the Simpler Society" which is to say an introduction to Social Anthropology. But he also had to do "Religion and Magic" and "Sociological Theory." The first was meat and drink, and for the second, between Spencer, Durkheim, Weber, and Popper, to say nothing of the philosophers of history, he managed. He even got a chance to vent his frustrations over Culture, and Values. The hardest task was a lecture series jointly with Political Science on "The Institutions of Law and Justice." This went along with a seminar for third-year honours students on the same topic. He did this with two interesting Pol. Sci. lecturers, Maurice Vile (American Federalism) and Derek Crabtree (English Liberalism), who were genuinely excited to have his cooperation. But political institutions had been one of the neglected areas in his undergraduate education, and he had to struggle madly to keep ahead. What little skill he had in Statistics was called on for there was no other statistician in the department—only a socio-logical historian. He cobbled together classes on social surveys and basic correlation and probability, and hammered away about the normal curve. He had as a co-worker Frank Oliver who was writing a book on the credit markets (*The Control of Hire-Purchase*.) Frank was happy to have him since the predominantly humanist arts and social science faculty had a deep suspicion of all things statistical. Science, they declaimed, was something any fool could do, it took no genius. Yes, he and Frank told them, that was precisely the point.

He was luckier with another assignment, perhaps peculiar to English uni-versities. There was no big demand for Sociology (it had not until recently existed outside the LSE) except from potential social workers. This necessary connection with social work was a bit farcical since not much of sociology proper was any use to them, except as background, any more than the largely Freudian psychology they were forced to ingest. They were potential almon-ers and probation officers who needed practical training in these vocational pursuits. They were nice girls from proper homes and good schools, but they had no intellectual curiosity on the whole—always the odd exception of course. But in the general rush to "professionalize"—something Marshall had a generation of LSE graduates study—they were forced to do Sociology degrees for the sake of academic respectability, and the sociologists were forced to accommodate to them. Many of them were shocked when they discovered that social work proper was only a part of their course. Their schools had never explained to them that sociology did not *mean* social work. Two positions in a five-person department were teachers of social work. The rest had somehow to find a way of adding some "relevant topic." His time served in Palfrey House was a godsend: what better than "Cross-Cultural Studies of Socialization"? All the Johnny stuff on tots-and-pots could be wheeled out and aired—once his notes and books found their way home from Canada.

It wasn't bad. He had six years of dense study behind him, and a photo-graphic memory for things that he actually committed to memory, so he kept pace. But it was, at first, full-time work to stay up with the lectures and classes, and this being the English system he also had a slate of individual tutees with their weekly essays. This was time consuming rather than difficult. But he tried to put as much as he could of his ongoing concerns with Pueblo kinship into the "simpler societies" lectures to keep some of the issues alive—under the head of "ethnographic examples." He developed the line of teaching he had started with his Leverett House boys, and began to move on from local groupings to forms of descent. And always, in the theory lectures, he harped back to the problem of "explanation" and used the incest taboo as his prime example. Why do we have incest taboos? The official line was: because if we didn't something terrible would happen. Exactly what terrible thing would happen depended on the theory you wanted to support: the family would collapse in sexual competition; primary narcissistic love-objects would be permanently cathected; the probability of deleterious homozygotes would increase; wider communal bonds would not form through exogamy. Or, as the natives themselves would argue: the crops would fail and you would breed monsters. As modes of explanation, he suggested, the behavioral science theories were no more secure than those of the natives. And they were all hypothetical; we really didn't know why societies forbade incest (those that did—there were the well-known exceptions) only why they said they did, and if that were the explanation then there would be no need for social science. The anthropological favorite: that wider social bonds would not be formed, seemed to confuse incest and exogamy, he thought. He was back to Freedman's question about why we could not have a sexual free-for-all in the family and then marry out of it. There was a difference between sex and marriage, as every teenager knew, but anthropologists seemed to forget.

So he blundered on. What of his scheming to get back into Philosophy? O'Connor was sympathetic, but was interested in him as a linguist rather than a philosopher. How did different languages handle causality, the philosopher wanted to know? Linguistic philosophers were bogged down in English: how would it work in Turkish, or Chinese, or Keres, or Navaho. O'Connor though, being Irish by descent and interested in his relationship with the senior line of the O'Connor clan, wanted to learn Irish Gaelic as part of his pursuit of language differences. He had the cumbersome set of old Linguaphone 78s, with the odd 1930s textbook. The Linguaphone plan meant that illustrations and texts had to be uniform for all languages. So it had Irish peasants visiting the jewelry shop and the fashion house and the elegant seaside resort. But it was intriguing to pick up the Irish again. He knew that returning to Cochiti was impractical for many years to come, so if he wanted to keep up the fieldwork thing, perhaps he could try the west of Ireland? Arensberg and Kimball had done it, and *Family and Community in Ireland* was one of the best-regarded ethnographies in the subject. Why not? There were language and culture issues to be sure, since most of the Irish Gaelic speakers also spoke English and he could compare this bilingualism with that of the Pueblos. For the time being he concentrated on "The Family in the Parlour" (Record One): *An líon-tighe sa bparlus.* "I have to go translate some Irish," he told Maurice Vile. "Like what?" asked the expert on federalism: "'sure and begorrah me boyos, we'll be a-peelin' o' the praties?'"

In his past incarnations he had always found a friend: Ken in London, Roy in America. There was not much in common with them, except they were a couple of years older than he was and had seen life outside the groves—both had done national service. Perhaps they were the older brother he never had, but sometimes had fantasies about, as he did about the younger sister who would stay home, marry the local dentist, and worry about the parents (her name was Susan.) In Exeter he soon found Ewart (Johns—surnames are creeping in; we must be getting closer.) Ewart was officially a lecturer in Geography, but unofficially the artist-in-residence, and definitely the prototype bohemian. He painted what he called "figurescapes"—nudes mostly, with a kind of application of Turner techniques of light painting to figures, done with a palette knife. They were delightful and striking and won our once-upon-a-time artist's heart. Smitten with Jack Yeats, J. M. Synge, and a bolt of Celtic romanticism, they agreed that they would venture together to the Wild West of Ireland, to paint and folklorize together. Ewart, being Welsh, felt the tug of the Celtic thing: once again there was the call to go west.

In the meantime, Ewart had a commission to paint a huge mural in the refectory. Most ceremonies were held in this room because it was the only space large enough. The vice-chancellor (read president) was desperate to have a great hall built since he was, he said, "sick and tired of holding ceremonies in a cafeteria." It was about all he seemed interested in as he cruised about in his big black chauffeured limousine, hunched in the back, talking to no one. But in the meantime he wanted the mural to dignify the otherwise bland eating hall. Ewart, with an artist's eye for popular culture, settled on "Modern Dance" as the subject (all college dances were held there), and asked our couple—thought of as "very American" by the faculty—to pose with some young Exeter people in various states of jive/jitterbug/be-bop. They remembered these very well from the jazz days. So there the soul-catcher was, immortalized in violent red and bigger than life—although, in Ewart's abstract style not personally recognizable—on the refectory wall. If no other monument was ever erected, this would do very well, he thought.

He definitely felt ambivalent towards the place. It was unbelievably pretty, and certainly very pleasant, and the people were polite and charming. He loved the countryside and the music in the Cathedral. He went with Crabtree, score in hand, to hear *Gerontius*. But he couldn't help feeling wildly out of place after the LSE and Harvard. There were a few bright souls there, like Ewart, with whom he felt an immediate rapport, but most of the older staff, left over from the university college days, were fabulous creatures out of an Agatha Christie novel. (She was a neighbor, and as Lady Mallowan appropriately graced the odd event, as did the Duchess of Devonshire and the Earl of Devon: like all good Englishmen the Exeter people loved their lords.) The older ones often carried their eccentricity to stupefying lengths. One lady lecturer (in French?) used to come to her lectures in a taxi, leave it outside with the meter running, and depart the minute the bell rang. Most of her salary must have gone on these quick trips; but then, it was rumored, she "had means"—true of so many it seemed. They were mostly simply schoolteachers, and were uncomfortable with the new demands of being in a "real" university. They never published, and were condescendingly proud of the fact, dismissing the new emphasis as another unwanted Americanization: "publish or perish" was equated with Coca-Cola and rock-and-roll.

The professor of English (there was, of course, only one professor per department, its chairman for life) refused to countenance publications by his troops. He had only published once and under protest: his inaugural lecture, automatically printed by the university and titled *Where Muses Haunt*—a disquisition on the beauties of English poetry. He didn't believe in "research" in literature: we could all read literature and form opinions; what was there to do "research" on? The business of literature departments was to "enhance appreciation through knowledge" and that was that. His underlings fumed and resigned. Our one-time poet—and skeptic about all "literary theory" - actually felt some sympathy. The classic eccentric was bachelor classicist Jackson Knight, brother of the (also bachelor) Wilson Knight (Leeds University) whose book on Shakespeare had been a revelation in the now distant-seeming schoolboy days. Jackson was a spiritualist who was convinced he spoke to the shade of Jack the Ripper. There was a little spiritualist church in Exeter where Jack evidently gave weekly sermons through this unlikely channel. Jackson got most of his opinions on difficulties in Virgil and Ovid directly from the poets themselves. Need we add it was hard for him to find outlets in the regular journals for articles citing these otherwise authoritative sources. He and his brother (who visited often) were reputed to go out at night with candles and nail scissors to trim the lawn. One cannot make this stuff up.

The resident intellectuals on campus (as he called it, to the amusement of the old timers) were the New Left Review Study Group. Nothing had changed in England regarding the oxymoronic status of "Tory intellectual." Intellectuals were, by definition, left wing, and the *New Left Review* was the bible of its bright-eyed vanguard. Their naïve utopianism was made bearable by their obvious decency and wish to do the right thing by everybody. The miserable pay of the junior lecturers was augmented by a one-time increment: Alan Williams, economist leader of the New Left—who sincerely believed that high taxation motivated people to work harder—gave his to Oxfam. Frank Oliver, the most studiedly aristocratic of anyone there, was, of course, as befitted an economic statistician, a confirmed Socialist also. But his real passion was the work of Ivy Compton-Burnett, who he claimed had invented small-group Sociology. Once you tasted Ivy you were lost; *Manservant and Maidservant* was the best thing since Jane Austen, all agreed, and he couldn't but fall in line. The little blue volumes by Gollancz were collected and chortled over.

So he stuck with the group even if he was constantly at odds with them, since this was the only place where any kind of serious and lively discussion of politics was possible. Stephen Fisher and Peter Fletcher, whom he remembered from the LSE, Vile and Crabtree, his fellow workers from pol. sci., and others who floated in and out, were the core. They wanted to discuss "super-structure" and the social derivation of ideas, so he gave a paper on "Marriage and Mobility in Modern Society" comparing *Lady Chatterley's Lover, The Card, Lucky Jim, Room at the Top,* and *Look Back in Anger.* He was looking for patterns of "marital mobility" in which lower-class males married up and suffered the varying, but generally uncomfortable, consequences of absorption into the middle classes. He could see at Exeter that the girls were mostly middle-class and the boys the sons of the sons of toil, come up through the scholarship system. More and more marriages, he suggested, would be of the type that was central to the plot of these works. It was hypergamy (male), and anthropologists knew about that. He could compare it to female hypergamy that characterized the Indian caste system. He felt good that he could contribute a new angle on society like this, and began to think that there may be something in the sociological obsession with social class. He was, after all, an exemplar of the pattern he was examining, even if he had never thought of it that way. He had professionally to accept what he had personally never believed: that in some things the group trumped the individual.

Exeter was seductive, but he had to keep up with the wider world. It was difficult though to find time to travel. The train to London took two hours, and if you attended evening meetings you had to stay over. He couldn't easily afford this, until he discovered that the National Liberal Club—that monument to self-satisfied Victorian munificence—had a very cheap "country membership" and even cheaper simple rooms (bathroom down the hall) with bed and breakfast. He found that they would serve tea and toast with a newspaper early in the morning, but that the real "full breakfast" was available until 11 p.m.. (These were - have we said? - simpler times.) So he would eat the toast, work until 10:45 in the ornate and comfortable library, then go for breakfast at the last minute: porridge, kippers, mixed grill, toast and lashings of marmalade. Finishing at around noon this sufficed as lunch and lasted him until he got home in the evening. It annoyed the kitchen staff, but it was a money saver, and his membership fee soon paid for itself. The spartan rooms after all looked out over the Thames (Embankment gardens). And you could take tea on the club terrace and look down river to the Houses of Parliament in one direction, and Tower Bridge in the other. Earth has not anything to show more fair, and at such a bargain price too.

He went to meetings at the Royal Anthropological Institute, and to those of the British Sociological Association, usually at the LSE. Everyone seemed glad to see him back. Firth insisted on putting him up for election to the Association of Social Anthropologists, and Macrae insisted he contribute something to the *British Journal of Sociology*—you must have learned *something* from the American experience, no? Well, there is this Balesian thing about incest avoidance—perhaps even a "law"—a true rarity in Sociology. Splendid. Work it up; send it in. When, for God's sake? It was not clear, but it would surely be done. Somehow things got done, even if the soul got left behind. Going back through the rain to the West Country, he opened his notebook and began to sketch the article out. The explanation issue first, then the "Westermarck versus Freud" argument, then the theoretical resolution (they were talking about different situations and so were not incompatible), then the "law," then the ethnographic examples to illustrate the variations it suggested. Yes: he could combine article and lectures and double up, thus saving time. This was still the days of the well-written lecture. Visual aids were limited to the blackboard, and you were supposed to have composed a literate address, and to read it, not to extemporize. It was a good school for writers, and before he published it, he could use it as a lecture at other universities when he was asked; he would be asked. He scribbled, surviving on tea and a currant bun, because there was no way he could afford the dinner in the dining car. The vice-chancellor was in first class (of course) and walked by to his dinner with some black-suited lackeys, loudly proclaiming that they would do very well because there was a good crew on that evening.

How the years blur. Chronology, as we know, is not his strong point. But one thing remains fixed: in that first year, under the combined influence of Dan O'Connor's interest and Ewart's desire to find inspiration for real landscapes, he decided to spend part of the summer in the West of Ireland, looking for a bilingual area to study. If he could inaugurate this, it might lead back to linguistics, which he felt was otherwise slipping away from him. He wrote to various people he and O'Connor had marked down as possible connections during their excursions into Gaeldom, and while most wanted him to go to Galway and County Clare, he wanted to try somewhere away from the already explored turf of the Connaught family farm. He was looking for a Gaelic summer school that would take beginners. This was hard because these schools usually took urban schoolchildren, whom they assumed had done some Irish in class. The summer school was to introduce them to "native speakers" on whom they could try their budding skills. Only one readily accepted him as an adult beginner: it was the *Coloiste Uludh*—Ulster College, in Donegal. It's secretary, Síleadh Ní Rúnaí (Sheilah Rooney), wrote in that mixture of Gaelic and English they seemed to prefer, that he would be welcome, and accommodation could be arranged with other adult beginners at the home of Bean Ní Churrain (Mrs. Curran) in *Gort An Chórcaigh* (Gortahork). On the map he saw it was at the extreme northwest of Ireland, in that county the boundary commission had excluded from Northern Ireland because of too many Catholics. Stuck up there like something forgotten by history, it seemed just fine, and he wrote to book his place. He noticed on the map, about nine miles out to sea, the oddly named Tory Island. Must be a large, uninhabited rock, he thought.

The world swirled on by. Harold Macmillan made a speech in South Africa about the winds of change that were sweeping that continent. The police in Sharpeville killed sixty people who were demonstrating in favor of that same change. United Nations troops were sent to the Congo to take sides in a civil (read tribal) war. An American spy plane was shot down over Russia causing the end of yet another futile summit conference. After a long trial the ban on *Lady Chatterley's Lover* was lifted. The prosecutor in the case demanded to know if this was a book we wanted "our wives and servants" to read. The nearest he had to a servant was Miss May, a small local lady of advanced years who came to clean once a week. Miss May had not read the book in question, devoted as she was to *Woman's Own,* which gave her, she said, all the reading matter she needed; but she listened patiently to his explanation of the plot and the obscenity issue, leaning on her broom. Her response was always the same to his lengthy explanations: "Funny ole world, i'n it?" It is.

Ionesco's *Rhinoceros*, and Pinter's *The Caretaker* rubbed that truth in. The staff drama group put on *The Bald Soprano*, with Cecil Jenkins playing the fireman as a droll Irish wit. Cecil, an Ulsterman who had spent time in McGee College in Londonderry, also became a firm friend. Jenkins had aspirations to novel writing, and amazed everyone when his murder mystery *Message from Sirius* was actually published and was actually a critical success. The murderer was an anthropologist who killed people because of their bad values. Cecil said he got the idea from our man's notion of the anthropologist as the eternally detached observer.

The detached observer was a bit ambivalent about his proposed jaunt to Donegal. He might be better employed using the time to write the article, or work on lectures, or even try to push his thesis forward, using the Liberal Club breakfast strategy to give him time at the Anthropological Institute Library. But then again, he was desperate to get back into linguistics, which was not, in England, the big thing it had become in the States. He needed a lecture series, perhaps "Language and Society" in the near future, and he needed a basis in ongoing fieldwork since there was no prospect of a return to New Mexico anytime soon. So the summer found him, aided with small grant from Exeter, taking the train to Liverpool (via Birmingham), the night ferry to Dublin, the train north to Belfast, then east to Londonderry, and the bus to Lifford, changing for Gortahork. He was hit with the sensation, the further he moved towards the coast, of the powerful smell of peat burning. From every chimney this rural incense spiraled to the sky and entranced the nostrils. Some smells have the ability to arouse us as profoundly as the taste of Proust's madeleine: burning pinyon in the New Mexican desert, and burning peat on the Donegal coast are olfactory wellsprings for him.

The coast there is very wild and very lovely in its wildness. He arrived at the college, and was taken to Mrs. Curran's house by students operating under a strict rule of Gaelic only: no English. *"Ná caint Béarla!"* he was fiercely ordered by an older student, which rather put an end to the conversation for he understood scarcely a word. If this was Irish they were speaking it was a mysteriously different Irish from that of the Linguaphone tapes. He caught the odd word, and they seemed to understand his simple greetings and questions, but he was baffled by the replies. Fortunately Mrs. Curran was not bound by the rules, and was herself, curiously, a speaker of Scots Gaelic who had married into the area. The two dialects were evidently very similar, but she was still regarded as a foreigner. The older beginners were sent to her since she had a big house for the district, with a large extra bedroom for these guests, which included a schoolteacher who needed to improve his Irish for advancement. Everyone addressed the teacher as *Máistir* McGoldrig—Master, like the Scottish *Dominie.*

All the beginners, old and very young, were thrown together in the one class, held in the basement of the college hall, which Mrs. Mulhern taught with crisp efficiency. Learning by recitation was the favored and effective mode, and the would-be Gaelicist rattled off the descriptions of *An Ait Seo*— This Place. These he copied into his exercise book in old Irish script, this being the preferred way to write for beginners, so they could learn to read the older books printed thus before the typewriter led to the use of Roman letters. *Tighe beaga, aol-nighte...*—little lime-washed houses... would stick always in the memory as the first phrase he ever took down from dictation. The fundamentals of Gaelic were the same in this northern dialect as in the Connaught Irish that was the basis for Linguaphone, but much of the usage and pronunciation had to be learned from scratch. The grammatical likeness to Latin was striking, and the mutations of words to indicate case were similar, in principle, to Welsh. The spelling, while often strange to an English speaker, had its own phonetic logic. It was not in that sense a difficult language, and unlike Keres had numerous grammars and a large literature to work with. They had to learn passages from Brian Merriman's *Cúirt an Mheadhion Oidhche* (The Midnight Court), an eighteenth-century satire on the marriage of young girls to old farmers, for recital in the nominal exam. It was like old times as he rattled off his memorized lines.

He had been referred to the local Folklore Collector for help and advice. Perhaps only in Ireland is this a civil service position, and Seán O h-Eochaidh (John Haughey) was its local incumbent. With all the charm and friendliness the Irish are rightly famous for, he took the apprentice under his wing, explained the dialect thing, and discussed the local *gaeltacht*—the Irish-speaking district, for which he was responsible. It differed throughout in the amount of Gaelic spoken, from half-and-half around Gortahork, to virtually monolingual on Tory Island. There were people on Tory Island? Oh yes, about three hundred of them. Tory stood off on the horizon, looking like a distant aircraft carrier with its high cliffs at one end. It didn't seem possible it was inhabited, but there it was: it was old in its history, the Folklore Collector explained, going back to the Iron Age, and having monastic establishments—including a round tower—going back to St. Columba (*Colmkille*—Dove of the Church, in the vernacular.) The helpful collector pulled out the first number of the

Ulster Journal of Archaeology (1853), in whose battered pages there was an article on the History and Antiquities of Tory, by a Mr. Getty. There must be something more recent? Not really. Tory was there for the taking.

Seán went on to explain that the people were "a breed apart" from the mainlanders; for one thing, husbands often didn't live with their wives. What did they do? Not sure, but it was something worth looking into. How to get there? A boat from Magheraroarty, past the inshore island of Inishboffin, out over nine miles of treacherous currents. When? When it felt like it. Boats came out from time to time, the only regular one was the boat that carried the mail, which was supposed to come once a week, but often didn't since the weather was often bad. How would you know? Get the people at the pub in Magheraroarty to call the post-office in Gortahork. A message would be relayed, but you must leave at once—get a lift down there and grab the boat. And don't pay attention if they try to get five pounds from you for the crossing: they take bird watchers over each summer, and they charge them ten shillings.

In class Mrs. Mulhern told them a story about Tory Island, got from one of the old men who knew the old stories. The island had a "king"—*An Riogh* (old spelling)—who was a keeper of the law and the secrets, including how to "turn the stones." These were "cursing stones" covered with runic writings and buried on a headland. Sometime in the nineteenth century, the landlord—a Jewish businessman from Manchester—couldn't collect the rents, and the county couldn't collect the rates, for the islanders flat wouldn't pay. So a British frigate, the *Wasp*, was dispatched from Westport in County Mayo, to land officers on the island. The king called all the islanders (there were more of them then—about six hundred) to the headland, and recited the curse. This "turned the stones" and a great storm blew up from nowhere and wrecked the *Wasp* on the rocks, with a total loss of life. The islanders were not bothered after that. They still didn't pay taxes, much to the disgruntlement of the mainlanders. Seán (pronounced "shan" locally, not the nasal "shawn" of the southern version) said the Admiralty put the loss of the boat down to "navigational error"—but the natives knew better. "They still sight ghosts from the *Wasp* out there," he added, "they have the best ghost stories around here." He was the Folklore Collector; he should know.

The call came in the middle of a class. "Go," said Mrs. Mulhern, "you may not get another chance. Although I wouldn't want to be going out there myself." The Collector drove him down to the little pier a few miles south, where a small boat—a half-decker—was waiting. They rushed down, but there was no hurry: the crew was having a few pints in the pub up the hill. They watched the fishermen from Inishboffin loading their little yawl, and helped load a few boxes onto the Tory boat. The weather was getting rough and rainy, and Seán took off his raincoat, found some rubber boots in his trunk, and gave them to the shivering voyager. "You won't be coming back any time soon," he ventured, "ask for Mary Doohan, she puts up visitors." The crew came back, and the boat pushed off. It was too rough to depend on the motor—the propeller would be out of the water half the time, the skipper, Johnny Dixon, explained, so they put up a tattered, red lateen sail, as they headed out into the rolling seas of the bay. "Well," said Johnny (they always started sentences with well—pronounced "wol") "sure the engine is a bit skittish anyway. We're better with the sail."

He was to make that voyage many times over the next years, but nothing would ever match the first. They rose to the top of one wave and the island was in view in the rainy distance; then they plunged to the bottom of another and there was nothing but a wall of sea behind and in front. He was sitting in the bottom of the boat next to a Franciscan monk, Father David, who told how he was sent over in the summer as a locum for the regular curate, off on his deserved furlough. It was hard, the good Father said, since the people didn't like to make confessions to the resident curate—they had to live with him all year, so they saved up their worst sins for the summer and laid them off on the locum. Like the old scapegoat from the Talmud, ventured the apprentice, remembering Holman Hunt from the Pre-Raphaelite days. This warmed the monk to him, and, finding out he was an anthropologist, the father started a debate about whether polygamy or polyandry was more contrary to natural law. Neither, he replied, although both may be contrary to canon law. Canon law, said the good father, should be consonant with natural law... It seemed to be his fate to tangle with Franciscans on the issue of marriage customs. They grabbed the heaving gunwale and prodded the air with emphatic fingers. An old man with a pipe and very few teeth (and the telltale white flash of cancer on his nicotine-stained lips), who had been speaking Gaelic to his neighbor, asked: "Will you be wanting the Gaelic, now?" He would indeed. "You came with O h-Eochaidh, did you not? So you'll be wanting stories of Balor of the Mighty Blows." "A cyclops," said Father David, "he had one eye in the middle of his forehead. Its glance could kill, so he kept it covered by a shield. In Donegal they still call the evil eye *Súil Bhaloir*—Balor's Eye." The old fellow addressed the priest politely in Gaelic, evidently establishing his precedence when it came to telling his own legends. The visiting holy man smiled and nodded.

The boat continued its gyroscopic lurching; the rain beat down. He was too busy being seasick to hear the old man's story, and asked to postpone it until they landed. He had already heard a version in Gortahork. Balor lived on Tory, in a castle—*Dún Balor*, on *Tór Mór*, the great cliff at the east end that you could see from the mainland. A local chieftain called Kineely envied Balor his famous white cow and eventually stole it, landing it on the little inshore island of Inishboffin (*Inis Bó Finne*—"Island of the Beautiful Cow.") Balor, furious, captured him, and cut off his head in Clochaneely. A battle ensued where the boy Lugh thrust a spear into Balor's eye as he opened the shield. The evil matter from the eye spilled down The Poisoned Glen (there on the map) where nothing has grown since. On application to the Folklore Collector, he was told that this was one of the many local versions of the great Celtic solar myth of the rise of the sun god—Lugh laimh-fhada (Lugh the long handed) who was in fact Balor's grandson. A prophecy told Balor that his grandson would kill him, so he kept his only daughter in his prison on Tory (see it when go to the east end.) It didn't work since the young Cian (original of Kineely?) came over and "there was a child." Balor threw the baby Lugh into the sea, but he was saved by the sea god *Mananán* (of the Isle of Man), and did indeed slay his giant grandfather (he of death and darkness) with a slingshot made of the brains of his enemies mixed with lime.

The various tales were told as if Balor and his chums had been there yesterday. The same was true of the patron saint, Colmkille. He parted the seas, changed Danes into rocks, blessed the soil so that it would resist pests. The boat had a little bag of soil tied near the prow. All the boats had one. It was "lifted" by the Eldest Duggan from The Grave of the Seven (shipwrecked nuns) and rats could not live near it. When Tory boats came into a harbor, the rats fled. And the potato famine never traveled across to Tory. The round tower of Colmkille's monastery was pointed out as they came nearer to West Town, the main port of the island, with the pier and slipway. Far off on the east end, at the foot of Balor's hill, was East Town, with only a beach for the boats. "You won't find much there," said the old man, "everything's in the west: the school, the church, the post office, the shop, the graveyard and the nurse's house." With difficulty the men got the boat secured at the pier. He proffered ten shillings and it was accepted without demur. One of the boatmen turned out to be Hugh Doohan, and it was his wife that took in boarders. Their house, right there by the slipway (with a tall T-shaped cross fixed into the concrete) was one of the only two-story buildings visible in the huddle of houses around the tower and graveyard. He stumbled into it, wet and shaking, and was immediately soothed by the warmth of the turf fire, the smell of cooking soda bread, and the incense of strong tea. Every nerve said "home."

He had nothing but what he stood up in, and would have been a total mess without the Folklore Collector's coat and boots. The rain lifted, but the seas continued to heave and swirl round the island, and they warned him he would not be able to leave for a few days at least. Mary and Hugh spoke English to him, but the rest was a riot of rapid Gaelic that left him helpless in its wake. This was not the careful Gaelic of the classroom; it was the fluid, fluent local speech, full of those word plays and idioms and double-barreled inventions that make this language a delight when you can pin it down, but a nightmare to follow for a beginner. But everyone he met was patient and he tried out what halting words he had mastered and they laughed and encouraged him. These were not at all the strange, suspicious people he had been led to expect. They had had Gaelic scholars there—Heinrich Wagner, the phoneticist from

Queen's Belfast, had stayed with the Doohans, and were used to being regarded as a precious asset by the government, ever anxious to promote the
dying language. So he relaxed and tried to get the measure of the place. First,
said Hugh, he must go see the King; it was expected.

Whenever they mentioned the King (*An Rí*—new spelling) they smiled,
and he didn't know if this was because they were themselves amused or if
they knew outsiders would be. But he knew from reading, for example, *Twenty
Years A-Growing* (about the Blasket Islands) that these small offshore islands
often did have a "King" who was a local arbiter of disputes and often had the
task of dividing up the common lands, like the shore, between the people. He
had to walk the length of West Town to get to the King's house, and was able
to take in the "street"—unpaved and with a drain running down the middle,
and the one-story houses with occasional thatched byres that Hugh said were
the last of the old cabins they used to live in, before The Board built the slate-
roofed dwellings that were now universal. The Board was The Congested
Districts Board, an institution that flourished at the turn of the century—part
of Balfour's attempt to "kill Home Rule with kindness." The houses, the
slipways and piers, the curing station and school of the West were mostly the
work of The Board, as was the knitting industry that introduced cable-stitch
and the "native patterns" now so prized as "Aran sweaters." The usual pattern
for the local ladies was no pattern at all: the sweaters they knit for themselves
were plain turtlenecks. Mostly they ordered plain sweaters from a catalogue,
as well as cheap material to make their own trousers and dresses. Very few of
the ladies still spun and wove, and there were few sheep left to provide wool,
for all the land was overgrazed and what was left was needed for cows. Some
of the grass turf was taken by the islanders for fuel, since the peat on the island
was mostly gone, some malicious people said for making poteen, but the
illicit whiskey trade had stopped years ago and the fields of barley were
intended for the chickens. Although the government had allotted them peat
bogs on the mainland it was the devil's own business to get out there, foot the
turf, pile it and dry it and haul it over in boats. All these things, and many
others, the King told him in a non-stop verbal onslaught.

The King of Tory was not a hereditary official, but usually the islander
most respected for fair decisions, and one who could deal with outsiders. The
previous King had been Paddy Heggarty, a dwarf. The current Tory monarch
was one Paddy Og Rogers (Mac Ruadhraigh), a diminutive, talkative, lively
man who was literate in both Irish and English, and prided himself on his
penmanship. He welcomed the supplicant in the vernacular, but switched
immediately to English for he obviously enjoyed showing off his command
of that tongue to the courtiers. "All scholars are welcome," said the little
royal, "so share a bowl of cold porridge with cream, or some poundings, or
tea, or some soda bread, or a cup of milk, or all the aforementioned items
should you so wish." He took the tea. The King had poundings—a pile of

mashed potatoes with butter and salt, and continued his monologue. Life would be impossible on the island were it not for "two salubrious institutions"—the dole and the blind pension. The dole (unemployment pay) was a sacred cow—no mean thing in this pastoral kingdom where the cow was the head of the house. No one wanted to "lose the dole"—especially those with full-time work, although that was not many for work was seasonal. In summer it was the lobster fishing, and most of the young men, and increasingly the young women, went away in the winter to find work in Scotland. The summer was the best time to be here because the young folk were back and there would be dances and singing and a grand time generally. The blind pension, mind you, now there was another thing entirely. You had to score below a certain point on the visiting doctor's scale to count as blind, and he was a good fellow—"a man of exemplary compassion"—who "always gave us the benefit of the doubt." He would put up the reading chart in English, and ask, "Can you read that?" and of course they could not, for none of them read English anyway. The entire island was legally blind.

The young scholar's head was spinning, but the King's sister offered more tea and bread and it was gratefully taken for the break it provided. He asked the King, "What is this I hear about husbands and wives not living together on Tory?" "Ah," said the King, "the calumnies and falsehoods that those in Ireland spread about us." The truth was, that often when people married "in their advanced years" they did not want to disturb already established family arrangements, particularly when the sisters had brothers to care for. The King was a widow, with a daughter, who had a baby (which was another story), and his sister was married to a man who had himself a sister to take care of him. The King's brother was married, but he lived still at home, and his wife had a brother and sister to care for—and so it went. No one lived far apart on the island, the King explained, and why would they want to be moving about and changing everything? For what? For the want of a common bed every night? At their age there was not the "same urgent need as when they were younger"; indeed it bordered on the indecent to suggest it. In the King's own case it was different: he was still, he thought, a young enough man, and had "known the marital state." If he married again he would want his wife with him, but he wasn't sure his sister would approve. That was one reason to marry an outsider: your sister had to accept her in the house.

The King suggested he could help the scholar by taking him for a walk and telling him the place names. "There's not a rock or hummock that does not have its appropriate appellation," he claimed, "and I know every one of them." Also, they should gather some people and teach him some songs and tell him some stories. There would be a dance in the village hall, which had been the church. One winter the men had used the hall to build a large herring fishing boat. Come the spring they had to break down an end wall to get it out and then build the wall up again. The King's son played the melodian in the

band for the dances. The musician was prevailed on—showing much modesty and protest, to give a sample, and the first interview ended with a merry round of tunes, which attracted several neighbors to an impromptu *ceilidh,* with a few clog dances, to show him the steps. He stumbled back in the dark to his supper of tinned meat, tinned peas and potatoes boiled in their skins. "Did you have a good *craic* with the King, now?" asked Mary and Hugh. He did indeed. "Don't believe the half of what he's tellin' you. Sure he got himself arrested with his stories. And isn't that one the best story of them all?" Sleep overcame him, and overloaded with bizarre information, he went off into dreams of one-eyed monsters with unreliable daughters, and islands of the blind where the one-eyed man was persecuted.

A wild morning saw him walking to the east end to East Town, with the boatman's brother Jimmy. Jimmy was renowned as an artist, and showed him some dazzling primitives of island scenes—the tower, the lighthouse. There was an artist called Derek Hill who came sometimes in the summers and stayed in the old Lloyd's signal station near the lighthouse and painted the scenes and the portraits of the people. He had given Jimmy some materials, and Jimmy had tried his hand. Hill was going to try to sell some for him in Belfast and Dublin. In the meantime he wanted to show off the all ruins on *Dún Balor*—and Iron Age hill fort. Jimmy explained that a lady had come to try to dig up Balor's treasure there (that he got robbing ships carrying gold to America) but the government had stopped her and the treasure was still buried. Surely she was an archaeologist? Had he not seen a reference to her article on the fort? Ah sure, that's what she'd be telling you, wouldn't it; would she *say* she was after the gold? Probably not.

They saw the stone rings of the fort and its big ramparts of earth—just like the same structures he had seen on Dartmoor at Grimspound (the Grimpen of *Baskervilles* fame, where Holmes had hidden in his search for the hound— drifting here.) From the hill he could look down on the East Town fields, radiating out like the spokes of a wheel from the little row of houses. Why were the fields so long and narrow? They didn't used to be said Jimmy. Way back in the old, old days they had been divided up all over the place and people had very different qualities of land. Then a landlord had "striped" the land, and the long strips had all qualities from the poor stuff on the hillsides to the good soil further down. They had been kept that way ever since, and always divided down the middle, so they became narrower and narrower. That was why they only used donkeys for ploughing. The strips were too narrow for a tractor to manage; not that anyone could afford a tractor. And the horses, which seemed to wander about the island like the donkeys, dogs and gaggles of geese? They used to pull kelp sleds, said Jimmy. No one collected the seaweed now (it was sold to iodine manufacturers) but the horses were just kept as pets.

The days passed with visits, potatoes and boiled fish, tinned fruit and jam on soda bread, and huge duck and goose eggs. Tea was like a constant lava flow, and was thick and stewed in a pot that was never taken off the fire. Mary's brother Patrick came over (she got the family house, he got the land and built his own house on it) for he knew "all the family histories" in which our ever-entranced scholar evinced an interest. What was the significance of the names, he asked? He remembered in Synge that the Aran Island heroine of *Playboy* was Pegeen Mike after her father. Mary, his hostess, was Mary Bhrianaigh Bhig (Wee Barney) after hers. But Patrick was Paddy Nábla John. Well, so was Mary, her brother explained, but she preferred her father's name "for the calling." In fact, said Patrick he was Paddy-Nábla-John-John-Iain-Nellie. It came out all at once, like one word, and they had to write it down— with its mixture of Gaelic and English names—to make sense of it. You never used all the names—although some people used three, and a few four: just enough to distinguish you from everyone else. But the old men knew them all, and for everybody on the island. Why? So that you knew of what *clann* you were: who you were the offspring of and exactly how. Why? "A man must know his people (*muintir.*) We are Clann Eoin-Neillí" he announced with pride. "Neillí was our great-great-great grandmother." And did he know all her descendants? "Oh indeed. All the Eoin-Neilí and the Liam-Neilí. These are the two *craoibh* or branches of the *clann* of Neilí. But we are also *clann* Hamish. We know all the *clanna*."

On the day before they decided the boat could leave, he went out alone to one of the cliffs at the north of the island (was it *Mór Ard*, or *Miodh Ard*?) and spent a while just staring out into the Atlantic towards Iceland. He thought of the centuries that were represented there, and that Mr. Getty had chronicled: from the pre-Celtic beaker people who left little but a few odd surnames; through the Bronze and Iron Age Celts with their cattle-stealing stories and Solar legends; through the Danes whom Colmkille had ossified and who may have given their name to the place (*Thor Eye*—Thor's Island); through Conan who built a great tower (a more likely source of the name—*Torach* - towery); through the Christian monks who left their ruins and their graves; through the Spanish shipwrecked there whose overflow of genes might explain the un-usual height and dark looks of the men; through the Scots who "devastated" it and the British who appropriated it but made so little lasting impression on the people, even if their work was stamped on the physical landscape.

They all came and went and the people endured. Like the Cochiti, they survived, and like the Cochiti they called. Could this be the next place? Could it be another act of the non-existent providence that had impelled him to this wild edge of Europe, this next stop before the infinite ocean? Was this what he really wanted to do? No. Not again. Not the questions; not the doubts; not the futility. The sea sucked and roared and lurched into and out of the gullies and fjords. Some boys came running up the hill to shout that the boat was leaving—"*Tá a' bád ag imacht*!!" He must leave, but he knew with a certainty beyond calculation that he would return; if not for professional reasons—he could scarcely muster those, then for those reasons of the heart that reason didn't touch.

> *Tomorrow, and, the pageant moved away*
> *Down to the poorest tent pole, we and you*
> *Part company: no other may pursue*
> *Eastward your voyage, be informed what fate*
> *Intends, if triumph or decline await*
> *The tempter of the everlasting steppe.*

The tumble back into fertile Devonshire gave little time for the soul to catch up, and things there rattled along. He had a long piece worked out on curing rituals in Cochiti, and Mitchell suggested the Tavistock Institute journal *Human Relations*. This brought him into contact with the dominating figure of John Bowlby, who was already famous for his work on autistic children and the "attachment" of mother and child so fragile and so dangerous to disturb. Bowlby is another of those figures whose importance at the time is hard to convey adequately in retrospect. His insistence on the traumatic significance of mother-infant separation had influenced his whole generation. The legal system was said to be "Bowlbyized"—it was fixated on "separation anxiety." No magistrate or judge would ever give custody of an infant—or even an older child—to its father for fear of the terrible consequences. When told about our hero's theory that it was the mother-child unit that was basic and universal, not the so-called "nuclear family," the avuncular Bowlby could hardly contain his excitement. You should look at some of the work of the "ethologists" said the great man, mentioning Tinbergen and Lorenz, whom he knew about, but also people he hadn't heard about—Harlow, for example, who had done amazing experiments with baby monkeys, and a young Englishman called Ambrose, who worked on smiling in infants. Perhaps. But wasn't all this emotional stuff to do with the psychology of the bond, something that a Freudian like Bowlby might be interested in, certainly? But our sociologist manqué was working on "social structure"—couldn't you take all this attachment and grief and anxiety and love for granted? No, said Bowlby, not if you believed that such attachments and their consequences were purely dependent on "learning" or "culture." It was important to show that they were not: that they were givens of the human condition, brought about through evolution, based on the mammalian substructure of human behavior. Experience was important: the baby had to have the right experience; if you failed to give it this then all the awful consequences followed. Culture messed up all the time. But it was important to see that if all these emotional things about the mother-child bond could be simply learned or unlearned, you could easily substitute something else for it. But you couldn't: look at the results of trying to do so. If it was the fixed point of turning social structures, the reason lay beyond the social structures themselves.

Bowlby sent him away with things to read: on the "critical period", on "imprinting" and an article by one M. R. A. Chance in *New Scientist*, called "What Makes Monkeys Sociable." It was their struggle for high rank in order to mate, it appeared. He was sure the great Bowlby was right about the basic issue, but there was a division of labor here, and he really was dealing with social structure. It wasn't his business to deal with the psychobiological basis of the bonds. Not yet anyway.

Still influenced by Vogtie, he wrote a brief piece for *Man* on the role of veterans in Cochiti factionalism: the men who returned from the wars were able to combine progressivism and conservatism, thus breaking down the barriers and bitterness of the factional struggles. Those barriers remained strong in divided England, and he fought a need to get back into the political struggle, but it was a losing battle: he could not play the outlaw here. He was still disillusioned with the Tories and they had not improved much in his absence, but there was no question of succumbing to Socialism; his adventures with the New Left Review had confirmed his prejudices there. But in the West Country there was still that lively tradition of Liberalism that survived in the Celtic fringe—or at least the geographical fringe, since the leader of the Liberals, Jo Grimond, was the member for Orkney and Shetland. There were a lot of Liberal voters, but few Liberal MPs, given the winner-take-all voting system. It had pretty much escaped his notice in the past, but here was a party that was anti-Tory but not socialist. He was a member, but a non-political member, of the National Liberal Club anyway. It looked promising; he plunged. He organized a campaign in the local elections where, in his ward, the Liberals were up against a sitting Tory with a huge majority who had been more or less unopposed in the past. They came within a handful of votes of unseating this complacent reactionary. It was a kind of satisfaction. He didn't tell his parents.

He was in the whirl of lectures and classes, and now was going up once a week to attend the LSE seminar on "Small Communities in the British Isles" that met on Thursday evenings. He combined this with his research reading and note taking at the Institute and the late-breakfast tactic at the club, to push on with his publication schedule. He sang G & S (*Princess Ida*) and tenor in the Madrigal Society, and began to feel that he might just get to like it here enough to want to dig in. He even joined the British Sociological Association, since he was officially a sociologist after all, and what he was proposing to do on Tory could double as Social Anthropology or Rural Sociology—undergoing a revival at the time. Manchester University was the seat of the revival, with Ronald Frankenberg in the department founded and still ruled by stern empiricist Max Gluckman. They had a fellowship there, and he was invited to go up for an interview for it. It would give him a year in which to do nothing but research. He had nothing to lose, except that it became clear that Gluckman had a candidate in place (Mervyn Meggitt from Australia) and only wanted to put on a show of "selection" for the university. He was told this on arrival, but, it was obviously assumed, he should be glad of the invitation anyway.

Gluckman was a bully. It's hard to find good things to say about him. To impress visitors he would send Frankenberg out for cigarettes with a curt order. He demanded that all members of his department go with him to watch Manchester United. It was their only chance, he joked, to shout openly "Up with the Reds!" Our boy's teeth-clenching: "I don't watch soccer" was greeted with a sneering: "Well *that* will have to change then, won't it?" When they got to Gluckman's house the great man threw the car keys to him and commanded: "Put it in the garage for me." "Put it in yourself," said the appalled candidate, throwing the keys back, "I'm not your bloody chauffeur." He did help with the washing up when ordered, since he felt truly sorry for Mrs. Gluckman. Pleasing the grownups was one thing; groveling to them was an unacceptable other.

There then came upon him a painful realization: he was henceforth a grown up; he had joined, while scarcely realizing it, the ranks of the adults. The people he now had to please with his dances—the people for whom he had to choose masks—were his quaintly named "peers." Life was now a prolonged peer-review process. You no longer got brownie points from the big people for being intellectually cute; you got cut down to size by your equals. This is how equality was maintained. The culture of contradiction ruled: any proposition, however self-evidently true, generated an automatic counter proposition. The academic favorite word was "however"; the favorite weapon was the book review. It was a jungle—a polite, polished, sherry-sipping jungle. The next major hurdle would be the Ph.D. thesis, where a committee of highly critical examiners—eminent, learned, powerful professors, would analyze, dissect, and ruthlessly disembowel his amateur efforts. My God, they might even put Gluckman on the damned committee! But now he could no longer divert them with his whimseys; he had to stand up and take it. In the meantime, he could get in a little practice by doing some book reviews of his own; the sherry sipping he had pretty much mastered, and if nothing else he could distinguish at first taste a manzanilla from an amontillado.

Sociology was becoming more popular; people now at least knew the word. The good folks who brought us *New Scientist*—a really very well presented weekly on natural science, wanted to start *New Society*, to do the same for the social sciences. It must have been Macrae who put them on to the onetime would-be journalist and ex-cub-reporter and columnist-about-town. It was hard to resist either the opportunity or the money, which, while being pathetic by any real-world standards, was a welcome subsidy to an underpaid don. The editor, planning the first issue, was an old Etonian, with the grand manner and clipped speech of that tribe, while his co-editor was of, one supposes, humbler origins, but had adopted the manner to which he ought to have been born. Different masks for different tasks. The Etonian was running for parliament on the Tory ticket, his compère on the Labour. They reviewed each other's campaigns and obviously got on very well. He liked them both and when they asked him to write reviews, articles and editorials (they had seen "Pueblo Baseball" and thought he had the touch) he plunged in. It meant sitting up all day Sunday late into the night to finish whatever the piece was, and also a lot of bluff since he had to write about this and that in the "state of the social sciences" and he was only marginally in control of this information. But he found he liked this writing to order. The earliest pieces in the "Observations" section of the new magazine were often his: he prepared an article on Cochiti and promised one on Tory Island. The Tory editor, Tim Raison, was much amused by the name: it was indeed the insult the Whigs had thrown at the King's party in the eighteenth century, and which had stuck as a badge of honor. In Gaelic, one of the meanings was "pirate, brigand, robber" and, yes, it was one other theory of the origin of the island's name. "Island of the Brigands"—plausible.

The events of these years go by in a whirl, and if you, dear reader, are looking for a coherent and chronological account, don't hold your breath. Such an account could be done with enough "research"—but to what purpose? We are writing of the development of a soul, not a history of the twentieth century. The soul in question was a ragbag assortment of emotional, intellectual and informational odds and ends that were spinning round like clothes in a dryer. It would have been nice to stop, like those Mexican bearers, and sort out the clothes into neat piles and assess what to keep, what discard, and what augment. But there was never time. On his repeat visits to Tory— every summer for at least three months in fact—he often had time alone as he sat on the cliffs and listened to the sea. But his head was filled with Gaelic idioms, the names of fields and cliffs and harbors, the twenty versions of the Balor legend, the difficulty of taking down genealogies, the attempt to memorize verses and songs, the failure to have brought the right valuation maps from Dublin, the problem of how to get off this isolated rock in time if the weather turned brutal again and the sea threw its shock of waves over the whole island, destroying crops with the salt. He never seemed to have time to stand still and let his soul catch up. Leaning out to watch the indifference of the sea only brought on the psychic vertigo again. The gross impersonality of the ocean, which created and destroyed life without judgement or even interest, seemed to represent Nature herself in her unconcern for either herself or her children. From her we came and unto her we must return, and no one is there to care one way or the other. She was the uncaring mother, and we yearned pathetically for the love she could not give. Perhaps that's why we needed God: to make sure someone is at least laughing at our fate, that something cares enough, even if it is only to despise our pretensions. Too much attention to ontology meant too little attention to Tory. Too much attention to Tory meant too little work on the thesis. Too much work on politics (would you run the general election campaign for your ward?: of course—ask and it shall be granted) meant too little attention to family, parents, and then, children.

They almost broke up over the children issue. He thought it would be unfair to children to bring them into this tumultuous life. Wait until we are more settled, until some necessary things have been achieved. When will that be? she rightly asked. It would mean her giving up work and they would lose that vital income. But she had virtually given up anyway, having broken her foot trying to kick-start the Lambretta they had bought to replace the old Ford which finally gave up on hills entirely. The journalism income would make up the difference. His mother would come down and help them get started. He relented, nervously. He knew he would love a child, but what kind of father could he possibly be? He was barely a grown up in his own estimation. He was being forced into some semblance of adulthood: he had grown more confident and easier in his manner with lectures and classes once he got used to being on that side of the podium and the desk. He tried to be as dedicated as Whatmuff and Friedrich, as provocative and tough as Freedman and Gellner, as considerate and supportive as Firth, as personally interested as Moser and Kluckhohn, as responsible as Vogt and Morris, as erudite as MacRae, and as intellectually challenging as Popper and Ayer. He had the best teachers if only he could stop thinking of himself as the eternal bright student out to please. But years of being the little dancer were hard to shake off; his dance had now to be that of the choreographer, and it did not come easily to him.

He left for the summer on Tory: this time to explore the sources in Dublin. He left wife pregnant, her foot still in a cast, but brave as always and with now some good friends around. He had, only half jokingly, suggested getting a baby chimpanzee so they could raise the two together and note the comparisons (memories of the Kellogs.) But there was no room, and in any case this was something where the woman had, and used, the veto. Nonplussed, he went for a while to Dublin, since he now knew where to hunt for sources. He had been in touch with Estyn Evans at Queen's Belfast, author of the definitive *Irish Heritage*, which, among other things, settled the issue of what island kings were for. Evans sent him a copy of an unpublished thesis on the social geography of Tory by one Jim Hunter—a B.A. honors thesis, which was rich in suggestions. He must visit the Valuation Office in Dublin to get the basic land maps dating to the early nineteenth century, and the maps at the Land Commission left over from the work of The Board (defunct since Irish Independence.) The Commissioners of Irish Lights had important stuff on the history of the lighthouse. The Ordnance Survey office had its own beautifully engraved maps showing changes over the years, augmented by records kept by the Central Statistics Office. Works on the general area of northeast Donegal were at the National Library, and experts in history and language were at Trinity and University Colleges, and the National Library, as well as the odd Institute for Advanced Study, dedicated to higher Physics and the Irish Language. Everyone, everywhere had that tantalizing Irish mix of learning and madness, that at once endears The Irish to foreigners and leaves the serious visitor in a state of subtle bafflement.

He was taken by the city's most eminent historian of Ireland, to the Register of Deeds, to get a copy of the 1861 deed of sale for Tory. This showed it passed (for six-thousand-five-hundred pounds) from the reforming landlord, Woodhouse, who had "striped" the land (and removed one hundred islanders) to "the Jew man" as they still called him: Benjamin St .John Baptist Joule, who was to receive no income or profit from his misguided purchase. The serious searchers after history ended at the Gate theatre, already a few pints of stout the worse, and afterwards in a scruffy local pub. Here the great historian lay on a bench reaching for his pint glass on the floor, and recited swaths of Steven McKenna's translation of Plotinus' *The Divine Mind,* between choruses of *Finnegan's Wake*—the song not the book.

> Tim Finnegan lived on Watling Street,
> An Irish gentleman mighty odd.
> He had a brogue both broad and sweet,
> And to rise in the world he carried a hod.

> Whack-fol-de-do, dance to yer partner,
> Welt the floor, with yer trotters shake.
> Isn't it the truth I tell yer,
> Lot's of fun at Finnegan's Wake.

The singer-historian had introduced our bewildered fellow to Lord Longford, the presiding genius at the Gate, Catholic humanitarian and friend of prisoners, who shuffled about greeting playgoers. His lordship hung on to the proffered hand for an alarmingly long time. The gate was the avant-garde theatre in the town, set up in conscious opposition to the more famous Abbey, where they only put on plays by Irish writers, and a Gaelic short feature after the main show was over. The fare was usually slapstick stage Irishry (*Put a Devil on Horseback*) and the smart set preferred the Gate (*Waiting for Godot*), which had in consequence acquired a reputation, deserved or not, as a workshop for homosexuals. The singer-historian-raconteur told of Brendan Behan's crack that the difference between the Gate and the Abbey was only that between Sodom and Begorrah.

The smell of the burning peat hit his nervous nostrils once again, and he stopped in Falcarragh, up the coast from Tory, to see a man who was to change his life there. Séamus O Rathallaigh (James O'Riley) was the local representative of the Ministry of the Gaeltacht, responsible for the welfare and development of the Irish-speaking districts. He was a Belfast man and had learned Irish in Catholic school, then become a civil servant for the Republic. He was a charmer but without the madness. He was a sober, tee-total, religious family man who worked hard to improve economic conditions for the Gaelic speakers. He introduced mink farming, with Scandinavian managers, which was a low cost (feed them on cheap fish), high profit enterprise, and employed many local native speakers. But Séamus had to be warned that they had tried mink farms in Devon and the little devils always escaped and then devastated the local small fauna. Mink were savage serial killers and took over from the badgers and otters, which they exterminated. Local otter hounds had been replaced by mink hounds, but these couldn't make a dent in the numbers of little killers. Séamus noted everything, and demanded more. All the social science information and methods he could soak up. He was working on county incomes and central place theory—something that had the attention of the social geographers, and the two of them drove deep into Donegal to find a calculator big enough for the statistics involved: at the Crolly Doll factory. Séamus understood his concerns and enthusiastically plied him with information. He helped him understand things like the naming system, since among his many talents he was a grammarian and had written an introductory grammar for Irish learners. Above all, the islanders liked him and trusted him as they did few outsiders.

A whole summer on the island gave him time to work with the King and Patrick on the genealogies, and he found a young man who had helped Hunter—Owen Whorriskey, who was willing to go over the fields with him, and pin down the current owners. Work back from this with the maps, and some help in working out who was whom since so many had, officially, the same name. Of two Patrick Duggans who was which? Well, there was Patrick-Eamon-Mary and Patrick-Ruari-Liam. Must get all the "strings" of names of everyone—see how they related themselves to the older generations through the names. What would it tell about their notions of descent? How would it tally with the genealogies? He tried taking down all Mary's relatives in approved fashion (as outlined in *Notes and Queries on Anthropology*.) This was not like Cochiti; you couldn't just look at the clan and then its lineages and households. But he was getting nowhere; it was just a spiderweb of ad-hoc relationships spreading over the whole population. Then the King told him to stop doing it that way. There were indeed clans, but they were not matrilineal clans (his observation, not the King's.) Indeed the very word "clan" was the Gaelic *clann*, misappropriated by the anthropologists to mean a unilineal group (descent exlusively through either males or females.) He may be the only person using the word correctly! It meant "children" in the sense of "offspring." The Cochiti for "clan"—*hanu*, meant, literally, "people"—so you were the Oak people, or the Fox people. On Tory you were not "of a *clann*"—you were "*clann* so-and-so": descendants of… whomever. And whomever was whomever you started with in the distant past; and *all* the descendants of that person were his (or her) *clann*. It had a plural—*clanna*—which he translated as "progenies" for want of a better way of putting it. And Patrick and the King announced that there were four main ancestors from way back: the Nellie (Doohan) he had already come across, then Séamus (McClafferty) who yielded the *clann* Shéamuis (Hamish—genitive, and vocative, of Séamus) that Patrick had already claimed; followed by the descendants of Feilimí (Phillip Mac Ruarí) and Eoin (Iain Duggan). Get these and you have more than half of the islanders, they said. He did, and his kind and patient friends walked him through the often seven or more generations involved, going back into the eighteenth century with definite links, but with mythological depths as deep as Colmkille and his sanctification of the soil and the Duggan family that welcomed him ashore. The Eldest Duggan led prayers in the absence of the priest, and was the only one who could lift the blessed clay.

There was so much more, with a complete household census (from Mary who knew everyone), a copying out of all the marriage records—from the completely cooperative and unsuspicious priest, Father O'Colm (and his successor the young Father Sweeney.) O'Colm was writing his own book on the folkore of the island, (*Toraigh na dTonn*—Tory of the Waves), so a division of labor was in order and agreed on. That the priest's book was to be in Gaelic restricted its usefulness, but it was on the record, and someone would translate it surely: he might do it himself. He figured out who was whom in the "living apart at marriage" arrangements. It seemed to be of two types: older people who married after thirty (like the King's brother and sister), and younger people, who had what in common? He must delve and delve. There were twenty people—ten marriages out of about fifty, involved in what he decided to call "natolocal" residence. Anthropology lacked a category to describe this—"matrilocal" described Cochiti's dominant pattern well enough, but if he had a coinage, a neologism, a new term to add to the vocabulary, what a coup!

Meyer Fortes had already described the situation among the Ashanti of "the visiting husband"—same thing: they lived apart and the husband was a "visitor" in his wife's house. But Fortes attributed this entirely to the matrilineality of the Ashanti. Tory was not matrilineal, descent was bilateral or cognatic: all the descendants of an "apical ancestor" were related equally, and the *clanna* so reckoned all overlapped endlessly. Yet they had the visiting husband thing. And in the past more than half the couples had lived this way. My God! Here was a test case, a classic natural experiment. Get more details; get the cycle of the household that Fortes had claimed was crucial. Was the natolocal residence part of such a cycle? One phase of the turning saga of birth, marriage, birth and death? It wasn't the "country divorce" of the south (nothing here was much like the south it turned out)—they *never* lived together. Here was a clue: the islanders firmly announced that the only true family was the "holy family"—parents and children under the same roof. At the same time, they regarded marriage as a kind of treason against the parents. To start a holy family you had to break up a holy family. Talk about cognitive dissonance: he should have had this example at Harvard.

But all was not paper and pencil. He had a small, poor quality, reel-to-reel tape recorder, all he could afford. But it drew the singers like a cache of poteen. They loved to hear themselves and used up his small amount of tape quickly. But it enabled him to study and learn the songs. This helped with the language learning but it was also important because of the high value the people placed on the ability to contribute a song at the weekly *ceilidh*. He had picked up some dances and joined in, and they obviously genuinely approved. Songs were the next. Father Sweeney had a great voice they all agreed, and was called on each week, early. Then he went home to the parish house to avoid embarrassment, for he had tried to get them to start the dance earlier than midnight and finish at a respectable hour, for the children at least. But this was not *béas an oileáin*, the custom of the island, and they politely ignored him. A tactful standoff ensued, and it was explained that the hall was built by Tory men, not men from Malin, even though they be priests, and the Tory men would decide on Tory matters. So the songs were learned and the word passed that he should be called, and he was, and sang, and they applauded, and he felt suddenly, sharply, unnervingly, at home.

> Buachaill ó'n Éirne mé's bhréagfinn fein cailín deas óg.
> Ni iarrfiann bó spré léithe tá mé féin saidhbhir go leór.
> 's liom Corcaigh 'a mhéid é, dhá thaoibh a' ghleann a 's Tir Eoghan.
> 's mur n-ath-ruigh mé béasaí 's mé 'n t-oighr ar Chondae Mhuigheo.

The lad from Eirne teases the pretty young girl: he doesn't need a dowry cow for her, he's plenty rich enough. He owns Cork and the two sides of the glen of Tyrone, and if he minds his manners he's the heir to County Mayo. On Tory the cow-boy from Eirne wouldn't have needed the cow; there was no dowry on Tory; it was different.

Shaking himself awake he landed back in the untroubled real world where the young Irish senator from Boston won his presidency in the USA. Nigeria and Ghana became independent, and a young Canadian sociologist improbably named Lionel Tiger went to see how the transition, under the dictator Nkruma, worked in the land of the Ashanti. Away on the island he missed all the events of the world, and was always a little surprised on his return to find that his absence had not hindered a thing. How solipsistic are our personal worlds. Regimes came and went, power changed hands, stock markets crashed and recovered, without his knowing anything about it. His missing these events, and his daily avid scrutiny of the papers to follow them, had made no difference. And the world seemed much the same.

But his own personal world took a heart-banging leap into a terrifying unknown: Kate was born. Tiny, perfect, beautiful Kate. Most babies look like all the others and mostly like little red mongoloids. Kate was elfish and smooth and totally pretty from the start. All doubts evaporated in the eye contact that seemed so well established even if the books said she couldn't focus. It was like falling in love to the nth degree several times amplified. He felt that total jolt of the system once again, and more blood-rushing than ever. "Life is for her now," he said to himself, and for a brief space all the doubts fell away and the meaning was revealed: this is what we are about; this is what we are *for*. He saw life steadily and saw it whole, and it was Kate. His soul caught up for a moment, but a moment he couldn't preserve for long, as the search for the hidden city sounded its imperative fanfare.

Kate's early life was a minor miracle of survival. Inexperienced parents should not be allowed to have children, or there should be practice children they get to make mistakes on. Kate was dropped into her bath and nearly drowned. Still over-influenced by the Indians, they decided she should not lie on her back staring at nothing more interesting than the blank ceiling, so they bound her to a cradleboard (brought back with the drum) and propped her up to take in everything. Fine, until the cradleboard, propped on the stove (unlighted) in the kitchen, tipped forward and deposited her on the hard floor. It was not easy to explain to the horrified doctor, who was all for calling in the social services. Some of these social workers were his students doing their training; given their introduction to the social institutions of the simpler society, they might have understood; one hopes. Driving north in the winter to see his parents in the mother-in-law's car, they skidded on black ice and rolled off the road. The back of the car, where Kate's carrycot was lying on the seat, was crushed. Kate, however, having been kicking up a fuss, was in her mother's arms, and since the front of the car was not dented, she was saved along with her terrified parents. Once Kate could toddle, she climbed up a stool-ladder to the top-loading washing machine to look in, tipped over, and disappeared except for two tiny feet kicking in the air. She was hauled out dripping and *laughing*. She spent weekends, early on, watching cricket matches from an infant chair, then, once upright, wandering uncertainly round the boundary. In a moment of not being watched she saw daddy out there batting, and tottered forward into an arena of ninety-mile-per-hour hard leather balls piping, "Daddy! Daddy!" The game was suspended while she was grabbed by the horrified daddy and placed under guard in the pavilion. He was out LBW the next ball, his concentration shattered. His concentration would never be the same again.

Cricket, which he had only played under protest at school, became a big thing because it was a way to get away from the Olivetti and the classroom, and out into the air at weekends. The staff team, known appropriately as The Erratics, had quite a history and a good fixture list with the local village sides.

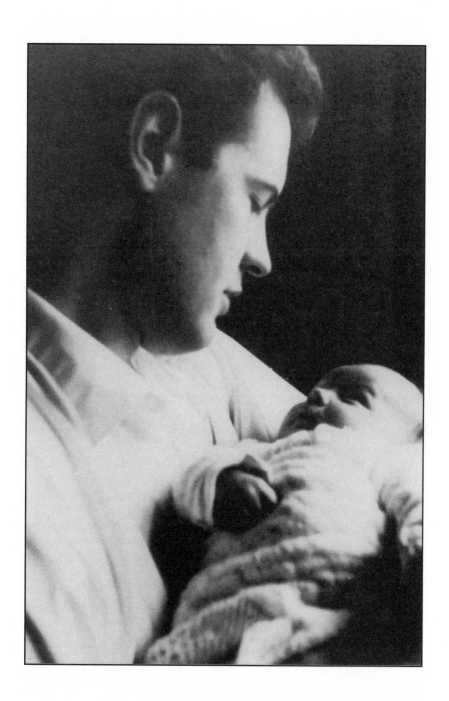

Its average age must have been in the fifties—the captain and opening fast bowler (John Lloyd the librarian) was 65. Thus youngsters like himself were welcomed not for their skills, but because they could run after the ball on the boundaries. (His fellow runner was Trevor Smith, ex-LSE, some-time Liberal candidate for Parliament, and later, from the House of Lords, Vice-chancellor of the University of Ulster.) The older players firmly monopolized the infield positions—preferably slip or point where no running was required.

Playing conditions were often primitive in the more remote villages—like Ide Monachorum—and sheep had often to be removed before the game could start. The leavings of the wooly tribe usually still littered the field; they required some imaginative re-writing of the rules for when a ball landed in them. The indignant animals would sit up on the hillside, bleating loudly with what sounded perilously like a commentary on the state of play. The village captain was usually the vicar, the fast bowler the blacksmith. The vicar would often ask, very politely, if the gentlemen would mind fielding first, since the villagers were bringing in the harvest and only had a few players available while the sun was still high. Of course, no problem. The whole point of the exercise in any case was to work up a thirst. Games stopped strictly at six when the village pub opened, whatever the state of the game.

That was Saturday; Sunday was back to the Olivetti, the carbon paper, the draft after draft. MacRae was pressing on the incest article. Surely it would be done. But he wanted to get it just right. Bales had set him to look for a regularity of interaction process, and Johnny had said it must be negative reinforcement. Freud, he had decided was talking about a situation, between siblings, where there was little or no actual physical interaction, but there was proximity: the claustrophobic sexually repressed Viennese family. Westermarck, on the other hand, was talking about a situation where the little pre-pubescent siblings tumbled all over each other. The outcome was the same—no incest—but the mechanisms were very different. The Westermarck Effect (as he happily called it) obliterated sexual desire between them; the Freud Effect might even have increased it. Drawing on the Palfrey House material he looked for the fullest descriptions of sibling interaction in the ethnographies, including the startling favorite by Mel Spiro of the Kibbutz *sabras*, who, despite the insistence that they should marry, resolutely refused to, and even to have sex in that otherwise progressive environment. How can you have sex, they said, with someone you've slept with, showered with, and seen on the potty? Spiro couldn't see the Westermarck wood for the Freudian trees, but our Balesian, adept with the language if nothing else, came out with:

> The intensity of heterosexual attraction between co-socialized siblings after puberty is inversely proportionate to the intensity of physical interaction between them before puberty.

Surely Bales and Johnny would be proud. Asher Tropp (LSE), whose belligerent personality had led him to be dubbed The Spartacus of Sociology, (by Robert McKenzie?) announced to the British Sociological Association meeting that this was the first real "law" any British sociologist had yet discovered. Of course it wasn't a sociological law in the strict sense, but who was counting? For better or for worse it became known as his law by his name, and MacRae happily took the manuscript for the Journal. There was a "Part II" with the cross-cultural comparisons and statistics, but Macrae didn't want this. He was suspicious of that whole enterprise, so it sat in a draw and was eventually lost. But for better or worse, *Sibling Incest* was launched. "You could get a chair on the basis of this," Asher said, exaggerating as usual.

There just weren't chairs in those days. This was before the almost lunatic expansion of the universities, which had them floundering about for enough professors (Asher went to Surrey, Alan Williams went to York—most of his friends ended up in chairs in the new wave of provincial universities in genteel cathedral towns.) The number of departments and chairs was then pretty fixed, and people assumed that Lecturer was the "career grade" - and that, or at best Senior Lecturer or Reader was where you would end up. He couldn't look beyond the next week's lectures, and his publication efforts and pieces of journalism kept him totally occupied. This was in embarrassing contrast to most of his older colleagues. Depressed by the continuing low salaries, they had a union meeting—they didn't often do that—and even recklessly suggested they might strike. It was actually considered, until one timid voice asked: "But how would they know we were on strike?" and the matter was quickly shelved.

A small raise was obtained, and the senior staff decided the total sum due the university should be divided among the juniors. They were pretty damn nice people, even if they didn't publish. How did they see him? In a history of the Erratics published many years later, an economist who had also been relegated to the outfield where they had numerous chats while waiting for something to happen, said he was "the resident intellectual" at the time. He was known for "not having a conventional opinion on any subject." He proposed, said the writer, that there was an almost perfect correlation between IQ and final exam results. If we were truly concerned only with this final outcome, we should give degrees at enrollment based on IQ testing, give those who wanted to learn something extensive reading lists, and go about our other business. However, noted the fellow outfielder, when it came to cricket he was of the opinion that anyone who had gone through an English school should be able to put a bat to a ball effectively; there was no excuse for messing up. Some things were sacred.

He did a lot with the student Folk Song Society, and this led to a memorable encounter. A guest speaker and singer turned out to be Dominic Behan, Brendan's younger and much smaller brother. Dominic had adopted the mask

of the eccentric, alcoholic bard, and wavered, drunk, through altogether cred-
itable performances of Dublin street songs. To him Ireland was Dublin and he
affected never to have heard of Tory and to despise the Gaelic speakers:
"aboriginals" he called them. He knew still more verses of Finnegan's Wake,
describing, in a chant-like version all his own, the resurrection of Tim:

> Mickey Maloney tried to duck, when a bucket of whiskey flew at him,
> It missed and landed on the bed, and the whiskey scattered over Tim.
> Bedad he revives and see how he rises, Finnegan rising on the bed,
> He says "Whirl yer whiskey around like blazes, thunderin' Jazus d'ye
>   think I'm dead!"

> Whack-for-de-do, dance to yer partner... etc.

Finn Again's Awake. River-run-down where are you when we need you?
Lot's of fun in any case. Our semi-Irishman told the Tory story of the drunken
wake there when, while they were taking snuff and playing cards, the men
propped up the body in the bed and dealt it a hand. The legend goes that the
corpse won. Dominic produced a tortured legendary genealogy, which said
that the Behans (O Beachain) had been bards in the Kingdom of Offaly where
the other bardic family was our boy's maternal lineage. Since the caste system
meant bards could only marry into other bardic families, this meant they must
be cousins, and yes he would accept any hospitality and another few pints as
was befitting between one kinsman and another of equal and exalted bardic
rank. Ah yes, we are indeed both *seanchaigh*. "What the fuck is that?" Never
mind, O Dominic, give us another story; give us the storyteller's gift.

So he told of how as a wee lad in the Dublin slums, he was used to the
daddy coming home late and drunk, and seizing him to fend off the angry
attacks of the mammy. One night she had been boiling his dinner for hours
and in the end moved the pan off the gas ring in disgust. The drunken daddy
burst in, grabbed the bare-arsed Dominic, and promptly sat him down on the
still glowing ring, his scream loud enough to rattle the whole city block.
Dominic displayed for the startled assembly the proof of his story; a proof he
carried throughout his life. He gave them his singer's gift of a song he made
up, satirizing Hugh Gaitskell, who was, to the annoyance of the real Left,
arguing for a British nuclear deterrent. Dominic included the withering lines:

> You can stick your Polaris
> Up your arse

This may not be, written down, an obvious rhyme, but if you have a truly
thick, and truly drunk, Dublin accent, it comes over with delicate perfection.
Dominic gave the finger to the neighbors, peed in the gutter, and went on his
way, singing.

Where was language and culture? It was there. An article comparing the use of more than one language in Cochiti and Tory appeared in *Man*. It was OK—it argued that language was more than a barometer of social change, it was an agent of change—but it was not a main thrust. He "kept up" but in Exeter he was isolated and lacking stimulation. Maurice Vile had urged him to look at the political situation in northwest Donegal—a marginal seat in which the Tory islanders had a block of votes devoted, except for one, to the Republican (Fianna Fail) cause. The identity of the one dissenter was an occasion for great gossip. But a sympathetic government meant a lot to the island, dependent as it was on subsidies. He began to explore the local politics and politicians, but found himself caught up in the inevitable intrigues and was in danger of becoming a pawn in Republican struggles. He couldn't risk his independent status by taking sides, and after some close calls decided to concentrate on domestic matters and leave the politics alone. Ignorance may not have been bliss, but it was relatively safe.

The next long summer had Ewart along for a few weeks, easel and all. The stark beauty of the island and the quirky character of the people inspired the artist, but the monotonous food (tinned meat and potatoes) and the unstable weather, drove him back to benign Devon. The intrepid ethnographer barreled on, with his field ownership survey. He began to suspect that despite the tendency to "ruinous fragmentation" that was supposed to accompany partible inheritance (every heir gets some land), there seemed to be a stability of holding size over time: about two and a half acres. There was something going on here; obviously not everyone with a right to inherit did so. One of the very old men in East Town dropped a mention, in Gaelic, to "the land of the marriage." This was the land that went to a child marrying, and theoretically every child had a right to some. But there was Mary's own case, where she got the house and brother Patrick the land. And with the King's siblings, some had, the monarch said, married into land, such that that they had no right to take land from their brother (him). Clearly some balancing act was going on, so that, despite the theory, landholdings did not infinitely fragment. Even so, some divisions were actually so minute it was almost impossible to show them except on a huge-scale map, and there were always mini soap operas for the telling about disputes over these fractal inheritances.

The inheritance of land was connected to the genealogies as was the curious system of naming. He had to tie this up with marriages; the whole thing with household composition; and then what about the sustaining economy? Traditionally this had been both farming and fishing. Unlike the coastal peoples of the West who had starved while within reach of plenty, the Tory people, like the Aran Islanders, had always fished. First in the *curragh* (coracle) and then small row boats, and in the nineteenth century in big herring fishing boats (the nurse's house had been a herring curing station—courtesy of The Board.) How did the boats and their crews tie in, if at all? He needed so much more information, and to tap the right memories. He would petition the King. If the King didn't know himself he knew who knew what and would recruit him to the team. People were introduced at Mass, where only the women went into church. If the weather was at all tolerable, the men stayed outside smoking and gossiping, until the elevation of the host—announced by a tinkling bell, when they would kneel and cross themselves. After that perfunctory gesture towards piety, they resumed the serious business of the Sunday morning: gossip and stories.

Derek Hill was there that year. The Hills were a noble (of the nobility) Anglo-Irish Donegal family. Lord George Hill had been the first to "stripe" the land and forbid fragmentation—in Gweedore. This was to put his lordship up there as the first "reforming" landlord, and he was assassinated for his trouble. Derek was already a well-known portrait painter, and liked Tory for the beauty of its landscape, and for the isolation it gave him to concentrate on nothing but painting. He rented the Lloyd's signal station—no longer used by the insurance company to let the London office know of the inevitable wrecks on the coast, and his one-room cabin became a retreat from the strangeness of Tory. There they could discuss painting, literature (Derek knew all the Irish writers) and the doings of the "finest Aristocracy in Europe" (Yeats)—or what was left of it, but Derek knew them all—Frasers, Butlers, Pakenhams, Fitzgeralds, Leslies, Gregories. Over Pimms No 1 Cup, they talked of Derek's family home and estate in Churchill, Donegal, on Gartan Lake where Colmkille was born, and where the celebrities stayed (including JFK and Jackie.) He had kept the house exactly as it was when his mother died—as it was in the last century. In the generous kitchen he had hung Tory primitives all round the tops of the high walls. It was like fairy music from a Yeatsian world (And let her husband bring her to a house/Where all is ordered, ceremonious…) He should visit. He would.

While he worked and gossiped, the world turned awkwardly on its always wobbling axis. The precession shrugged off the death of Dag Hammarskjold in the Congo, Russia's break with China, South Africa's withdrawal from the Commonwealth, the stupefying foolishness of the Bay of Pigs invasion (what was that young Associate of Leverett House doing?), and the even more egregious idiocy of the Berlin Wall, erected by the vulgar peasant Kruschev to keep his pigs from straying into greener pastures. The stupidity of men seemed to him fathomless: whenever you thought "they can't possibly do anything more stupid" they inevitably did. It was the condition of a creature endowed with intelligence, foresight, imagination and the capacity to embrace ideas, convert them into reality, and die for them. He had been in the company of men who were quite willing to die for an idea, or for revenge, or for no reason at all that they could articulate. The whole business of dying seemed to hold a fascination for them as a thing in itself. And the pernicious impetus of superstition was its life-blood. The blood of Christ, shed for you… There were no ideas worth dying for, only those worth living for. On Tory one really did feel on the edge of the world looking in. And it did not look good. The Russians were said to have a super-bomb, a doomsday bomb, fifty times more powerful than the atomic bomb. If exploded, it would end life on earth. But they would never use it, would they?

He came back to the pressing relevancy of the New Left discussion groups. The Labour Party had lost its latest election. His Liberal candidate came close in Exeter—beating Labour into third place against the entrenched Tories. Father figure Macmillan was back in office at 10 Downing Street. The comrades had an emergency meeting to express their deep upset at the electorate's disgraceful failure to grasp the obvious superiority of the Left's arguments. You present them too arrogantly, he told them; you should try more persuasion and finessing of the voters rather than intellectual bullying. They were deeply shocked: this was to suggest Goebbels' tactic of "the big lie." No, he wearily countered, it was to suggest some respect for the people's healthy skepticism. We told them the truth, and they rejected it, was the reply. They don't *deserve* an enlightened left-wing government. In the meantime, the lofty discussions had to continue. The talk must go on.

They insisted on doing Marxism, so he took a tough Popperian line (the impossibility of Historicism) which caused them to cluck at his stubborn refusal to face the obvious truth. It was impossible for these good people to imagine that someone might have a genuine intellectual disagreement with them. Like the Freudians, they had to believe that you were somehow perverse or in denial, otherwise it was too challenging to ideas they saw as self-evident; ideas that were as essential to their mental and political lives as sap is to the tree. Theirs were not propositions that could be operationalized and tested; they were articles of religious faith. Consequently, it was some kind of diversion to bait them. He gave a paper on "Disraeli or Engels?" He showed how the former, in *Sybil, Or The Two Nations*, and the latter in *The Condition of the Working Class*, had both drawn from the same sources (the government Blue Books on the state of the poor), and they agreed on the diagnosis. But Disraeli's conclusions and solutions were sounder—an alliance of the aristocrats and the proletariat against the capitalists. It is a measure of our distance from these times that no one now will probably understand why this was seen as, well, almost uproariously obscene.

The collegiate comrades of the New Left were, of course, never less than polite. But they were deeply shocked, and took refuge, like the Freudians, in denying his seriousness. And he was only half-serious; he totally lacked the potential Lord Beaconsfield's deferential faith in the aristocracy. But he persisted that any solution was better than the revolutionary one Marx and Engels had proposed (on the one hand) or unbridled capitalism (on the other.) Look where they had got us. The New Lefties agreed, but the answer, if not Communism, was some form of state Socialism, the welfare state, and the abolition of privilege (particularly the poor old House of Lords, and, for some reason that had nothing to do with the supposed suffering of the animal, fox hunting.) Alan Williams tried to get them to discuss how to raise the GNP while still holding to punitive progressive taxation, wealth confiscation, and nationalization. The economists favored this topic, but it was not pursued since the tweedy-corduroy hard-core conscience of the group insisted that Socialism was not about money, but about "the relation of man to man." They were all very uneasy about Hugh Gaitskell's stubborn efforts to purge Labour of its addiction to nationalization. They were even more uneasy about criticizing Russia.

It all became irrelevant when Ellie was born. An only child was not a good idea; that was agreed on. So Ellie was welcomed as a daughter and a sibling. She was born at home with the midwife, an experience that shook and bonded him. But the poor mother was not yet recovered when it was discovered she had a tumor and had to go immediately into hospital. Her grief at leaving the babies, particularly the new one, who was untimely ripped from the breast, was unbearable to watch. But practicalities demanded he buckle down and care for the tiny creature. The Bowlby thing scared him; he would have to be as much like a mother as he could. Ever dependable grandmother left long-suffering grandfather to his own devices once again, and traveled down to help. She more or less took over Kate who was old enough to know that she was without her mother, but not old enough to understand why. Her sad, repeated question: "Mummy coming soon?" left him helpless and hurting. It would not be soon. There was no in-and-out then. It took weeks to recover from a major operation. So he had to dash back and forth from the campus, rearrange classes, and get up in the night to feed the demanding little creature, who as yet had no personality or identity other than that of needy baby.

She was difficult. He did not know how to feed her. She wouldn't take the bottle; she spit it out and yelled, and resisted all coaxing, rocking, singing and simple persuasion. He was not a patient man. At some point his fragile self-imposed calmness broke down. He thrust the nipple into her protesting mouth, held it there firmly and yelled back: "Drink, damn you! Drink the bloody milk!!" She stopped the noise, stopped the protests, burped once, and drank. He didn't think she drank "contentedly" as they used to say, but she drank, and lived, and eventually they got into that rhythm of changing, bathing, holding, feeding, burping and lulling to sleep, that is one of the profoundest human rhythms: one only the mother usually knows in full. But night after night Ellie looked over the bottle with her bright, curious blue eyes, and sucked vigorously, and he sang her Gaelic lullabies and Cochiti children's songs, and little things he made up for Kate and now sang for her. He knew, despite the weariness and dread of facing a busy day, that what had been granted was a privilege almost beyond comprehension, a glance of the Grail. The kingdom of his soul would never be a Waste Land now. The vastations would never have their old force: two little girls would defeat them.

There was no time for his own music, or for much theater or cinema or reading outside the stuff needed for lectures, classes, papers and research. But on trains he read; it was his only chance. A paperback hurriedly picked up at a station bookstall (in Birmingham where he gave a lecture and where Charles Madge told him he must "try to get into the matrilineal mind") reintroduced him to the perfection of writing in Jane Austen that he had so easily dismissed in school. He read William Golding for the first time and something was stirred up that went back to his parrots in the winter jungle and the ring stones on the moor and the guilty sense he had that primitive societies really were a glimpse into the past of humanity. Was his attempt to get into the matrilineal mind just a psychological exercise, or comparative sociology, or idle curiosity? Or was it a window into a state of society that lingered among the Pueblo Indians and that had been lost in the modern (developed, civilized, industrial) world? If not matrilineal kinship specifically (he knew enough know that there was no "matriarchal stage" of development) then the world of moieties and clans, shamans and magic?

The old Lord Raglan, grandson of the destroyer of the Light Brigade, author of one of the odder books on incest, *Jocasta's Crime*, and former president of the Royal Anthropological Institute, visited Exeter. His lordship was an endearing representative of the established intellectual aristocracy (like Bertie) and the old diffusionist school of Anthropology. "No savage ever invented anything," was his conclusion; and although one knew he was using the term in the old technical sense—a member of the stage before barbarism and civilization, it was jolt like hearing a swear word in church. In his highborn way the Earl announced forcefully that it was important to study Tory Island as "a representative of the village societies based on common ownership that had flourished in Europe before the coming of industrial capitalism." It was a "social fossil", he said without a twitch of guilt. Our structural-functionalist visibly blushed and tried to change the subject. Secretly he wondered about it, but could not pursue; he had a thesis to write, and functionalists to please, and miles to go before he slept. Even so, while Tory and Cochiti were physically contemporary, to go there was, in a sense, to step back significantly in time. Even so…

He ran through Naipaul, Anouilh, Heller, Solzhenitsyn and Fuentes, and marvelled at *Lawrence of Arabia*. David Lean was confirmed as the greatest, and the fellow with the Irish name at the Holland Park party, hair tamed and died blonde, turned up as a stunning Lawrence. He suffered a serious disappointment over Kubrick's attempt to incarnate the nymphet *Lolita* in a nubile teenager—despite James Mason's perfect (of course) Humbert Humbert. The four ex-skiffle-group boys from Liverpool, with their new girlie hair-dos and electric guitars, had a hit record called *Love Me Do*. He really didn't like it; in fact he barely noticed it. He played his guitar at the occasional party, usually given by the bohemian Ewart in his sprawling Victorian cliff-top house in Dawlish. Just to show how cool he was, he ran off sprightly versions of *Behind the Green Door*, *Singin' the Blues*, and *Little Blue Eyes*. The students, mostly girls, and many of them pretty enough, liked it and flirted with him.

He wasn't all that impressed with them as students. They were a party crowd, and while conscientious enough at their work, showed very little interest in it except as a means to the ends of job and marriage. It was stuff to be learned, and they learned. Of course the majority of students were always like this, he had to admit, even at his precious LSE. But these students had no sense of politics, no sense of injustice and the need to right it, having come from comfortable homes and settled backgrounds. The nearest they came to a mass protest was when Princess Margaret visited and they reckoned that not enough students were to be on the receiving line. The nearest they came to a riot was when groups of them fought over her discarded cigarette butts. But something had happened on the sexual front; it was palpable; you could smell it.

One of his colleagues, a little bit older than he and also married with children, reflected bitterly that the system brainwashed us into marrying immediately we graduated. Soon enough we discovered (a) how attractive we were (at least as young authority figures), and (b) how willing were the eighteen-plus hordes of pretty students out there. It was discomforting, disturbing, even exciting; but he was a new father and took the protective roll seriously, and even if they had thrown themselves at him he was still wrapped in a protective cocoon of incapacitating shyness. At the same time the country was nastily divided over the implication of the Profumo affair. It seems so trivial now, but the genuine extra-marital love affair between the Minister of Defense and the high-priced call girl Christine Keeler, had the English foaming at the collective mouth in what Macaulay had called: "One of their periodical fits of morality." Profumo's serious error of judgement was—it was universally agreed—that he shared her with a Russian air attaché; the affair otherwise was his own business, said the enlightened. No, thundered the *Times* editorial, it *was* a moral issue. The unfortunate go-between, Stephen Ward, was hounded to suicide by the police, the press, the public, and the law. Sometimes the prudish mainstream could look hypocritically unlovely, and Macaulay had their number. But it was certainly a time when any similar affairs went into their holes like frightened field-mice. The cynical wits said that the Tory government (Public Schoolboys all) was only upset because Profumo had been caught with a woman rather than a man. Either way the Minister had definitely let the side down, and poor Macmillan's government looked shaky. Unshakably skeptical father thought Profumo was a bloody fool.

Gluckman came down to give a lecture, a rather good lecture on the social anthropology of gossip. The domineering Max announced himself to be an expert on Jane Austen—the source of his illustrations about the social uses of gossip. Max, however, also announced, at the start of the lecture, that Emma (in the novel of that name) contemplated a day of boring gossip on her way to the fateful picnic (where she would insult poor Miss Bates) to be held at Box Hill "in Middlesex." Our cautious lad, once bitten, hadn't meant to quibble, and he didn't do so publicly (will the recorder of these things notice and perhaps give him half a point?) He told Max quietly, after the lecture, that Box Hill was, of course, in Surrey (or "Surry" as Jane spelled it.) Max scoffed and sent the amateur to check his facts; he, Max, was never wrong about Jane. Well, he sent the page references to Max, who, in reply, said the problem was that he, Max, knew Jane so very, very well, that he never bothered to check such minor details.

Men, meanwhile, were orbiting the earth; quasars were discovered; Fred Hoyle had a confident new theory of gravity (he dismissed the big bang); there was a sense of endless expectations. The young President from Harvard said they would put a man on the moon, and it looked like happening. Fears of the bomb began to recede after the Cuba thing was settled (the Harvard man was really in charge by now.) De Gaulle snubbed Britain on Europe; the Congo crisis was resolved. The girls had their mother back. He was still waiting for his soul to catch up, but there was no time. He went once a week to a seminar at the LSE on small communities in industrial societies: the School's answer to the Rural Sociology movement in Manchester. Firth was doing his survey on urban kinship with Anthony Forge and Jane Hubert. Old teacher John Barnes had been working in Norway; Jimmy Littlejohn, from Edinburgh, in the Cheviot Hills; Bill Williams, from Cardiff, in the West Country; and Isabel Emmett, a doctoral candidate, in Wales. Michael Young, of meritocracy fame, was doing family and kinship in the East End of London. There were others; it was a lively, argumentative, but supportive little group, with Firth as the wise president. It was so LSE, and he so missed being a regular part of that world, from which Exeter sometimes seemed as removed as New Mexico had been. Firth was concerned that he not become too sidetracked with Tory to the detriment of the thesis. "Don't let these new enthusiasms distract you from that purpose," Firth told him. "Don't let the Pueblos slip away."

The kind and concerned mentor was doing more than just offer advice. He said that being in London, in touch with the libraries, the Institute, other scholars like Daryll Forde interested in the Indians, and all the others, like himself, interested in kinship, would be the right stimulus. "It is where you should be." Fine. But how? Be patient, he was told, be patient; something will turn up. This was an appeal to his basic philosophy of practical exist- ence, as we know by now. Micawberism ruled. Meanwhile, he went back to Lévi-Strauss and the "atom of kinship" that the French master had said was the basis for all kinship (and not the much touted nuclear family.) It had all started (when?) with the incest taboo, which led the brother to "renounce the sister" as a marriage partner. This renunciation therefore involved "giving" the sister as a partner to someone else, making the relationship with the brother-in-law the most primitive truly human relationship. The brother's relationship with his sister's son—the product of the fundamental renunciation—was the other equation in this basic "atom" of kinship.

All very ingenious, but somehow it seemed to be missing the point that the real basic unit of human society, the one that it had in common with all mammals, was indeed, as he agreed with Bowlby, the mother-child unit. Pause. Gentle, patient reader, you must have a little sympathy with an ingrained academic who is unnaturally forced to do without his favorite trope: the footnote. Inserting these precious asides into the text leads to all kinds of stylistic clumsiness, but what can we do? For we should note that the theory of the basic mother-child bond came not from any psycho-biological, or ecological reasoning, but from plain logic. In trying to figure out the logic of matrilineal systems—where they fit into the continuum of kinship systems, he firmly decided that the nuclear family was not the appropriate starting point; it was one outcome of more basic processes. Matrilineal societies arose when the brother's claim to the sister's children outweighed those of the father; patrilineal, when the father's claim outweighed that of his wife's brother. The constant here was the mother and children: the variable was the way the males were attached to this unit. There. Enough. The truly curious can read the details elsewhere.

But Bowlby had added his forceful insistence that the "basic" nature of the mother-child tie went beyond the logic of kinship systems. At least in the days before feeding bottles—the days when the rules were laid down—the mother fed the child from her own body or the child died. This was the rudimentary given, and Bowlby had shown the depressing consequences of ignoring it. What was variable and "human"—in both logic and psychology, was the variety of ways in which males were assigned to the base unit. Mammals only seemed to have one way per species: some were monogamous, some polygamous, some mated by season, some barely mated at all, and the unit managed very well on its own. But in humans you could either attach the mother's mate, or you could attach several units to one male (polygyny)—or, as in polyandry, several males to one unit. More interestingly, you could have the mother's brother be the "responsible male adult," with the father often a shadowy outsider—in some cases little more than the propagator of the children, and even this role was often denied. This process of the variable attachment of males was the hub on which Tory and Cochiti turned, their variations being variations on this theme: how did you provision and protect the basic unit?

In Cochiti the "responsible male adult" role was shared between the "father" and the "mother's brother." On Tory the tradition of the "visiting husband" had once ruled and was still common: the brother-sister tie trumped that of husband and wife. He would get around to following up Bowlby's leads into the evolutionary psychology of the bond; for the moment it was enough to doubt that the non-mating of siblings was to do with Lévi-Strauss's "renunciation" based on the benefits of "organic solidarity" (pulling in the sister's husband's family.) It was probably as built-in to the mother-child unit as maternal care itself. This is what his "law" was all about: left to their own devices, siblings would not want to mate. But these thoughts were almost too heady. This was to stare into the nuclear big bang that was the whole basis of human society and culture, and to link it to the processes of life itself (his mind ran back to Jim Watson at Harvard.) He didn't really know how to do that. He couldn't take on the world. It was scary. It could wait.

The call came, and in the most astonishing form possible. Not only was he called to London, but, by the miracle-working Firth, to the LSE itself. There had been other probes. Rosemary Harris, from Queen's Belfast, had been working on Rathlin Island, and had invited him to Queen's to lecture on Tory. There was a Senior Lecturership open at Queen's; why didn't he apply for it? He thought about it—it would be an accelerated promotion to say the least, but it would also be to swap one provincialism for another. He needed to be back in London; it was his natural environment. Belfast was a strange, cold, dangerous place. Not the place to take little children and bring them up in that atmosphere of sectarian hate. It was like stepping back into the seventeenth century; being Protestant or Catholic was literally a matter a life and death. "Are you a Protestant or a Catholic?" they would ask. "I'm an atheist." "Well are you a Protestant atheist or a Catholic atheist?" The correct answer was, in fact, a Protestant atheist, but it wouldn't have helped. He was horrified by fanaticism of any stripe. He didn't want a part in this archaic quarrel; he had battles of the mind to fight.

He went up for his interview in a dream. It was almost a death trance, since he had been given oral penicillin for a nasty infection, and it turned out he was seriously allergic. After several public faintings and suspicions of heart attacks, a clever young doctor figured it for what it was and switched him to antibiotics. But he went through the interview in a daze of sweat and pain. The new director—Sir Sidney Caine—was there, and to his relief, so was MacRae—and the always-gentle Firth was at the steering oar. What research are you going to do other than the fieldwork? Caine asked him. To his own surprise he heard himself say, echoing Bowlby, that he wanted to look into the animal roots of human mating behavior. There was a lot of animal evidence that bore on the incest issue. He had handled the sibling thing, but that left the puzzle of the other two equations: mother-son and father-daughter. Then, said Caine, you will be in close contact with the Zoological Society? He supposed he might. You should, said the Director, an ex-colonial civil servant with lordly manners and diction, since the school once had a chair in Social Biology, held by Lancelot Hogbin. It was in abeyance now, but it had once been part of the school's grand design. The Director was into grand designs, the way directors of things are. They all seemed satisfied. MacRae said it was a pleasure to see younger scholars willing to tackle the big issues rather than getting bogged down in trivia. Firth was quietly pleased, but said carefully that interest in these wider issues should not detract from his work on the thesis. They were all delighted with his resurrection of the school's own Westermarck. The Director shook hands; the deal was done; the pain receded. You *can* go home again.

Oh foolish young man to be so smug. You can go back to a *place* where you led a former a life, but "home" is a state of existence, not a place, and you can't go back there: the man (whatsisname) was right. You can try, as you are now, to burrow back through the dense sorrows and regrets of personal memory, dig back through the detritus of the evolving soul, to try to re-experience the state of "home"—but you can't relive it. It is forever in the third person; it happened to someone else. There might be flashes of connection with the past, when you feel a little closer, but you can never *be* there, never *exist* there, never. For one thing you can never return to your same place in the social hierarchy. He was struck by Chance's description of primates—monkeys and apes, who lived in hierarchies, but only ever in one hierarchy. They worked their way up it and won or lost in the mating stakes. But human young males, as his studies of initiation and his own experience showed him, often had to make it to the top of one rank order only to be then thrown to bottom of another. This could happen several times in a bruising lifetime.

You rose to the top in your junior school only to be ruthlessly cast at the bottom in grammar school, then, hung about with all your honors, you moved to university where you went back to the anonymous bottom again. Once magnificently graduated you hit graduate school and down to the bottom of perhaps the worst hierarchy of all. Once out of that exhausting climb, you went back down to the bottom of the faculty ladder, and you had still to climb the rungs to tenure before you started on the promotional stairway. He had skipped a few rungs here and there to be sure, but the general principle held. He had come some way up the ladder at Exeter—even being an elected member of the Board of the Faculty of Arts. But now he was to return to the LSE on the bottom rung of the toughest ladder of all, at the top of which stood the great ones who had also been his teachers, his gods. Once again he was bottom man on the totem pole, and the top was lost in the clouds. In moments of panic he looked hard at the comfort and safety of Exeter. But somehow it seemed that four years was his maximum in a place. He had to move or he would take root in the rapaciously fertile Devon soil, becoming a florid and overgrown shrub.

He would miss so much: the sheer beauty of the place, the gentility of the people, the quiet but fierce games of croquet on the faculty club lawn, the Thursday evening poker game with the economists. Just once he would have liked to win, but he was too impatient and they outclassed him. Fortunately they only played for pennies. He would miss the New Left Review group, despite everything, although the LSE would have plenty of substitutes. Above all he would miss the cricket and the madrigals. He did not see having time for these in London. The press of events and work had not left much time for any of these side dishes, but they had been sustaining, and he had needed them when giving time for the soul to catch up. Life in London was going to be very different. For a start they needed a house, and these were hard to come by. He had to skimp on Tory that summer for time was needed for the move. A student's parents, in an act of overwhelming generosity, loaned them a house for a week in Ewing—in the stockbroker belt south of London. He didn't want to live there, but it was a good place to start the search from. Inner London was too expensive, and perhaps not too good for little children. The southwestern area—Wimbledon, Richmond, might be better. It was a rush, and, armed with a small loan from the LSE for a house deposit, he found an Edwardian row house, with a nice long garden including a hedge of wild roses. It was in Kingston-upon-Thames, the county town, then, of Surrey, next to Richmond with its rolling deer park (where Bertie had grown up), and opposite Hampton Court on a beautiful stretch of the Thames. It was a forty-five minute commute by electric train to Waterloo, then a bus or long walk over the bridge to the Aldwych and the workplace. But it was the best he could find at short notice, and he grabbed it eagerly. It was a home base.

In the midst on the rush (the rush was not new, only the content and context of it) he had little time to pause and reflect. He couldn't remember when he had last had the luxury of reflection, and to be truthful, he wasn't much of a reflector. He moved from impulse to impulse and rationalized rather than reflected. We have exhausted the metaphors: he danced for the appropriate ladies, he donned his masks, he roller-skated, he ducked into his foxholes, he consumed the juice of knowledge, and he searched for the hidden city without waiting for his soul. Something always turned up, and was the catalyst for a new impulse that drove him onwards. He took on the appearance of adulthood without much conviction. He was a quick learner of the superficialities of new situations, even if he stubbornly persisted in most of his more annoying settled traits. He veered between treating the deservedly solemn with sarcasm and cheap wit, and investing the undeniably trivial with outrageous significance. His breathless indignation at supposed injustice spoiled many a night's sleep and aborted many a friendship. But in one of those moments of rare insight, he saw both how he was, and how he might be. He saw George Peppard in *Breakfast at Tiffany's*, and his life took one of those major lurches that were his substitute for careful navigation.

Who invented cool? We shall probably never know, but George Peppard as Paul Varjak certainly epitomized it. He was the writer, the observer, the outsider looking in. It wasn't that he was without feelings: he was not one of the "low affect" personality types much talked about in Clin. Psych; he had quite deep feelings for the hapless Holly Golightly. But his emotions were always in complete control; he was never ruffled or indignant or angry or outraged or helpless with embarrassment. He maintained a calm in the midst of the emotional turmoil of others; he was rational to a fault. His ego, as Roy would have said, was strong, but it was far from hard; he was not even remotely arrogant, but he was sure of himself, and conducted himself with a confidence that came from within. It was not the aristocratic confidence of the Bertie or the Raglan that came from knowing you were superior from birth, and being treated so by others. It was not the mannered outer shell of confidence, in imitation of the natural bearing of the true aristocrat, which came from the much-vaunted Public School education. It was something that came from who you were as a person, not from what you had been taught as a strategy. Our much-confused young man, thrown into a demanding new world by a series of accidents, longed to have Peppard/Varjak's inner confidence and calm, or to know how to develop that immaculate cool. He felt his soul was bouncing along behind him like tumbleweed in a desert wind, but he had to keep urging the horse forward through the Waste Land. He was straining upwards, up to the hidden city, where the Grail was waiting with its life-defining question; waiting for the supplicant who had nothing but his own questions to offer in return.

8

The Idea: Challenging the Dominant Males

Michael Chance's little essay had prompted him to look further at those primates that lived in social groups. He looked mostly in the work of C. R. Carpenter, which had been on the indigestible reading list the dragon lady had given him for physical anthropology, and had been handed out as "reprints" in a class by William Howells. Howells was another Boston Brahmin, the top layer of that local hierarchy, who lived in a grand house overlooking the Charles River, and gave generous dinner parties for his students, where finger bowls were actually provided after the fruit. The group-living monkeys and apes were also arranged in a "rank order"—at least the males were. This was a hierarchy of power and prestige in strictly simian terms: no finger bowls. The big male, or males, at the top got the space, the attention, the pick of the food, and, most important, the females when they came into heat. Human females were not mentioned, but we remember "unrest"—our females are sort of mildly in heat all the time. Despite the poets' love affair with springtime, humans can and do mate and conceive at any season of the year. The human female's monthly period of "estrus" is cleverly concealed, so the male has to keep after her all the time—just to be sure.

The young male monkey, faced with a phalanx of hard-faced elders, had to work his way up this hierarchy if he was to breed; many didn't make it. They had to pick their way carefully, always paying attention to the dominant males, grooming parasites and showing deference by "presenting" the rump. It is as if the threatened juvenile male were saying: "I'm really only a female; sniff me, don't bite me." The big guy would, yes, *mount* the youngster, as if to emphasize this interpretation. The subordinates were constantly getting out of the way of food, and particularly avoiding the "estrus females" who often declared their receptive state with red and swollen genital areas. Lord help the careless little fellow who tried romancing one of the courtesans-in-heat when her master was around. He would be beaten and sometimes fatally bitten. After a few beatings, a ritual baring of the red gums—showing up the heavy white canines - would be enough to keep the youngster in his place.

Some young males were so busy paying attention to these details that they hardly ever ate, and died of malnutrition. One day, if the growing "peripheral male" played it cannily, he would get the chance to oust the oldster and take over the females. The young and rejected "peripheral males" would often hang about in bachelor groups at the edges of the troop. They could try their hands in another group, where novelty might (or might not) be an asset. Chance didn't say if any peripheral male, having made the move to another group, made it back to the original group and succeeded there. It seemed unlikely.

It would not have been most people's idea of the empyrean. The tiny room was little bigger than a closet; if you pushed back your chair from the desk it hit the wall behind. The window looked out onto a yard enclosed by other buildings of the school with not even glimpse of the patch of blue we prisoners call the sky. Crashes of coal down a delivery chute to the cellars punctuated the day, along with the constant whine of concrete mixers and the racket of jackhammers. The LSE was, after all, "the empire on which the concrete never sets." (Who said that?) But the room, if ridiculously narrow, was impressively high (it was obviously portioned off from a larger room) and when the always-inadequate daylight faded completely, there were long heavy curtains to be drawn, and a cozy glow from the heavy desk lamp made the malformed niche seem almost comfortable. It was next to the Shaw Library, so he could hear the musical concerts and remember his own satirical triumph as the male Webb from the famous portrait. In the senior common room, with its crowded lunchroom (waitress serviced) he could drink and eat and talk with the Olympians, if not as an equal, at least not as a student. Whatever their insistence, there was still no way he could call Firth "Raymond" or MacRae "Donald" or Gellner "Ernest." He just avoided the issue if he could. Moser, Popper, Ginsberg, Oakeshott and the other gods all called him amiably by his surname, as was the style then. It was a definite step up from student status where the polite (but unfamilar) "Mr." had been de rigueur. It was hard to explain to Americans—that the surname was used as a sign of intimacy. But could anyone imagine Holmes calling his dear Watson "John," or for that matter, Col. Pickering calling Professor Higgins "Henry"? Bertie, with his self-conscious aristocratic egalitarianism, had been the excusable exception. Bertie was always slightly ashamed at being a lord, and even more ashamed at not being able *not* to be a lord.

The new boy did not get to pick and choose what he taught. Had he stayed at Exeter he might have been in that position. But here, at the bottom of the heap yet again, he received his assignments. The new boys basically got to do the things that those who were one rung higher were happily ditching, and these were usually the things that the students liked the least, because they were the hardest. Our eager young junior immortal was anxious to get to his language-and-culture enterprise, but Firth was having none of that. Here he

was—the lad—with all these bright-eyed notions about the basis of kinship,
and fresh enough from his own experience and his "thorough grounding"
within these hallowed walls, that he was the perfect person to take on the
grandly titled "Advanced Kinship." He went into his usual whine about his
inadequacy, but Firth wouldn't have it. It will help you enormously with the
thesis, was his argument; you are the perfect person. What he didn't say was
that everyone else was tired of slugging through lineage systems and kinship
terminology, an odyssey that required the kind of concentration from students (and teachers) more usual to symbolic logic or statistics. Firth's tactful
approach was that all the "old hands" were "a bit jaded" and a fresh approach
would be much appreciated. Lucy Mair was more delicately direct: "I see
Raymond's dumped kinship off on you," she said with no suspicion of a
smile. "Good. I was damned if I was going to do it again."

Lucy was one of the women who had lost their men in the First World War,
and had been condemned to spinsterhood, and were married only to their
careers. She was one of the School's aristocrats, being the stepdaughter of
Lord Beveridge, and the daughter of Jennie Mair, the long -time secretary and
eventually Beveridge's (chaste?) wife. They were people out of Bloomsbury,
out of the twenties, out of the Fabian past. Lucy had a reputation as a bit of
schoolmarm. He hadn't known her as an undergraduate, since Applied Anthropology was something he didn't even recognize. But she wasn't, as his
father would have said, "a bad old stick" at all, once you got round the
prunish exterior. He shrugged off her treating him like a naughty schoolboy;
there was clearly no changing her, and she more or less treated everyone like
that anyway. She was always ready with a barbed, suspicious comment, but
often on the mark. And he liked her punctilious manners: hat on for lunch, off
for dinner, gloves at all times.

He took quick stock; it was doable. For the year he had to find twenty
lectures. The introduction was, well, introductory. You had to define the topic
and say how you were going to deal with it. He had his way in: the relation
between local groups and descent groups that he had worked out for the
Leverett boys in response to Roy's challenge. Before that he had to get the
"nuclear family" out of the way, and explain his own different starting point—
and contrast it with Lévi-Strauss's "atom of kinship." This led into the incest
taboo and all related problems: no difficulty there. He had, in fact, pretty
much got one term's lectures. The Christmas break would give him a chance
to work on the details of descent systems. The Pueblos, naturally, would be
his primary matrilineal examples, and his South African notes, and what he
remembered of Freedman on China, had plenty of patrilineal cases, with Tory
giving him an ongoing "cognatic" system. As he went forward, he could work
up his notions about kinship terminology—but that meant a lot of new homework on such things as the Australian systems, about which, despite Radcliffe-
Brown and Lévi-Strauss, he was hazy at best. He saw his task as leading the

students over one pons asinorum after another, for, even if the course was called "advanced" it was introductory to many.

This was the great democracy of the LSE again. Out of an audience of about one hundred, a quarter was graduate students (he had to relearn "post-graduate" which was still insisted upon), and at least half were not anthropology students. Many of his old teachers in other social science subjects had told their students to go to his lectures; others came, in the School fashion, because they really wanted to know things, and he was a novelty. Much was obviously expected of him; the terrors returned and he fought to keep his Peppard cool. It was to be a long slog, and the ultimate rewards were very ultimate indeed. At this point he could scarcely envisage them. But even if there were no moist, bright-red rumps waving in his immediate area, there was a perhaps a dim, encouraging light at the end of the steeply sloping tunnel. He really did have to do something about this mixed metaphor thing.

Two other of his colleagues were equally glad not to have to do the kinship lectures. He had moved Anthony Forge and Burt Benedict up from their bottom-rung spots, and they rewarded him with friendship and more of their unwanted chores. John Anthony Waldo Forge betrayed by his name and appearance his Huguenot lineage. Very tall, imperiously handsome, Public School and Cambridge, meerschaum-pipe sporting, back from New Guinea and an expert in its tribal art, he handed over the Anthropology Club with a cheerful: "Thank God there's someone else to do it." Burton Benedict was equally delighted to dump the running of the departmental library, named after the founder C. G. Seligman (*Pagan Tribes of the Nilotic Sudan*), onto the glum new boy. It really needs re-cataloguing, the reprint section re-filing, and a lot of old stuff weeding out, selling (call in Routledge-Kegan Paul) and replacing with new stuff from the proceeds, he casually explained. And what the hell have you been doing all these years, Burt? thought the disgruntled one. Burt was from Harvard, where he had been one of the few Jewish students, and felt it. His parents had been something in the film industry, and he had grown up on the lot in California. When he went to Harvard it was to study natural sciences, particularly zoology, and they told him he would have to learn German—as they did in those days. This was after the war and the revelations of the camps, and Burt found that he simply couldn't stomach the German; he physically could not form the words. So he switched to anthropology. He had been studying Mauritius and the Seychelles and was interested in "smaller territories" on which he ran a seminar at the Commonwealth Institute. He thought Tory would be a good subject. It's scarcely a small territory, said the overwhelmed newcomer; technically it's a "half parish."

Burt had grown up in a wealthy family, and one of the benefits was that, as a potential zoologist, he was allowed to keep a collection of animals and birds. His pet fox had driven the family out of the house when its thousands of fleas migrated in a cloud into the kitchen. So despite his reluctant transfer to social science, he kept up his interest in the natural world. To this end he was a Scientific Fellow of the Zoological Society of London, which sounds grand, and indeed you had to be elected by the other fellows, but they liked non-zoologists to join evidently. Burt's "contribution to zoology" - which you had to cite—was: "Some Immigrant Birds of Mauritius." Burt had been impressed by the incest article, and suggested he apply, citing that as his contribution to zoology. Why not, said Burt—it contained a law, which, if true, applied to all sexually reproducing organisms, did it not? True, and he did want to follow up on the Director's suggestion. So the decision was taken: he would go with Burt to a meeting at the London Zoo, in Regent's Park. He had always seen this, as most visitors do, as simply The Zoo, and essentially a place of public entertainment. But it was, officially and in fact, the "collection" of the Zoological Society, and was there for scientific purposes. The entrance fees paid for its upkeep, for research, and for the worldwide collecting enterprise. There was a beautiful dining room overlooking the gibbon cages, for fellows and members. Lunch was in order. The gibbons called.

It piled on. He was proposed and elected to membership of the Board of the Royal Anthropological Institute, and (was it then or later?) he was enthusiastically elected as Program Secretary and asked to produce, yes, a program. Something else a less peripheral member wanted to dump? Did he agree to do it? Yes he did—what else? His neighbor, in the next biggest room by the Shaw Library, Paul Stirling, was in a constant dither about whether to call the feuding units in his Turkish village "lineages." Preoccupied with the book, Stirling didn't want to continue with the evening class. The LSE, still true to its socially conscious original mandate, took working students who did their degrees as a mixture of day and evening courses. This was a very hard road for them, and they needed a lot of help. There was no mechanism to refuse, even if it meant staying very late one night a week. He could, probably, have complained to Firth that it was all too much, but he had, he reckoned, whined enough, and didn't want a reputation as a shirker. Anyway, he knew his own rule: when asked, comply; he hadn't changed on that front. Graduate (post-) students fell on him like leaves in autumn. He was suddenly discovered to be "more suitable" as an advisor than the perfectly competent staff already in place. They could scarcely give him those students who fell under another "area" rubric, but he got all the marginal cases, particularly students doing MA degrees without specializing in an area—many of them Americans. "You seem to understand the Yanks," said Lucy Mair, handing him a couple. "If they're female," added Schapera, "always keep the desk between you and them."

Schapera, ('Schap" to his intimates) the professor of South Africa (Ethnographic Area) days, a precise, reclusive, sharp-tongued, confirmed bachelor, who lived in a book-lined hotel room, asked him to take over an MA student who didn't fit any known category. His name was Attenborough, and he made zoological films. He had recently turned to making ethnographic movies, for the BBC, and had done some about Australian Aborigines, claiming gleefully to be the first person to present full-frontal male nudity on television. Attenborough had a charmingly easy manner, and one could see why he was a success at drawing people into his programs, even if unkind critics did call him a bit of a scoutmaster. Actually he was more like an earnest curate, with frequent flashes of humor, but he was a serious and conscientious professional, who decided he needed to know some Anthropology to do the ethnographic filming properly. Also, his father had been vice-chancellor of Oxford, and something of him hankered for academic recognition as well as popular fame: another H. G. Wells.

He's a Darwinian, Schap explained. Perhaps you could find him some group of islands, like the Galápagos, and study the minute adaptations of the people to minutely different conditions; do a re-run of Darwin's finches on people. (Terms like "micro-eco-systems" were still in the future.) What about some of the Irish or Scottish islands? There was a sudden flashback to when, as an eager novice, our undergraduate had actually suggested to MacRae that they could do a sociological experiment by converting one of the Catholic Gaelic Outer Hebrides to Protestantism, and seeing how long it took to become capitalist. It was the only time he remembered the wise and usually unruffled Scot using the word "daft." He agreed to talk to the filmmaker anyway. He remembered his brother Richard, as a child star playing the scholarship boy dealing with bullies at a Public School in *The Guinea Pig.* He could fit him in, somewhere, between the classes, seminars, lectures, supervisions, meetings, committees (oh yes, there were those) and undergraduate tutorials.

The long train journey each morning reminded him of his first undergraduate year and the misery it had caused. But he tried to use it constructively, for reading and revising. Jammed in a stuffy smoking carriage, he would carefully scrape, clean, and fill up his pipe (Three Nuns or Balkan Sobraine), light up, and through the fog of his and his companions' smoke, diagram some of the Australian Kinship systems on a sketch pad (working from Radcliffe-Brown's *Social Organization of the Australian Tribes.*) He was searching for a way of giving it to the students from the perspective of an Aborigine rather than an observer. What the observer saw was something very complicated to do with four or eight lines of descent, and marriage to specific category of cousin. What the young Aborigine saw, however, was a simple rule like: "Always marry where your paternal grandfather married"—and that would do it. He drew and pondered and puffed. His neighbors, not given to comment, English style, sometimes broke through their reserve and asked if these were electrical wiring diagrams. It was good practice, he decided: if he could explain mother's mother's brother's daughter's daughter marriage to an accountant or stockbroker, perhaps there was a chance for the students.

The electric train had regular carriages with doors that had to be slammed to close them properly. He remembered his brief days as a railway porter, when his job had been to check that all the off-side doors were properly slammed. One evening, as autumn was moving briskly towards winter, he disembarked at the little station (Norbiton) with the other city workers anxious to get home to supper and family. He heard the doors slamming and thought, for no reason, how it sounded like rapid rifle shots. As he began the walk along his street of redbrick houses with their tiny front patches of garden, he was amazed to see people collected in the gardens, talking to their neighbors. They never did that normally. Not so many. Not *all* of them, in every little garden: in the street even. Some were crying, and people were holding each other. What was the matter? "Oh, they've shot the American President! They've killed him in Dallas!" Rush home; wife crying uncontrollably; little girls frightened. "It's all right. Everything's all right." But what was all right? Nothing was all right. *Who* had shot him? Didn't know. Why had they shot him? Didn't know. They would never know. He remembered the smile, the eyes, the hair that always looked a bit ruffled. He remembered the close election and how happy he had been that it was the Leverett House, the LSE man, and not that shifty Californian who had won. Now a bullet had cancelled out democracy. Just like that. Nothing made any sense at that moment. Nothing at all. They went outside with the babies, for a minute, just to be with the other people. It was a street, a nation, of broken hearts.

He had always assumed winters in the south would be easier than those in the cold north, but there had been a string of vicious ones. Not as bad as Boston—nothing could be as bad as a Boston winter, but bitter and long and very wet. He was bedeviled by repeated colds and flu, with the constant reinfection that crowds and poorly ventilated buildings breed. Wife was pregnant again. They had not deliberately sought it, but they had not evaded it either. With all its problems the house was a happy home. It was big and welcoming in its Edwardian way. They had found old pieces (not yet officially antiques) to furnish it, after painting the walls white as was the style then—to give more light to the rooms. Something about it said "family." They had enlarged the kitchen to hold a big oak dining-table—gift from old family house of ma-in-law, and family meals, sometimes with guests, were jolly if haphazard affairs. The outside cold and the inside damp could be forgotten with roast pork and cheap Chianti (in the bottles you could make into a lamp) and the cries of glee over Christmas presents as simple as hand-painted hobbyhorses and colored building blocks.

They had made friends with a couple met by the pond in Richmond Park: Tony and Rita Cattaneo. The whole world of "couples" as friends was a new thing, but they hit lucky with this pair. Tony was an animator, successful in advertising (the Typhoo Gnu as well as Coffee, Butter, and Bread commercials) but also doing art films and paintings. Rita was a beauty, a calm Urmutter, a dead ringer for Glenda Jackson. She worked at the local posh department store in Kingston where she had been courted by, among others, the Bedser twins: England cricketers of outrageous popularity, who gave demonstrations in the sports department. But she chose the amiable, talented Tony, who had survived a childhood in Mussolini's Italy (uniforms and all) and grown up in Soho. Tony would do wonderful cartoons of their chaotic life at table, and these would add to the presents, while exquisite Emma and baby Pete would join in the fun, and the songs. The next baby would be very welcome. But wife tired and got migraines, and struggled to cope. The solution was au pair girls, but they mostly proved more trouble than help. It was like having a ready-made truculent teenager in the family. He wrote frantically at the book reviews and editorial pieces for *New Society* to raise the money for the foreign girls. He was up until after midnight each Sunday, and up early Monday morning to take the copy in to the office in High Holborn before starting his weekly workload.

They spent so much money heating the leaky, drafty old house that his overdraft reached the limit, and his parents, with what meager savings they had, came to the rescue. He hated this situation. He was supposed to be "doing well for himself" according the world. The relatives boasted of his "big job" at the "big university"—but most of them, in their less prestigious occupations, were making more than he was. For the first time he began to be bitter about money, and tried to understand why he should be so poorly paid when he was so dearly wanted. The job, Firth and other old timers told him, was its own reward. At his age they had been paid proportionately less. There was a kind of Monty Python competition to see who had suffered the most misery. He got the point. He was doing what he wanted to do and getting paid to do it, and he couldn't see himself doing anything else. But his relatively-less-misery-than-theirs was cold comfort as the wind sneered at him through ill-fitting windows, the roof leaked without mercy, the damp sullenly kept rising, and his parents were paying for the heat. He thought of the howling winters on Tory, where, they had told him, they whiled away the long dark nights by gambling. The men would move from house to house and play cards for what beef was left to butcher. They did not play for joints, or parts, but for a whole cow at a time. Was this wise? He asked them. Reverting to applied Anthropology he suggested they cut up the cow and then play for the pieces so that it might be more evenly distributed. "Aw sure," they said, "what would be the fun in that at all?"

With the spring came the Zoo, and Burt, who knew everybody, introduced him to them all. As a new member he was welcomed to the meetings, most of which were technical and not interesting. But he found a delightful surprise in a whole seminar on animal behavior run by the then famous curator of mammals (he did *Zoo Time* on Television), Desmond Morris. Morris was a chubby, balding, ebullient, bright man—a kind of animated Humpty Dumpty. He was enthusiastic about everything, welcomed a paper on incest, and set his seminar to finding animal examples, and to take on the whole topic of the control of inbreeding. What they were doing otherwise was "ritualization"— in which they took off from their own Julian Huxley (concentrating on court-ship) rather than the continental Konrad Lorenz (concentrating on aggression.) In looking at the Great Crested Grebe in Northern Ireland, Huxley had raised the interesting question of the evolutionary purpose of the ludicrously elabo-rate, Bugs Bunny kind of courtship antics the birds indulged in. The word at the time was "communication"—behavior evolved from simple utilitarian gestures to elaborate strings of sounds and movements meant to communi-cate "intentions" to others of the species. At one point the male Grebe dives down to the bottom of the lake, comes up with weed, and dances on tiptoe with it across the water. He is saying to his potential mate: "Look, kid, stick with me and I'll build you a hell of a nest." It was, Morris said, the Grebe version of paying for an elaborate dinner on the first date: the sign of a good provider. Morris was good at pointing out these parallels. The topic in the current seminar series was "play" as a form of ritualization, and the young lady presenting the paper would have been worth a lot of weed diving. She was introduced as Caroline Medawar - instantly recognized as daughter of Sir Peter Medawar, the famous biologist and public intellectual. But she was in fact Caroline Loizos, by marriage, and husband Peter wanted to get into the LSE Anthropology doctoral program, could he help? He did, and Peter is still there. It happens like that.

Morris and Attenborough joined forces to introduce him to the Tetrapods Club. An informal association of vertebrate zoologists, it met in rooms over various taverns, and in a grand English tradition, over beer and food, listened to speakers—the more controversial the better, before an always-lively dis-cussion. Of course, incest was put on the list, and he got a marvelous battering of skepticism of a kind he had not experienced from the social scientists. One rotund member in particular, who always introduced himself as "W. M. S. Russell—and my wife, Claire Russell" insisted that all these taboos among humans, and conventions among animals, were to do with population con-trol. He insisted (as did his wife, Claire Russell) that a recently issued large tome be read: *Animal Dispersion in Relation to Social Behaviour*, by V. C. Wynne-Edwards (Regius Professor of Natural History, University of Aber-deen, it said on the title page.) Inspired by studies of the combative mating habits of Red Grouse on the Scottish moors, V. C. had undertaken a visionary survey of "conventional competition" across all species. The point of all this male posturing was to produce the "dispersion" of the title, and this in turn kept population in line with resources. It also, pointed out W. M. S. and Claire, cut down on inbreeding. There was some connection forming in his head between rank, competition, mating, dispersion, and the avoidance of incest, but he didn't know how to handle it. What had it to do with Culture? Malinowski, with his theory that culture must be seen as a response to human needs, had always been interested in what he called "the gray area" between animal and human behavior, and Firth had even had Huxley to the weekly staff seminar to talk about the Grebes. But it was all polite interest and no really serious thought that this natural history stuff could be more than suggestive or entertaining. (This part of Malinowski's thinking was generally ignored.) And, like a memento mori at the ear of a Roman emperor, Firth kept up the pressure: Remember that thou must write a thesis!

The third term (semester) that came after the Easter break, was always truncated because of exams. Usually lecture courses only ran for six weeks, and this time was used for special subjects, as opposed to the basic stuff in the main body of the year. Firth (he was slowly becoming Raymond - very slowly) had the inspired idea of six lectures on "Pueblo Society and Culture." There was nothing on the books at the School on American Indians; this would be a true novelty and "good for the students." It would give them a look at a classic case that was not otherwise taught. More to the point, it would force him write the necessary introductory chapters for the thesis. Raymond was relentless.

Over the break he worked on Fred Eggan's theory about the supposed "decline" of truly matrilineal kinship (called after the Crow Indians) from the Western Pueblos, to the "acculturated" version in the East. Looking at his Cochiti stuff, and reanalyzing the Eastern Pueblos from the literature, he came to a different conclusion. Eggan, he told a worried audience of Firth and Freedman and the staff seminar (every Thursday, late afternoon) had imposed Radcliffe-Brown's model on all the Pueblos, and where they departed, decided they were acculturated and in decline. But the Keresans, including Cochiti, didn't fit because they were not designed on the Crow model to start with. Eggan had had to sweep under the carpet—relegate to footnotes in fact—all the features of terminology that didn't fit his Crow scheme. But there was another scheme that they did fit. Our little forensic ethnographer was ferreting away at that, although he wasn't there yet. But the two mentors, while supportive, worried that he might write this up in a way that would look like an "attack on Fred." Eggan and Chicago were the best friends of British Anthropology in America; this would never do. He calmed their fears. He was standing on the shoulders of a giant, he assured them. Without Eggan's fundamental work he wouldn't even be able to make this correction. "Make that very clear," said Raymond.

In the midst of this cerebral rampage, Anne came into the world. A third child is always at a disadvantage. The first is the miracle child whose every word is a wonder, an act of spontaneous creation. The third is something of a known quantity. How many people who tell you proudly how exactly they remember the first child's first phrase (Kate's was "fwitty twee"—for the lighted Xmas tree) can do the same for number three? But she was still lovely and delicate, and had the advantage of being the baby with two "big" sisters: she was, to them, always "babyanne"—and they were touchingly protective of her, without a trace of jealousy. She needed all the help she could get, for she was, from the start, riddled with inherited allergies, not least eczema and respiratory illness. Test after test was inconclusive; foods were systematically excluded; wool, cotton, dust and other substances were suspected. Goat's milk was ordered tried, but where were the goats? No one seemed to keep them. Expeditions all over the south finally turned up canned goat's milk somewhere on the Sussex coast. It came from California and was hellish expensive. It didn't help. Nothing seemed to help. He thought of Juanita dismissing the idea that a kind and just God would require the suffering of children. He didn't have a God to blame; sometimes he thought it would be better if he did.

With an au pair girl and a cleaning lady installed by grace of *New Society* earnings, and with a fine German tape recorder and a grant from the School (Anthropological and Geographical Research Committee), he was set to return for most of the summer to Tory. He figured he could take some of the thesis dog work (like the many kinship diagrams) with him, and use those hours when everyone on the island was busy with other things to catch up. One stone, two birds, time saved, press on. He never got over the lift of the heart that returning to Tory gave him. The smell of the burning peat along the coast road, the little white cottages, the sheep everywhere, the smell of stout and sawdust in McClaine's bar, the huge sky behind the island and the suspiciously calm sea in front. Then the little speck of the boat sail as passed Inishboffin and Inishbeg and docked at the little pier at Minlarach. The chatter of Gaelic as the crowd came up the hill; the friendly greetings: "*Caidé már atá tú, a chara*?!" The enquiries, the catching up: a new baby; what a blessing! The winter was as bad as usual; we ran out of peat in February; there was no mail for six weeks; two of the old ones died. But we had a devil of a time at the wakes. No one revels in the death of a young person, but when an old one dies, having lived a good and full life, you do not mourn the death, you celebrate the taking on of eternal life and rest. And you have to have the wake anyway, to sit with the family until the ghost is well and truly gone. So put the snuff in the saucers for the ladies; bring out the whiskey for the boys; lay out the cards for the old guys—the *seandaoine*; fill a clay pipe for each *caileach*— each crone; rosin the bow for the fiddler, and kick up a row to keep the *bean sí* (banshee—fairy woman) at bay.

The hours spent smoking with the old men were paying off. They would tell their tales and answer his incessant questions patiently while chipping away at their bars of solid tobacco—appropriately called Crowbar. The fingers of their left hands were black, and the palm marked as if by the dark blood of the stigmata, as they rolled and rolled to make the chips soft. He joined in—what was this but participation? It took him years to get the nicotine stain off his own hand. But it was coming together. The form of the genealogies and the system of personal names jibed perfectly. Both could be correlated with the documents on landholding—starting with the Tithe Applotment Rolls in the early nineteenth century (from the Records of the Church of Ireland) to those of the Congested Districts Board and eventually the Department of the Gaeltacht. Against these he could put his own field notes, with the recollections of the old ones, and the careful notation of each field and its current and recent ownership. By looking at cases where land had "reverted" to relatives in the case of a lack of immediate heirs, he was able to see the principles on which inheritance worked. And he saw that you could not impose an outside notion of "ownership" on the island. Official lists of "owners" never told the whole story: for a start they completely underestimated the number of women owners. This was a system inherited from the ancient Irish "rundale" where land was held by "groups of blood kin" and distributed amongst them. (Legally, of course, after the plantation, the landlord "owned" all the land.) What he was getting at was the way this worked to pass land from holder to holder over the generations—with others of the "blood" kin—in fact the *clann*—always waiting in the wings as possible recipients.

One rock hard fact stood out: that at any period in its history, including the present, every household on the island had owned about the same amount of land as every other—currently just over three acres. Theoretically this shouldn't happen: with many heirs to land it should "fragment"; with fewer heirs it should accumulate. This didn't happen. As we have seen, "the land of the marriage" intervened, and, without any central planning or conscious overall scheme, land was evenly distributed, over time, among the households. He made a note to himself: "Society knows better than planners; custom is wiser than science:—when it comes to adaptation there is no substitute for centuries." He would use that. Edmund Burke would have been proud of him. But such insights were few, and the details were many. He sat up in his bed on the cold nights, clutching a hot water bottle that Mary thoughtfully provided, and made tiny notes on the margins of small maps, acre after half acre, after each "cows grass" and "cow's foot" of poor but precious soil.

When his brain was spinning too much to go on, he would trim the wick of the oil lamp, or pump up the Tilly lamp with its glowing mantle, or add a candle for more light, and work on the kinship diagrams for his thesis. They had to be "photo ready" so he used a plain nib and a bottle of Indian ink and a ruler, putting everything lightly in pencil and then inking in the outlines. He had made a template for the triangles and circles representing male and female by tapping-out the shapes from a flattened piece of tin. With a plywood board on his knees, he and his primitive tools patiently reduced the Cochiti to letters and numbers: letter for the clan, number for the person. He swore that for Tory he would use the names and be damned. The anonymity achieved by letters and numbers was pointless here, since many of the names were on public documents (rating valuation records, for example) so such things were public knowledge anyway. The dying lights cast longer shadows, and it got too cold to stay above the covers. The internal debate ended under the heavy pile of blankets and the ongoing battle to fall asleep. But he never felt alien here. This bedroom was too like those on the simple farms in Yorkshire and Somerset where he had spent so much of his wartime childhood. In the glow of the dying oil lamp flame he could sometimes hear the planes overhead, the terriers barking at rats, and the distant chatter of the grownups in the parlor...

Watching the colonies of puffins on the high cliffs above East Town, he was reminded that Julian Huxley had been drawn to Ulster birds—on Lough Neagh. He thought about the things Bowlby and Morris, Attenborough and the Tetrapods had introduced him to. He had been amazed by the sophistication of Lorenz's work on "Companions in the Bird's Life" (it said the bird's *umwelt* in the German.) It was so like the anthropological concern with the "life cycle" in primitive societies. At each unfolding stage of the life cycle, birds were pre-disposed to act differently to different "companions." While this was instinctive behavior, it assumed a certain environment (in this case other birds) for its completion, just as Bowlby had insisted that the infant "assumed" the environment of "mother." This seemed the perfect solution to the famous "nature versus nurture" conundrum: *nature assumed a certain environment of nurture*. They were not different, certainly not opposites, but part of the same adaptational system. If nature didn't get it its assumed nurture, as Lorenz's and Harlow's experiments had shown, things could go badly askew. He pondered the ideas of "imprinting" and of "displacement" and of "releasers" and of how ritual held the societies of animals and birds together. So what was new? Without our rituals where would we humans be? Hadn't Meyer Fortes told him that if you want the secret of a society, you'll find it writ large in ritual?

First recognize your rituals. They didn't always involve gods and masks, sacrifices and prayers. The Tory men did not seem much interested in formal ritual. They largely left this to the women. There was an island *turus*, a "tour"—a kind of stations of the cross, which involved the women going round a series of shrines at various places, saying rosaries and lighting candles. The women liked this kind of the thing; the men regarded it as women's work entirely. When the priest was not on the island, or was sick, then The Eldest

Duggan—the oldest man of that *clann,* would hold prayers at St. John's Altar: a ruined cross by the round tower that was part of Colmkille's old monastery. It was a Duggan (*O Dubhgain*—the dark one) that invited Columba onto the island; it is not forgotten. But only women and girls and a few old men attended.

But some things the men would not miss. The Saturday night dance was officially an evening of pure entertainment. Held in the church hall, with a small band of melodian, fiddle and drums, it drew everyone, including all the men, even if they didn't dance. There was always a long interval for singing, and this was largely a male affair. One woman sang, but she only knew "She Moves Through the Fair" in English, and the men affected to be bored by its repetition. Yet each man, when formally called on to sing with the full Gaelic version of his name, usually sang the one or two things he knew. They were regarded as "his" songs and no one else sang them ever. These were mostly Gaelic, with their themes of lost love, teasing courtship and shipwreck, but some songs with English words were used, especially Rebel songs and songs about emigration. Losing love and losing Ireland (especially Donegal) dominated.

He noticed how, at the end of a song, the men would not sing the last line but just say it, almost offhand, as though throwing the whole effort away. Any praise would only meet the standard denial: "Aw sure 'twas but a poor thing anyway." The men sat rigidly on one side of the tiny hall, the women and girls on the other, the young boys ran hither, thither and everywhere, imitating their elders. Crowds of men would gather outside to smoke and pass drink around. Alcohol could not be legally sold on the island, but it got there somehow. It tended to get consumed quickly. At some point in the proceedings a couple would slip out and come back having swapped clothes. This was the hilarious high point of the night. The pair were old hands at the cross-dressing game, and each mimicked the mannerisms of the other sex perfectly to the delight of the assembly. This was usually after the priest had left, having sung his much-appreciated Gaelic song. It was harmless, they said, but he wouldn't like it. They were protective of the singing curate's sensibilities.

The hilarity inside was often disrupted by drama outside, on the street lit only by such light as leaked or gushed from the hall when the door was opened. Long-simmering feuds were always close to the surface, and drink and excitement caused these little social volcanoes to erupt. The first such "fight" that he saw seemed like a genuine scuffle, and for while the road descended into chaos. Eventually it would die down, usually when the mother of one of the protagonists appeared with tearful imprecations and drew her angry boy away. But, as he was to tell in many ways at many times in the future, after three or more such episodes he began to discern a pattern. There were always three blocs of participants, not including the women and children spectators: there were the supporters of each participant, and the supporters of neither, the latter usually strategically placed in between. The "neutrals"—waving pipes and talking a lot, would interpose themselves and call on both sides to calm down. The two contenders would make wild rushes at each other, rarely landing more than a glancing blow, since they were pulled back by their supporters, and faced with a wall of neutrals. This rushing and pulling, holding and blocking, would go one for as much as a half hour, accompanied by stereotyped cursing and threats, and then a crisis would be reached. One of the combatants would start to take off his coat.

This was a major escalation: "I'll take off me coat" means, to any Irishman, a serious intent to fight. Men by the thousand offered to "take off their coats" for Parnell. The Tory fight here took a strange turn, since most of the action was between the combatant trying to take off his coat, and the supporters trying to get it back on again. By this time everyone seemed to be tiring, and the two heroes went through the formula of "hold me back or I'll kill him"— begging their supporters to stop them from inflicting terrible damage on the opponent. It was around this point that the mother, sister or aunt, was presented with the standard weeping and imprecations of the saints, the Holy Mother, and the spirits in the graveyard next door who would be unkindly disturbed by such doings. Unable to continue the battle in the face of these pleas, the simmering hero would slowly depart, hustled by his merry men, led by the female peacemaker, and it would be back to the dance.

After a while he knew the script so well, he could predict with an embarrassing accuracy what would happen, when, and to whom. Liam Rogers (he of the great herring fishing legends, and with only one arm from a terrible accident much celebrated in stories) explained how the three blocs were "the kin of each and the kin of both." No one was the kin of neither, except the anthropologist and the priest—and fights never started when the priest was there. With his knee-jerk attention to such details he now had a rough list, from the last few fights, of those variously involved, and could work out the relative density of kinship that was the focus of each group. It was exactly as Liam said. Where the network of ties was densest, there were the neutrals with their pipes and proverbs. The rest was scripted by the invisible hand that writes the rules of all such extraordinary social ballets: convention, custom, culture… or something beyond and beneath that had more to do with the Great Crested Grebe than he could fathom.

What should have been chaos was structured, even orderly, once you knew the rules: rules that were, like the rules of language, unknown to the speakers who nevertheless used them perfectly. We don't like the unknown; that is one reason we invent religion and grammarians. This non-religious grammarian was sitting on the hillside outside West Town the afternoon after a fight, when the two bold antagonists with the unsettled grudge walked towards each other, down the road. He waited for the explosion. Each looked the other way, one to the cliffs, the other to the bay, and passed without word or incident.

They had made the gesture at the great fight; they did not need to repeat it. They had not backed down; they had shown they were men, etc... Annie Rogers, a smart and cynical young woman who had worked in Scotland, cut off his earnest questioning: "Och, those lads," said she, laughing, "always heroes when there's a crowd."

His thirtieth birthday fell on Tory that summer. The incident in the Gulf of Tonkin went totally by him. Something called the Palestine Liberation Organization was formed. A Civil Rights Act was passed in the USA. They didn't celebrate birthdays on Tory. They didn't celebrate much except the death of the old ones. They certainly paid little attention to marriage. In one case, two young people married briefly in the morning and were back to their work before lunch. It was perhaps something to do with the "marriage is treason" thing. In one case of older people—involved in one of the "natolocal" marriages - who married much against the wishes of their widowed parents, each set off as if for a walk around the perimeter of the island. One went east, one went west; they met up at the church and again were married quickly, and then went back, their separate ways, to their natal homes where they stayed thereafter, not mentioning the marriage to their old parents.

He took some bottles of stout and some decent pipe tobacco sent from home, and went up on Tór Mór in an effort to contemplate the totality of things. It didn't work. Any such attempt was bound to send him into the usual blue funk. He simply couldn't tackle the "where is my life going?" questions. He was where he was. As long as he kept going at whatever he was doing, he could maintain an interest, even work up enthusiasms. But, with the exception of the connection to life that his daughters gave him, he could find no sense of ultimate purpose. Perhaps this was how it should be. Life is not directed towards any end but the living of it. Be thankful you are not bored to death, and plough ahead. Intense reflection was not a good idea. He felt sometimes like a juggler with ten Indian clubs in the air: if he stopped to examine any one, the whole lot would come down. Keep juggling boy!

> *...forth Sordello came, older by years*
> *Than at his entry. Unexampled fears*
> *Oppressed him, and he staggered off, blind, mute*
> *And deaf, like some fresh-mutilated brute,*
> *Into Ferrara...*

Once back in cheerful Kingston he found his teeth feeling loose and his gums bleeding and painful. His dentist confirmed that he had scurvy, ordered large doses of vitamin C, and cut away the bloody tissue. "Don't they have citrus fruits in Ireland?" asked the dentist, appalled at his sorry condition. Not in his little corner. But gums heal and life grinds on. Two young women in his kinship lectures asked if he minded their taking some of them down in shorthand. Just leave out the bad jokes and even worse puns, he suggested. They told him he had quite a reputation in the School for the rapid way he drew very precise and complicated diagrams as he spoke. They couldn't keep up with both text and diagrams. Could he slow down on the speed-drawing a bit? It was hard. He drew as he thought—as he explained. He couldn't adapt to drawing, then thinking, then speaking. So don't rub anything off while you talk, they said. Use the whole board and we'll copy them after the lecture. Of course he forgot, and the lecture was totally disrupted as, when he applied the eraser, one girl shrieked and the other shouted "No! No! No!" Too late; I'll re-draw it for you after class. It seemed a small thing at the time.

The big thing was his rash offer to an audience genuinely keen to learn to walk them through the Australian systems—fruit of his damp, smelly journeys in the third-class suburban electric-train smoking carriage. Remembering to leave the diagrams intact he did just this for his final four lectures, introducing the complexities of two, four, eight and sixteen class systems, from simplest to most baffling, diagrams flowing from the descriptions, from conception to blackboard in quick strokes of the chalk. He finished, saying that the next question was that of Lévi-Strauss, strangely neglected by the profession: how did these elementary structures evolve into the "lineage systems" like the Crow so beloved of Eggan? Look for further installments on the Pueblos. Then, Peter Loizos and David Attenborough, with some others of that remarkable audience—Alan Macfarlane, John Davis. Elliot Leyton, Krishan Kumar—stood up and began to applaud. "Give him a cheer," shouted Peter, and there was a ragged "Hip, hip, hooray" and some prolonged clapping. Never good with this kind of thing, he rushed to his Lilliputian grotto, and sniffed for a few minutes. His neighbor, the very proper Stephen Morris (Indonesian agriculture) came in: "What on earth was that noise?" Applause. "What for?" Lectures. "What on?" Australian Aboriginal kinship. "Good God! What next?"

Was it this term or the next that Lévi-Strauss gave his lecture at UCL? Dear, long-suffering reader, we could "research" these things, but this is not our method—or rather lack of method. It is remembered, vividly, and probably more or less accurately. But by now we know that chronology is a major weakness of the local memory system. It really doesn't matter. What matters is, always, the degree of impingement on the soul-in-development. The Master was in there as a master fermentor: he was a miracle of ideas, even when you didn't agree with them. He was, to our star-struck young male, one of the great living masters of ideas—surely they would rank him with Darwin, Marx and Freud in the ultimate history of knowledge? Our inveterate reviewer had tackled the English translation of *The Savage Mind* (for MacRae and the *B.J.S.*) with the proper Peppard cool required of the sober academic reviewer. But he really wanted to say that when he read L-S the ideas "ripped the top of his head off," which was Emily Dickinson's definition of how you recognized genius. He disagreed with much of the fundamental position, as we have seen over the "atom of kinship" and the like. And his newfound enthusiasms were making him suspicious of L-S's dramatic proposition that the incest taboo was "Culture saying to Nature: Thus far and no further!." But even so, L-S remained The Master, and a huge audience assembled to hear the Huxley Lecture. The Master gave no quarter. His lecture was largely technical, and dealt with the very Crow-Omaha kinship systems that had been a vital part of the argument with Eggan in the thesis. Raymond said, with his usual encouraging exaggeration, that there were only six people there who understood the lecture, including the speaker, and, of course, themselves.

There had been a dinner before the talk for the other alpha males (he was not invited), and they were about to let the guest go off to his hotel. This didn't seem right. What about a visit to a typical London pub? Raymond tried to signal no, but the quietly impressive Frenchman (a real alpha male in his reserved confidence) brightened up. It would be a great relaxation he said, and off went the little troop of them, for beer and chatter. The fan blabbered on about his thesis. Send it to me, said the indulgent alpha. When it comes out as a book, and I've had more time to rethink these issues. They conspired against Floyd Lounsbury and the "extensionist" school of the meaning of kinship terms. "We must oppose Lounsbury," said L-S, and for years after he cherished the memory of the "WE"—sure as he was that it was exclusive. He abandoned his text for the next kinship lecture (which was on the next day) and gave an account of the L-S argument, which had to be from memory; he had no notes. It was maybe the best lecture he ever gave, and nothing remains of it except the student memories.

The Tetrapods introduced him to John Napier who taught Primatology and human evolution at The Royal Free Hospital School of Medicine. True to the European tradition of Anthropology, human evolution was largely taught in Anatomy departments in medical schools. Napier, a small, assertive, Byronic man, with even Byron's club foot, was unusual in insisting on the Primatology bit. While he was basically an anatomist, he was, by his own description, a "functional anatomist" in that he saw that anatomy could not be divorced from the behavior it served. The opposable thumb, the precision grip, the rigid anklebone, the striding walk—all became part of an absorbing focus on the radical anatomical change that made ape into man. But it was a still a bit mentally chaotic. He had no framework for all this intrinsically fascinating information. Even so it was at the Royal Free that our increasingly amazed young hominid saw his first monkey movies (macaques on Cayo Santiago?) and absorbed the motto Napier had ordered carved into the balcony of the lecture hall in gold capitals. Derived directly from the most famous remark of Terence, it said starkly: *PRIMATUS SUM; PRIMATI NIL A ME ALIENUM PUTO.* Nothing primate was ever alien to him again.

The Zoo found him the young Vernon Reynolds who was back from studying chimpanzees in the wild. Yes, believe it or not, before Jane Goodall there were people who studied wild chimpanzees. Jane's study was already in progress, and Louis Leaky, who had passed through and been part of a gathering at Kenneth Oakley's, had been enthusiastic about her. She had no undergraduate degree (she was basically just a girl who liked animals, and Leakey took a chance on her) so there was a problem with registering her for a doctorate at London. Oddly, Cambridge had more flexible rules, and Jane (whose soul otherwise was now wholly owned by *National Geographic*) would do the degree there, with Robert Hinde who was doing experiments that seemed to confirm Bowlby's findings on the traumatic effects of maternal deprivation.

Miss Goodall was actually living with a band of chimps, Leakey told them, doing a kind of participant observation. It had taken her three years to get this far. Reynolds had just not had that time. But his one-year study, conducted at a respectful distance, had been valuable in giving an overview of the composition of several groups and their movements in the forest. This showed a breakdown into groups of mothers and children, and groups of roving males, coming together from time to time. Reynolds was now working on macaques at the Zoo's facility at Whipsnade Park: one of the first great experiments in natural conditions for captive animals. Morris brought them together in his seminar, and then broached the idea that they should contribute to his television program, *LIFE: In the Animal World.* This was produced in the BBC Bristol studios, where Attenborough and the brilliant BBC natural history team had perfected the art of the animal documentary, although their greatest years still lay ahead.

Morris (he quickly became Desmond) was working on an idea for a series in which animal and human behavior might be compared and contrasted—especially the former. "I keep telling my colleagues," said the ebullient Desmond, "that we have all the things they describe for animals: intention movements, displacement behaviors, mating displays, territorial marking. They tell me to put up or shut up - demonstrate that they are the same in each case. So I'm going to write a book about it. I'm thinking of calling it *The Naked Ape*." "Don't you mean *The Hairless Ape*? Desmond?" "Strictly speaking, yes; but try telling that to the publishers."

Desmond did a lot in his seminar, but wanted to put some of the ideas, with appropriate film, on the air. An anthropologist and a primatologist were just the people to act as commentators. Why not? It even inspired the purchase of a small television set (Xmas present from the grandparents) so that the strange phenomenon could be studied at first hand, in the home. It was strictly rationed because it was too seductive, but they watched *That Was The Week That Was,* Peter Cook and Dudley Moore (from the Cambridge review which took up where the LSE team left off) and of course any Attenborough specials. The little girls could catch up with *Blue Peter, The Wombles,* and *Noddy* (accompanied by Big Ears.) He always watched *Top of the Pops* with Ellie, since it was her favorite, but her big sister teased her devotion, and her mother faintly disapproved.

In the meantime the thesis loomed. He worked frantically over the Xmas vacation, battling the inevitable flu and coping with three sickly infants and a wife more harassed by the au pair girl than the kids. Tony and Rita had bought a new, bright red, Volkswagen bug, and they went on trips around Twickenham, Richmond and Hampton Court, packed in like students on a fraternity prank. All he could afford was a converted, ancient Post Office van (Morris Minor), with windows cut in the sides and old bus seats bolted into the back for the children. Anne's carry-cot rested on the floor and they swayed and jerked dangerously through the Surrey countryside in search of new sources of goat milk. He typed chapters on the now battered Olivetti, with a hot water bottle to keep his feet warm in the insidious draughts, a pipe stuck firmly in his teeth, and one or another of the girls on one of his knees, demanding to know what Daddy was doing and how she could help.

Daddy, he explained, is trying to make clear just what a man called Fred ("Is that Frederick?" No, precocious Kate, just plain old Fred) Eggan meant by "The Keresan Bridge." "Is that a bridge like the one at Hampton Court?" No. It is a string of Keresan-speaking Pueblos from western New Mexico to the Rio Grande. He pointed out the Pueblo water pot with the orange geometrical designs, which they had nursed back across the Atlantic and somehow kept intact: that was from Acoma, one of the westernmost Keresans at that end of the bridge. Let's look at the postcards, and the picture book of Indians. "Play the Cochiti drum!" Go bang it yourself. "Does that mean we'll get rain?" We already have too much. "I'd better not bang the drum then, had I?" Shut up, he explained. (Borrowed from O. Henry, but too good to waste.)

Daryll Forde asked him to talk about the thesis of the thesis at University College. He had always liked UCL, the oldest institution of London University, its mummified Jeremy Bentham sitting in a glass case in the main lobby. With its neo-classical façade it actually *looked* like a college; the LSE looked more like a bank. Forde was fascinated by his attempts to integrate archaeology and lexico-statistical dating into his arguments about the true nature of the "bridge"—and Mary Douglas, sharply critical but always encouraging, thought it was "daring." He had never thought of it as such, but people like Mary were trying even then to break out of the "stuffy mold of Functionalism" (as she called it), and she sensed a fellow spirit, even if they were breaking out in totally different directions. She was about the only person really interested in his interest in Chomsky and the whole linguistics impingement. As part of his job as program secretary at the RAI he organized a symposium on "Classification" and did his number on the componential analysis of kinship terms—which he thought, perhaps wrongly, that he now understood. But he was as baffling to his fellows as Duane Metzger had been initially to him.

He had started a faculty-student seminar on "Language and Society" and they had visitors like Roger Brown, and a bright cockney genius called Basil Bernstein who was the nearest to his own idea of what social scientists could be doing with language. (The lack of interest was such that Basil only got his research going when MacRae gave him five pounds to buy some recording tape.) Basil was one of the few people looking objectively at class-differences in usage, otherwise left to the superficialities of spotting U versus non-U ("looking glass" vs. "mirror," "napkin" vs. "serviette," etc.) Basil's analysis of the different "codes" (restricted for the working class; elaborated for the higher orders) was the nearest local thing to what Dell Hymes and the others were doing in the States. The earnestness got an occasional lift. A French linguist came and gave a talk on "The Negative." Everyone thought it was very dull. No, no—it had a certain "*je ne sais quoi*" said our smart-alec. Basil was the one who laughed aloud. He liked Basil.

He was dangerously diverted. Freedman had a colleague from Cornell visiting. Arthur Wolf had studied a form of marriage in Taiwan, where the daughter-in-law was adopted into the family as a child and brought up as sister to her future husband—with lots of physical contact. The result was disastrous to the marriage. Wolf told of how the father-in-law would have to sit outside the bridal chamber with a stick to make sure the couple did their duty. Most of the marriages collapsed, the pair being hostile and unwilling. "Adopt a daughter-in-law; marry a sister" Arthur said. It was the best corroboration of the "Westermarck effect" after Spiro's kibbutzniks. Arthur said come to Cornell for year and we'll work on this and you can work with Hockett and the linguists. Hockett was anti-Chomsky (an old line Bloomfieldian) but at least he was willing to argue about it. Why not? It would be a way back into linguistics. Freedman—who had spent a happy time at Cornell, agreed to set things up. It would mean a chance to revisit Cochiti. It was dazzling. He was owed a sabbatical in one year (the years at Exeter counted towards it) and this would line up nicely.

Then out of the blue he heard from an Israeli sociologist, Yonina Talmon-Gerber, who said she had a student (must get his name) gathering data on all the kibbutz marriages ever. The *sabras* evidently never married, despite the ideology that said they should. Spiro's observations on one kibbutz were true for them all. How good does confirmation get? Popper heard him out, in the senior common room, over tea and scones, and agreed that he had a genuine disconfirmable hypothesis. What he needed, said the Great One, was "a more general theory" in which to embed the hypothesis: otherwise it was just "an acute observation." A more general theory? He'd get to it. Keep those clubs in the air!

Reader, ever patient, this could devolve into a meaningless exercise in namedropping. But the impingements on the soul at this point were largely in the shape of people: people with ideas and acute observations of their own that stuck and struck and bent the curiosity-driven twig. Through the bubbling enthusiasms of the Tetrapods Club he was buffeted by the encyclopedic J. Z. Young, the most knowledgeable biologist he had met since Ernst Mayr at Harvard. He knew Young's *Doubt and Certainty in Science* well, and heard with fascination as the great one spoke about a new model of the brain. He met Niko Tinbergen of instinct fame, who thought animal signals evolved from practical actions into gestures into symbols. There was John Tanner—who wrote *Growth at Adolescence* and was making testosterone famous—in boys it went up forty times at puberty. Tanner's prize student, Nicholas Blurton Jones, was doing ethological observation-type studies of pre-schoolers. Peter Jewell knew everything about territory in mammals, and worked on wild sheep in the Scottish islands. There was J. S. Wiener, G. A. Harrison, Bernard Campbell, M. H. Day, W. H. Thorpe—who found that bower bird pairs in East Africa each sang unique duets. There were many other wonderful and often baffling people in the world of biology and paleontology. These were impressive minds dealing with problems that were crucial to a general understanding of behavior, but problems that were open to measurement, experiment, proof and disproof, as opposed to the incessant quibbling about definitions (What is marriage? Is the family universal? Is a sept a kindred?), which clogged the mental arteries of Social Anthropology.

He spoke at a seminar organized by Reynolds for E. H. Gombrich and Peter Ucko at the Institute of Archaeology—topic incest of course. There he had met Kenneth Oakley, from the Museum of Natural History, who was to become generally famous for exposing the Piltdown fake. Oakley carried around a pebble tool, half-a-million years old, from East Africa, with markings on it that looked vaguely like a face: a low-browed, ape-like face. He was going to show it to some mongoloid children to see how they reacted, since their brains lacked most of the frontal cortex and were the nearest living example we had of something like an Australopthecine brain. A what brain? Oakley gave him a reading list on East African paleontology, but wisely said, "Given your interests, you should look at Washburn's *Social Life of Early Man*." Now that isn't a sentence of advice as memorable, as say, Basher Birrel's "Never marry a woman just because she looks good on a horse." But it is remembered, because the effects were... Well, let's just say there were effects.

A cinema manager in Piccadilly Circus, perhaps by accident or perhaps with a black sense of humor, had put on one bill *To Sir with Love* and *Lord of the Flies*. Peter Brook's little masterpiece brought out Golding's dark vision of human possibilities, especially at the end where a British naval officer, in impeccable tropical whites, framed by his well-armed warship off the island, rebukes the battered Ralph and the war-painted choirboys-turned-savages. We would have expected better from English boys, he says. Golding's questions pounded away at him: why had we become the creatures we were? Why was there this fatal attraction to armed aggression—not just the punch up (the

Tory Islanders handled that quite well) but the deliberate, organized, form-a-group-dress-up-and-kill-the-other-similar-groups kind of violence? We had culture, language, symbols, intelligence, consciousness: is this what they were for? To use our best achievements to help us orchestrate mass murder? That battleship, that officer, said it eloquently. A copy of Washburn's book was obtained—the English edition. From the library he borrowed another book edited by Washburn: *Classification and Human Evolution,* and Roe and Simpson, *Behavior and Evolution.* His smoking-carriage reading was set for a while.

It should not have been a surprise to find that Washburn's book (SLEM as he called it to himself) was the result of a Wenner-Gren symposium that Raymond Firth had helped to inspire, through Paul Fejos, director of that odd New York foundation devoted entirely to Anthropology. It was part of the Malinowskian mandate, and the old Pole would have welcomed a look at serious evidence of the origins of human society and culture—as opposed to conjecture, of course. Washburn was in there with a younger colleague, Irven DeVore, looking at the social life of baboons. Early man was a primate who lived in small groups on the East African savanna, so why not look at the baboons which did the same? Irving Hallowell was in there, the Hallowell he had read for C & P at Harvard, but here looking at "proto-cultural" foundations. Hallowell did not, like most of his colleagues, content himself with saying that humans had culture and this made them different (ipso facto no material from animal studies was relevant)—he wanted to know why we had culture and why it was like it was. We could only have acquired the capacity for culture through evolution, so we must look at evolution. What is more culture could not just be anything. It was remarkably predictable in its basics. We did not acquire any old behavior during socialization, we acquired human behavior, like language and incest taboos.

Chomsky seemed to be saying something similar for language itself: it couldn't be learned simply through general rules of learning: the basic rules were somehow in the beast. Oakley was in there—fire, tools and hunting; Washburn was big on tools, and several Frenchmen pitched in with primates, cave art, and "primitive mentalities"—their special thing. Two Americans, David Hamburg (NIMH) on evolution and human stress biology, and Ernst Caspari on genetics, were impressive. Hamburg emphasized that much of human physiology evolved under conditions very different from those we created for ourselves today; much of our "stress response" was a consequence of this mismatch. Caspari gave a neat summary of how natural selection shifted the distribution of genes in a population. Genes were obviously important, but our would-be neo-Darwinist was poorly informed about them, despite his lunch encounters with Jim Watson. He figured he must try to learn some basic genetics. There were "programmed texts" that helped with self-teaching. When? In the railway carriage, of course; there was no other available time.

Most importantly, in the chapter on "The Nature and Special Features of the Instinctive Social Bond of Primates" he found Michael Chance's theory spelled out for the first time. The basic social bond, said Chance, was that between males—they had a strange attraction for each other compounded of fear on the on hand and a need to be close to a dominant animal on the other. Those thrown out of the hierarchy formed bachelor bands. Those who stayed in had to play a dangerous game of threat, flight, proximity and mating. They had to play it right: those who were not quick were dead—or exiled, which was often the same thing. This kind of pressure to assess the situation rapidly and to control one's responses accordingly, Chance called "equilibration." It required considerable mental powers, and explained the relatively large cortex of the social primates, and their obvious intelligence. Just being big and aggressive was not enough; too much aggression against big males—angered by pursuit of their females—could result in wounding and death. *Self-control* was the key: timing was everything; cunning would win out over mere brawn, although a combination of intelligence and physical ability would be the trump card. The potential alpha male sounded suspiciously like the perfect English school captain.

Then Chance made the great connection. The human brain, Oakley and Washburn had pointed out, trebled in size over the last half-million years. This was a rate of evolution for the brain one hundred times faster than the evolution of the leg of the horse (Ernst Mayr's calculation.) This could not have happened, Chance said, unless there had been "a special breeding system" based on dominance and equilibration. Our particular young primate, equilibrating like mad himself, immediately recognized the condition of "delayed gratification" they had drummed into him in Soc. Rel. What is more, he recalled Freud's point in *Totem and Taboo* that incest regulations and sanctions were "primarily directed against the growing male." And had been for at least half-a-million years (50,000 generations) if Chance was right. He still had a great respect for Freud, despite having rejected Freudianism (much like Christ and Christianity.) He was inclined to pick up the much-despised theory of the primal horde and look at it again, with the help of primate material from those Chance cited, like Hans Kummer, and the Japanese, Itani and Imanishi. Sometime. Soon. Perhaps. But most of what he did after this would be a long footnote to Chance.

That was when cousin Michael came back into his life: the Michael whose temper tantrums had so impressed him. (Chance said temper tantrums were basic primate attention-getting behavior. Reynolds said young male chimps have them every few minutes.) The cousin was younger than he, and he had not kept up any relationship. He knew that Mike had been a "problem"—a difficult child, and he sympathized. Mike had been a prodigy who played truant in order to read his favorite Latin authors. But Mike had left school early and done his national service in the RAF, where he applied his talents to electronics. He could do anything electrical, and having married a dancer found his way into the theatre as a lighting man, rose to the top, and became the darling of Franco Zeffirelli's Old Vic company with his lighting of the maestro's *Much Ado about Nothing*. Was it two thousand light bulbs? Something like that. Through a friendship with Robert Stephens and his then wife Maggie Smith (Benedick and Beatrice in *Much Ado*) cousin Mike was now at the Royal Court Theatre, as lighting director for one of Arnold Wesker's latest efforts. Some of this play of intense social consciousness (much talk of "my rageddy-arsed brothers" and the like) took place in the nave of Durham Cathedral, and was evidently challenging from a lighting perspective. Since the cathedral could not be reproduced on stage, the lighting had to suggest its vaulted vastness. Mike was re-met in the pub next to the theater, and found to be very smart, and curious about anything and everything. He thought Wesker had "the whiff of greatness." Mike asked what his long-lost cousin was thinking currently. When the latest enthusiasms for Zoology and early man were outlined to him, Mike said, "You must have read *African Genesis*." No. What is it? "Book by an American playwright called Robert Ardrey. It's about all that stuff. It has a great opening. Quite dramatic."

He made a mental note to find it. But a book by a playwright? There was no time then, for the thesis had to be typed (a nightmare for the typist) and bound with the numerous diagrams, maps and genealogies organized in a special fold out section so they could be seen along with the relevant text. He didn't envy the examiners; but he wasn't going to waste sympathy on them. He was firmly reminded of his low place on the academic totem pole; of his peripheral status in the primate hierarchy; of his continuing tendency to mix metaphors. The thesis was duly submitted—as an external degree, let us remember - to the University Registrar, and thence to the Faculty of Economics, which, for some reason, was the operative examining body for Anthropology. It ended up with Raymond, who naturally recruited Daryll Forde as the other "internal" examiner. The big question was who would be the external? There was no one else specifically in Amerindian studies, so Raymond called on Edmund Leach, (ex-LSE now King's College Cambridge) as the recognized man in kinship theory and its intricacies. If the thesis could pass Leach, it would have an impeccable imprimatur in kinship studies. But Leach, who could be arrogant and irascible, was by no means predictable, and in those days no one hesitated to fail a candidate. Grade inflation was a thing of the future, a future that was growing weirder by the minute.

Malcolm X was assassinated, and the black inhabitants of Watts in Los Angeles went on an extended rampage of destruction, despite a belated Voting Rights Act from Congress. The first official U.S. combat troops (as opposed to advisors) arrived in South Vietnam; white Rhodesians declared independence of Britain; war broke out between India and Pakistan; his thesis committee assembled at the LSE. Leach, whom at that point he did not know, was remarkably affable and benign. The expert on matrilateral cross-cousin marriage was notorious for being very wealthy, and supporting Anthropology with his wealth—money made by his family in Argentina. He said he admired the kinship diagrams: "intriguing and ingenious" was his comment. But where was ego (the usual personal center of any chart of kinship terms)? There was no ego; this was a chart of the relationships between the terms themselves, not of their relationship to an individual ego. Puzzlement. It's a kind of componential analysis, he added helpfully; based on set theory, he ventured, knowing that Leach originally had a degree in mathematics and engineering before his war experiences with tribes in highland Burma led him into Anthropology. "So," said Leach, "it's a kind of topology. Do you know the mathematics of topology?" No he didn't: he always thought of it in terms of geometry—fixed relations between points, differently expressed in different dimensions, he explained defensively. "You should know the mathematics of topology," said the Fellow of King's.

Raymond was playing his cosmic chairman role and prodded Forde to comment on "the Pueblos as such." Forde continued to be fascinated by the historical and linguistic arguments. How did you put together history proper and lexico-statistical dating? Especially, how could you include long time-depths, as with archaeological material? Well, if an argument about present distributions, like Eggan's, depended on a notion of which Pueblos were older than others, and particularly on the order of their founding, then all this evidence came into play. Raymond pitched in with some Oceanic examples, and the three examiners had a little debate among themselves, quite forgetting the candidate. "How would you relate archaeology and social anthropology in general?" He was drifting, and Forde's question caught him up short. He thought of the social life of early man, but decided this was not the time to start on that, and bumbled some generalities. Raymond decided this was a good place to break off. Too true.

He went for tea to the senior common room to calm down and wait for the decision. MacRae was there with a coterie of social scientists, sitting, appropriately, under a painting of the lighthouse on Tory Island by Derek Hill. Pure coincidence. They got into their usual conversation about Gaelic, MacRae being a native speaker of the Scottish variety (he pronounced it "Gallic"), from the island of Skye. MacRae's family members were still convinced Jacobites, and always kept, he explained, a thousand pounds in a foreign bank in case they had to flee the country. The bespectacled, erudite, scion of the clan, hearing that our man knew the artist of the Tiger in the Tank (cartoon version) remembered seeing a billboard in Donegal with "Put a Tiger in your Tank" in Gaelic. In his wicked way he asked if our man knew what that might be? Everyone listened. It was worse than the thesis situation. Well, he wasn't sure what the official Gaelic for "tank" was (although he did know tiger was *tighris.*) On Tory, he thought, they just said *tobar*, "well," for the petrol tanks on the boats. So it would be (imperative of "to put"?—quick); it would be *"Chuir an Tighris' i' do Thobar."*

MacRae's smile and nod, and the little burst of applause from the company, was some comfort for the anxious soul, wondering if his failure to master mathematical topology or the relevance of archaeology, would be his undoing. So he was swept with embarrassment when Raymond turned up, somewhat huffily, looking for him. He had thought they would be much longer, he stammered. "We've been forty-five minutes." But it was forgotten, and he was passed. Forde thought, for publication (publication!) he should leave off some of the "more detailed" kinship stuff and expand the archaeology and linguistic analysis. Leach thought he should leave that out and expand the kinship material. Raymond declared himself delighted that our tactful lad had said, with perhaps overdone politeness, that his work was "merely a long footnote to Eggan's." He was beginning to overuse that phrase, but one had to present to the dominants—for now.

As he came out of the room, they were mostly there to congratulate him: Freedman, beaming and pleased, told him to start work on a version for the London School of Economics Monographs in Social Anthropology series, of which he was the current editor. Publication! It pleased him to see Freedman so pleased, and the mentor pointed out that this was the first Ph.D. by someone who had gone through the undergraduate Social Anthropology program. Benedict, Forge, Schap, Lucy, Morris, Stirling, all saying nice things, with proper restraint. Burton-the-Yank, protected from embarrassment by his alien status, gave him a hug. MacRae and Gellner caught him in his room and added to the chorus. The secretary rushed to replace the "Mr." on his door with "Dr." It was warm and lovely, but it was hard to take it in. He phoned wife and parents quickly, then left in a hurry to wander some of his old routes and let his metabolism settle down. Through Covent Garden, through Soho, to Charing Cross Road. At Smiths Snuff and Tobacco shop he bought an ounce of Golden Cardinal for his horn snuffbox, sniffed mightily (a habit picked up at Tory wakes) and sneezed volcanically. It helped. He bought some Schimlepfenninck cigars and did the unheard of thing of taking a taxi to Waterloo. Once in the third-class smoking carriage he had calmed down enough to find a way to celebrate: *he read nothing.* He puffed and sniffed and just gazed out of the window at the dingy, suburban, redbrick landscape. For a moment there it looked, not like the Waste Land he had always thought it, but like a bustling, fertile, cheeky, cockney land of noisy life and perky vitality. He was glad, for a moment, to be a part of it.

Before departing for Tory he took a plunge. Freedman (he managed Maurice, but it did not come easily) had been teaching a course he called "Man, Race and Culture." It was mostly about "Race Relations"—a popular topic at the time. Freedman wanted to drop it, and the unwilling kinship expert wanted to unload his burden too. A new appointment was to be James

Woodburn from Cambridge, who worked on the Hadza of east Africa—a hunter-gatherer people. Woodburn was willing to do kinship if he could talk about "the father-son relationship." Sounded ominous, but that was their problem. He was delighted with the appointment since it meant he would get Paul Stirling's room. Paul was leaving for a chair in Sociology at the new University Of Kent at Canterbury, so Woodburn would be dumped in the closet - and have a few chores dumped on him, perhaps. He was learning the ropes of the hierarchy. The possibility was then mooted that Advanced Kinship could be traded for Freedman's old course, which could then be re-modeled to include some of the ethological, zoological, biological, paleontological and related concerns that were a growing part of the soul's development at this point. A lecture course was a wonderful way to get you to organize and concentrate on a topic. It had worked with kinship, and he now had the confidence—misplaced perhaps—that he could do the same thing. He had done one more thing to inspire this jaunty certainty that there was scaffolding here on which to erect an approach to those big questions: he had finally read cousin Mike's Book-of-the-Month: Robert Ardrey's *African Genesis.*

It wasn't anything specific in that remarkable book that hit him; epiphanies are not like that. He had absorbed a lot of the information through his ongoing contacts, although this was the first time he saw the whole Dart-Washburn controversy about whether or not early man was hunter or hunted laid out, and it wasn't as clear cut as Ardrey thought. It was not the playwright's purple prose ("Not in Asia and not in innocence was man born…"), which had so impressed cousin Mike, although he had to admit there were nice, sonorous, iambic moments: "Time, and death, and the space between the stars, remain still rather larger than ourselves." It was not simply that no one else had put together the material on human evolution and animal behavior in a way that made it obvious how they buttressed a theory of the evolution of human behavior. It was not that you necessarily agreed with him: human aggression did not seem to need a special explanation in primal murder. Baboon males would obviously *like* to murder each other, but killing another male was a difficult thing. Give them weapons and they would. The aggression was the same; the means differed. We were baboons with hand grenades. What then was it? It was partly the sudden realization that everything his friends were doing in the analysis of the evolution of behavior made sense, and not just as cute analogies. As we (the species) were crossing the human-animal frontier, we did not check in our animal badge and gun at the border: we brought an enormous animal baggage with us.

It was Bradley's insight about Darwin: society was older than man; we did not invent it, we inherited it. This animal heritage could only be understood by putting together the knowledge of animal society (territory, mating, dominance etc) with the knowledge of primate and human evolution. It was what would make sense of the whole incest and inhibition thing, and hence the origins of kinship systems out of animal mating rituals. But linear lists do not convey the immediacy of insight. This was more like his religious revelation; it was like his religious de-revelation; it was like Ayer and Popper; it was like first sex. It was that scary feeling suddenly in the pit of the stomach, like when you took a pass in Rugby and saw before you three moves all at once that would put you over the line. It was non-rational; it was a feeling; it was a flash that announced the whole future, like the passing of a lifetime the moment before death. This is it; this is the way to go; the world will be different now.

That summer he spent more time in Dublin, at Trinity College, which he fell in love with and wished he had attended, like *The Ginger Man*. David Green, the professor of modern Irish there, turned him to a treasure of a book, Daniel Corkery's *The Hidden Ireland*. For the first time he appreciated that he only knew the tip of the iceberg of Gaelic literature, and that poets like Aodhagan O Rathaille (Egan O'Riley) were the equal of their English-writing counterparts. He found a second-hand copy of *Dhá Chéad de Cheoltaibh Uludh (Two Hundred Ulster Songs)* where he found that many of his Tory favorites were recorded. The copy he found had been given by the collector and editor, Enrí O Muirgheasa, *"do mo shean-charaid"* (to my old friend), Seán bán MacMenaman—a famous Donegal writer, and all in brown ink in the old Gaelic script. He felt oddly in touch with these devoted linguists and their love for their old tongue. Douglas Hyde, the first president of Ireland, and a Protestant, contributed his *Love Songs of Connacht,* and many more. He could happily have settled in Dublin: it suited his spirit; no one there would have found him odd. When the singing started, he was transported and trans-lated like Bottom; no one noticed the donkey's head. All he lacked was Titania; the King, he figured, was his Puck.

He paid a brief visit to the King, whose phony ads for marine engines had landed him in Portlaoise prison. The little monarch, in a desperate way, said he was to have an operation, and would his subject give him fifty pounds to pay for it. Fearing it was more marine engines, the courtier suggested he have the operation and then see what it cost. The island would be lonely without his quirky little friend. He realized how dependent he had been on the wee man. No harm; he would expand his net of helpers, that's all. He needed to get the names of the crews of all the boats and their kin connections. The inherit-ance of land unfolded over the centuries; the *clanna* were the appropriate vehicles for that. But boat crews were recruited afresh every season: there had to be a different mechanism. He was further into the mystery of the couples who never lived together. There was an older group whose parents were dead, and a younger group, with one parent alive. It was a probable clue to the cycle: he must correlate type of household with form of residence at marriage. He was almost there.

But first he went with Derek Hill to Londonderry (Derry to the natives) to visit the Cathedral clergy (Anglican) who were Derek's friends, and probably relatives. The Anglo-Irish coterie was very tight. The Dean told of his problems with an aging verger, who carried the cross, by tradition, at the head of the procession round the church that started matins. "He's fine on the straight," said this Dean Swift of the north, "but his cornering leaves something to be desired." Elizabeth Bowen had written a nativity play for them, and they made a significant gesture by putting it on as a joint production with the Catholics. It was a great success, but, complained the Dean, the partisan press on both sides refused to report that it was an ecumenical effort. "At least they didn't bomb us."

This year on the island he concentrated his efforts since he knew what he wanted. The older men with the long memories—Roger and Eamon Rogers, Patrick Whorriskey, Patrick McClafferty—gave him the boat crews, and the connections. He tried his hand at baladeering with a song about the mail boat to the tune of *Nine Miles from Bangor to Donaghadee*. At first Johnny Dixon, the skipper, was a little miffed, since he thought it was too satirical, but he came around, and the rest loved it. Johnny was notorious for using the state of the tides as an excuse to go back to Jimmy McClaine's pub for another nip or jar.

> The crew has come down and we've started to cheer,
> It may be that we'll get to Tory this year,
> When the voice of the skipper is heard far and wide:
> "Now just take your time lads, we'll wait on the tide."

Taking a hint from something Owen Whorriskey said about the unreliable car engine that powered (if that is the word) the boat, he added:

> The engine has stopped and we're just three miles out,
> So fill up the tank with a gallon of stout.
> A boat's like a woman, well that's what we think,
> And she be the more lively for having a drink.

With a glance back at the rules of fighting, the ballad ended:

> There's Johnny and William and Willie and Hugh.
> In all of auld Ireland there's no finer crew.
> If a man should deny it, then take off yer coat,
> And defend the good name of the Tory mail boat.

> Fal da dah, fal da dee,
> It's nine miles from Minlarach to Tory *mo chroí*

On the way back he went with Seamus to Lifford, the county town, to look at some land records from the beginning of the century. They had a grand lunch at the grand hotel, of pork chops and spuds boiled in their jackets, and made plans for next year. Then he went up to Derry and met with some of the Tory boys and girls on their way to Glasgow for the winter. They took the night ferry and sang the old songs all the way across, landing at dawn. This was his first time in the land of the uncompromising Scots, although Glasgow was half Irish, and each year Rangers and Celtic replayed the wars of religion on the soccer field. It was a grim city, notable for its extremism in politics, its severity of public morals, and its devotion to learning and drink, more or less equally. Boys from the Highlands, MacRae had told him, used to come in with two bags of oats and a haggis to last the winter in an unheated garret, there to study classics or medicine and become a dominie or a doctor. Most of them, as Dr. Johnson noted with scorn, then came south. Of those who stayed in the untouched grandeur of their natural surroundings, MacRae told the tale of Professor Murdock (a pseudonym) devoted equally to Plato and straight malt whisky (the Scots version, without an "e")—and a man feared by his intimidated students. Two of these, desperate to know their exam results, plucked up courage to go to his big, gray stone town house and knock timidly on the door. The gaunt butler answered. "Is this Professor Murdock's house?" they asked. "Aye," said the butler wearily, "bring him in."

Six in the morning was not a good time to land. He decided to stash his cases at the railway left-luggage depot while he went in search of the general post office where he expected some money to be wired. The Scot behind the counter must have been a relative of Professor Murdock's butler. He took the cases in dour silence and handed over the checks. "I'm sorry to trouble you," said the fey sassenach, "but I wonder if you could tell me how to get to the general post office?" The man frowned, and from a long distance replied, not unkindly, "It doesnae open 'til eight o'clock." And went back into his warehouse. It was all true. They were logical to the point of idiocy. He crept round Galsgow until eight o'clock, speaking to no one until he got his money and found the boarding house where some of the Tory boys stayed, and where he put up for a few nights. The point of the visit was to get some idea of how the Tory colony in Glasgow functioned. But on the first night they took him to a local Irish dance hall—a huge cavern with a noisy awful band, and more drinking than dancing going on. People gathered in their local groups, and it was, they said, inevitable that a fight would happen between old rivals. It did.

There was nothing orchestrated about his one. Drink and old hatreds fueled an all-out brawl, heads were bashed, the police were called and bashed heads in turn. Our reluctant participant had been knocked down, and when someone tried to kick him he had grabbed and twisted the foot and brought the kicker down howling in pain. As the police arrived, and he was rehearsing his speech and hoping to pull rank, such as it was, he found himself helping his hobbling attacker out through a side door and into a taxi. He turned out to be an LSE student, an ex-IRA man who had done time for trying to spring a comrade from hospital in Belfast. "I had a gun," he recounted, "but when the copper arrived, he was an older fella and looked like he was just ready for the pension, and had grandchildren and a nice little wife. I couldn't pull the fuckin' trigger. 'Give me the gun lad,' says he 'and don't be makin' it worse for yourself.' At the trial I said me piece about not recognizing the court's juris-diction, in Gaelic. The beak asked me, 'Would you like an interpreter?' He was decent old fella for a magistrate. But I got three years." They swore eternal friendship over pints in a safe pub, and the gunman signed on to give Gaelic lessons back in London, with a spit and handshake, as they would for buying a cow.

The new course worked out very well, since Burt came in on it with him. There was some obligation to the "Race" part, and Burt, who dealt with race relations, could handle this. Burt also suggested bringing in Michael Day, on human evolution, and they got Napier to give part of it on primate anatomy and evolution, in return for some lectures at the Royal Free Hospital. Napier showed monkey movies and a lot of slides. It was an introduction to "visual aids" and he took it to heart, although some of his more prissy colleagues thought that anything but a well-written and well-delivered lecture was some-how letting the side down. But the School was under pressure from the Uni-versity Grants Committee: limited funds were more likely to be given to "science" rather than these "soft data" subjects. Freedman and Firth thought it was a good idea to push this zoological and anatomical stuff and parade it at the next quinquenium assessment to show how scientific Anthropology was. There was even talk of starting to teach the full B.A./B.Sc. in Anthropol-ogy—taught only at UCL.

There was at the same time much hesitation at the School because "social Biology" still resonated with the unpleasant memories of Lancelot Hogben, who had held a chair with that title in the thirties. It had been part of Lord Beveridge's plans for the School that at least a quarter of its efforts should go into Social Biology. Hogben was appointed to this end. He was a man of popular reputation. His books *Mathematics for the Millions,* and *Science for the Citizen*, had a big following. (Indeed, our eager reader had gobbled up the latter in the rationalist schooldays.) But the sarcastic Hogben got on with virtually no one, and some of the work, involving smelly truck-loads of giant frogs and small mammals, seemed totally unrelated to anything else done at the School. Chromatological analyses of frog skin colors didn't fit the scheme of "economics and political science" and persuaded the faculty, for years to come, that biology and social science had nothing to offer each other. The only lasting legacy, after the Rockefeller Foundation withdrew its support, was the firm establishment of Demography, since this was Carr-Saunders' research topic, and incidentally, the Director's own book, *The Population Problem*, had been the source of Wynne-Edwards' ideas. The links were there, but they were ambivalent links, and Hogben's supposedly dead frogs that revived and jumped all over Houghton Street, still evoked shudders, and blocked rational discussion.

But, despite these unhappy memories, now part of LSE folklore, something then happened that helped to cement into place the seismic shift in purpose that Ardrey had initiated. Burt Benedict had been his faithful companion in Zoology, and they went together to a lot of meetings at the Zoo. Burt announced that Julian Huxley was organizing a big symposium on "Ritualization in Animals and Man" and bringing together an international cast of behavioral zoologists ("ethologists" as they were becoming called, in the continental fashion) and anthropologists. This symposium would be held at the Zoo, and of course they would be there. It was a splendid, mind-spinning intellectual think-fest. Konrad Lorenz was there, Eric Erickson was there, and from British Anthropology, Victor Turner and Meyer Fortes. But the ethologists did their thing, and the anthropologists did theirs, and the twain did not meet. No matter. He had made slight friends with Francis Huxley, son of Julian, and a character more or less out of one of his uncle's novels. (We mean Aldous—perhaps you didn't know the family connection? Never mind, read on.) Francis was just back from Haiti where he had been studying voodoo, and was a sinister fund of strange stories about the latest in gory sexual perversions—"Fishing about in there and pulling things out." Francis and he and Anthony Forge were having a drink in a Regent's Park pub near the Zoo, when Anthony casually asked: "Do you know Lionel Tiger?"

Lionel *who?* Surely you jest? said Francis. No. He was the Canadian sociologist who had been in Ghana doing a Ph.D. on Kwame Nkruma (another LSE alumnus) and the founding of an African bureaucracy. He was back in some capacity or other at the Zoo (courtesy of Desmond Morris), and working, said Anthony, on "male bonding." What's that? Presumably what we're doing right now, suggested the two almost in unison. Anyway, Anthony would point Tiger out. He actually made the introduction on the way to lunch, by the gibbon cages. Gibbon males were intensely territorial, and didn't much like each other. This was relatively unusual in the primates, however, and here was a living example.

He was taken immediately by this funny, smart, talkative, small but confident son of the Montreal ghetto. He listened in amazement as the animated fan of the Canadiens told of his interest in "the biological substrate of social behavior" and rattled off the same reading list as our thirster after strange knowledge had stumbled on through casual contacts and odd perusals. Tiger had it all the information organized, in his head. He had an idea and a program. This Tiger was one to put in your tank: he had the energy of ten people, and ideas bubbled over and spilled about the Zoo like champagne as the two yeast enzymes fermented. "Male bonding" originated in human evolution as a result of "the transition to hunting" said the carnivore-named sociologist. Men had to have this bond to hunt and fight successfully. But, riposted the enraptured Englishman, it surely goes back further than that: Chance says the male bond is essential to primate society. But what about the gibbons? They're not social; they live in nuclear families. Burt Benedict, who had been listening equally entranced, interjected that Chance was lecturing at King's College. They should all go to hear him. The three musketeers, bonding away fiercely, went happily off to lunch. The gibbons were unimpressed.

Michael Chance was a maverick and a bit of a genius. He had been in the department of Pharmacy at Birmingham University, working on the effects of drugs on the "normal behavior" of animals—mostly primates. Chance had his own epiphany: all the work done in this area was useless, because no one knew what the normal behavior of these animals was. It was defined as the behavior of the animals when they were *not* on drugs; but this was the behavior of caged, imprisoned animals, which were normally social and free ranging. Chance began a one-man campaign to reform pharmaceutical investigations by starting with observations of free-ranging animals to establish the norm. He worked at Whipsnade with macaques and chimps. He was now Reader in Ethology at Birmingham, but still in the Pharmacy depart

His lectures at King's were about what he called "attention structure"—the fact that you could pinpoint the group hierarchy simply by counting which animals paid attention to which others. The alpha male rarely paid attention to anyone unless he got angry or wanted to mate. The hoi polloi paid attention to *him*. He just stared loftily into the far distance, totally unconcerned, like that ideal school captain, or like Macmillan in the rowdy House of Commons, or even better in the United Nations telling the shoe-banging Krushchev, in his wonderful bored voice, "Bang away. Bang away." The peripheral males paid the alpha such constant attention that they often didn't eat. Everyone was looking to this hypnotic center. When trouble came, they wanted to crowd round the alpha male. The females groomed him; the lesser males observed him carefully; the babies stayed in his protective presence.

This was meat-and-drink to Tiger the political sociologist. He had been fascinated with the powerful attraction a dictator like Nkrumah had on his followers. The word "charismatic" (literally "endowed with grace") was still largely the province of theology then, but Max Weber had used it to describe one of his types of authority (as opposed to traditional and legal.) Weber had also added, enigmatically, that it was in charismatic authority that "the social faded imperceptibly into the biological." Tiger supposed he meant that there were things about the magnetism of a powerful leader that could only be explained by the nature of the beasts (followers as well as leaders.) A whole page about this had gone into his thesis, advocating a suitable inquiry into the "natural history" of leadership. His thesis had been enthusiastically passed, but his committee (including Gellner and Bottomore) had insisted that he remove this page.

Now, faced with Chance's observations, he felt vindicated. This was a place to start indeed. Burt, ex-boy zookeeper, was equally enthused. "He's talking about roles," he cried out loud. Role theory was a big thing still in the social sciences; Burt saw a chance (no pun intended) to contribute some thoughts here. Society preceded man; roles were there before language and definitions. Burt had become involved in the reorganization of the Anthropological Institute publications, which had been boldly merged into a quarterly: *MAN: the Journal of the Royal Anthropological Institute*, with Burt as book review editor. Why didn't the now-bonding pair, he asked, do a general think piece to help launch the reformed journal? Burt himself would do a piece on roles in primate society, and they would ask Chance to do one on attention structure. Chance, who turned out to be an agreeable, somewhat fussy, slightly daffy, very English eccentric intellectual, agreed to do his part, and the peculiar quartet went off, arm in arm, down the yellow-brick road, to the fabled city of Öz. (This is Zö spelled backward. Keep up here.)

The two boys, in a fit of bonding madness, talked and talked and talked, and with brief intervals for food and sleep, talked for three days. Apart from the intellectual content, they took moments off to compare notes on a mutual devotion to the Goon Show. For Lionel there were only two kinds of people: those who knew and appreciated the Goons, and those who didn't. It was like all cults, a matter of faith; you got it or you didn't. If you didn't there was no explaining it to you—like bullfighting. When Lionel discovered that his newfound friend could do whole Goon shows, voices and all, from memory, a bond stronger than blood brotherhood was formed. The talk went on. Life was put on hold. Wives became distraught. Colleagues shook their heads and tut-tutted, as the likely lads, gesturing and chattering, ignored the world outside their charmed circle of ideas.

Tiger's wife, Virginia, was a beautiful, aristocratic Canadian (lieutenant-governors in the lineage somewhere), who was writing a book on William Golding. They were an odd but oddly exciting couple, and the Golding thing was just too coincidental. She was well used, she said, to Lionel's "whirls on the cerebral roundabout"—she tolerated, encouraged even, and was always gracious. The three little girls became very excited when told "Mr. Tiger" was coming to see them in Kingston. "Will he be like Tony's tiger?" they asked. "You'll see." When the tiger visited them at bedtime, they were officially disappointed, but soon succumbed to the Tiger charm. "You have a smile like Tony's tiger," said Kate. "And you do have a stripey tie on," said Ellie. "But your name is *Lionel*," protested Anne. Firm friends forever. It was love at first quip.

Down to business, the boys hammered out, over another marathon session, a piece for Burt's new venture. Burt was a tough reformist and had insisted on some new policies. For a start, he abolished the practice of requiring reviewers to send back the books to stock the Institute library. Burt thought this was just plain cheap and embarrassing. Also, he objected to the practice then common with journals of accepting everything then taking up to two years to publish it. Burt encouraged the editor, Adrian Mayer, to adopt a much more rigorous acceptance policy, but to guarantee publication within six months. This was truly a revolution in academic publishing. The boys pushed on with their piece. It included the first news of the tying together of the incest, equilibration, dominance and initiation argument, and of the male-bonding hypothesis. Little could they have known that the argument about the relationship of "female exclusion" and even "female degradation" to the cementing of the bond, was a serious hostage to fortune. These were (did we mention?) more innocent days. The possible opposition they anticipated was purely professional. This was, of course, no problem: rational argument and evidence would take care of that. They were Popper's boys: they would avoid metaphysics and provide refutable hypotheses. They had found the way for the social sciences to tap into the huge resources of the natural sciences—Marx's great dream. The whole force of Darwinian science was with them. With rash confidence in their connections to Regent's Park, they grandly titled the piece *The Zöological Perspective in Social Science,* and sent it to Burt.

Some moments in time have their peculiar flavor, which pervades the ideas and movements and passions in a way that is hard to appreciate later. This was the Swinging London of the late sixties: the London of fashion and fun and a kind of almost un-English, classless, talent-dominated exuberance. The land of austerity had become the land of prosperity. A new class dominated the attention structure of the land, what Jillie Cooper (another chum from school days—from Ilkley) called "class-X"—the class that was not a class in the traditional scheme: the class based on talent alone, that embraced entertainment, business, politics, sports and the universities. It was the class he and Tony Cattaneo exemplified: your background didn't matter as long as you had a talent that was in demand, and you could get and hold attention. "You've never had it so good," was fantasy-father Macmillan's political rallying cry. (So goes the myth. What the Conservative poster actually said was more like "Life is better under the Conservatives. Don't let Labour ruin it.") Relatively, this was true: pretty much everybody was better off than in the years of austerity, even if wealth had not trickled down to the mass of the workers, and certainly not to miserably underpaid university lecturers.

But the new sense of prosperity was just that: a sense. This was the London of Carnaby Street, Mary Quant and Bibi, and the new British flair for flashy fashion, which effaced the somber and sober traditions of Saville Row. It had its own kind of elegance. Lionel sported suits with full-waisted jackets and trousers cut tight around the thighs and bell-bottomed over the shoes—some in velvet cord. Lionel was quite the dandy. Union Jacks decorated shopping bags and toilet seats: a thing that would have been unthinkable in the days, not long passed, when cinema audiences still stood for the national anthem.

London pop music helped the scene to swing: Cliff Richard satirized himself nicely in *Espresso Bongo,* where the coffeehouse cult got its famous film airing. The anorexic Twiggy and the cheeky Michael Caine (as the amoral *Alfie*), two out-and-out cockneys, were the darlings of modeling and film. Julie Christie, in *Darling,* approached our unformed hero's somewhat un-formed idea of the perfect woman: a simply dizzying girl, whose untouched beauty exemplified the new era's new aesthetic.

When he saw his old school chum, Billie Whitelaw, with Albert Finney in *Charlie Bubbles,* while she still stirred his unfulfilled adolescent yearnings, she seemed already a lovely memory of a past age—a provincial, serious, stubborn, puritanical age that was dissolving like the shots in Antonioni's definitive *Blow-Up.* Vanessa Redgrave, in that movie, and her sister Lynn in *Georgy Girl* (with the ever-sinister Mason) were twin-like, already almost mythical representatives of that revved-up time. The dramatic and really quite beautiful funeral of Winston Churchill, with the gun carriage of the Duke of Wellington, the massed pipes and drums of all the Highland regi-ments, and the spontaneous dipping of the cranes over the Thames as the barge went by, was an overwhelming signal of the ending of an age. The four lads from Liverpool, with their humble skiffle origins well behind them, and *A Hard Day's Night* just in front of them, were to become the ultimate icons (another word not yet on the buzz list.) The Rolling Stones were Lionel's favorites; The Kinks and The Who joined in. Personally he liked Rod "The Mod" Stewart, who, dressed almost as well as Lionel, with Long-John Baldry and his Hootchie Cootchie Band, had just made his first disk, *Good Morning Little Schoolgirl.* No one much noticed at the time, but Stewart went on, singing a decent version of the Chicago Blues style, with The Steam Packet and Shotgun Express, to ultimate fame.

Lionel was so much part of this time. He truly enjoyed it and reveled in its swirl and promise. The self-made son of immigrant Latvian parents, he had waltzed through McGill (friends with Trudeau and Leonard Cohen), courted and won the divine Virginia, got his grants from the Canada Council, stormed the citadel of the LSE, taken on the immense task of understanding modern Ghana, landed a tenure-track job at the University of British Columbia, and ended up the golden boy of Desmond Morris's Zoo enterprise. But the list of achievements does not convey the brightness and the charm, the sheer fun of the man. Lionel was worldly in a way our developing soul had yet to appreci-ate. Lionel really believed that living well was indeed the best revenge (re-venge for what?) He and Virginia were the original DINKS, and with two salaries and supporting grants they were able to take smart advantage of a London not yet beyond the pockets of the average academic. They sublet a flat in Knightsbridge from Richard Harris, and entertained like minor royalty.

Lionel was horrified at the genteel poverty in which his British academic friends lived. Come to Canada, he said, and live like a human being. Canada!

All the wide-open memories; a magic word. But Vancouver? It was a distant and unknown thing to him; might as well have said Siberia. Leave London? He would never do that. But then he felt, sometimes, in danger of having succumbed to the temptations of a comfortable mask. With his D. H. Lawrence beard, his waistcoat and watch chain, his wild rose buttonhole (in season from the garden), and his horn snuffbox (all in fact very cheap items, but a convincing ensemble nevertheless) he cut a kind of figure in the London circles in which he moved. He was the eccentric Edwardian, the academic-public man, the literary-scientific man out of H. G. Wells, with, when he remembered and didn't chatter too much, a dash of the Peppard cool. It was dangerous. He was melding with the mask again. He had to snap out of it. But they liked it on television, and that was seductive.

He became a regular on *Late Night Lineup* with hostess Joan Bakewell, notable for displaying brains and legs in equal proportions. She was affectionately known as The Bakewell Tart, and regarded by academics as the thinking-man's bimbo. The impeccably monogamous Raymond (married to the formidable but certainly attractive Rosemary) had a soft spot for her, although he confessed to liking Honor Blackman best. It was a talking-heads show, commenting on issues of the day, and he usually found something quirky to say about why people couldn't resist looking at public disasters, and the like. He got to meet Hugh Trevor-Roper, Kenneth Clark, A. J. P. Taylor and other of what were becoming known as Tele Dons. But it was the trips to Bristol with Desmond and others to do the LIFE series that really hooked him on the medium. This little team introduced Ethology to the public—and a lot of the uninformed academic world as well. He did ritualized fighting, and, with Peter Jewell, territoriality. They had Vernon Reynolds of course, on the chimpanzees. They brought Ardrey and Lorenz graphically to the screen. Lorenz's *On Aggression* was enjoying popular success, but made a serious point about the constructive role of aggression in adaptation. They had Lionel in and did the evolution of hunting.

They traveled down by train. The BBC would only pay for third class, but Desmond always went first class. He would in fact sit with them, except at mealtime, when he went to the first-class diner. Desmond too liked living well, and he and Lionel fully understood each other, even though Lionel was scornful of the curator of mammals' penchant for unadorned steak and potatoes. Desmond hated to go abroad, but was forced to go to Moscow to try to get the Pandas (An An and Chi Chi?) to mate. The rest of the crew was of the opinion that any species so unwilling to reproduce itself, deserved to be extinct. But Desmond had his duties. On leaving the plane at the Moscow terminal, he took a deep breath and nearly choked to death, as the air literally froze in his mouth and nostrils. The news came that the Pandas had not mated. The merry band sent him a telegram - "If you want something doing well, do it yourself."

The BBC Radio Third Programme had got wind of all this, and wanted some kind of discussion and debate series. Would he organize it? His old love affair with the Third Programme had matured into a relationship. Of course he would. He organized a six- program series of half-hour discussions, which he called *The Animal Society*. Lionel was naturally included in each session, and all the usual suspects, including some skeptics like Ronald Fletcher (*Instinct in Man*) were drummed into service. The Radio Times ran a nice advertisement. Since he rarely kept such things—too busy moving on to the next thing to want to preserve the past, the details are dim. But it did have a little statement about how, if you looked at the basic things a simple human group had, then animal groups had them also. It was the "society preceded man" theme, and was perhaps the first public discussion of the relevance of animal studies to social science ever. No. In a forgotten, but significant Third Programme debate, V. C. Wynne-Edwards had been challenged by no less than Ernest Gellner, who saw many of the flaws in the argument that later critics were to re-discover. Wynne-Edwards got quite ratty. It was good stuff. Our budding media don was quite enjoying it all himself. Without almost recognizing what was happening, he was becoming a minor "public figure." It was like being a politician without all the grubby necessity of kissing babies and soliciting votes.

The air of confidence was everything. But by the same token he had some real opinions. He was in favor of reforming the licensing hours, having seen in America a society where you could legally drink twenty-four hours a day, and where violent public drunkenness, on the scale it was found in England, was unknown. He still had bad memories of too many pints guzzled down between "last orders" and "time." He was, remembering his experience on the geriatric ward, pro-euthansia, which brought him head on against Leo Abse (brother of the gloomy poet Danny from the coffeehouse days.) He was for homosexual law reform, which had him in uneasy alliance (ideological not personal) with the same Abse. There had been a big homosexual scandal with Lord Montagu of Beaulieu, the unfortunately named Peter Wildeblood, and his friend Michael Pitt-Rivers. The latter was a relative of the anthropologist Julian Pitt-Rivers (an unquestioned heterosexual we hastily add) whom he knew from the Institute. These cousins were in turn relatives of the Pitt-Rivers who founded the anthropological museum of that name at Oxford. The General had been originally a Lane-Fox, adding Pitt-Rivers to get an uncle's inheritance. These were his putative, and certainly untraceable relatives, from the family legend (the Guy Fawkes thing.)

In this roundabout, quasi-kinship way, sympathy for the plight of consenting adult homosexuals, including his old choirmaster of female impersonation fame, was kindled. He was with Mrs. Patrick Campbell on this: as long as they didn't do it in the streets and frighten the horses, it was no business of the state what they did. The state, as Lionel's friend Trudeau aptly put it, should stay out of the bedrooms of the nation. Reform was impossible though, because no politician who wanted to get reelected could afford to back it. It was going to take the House of Lords, and the wacky but courageous (and Liberal) Lord Arran, to sponsor a bill. The House of Commons could then defer to the Lords. That was the good thing about not being an elected chamber: you could do the right thing without bothering about whether or not you pleased the electors. He was pro-foxhunting, seeing, like Macaulay, the anti campaign as being less about the suffering of the fox than about the pleasure of the hunters: a kind of sanctimonious Puritanism of the Left.

He was dubious about abortion "free and on demand"—about it as a substitute for birth control, so horribly abused in Eastern Europe. This got him into the first issue of *Penthouse*. A character called Bob Guccione, his hairy chest hung about with gold chains, was starting the magazine in obvious imitation of *Playboy*. How, our experienced journalist asked Guccione (and his super-tanned, bleached-blonde assistant) do you propose to challenge the very successful incumbent? By putting our girls in natural poses, said the hairy one. *Playboy* uses artificial poses; male readers will prefer the natural. "We're gonna show anal hair," said the publisher, chains clashing as the hairy breast heaved with sincerity, "they never shown anal hair."

His contribution to the discussion was a recital of the cross-cultural findings on abortion in primitive societies (some for, some against), and most of it was cut out of the final version anyway. He thought he was going to get paid for participating, but Guccione said no because it was a "public service." But what about an article on incest, as long as it had "lots of detailed case histories." That brought him up short. The anthropology of incest was about taboo and avoidance. The behavioral sciences had trouble enough explaining what did happen; he was busy trying to explain why something didn't happen. Except that it did sometimes happen, and he started to look at statistics and accounts of "consummated incest." If we saw why the avoidance broke down, perhaps we could understand better why it was there in the first place. He found the order of occurrence was: father-daughter most common; brother-sister variable, but next most common; mother-son very rare and definitely least common. He realized with interest that this was pretty much the same as in primate troops. Freud was right: the older males got the females, while most of the "sons" were killed, subdued, or dispersed. Some survived though. What were their qualities? Being tough, yes, but, following Chance, being smart and self-controlled: having real Peppard cool? Sort of.

He had supported the Liberals in the last general election, campaigning in Kingston and doing his bit at the exit polls on election day. But that was about the sum of it. There was a not a lot of enthusiasm in his Liberalism, but he felt the necessity of taking part, however minimally. Labour had squeaked home by was it four votes? David Glass, in a Common Room tea time session, bewailed Harold Wilson's decision to ignore his advice and to present Labour as the proponents of the "new management" and push the agenda of the science and technology élite. This was "deserting the working-class base" of the party, said the angry Glass. The Liberals, under the likeable Jo Grimond, garnered a record six-million votes, but only hung on to their nine seats (all these numbers are suspect.) Still, it looked as if the voters felt as he did: that if they didn't want Labour, they didn't want the Tories either.

Being a Liberal, for a brief time there in the late sixties, actually seemed like the progressive place to be, although the self-proclaimed progressives of CND would not have agreed. The latest incarnation of the sanctimonious Left, they dominated the self-destructive internecine warfare of the Labour party. They were morally superior people who were "anti-nuclear" and "anti-war," as though the rest of the world just couldn't wait for atomic destruction and Armageddon. They were the people who thought the evils of fox hunting were "self-evident" and whose "anti-violence" had them working to ban boxing. They were Rousseauians who believed people were innately good, and it was only wicked societies, and particularly the wicked capitalists (and their lackeys) in those societies, that made people evil. Thus everybody in Russia, where there were no capitalists, was good - except Stalin, of course, but he had been warped by the tsarist society in which he grew up. (This was actually argued; you can't make this stuff up.) He ignored the fanatics, and, warmed by the ongoing presence of Popper at tea-time, pushed on with his own piece-meal social engineering agenda. His views on the mother-child bond, had him, along with John Bowlby, and again for an historic moment, looking like a hero of reform.

This was the time of the first stirrings of the women's movement. Word had come across the Atlantic of one Betty Friedan and *The Feminine Mystique*, but European women were not much interested in this new-fangled "feminist" theory; they were more interested in practical reforms. It was a time of disillusion with the bourgeois ideals of the nuclear family. Hannah Gavron wrote *The Captive Wife,* bemoaning the imprisonment of wives in their "little boxes" in the suburbs. The British Women's Medical Association was campaigning to get equal rights for unwed mothers and a removal of the stigma of illegitimacy. They asked him to address their annual convention on the subject of the family. With a blackboard and a lot of examples (this was expected of anthropologists) he outlined his notion of the mother-child bond as the basis of all systems, and first expounded what was to become "the law of the dispensable male." The bond was basic: societies varied widely in how they attached males to the bond for the purposes of protection and provision. Cochiti and Tory provided examples, but he weighed in with polygamy and polyandry, and "matrifocal families" and all the weight of argument from Bowlby and Rheingold (*Maternal Behavior in Mammals*) and the course of evolution to make the argument. A mother-child unit could never be an anomaly, and certainly not an immorality. Unwed (or as they rapidly came to be called, "single") mothers should be cared for by all of us, just as primate mothers were the responsibility of the whole band, and in Cochiti and other matrilineal societies, of the whole clan. The lady doctors gave him a rousing ovation. The chairman (it was still "madam chairman" then—did we mention that these were simpler...? Never mind) thanked him for his review of "the protean forms of the family" and invited him next to tackle the issue of mothers and newborns in hospital and the newly recognized syndrome of post-partum depression. He promised.

What happened to sitting on the fence, to being the eternal observer, the man from Mars, the Outsider? It proved impossible at home. Indignation at injustice was too strong, and her lessons in vocal resistance to it were too powerful. And this was home; you had to care about it. At the same time, the perspective of millions of years of primate and hominid evolution gave him a view of human history that was dizzy with distance. "History" was reduced to a couple of flickering frames at the end of an hour-long film. It was an experiment whose result was in doubt. (Toynbee's conclusion that civilizations existed only to produce the ultimate mish-mash religion, made the thirteen volumes of *The Study of History* the longest shaggy-dog story ever.) If one wanted to know the constants of human nature, history was a poor clue. It was what we brought to history that mattered. History—all that mass of detail so carefully carved into shape by Toynbee—was simply a record of our misuse of nature, including our own. But history was also what we lived in; we had no choice but to participate, however lofty our feeling of distance. So he participated without much hope of reversing the course of human folly.

Back at the LSE there was the phenomenon of Derek Freeman to tackle. Derek was a living legend in the Department. While doing his Ph.D. there he had been missing for days and people got worried. They searched through the warren of dusty rooms that was the library then, and finally found him way back in some recess, unshaven and glassy eyed, poring over volumes. "I've been reading backwards through the *Journal of the Royal Anthropological Institute*," he explained, "I'm at 1907." A good story to tell graduate students complaining about "direction" in their studies.

Derek, an Australian, with the size, manner, and appearance of a hardened rugby forward, had been brought up in some religious cult to believe he was the next Messiah; he never fully recovered from this overzealous version of the wonder-child experience. There had been all kinds of odd episodes and scandals, but he had completed his doctorate—on the Iban of Borneo (headhunters), and was here for a sabbatical. He had converted wholesale to Psychoanalysis, and as was his way, was ruthlessly trying to convert everyone else. He would have been happy at Harvard, but in London, among the anthropologists, he got little sympathy. He spent days wandering around the Bloomsbury squares, photographing the big brass door knockers on the townhouse doors, which were, according to him, blatantly phallic. Plausible.

That lower down on the door was always a big brass slot where you put the "mail" was, to him, just too much. They would have loved this in Cambridge Mass. At the LSE it was just plain nutty.

Quite outside all this, our little mister kinship had taken on Derek in the heartland of the Messiah's country, the nature of the kindred. Derek had written, back in the early sixties, what was reckoned to be the definitive study of kindreds, with the Iban as a prime example. When Julius Gould wanted a contribution to the annual *Penguin Survey of the Social Sciences*, the outcome was a pretty searching dissection of the logical failings in Derek's analysis, as "Prolegomena to the study of British Kinship." The Anointed One took it hard, but they ended in a respectable standoff. Derek himself had taken on Leach, whose *Rethinking Anthropology* was just out. It was a pipsqueak sort of rethinking, said Derek: what Anthropology needed was a complete rethinking about its position on the autonomy of Culture. He had written on evolution and aggression, making the same point. They got him to contribute a piece on how Social Anthropology should be rethought to Burt's reformulated *Man*. Derek should have been the perfect ally, but it's hard for Messiahs to master the finer points of teamwork. You couldn't take Derek with any reservations; you had to swallow him whole. A Messiah is one hell of a mouthful.

The Light of the World seemed to have a special place in hell reserved for Margaret Mead, for reasons not all that clear at the time. The rest of the British school seemed to see her fault as a case of whoring after cheap fame instead of doing a professional job of fieldwork. When he was invited to join the ASA, Meyer Fortes had explained that one point of having this organization was "to stop people like Geoffrey Gorer and Margaret Mead from calling themselves social anthropologists." But for the anointed one it was more a matter of her being an ideological lackey of Franz Boas. The crime of Boas was the enthronement of Culture and the rejection of Nature. Mead had dutifully gone out and "proved" this with her "Samoan fantasies" as Derek called them. For now Derek was flourishing the latest in the book of revelations: Irven DeVore's edited volume, *Primate Behavior: Field Studies of Monkeys and Apes.* This held one of Jane Goodall's first long pieces on her chimps (Morris had enthusiastically shown him a couple of her earliest articles), and the other primatologists who were to become household names in anthropology were there. The book became, along with the Washburn and DeVore *Social Life*, the text for his lectures. He was particularly taken by the chapter by Jane Lancaster and Richard Lee on the reproductive cycle—that business of estrus, at whose quivering peak of ovulation, insemination produced conception: the goal of all that dominance hysteria in primates.

Even so, he was still a working social anthropologist, and that little life went on. He was flown to Queen's Belfast where Rosemary Harris was the lone lecturer in social anthropology, to give a lecture to Estyn Evans' seminar on landholding on Tory. They liked it well enough to publish it in the *Journal of Ulster Folklife*, and then to re-print it as a publication of the Institute of Irish Studies and the Ulster Folk Museum. He never listed it as a book, but it was his first such publication, in a museum series, and he was happy because he felt it was the best thing he had done by way of empirical social science. All the ethological stuff was at the level of theory; we still, he insisted to his dubious colleagues, needed all the ethnographic material we could get. We just might interpret it differently. Anthropology had been certainly very good at exploring the variations; now was the time to start looking again at the constants, just as Chomsky and Greenberg were doing with language. Lionel told his audiences that the "male bonding" theory was essentially a contribution to the study of human universals. Clark Wissler, dean of Plains Indian Ethnography, was invoked: if you wanted to look for universals, he had said, you were going to end up looking in the genome.

Australia provided other allies, most notably Les Hiatt. Les, from Sydney University, was a converted dentist. He explained how his mother had made him shave under his arms and use deodorant—which left him sticky and in pain—so that he wouldn't offend the patients. He was happy to change to Anthropology and had done original work with Aborigines in Arnhem Land, but was unhappy with the limitations of functional explanation. He couldn't, however, have been more different from Derek. Les was an Aussie's Aussie, a true cobber, who lived with the mates and Sheilas in the Aussie colony in Notting Hill, known affectionately as Kangaroo Alley. He was amazed at the sexual freedom in London, which contrasted with the prurient repressive regime back in cobberland. His favorite hobby, apart from booze, was singing ambitious rounds, and mildly obscene versions of Anglican hymns:

> Virgin Mary meek and mild,
> Got herself a little child,
> With her finger! Hallelujah!
> With her fi-in-ger!

His was probably the first version of *Tie Me Kangaroo Down Mate* ever heard in London. Like Derek he had been much influenced by fellow Aussie Glen McBride and his work on dominance in chickens: dominant hens, McBride found, laid bigger eggs. The "pecking order" in hens (discovered by Schelderup-Ebbe in the 1930s) was one of those striking discoveries that evoked the "ahah!" response in the laity, and has hence passed into popular phraseology. Pecking orders were ubiquitous: Nature was not egalitarian. Les looked at the truly primitive—technically Paleolithic—Aborigines, and saw a male pecking order where the rewards were wives and hence "reproductive success"—the Darwinian criterion of "fitness." Our very own young male, struggling with his own rather benign version of the pecking order, saw, through Les's eyes, the elaborate Aboriginal cousin-marriage systems as a way the older males controlled the reproductive behavior of the young males. Such controls were built into the rules of the system: the marriage "choices" of the young would always be determined by the previous marriages of their elders. They would have to wait a long time to gather their wives, and in the meantime there would be those savage initiation ceremonies to remind them who was boss, and genital mutilations to let them know what it was all really about.

They were all obsessed with Lévi-Strauss. Les had written a song to the tune of *Jimmy Crack Corn,* about a mythical figure from the outback called Leddy Straws, who disappeared into the bush. Here is some of it.

> Verse: Old Leddy Straws is a *bricoleur,*
> His myth machine makes the Oedipus purr,
> He solved the riddle of sphinx,
> But Baudelaire's cat just sits and winks.

> Chorus: Old Leddy Straws ain't my uncle at all,
> Old Leddy Straws ain't my uncle at all,
> Old Leddy Straws ain't my uncle at all,
> He's my old man's brother-in-law.

He used to set the whole thing as an exam question. Really good students could explain every allusion and reference, even to Baudelaire's *Les Chats* and L-S's desire to exchange a wink with same. It was like that then.

Still living in the glow of Leach's approbation of his kinship diagrams, he was pulled into the annual conferences of the Association for Social Anthropologists. He had been a discussant in a previous year of a paper by Marshall Sahlins, and on the continuing theory that he had some special insight into the Yanks, he had been assigned this time to discuss David Schneider's paper on "Some Muddles in the Models." Schneider, knowing no French, had teamed up with Homans, who knew only a little, in the Harvard venture criticizing Lévi-Strauss that had plagued the graduate-student years. Back then he had told them, "some person at Oxford is doing an extended critique." He didn't know who that was, but it turned out to be Rodney Needham, and the elegantly dismissive *Structure and Sentiment* had indeed appeared and pulled the rug out from under the Harvard duo.

This dispute became one of the most celebrated of its day (is it even re-membered now?) and with his penchant for sticking his nose into messy disputes, our lad got in the middle of it: literally in the middle. The details, exhausted reader, need not concern us. To explain would be to create one of those Borges maps that is only perfect when it is the same size as the country it covers. But the characters are interesting. He became a friend of each of the duelists. Immediate qualification: no one became a friend of Rodney's. One might think he was a friend, but Rodney did not suffer friends gladly. He could be amiable and charming enough, but sooner or later he would find some reason to be fussily punctilious, or downright unpleasant. He was, in the language of a later time, uptight. He had notions of perfection that were hard to live up to, and no notion that they might be relative.

Dave Schneider, on the other hand, was a tough kid from Brooklyn. Harvard (and the LSE) had not softened him. He was perhaps the funniest man with a pen our appreciative punster had ever encountered (in correspondence - one still did not exhibit wit in publications for fear of appearing unserious.) Dave's introduction to his edited volume on *Matrilineal Kinship* was perhaps the best thing written on that subject. But Dave's ego was bruised by Rodney's very Oxonian onslaught. Homans just retired from the field and was not heard from, but David began a long, strategic retreat, in which he tried to change the rules of engagement as he went along. If he hadn't been right about kinship, as Needham and Lévi-Strauss—and indeed most everyone, defined it, then the problem lay not in his analysis (which was unacceptable to him) but in the definition of kinship. Dave ruthlessly set about his various re-definitions, and in the end the result of this intellectual smokescreen was absolutely a new version of what the study of kinship was—a "Cultural Account." Very Harvard. What now passes as the study of kinship in Anthropology (and indeed a large part of Anthropology itself) is partly the result of Schneider's moving the goalposts once the game was started. Without wholly sharing either view, piggy-in-the-middle kept up a running relationship with both protagonists, and sort of liked the role of mediator, which was as well for it was to be frequently thrust upon him.

The next thing Leach pulled him in on was a symposium on "The Structural Study of Myth and Totemism"—an *hommage* to Lévi-Strauss. Leach wanted him to do something on Pueblo totemism—a kind of exercise in the manner of The Master. But there was nothing much this could have added except more examples of animal and plant names being "good to think," which they undoubtedly were. But they were much else besides, and Leach himself had said that the theory did not explain why, in so many cases, "the totem was still taboo." So he said he would contribute if he could talk about his old love, *Totem and Taboo*. Leach agreed as long as he promised to say something about the contrast between Freud and The Master. Done. This was his chance to take the incest issue beyond siblings and try to get his own thinking straight. But it was put off until the summer, which meant less time on Tory, but it was something he had to do. He felt the argument getting firmer, and he had to follow the lead. Derek was flourishing George Schaller's *The Mountain Gorilla*, and pointing out, quite rightly, how this modified Freud's account of the Primal Horde. Put it on the list. Keep the clubs going.

Lionel was agitated by the fall of Nkruma in Ghana; the U. N. ordered sanctions against Rhodesia; Harold Wilson blustered like an old gunboat Tory, but didn't do anything. (The father thought Harold Wilson was a bloody fool. He wasn't a fool, but he was a wily and unscrupulous manipulator and opportunist.) The Ibo were massacred in Nigeria; Africa was falling apart. He knew Roy and Diane were in Nigeria and was deeply worried until he heard that, thanks to the intervention of friendly locals, they had escaped unhurt. He heard Segovia at the Festival Hall and marveled that the little fat man with the pudgy hands was able to weave such silver threads of sound. The young ladies who had taken down some of his Kinship lectures had evidently shown them to a lady editor at Penguin Books. She appeared at the LSE full of enthusiasm: you must make this into a book. A *Penguin Book*? No less. Like the Penguin Philosophers? Just like. But this was impossible. He really didn't know all that much about kinship, he protested. He had figured out how to introduce it, and, yes, his figuring did have some sort of logic to it, but there was a massive amount of stuff out there he just hadn't read. Come back later: he'd talk to Raymond.

Raymond was in accord: a "textbook" on Kinship and Marriage was something for the much older hands with far more knowledge, said the sage one. Then why haven't they done it already? Malinowski was always saying he was going to do it, but he never did, said Raymond. The fact was, that since the abandonment of Morgan's evolutionary hypotheses, no one really did have an overall "theory of kinship." He didn't say "well I do." Raymond hadn't heard his lectures, although he had "heard good things about them" from the graduate students, but he had no idea of the logical structure that hung it all together. A brief time to brood, then: call the Penguin lady. Let's talk. No harm in talking. He was always ready to talk. A *Penguin Book*?!

The summer came too fast, and Freud and totemism called. One or the other of the girls was always ill, and they were poor sleepers. Wife had terrible migraine headaches, which put her out for days, while he was hit with the inevitable flu and a bad dose of glandular fever—the "mono" so popular with Harvard students—a result, they said, of stress. Doctors had discovered stress. Since they rarely knew the causes of any of your aches and pains, they were happy to attribute everything to stress. "Is there any stress in your life?" they would ask. How do young parents manage? They must be endowed with some special parenting juice to endure the battery of much illness, little sleep, and constant attention. Yet these are the years when careers have to be built, a major effort put forth, and not much sympathy from the dominant males for the vagaries of family fortunes or personal health. Home was chaos; work was relentless. Yet the glow that came from the happy moments was almost over-compensation. Look at the photos: three little girls in identical Liberty dresses, looking at the flowers in the Richmond Park gardens; Anne sitting on Granddad's shoulders—her favorite place in the world. Nana paying, as always, careful attention to Kate. Ellie paying equal attention to Anne. The first day at her infant school, Anne cried, so they took her up to Ellie's class and she sat with her sister for the rest of the day. Ellie was maternal from the start.

Personality is largely in place at birth, he decided. Put on the light in the darkened children's bedroom, and of the sleeping babies Kate would start and twitch, Anne would murmur, and Ellie lie still and tranquil as a hibernating bear cub. Birth order? Very likely. Kate was a prototype first child; her self-confidence was intimidating. She always seemed to have talked. She hated to wear hats—could never bear to have anything in her head. When she started a new school (Robin Hood School in Wimbledon) they required a straw boater. There was a big flap about how to break this to Kate; what a scene would ensue. On the fateful morning, they told her what a wonderful school this was (it was) and how she would love it (she did) and how, oh dear, they did require you to wear this very nice, very smart, straw hat. Kate stared at the hat, shrugged, plonked it awkwardly on her head and declared: "Let's go then."

There was no news from Cornell. Freedman appealed to Wolf, who said Allan Holmberg, the Chairman, was dealing with it, and had assured him all was fine. But time dragged on and there was no word. Holmberg was famous for his daring and dangerous fieldwork in the Amazon. But he had contracted some awful tropical disease along the way (the Indians led him blind and helpless back to safety) and was dying of it. It was only after he died that they discovered drawers full of letters that he had just filed and forgotten, the LSE correspondence among them. Perhaps the disappointed lad should have been more sympathetic, but Cornell had let him down once again, and again thrown his life into confusion. It was too late to rearrange the sabbatical, so he would have to take a rain check and keep on teaching.

His continuing dream to get back into Linguistics was fading. Chomsky had published *Aspects of the Theory of Syntax,* and Floyd Lounsbury, at Yale, was applying "rewrite rules" to kinship terminologies—the very thing that L-S wanted them to oppose. Things were happening on this front, but they were only one of the clubs in the air; he couldn't pay them more than peripheral attention. Burt wanted an article on Tory for a book on smaller territories, an outcome of his seminar. It was a good chance to write a general description and to rework some demographic skills forgotten since abortive undergraduate days.

They asked him to give a talk to the Cambridge Anthropology Club. He talked about dominance, inhibition, initiation, evolution and the origins of kinship systems. They were suitably unimpressed. "How does this affect how we do fieldwork?" they asked. "Not much," he told them, "fieldwork is not the goal of Anthropology; it is one means among others of obtaining data." He was the man who shouted in the quiet of the library, who yelled obscenities at the garden party. But at the reception afterwards the students admitted to enjoying the *frisson* of flirting with the forbidden. He met the reclusive Reo Fortune there for the first time. Fortune's two claims to fame were as the ex-husband of Margaret Mead and the author of *Sorcerers of Dobu*, in which he portrayed the natives as just about the nastiest people imaginable. This had been very worrisome to the C & P people at Harvard, who could not figure out what horrific child-rearing practices might have produced such a painful result. Their answer was that the natives were OK; Fortune was paranoid. He had pooh-poohed this suggestion at the time. The ex-Mead-spouse now cornered our reluctant visitor, and told at some insistent length the story of how Malinowski had not only cruelly abandoned him on Dobu, but plotted to poison him as well. It was not clear why, but the chemical composition of the compound was known and would be revealed. Fleeing to the relative sanity of the LSE, he relayed his tale to the Senior Common Room tea group, telling them firmly that it had happened at Oxford. "Who came to hear you?" Raymond asked. Oh, everybody. Jack Goody was there, Edmund Leach, Meyer Fortes, Reo Fortune… "They came all that way?" They're only round the corner from the lecture hall. "I think," said Raymond gently, "you were in Cambridge."

If his notions of where he was in space were as hairy as his sense of place in time, he was definitely in London (and in June, when he should have been on Tory) for the Leach symposium on Totemism. He held off on Ethology and evolution: slowly, slowly, catchee monkey. He did his number on Freud's opus alone, pointing out how almost all commentators from Kroeber and Marrett to Goody and Parsons has misrepresented the argument. Freud had (contra Goody) fully understood the implications of unilineal descent - taboos were a property, not of the family, but the totem clan, and, contra Kroeber, was not arguing about "recurrent psychological events" but about historical events. It was the inheritance (Lamarckian or otherwise) of attitudes laid down in the dawn of humanity. He pointed out how prototypical patrilineal ideologies of procreation deny the role of the mother, and their matrilineal opposites (like the Trobrianders) the role of the father. He worked in Johnny Whiting's theory of mother-denial (linked to the post-partum sex taboo) and wound the whole thing up by hectoring the gathering on the fatal mistake of assuming that "rules are more stable than emotions." Not so, he pounded on: rules can be changed overnight, but strong motivations are often ineradicable. We have to heed Freud and understand that emotions underpin social structure. It is not enough to reduce everything to the power of the intellect— this was how he got L-S in there. The gathering was politely puzzled, but there was not much discussion because Derek Freeman took the opportunity to sermonize them at length on "the return of the repressed" and how they were all suffering from abreaction. It was just like old times in Cambridge Mass.

Tory was very abbreviated. He spent most of the time on boat crews, where Mary and her friends laid out all the marriage relationship between crew members, something the ladies knew by heart and constant gossip. The yearly negotiations for crews showed up both the constant bonds over time, and the shifting allegiances over the same time. The notebooks and sketchpads filled, and the merry times sped by. For Xmas his parents had bought him a ukulele, and not just a ukelele but a George Formby-autographed banjo ukelele. For the few who do not know, Formby was the Segovia of the banjo-uke. His classics like *When I'm Cleaning Windows,* and the sadly whimsically, *Leaning on a Lampost* (on the corner of the street, in case a certain little lady comes by), are still cherished by aficionados. Our enthusiast's personal favorite was the wittily risqué *With Me Little Stick of Blackpool Rock.* The islanders loved songs with the uke: this miniature banjo fascinated them. He plunked away at the chords to his Percy French favorites, especially *Eileen Og* and *The Star of the County Down,* and the lads joined in the choruses of *Kilkarra Mountain.*

Time passed too quickly, but he didn't worry. He would be back again and again. He would be back to feel the slight thrill of danger in the rough crossing, the first sight of the gray roofs of West Town, the green-gray fields set like a turquoise in the dull silver of the rocks. He would be back to see the straggle of people leaning against the wind as they walked along the pier to meet the boat, to smell the cows and stout and wet wool, to hear the dark tea brewing on the hob, and to breathe in the new soda bread. Above all the singsong nasal lilt of the Gaelic would be there to draw him in. *"Dia, 's Muire, 's Pádraig dhuit!"* He would be back. There was no need for farewells.

He always felt the jolt of returning to rainy, foggy, exciting London. The cultural distance (as we now say) gave him a case of the ethnocentric bends as bad as that felt on the return from America. He sometimes used the opportunity to call in on his parents—another kind of emotional decompression chamber to break the sentimental journey. (Tory to Lifford; Lifford to Derry; Derry to Belfast; Belfast to Dublin; Dublin to Liverpool; Liverpool to Manchester; Manchester to Bradford.) While he had been away they had rented his room to a Welshman, Harry, who had grown up speaking Welsh, and who even now, when teaching English at a local grammar school, kept a dictionary in his pocket. Harry *bach* became the son-who-never-left-home for them, taking them for holidays to his farm in north Wales, and to the Eistedfodd to see the crowning of the bard. Harry was tactfully away for this week of the summer, but his presence was heavy on the place: the Welsh dictionary and Welsh bible sat on the bedside table. It added to the sense of alienation.

He saw his old mates who had done their degrees and returned home (or had never left), and they were happy rising up the local hierarchy, and were deep into local things. It had never occurred to most of them to do otherwise. You got your advanced education somewhere else to enable you to come back and do just this. Many of them, having done their teacher training courses, even tried hard to get back into their old schools. Whatmuff had done this; others were to follow. How easily he might have gone that route, and how utterly inconceivable it now seemed. Harry yearned to go back to his village in Wales—if only there were jobs. While in exile Harry *bach* went twice on Sundays to the Welsh chapel in Leeds, to sing and pray in his native tongue. Our Branwell-who-made-it-in-London had no native tongue, and no local chapel to pray in. He was as adrift as on the Tory mail boat with a failed engine and a flimsy sail. He made his quick secular pilgrimage to Haworth, and said a secular prayer for the soul of Branwell. There but for the grace of ... He listeth as the wind bloweth, and he hopeth for the best, without knowing really what that is.

Once back, in his nice big room (vacated by Paul Stirling) John Napier called in to see what he thought of Desmond's latest venture. Desmond, himself a television star, knew the film people, and when Stanley Kubrick was planning *2001: A Space Odyssey* (after the book by Arthur C. Clarke) he approached Desmond. The subject was the ape-men at the beginning who, to music by Richard Strauss, discover (shades of Ardrey) that animal thighbones can be used as weapons. What would they look like, these half-ape/half-man creatures? Desmond could handle the gestures and noises, but the appearance question was passed on to Napier. The result was little actors in "monkey suits" that were really quite convincing. Baby chimps, which look disconcertingly human, were used for the infants.

Another Tetrapod, Alex Comfort, also had a project. Alex was a bright little man with a withered arm, like the Kaiser. They got on particularly well, while disagreeing about most everything. They had both contributed something to a "World of the Future" symposium, with Alex preaching his own brand of egalitarian anarchy, and the newly confident commentator-on-things-of-importance-to-mankind advocating small national states protected from themselves by some form of World Government—anathema to Alex. The anarchistic Alex had a unique twist on the keeping of mistresses: every time he took on a new one, he wrote a book and dedicated the royalties to her. It was really rather responsible of him, and certainly the most interesting attempt to meld literature and polygamy so far known in the Western World. Alex had been sent some graphic drawings of attractive people in various sexual positions. An American publisher asked him to do some accompanying text for them, to make into a book that would do for sex, it was explained, what *Joy of Cooking* had done for food. Alex thought it a good scheme—he could probably see a couple of mistresses supported by this one. But our little-man-of-the-world demurred. The long-suffering public does not need another self-help book, particularly for sex, he opined gravely. That market is saturated; you'll be wasting your time. Words that should, he insisted, be marked. Alex marked them, but, muttering that the drawings were pretty damn good, went his own stubborn way.

Peter Watkins came to see him. Watkins made startlingly odd docu-dramas, where television intervened in historical occasions as though they were contemporary events. In *Culloden*, an interviewer, in the heat of the battle, pushes a mike into the face of an English redcoat and asks his opinion of the screaming, bagpipe wailing, kilted Highlanders, about to charge with their claymores and targes. "Bloody savages!" says the soldier. Very effective. It hadn't been done before. Watkins came to him for his supposed expertise on American Indians, but like everyone else the producer was only interested in the Plains (real) Indians, and particularly the Sioux. The idea was to make the definitive docu-drama, in the Watkins style, of Custer's last stand. The filmmaker, undoubtedly a sort of cinematic genius, was also oddly nervous. Throughout the conversation he repeatedly tied and untied his shoelaces. He wanted, he said, to take the whole Sioux tribe (as extras) and ship it to Spain, where it would be cheaper to make the film than in the States. Even hiring an ocean liner to ship the extras? Even then. They would use the Spanish army as cavalrymen. But Watkins wanted the Sioux for authenticity. It was out of our Southwesterner's league. Try the Apache; do Geronimo. No. It was Custer or nothing. Go see Sol Tax in Chicago: he will know the appropriate people. No such film ever emerged, so it must have been nothing. But such visions he had: South Dakota half emptied, and the QE II entirely taken over by the Sioux nation, with Sun Dances on the poop deck, dog stew in the restaurant, counting coup on the cabin boys. Had he pursued the visions in print, the post-modern novel might have been born before its time.

It was hard to explain to people that you were only an "expert" (if that) on one culture area of a vast continent. All Indians looked alike, even to the anthropologists. The department had never offered North America as a special ethnographic area; now it decided was the time to take advantage of a resident expert. He could give his own classes, but the exam (a University of London affair) would be done in conjunction with Daryll Forde at UCL. He had spent a mad time adding to his inadequate knowledge, and was only able to manage because he was his own master in this, and, while doing a survey of North America (on the culture area principle) he was able to specialize in the Southwest. This suited Forde too. He had about five takers, and it went very well. Students were relieved to get away from Africa. He concentrated on kinship for obvious reasons, and on religion because an international encyclopedia had asked him to do their entry on North American Indian religion. Two birds with the same stone again.

This was also when the University decided to let its larger colleges have more autonomy in their degree programs, and the Department weighed in a with a proposal for a B.Sc.(Social Anthropology) degree. This was to be on the "modular" system: essentially the American "course" system. One course had to be "Kinship and Marriage" but they also put forward his "Man, Race and Culture" series as a course. Students would take it and be examined at the end. It was Harvard all over again. He wasn't sure he liked it, but it was the way things went. Whatever the Yanks did would be initially disparaged, then imitated a decade later.

Robert Ardrey's *The Territorial Imperative* came out in its English edition. He gave over a whole lecture in his new course to it. Ardrey, he felt, had made a good case for the continuity of territorial behavior from animal to man. Territorialism could take many cultural forms, but some atavistic urge to defend one's own ground, closely connected with dominance and sexual potency, did seem to be ubiquitous. Those grouse of Wynne-Edwards that did not get territories, clustered in their all-male impotent group of losers, and their genes were lost to the pool. The formula "territory + dominance = reproductive success" seemed to work. The only snag was Ardrey's equation of territory with property. This didn't work. The whole point with human property was that it could be exchanged. Animals never "exchanged" territories; humans traded real estate all the time. There was an overlap: once property was defined as sacred home turf, it would be treated like animal territory. But it could equally well be treated as an economic asset to be traded. Our boy was, after all, too imbued with Economics and the French school (Marcel Mauss and L-S) not to see exchange as something fundamental to human social life—so fundamental it required its own evolutionary explanation.

Morris arranged for Ardrey to appear on LIFE. They all traveled down to Bristol to meet him, high with expectation. Lionel had met him already, and said "You'll like him. But give him time. He's a slow speaker, and you tend to finish off sentences for slow speakers." "It's my way of showing I'm interested and following the argument." "Bite your tongue anyway." But there was no problem. Ardrey was instantly likeable in his no-nonsense, tell-it-like-it-is fashion. Another small round man ("I haven't seen my thing, except in the mirror, for a decade"), he had an easy manner and a witty delivery, with a wicked line in sarcasm. "Every time Solly Zuckerman makes another elementary mistake, he gets another promotion. It obviously pays to be a friend of Winston Churchill." No one seemed to like the Nibelung figure of Zuckerman—Secretary of the Zoological Society—very much. But while he was a very small man, he was a very big target, and clearly Ardrey had no fear of such. A failed marriage and unpleasant divorce had left the combative playwright (*Thunder Rock*) broke but undaunted. These were still the days when husbands had to buy their way out of failed marriages by mortgaging half their future incomes. Bob (he was immediately Bob) explained how his publishers helped him by paying a lot of royalties as "expenses" thus dodging the divorce accountants. "Remember that when the time comes," he suggested. Such a time, they assured him with all the silly optimism of relative youth, would never come. "Remember it anyway." They got on with the lively TV program, firm friends forever.

Bob had an apartment in Rome, sublet from Fellini (Bob was a screen-writer still—*Khartoum*—to supplement his divorce-depleted income, so he knew the movie people.) Bob liked it because it was half way (more or less) between London and South Africa. While in South Africa tracking down Raymond Dart and the Australopithecine murderers, he had met a beautiful actress and lost his romantic head over her. It was one of those true-life love stories: out-and-out unabashed passion and pursuit. Berdine was secured, and a wandering life between the Algonquin in New York, Brown's in London, the flat in Rome, and the house near Capetown, ensued. It was hard to know whether to envy this life or be sorry for them. He called Bob the Flying Dutchman. But they were happy: Berdine was anchored in South Africa (where her *Marie Stuart* is still remembered with reverence), and for her any sacrifice was worth it. For someone who always wondered if he had any real feelings (except for the girls—there was no doubt there) such unqualified devotion was both alarming and very touching. You had to be impressed.

He was losing and gaining people. Anthony Forge went off to Australia to the chair at the Australian National University in Canberra. He would miss Tony and wife Jane and the two boys. He had become used to visiting them at Passfield Hall where Tony was the warden, and drinking a coupe of bottles of Pomerol, their favorite. He would miss the dinners at Bianchis, in those days when good Italian food in Soho was still reasonably priced. But Australia was near to New Guinea, and a chair was a chair. New people came in to his life to compensate. Keith Hopkins came from Cambridge to revive the moribund Greek and Roman Society option for the Sociology degree. Keith, a hand-some cricket captain type with a permanently hoarse voice, had studied Roman society in Egypt, and found that the colonials had adopted the practice of brother-sister marriage. Did they raise the siblings together in intimate physical contact? Keith didn't know, but promised to find out. John Hajnal, the demographer who had discovered the "European pattern" of traditionally late marriage, had also worked out why, given a free choice of cousins and an age differential at marriage, the mother's brother's daughter would be most likely to be married. Armed with this, our boy entered the debate so far mo-nopolized by Rodney Needham and the elders, and he annoyed the aristo-cratic Leach by "calling his attention" to the finding. You didn't *call* the attention of the elders to things. You *paid* attention to the elders. Leach bared his fangs, and there was a ritualized stand off.

Michael Mendelsohn, who had done the definitive work on Burmese Buddhism, gave a talk on Mexico, where he was now working. It consisted of readings from a translation of the *Popol Vuh*. The department didn't like this, but it turned out Mike was a poet, writing under the name of Nathaniel Tarn, and this warmed our ex-poet's heart. They met, with other sympathizers, at Mike/Tarn's Hampstead house filled with oriental rugs and icons and back-lighted Buddhist statues in niches, to discuss the stuffy state of British. Soc.

Anth. Meyer Fortes had told Tarn/Mike, while he was at Cambridge, that he must "drop this poetry nonsense" or have no future in Anthropology. Tarn/Mike had been at Chicago for his doctorate, and was convinced that the States had a more tolerant atmosphere. "We should all go there," he said, gloomily, "set up our own place."

One day David Attenborough came in, and seemed particularly nervous and more shy than usual. Of all the students he most truly liked the talented and modest David, who was not really a student in the usual sense of course. Plans for the island fieldwork had never materialized because film projects kept interfering. This day David was more apologetic than usual. What's wrong? "I have some news," said David, "I'm afraid I'm going to leave the graduate program." Shock. What's the reason? Better be a pretty good reason. "Well, actually, you see, I've been offered a rather good job." Better be a damn good job, what is it? "Head of BBC 2 Television." Oh well, yes, that's a pretty damn good job. But one day you'll regret not completing the M.A. The stern mentor—several years David's junior—suggested that his words be marked. David guiltily promised to mark them. They parted with mutual agreement not to lose touch. There were tender recollections of visits with the children to the Attenborough's house on Richmond Hill, where little black siamangs swung around the draperies, and bush babies peed on their hands to mark their territories, and the girls giggled and wondered at this close contact with the gentle wild things. But they wouldn't lose touch. There was always the Tetrapods.

Burt Benedict, good friend that he was, was leaving for Berkeley: sunny southern California. Burt had a farewell dinner and showed off two paintings recently bought in Birmingham. They were unsigned; what did he think they were? Our one-time artist *in potentia* had no particular hesitation. His love affair with the Pre-Raphaelites left its mark in memory, and he pronounced them as either Burne-Jones or mostly Burne-Jones. Burt was delighted. They had been advertised as "from the studio of Burne-Jones." Birmingham was the manufacturing center of the Arts and Crafts movement, and they were B-J nuts there. It would figure. Burt, perhaps unduly impressed by his chance connoisseurship, told him to consider coming back to the States. They'll like your ideas over there, he insisted. It's too stuffy here; they like going on the way they are; they don't really trust new ideas. In California they like new ideas just because they are new. Of course, Burt added wistfully, ideas there have a short shelf life; but it would get you off the ground. It sounded good. He wanted to go back to America; he felt that America was unfinished business, something calling, even inevitable. But he was not yet ready to leave London, and to make that considerable leap of faith.

He was in the middle of two tasks. He had, despite Raymond's misgivings—or perhaps because of them, agreed on the Penguin Book. They offered him an "advance" which was somewhat more than his miserable year's salary, and a royalty deal which involved an equally miserable few pennies a copy. He scarcely paid attention. It was a Penguin Book for God's sake. He would have done it for free. It had written itself. It needed an introduction, and maybe a conclusion, but the lectures fell naturally into chapters, and the editor told him to keep the chatty style since it would help to make it easier for the readers. The Penguin editors were quite ecstatic about it. They talked about its "architecture" and its "clarity" and such. He worried about the cost and effort of making a clean and perfect manuscript, but they took his typed and overtyped and altered and scribbled text as it was. The typesetters have dealt with worse after the copy editors have finished, they told him.

But there was to be no copy editing. His text was fine as it was; why waste time (and presumably expense) on copy editors? He didn't know whether to be flattered or concerned. But this was a Penguin Book, these were the Penguin editors; he was barely thirty and he was in the club. They had fixed on a title: *Kinship and Marriage: An Anthropological Perspective*. He was dizzy with too much effort and too little sleep, but he reckoned this was some kind of sign, and the adrenaline boost gave him enough nervous energy to press on. He could no longer feel such a sign as the work of a good angel, but the feeling he had was not all that different. Good angels come in many guises.

At the same time he was reorganizing the thesis for publication, and what had been only a footnote in the thesis had become a chapter in the book. He was reconstructing the history of Keresan kinship terms, something no one had thought of attempting since Radcliffe-Brown had more or less banned "conjectural history." Had he done it in the thesis itself, it would probably have been ordered out. But for him logic demanded it, and logic—stern mistress—was there to be obeyed. The only way the current use of terms could be understood was as an "unfolding" of an elementary system into a version of a Crow system. The variation in Crow systems could only be understood this way. It was what L-S's difficult lecture was really about, although he couldn't convince anyone of that. "You're doing 'ethnology,'" said Freedman, "we don't do that anymore; leave it out." Wrong thing to say. Not only did logic's child leave it in, he called the book *The Keresan Bridge: A Problem in Pueblo Ethnology*. The "reader" for the series was Lucy Mair, which was lucky in its way. She confessed to not understanding the maverick chapters and concentrated on correcting the English, which surely needed it. Her corrections were precise and numerous and he learned a lot from them: "none" is singular; never start sentences with "hopefully"; no dangling participles! The only trouble was that in her zeal Lucy had corrected the English of everyone he quoted: Eggan, White, Service, Murdock... He had to restore the original surreptitiously, while loading genuine praise on Lucy for her thoroughness.

Mary Douglas was to ask him how he "got away with such a thesis at the LSE." He had to explain his "external" status, which meant no ongoing "supervision." Then there was Lucy's indifference to the "technicalities." Mary was still amazed that they let it into the series. She never appreciated how indulgent they were with one of their favorite sons. Tony Forge had taken over as editor of the monographs. "*You* can get away with it," was his judgment—and his usual smile and shrug. But he knew that this really was just an indulgence. They thought his ethological and evolutionary interests were, as Burt would say, cute. By all means indulge yourself. But he knew that no one, except the peculiar Aussies and the odd surprise like Harry Powell at Newcastle, would follow him down that path. (Michael Banton, now at Bristol, had edited *Darwin and the Study of Society,* but it had been a strictly editorial responsibility; he wasn't really interested in the issues.) Gluckman had written of "Closed Systems and Open Minds"—but the minds were as closed as the systems when it came to any fundamental rethinking of the foundations of the discipline. They saw him as something of a Trickster—the shape changer, the mischief-maker. Trickster, however, was always on his own. Tricksters are no more team players than are Messiahs.

But they were indulgent. Max-the-Bully had been an external examiner and had shown extreme prejudice towards the American student concerned, whom he threatened to fail. This caused a big row between them, and Max lied freely about what he had actually said. Both Freedman and Firth had heard the pompous utterances, but would they support a junior against his powerful elder? They did. They told Max to back off—or very polite words to that effect. Freedman even got quite heated. The student was passed, and Max immediately began to re-write the episode to his own advantage. Max-the-Dominant simply couldn't help himself. He tried to have some of the lad's editorial pieces for *New Society* censored because he didn't like the views expressed. He wrote that he wanted future such pieces to be "submitted to him for approval." Even Firth's imperturbable calm was shaken by this, and it was the first time he had ever uttered an impolite expletive in public. Even so, they warned him not to keep provoking Max-the-Terrible; it would do no good in the long run to make the old male mad like this. Well, he told them, it's the business of the young males to make the old males mad. That's what they're supposed to do. It's part of the test.

There was an annual Malinowski Memorial Lecture, given by a younger member of the profession. The previous year it had been given by Godfrey Lienhardt from Oxford, and no one was very happy with it. They respected the ethnographic skills of Evans-Pritchard and his people, (including Mary Douglas) but were deeply suspicious of their anti-scientific bias and their quite conscious attempt to treat Anthropology as another of the humanities. Firth, a Rationalist to the core, saw it as a faintly disguised attempt to smuggle their Catholicism into the discipline. Gluckman referred to the Institute at Oxford as "the Oratory." They all sighed when Victor Turner—an ex-Gluckmanite, now a Catholic convert from Marxism—referred to stages of

Ndembu ritual as "stations." A bit blatant, said Raymond. Anyway, they saw it as all very reactionary, and as an antidote they asked the devoted son of science to give the next Malinowski lecture. His Popperean credentials were sound; there would be no danger of covert Thomism, even if he did insist on talking about monkeys and fossils.

Among the Tetrapods various names circulated as the next big thing. There was Anthony Ambrose, a Jungian analyst who had done the work on smiling in infants: it was spontaneous and not a result of experience—blind children smiled. Ambrose was working on the ethological idea of "critical periods" and thought this was when the Jungian archetypes were learned. There was a kind of inbuilt template but it was activated by "releasers" in the environment: the basic ethological model for behavior. Ambrose suggested that the learning of incest avoidance could be a critical period phenomenon. John Hajnal mentioned a young geneticist at Imperial College, Bill Hamilton. He'd solved a basic Darwinian conundrum, they said, and it had implications for the genetics of social behavior. Bill was undoubtedly a genius, John said, and so far ahead of his time that the academic geneticists didn't understand what he was doing. The LSE Demography department, in the true spirit of Carr-Saunders, had given him a home: he was doing population genetics, they reasoned, and population was their thing. They gave him a scholarship and saw him through his Ph.D.

A visit to South Kensington was arranged, and while they were feeding pigeons with crusts from their sandwiches on the steps of the Albert Memorial, Hamilton enthusiastically poured out his theory about the "altruism" of sterile castes in insects. The hours spent with "programmed learning" workbooks on genetics in the third-class smoker just, and only just, enabled him to keep up with Hamilton on haplodiploidy and the arithmetic of "altruism"—which he thought was a dangerous misnomer. Surely "altruism" suggested intent? Insects and bees had no intent; they just did what their instincts told them to do; they could do no other. Bill went on about hypothetical genes for altruism and how they could multiply in a hypothetical population under hypothetical conditions. I'd better get your paper and study it, said the increasingly baffled layman. "I'll send you one," said the altruistic Bill. Hajnal might have been right that Bill was a genius, but at the moment it all seemed a bit, well, hypothetical. Thus do great moments in intellectual history sometimes just not occur.

Out of the blue. Somehow that oddly named university in New Jersey kept dogging him. There had been inquiries from the States. The president of Smith College, a tall bald dignified man called Mendenhall had taken him for drink to a bar in Piccadilly, where, to the bafflement of the barman, the stately Yank had asked for "a pint of old and mild." Settling for brown ale, the president said that the students were "demanding" anthropology. Why on earth would they do that? It was an esoteric subject meant for the eccentric few. Well, they did. It was "something in the air." The president obviously didn't know what, but he knew demand when he saw it. Polite refusal was the order of the day. But it had been Kluckhohn's prompting that had sent Mendenhall on his quest, and Kluckhohn was persistent. There were just not enough "qualified" people in the States to keep up with this new demand. Theirs was a small generation. The depression had not been a time of reproductive exuberance. The post-war "baby boom" was now threatening to flood the colleges, and the social sciences were booming along with it. So the Yanks were recruiting in England: it was the start of the notorious "brain drain." In New Jersey the legislature had voted forty million dollars to add a new college to Rutgers University, and appointed as Dean a physicist with a humanistic background, and the Dean was on the hunt for brains to drain.

"You probably won't have heard of Rutgers," the Dean began his letter. But he had. He had seen it even, however dimly, in his confused state at the New Brunswick railway station. It was Roy's university; it was Robeson's university. And it was the State University of New Jersey—whatever that was. But he told the Dean no, and at the time he meant it. There was simply too much happening in London, and he wanted to remain part of it. The Dean was persistent. The new college, named Livingston after one of the founders of the original Rutgers College, was to be the "the MIT of the Social Sciences" he declared. Entrance standards were to be of the highest. They would get the best of the new large crop of students applying. Our new minted "full professor" could have a department and a blank check/cheque. What Kroeber was to Berkeley, Boas to Columbia, and even Malinowski to the LSE, he could be to Livingston. The pay was good too. Even the opening negotiating salary the Dean suggested was six times what he was earning. He thought of the discussions at Xmas about whether they could afford new heavy coats for the winter, or whether they should use the money as a down payment on electric night-storage heaters for the girls' bedroom. The converted post office van had to be dangerously hand-cranked when the engine froze up. He thought of Burt going to the California sunshine, of Tony Forge and his chair in Australia, and of Lionel's comment that high thinking didn't require low living.

He decided to keep the lines open, but didn't think of it too much since he was working on the Malinowski lecture. Lionel was back—he always had some grant or other, and they went through the lecture together, word by word, idea by idea. The whole thing about the origins of exogamy, incest taboos, and guilt (all in one package) was not Lionel's thing, but he was the best listener, and Burt leant a friendly ear. Burt wanted the lecture for *Man*, once it had been delivered. What is more, Thomas Nelson, the publisher, had approached them about doing a joint book: something like *The Evolution of Human Social Behavior*. Its premise was the simple ethological one: that natural selection acted on behavior, and the behavior of any species, including our own, could be understood by tracing its evolution. In principle they agreed, they even signed a contract (without thinking too clearly about the logistics,) but in practice they thought it premature. What Nelson wanted was some kind of textbook. But you could only write a textbook for a subject that already existed. What they were doing was creating a subject, and that required something other than a detailed guidebook; it required a preliminary sketch map of the territory.

It didn't matter; everything was put on hold by the Troubles. The Troubles (as they came to be called by those recollecting them in anguish) had been simmering for a few years. There was a new wave of students—the first wave of baby boomers—who displaced the lethargic, conformist crowd that had characterized Exeter. These new kids on the academic block had a new vocabulary. "Malaise" was on the list, as were "governance," "participation," and particularly "power." Like all adolescents they saw life as a matter of being unduly "controlled," but unlike most they wanted, not to struggle for their eventual places on the higher rungs of the ladder, as his generation had done, but to gain places there immediately. This was a generation that did not seem to have learned, or at least seem to be interested in, deferred gratification. "Now" was the other big word on the list.

This was not just a personal agenda for them. They saw it in political, collectivist, terms. The "youth movement" was seen on the analogy of the proletariat; the older generation was the "establishment" that practiced or condoned "militarism" and "racism"—the list was to lengthen. The movement was Left without being socialist. It wanted "civil rights" and "free speech," a banning of the bomb of course, and particularly an end to apartheid. But apart from a vague utopian egalitarianism, it had no clear idea of the future. Its inspiration was the "free speech movement" at Berkeley, and American students were to play key roles. The word "hippie" had not yet become common currency, and the pejorative "beatnik" was most often used. Its driving forces were to be its sheer numbers, which changed the rules of the hierarchical game, and the birth-control pill, which freed it from the moral constraints of the elders, and so changed the rules of relationships between the generations. Like all movements of underdogs it was rife with conspiracy theories.

The catalyst of The Troubles was the search for a new Director, Caine being due to retire. Caine was a very decent man, and would be missed. But he was also stiff and formal and a bit of an old-school-colonial; this would tell against him. The selection committee included MacRae, Oakeshott and Titmuss. His favorite candidate was Alan Bullock, then Master of St. Catherine's, son of that Unitarian minister who had educated him in the true meaning of T. S. Eliot, and so perhaps started the soul on the most crucial leg of its journey. But Bullock, who had risen to fame for his *Hitler: A Study in Tyranny*, declined, and the committee chose the head of the University College of Rhodesia, Walter Adams, and all hell broke loose.

The details have been raked over from every angle: there is a huge, largely self-serving, sub literature on the Troubles and their aftermath. In retrospect it looks as if Adams was an excuse: the eruption would have happened over something. Adams was not a bad choice: he had done a lot to integrate the College in Rhodesia for example, but he had been criticized in several reports, one of which, it appeared, the committee knew nothing about. This sin of omission, plus resentment at a perceived lack of wide consultation, irked some of the faculty. The students began their round of now familiar, but then shocking, boycotts, sit-ins, teach-ins, demonstrations, and hunger strikes, tutored by their transatlantic cousins. It all took a tragic turn when a student protest meeting resulted in the death, by heart attack, of an older porter. The porters, old-fashioned Londoners, whose life was the School, were universally liked. The students were appalled and disbanded their meeting in genuine sorrow.

The Director had banned the meeting, and the School secretary, Harry Kidd, became dead set on "discipline"—the favorite buzzword on their side. Meetings of the Academic Board showed a shockingly divided School. MacRae, Oakeshott and Titmuss, partly in self-defense as members of the guilty committee, were firmly in the ranks of the disciplinarians. Caine grew more rigid, prompted by Kidd, his evil genius, who popped up, peering and weaving like a bespectacled Puck at every crucial moment when compromise was in sight. Without Kidd there might have been a settlement. The man was a decent administrator—they were all decent men—who got carried away by the events and became the local hanging judge, along with Ben Roberts, who denounced the student actions as the worst thing to happen since the Brown Shirts took over the German universities. It was like that. Subdued but determined the students continued their sit-in. One of his girl students from the Man, Race, and Culture class, a frail, pale pretty thing, joined the hunger strikers with a big Red Cross armband (another Berkeley import.) "I don't each much anyway," she told him. Why are you doing it? "Because you have power over us." What power for God's sake? The only power he had, he protested, was the power to mark exams, and that was inherent in the situation. Education was not egalitarian; teachers knew more about the subject than pupils. "It's all power," she said, sipping her sugar water and lying down on a mattress.

Egos are always bigger than issues. The student end of things was taken over by a paranoid narcissist called Marshall Bloom, an American graduate student, not even at the LSE. Several faculty committees were formed to try to mediate. Firth, to his credit, formed his; Gellner formed another. (When in doubt form a committee.) Our growingly anxious lad, who saw his beloved School falling apart, was on both. They tried to talk with the excitable Bloom, but he spent the whole time haranguing them about how *he* had been treated, yelling that they were all McCarthyites, and that nothing would be solved until the wrongs done to *him* had been righted. The Gellner committee took the action of ultimate gravity and wrote a letter to the *Times*. (When in doubt, write a letter to the *Times*.) They tried to talk to the Director, who gave them tea and scones. Not even a prison, said Terry Morris, could be run by coercion; they had to work for consensus. But an alarmed Kidd rushed in and stopped the whole thing short with his insistence on even more discipline.

In an episode worthy of Evelyn Waugh, our busy mediator went on a late night taxi ride to Smith Square with John Griffith. Griffith was the professor of law who had defended the students at the hearing on their behavior. He was famous for getting students off charges, including one boy who had taken a police car for a joy ride, then delivered it back to the station. The charge was theft, and Griffith got it dismissed because, he argued, theft meant taking something permanently, and the boy had returned the car. It might be something criminal, but it wasn't theft. He and Griffith were on all the committees: the hard-line faculty, particularly Roberts and Oakeshott, called them "student lovers." Oh God! It was like that. The aim of the expedition to Smith Square was to try to find Jo Grimond, the respected Liberal leader, at the party headquarters. Perhaps he could be persuaded to be a mediator? They went to the Conservative central office by mistake, and were told that the Liberals were "a little bit further on the left." Grimond was not there, and the next day he issued a harsh condemnation of the students that warmed Kidd's icy heart.

Some sort of compromise was eventually reached. He was having dinner with Raymond and David Attenborough at the Firths' house in Highgate, when a porter called to tell of the settlement. The details grow murky with distance. Does it matter? Nothing would ever be the same. The Director promised "a new start" with definitely "no reprisals." But at the next Academic Board meeting he made it all an issue of "obedience" to him and "loyalty to the office of Director" and specifically attacked the committees and the signatories of the letter to the *Times*, by name, as the worst sinners. Depressing. Given the cast of characters it probably couldn't have come out other than it did. There were endearing moments. At the peak of the trouble, Gellner stopped the Academic Board dead with his self-described "ethical argument." If we asked the students to stop the boycott, when their leaders were in peril, we would be asking them to be disloyal to their friends. The Director could not, on the one hand, ask for loyalty from us, and on the other deny it to the students. To its credit, the Board seriously considered this issue for a while.

It was never going to be the same after this. In the department, he and Firth stood together, but Freedman and Morris were two of the hardest hard-liners, and there had been harsh words between him and them. Schap and Lucy were consistently cynical, but made it clear they disapproved of his active role, even if it was as a mediator. As a junior he should have kept his nose to the academic grindstone and let his seniors in the hierarchy take decisions.

Raymond didn't feel this way, but Raymond would be retiring soon. The times in general they were a-changin' too damn fast. The cost of caring about it was heavy in time, energy and emotion. The new policy of "expansion" consequent on the report by Lord Robbins on higher education—another serious intrusion by the School into the affairs of the nation—meant a huge influx of students, taking them from two percent of the age cohort to nearly forty. This meant the School would get much bigger, thus changing its character to a large, primarily undergraduate, university. The push to provide more university places that had bothered them at Exeter was inexorable. The baby boomers wanted to "go to college" on the American model: the next thing you do after high school. "Elitism" was added to the list of boo words. In the new dispensation everyone would be elite.

But in England they were trapped in the elitist web. Rather than expand the already excellent redbrick civic universities, perhaps on the model of the City College of New York, they started new little Oxbridge imitations in cathedral towns (Bath, Canterbury, Guildford, York, Colchester...), draining the existing universities of staff and resources in needless duplication. He didn't want one of these "greenbelt" chairs, with a converted manse and two spaniels, and he was pessimistic about the future at the LSE. The tone of the times was set by Anthony Crosland, a private school product who clearly hated his own class, like so many left-wing public school boys reared in the thirties. As the Labour government's minister of education, he announced, as part of the campaign for "comprehensive" education, that his aim was "to destroy every fucking grammar school" in the country. This campaign was part of the current passion for equality in society, and had nothing to do with quality in education. The Crosland plan was ninety-percent effective in the end: the worst piece of iconoclastic vandalism since Henry VIII destroyed the monasteries. The Minister's language confirmed his mother's worst fears about Labour; his father thought Crosland was a bloody fool.

The offer from the Rutgers Dean was starting to look better. It would be a chance to start afresh without all this emotional detritus and despair. The Dean came over. He had been in touch with Bob Guttman, a Rutgers sociologist at the LSE, who had reported Gellner's opinion that the prospect's exam papers were "the best he'd ever seen." The Dean was impressed, and with the two books in the offing. He had evidently flirted with Mel Spiro, but the ethnographer of the Kibbutz had gone to San Diego. The Dean was of Dutch extraction and education, and multilingual like all educated Hollanders. He was a smallish man with a hairy wart on his nose, but he was jovial and smart. A physicist who taught classes for non-scientists, he expounded his notions of "elite education for the masses" as the goal of American higher ed. He wanted "a young department that would grow with the college." It was a perfect chance for "new directions" - he welcomed the idea of Lionel joining them. Lionel was certainly interested, as was Virginia. The already glamorous pair would get to live in chic Manhattan—preferably Greenwich Village. It would solve the boys' logistical problem of how to write a book together. Their attempts so far had been a bit like playing chess by mail. They worked better when turning things over in constant conversation.

Your family would like living in Princeton, the Dean suggested. It was just down the road: a beautiful place "like Cambridge" and had "good schools." Just one bothersome thing, he told the Dean: don't you already have a department, and isn't Ashley Montagu the head of it? It says so on his books. The Dean was embarrassed. It's a long story, but no. Montagu was there for a year, back in the fifties, then went on indefinite leave of absence, but continued to bill himself as head of the non-existent department. It was a sore point. Perhaps it should have sent up a red flag, but the Dean's enthusiasm was contagious, and they parted with the lines of communication open. He was playing cricket at Brighton when the Dean had a transatlantic call put through to the pavilion. Come over and visit us, he said, if that will help. Any remaining resolve crumbled before this persistence: don't worry, he said, I've decided to accept. It was so nice to be so wanted.

In the wake of the Troubles he delivered his Malinowski lecture. It amounted to a farewell dinner for him—in the Director's dining room, after the talk and reception, and everyone put a brave face on it and wished him well. He made his little farewell speech, saying that the occasion demonstrated the truth of Freud's theory of the Primal Horde: fist the brothers demolished the father with polite criticism, took over the "mother-matter" (the *materia*) of the discipline, then gathered for a totem meal to wallow in collective guilt. He dubbed the goulash they were served "Boeuf Bronislaw." Everyone laughed politely. He had called the lecture "In the Beginning: Aspects of Hominid Behavioral Evolution." Its publication in *Man* was to mark Burt's swan song as an associate editor; a pretty remarkable editorship between him and Adrian Mayer, that future so-called historians, with their usual sloppiness, were to miss entirely. Lucy introduced him and surprised him by her warmth. They would miss him, she said, but they were proud that he was to be the youngest ever Professor of Anthropology. Was he? No matter, it sounded good. There was a fee for the lecture, fifty pounds. Lucy had told the wife that he must spend it on a new suit; he couldn't deliver the lecture in his elbow-patched tweeds and faded corduroys. Riddled with guilt at spending this money on himself, but not daring to offend Lucy's sense of propriety, he bought a charcoal gray business suit off the rack at Liberty's, rationalizing that he would need it to enhance the dignity of his new position.

The title of the lecture, given late afternoon in the Old Theatre to a surprisingly big audience, was taken from the last words of *Totem and Taboo*, which were themselves from Goethe's *Faust*: *Im Anfang war die Tat*. In the beginning was the deed. Some deed of nature, over a considerable period, had made us over from ape into human, and we bore the scars of it today. As in Freud's drama, the young males confronted the older in a constant battle for dominance. The old found many ways to control the rambunctious young, but the guts of it was to control their sexual access to the females. Already he had sensed that the young of the Troubles had started to ignore the sexual conventions in a very open way. The advent of the pill had removed the fear of pregnancy, and virginity was no longer at a premium. Sex was no longer surreptitious; it was taken for granted. Girls were already beginning to argue that, once they were on the pill, not to have sex was to "waste" their investment. There was no more male-initiated fiddling with condoms; girls slipped out of their clothes and into sex like otters into the river. There were no longer any serious initiation procedures to curb the youngsters. The new comprehensive schools seemed to lack the means to instill deference in their pupils. The older generation was losing its grip. The Latin requirement for university entrance had been abolished. You could no longer force the young to slave away at dead languages to keep their minds off sex. There were so many of them. In the words of the popular *Marat/Sade*, they wanted their revolution NOW.

He didn't deal directly with this in the lecture; that just wasn't done; it was too Margaret Mead (or Geoffrey Gorer for that matter.) But he did try to tie in the Chance hypothesis with incest avoidance, and tie both to the evolution of the brain via hominid adaptations to changing African environments—an idea developed from the work of John Crook at Bristol. The young males had to develop a capacity for self-control if they were to survive, a development made more vital by the advent of hunting and weapons. The upshot of this, over the generations, would be an expansion of cortical control over hormonal behavior, so that emotional responses like lust and anger could be controlled and timed. The rapid growth of the hominid neo-cortex suggested that fairly rapid selection was indeed taking place. It was taking place in the evolving primate horde, and here the basic lessons were learned. They were learned in the context of a struggle between older males and younger males for control of the females. The young males that won out were the ones with greater powers of equilibration, on the Chance model; that is, the ones with slightly better cortical control. Given the selective breeding system, this would cumulate, producing animals that were, not less sexy and aggressive, but that were better able to control their sex and aggression. Almost as a byproduct, the brain that expanded to exercise control, would also develop those other human attributes of memory, intelligence, foresight, and eventually language and consciousness, probably in that order.

The important connection he felt he made was that this was the context in which incest inhibition and avoidance were evolved. Thus everything human was indeed the result of the avoidance of incest, but not as some hypothetical act of renunciation; it was part of the adaptational process. The evolving males in particular would become increasingly sensitized: those that bred and passed on their genes, would be those that were most able to control their sexual impulses to related females, and rein in their aggression towards older related males. This is what was added to the physiological tendency to avoid siblings: it was what made for restraint, but not in something called "the family." It was learned in the context of the total group, which would include the biological family members. Young contemporary males contesting the power of the old, had been diagnosed by psychiatrists as having "unresolved Oedipal conflicts." This, he thought, put the cart before the proverbial horse: Oedipal issues were simply those general issues the young had with the old, compressed into the "nuclear family," itself a later development.

We humans are thus "primed," as it were, to develop inhibitions, but as with other innate propensities (language for example) we need the releasers or stimuli in the environment to realize them. Initiation, whatever its form, is our way of reinforcing these evolutionary lessons for the young: it taps these deeply lodged motivations and turns them to the service of group solidarity. The trick is to make the young concur, and by making the rewards so obvious, cause them to defer to, and identify with, the elders and the system. In fact, as Johnny Whiting had taught him, having had their largely symbolic rebellion, the "aspirants" would be all too willing to dish it out to the next generation in their turn. The Grammar/Public Schools understood this perfectly; where were we now heading? He didn't say that.

His parents had come, and they were at the reception in the Shaw Library, puzzled, but proud of the occasion. Before he received anyone he went and kissed them both. His mother said his suit was very smart; his father said that it had been a long talk. Lucy, standing with him in the reception line, was almost unnaturally pleased at his attention to them. But she pointed out that "humans" was not a noun: human was an adjective: he should have said "human beings." He would miss Lucy. He would miss the Shaw Library, he would miss Raymond, and the Institute, and the National Liberal Club, and the Tetrapods, and the Zoo... But the die was cast, the Rubicon crossed, the clichés exhausted; he could only look forward.

At least this time he would not be condemned to the bottom of yet another hierarchy. The Dean had pointed this out. He would, at one blow, put the whole promotion thing behind him. He would be freed from that pressure, and could get on with his ideas and department building. Fine, but did he really want to build a department? Was he an administrator? What did it even involve? Vogtie had been off-putting: there were simply not enough qualified people out there to build a department with. This is why they were aggressively recruiting Europeans. Well, he reckoned, starting with the Canadian Lionel, he too could perhaps find some brains to drain. But he had to build a whole department, covering the "four fields" of American Anthropology: Cultural, Linguistics, Archaeology and Physical. And he had little idea what the local set-up was at Rutgers. There were "autonomous undergraduate colleges" and separate "graduate programs" but he wasn't clear what this all meant or how it worked. The Institute of Animal Behavior, under Daniel Lehrman, which Desmond had praised, was "on the Newark campus." What did that mean?

Once again he had blundered into something with dangerously low information, and too much of a sense that things would somehow work out. Once again it was as much a negative decision as a positive. But at least the hierarchical thing would be, as the Dean had said, behind him. And something would turn up; something always did. Mr. Micawber had never let him down yet. And if there wasn't some element of chance, where was the thrill? The Tory cow-gamblers understood this, in the face of possible starvation in the winter. At least in this life-gamble (he thought, in a flood of truculent self-pity) he would be able to buy warm coats for his children, rent a dry and heated house, and get a car that he didn't have to crank on icy mornings. The rest would take care of itself.

9

The Career: Telling God Your Plans

"S*i quieres hacer reir a Dios, cuentale tus planes.*" This was the most memorable line from the monumental film, *Amores Perros*, by Alejandro González Iñárritu; a film whose portrayal of moral confusion and complexity probably defined the beginning of the twenty-first century. Two characters survived the physical and moral carnage with any dignity. One was an intellectual, turned radical, turned guerilla, turned dog-keeping wino, turned hit man, who finally meted out rough justice to those who hired him, and showed a redeeming love for his estranged daughter. The other was the Rotweiler, the champion fighting dog, finally called Negro, which had been taught killing for profit by its original human owner, but in the end was accepted by the reformed assassin as a suitable, and only, companion—despite its savage mangling of his other dogs. None of the protagonists in this movie without heroes is free from moral taint, and none is wholly bad, including the adulterous model, mutilated in a car crash, whose pampered lap dog disappears through a hole in the floor and is almost bitten to death by rats.

The beauty of the movie is its subtle portrayal of moral ambiguity, with the inextricable mix of good intentions and bad actions that characterize the moment-to-moment reality of human life. It is a kind of Mexican Iris Murdoch. Against the theme of human confusion is played the brilliant counterpoint of the innocent, but potentially deadly dogs, helpless against the corrupting forces of human love and greed. Here we suspend this review (and any review should mention with awe the writer—Guilliermo Arriga Jordán) to relate the minor moment that led to the memorable line. There is an unhappy widow whose husband has been shot in a bank robbery. She meets, at the funeral, her husband's brother, with whom she has had an adulterous affair, and from whom she had stolen (or had she?) the dogfight winnings, after he had arranged to have his wife-beating brother beaten up in turn. Her guilt will not allow her to join him now she is free, and she quotes to him an old Mexican proverb, which her grandmother used to tell her: "If you want to make God laugh, tell him your plans."

First, you have to have plans. Start a department—what did that mean exactly? Set up a new home near "good" schools. How did you know the schools were good? Start a "graduate program"—how did that differ from a department? Bring Lionel in at some point and write the book—how would that jibe with the other stuff to be done? This stuff included developing a "working relationship" with the Institute of Animal Behavior in Newark. He didn't even know where Newark was and how you got there. You will start to build, the Dean said, a "stellar reputation." The Dean was given to such phrases. The books, and the numerous papers you give around the country, would do it he said. There were already invitations to Harvard (Vogtie), Pennsylvania (Dell Hymes), Chicago (Fred Eggan.) Of course, the two books were coming out in England precisely as he was leaving. He had signed off on "world rights" with Penguin, but he didn't know what that meant or how it translated into sales and timing in the USA. He had wanted to claim his sabbatical and go to Tory, but the Dean said no, come over and help us plan the college; we can use your input.

Input was a big Dean word. He wasn't sure what he could put in; he had never planned a college or anything like it and wasn't sure he wanted to. But the Dean was a hard man to say no to. You can take your sabbatical later, once the college is up and running, the Dean promised. In the end he not only went over for that year, but was persuaded to go over for the summer. This meant leaving the family behind to sell the house and furniture and come over on its own. They had good friends: Rita and Tony helped, and Alan Williams from Exeter (now a professor at York) pitched in, and of course the parents. He had not thought about how they would see the departure of their grandchildren. There would be visits back and forth; not a year would go by, he promised, without a visit. They were brave and said, yes, they would love to see America. But he could see how sad they were really, and again was puzzled by his lack of appropriate feelings. Their emotionalism simply irritated him. They should be pleased with his plans.

He arrived at Idlewild (later christened JFK) airport on a muggy June day, with smog lying dense and oily over the city in the background. His English bank had given him some dollars, and he tried to use them in a change machine to get a dime for a phone call. They were spit back contemptuously. He appealed to a uniformed person, who looked at his bills and pointed out that they were "silver certificates" and the machine wouldn't accept them, only "regular dollar bills." The guard thought they must have been sitting in British bank vaults for a lot of years, since silver certificates had long gone out of circulation, even though they were still legal tender (except in vending machines apparently.) The guard and a newspaper vendor took pity on him and gave him a real dollar for one of the certificates and he made change. The Dean told him to take a taxi to the American Airlines terminal and take a Princeton commuter plane from there. When he told the cabbie where he wanted to go, he was hit by a creative string of expletives. The angry little man had been waiting in line for a fare to "the city." Now he would have to go back to the end of the line and wait again. There seemed to be no way to make the situation easier for him, and he cursed more and at length. Our bewildered traveler paid him off in silver certificates. He didn't seem to notice or care.

The single-engine plane shot off into the smog, and when they were clear of that he saw an ocean of woodlands with settlements here and there and long strings of roads. New Jersey was mostly forest where they were flying: "west of the turnpike" the pilot said. The pilot banked for him to get a view of New Brunswick, but it was too quick to see much. There were some church spires and large buildings and a lot of suburban sprawl. The Dean greeted him at the toy airport, and whisked him off to Princeton, where again the impression was of tall, very leafy trees, big houses in the colonial style, and slow-moving large cars. Over the treetops loomed a ghost of Magdalen Tower and the roof of King's College Chapel. How did they get there: this gothic fantasy in the northeastern woodlands? The tower was the "graduate school" of Princeton University. They had decided, like Yale, to "go gothic" the Dean explained. He also dropped the news that Israel was at war with Egypt (again) and that there had been riots in Newark. They would discuss these things at a dinner that night to which he had been invited.

Groggy with jet lag, he tried to keep up with the crowd at the dinner. When the Dean explained what he was doing there people inevitably asked, "Why did they pick you?" He was tempted to reply, "Because they wanted the worst anthropologist they could find of course." But he decided it was because he looked so young. He had shaved off the Edwardian beard in deference to what he assumed was the ongoing Yankee horror of facial hair, and probably did look ridiculously young to be doing what he and the Dean claimed. The crowd of talkative bright people took in a huge amount of hard alcohol before dinner was served after nine-o'clock. Everyone was overtly sober, but they could hardly have appreciated the wine or the food at that point. This was to be the way with dinner parties. It was a blur. He told his silver certificate story, and a collector bought his remaining notes from him at a profit. He was overheated in his waistcoat ("love your vest") and slurred in his speech ("love your accent") and couldn't keep pace with the speed of conversation, much of it about Israel. It was then that he realized, foggily, that they were all Jews.

The Dean was a Jew (he must remember "Jewish"—and never, never, never "Jewess") and so perhaps it was not surprising that the Dean's friends were likewise. Jews were way over-represented in the academic community (in proportion to their numbers in the population) he had read somewhere. While this wasn't true at Harvard, it was true at the LSE—Popper, Freedman, Ginsberg, Gellner, Schapera, Gould, Benedict, Moser, Morris, etc, all Jews. But he never even thought of them as such. They were secular Jews, rationalists to the core, and made no big thing of their Jewishness. Apart, perhaps, from Gould, who edited the *Jewish Journal of Sociology,* and Freedman, who collected signatures for a petition once, none of them was active in Jewish causes, or particularly self-conscious about his race. But these Princeton people were different. Being Jewish was obviously a major reference point of their existence, even if they were sometimes skeptical about themselves. One shrewd looking commentator told him: "We don't have a synagogue in Princeton: we have a "Jewish Center." We're "reformed" Jews. Some orthodox Jews came in one Saturday and thought they'd disturbed the Unitarians." It turned out the shrewd commentator was the Rabbi—"Just don't call me that." What should he be called? "I'm the Director of the Jewish Center." There was a lot to be learned here, but if his undergraduate experience was anything to go by, the food would be outstanding and the dark-eyed girls gently dangerous.

The Princeton physicist whose house he was going to rent was also Jewish. The house was right in "downtown" Princeton, only a walk from the good schools. They were very proud that it was only a few doors from the famous pianist Robert Casadesus. The Bloomenfields were an oddly assorted couple: he a reclusive scientist, always at the lab; she a flamboyant ex-Vogue model and talent scout. The father, Irwin Bloomenfield, had pretty much invented magazine color photography. They had a boy who was an *enfant prodige* (their words) and whom they were taking to school in Switzerland, where he would be with intellectual equals. What about the "very good schools" for which Princeton was famous? Didn't he know? That was a euphemism for "very few Negroes."

The Bloomenfields had a big visiting extended family, some of whom were concentration camp survivors. He was fond of brown as a color, and one day wore brown boots, brown trousers, and a long-sleeved brown shirt, with a dark brown tie—no coat in the hot summer. He entered the house with the sun behind him, tall (by their standards), fair-haired, slim, and brown, brown, brown. An old lady looked up, screamed horribly, and fainted. He saw the numbers tattooed on her arm. Everyone was embarrassed, no one more than the old lady when she recovered. Her tearful apologies only made it worse.

The Bloomenfields were to leave shortly and sell him (on the installment plan) their two Ford cars: a large "station wagon" and a small "sedan"—both of which had an automatic gear-shift, and didn't need cranking. In the meantime he was borrowing an MG from the Dean, and driving up daily to New Brunswick. The Dean drove a Citroen and his entourage drove Volkswagens and Volvos and even Austin Princesses. No one drove American cars, except the Englishman, who was excused on the grounds of allowable eccentricity. The Livingston campus was actually in the exotically named Piscataway Township. (The founders had migrated south from the Piscatawa River in Massachusetts in the 1640s.) The site was the old Camp Kilmer. Ask a serviceman from World War II where he spent his days before being shipped out "over there" and it would probably be Camp Kilmer.

The city of New Brunswick had been overwhelmed with the troops and the camp followers who took over the downtown. It was a very run-down light-industrial city, kept alive by being the headquarters of Johnson and Johnson. Part of the genesis of Livingston College was that the federal government had given the camp to the state, which had given it to Rutgers, adding hundreds of acres to a university that already had more acreage than any other in the country. It sprawled over five townships, at once a luxury and a problem. It needed a town-sized bus service to connect all parts, among other things. Camp Kilmer was named after the local poet Joyce Kilmer, known pretty much for one lyric: the words to "Trees." Our warbling boy soprano had, with his father, sung along with Nelson Eddy's scratchy 78rpm version:

> A tree that may in summer wear
> A nest of robins in her hair...
> A tree that looks at God all day,
> And lifts its leafy arms to pray.
>
> For poems were made by fools like me,
> But only God can make a tree.

But the Camp itself was devoid of trees. It was an appalling site: rows and rows of dirty yellow Quonset huts with barbed wire and stockades and guard towers. It looked like a mid-Atlantic version of Auschwitz. One of the big questions was how to get rid of the sordid square miles of huts. The local fire brigade wanted to burn them down for practice. The expense of demolition was daunting, the drive through them depressing.

The makeshift college buildings were the former officers' quarters in the camp HQ. The rooms still had the ranks over the doors. The Dean had the general's office; the new boy was a lieutenant colonel. He was, after all, the first appointment to the college (from outside—some Rutgers people were to transfer.) He had a secretary, a mousy young woman with a Polish name, who never seemed very happy. Time was consumed with plans, plans, plans. The Dean wanted whole "programs" detailed, when the unwilling planner had no idea whom he might hire. He hated these exercises in make-believe, but they were a necessary part of the process. Most of the state's money was going into the bricks and mortar (with a substantial kickback, he was told, to the Mafia, who controlled the bricks and the labor unions.) There was not much left over for other things—like faculty and supplies etc. So there was a constant harping on "funding." He had to take a crash course in "funding agencies"—state, federal and private. He hated this grubby, time-consuming, money-raising function; why hadn't they told him?

Then there were the endless "policy" discussions, particularly the "philosophy" (every program or plan or bunch of loose ideas was a "philosophy") of "grading." The Dean and his cohorts were in favor of a "pass/fail" grading system, instead of the traditional "letter grades." Why? It was unclear to the newcomer: something to do with taking competitive pressure off the students and allowing them freedom to discover themselves and develop intellectually? Also the college's "role" and "mission" were on the agenda. It was to have an "urban emphasis." So why were they putting it out here in the country rather than buying up run-down areas of the city and building it there? And why were they calling it after one of the slave-holding governors of New Jersey rather than after Paul Robeson? And, looking at the plans, why were there no quadrangles?

He had been put on the Design and Architecture Committee, among many others. This he liked. The "team" of architects would come in, all wearing pastel-colored blazers and identical polished-silver hairdos. They would be asked to "come up with solutions" for this and that (garbage, policing, lighting) and they would protest that they needed firmer guidance about design. The Dean told them to "come up with a high-rise solution" to the problem of what kind of dorms to have. The neophyte college planner was asked for his anthropological input, so he put in his opinion that they should keep the buildings low; high rises promoted anonymity and even anomie. He had learned this from Michael Young and the East London experience as an undergraduate. "Council flats" were inevitably a social disaster. What about the quadrangles, he insisted? The college as designed was strung out along avenues (the planners were drunk on the almost limitless space available) and on a cold winter day a student moving between dorms, classes, and facilities would end up walking a couple of miles in the icy wind.

The buildings should be clustered around quads. Since the Middle Ages (since the original Moorish universities even) no one had come up with a better way of promoting "interaction" than the quad. He rearranged the models of the main academic buildings and the dining facilities to form, not a quadrangle, but more of piazza. Pave it in the Florentine style, he told them, and leave the bottom floor facing the river open so that there is a vista. The buildings had to be rearranged to go round the square rather than in the long line, and later generations, finding their way like untrained rats round the mazes of Lucy Stone Hall, would curse the complexity of corridors produced. But it was a really nice piazza.

He was getting into the swing of these design things. He had, he discovered, a "philosophy"—(something like): Academies are sacred places where very special things go on; they should, as the Princeton and Yale builders understood, be made to look like sacred places, like churches, not like the latest municipal airport or office complex. Livingston was going to be hard to save. But even if they meant largely to ignore him, they liked the input. The men at the top were pleased to have this kind of comment; it was what was expected from their brain drain Englishman. Mason Gross was the president, a man of dignity and humor, who had rowed for his college when doing philosophy at Oxford. Richard (Dick) Schlatter was the provost, a Renaissance man whose house on College Avenue was the best venue for talk and parties on campus. (Jean Martinon, then conductor of the Chicago Symphony, demonstrated Yoga at one of these.) Henry Winkler, who later became president of the University of Cincinnati, and Henry Torrey, the graduate dean, were equally men of scholarship and science first and "administrators" later. They were perhaps the last of their kind. But at the time, he felt very at home with them, particularly the shrewd Gross with his deceptively genial manner and his perpetual Rutgers tie.

Not so with the Dean, who despite being a smart and generous man, was dangerously slippery and hard to pin down about things, and who eased over into sheer deception at times. As they might come to say in future years, the good Dean was veridically challenged. Little things, then not so little things. He was to get a bigger room—the Dean showed it to him, more tree shaded, which mattered in the sticky heat barely dented by the small air conditioners the army had got by on. Then a new hotshot English prof. was moved into the room. What happened, he asked the Dean? Oh yes, I should have told you about that. Special circumstances; college needs; recruiting priorities...

Then there was the matter of Helen Safa. The Dean had written to him at the last minute before he left the UK, saying that, because of the "urban emphasis" he "had a special slot for" an urban anthropologist. Dr. Safa was available. He sent the Dean a telegram saying don't make appointments until I am there. I don't want an urban anthropologist—whatever that is. When he arrived, Safa was there. The Dean, who had received every other communication, said he never got the telegram. Western Union said they delivered it, and had phoned it in. The Dean blamed an unnamed assistant dean. Safa was a nice lady and did good work of its kind, but he was stuck with a faculty member he didn't want, and no way immediately to rectify the situation. He gave the Dean the benefit of the doubt, and they went ahead with their fantasy-spinning of plans, plans and more plans, including an unbelievable one for "college four" to be built next to Livingston on the unlimited and infertile plains of the Piscataway concentration camp.

The family came over on the busiest day of the flying year. He hired a Princeton student to drive the station wagon there and back to JFK. He was, as usual, riven with guilt about leaving them, and bought large woolly toys—a lion, a monkey, a puppy. The drive down the turnpike was relieved with songs, including those he had made up for them:

> The lion and the bear and the elephant
> Were walking to the zoo,
> When the lion and the bear and the elephant
> Met a kangaroo.
> Said the lion to the kangaroo "Good day,
> Would you like to hop along our way?"

> So the lion and the bear and the elephant
> And the Kan-ga-roo (Pom! Pom! Pom!)
> Hopped to the zoo.

He swore he would never leave them so long again, and probably meant it at the time. But they took to Princeton, and with the extraordinary resilience of kids set about enjoying the new place. The wife said she was happy with it, but he could tell she was tense. He put it down to anxiety—lord knows he felt it himself. But now they could start making plans.

The term started with bustle and exuberance, and he was delighted to see the Rutgers College freshmen wearing their little skullcap "beanies" and signs around their necks. Initiation was alive and well on campus. The Douglass College girls were practicing cheerleading, and practicing courtship rituals by the ornamental pond known as the "Passion Puddle." College Avenue was ablaze with signs about the forthcoming football game with the archrival Princeton Tigers: "Beat the Pussycats"—posters of a Rutgers Scarlet Knight mascot drubbing a Tiger mascot. The agricultural college was having an exhibition on swine production. The glee club was recruiting (men only) and the University Choir (mixed) wanted tenors for Verdi's *Requiem*; he put his name down. The two chapel choirs—men's and women's—were arranging a joint concert for Christmas. The Philadelphia Orchestra (Eugene Ormandy) was giving a concert in the gym. "Mixers" were advertised; rock and roll was promised. The fraternities were getting ready for "hell week" when new re-cruits would be "hazed" in a flourish of tribal savagery. The Corner Tavern displayed, over the bar, crossed oars marked with rowing victories. The bar itself was hung with College beer mugs bearing the names and graduation years of regulars. A plaque in the car park showed where Alexander Hamilton had placed his gun battery to protect Washington's forces retreating over the Raritan River on their way to Valley Forge.

When the makers of the Mr. Magoo cartoons had wanted to portray their myopic protagonist as a rah-rah super-loyal alumnus type, they decided he should come from Rutgers. "When I was at Rutgers, Waldo" became a catch phrase of its time. It was because the shortsighted Magoo couldn't tell foot-ball players apart, that large numbers were put on the backs of their jerseys. The College had invented "inter-collegiate" football. In the first game ever played (1869) they beat Princeton, and had lost pretty much every year since. But they always gave it the old college try. "I'd die for dear old Rutgers" was supposed to have been said by an injured football player, and as "Nobody's Gonna Die for Dear Old Rutgers" became a hit song in the Broadway musical *High Button Shoes*. He liked the old college spirit, but there were signs of uneasiness. There were "hippies" on campus: longhaired, bearded males (surely not?) and "easy" females, who "protested the war" and held "happen-ings"—and a cell of the Students for a Democratic Society (SDS) who protested everything and threatened violence. But these were rumblings; basically the fifties hadn't died yet. One of the boys told him they were planning a panty raid on the Douglass dorms. Happy days!

The Dean had talked him into giving a course at Rutgers College in the Sociology department. He hadn't wanted to, but the Dean said it would be good practice, and get him used to the students, examining etc. There were some six hundred plus students wanting anthropology, so he would have to give one course each semester to accommodate them. Douglass girls, and agriculture students could "cross register" for the course. There had been the odd anthropology course taught, since the Montagu debacle, and they gave him the current teacher, a young oriental woman from Columbia, as a teaching assistant. He had never faced such numbers, but drew up his reading list for the bookstore and the library reserve. He was surprised to see the library well stocked with anthropology; someone had been buying stuff for a long time, and runs of journals went back to the beginning in many cases. He discovered that Rutgers was a "government depository" library, and received all federal publications, which included publications of the Smithsonian Institution and the Bureau of American Ethnology. Not that these "intro" students would read these things, but it boded well for the future graduate program.

The university bibliographer, Francis Johns, was an Englishman, a student of the works of Arthur Waley, who had fought with partisans in China. They discussed *The Tale of Genji* and how to plug gaps and keep abreast of publications in the field. He had a new friend in the quiet Francis, and wondered at how these scholarly, mild Englishmen had so often been the "special forces" dropped behind enemy lines to kill and cause chaos. How was he to examine these three hundred (and) fifty students when the time came? A mid-term was due, then a final. The sociologists told him not to give essay questions; the students weren't really up to that anyway. He would have to devise a multiple-choice test: the TA would help; that was what she was for. Faced with these numbers he had no choice, multiple or otherwise. The large audience seemed attentive enough, and he gave of his best, doing the genuine "four fields" approach, although he skimped on the Archaeology, and perhaps overdid the Linguistics. They particularly liked the lectures on evolution and primates, where he used a lot of slides and bits of film. The mid-terms were a bit of a shock. The best students had obviously got it, but there was a long tail of C and below. These were the days before grade inflation; a C was still an average, not a failing grade. You got what you earned.

He had reviewed a book on human ecology by Vayda and Leeds (*Man, Culture and Animals*) for *New Society*, and been pretty complimentary. He liked to be positive in reviews and usually tried to find something good to say about a book, but this was genuine. A surprise letter came from Peter Vayda, at Columbia, who had heard he was over. It invited him to become a member of the Columbia University Seminar in Cultural Ecology, which met once a week on Monday evenings. Membership in one of these seminars carried with it "the privileges of a faculty member" at Columbia. He could stay at the Faculty Club near the campus, use the library, join in events. It was such a welcoming and welcome gesture; he had circle of anthropologists (Marvin Harris, Alexander Alland , Paula Rubel, Conrad Arensberg of *Irish Countryman* fame…) ready made, in New York City: his very own slice of the Big Apple.

There were a few anthropologists at Princeton: they were not a "full department" but wanted to be. They liked his kinship, Indian and Tory stuff, but were not much into Ethology. They were "symbolic anthropologists" and enamored of Clifford Geertz, another Harvard Soc. Rel. product, who was an expert on Java and wrote long Soc. Rel. type disquisitions on his own long definition of religion: a bit like Kluckhohn on Culture. The whole trend, they told him, was towards a "humanistic" approach rather than a "scientific" one. Then why bother? he asked. You will end up floundering around like the rest of the humanities in a constant state of anxiety over where your authority comes from, why anyone should believe you; constantly looking for saviors to validate your opinions. How, they asked him, would your approach help in the analysis of man's symbolic capacity? Good question.

Ethology was very concerned with the evolution of behavior—and communicative behavior at that; he argued it should equally concern itself with the evolution of thought: with the origins of symbol using, and the a priori categories of consciousness, à la Kant. It all lay in the origins of language, a subject more or less taboo since the Linguistic Society of Paris banned the topic in the nineteenth century. He did give them a paper on it, based on the idea that language was born of social communication, and hence would have reflected a basic hominid form of society. What that form of society was, he was still pondering. They were polite, but went back to discussing the meaning of religious symbolism in their various "people"—something they were happy with.

Even so, they tried to get him to defect, so that their claim to "full department" status would be strengthened. He liked Princeton a lot, but not enough to change. There would never be a large-scale department here, he saw. This was a small, beautiful and mannered, gentleman's school, devoted to sound scholarship and the production of mandarins: he was already half way somewhere else. They had a lot of meetings to plan a "joint program" in which Rutgers would supply the "physical and archaeological" and Princeton pitch in with its "cultural and linguistic." It never came to anything. The symbolists used the plan to help prize an independent department out of their administration, then dropped it.

The "good schools" issue was resolved: they were not. They may have had very few colored students, and they were furnished lavishly and had small classes, but the teachers… He was just not used to dealing with "teachers" who seemed to be only semi-literate and barely half-aware of the subjects they were supposed to teach. The Dean told him that there had been frantic teacher recruiting after World War II, and a lot of under-qualified people were let in just to put bodies on the podiums. This was the residue? What about the good schools? Well, there were good *private* schools. And they cost? They weren't cheap. Something had to be done. The girls, who were getting restless with the Dick and Jane nonsense, were transferred to Miss Mason's School, a truly good school by any standard, and one where most of Princeton's well-heeled sent their kids. Princeton doubled as a college town and an expensive dormitory suburb for New York businessmen and old money families. The school reflected this character. It was good, but it was not cheap.

Back at little Auschwitz things were heating up. With an irony that no one noticed at first, the accumulating staff of sub-deans and mini-deans and faculty that crowded the military HQ, were to a man (and woman) Jewish. When he did point it out, an amused demi-dean told him, OK, then he was the *Shabbas Goy*. He found out that these were the gentiles (*goyim*) employed in orthodox Jewish households to do chores on Saturdays, when no work was allowed for the faithful. The words of his childhood came back strongly as he heard the little boy reciting, with fervor but without understanding, "Remember that thou keep holy the Sabbath day… In it thou shalt do no manner of work, neither thy manservant nor thy maidservant, thine ox nor thine ass…" But wasn't that Sundays? He was getting to know, and like, his American Jewish intellectuals, but he couldn't figure them out, and never did until Phillip Roth wrote *Portnoy's Complaint*, when all fell into place, particularly the mother thing. They were all "liberals" by philosophy, and this pretty much meant Democrats of the northeastern stripe. They were understandably upset by the continuing race riots in Newark, a dreary drive northwards through an ugly and depressing industrial wasteland.

He went there to the Institute of Animal Behavior, and had a good meeting with Lehrman, Desmond's friend (and antagonist of Konrad Lorenz), and Colin Beer, a British ethologist who studied the behavior of shore birds. But they warned him that there was not much effective contact between their campus and the mother ship in New Brunswick. He'd work on that. But driving back from Newark he was stopped by the National Guard and had his car searched for weapons. He had his New Jersey car registration, but still an English driving license, which caused momentary panic and suspicion among the young guardsmen. A foreigner: something to be suspicious of. He showed them his green card and this seemed to calm them down. He didn't like the nervous way they fingered their triggers as he drove away.

There was the weekly meeting about "recruitment and standards" in the Dean's office. The day was stifling, the air conditioning was out, the windows were open, and every one was tetchy. They were still aiming to be the "MIT of the social sciences" and there was much talk about how high the SAT scores should be set. Then the philosopher lost his temper. "Look" he yelled (he really did yell) "they're burning down Newark and we're here talking about elite recruitment. Who will that be? It will be the same as the faces in this room: middle-class white males." The Dean slammed the window down in anger: no one was going to out-liberal him. This college was going to be "relevant." The word was gaining buzz status; it soon became the measure of everything. But the next stage was a series of weekly meetings about "non-traditional recruitment" and the appointment of a colored—except that now the correct word was "black"—recruiter, called Kwame Macdonald. Kwame was put in the next office (a major.) He was a mild guy, very pleasant and serious, and reputed to be a poet. Show me something, Kwame. It came as a neatly typed manuscript under the door. There were some free-verse doodles on various domestic subjects, but every poem ended the same way: several lines of:

> Get a gun and kill whitey
> Get a gun and kill whitey
> Get a gun and kill whitey…

Finally the copies of his two books arrived. No fanfare. No publisher's parties. But they looked so good, even if Penguin had put a meaningless design on the cover. He had dedicated the Penguin Book "To my Parents" and the parents would be pleased; it was so little to do. And there it was: one book in an academic series of impeccable respectability, and *a Penguin Book*. It came with the news that in Paris, Gallimard, having seen the proofs, wanted to do a French version for their series *Les Essaies*. My God! With Sartre, Freud, de Beauvoir, Camus, Russell, Paz, Toynbee and Wittgenstein. It was too heady, and he went to the Corner Tavern and drank a pint of ice-cold thin lager with the students, to steady his nerves. They were preparing for the big game and that put things in perspective. Here were other people with very different priorities: beat Princeton; steal panties. They sang the "alma mater":

> My father sent me to old Rutgers
> Resolved that I should be a man,
> And so I settled down,
> In that noisy college town,
> On the banks of the old Raritan!

He grinned at the sea of young, white, middle-class male faces. "For has she not stood/ Since the time of the flood/ On the banks of the old Raritan?!" Oh yes. And when is the next flood due, my young masters? Look to your plans.

Thanksgiving, was a warmly family time of roasted turkey, New Jersey cranberries, elaborate stuffing and pumpkin pies with ice cream. They threw themselves into these native festivals. The girls had loved the whole Halloween thing—the local version of the Night of the Dead, of the Eve of All Souls, with the children playing the ghosts of the ancestors, rounding the cycle of life-death, and demanding treats of the living adults stalled in between. He got used to the rate of alcohol consumption—mixed drinks being demanded of and provided by attentive hosts: Whiskey Sour, Brandy Alexander, Manhattan, Tequila Sunrise, Old Fashioned, Piña Colada, Mint Julep, Bourbon and Branch Water. He fought to keep ice cubes out of his Scotch. The Dean explained that only "truckers and rednecks" drank Scotch neat. The hostesses preferred to believe they had not heard him right, and plunked the big cubes into the generous glasses anyway.

This was also the time of annual conventions of the professional societies, and subsidized by the university, he went off to the Hilton in Washington DC to his first meeting of the American Anthropological Association. It was a bigger affair than anything in England. There were many more anthropologists in the USA, but not all that many, and he tried to get to know them all, which meant a prodigious amount of drinking. The main aim of the convention seemed to be to locate the best parties and get invited. The Harvard party was rated the best, and of course he had a standing invite there. It was good to see all his old friends. We shall not list them, but Roy was there—with his new job at Stanford, and Johnny, and Paul Friedrich, and Vogtie was warm and forgiving. He met Irven DeVore, who, with his little Van Dyck beard, looked a bit like a dark version of Ewart. The elegant DeVore was Washburn's ex-student and collaborator and the coming man in primate studies. His collaborator Richard Lee, had moved to human ethnography and was back from the Bushmen with news about the high homicide rates among the Harmless People. Come up and give us a paper. He was to hear that a lot. Roy had a great idea. Come and visit the anthropology committee of the National Institute of Mental Health—Roy was on it. You will see how it works and how your students should prepare grant applications. Excuse for a trip: sell it to your Dean. The Dean was begging them to cut back on pencils, but he'd try.

Not that much stayed in the memory except Margaret Mead striding through the lobby with her forked stick, and police coming to the Columbia party to break up a riot in the corridors, and the hotel being snowed in and running out of liquor. Then there was the consuming of dozens of oysters and several bottles of Muscadet with Alan Lomax, the folklorist, in a DC oyster house. He never did remember how they got together, but they swapped folklore wisdom, and sang songs they had in common. They played a game of each singing a British Isles folksong and asking the other for the American derivative. Thus "The Young Trooper Cut Down in His Prime" became "As I Went Out in the Streets of Laredo," and "A Frog He Would a 'Wooin' Go (hey ho

says Rowley)" became "Froggy Went A-Courtin' (and he did ride, Mm Mm!)"—
and so on. Finally the waiters, who had applauded the first few, and were even
taking bets on how many more dozens of oysters they would down, became
weary and threw them out. And were there really those glamorous, flirting,
smart, elegant and almost predatory young women, graciously applauding
the benefits Karl Djerassi had wrought with the pill? He'd never seen their
like at any English function of a learned society. At first he thought it must be
a mistake and they were expensive hookers (as he was learning to call the
ladies of the evening.) But no, they were colleagues, and clever, ambitious
colleagues at that. He was in at the deep end, and swimming for his life.

Desmond's promised *The Naked Ape* came out and the zoo man came over
for a publication party in New York, and remembered to include the exile.
The book had become a runaway success. It was informative and funny and
written in that easy style that Desmond was master of. The Provost had liked
"the sex bits" and wasn't much moved by out little critic's insistence that
Desmond's descriptions were ethnocentric, and if he wanted to do this right
he should have done a thorough cross-cultural survey. "That would have
been a very different book," said the Provost. Yes, I'm going to write it—
maybe. Desmond was on good form. He was dismal at his own success, because
he was going to have to live outside the UK for two years to escape the worst of
the tax consequences from his considerable gains. Desmond hated the idea of
living abroad, but no one was too sympathetic about his exile to Malta in the
winter. He was already at work on a sequel, and he came to love Malta.

Term ended. He had put in an essay question—a paragraph or two really,
for "extra credit" on the exam, which he marked himself. Some of the answers
were as good as he had ever seen, but most of them were not so much wrong as
illiterate. He thought of the hastily recruited teachers and was not surprised.
These kids had good native intelligence, but their English was sloppy at best.
They told him it was unusual to read a whole book in High School. They had
"readers" with excerpts from lots of books. That way, they told him, you get a
bit of everything and you don't waste time reading a whole book on one
subject. They didn't do "essays" in High School, they told him; they had
"writing skills development" classes. They came and complained about their
grades, which was odd, since on the multiple choice they were either right or
wrong; there was no argument. They argued anyway, especially about low
marks on the "essay." So he said, OK, I'll reconsider the grade, but I reserve
the right to put it down as well as up. Or you can take the one I've already
given. Most took the established grade. There were always a few gamblers. He
tried to be generous: to temper justice with mercy, and mercy with common
sense.

At least the year ended on one good note. The gloomy secretary left, and
he won his first serious battle with the Dean. He had, while the gloomy one
was off ill (she often was) had a temporary: Merle, an older local lady from the

typing pool. She was putting her kids through Rutgers by working as a typist. He liked the motherly, brisk Merle, and asked for her when the time came. Even though the Dean had agreed in principle, true to form he now said it was impossible, and produced the usual string of excuses. She was in the typing pool; she was several "steps" below the rank of secretary; she couldn't be promoted over the heads of others... She did shorthand and typed fast and was damn nice and well organized. What did they want? He hung on. The Dean, with bad grace, relented. He got Merle. Life was good. Now to make plans.

Kubrick's *2001* came out with the Morris/Napier ape-men a great success. The Tet Offensive shook America and roused the anti-war protests to a new pitch. He had tried to avoid any comment on the war, figuring he was an outsider and it was their affair. But all his colleagues were against the war, and obviously expected him to be against it as a matter of course. He was, but not for the same high-minded reasons they espoused. He thought it was a stupid war; his father thought it was a bloody stupid war. The Vietnamese had been throwing foreigners out for centuries, and were sworn enemies of the Chinese. We should have had them as allies, not enemies, if we hadn't been too busy supporting the French imperial ego. What if the South did fall to the North? It couldn't be worse off than it was under the bullyboy dictators. And as fought (his father's opinion) it was just not winnable. They could bomb and napalm all they wanted, but unless they put in two or three million men they couldn't win, and even then, unless they kept them there indefinitely, they couldn't hold it. "Never get involved in a land war in Asia," his father repeated. Someone had said that. The defeat of the communists in Malaya didn't count as a war; that was counter-insurgency. It wouldn't work in Vietnam, since the North was a viable sovereign country with an army, not a bunch of irregular guerrillas. Tet proved this to be all too true, and it proved the end of Johnson and his Great Society.

Things rolled horribly on. The ill-fated House of Kennedy took another hit, and Bobby, the other of the Borgia brothers (so Macmillan had described them), fell to a second meaningless act of random violence. He'd never liked Bobby, McCarthyite that he was, but he was a Harvard man, and didn't deserve this. As the sense of horror grew, Martin Luther King was gunned down in Atlanta. He had always liked King's "content of character not color of skin" remark: it summed up so much. Now the greatest black hero since Robeson died the random death. Robeson was in a New Jersey nursing home, not receiving visitors any more. When the champion of his people had gone to Truman to ask him to stop the mass lynching of blacks in Mississippi and Alabama, the old Missouri political hack had told him it "wasn't politically expedient" to intervene.

The conspiracy theorists came out of the woodwork, and J. Edgar Hoover, the CIA, the Mafia, the Unions and the Klan were paraded along with the other usual suspects. No one could bear that it was what it seemed to be:

random. Conspiracies restore one's faith in rationality. The liberal academics started doing things like wearing love beads to meetings, sporting "make love not war" buttons and the "peace sign"—which was the old CND logo, growing their hair long and, lord love us, growing beards. Everyone listened to Dylan records. The curly-haired boy was becoming, as they were starting to say, "an icon." The Beatles sang melodically of peace, love, and optimism. "All you need is love…"

He made a visit to DC (actually Bethesda, Maryland) and sat as an "observer" on Roy's committee. It was so formal and so much work, with everyone reading out opinions on the applications that were as long as the applications themselves. Why would anyone want to do this? Because, Roy explained, they all feel the need, from time to time, to get up in an airplane and go somewhere different. Roy had daughters of his own now, but was unhappy with California. It was too full of easterners escaping, but they had nowhere left to go, and this made them very nervous. But there was a standing invitation to go there. The David Hamburg whose work he admired was head of Psychiatry at Stanford Medical School, and wanted him to visit. They wanted him at Berkeley too—Burt of course was waiting for a reunion. He got invitations from all over the place. This was what the Dean had meant about the reputation. This is what you did: went around giving lectures all over the country. The hosts paid most of the expenses and the Dean the rest, because it was good for recruiting and for "the image" of the new college and department. Get up in an airplane and go places. I got a ticket to ride.

It was while with Roy and Hamburg at Stanford that the first serious pains began. He had always had this and that sort of muscle and joint pains: "growing pains" they had called them when he was young, then "rheumatism" when he got older. No one could do anything. They got worse in his late twenties, but out there in the California sunshine a sudden set of sharp pains hit the soles of his feet. He couldn't bear to wear his shoes. Diane gave him alternating hot and cold footbaths, but despite her kindness, nothing helped. He hobbled back onto the plane and returned east in misery. The Princeton doctor took a uric acid test. It showed only a mild elevation but it was enough to diagnose gout and ban all purine from the diet, which meant anything worth eating. He took Colchicine in the approved doses, and it didn't work. This should have told them something, but they persisted with the wrong diagnosis.

He looked it up: there was no real evidence that exogenous purine could even get into the system. The banning of purine was homeopathic magic—pure Frazer. Excess purine in the body causes raised uric acid, which, when deposited as crystals in the joints, causes gout. Ergo, ban purine in food: like causes like. He called them witch doctors, but that was unfair to the medicine men. Finally, he "went to New York" which was the solution Princetonians had for all medical difficulties. The specialist at Columbia Presbyterian said he had "plantar faciitis" and recommended crutches. He looked it up. It meant the soles of your feet hurt. This brilliant diagnostic effort cost him several hundred dollars. Finally, a truly smart New York rheumatologist did a very careful history of all his aches and pains and particularly the associated symptoms, and told him he had Rieter's Syndrome.

Dr. Reiter served in the German Army Medical Corp in World War I, and discovered this pattern of symptoms in even young soldiers after epidemics of dysentery. So Reiter thought it was an infectious disease. Current wisdom had it as a venereal disease, although this was disputed. In fact no one was certain. The medical journals were mostly enamored of its correlation with the gene HLA B27, on the short arm of chromosome six, along with its fellow human leukocyte antigens including the closely related one for psoriatic arthritis. The smart doctor had looked for and found patches of psoriasis on the skin. The genetic connection caused many to think it a congenital ailment—perhaps triggered by things like infections. It sounded like the ethological formula for inherited behavior patterns. Now there was a wicked irony. (It is in fact a deficiency of the auto immune system; a kind of backfiring of the system against itself.) But no one knew what to do. It was a relatively rare form of rheumatoid arthritis, and there was no known cure, only an ongoing quarrel about how to relieve the symptoms. He hobbled about as the pains spread from feet to ankles to knees to wrists to spine; wandering through the body at will, like an alien presence that found it interesting to torture him at random.

The drugs had unhappy effects on the central nervous system; his natural manic-depressive behavior was startlingly exaggerated. When depressed he would exude paranoid fantasies but drown them in Irish whiskey; when manic he would write bitter diatribes against his persecutors. He should have known not to mail them, but he didn't like to have all that effort go to waste. It was a sure formula to lose friends and alienate people. He tried to make light of his condition to the girls: he didn't want to scare them. When they saw a blue and swollen toe or knee or hand, he would tell them to ask, "What is a nice disease like you doing in a joint like this?" But wife didn't laugh. It added to her other tensions—being away from familiar things, not having close friends, continuing migraines, difficult cleaning ladies, kids' asthma getting worse; she didn't need this.

Through Helen Safa (with whom he got on very well) he met Mike and Gloria Levitas. Mike was an editor for the *New York Times,* currently in charge of the magazine section. Mike was a character out of *Guys and Dolls*: a thorough New Yorker, witty and worldly, with a bit of the sound of Howard Cosell in his voice, and a very Times-Broadway sense of being at the center of things. Gloria was a graduate in anthropology, an editor of popular anthologies, and wanted to do a doctorate. She was anxious to join the new graduate program, but that, he explained, was still a bunch of optimistic plans. She would wait; she liked the idea of a new program; Columbia and NYU (its satellite) were, on the Harvard model, heavily into examinations and massive factual examinations at that. Columbia took in large numbers and then failed half of them. It was like that then. Mike, who amazingly knew about his *New Society* contributions, asked him if he would do an article for the magazine on "race." What about race? Everything or anything—just aim it at a general reading audience. He could do that; and it paid. The result was a flurry that genuinely surprised him. He had no idea how influential and widely read the *NYT Magazine* was. His doctors were positively deferential; people asked him to pool parties.

At one of these he met the grand Ashley Montagu and the sweet, funny Marjorie. Ashley told his own version of the Rutgers thing—very different from theirs, and commiserated with him on trying to deal with the place. Like Topsy, said Ashley, Rutgers had "just growed"—no overall idea of what it was doing; they just kept sticking new things on to an already inchoate mass. Ashley had chosen to work outside the academy and preferred it. He wrote a couple of books a year and made a small fortune from the lecture circuit. He was a subject of endless gossip and spite in the town, and was perhaps a bit of a poseur, overdoing the lordly Englishman (particularly since he had been born a poor Jewish boy—Israel Ehrenfeld—in the East End of London.) But he was a polymath with an alarming store of knowledge about everything. He disliked Ardrey and "the new litany of innate depravity." He said our innocent boy should not be seduced by Ardrey's arguments. But Ashley was still very likeable. He insisted he could teach anyone to swim, and was truly pained when he failed miserably with the thrashing child of the wonder birth. But he was nice with the girls, and became a kind of adopted grandfather. They were told to "say goodnight nicely" to him, so they called him "Mr. Nicely," and that he was from that time forward.

He used to go up to New York for the seminar and would meet Mike Levitas in the old Toots Shore's, Michael's Pub (Woody Allen on the clarinet), and McSorley's Old Ale House (still all male.) But mostly they met in Jack Dempsey's bar, where the champ was to be seen talking to his regulars. They shook hands and Jack recommended the cold lobster salad, and pointed out Joe Namath across the room, holding court. Mike wanted another article since the response to this one had been so good. What about the evolution of sex? Perfect. But, our jaded journalist insisted, this time no messing with the title. He had proposed "The Abolition of Race" but it came out as "Chinese have bigger brains than whites: are they superior?" Mike said that's how they did titles. It was like headlines where they stuck "says" in front of everything: "Says Quality of Mercy Not Strained."

In the meantime Mike had a plan. Margaret Mead had said the article was "the best short thing on race" she had read to date, and was sad it came too late to put in an anthology she was editing. Mike wanted "an interview with"

Maggie. No deal. He wasn't an interviewer. How about "a conversation with" the Queen? OK. She agreed. They met with a tape recorder in her apartment. It was not a success as an interview—too rambling and conversational—but he and Maggie got on. She obviously liked the attention of young males and flirted shamelessly. They discussed the "generation gap" and "future shock" and relations between the sexes in the post-pill period. She was such a smart lady, and so witty that he quite forgot he was supposed to look down on her impressionistic fieldwork (and he had used her acute observation of the Arapesh at length in the incest paper.) She invited him to the American Museum of Natural History to give a paper. He would try out his evolution of sex thing. Maggie liked that.

Despite impressions to the contrary, he was still gulping down information, particularly from Primatology, which was rapidly becoming the coming thing in the discipline. Just as in the forties and fifties every department had to have its Freudian and C & P mavens, and in the late fifties and early sixties its structural linguist, now each had to have its primatologist. The work of the Japanese was at last being translated, and the complexities of macaque society astonished everybody. They had kinship, and what looked like ranked matrilines, and their societies would break up into two groups which then "exchanged" males. Mothers helped determine the rank of their offspring: high-ranking mother, high-ranking son. As with the Kennedys, the best way to get to the top was to start there. But this modified his notions of dominance, breeding and genetic success. There was obviously a big female input here that Chance had not seen. It was still a bit early for this lacuna to be put down to "male chauvinism"—but somewhere some angry female brains were storing this possibility for the future.

Also, the work of Hans Kummer and John Crook was showing a system of baboon social behavior that contrasted sharply with both macaque and chimpanzee. He labeled the multi-male system of the macaques and common baboons "Baboon I" and that of the gelada and hamadryas baboons (the desert baboons) "Baboon II." The question became: since Chance based his observations on Baboon I types, how was this modified by our knowledge of Baboon II, where breeding was seasonal and males kept harems rather than having short consort relationships with females in estrus? He was still Popper's child. He had set up a hypothesis, now he should challenge it. Despite the differences, he concluded, there was still hierarchical competition for breeding success. But he was quick to note that these systems (and the chimpanzee's) were only suggestive. Insofar as *Homo* came out with a different end result, it must have been doing something different. We were, loosely, a kind of bipedal chimp that had emerged onto the savanna, and made baboon/macaque adaptations, but with a better cortex to start with, and the complications of hunting and language to speed things along in a "reciprocal feedback interaction" (Ashley's happy phrase.) He pounded away at it. The picture was coming together. The hypotheses were vulnerable. He should know more about the brain. More fossils would help put it all together.

He went on the Alan Drake show—his first stab at American TV, where the subject was race. They smoked a lot—Drake's cigarettes, his Schimelpfenninck cheroots, and he was asked loaded questions about Negro and Chinese intelligence. He found that his views were "liberal" and that this meant either praise or vituperation. White "racists" assailed him on the one hand, and "black power" advocates on the other. The latter were as upset as the whites at his suggestion that race be bred out rapidly: he had called his proposal "massive miscegenation" but Ashley pointed out that this was an unfortunate way of putting it, so he used "vigorous interbreeding" instead. The Black Panthers logically attacked him, because you can't have black power if everyone is light brown. His answer that this was a kind of black racism made things worse, so he left it alone. He was surprised that the TV program didn't pay him; British television always paid. They were equally astonished at the suggestion. We give you half-an-hour of free airtime, and you want *us* to pay *you*? I don't want to advertise myself, he protested. I'm not a commodity or a service. Oh yes you are, they said. He really had to learn that he was in a commercial civilization, and that things were evaluated differently here. Life was a market; everything was negotiable.

Meanwhile, back in Princeton he made friends with the Rortys, Richard and Amelie. She was one of the internal transfers to Livingston, on the grounds that "it seemed to be where the most interesting people would be." Richard taught philosophy at Princeton, and bemoaned the fact that no one was as interested in the Idealists as he was. Our boy trotted out Bosanquet and Bradley and his argument, derived from Macrae, that social science would have been better off following their collectivism than the individualism of the Utilitarians. You must read Josiah Royce said Richard, and he did read him. At the time he thought Amelie, a realist and empiricist, was the real brains of the outfit, but it was Richard with his neo-Idealism who went on to academic fame by arguing philosophy out of existence.

Through them he met Tom Kuhn, who moved into Princeton just round the corner from their rented house. Tom, like David Attenborough, kept monkeys in his house: but in a big cage. This was a great attraction for the children who fed the dominant male, Singe, while daddy chatted about scientific revolutions and normal science with the host. Tom thought *Kinship and Marriage* was impressive normal science, while the "human ethology" had the smell of revolution about it. Push the established paradigm of Behaviorism to the wall, said Tom, and see where it fails. It was not quite the sedate Popperian picture of the logic of scientific discovery, but it might be a more realistic portrait of what actually happens. Was it Max Planck who said that theories only changed because their proponents eventually died out?

The end of term brought the usual multiple-choice exams. They were a good device to find out what facts the students had amassed, but they gave no indication of whether they had learned to think about the topics. But nobody seemed all that concerned with whether undergraduates could think or not. Just make sure they get the facts. They can start thinking in graduate school (if then—certainly not straight away.) He was interrupted in his pedagogical ruminations by the shock of his final pay total for the first year. It was some four thousand dollars short of what he thought had been agreed. Back to the Dean's office. Where is the X dollars we agreed on; I seem to be a lot short? "Oh, didn't you understand? That was the total I assumed you would have including any grants you got." What bloody grants? I haven't got any grants. "Don't you remember my saying that everyone depended on grants to provide "summer salaries" and hence make up a living wage?" He remembered an agreed upon salary for year one, and the one he received was four thousand dollars short. He waved the letter: grants were mentioned, but not as a necessary component of the salary.

On it went, on and on. But the private school bills were piling up, and he had to get a house during the summer. Before he had a chance to transfer his accumulated pension fund from England, the panicked government devalued the pound, and he was down below what he needed for a down payment. Rutgers had no scheme for helping buy houses. Rugged individualism ruled. You were on your own. But he couldn't give in on the salary thing. "It will mean asking for four jumps on the scale for you. This is never done." Because you set the salary too low in the first place. Fix it. It was fixed, through the good graces of Gross and Schlatter, who didn't want to disbelieve the Dean, but equally didn't want to lose their slice of the brain drain. He was indeed a commodity; he was negotiable.

He went to England in the summer to see the parents and look for possible recruits. He'd been looking for recruits, and Vogtie was right: they were difficult to find. Supply and demand. The Dean had been talking with Yehudi Cohen then in California, and he expressed a renewed interest. He came over and made an impression with his beard and his pipe and his serious manner. He had grown up in New Jersey in Perth Amboy, in an orthodox Jewish family. His brother was chief orthodox rabbi somewhere, and his name, Lionel pointed out in a letter, meant, with nice redundancy, "Cohen the Jew." Well, he would be in good company. Goyim were in short supply. But Yehudi was a secular Jew, and, while he studied Israeli society, he disliked Israelis intensely. He had though written an excellent book (in the C & P style) on initiation: *The Transition from Childhood to Adolescence,* and was thinking of working on a "reader" about "Man in Adaptation" with a first volume as "The Biosocial Background." Good word that, "biosocial." So Yehudi was a definite prospect, although the Dean thought he would be "expensive." We need young people, the Dean told him, to grow with the department, and not cost too much.

Such a one was Warren Shapiro, back from working with Australian Aborigines, also teaching in California, who wrote out of the blue. He had been working with a Murngin tribe, and *Kinship and Marriage* contained a solution to the knotty "Murngin problem" that even the fastidious Rodney Needham had described as "elegant." Well, said Warren, it was wrong. He would use the book in his classes, but only to show how wrong it was. This was delightful: here was a feisty (need we say Jewish) boy with fieldwork on hunters and gatherers and a wish to get back east. He was from Brooklyn and apart from kinship his only other interest was baseball. Keep him on the list. Others came and went, but there were no real prospects. However, potentially there were four of them, and it could be just enough to get things started. Now to make more plans, and to ignore the sound of Olympian chuckles in the far, far distance.

Apollo 8 circled the moon and outer space seemed full of promise. On earth things were as unpromising as usual. The Chicago convention and the "police riot" had unnerved every one of his liberal friends. The students in Paris took to the streets, invoking the "worker student alliance" and tore up paving stones to make barricades. "Danny le Rouge" dominated the charisma scene, and he and his simulacra in other countries presaged a new kind of violent fanaticism that made the LSE troubles look tame and rational by comparison. But even there, things had deteriorated and the violent destruction of gates put up by Adams and his new administration led to police intervention—something they had avoided even in the worst of the Troubles. After seeing the parents and assuring them that once there was a new house with room, they could come over, he went on to Austria, to the Wenner-Gren castle at Burg-Wartenstein, for a conference.

Wenner-Gren may have been the only foundation to be devoted to one discipline, and anthropology was ridiculously lucky—among other things to have the use of the splendid Austrian castle for European meetings. The headquarters in a gracious town house in New York had been home to a number of meetings he had attended, including one of the last in the States addressed by Evans-Pritchard, who was wistful and personal in his Oxford-Catholic way, foreseeing his own demise and nostalgic about Oxford anthropology. The director was the beautiful (and she was) young wife of Paul Fejos, who, like Maggie, enjoyed having young men around her. Unlike Maggie, who also had her retinue of adoring female disciples, Lita Osmundsen retained attractive girls with official-sounding titles, who no doubt performed important professional functions, but who were there essentially as geishas for the male guests. The girls took them around Vienna, and they did the coffee house and everything *mit schlagge*, the Kuntshistoriches Museum, and a sumptuous, very Viennese production of *The Merry Widow* in its original setting at the Theatre am den Wien. They had a sing-along in a musical café, where his English version of Tauber (pitched in the high tenor range) was a surprise, but got polite applause from the friendly Viennese audience, and the geishas:

> Girls were made to love and kiss,
> And who am I to interfere with this?
> Is it well? Who can tell?
> I'm a man. I'll kiss them when I can.

The castle, in northern Austria, was only a few miles from the Czech frontier. The idea was a rerun of the "Social Life of Early Man" conference that had spawned the book that had so influenced his thinking in what seemed now to be dim and distant days on that other planet, London. Roy was there, it was not clear why, since this was not his thing at all. But ever on top of the situation, he took George Homans' list of the "elementary forms of social behavior" and looked to see if they were there in primates. Mostly they were not; they were peculiarly human.

David Hamburg was there. He had become totally smitten with Jane Goodall and her chimps, and even become her U.S. mentor and protector. He talked only about anger and emotion in chimps these days, but interestingly so. Two Japanese primatologists came, and were irreverently christened Ying and Yang, because they did everything together and in sync. Cameras came up at exactly the same time to snap exactly the same thing. They bowed often and in perfect unison. Each read the other's paper because each deferred to the other's better English. They were equally unintelligible. It was only half way through the first paper that he realized they were talking English at all. The words "SHIMazhee" and "go'I'a" were the clue. A philosopher from Berkeley tried to push the use of lightweight dirigibles to follow desert primates, and the bewildered new boy gave his revisions of the Malinowski lecture an airing. There were others, but all was overshadowed by the sound of guns to the north and the stream of refugees pouring south past the castle. They went out on the walls and looked at the smoke and flashes on the skyline and examined the suits of armor and halberds with the stupid thought of defending the walls from the Russians, if they came. But the Russians were only interested in establishing dominance in their own territory, and the halberds and maces were replaced on the walls, where they had hung impotently for centuries.

Back home they did find an affordable house, but it was not in Princeton. It was north, on the Millstone River, and was in fact the borough of Millstone itself. Millstone, which was originally Somerset Courthouse (burned by the British in the revolution), was one of those leftover enclaves that had never been assimilated into the larger townships, and with some 280 inhabitants was its own borough, with a mayor, officials etc. It did not have police and schools. The house, with some acres of trees and a barn and a big river frontage, had been built in the early eighteenth century. On the march north to

Pluckemin after the battle of Princeton, Washington had stayed there. He slept in the house over the road, now the home a Princeton art professor who was an expert on fakes, but his officers and horses were quartered in the house and barn by the river. They were buying a romantic piece of history, for a decent price, and giving the girls some room to breath and run. Except that it was a damp house, for the river flooded in the winter and came up close, and there must have been mould and mildew. They didn't give those things much weight in those days; even smoking was not connected with asthma. But the big trees, the wild animals, the "Indian trail" with trees grown in a horizontal "s" shape after being tied down as a saplings by the Delaware tribes to mark the way to the river, were the stuff of autobiography. It was an "I was brought up in..." house. Perhaps they would be happier there. Perhaps wife, installed with cleaning lady and some good friends, would be happier there. That was the plan.

The sit-ins at Columbia continued the theme of bad behavior on behalf of good ends. John Lindsay ordered the police not to hurt one hair of any black student head, not out of compassion but out of fear of further Harlem riots. Mike Levitas and the *Times Sunday Magazine* published his "Evolution of Sex" article (title intact), and he drew the first accusation of "male chauvinism" from a female letter writer to the next issue. He made the first of many riposte's of the "don't blame me, I just work here" kind. There was a growing chorus of such stuff at talks and meetings. He didn't understand the logic of it. It seemed a typical case of blame the messenger. Male dominance was undoubtedly there; this is what they were complaining about, surely? What bothered them was that his attributing it to "evolution" (he never mentioned genes) might make it seem "natural" and hence unavoidable. It was Locke's and J.S. Mill's classic objection to the doctrine of innate ideas: that if they were innate they were ineradicable.

Fair enough, but he never made that step. The proof of that pudding was in the eating. Things may be established by the evolutionary process, but whether that made them unmovable by human imagination and intelligence was an open question. Some things might indeed be ineradicable, but that didn't mean determinative of all consequences. It did mean you had to take the ineradicableness into account when trying to pursue social justice: as with the mother-child bond, for example. But that latter got him no credit with the angry women who were now calling themselves "feminists." The mother-child bond, from being a basis to argue about equal rights for mothers, had become another sinister weapon in the male plot to keep women trapped in subservient roles... or something. There was a lot of talk from the American bourgeois women (who were the envy of the women of the world) about men doing housework, and babies being dumped in child-care centers so that their mothers could go out and double the family income. Who would care for the children? Women who liked to do it. Who would do the housework? Poor black ladies presumably; that was already in place. It was all a bit inchoate, but the anger and outrage were real, as was the conspiracy theory that inspired it all.

Two odd outcomes. Time-Life wanted to put out a series on evolution, and wanted him to do the volume on human evolution. He did a sketch, which they didn't like; it was "too intellectual." They wanted a book with, the editor said, "heroes along the way." *Ramapithecus* started the line, *Australopithecus africanus* was the next hero, *Homo habilis*, the next and so on, up through Neanderthal and Cro-Magnon man, to the ultimate hero: our white, tall, confidently striding, trim-bearded Caucasoid selves, *Homo* doubly *sapiens*. They had a neat drawing showing this evolutionary progression as an actual procession of creatures leading onwards and upwards. He said no, he wanted to deal with it ecologically in terms of successive environmental changes. He drew his own picture of a cross section of Africa taken from the work of Napier, Campbell, Crook, and others. He showed a profile going from the dense forest canopy, to the trunks of the trees (where the lemurs stayed), to the forest branches, to the forest fringe, to the tree savanna, to the dry savanna, to the desert. He showed how this journey in space could be translated into the journey in time through the gradual drying out of Africa in the Pleistocene epoch. The heroes would be placed in their appropriate ecological slots along the way. But Time-Life preferred its heroes up front and strung out, and went with that.

Then he received an enthusiastic letter from Maurice Girodias, who had been the publisher of the Olympia Press in Paris, and responsible for *The Ginger Man* and *The Story of O* among other delicious things. At a lunch in New York, at the very French Fleur de Lys (where you could still get a nice *tête de veau vinaigrette* without provoking a demonstration), Maurice told how he had reached these tolerant shores a few steps ahead of the Paris vice squad. The dark, and very Parisian Frog Prince (as he called himself), explained that he was writing a book with a collaborator, to be called *Sex On Earth*. He could do the writing—and he produced a delightfully pornographic first chapter about aliens abducting humans for sexual experiments, and then wanting to know how they came to be such odd creatures: cue for evolution-of-sex stuff. The collaborator had amassed a huge amount of material, but had no idea what to do with it. Maurice had "bought" all this research material. Help to turn it into intellectually respectable but readable stuff, and fortune would follow.

He thought of Alex Comfort, and again decided the world didn't need this, and he felt too much in pain and too overwhelmed with the coping he had to do to want to take it on. He wanted to say he would do it in return for an introduction to Pauline Réage, but he dithered, then backed out. Only just in time perhaps. An angry woman (what was her name?) later shot Andy Warhol, for crimes against women that she documented in her book *The SCUM Mani-*

festo. (SCUM = Society for Cutting Up Men.) The police found her list of future victims which was evidence at her trial and helped send her up for a long period of secure care and treatment. Third on her list was Maurice Girodias.

Al Ortiz had come to join the symbolists at Princeton. Al was a half-Tewa Indian, from the Pueblo of San Juan. He had grown up there, gone to college, got an Anthropology Ph.D. and was writing it up as a book—*The Tewa World*, which would be certainly the best book on his own tribe any Indian ever wrote. Al was like a warm memory of things New Mexican, with his understated humor and his hair in a ponytail. He operated on Indian time, which drove the local Puritans nuts. He affected great disdain for the Keresans. The winter weather in New Jersey, was, he declared, "colder than the north side of Cochiti witch's tit." But they could swap songs, and even roll some cornhusk cigarettes, while they downed Margaret's green chili stew, and shocked the kids with gory folk tales about the buffalo husband.

Lionel had sent a Canadian student, Ray Larsen, who stayed with them for a while. He wanted to work with Lionel on a Ph.D., but that would have to wait for a year. Meanwhile, he registered for a sociology Ph.D. from which he could transfer courses later, and was to be the teaching assistant for the current course. He went everywhere with his dog, including to class; a kind of Huck Finn character with blond hair and a Nordic beard. He added a bright touch of gentile youth to the scene, and played Leonard Cohen records in the office, to Merle's annoyance.

> I know that all the men you knew
> Were dealers who said they were through
> With dealing every time you gave them shelter...

Students from the Rutgers College campus came up to see various Livingston faculty. One black student asked for help from Merle on some point, and she rang the Dean's office, saying, as she would have said for any student, "There's a boy here who..." The student created an instant uproar, demanding to see Kwame, shouting "racist insults" and demanding apologies. Kwame wasn't there; and the startled chairman emerged, ascertained what had happened, told the boy he was being ridiculous and suggested it was he who should apologize to Merle. This led to an "enquiry" by the Dean who positively begged him and Merle to apologize, "to avoid more trouble." That teaches the kid nothing, he insisted. What are we here for, just to avoid trouble? The Dean apologized on their behalf.

They had numerous meetings on "non-traditional recruiting." The recruiters told of their methods. If a non-traditional student had insufficient traditional grades, they would interview him and ask him questions about baseball to see how original and sharp he was. But what if he lacks basic skills? He can acquire those at college. How so? We are not equipped to do high-school remedial education. It is bad enough with the current students whose literacy is seriously below standard. And what do you say to the white "inner city" kids who come from poor homes but are not being given any consideration. That isn't our problem, said the non-traditional recruiters. The Dean and his entourage hurried on to the next item.

They had a meeting with black students about their special needs. One impassioned student complained bitterly about how the teaching of English was not "relevant to his life experience." They gave him poems about palm trees to comment on. He was from the Newark ghetto; what did he know about palm trees? They should give him poems that were relevant. You come to college, the denizen of the Yorkshire moors and mill-towns told the student, precisely to learn things you don't already know about. If he had been the instructor, he said, he would have had the student write poems about his personal ghetto experience, but would have insisted he learn poems remote from that experience. Very few of us have any experience of palm trees, or of blessed damozels, or lotus eaters, or the shield of Achilles; we come here *to find these things out.* The English professor rebuked the ignorant foreigner for not understanding the "dynamics of the local situation": we have to teach things "relevant to the black experience" he said sternly. Anything less, he implied, was indeed racist. Most things were becoming racist. "This is a racist institution," one student said. Why particularly? "Just by existing." Couldn't win that one.

The self-appointed student "militants" pointed to the dread experience of Columbia. That is what happened to institutions that were only concerned with "credentials." Degrees were a political device to stop blacks rising in the world. They seemed to want degrees to be given to them as a kind of reparation for the wrongs they had suffered. The Dean cut off his, perhaps obvious, reply to this suggestion and explained that Livingston was going to a "pass/ fail" system of grading to get rid of the "invidious comparisons" implied by the letter grade method. What is more, students could take a failed course over until they passed it. The failure would never appear on their transcripts. Failure was becoming a bad word. The gesture did not satisfy the militants. They demanded to have "control over the content" of courses to make sure no racism was preached therein. As examples they cited "saying the brothers had lower intelligence than whitey" and "saying black kids in families without fathers are cheats." The Dean, in almost angry desperation, cut him off from replying. There would always be consultation, said the Dean; extreme sensitivity was promised.

The students demanded the right to grade the performance of teachers as a check on their racist tendencies. Student evaluations were being considered, said the Dean. A few days later a group of black students appeared in the HQ building and sat in the corridor outside his office, to block the way to the "racist Dean." Merle was alarmed and called him out. What do you want? To see

Kwame? Kwame isn't here, come back tomorrow. "This is a sit in." Well, you can't sit here; Merle has work to do. Come on, chop chop, clear out or you'll miss the last campus bus. Puzzled, they went, looking back and shaking their heads a lot. A bit later one slightly abashed black student knocked on his door. "I've missed the bus anyway, can I get a ride back across the river?" Sure. It was on the way home. The Provost told him at lunch the next day that word was around campus that he had "successfully diffused a tense situation" and congratulated him. How had he done it? I just told them to go home and they did. Well, would he like to be on the committee that dealt with "confrontation policy." He would not. He was off to DC with other fish to fry.

The Northern Irish "Troubles" had erupted. The usual mix of inept governance and religious/nationalist fanaticism had boiled over. The British troops had been called in to save the Catholics from Protestant wrath, giving the IRA perfect "legitimate" targets, and the whole thing snowballed. China was fighting Russia on the border, and the terrorist Yassir Arafat became president of the PLO. Ibos were being slaughtered still in Nigeria—almost a million of them, and Stanley Diamond, anthropologist at the New School in New York (and no mean poet) was organizing petitions and funds. Violence continued around the country, anti-war, anti-black, anti-white, anti-establishment, anti-everything.

A Presidential Commission on Violence had been formed, with Milton Eisenhower as its chairman. Such commissions, like the English Royal Commissions, were ways the government gave the appearance of doing something about the problem while actually sitting on its hands. But he was asked (by the sociologists at Princeton who were organizing the presentation of evidence from the social sciences) to appear—and do what? No one was very specific. He was to "give testimony"—about what? Violence. What he said was up to him. Perhaps the state of play in the ongoing debate about the "naturalness" of violence and aggression: Ardrey versus Montagu perhaps, or the current excitement about the XYY chromosome debate? OK. He could do that. So off on crutches, for the enduring insanity in his feet, he went on the commuter plane to "our nation's capital."

He went into the Commission brandishing a copy of Ashley's *Man and Aggression*, with a suitably neutral beige cover, and Anthony Storr's *Human Aggression*, with its equally suitable violent red cover, and gave them a brisk run down on the debate. He gave as his own opinion that while aggression was indeed innate, indeed necessary for evolution to take place at all, stimuli from the environment could either raise or lower levels of it, so there were things that could be done. They seemed pleased, but did not seem that interested in the theory. A cardinal asked him, since he came from a country that did not have armed police, if he thought that disarming the police might reduce violence. He didn't have a theoretical take on this. He said common sense would suggest it couldn't be done unilaterally, and the criminals were not likely to do it first. Eisenhower asked him if he thought taking guns away from people would reduce violence. No, he said, but it might mean fewer people getting shot.

A letter had come for him from DC, from one Joseph Alsop, inviting him to lunch when he was down there. He asked Merle if she knew who Alsop was. He's a columnist, like his brother, Stewart. They're "syndicated"—they appear in lots of newspapers all over the country. What do they write about? Anything they want to. Nice. Alsop took him to a men's club, on the London model. He explained, quietly, that neither women nor "persons of color" could be members. (The National Liberal Club, in which our exile retained a membership, had a ballot on the women's membership issue, and he had voted "yes.") While the exclusion of women, said Alsop, might be natural enough—men wanted to be apart some of the time, he wasn't sure he approved of the color bar; but one had to remember that "Washington was in the South. People tended to forget that." The waiters were all black, however, and when the Virginia ham was ordered, one of them brought plain boiled ham, and Alsop sent it right back. It was something he was particular about, although his guest would not have known the difference. He soon learned. Alsop, a dapper, neat, precise, confident man, confessed that he had once had a terrible weight problem, but had overcome it with calorie counting and exercise. Hence the ham-and-salad regime. Dining out in DC was a hazard for those with a tendency to obesity. You had to dine out to find out what was happening. No one could afford not to know what was happening, particularly a columnist. The result had been "a ballooning body with little tiny feet."

Not now though. Quite the dandy was Joe: pinstriped tailored suit and silk pocket-handkerchief to match his tie. Joe wanted to be updated on the race and intelligence issue. He did not want bibliography and references; he wanted the scoop. Well, standard tests always showed a difference between the means of blacks and whites as a group, but the curves overlapped. You could not use this as a basis for individual assessment; you had to take it one case at a time. Were the tests biased? Probably. The differences between races here were echoed by the differences between classes in the UK. They were trying to devise "culture free" tests, but he was skeptical about this. How much of intelligence was inherited? Twin studies suggested about eighty percent. Then were the differences between the races "fixed." As averages, as means, probably, but again the overlap of ranges was large.

And the whole definition of it as a "racial" issue begged the question. The whole point of his article, and of Ashley's life work, had been to deny the realities of races as homogeneous genetic groups. There were in reality only clines or gradations fading off into each other. There was no "Negro Race." What about the influence of environment? Strangely, this was more murky than the influence of genes. We really didn't know much about what the environment contributed. What exactly was a "rich environment"? Black middle-class boys who had been placed in Groton (Joe's alma mater) were not doing very well. People were concerned. That could be for a lot of reasons not to do with native intelligence. "Black middle-class" might still be a very different "environment" from "white middle-class."

Joe said they must definitely correspond and meet again. He thought the visitor was, like him, a natural "progressive"—meant in the technical sense as a sympathizer with the Progressive Movement. Be careful, he told Joe, like their European counterparts (including the young Julian Huxley) they had been sold on eugenics, yea, even Teddy Roosevelt (whom they both agreed to admire nevertheless.) We know better now, said Joe. Replete with martinis, Virginia ham, and cherry pie, the dabbler in public policy hobbled back to the airport, feeling he had done something about something, although not quite sure what.

He took the girls to see a matinee of the whole of *Gone With the Wind*, thinking it would be good for them to see some American history. Kate was unreservedly for the North because they were right; Ellie was sorry for the Southern women, particularly Melanie; Anne was deeply upset by the scene of the army of Southern wounded outside Atlanta at the end of part one, with the screams of the dying, the blood and smoke. She cried and said she hated him for bringing her. He sat her in the foyer with an ice cream and chocolate and tried to tell her that, yes, it was awful, but that it wasn't a sick fantasy, it had really happened. You had to face up to things that really happened; you couldn't just have daddy hide them from you forever. She was too little for such a lesson, but she was as always brave, and when assured that there was nothing like it in part two, they joined the others and watched to the bitter end. They had no idea why Rhett Butler's parting words were such a scandal; they heard, said Kate, far worse at home. One of her first complete sentences was: "Chwist all-bwoody-mighty, there's that bwoody doorbell again!" But they played at Tara for weeks after, when they weren't singing the songs for their favorite, *Finian's Rainbow*. Lovely, sad, Fred, who had so little dancing left in him, and certainly no roller skates.

His Unitarian connections took him to a local church that was without a minister temporarily. Would he come on Sunday mornings and give them talks until they got a new minister? These Unitarians (and their Universalist allies) were different from their English counterparts, and they recognized it. One told him that he was surprised, on a visit to his UK brethren, to find they were so much concerned with God. One heard Him well spoken of on Sundays, certainly. These were people who had essentially lost their Christian faith, but still needed something earnest to do on Sunday mornings. They told Unitarian jokes: they prayed "to whom it may concern" they told him. They didn't wear a cross on a chain, they said, they wore a question mark. But they were nice serious people, and the girls liked to go to the service, so he told them to put their fifty dollars back in the funds and gave them talks on "Whither Man?" and "What is Human?" and "Unoriginal Sin" and the like. He figured if anything went wrong with his academic career, he had a shot at a Unitarian ministry. He gave a talk on "The Waste Land Reclaimed" and Mr. Bullock's sermons were fondly remembered.

Bob Ardrey came across to see his publisher and they met at the Algonquin, where our boy, who worshipped the wit of Dorothy Parker, was disappointed to find the actual Round Table was not a permanent fixture. It was always good for him to be with Bob, who kept a steady perspective on things. When the youngster started to criticize some findings or theories of fellow workers in the vineyard (like Desmond for example) Bob would stop him. Is this a deep and desperate issue, he would ask? Is it something to get into a big fight over? Not really. Then remember, said Bob, you are on the same side in the great struggle: the struggle to get the evolved, biological aspects of behavior recognized and incorporated into a scientific view of human behavior. Unless it is an absolutely fundamental matter, don't start picking fights with your fellow travelers, try to boost and encourage and promote them. Always remember the big line drawn in the sand: on one side are the Darwinians, devoted to the same general ends as you; on the other are the Creationists of whatever stripe, including the "superorganic" anthropologists, who feel threatened by Darwinism and will resist and attack any manifestation of it. Stick together, said Bob.

Tell that to the academics, said the already bruised neo-Darwinist, they only know how to climb over each other's bodies on the way to personal fame and power. They basically don't give a damn about anything but their own success, their own careers. You're getting too bitter too young, said Bob; they're being consistent with their own Darwinism: they struggle for existence, for the reproductive success of their own ideas. But that's the reason Bob stayed well out of the academy. The two of them had one of what was to become their many ritual dinners at Sardi's, where Bob knew all the theater people, and loved the company while deploring the food. They went off replete, and Bob suggested several messages he might deliver to Ashley Montagu. Sure.

The AAA meetings were in Seattle, and he welcomed the break and the hilarity of the drink and the parties and the attentions of the hetaerae. As "women's liberation" moved into its own militant stage, the fanatical ones were burning their bras and butchering the language. But it spilled over. Even those not devoted to "feminism" as such were affected by the new "assertiveness." Women, being exactly the same as men—except that they took the odd time off to have babies—should not be coy mistresses, but take the initiative and let potential "partners" know directly what their "needs and preferences" were. They had a "right" to satisfactory orgasms that the Constitution had somehow missed. The hell with the *pursuit* of happiness, they wanted happiness up front. Securely on the pill, they could drop the "games and hypocrisy" of the dark ages of sexual repression. It went on and on, but the upshot was a sexual frankness and availability, a kind of modulated raunchiness, that bewildered the child of provincial fumblings and evasions. But he learned fast enough.

The thing to do was to fend off the embarrassment of choice by fixing on one, and then making the exclusiveness obvious. She would do the rest. The sisterhood was fragile when it came to sexual competition. He took her to dinner in the Marine Room Restaurant at the top of the Olympic Hotel, and to his amazement, the poetic facility, banned and banished with Platonic distaste on the home planet those eons ago, returned with a jolt. He was contemplating the maraschino cherry in her drink and the green olive in his, when the bolt struck. He saw the room with its walls of tropical fish tanks as something the sad Ludwig II of Bavaria would have liked. Ludwig had made a lake on an upper floor of one of his palaces, with Wagner piped in from an orchestra and chorus below. He fantasized that he and the mad king would reproduce this room on a mountain top, where they would have flooded it, and drowned its vulgar, chomping, noisy inhabitants:

> Then in the swan boat on the lake we'd sit
> and call up Parsifal from hidden choirs
> eat cherries from a shallow silver dish
> and olives from a bowl of ivory
> We'd scatter lilies to the mountain folk
> who came to us for bread—but loved us more
> for flowers—and would die for us because
> they know we are not mad but half divine
> princes who ripen olives with our gaze
> who feed wild cherries to our hunting dogs
> who feel the colored fish swim through our blood

It was a strange moment and the product an uneasy one, but genuine. He could not deny it even if he did not particularly approve of it. But he was not in charge. The unconscious is diabolical; it knows you better than you know yourself.

He had what became an annual lunch with Dave Schneider, who was now re-defining kinship virtually out of existence. Dave was as funny as ever. He thought Rodney was getting more and more brittle, and that very soon he would shatter. As they parted Dave passed on a few choice comments he hoped would be transmitted to Rodney. Johnny and Roy, over many mixed drinks and pretzels, told him that he should make some kind of "programmatic statement" of his views about Nature and Culture. He told them he had been toying with a piece on "The Cultural Animal"—the title making the point. Bob had been asked to give a talk at the University of Toronto but didn't want to go and had recommended him as a replacement. He would give it as a talk there, first practicing with it at Drew University in New Jersey, where he was also contracted to speak.

Drew was a Methodist foundation, and still had the look and feel of a seminary. The talk was well attended and well received, but the most vivid memory of the place was a graffito in the gothic, somber men's room. Someone had written, in careful calligraphic script, "Andrew Wyeth uses tracing paper." This beat his previous favorites, "Down with Logical Positivism" in the stalls at the LSE, and "Keep the Pope off the Moon" at Queen's University, Belfast, under which someone had written: "No. Keep the Pope off Uranus"— which puritan America, he noticed, was busy repronouncing with the accent on the first syllable (and a short "a" for good measure.) He mooted the idea of the talk with Lionel, who agreed that it would be good practice for the opening chapters of the book. They had been writing back and forth on this and definitely decided to drop the idea of a textbook. They talked about it on a visit to Vancouver while they drove in Lionel's Alpha Romeo up into the mountains along the seacoast towards Alaska, with the top down and the heater blazing. They ate huge salmon steaks, drank Columbia River wines (damn the purine!), and made plans. The only laughter they heard was their own.

As it happened his ruminations on Lévi-Strauss and his vacillations over the Nature/Culture divide—was it a part of reality or part of our persistent thinking about reality, not that thinking was not part of reality...—could be put to some use. The Smithsonian Institution was planning a grand think-fest on the subject of "Man and Beast: Comparative Social Behavior" and had invited him and Lionel to take part. Wilton Dillon was organizing it, along with Mathew Huxley (brother of Francis, son of Julian, nephew of Aldous— let's keep the Huxleys straight.) This whole "Comparative Social Behavior" thing was taking off. The intellectual world was taking notice, if not always friendly notice. Part of the problem seemed to be the false identification of the enterprise with eugenics and the horrible consequences of racial thinking in Germany. There was much rumbling about "genetic determinism" even though no one talked much of genes: nor was there much to say, except that you had to end up there because there was no other known way to make an organism.

As to the racial thing, he continuously pointed out that the ethological view was not interested in sub-species differences, and human races did not even rise to the level of sub-species. In fact, to use the Tinbergen term, the interest was in "species-specific" behavior; individual or group differences were not of interest in this view, it was what was common to the species that mattered. But while these objections were not more than rumblings, there was obviously distaste in some quarters at the question even being raised. He ignored them. His business was to reshape the social sciences—or at least to

get them to take some notice. That was enough without taking on the progressive liberalism of the western world (at least for now.) In any case, the facts
would speak for themselves, would they not?

At some point they moved into new buildings. Delays had heaped upon
delays, but at least a few blocks of dorms had been completed (the yellow
huts were happily gone) and they moved offices into these while the re-
juggled academic building round the piazza was finished. He was getting
more familiar with the local scene. The only wandering possible here was in
a car, but there was, contrary to popular myth, much driving possible other
than on the turnpike. The Millstone valley where they lived was still rural
and undeveloped, although to the north of them the Johns Manville asbestos
factory was doing its unrestricted worst. No one knew the cost, anymore than
they knew about secondary tobacco smoke. To the west, the state was really
an extension of Bucks County, and the whole Delaware valley up the Water
Gap was a splendor of autumn color and spring dogwood blossom. To the
east, you crossed the rich farm plain with its colonial villages like Cranbury,
and hit the lively Jersey Shore, from the Blackpool-like Asbury Park with its
fun houses and carousels,

> I smile reluctantly to see
> the carousel go spinning by
> the children calling out to me
> to get aboard at least to try
>
> But then I am afraid to look
> afraid because I know I'll see
> the phantom from the story book
> the ghostly child who looks like me

south through the Baptist bible-camp of Ocean Grove, with its superb pipe
organ, the elegance of Spring Lake (where the New York Irish who had made
it, built their summer homes and flew their tricolors), through the fishing
towns of Manasquan and Tom's River, and marinas with Californian laid-
back carelessness, past deserted promontories with their dune-and-coarse-
grass beaches and slim gray lighthouses, through the vulgar energy of Atlantic
City where Miss America reigned, down to the Victorian calm of Cape May,
with its gingerbread "cottages" for the Philadelphia wealthy (a cottage could,
by law, have no more than thirteen resident servants.) Drive back through the
almost wilderness of the Pine Barrens, where Civil War cannonballs had been
made in scattered smithies from the local iron, through the State capital of
Trenton, home of Campbell's Soup and the motto "Trenton Makes, the World
Takes." Trenton hadn't made much for a while and was a classic northern city
in decline. But Paul Bohannon, African ethnographer who had taught at
Princeton for a while, had preferred its gritty urban reality to what he saw as
the precious fantasy life of the rich little university town.

Rutgers itself was an odd mix of brilliance, even sophistication, set like islands in a mediocre sea. One of the accepted centers of brilliance was the English department, which housed the *Partisan Review* and was headed by Richard Poirier. Poirier was the friend of Lillian Hellman, and the one-time boy friend of Gore Vidal, with whom he used to cruise the streets of Rome, before Vidal, like a shade from *La Dolce Vita*, went off to his villa and lazy weekends with the Paul Newmans and Princess Margaret. The university was not a notoriously liberal place, having ejected Marcus Finlay during the red-baiting McCarthy years; it was even a bit stuffy and provincial. But it was forty minutes by bus from New York, and hence attractive to the city sophisticates. Poirier lived in a modern block down by the river, the attraction of which was that he only had to walk downstairs to a convenient express bus stop and be whisked off to the city.

The department seemed at once hospitable and suspicious. Since English was their business, and him a native speaker, they probably felt some mix of curiosity and obligation. They invited him to gatherings, and were genuinely attentive, but at the same time some of them appeared to see him as a threat to their monopolization of the subject matter, especially since he was happy to talk about English Literature (which was still the subject of their discipline then.) The only place in England or America that he ever ran into overt, out-and-out, unpleasant social snobbery, was in the English department at Rutgers. It was the only time not being from Oxbridge was held against him: how could an LSE graduate claim to know anything about literature? Apart from the scrupulously polite, genuinely old-money WASP, Paul Fussell, who was too comfortable with his status to feel threatened, they all seemed thus ambivalent.

Why do these minor social discomforts —probably his own fault anyway, with his annoying commentaries on everything and anything—sit so heavily on our mental digestion? They are only recorded because they do raise this question so fundamental to the issue of what does or does not go into a "memoir." We know the local rule: if it is not in memory it does not go in (no records, no journals, etc.) But even of what is remembered, what goes in? Only that which is burned into the memory: the events that impinged. But then not all of those. He could not always account for the burn of the memory, but there it is.

People would later ask, "why did you stay so long at Rutgers?" He ponders this himself, and so looks for clues as to how he felt and what really mattered. Not that the decision stayed for long in his conscious hands (if hands can be conscious.) This is an accidental life. He pursued his rational path, worked out his ideas, accepted his successes (good reviews and more foreign translations—Hindi, Malay, Japanese) and bemoaned his reverses, but it was out of his hands. Forces set in motion from his cradle (the cradle he never had) were working themselves out. He was recreating his parents' marriage in his own, just as she was living still in the shadow of the pain of losing her father. It was a recipe for doom. Neither was to blame—what is the use of blame in such things? It stems only from that very deep human desire to blame that he was beginning to think was the worm i' the bud of human nature. But the ship of life sailed on, uneasily, with the rudder missing the indifferent waves half the time, and the sail flapping with metaphorical uselessness. One still made plans.

Lionel's *Men in Groups* came out to much applause and abuse. The publishers had wanted him to do a "popular" paperback version, but the original was popular anyway so they left it at that. He had told Lionel that *men* would never forgive him for writing the book, since it blew their cover and showed them up for the silly, vain, dangerous creatures they were. But it was the strident spokesmen (-persons?) for all women who made the most abusive attacks. "Male bonding" could not be something natural and vital to males, because that would make it ineradicable, and *it had to go!* Yehudi Cohen moved in, first to Princeton, then to a house just up the road in Millstone. He had a large screen television, so they all went and watched the moon landings there. It was midnight and they had to wake the children up to see what seemed to them no more than a poorly filmed episode of *Lost in Space* (the only program besides *I Love Lucy* that they were allowed, at that time, to watch.) They kept expecting Dr. Smith and the robot to appear stage left. He made them a song about the robot.

> I wish I were a robot
> To know just how it feels,
> I wouldn't walk around on legs
> I'd roll around on wheels.

Children are such a wonderful audience. Anything will amuse them if it's made up just for them.

> I wish I were a robot,
> Oh wouldn't I be cute?
> I'd never say I didn't know,
> I'd say: "does not compute."

The CIBA Foundation had a conference in London, so he got another ride across the Atlantic at someone else's expense—something he realized was perhaps the major perk of his new status. "The Family and Its Future" brought him together with Leach for the first time in a long time, and his external examiner was brimming with good fellowship and thought well of his paper—a revision of his talk to the Women's Medical Association. He linked up with Mike Mendelsohn, now definitely committed to fleeing to America, changing his name, and his profession. What was his new profession? "Lyric Poetry." Come to Rutgers. Would they have me? Mike/Tarn had translated

Pablo Neruda, who had in turn won the Nobel Prize. The English Department won't be interested, you'd be much too much of a threat; what about Comparative Literature? Such things did not exist in the UK, but Comp. Lit. was a graduate program at Rutgers, and Francis Ferguson had been its chairman (the department had been created more or less because English wouldn't have him either.) They would like the poet-anthropologist-translator perhaps. "There must be no administrative duties," said Tarn, "they are incompatible with lyric poetry." You bet.

He flew back with his parents for their first visit, and was again stricken by and appalled at their emotionalism on being reunited with the girls. Would he live forever with this guilt? But they loved the house and the woods and the river. Anne, wheezy as ever, rode happily on granddad's shoulders again. He took the father to see some boxing in New York ("the city" as he was learning to call it) and to dinner at Sardi's, where they could pick out the caricatures on the walls and discuss the old films. He suggested they have steak, and they brought the father's first. The old Spartan looked at the huge oval plate with the great slab of meat on it (little pots of vegetables on the side) and asked, "Shall I carve?" It's all for you Dad. "Bloody hell!"

Peggy Lee sang "Is That All There Is?" It hit him in that undefended place where popular song is so potent (thank you, Noel.) Perhaps it was because it opened the floodgates of personal memory: the Grammar School lads with their comb-and-paper band with its single-string-broom-handle-and-tea-chest bass murdering *Goody Goody.* The Mariner Probe sent back the first pictures of Mars (not at all like Edgar Rice Burroughs said it was.) *Oh Calcutta!*—brainchild of Ken Tynon, brought full nudity to the stage. Woodstock reveled in mud, rain, sex, noise and psychedelia, with Bob Dylan now eclipsing Burl Ives for good and all.

Seismic shifts, funneled by the pig-in-the-python baby boom that was increasing its grip on lives and imaginations. The summer of '68 had been to the twentieth century what that of '48 had been to the nineteenth. The world changed overnight. The fifties disappeared suddenly. The old proprieties were swept aside and co-ed dorms and bra-less coeds took over. Beards became the norm (so he never re-grew his own) and male hair was grown to biblical lengths and styles. ROTC was boycotted; MASH fueled the growing and gripping anti-war, anti-system firestorm. Kurt Vonnegut added *Slaughterhouse Five* to the fires of Dresden, and Mario Puzo wrote the definitive ethnography of the Mafia in *The Godfather.* He saw in the Mafia "family" some evidence of the subversive persistence of kinship values that he hinted at to CIBA, and that had to do with those underlying verities about the continuing need for such unqualified bonds, despite the demands of impersonal bureaucracy. Weber had understood. He would work on this, on so many things, if only the pain would stop, and if only he could figure out where to fit feelings into his busy plans.

The college was officially up and going with its first students. There was not to be a "core curriculum" for them, but series of "college course" of which they had to take a certain number in their first year. These course were supposed to be broad and general introductions, so he did his "Man, Race and Culture" number, while Lionel tackled "The Biology of Social Bonds." When justifying his courses to the numerous committees, he had met some unpleasant opposition from the biologists over his title for this one. You can't use "biology" in titles, they insisted; that was the privilege of the Biology department. There was a lot of this turf-defending behavior, because departments "competed" for students, and funds depended on "registrations." But he spent a couple of hours reciting the syllabus for physical anthropology, evolution, primatology and the like, and the biologists backed down. They had honestly thought, citing Margaret Mead on Samoa, that anthropology was a "humanity." Well, shame on them.

The psychologists were easier to live with, welcomed his program even when he threatened courses on "Evolutionary Psychology and Psychiatry," and even liked his paper on classification and linguistics. Chomsky's *Language and Mind* had come out, the clearest statement so far of his views on the innateness of universal grammar. Chomsky's invocation of a "language acquisition device"—without which no child could learn language, immediately suggested a "culture acquisition device" which directed the learning of culture. He told them about Earl Count's coinage of "biogram" to parallel "ethogram"—what the culture acquisition device was, was a basic *biogrammar*: an online general manual that allowed the user to learn any specific, cultural grammar, as long as what was presented was compatible with it. If you talk gibberish to a child, it will not learn a grammatical language. Too much of the time, he thought, remembering Hamburg, we are talking behavioral gibberish to children, then wondering why they have speech problems. The psychologists said his grammar analogy would only cause confusion, so he dropped the coinage. But he fished it out again later, for the book, since despite technical objections—rules of grammar and rules of behavior were different—he thought it was too good a metaphor to waste.

The psychologists were mostly behaviorists, and skeptical; they preferred to treat "human nature" as a black box and get on with the reinforcement schedules. But they directed him to "cognitive psychology" and even "ego psychology" where they said he would get a friendly reception (mostly.) On the whole he got on well with his colleagues, once he learned what toes not to step on. But he didn't like all this diplomacy, this administration, red tape, committees, memos, reports, accountancy and filing everything in triplicate. He was discovering that he was not one of nature's bureaucrats; he did it well enough, but with very bad grace and many sleepless nights. Without Merle he wouldn't have survived it. It's the Merles of the world who keep the world turning, in spite of the plans of the visionaries.

But it was filling out. The Graduate School accepted his proposals for a graduate program, and interviews with prospective students were encouraging. The Israeli who had all the data on Kibbutz marriages, Joseph Shepher, wanted to take leave from Haifa University (and his Kibbutz) and work this up into a thesis. Gloria Levitas happily signed up, as did Roy's sister. A student from New Mexico, Jay Miller wanted to work with him on "The Archaeology of Keresan Identity." Things were cumulating. Warren was teaching "Social Organization" and dismantling his theory of the Murngin system. Good. He didn't want to go on with the details of kinship and marriage. Given the usual "career path" of a young academic this was perhaps not wise. The book was doing well; translations were pending (Dutch, Italian, Malay.) A request came for a Hindi translation, but with a rider that Indian students could not pay much for the book. He agreed to waive any royalties to help reduce the price. He was receiving a lot of mail, including attractive "offers" from other universities (Cornell, Georgia, Arizona State, Illinois at Chicago.) You were supposed to go to the Dean with these and bargain for—whatever you could get. He never did this. He knew he was a commodity and had a market value determined by supply and demand, but he had no intention of leaving and couldn't put up the necessary front.

Yehudi was exasperated with him; he had no good sense of his own survival, said the older hand. You had to know how to play the game. You had to "build up a career" which included doing more of what you had been successful at. But I never wanted to be a success at "kinship theory," he whined. I only did it because Raymond left me no option. I want to look at the primate origins of kinship now, at the origins of mind and categories. Yehudi said that was all very well, but he had to use his position to develop a "plant" by "bringing in grants" and to build up a "following" by fathering disciples and starting a "school." He found it difficult enough handling one secretary and a teaching assistant. But Yehudi, waving his pipe and shaking his gravely bearded patriarchal head, detected a pattern: you are quickly bored with things; you have a short attention span; you are restless by nature. Lévi-Strauss had said the same about himself: he had a "slash and burn" mentality; he devastated an area, then moved on. What L-S didn't say was that he was appalled by the prospect of such responsibilities and had fantasies of joining a band and writing lyrics and living on the road.

The New York Jets under the flamboyant Namath had won the Super Bowl against all odds, but that was nothing compared to the upcoming centennial game against Princeton. The annual game with the oldest rival was usually held in the Princeton stadium because it held so many more people, and the gate receipts were shared. He'd watched one game, with some Rutgers fans. Their team was winning until the last minute, when it seemed to lie down and let Princeton walk all over it. "These guys don't need a coach," wailed one despairing fan, "they need a psychiatrist!" But the memorial game had to be held on the sacred spot where it all started, and what is more, Rutgers had to win, which would certainly be against the odds.

It was hard to do anything on campus during the game week, and he succumbed and accepted Mason Gross's invitation to watch with the Presidential party. He liked joining in such things; loyalty was a good feeling. The packed stadium went crazy when Rutgers did win. They tore down the goalposts and paraded a large banner: "Bring On Ohio State." He was quite entranced with the game: with the delicate skills of the quarterbacks and receivers, the smash-tackling of the defenders, the cheering rituals of the crowd, the cannon sounded by colonial soldiers when the home side scored, the healthy pink cheerleaders, the Ruritanian band (The Marching One Hundred) with the prancing drum major. This was the real religious ceremonial celebration of America, not the sectarian separatism of the churches. In an away game the team actually beat Harvard. Did the white handkerchiefs still come out?

Vogtie had him up to Harvard to give the ritual paper. He had just read Karl Pribram's *On The Biology of Learning,* and was all fired up. The opposition of "learned" and "innate" was just another of those tiresome dichotomies that L-S had seen as basic to human thinking. But there was no dichotomy in the real world. Even Pavlov and Skinner had understood that the conditioned response only worked because the organism was designed that way. Learning was not arbitrary: we learned things in ways that were laid down in our biology as much as our flesh and bones were. They were, as Tinbergen had taught him, in the central nervous system. The seat of all learning was an organ, the brain. Pribram, the great brain scientist, was at Stanford with Hamburg; maybe that's where he should be? Off in the California sunshine and the orange trees, near to Burt and Roy, Washburn and even the Southwest. He kept trying to fix time to go back to Cochiti, but when? Everything was too pressing.

Things at Harvard were changing. I. M. Pei was designing a new tall building for the social sciences, but Soc. Rel. was threatening to break down. Parsons was aging, and the new generation was not as sold on his theory of action as his contemporaries had been. DeVore, the primatologist, was chafing under the restrictive demands of the social scientists. He wanted to cooperate with the natural sciences, particularly the zoologists like E. O. Wilson, who were engaged with the Ethology-Ecology "paradigm." (Wilson, an entomologist who hailed form Alabama, came to the lecture, and was friendly and enthusiastic.) The anthropologists had never been happy with the arrangement, and they didn't like being outvoted on appointments by the other three wings. Johnny had moved from Education to a chair in Anthropology proper at the Peabody Museum. Kluckhohn had died: the first of his older male mentors to go. Leverett House had built a tower block over the Charles that had made it, from being the Cinderella of the Houses, the chic place to be. No foot in the same river twice.

Vogtie was "bucking" for the Mastership of a House. They'd like their cowboy Master, especially when he grew-out the crew cut to shoulder length locks, and abandoned the bolo ties for tie-died tee-shirts. Vogtie was alive to the winds of change, and trimmed his sails accordingly. Everyone there was violently anti-war, except Ernst Mayr, who could not understand why young men resisted the draft when their chances of dying were a hundred times less than in the two previous wars. Cora Du Bois, who thought he was an undergraduate, asked him if he'd burned his draft card. He had one since resident aliens had to register. No, he told her, he'd just singed the edges.

Lionel and he tried to squeeze in time for the book, but it was hard given the press of things. The first chapter was to be extracted from "The Cultural Animal"—in progress and rehearsed. The chapter on bonding was split into two: one on the male bond, courtesy Lionel, and then one on the mother-child bond from the coffers already filled. But the tone, the strategy: what was it, what kind of book, for whom? If it was not a textbook, it was not a *Naked Ape* either. They wanted to proselytize the social sciences, but they saw here a message for mankind as well: we were an endangered species, but endangered by our own actions. If we did not understand ourselves as a species we were in serious trouble. The means to this understanding were at hand, but a lot of shibboleths would have to tumble first, and a new humility cultivated. This was surely something of importance to tell the world at large? Not for the first time they decided to aim for the middle ground, and not for the first time fell between the two stools (the mixed metaphor habit is so hard to kick.)

But the initial success of both their books brought them to the dangerous attention of ambitious publishers, and Lionel insisted on the protection of an agent. Lynn Nesbit ran the International Famous Agency—sounded propitious. (It was to become International Creative Management, and organize the lives of film stars as well as authors.) Lynn was another of those beautiful, smart women, who didn't need "liberation" and had done brilliantly in the corrupt masculine world as it was. She seemed to understand better than they did what they were doing, and said there was a market, not only among professionals, but among the "intelligent lay public" that was eager for such information and ideas. Who was this public? The people who read your *New York Times* articles, she said. They are literate, educated, not afraid to tackle a difficult subject; you don't need to write down to them. If fact, she announced proudly, I'm one of them: if you can persuade me, you can hook them.

The Tigers had moved to Manhattan, in Greenwich Village, close to Balducci's where you could get then exotic things like Perrier water, balsamic vinegar of Modena, and *prosciutto di Parma*. They were near Bradley's Bar and The Village Gate, for the best soft and big band jazz respectively, down the road from Nathan's Famous Pizza and across Washington Square Park to the inviting bistros of Little Italy, each with its own story of its own Mafia hit.

The apartment was, naturally, magnificent, in a brownstone on West Ninth Street (Jane Curtin lived on the top floor.) Virginia had landed a job at the Newark campus, Lionel found a garage for the Alpha, which cost almost as much as the flat, and they were set for the city "lifestyle" (as it was becoming known—Lionel hated the word and banned it from his classes.) They already seemed to know everybody. Their parties soon became the place to be. Virginia complained, however. "We are supposed to be attracting the 'beautiful people,'" she said, "but look, *we are* the beautiful people."

Lionel was better at handling the Dean. They actually both liked the Dean enormously. His enthusiasm, his capacious learning, his genuine desire to "make something happen," his generosity and humor, were all endearing. But it came unhinged when trust was involved. He was so devious he often double-crossed himself. But the worst row yet came over the first lot of pass/fail grades. Only by accident was it discovered that from the college course there were no fail grades at all on the "official transcripts." Everyone had passed. Now our reluctant disciplinarian had in fact failed about thirty or so students out of the three hundred plus. He thought he should have failed more, and had been excessively lenient, but they were all new at this, and he decided to go easy at first. Most of the failures were black students (although other black students had done very well.) They had failed both the multiple choice and short answer questions. Even the "identification" questions required a sentence or two, and some of these students literally didn't know what a sentence was. This was not the general poor level of English he had found earlier among all students; it was total incoherence. It was as if they had never been taught to write at all, and didn't know what to do apart from forming letters and stringing words together. How had they been admitted in the first place? The non-traditional recruiters presumably.

He had tried talking to the students to find out if they could speak what they could not write. It became clear that some of them could not read very well either, which is why they had failed the true-false questions. But it was hard to talk to them. He found himself up against a psychological barrier, a kind of truculent denial, a refusal to accept there was any problem, a blizzard of blame, an anger at any kind of criticism. He couldn't see how he could help them. He had tried pointing out to his colleagues that the college was doing these students no service by throwing them into a situation they couldn't handle. They needed remedial English courses (no—they needed *basic* English courses); they couldn't be taught anthropology or anything else if they couldn't read and write to start with. Not to worry, he was told, they would mostly be doing "Black Studies" anyway. How would that solve anything? The people in the black ghettos didn't need Black Studies; they knew all about being black. What they needed was doctors, entrepreneurs, and most of all *teachers* to get them started on the right route to college from an early enough age to compete. The universities couldn't do this job; it had to start in the homes, the neighborhoods, the schools. But no one was listening to such hopelessly reactionary advice. They had other, loftier plans.

How did it come about, he pressed the Dean, that there were no failures? The Dean explained that he, the Dean, had the right to revise grades. On what basis had he revised them; had the students re-taken the exam and passed? No, they had been "counseled." By an anthropologist? No, by their "student counselors." And these counselors had brought them up to an acceptable level in their exams? No, they had advised them on study techniques and time management, and how to improve their self-image. And who was working on their English? But the Dean had phased out with that glassy look he got when confronted with these things. I can't teach under these conditions, whined the outraged one. The Dean smiled and shrugged. It's how things have to be...Do you have your outline plan of the proposed honors program? I have so many plans, *Decani*, that God is choking on his guffaws.

Up again on an airplane, and off to San Francisco for the meetings. It was his first encounter with Irving Goffman. While in London he had received an odd manuscript from Michael Banton, then at Edinburgh, with a request for an assessment. Once again it was assumed our ex-Harvard man "understood the Yanks" (oh yes) and the author was an American. It was supposed to be about fieldwork in Orkney and Shetland, but was about something else, and Banton didn't know whether it was a work of genius or the product of a deranged mind. It was in fact *The Presentation of Self in Everyday Life,* a look at the symbolic content of moment to moment interaction: what we now casually call "body language" as though we always knew about it. It was in its way curiously ethological, and the fascinated assessor said it was probably indeed a work of genius, and yes, the university press should publish it. It was as though Goffman had taken Iris Murdoch's analysis of character, only applied it solely to the externals, the appearances.

In its paperback popular version it had become something of a cult classic, and its author, a bright, sarcastic leprechaun of a little man, became an instant adversarial friend. He "believed in cultural relativism as in mother's milk" he said, and would have no truck with "species specific" traits whatsoever. But he hated "feminists" in a way that was almost frightening. The two of them came out of a session on "gender roles" with Goffman fuming: "Gender is a grammatical category, for Christ's sake!" Our man suggested that the new buzzword, despite the rationalizations, was yet another product of genteel Puritanism: they really wanted to avoid saying "sex." He used to ask them if they were practicing safe gender. Goffman snorted and headed for the door of the nearby men's room and held it open, shouting to the startled ladies as they exited the lecture hall, "Come in here you bitches; if this is what you want, come in and use it!"

A surprise invitation to lunch found him with Richard de Mille. Son of the film director, he was the opposite of his powerful father (who turned out to be his uncle—long story.) A quiet, scholarly man, he was on an almost obsessive crusade to expose as a fake the work of Carlos Castaneda, and to make Castaneda's thesis committee at UCLA accountable for passing off this fraud as genuine ethnography. De Mille had heard that our resolute Southwestern ethnographer had spoken out on the subject. Yes. It had been at one of those discussion sessions ("The Shaman as Visionary"?) on Amerindian religion, which had been taken over by hippies—now commonplace at the sessions, with their own agenda for appropriating Indian mysticism. They had taken over large areas of San Francisco, and had become institutionalized to the point where you could buy hippie outfits from the Woolworth Ladies now. They had been waxing ecstatic about the "philosophy of Don Juan"— Castaneda's supposed Yaqui Indian sorcerer. Asked to comment, he had said that Castaneda's Yaquis were unlike anything described in the not inconsiderable literature on that tribe, and that the author's statement that on his first outing as a peyote initiate he had chewed twenty buttons was simply unbelievable. No one who knew the potency of peyote would make such a ludicrous claim, which suggested that, like so much else, it was made up. He told de Mille how he had been howled down, and how a distraught devotee, bombed on the easily available grass, had threatened him with a knife, being held back by his less-stoned, and more consistently passivist, neighbors.

De Mille was bringing out an anthology to refute the claims to authenticity. He thought the trickster of the piece was Garfinkle at UCLA, one of Castaneda's committee, who had his own ideas of society as theatrical "happenings" and had delighted in this fakery as an example of the theory. The contributors were unearthing all the sources in fantasy literature that Carlos had cribbed. Would he write something for the book? He had a satire in which a fat journalistic faker, desperate for a new volume, sat in McSorley's Old Ale House in The Village. The desperate, seedy character was making up stories and asking people if they had had any funny experiences he could use, including *broujas* who raised a *broujaja*, all the while sending kids to get him a "little smoke" (panatela) or a "big smoke" (corona) … and so on. De Mille loved it, but wasn't sure it would fit with the serious tone of the proposed volume. They parted vowing to keep each other informed, and to keep in touch. The crusade was a qualified success, but the Library of Congress never changed its classification of Castaneda's work from "ethnography" to "fiction" as they demanded. UCLA never officially apologized.

He loved San Francisco. It was like landing in a different world. The mix of types, the beautiful women, the food: description cannot match the wonder of the town. It was the homosexual capital of the world, but he liked their attentiveness and skill at services. They really enjoyed taking care of people, and so waiters and hairdressers were a delight rather than, as in New York, a trial. (They were already beginning to call themselves "gays"—thus robbing the language of another perfectly good word.) He really wanted to spend time there. David Hamburg and Roy came up with a plan through their NIMH connections. There were "Special Fellowships" for faculty who wanted to make career changes or learn new skills. Stanford Medical School would back him for one of these. He could spend the better part of a semester there—and come over to the Bay and Berkeley whenever he wanted.

This was opportune, because in his worst run-in with the Dean yet, he had asked about the promise to give him his delayed sabbatical. He had given Livingston a year of his life, and he wanted it back soon. Well, said the Dean, straight-faced, you must know that we don't have a sabbatical program here. You have to apply for research leave, present a proposal, then if it is granted, you get leave with three-quarter salary. Oh reader, you may be gentle, but even you are wincing surely? There was nothing on paper. What did this man want? How did he imagine one would take such a thing? He had probably convinced himself that there was no such agreement. The truly devious have to be adept at self-delusion; the Dean was a master.

But he was learning to pick his fights. For the record he wrote a letter of protest with copies to everyone concerned, staking his claim to a full-salary sabbatical in the future. In the meantime he took the generous offer of the NIMH, with recommendations from Vogtie and Leach—who very cordially agreed to supply one. "Send those forms!" he wrote, "we'll get you to Stanford." So to Stanford he would go, after a Christmas which included log fires in the two stone fireplaces, punch parties at the Provost's, and decent presents for the kids, including a "big wheel" for Anne who careened about the place endangering everyone's ankles. The Christmas service in the college chapel had the glee club in the balcony singing antiphons with the choir in a setting of great beauty. The deep scarlet walls were hung with portraits of past presidents; the whole delicate, gothic place, with its fine, carved-wood pillars and tracery, lit only with candlelight. He could get to like this.

But between the beauty and the music walked the shadow. Kate's asthma was getting worse, and the shots didn't seem to help. Anne had always been bad, and continued to suffer horribly. The poor wife was torn between pleasure at the house and her new friends, and fright over the fate of the girls. She moved further away from him all the time; he was never sure why, and they didn't talk about feelings: they didn't know how. He would read for long hours to Anne to take her mind of the wheezing and get her to sleep: *Charlotte's Web, The Cat in the Hat, Right Ho! Jeeves.* She would eventually fall into exhausted sleep, with her hand gripping his finger. He would lie and look at her white, tired face, unable to cope with the emotion and the feeling of helplessness. Then he would disentangle himself, and go unhappily to that other bed where he knew he was not wanted. And the pain got only worse in his extremities as he dumped the program off (temporarily) on the kind and competent Yehudi, and made his ambitious plans for Stanford.

Two things: holed up with few distractions and a good library he would do some heavy reading and research for the book, and at the same time he would pick the brains of Hamburg and Pribram on hormones and brains respectively. He could attend any lectures, and he would pick and choose those. Buried in work he would forget health and troubles, deans and departments. The warm air of California washed over him as he walked down the steps from the plane. NIMH provided for "transportation" and he had a yellow Mustang convertible waiting for him. As he drove out to Palo Alto, over the Oakland Bridge to the Junipero Serra Boulevard, life for a moment seemed relieved of pain. The soft air was like the kiss of a young girl; all would be as promising and as gentle as that kiss. And he thought (not being very much given, as we know, to morbid introspection) that he had not for a while worried about the dangers of the mask. He had been too busy dealing with real difficulties to indulge in such existentialist luxuries. The self had been too occupied with everyday life to worry much about its mode of presentation. Whatever he was, it was now something he would have to live with, for better or for worse.

Set up in a motel next to a strip club, he got to work. Hamburg was way too busy to be bothered. His department was like a small university, and he was the president. He walked his charismatic way, and you got, occasionally, to touch the hem of his garment. But he did give good advice on the endocrinology of moods, including the post-partum depression ("baby blues") that the lady chairman of the British medical Association had made him promise to study: he did. Hamburg was busy working on the biology of grief, and the "coping mechanisms" that enabled one to survive it. This was the beginning of what was to become one of those psychological industries dealing with grief and how to handle it.

Busy as he was, Hamburg took time to assign suitable mentors to the visitor, and Karl Pribram in particular took him under his wing. They did a crash course on neuro-anatomy and -physiology, and at some point Karl said, you can't do all this from books; you have to dissect a monkey brain. They were working on the memory circuit, for somehow he knew that if he were to do anything on the origins of thought and categories, he would have to know exactly how memory worked. He was surprised at how controversial this was in the neuroscience world. No one really knew how memory was stored or retrieved, or what part dreaming played, although it must play some. But in the meantime he could get the mechanisms.

The lab personnel were tactful with their tame amateur, and helped him slice and chop and prepare specimens and slides. He actually made a good job of isolating the hippocampus and locating the mammilothalamic tract. He looked at the amygdala with awe and remembered Michael Chance's momentous statement about its importance. Remove the amygdala in live monkeys, said Karl, and they behaved as if they were drunk: very little control or coordination or anticipation. The lateralization of the brain amazed him: everything on one side exactly mirrored on the other. But in human brains, the hemispheres were specialized: speech especially was firmly lodged in the left side, in Wernike's area, although its exact location was another cause for dispute. Karl was right: all the stuff about brain size and function in evolution he was reading came alive in the dead tissue he examined. Why had it tripled in size so relatively quickly? Press on, press on.

He used to drop in to the bar at the strip club for a drink on his way "home"—usually late at night. The club was misnamed: the girls did not really strip. They were go-go dancers who started in a tight dress, at some point undid the zip, then went off-stage and took it off, coming back to reveal nothing more alarming than tank tops and hot pants (and of course the standard high boots.) When they finished a set they circulated among the (male) audience to encourage drinking. One found him at the bar reading *Catcher in the Rye*. "We read that in high school," she commented. He explained that he had never been in high school, so he was trying to find out what the fuss was about. What did he think of it? As an anatomy of what was most unlovely about spoiled adolescent males, it was OK. She was reading John Barth, and offered to lend him one—*Giles Goat Boy*. It had a translation of *Oedipus Rex* where Oedipus was a dean, she said. He'd really like to see that. She was a graduate student—most of the dancers were—putting herself through law school. She wanted to specialize in family law and help "mothers in trouble." Was she a feminist? No, she was a lawyer, she said. What was he? I'm a sort of medical student, he offered. At which point the manager told him to buy a drink and her to circulate. He would come back for the book.

Hamburg urged him to see the local specialists about his condition. They were convinced by recent findings on a similar disease in sheep that it was indeed infectious, and that the answer was therefore mega-doses of tetracycline. He took them and became seriously ill with the side effects, since the antibiotic killed off all the good bacteria in his gut. They told him to take Pepto Bismol and stick it out, but his gut told him otherwise. The infection theory was later abandoned. Of course he saw a lot of Roy and his daughters, and went across to Berkeley where Burt introduced a lecture by him to a big audience. Burt told them he was "very funny." He had to live up to that. He described the emerging alpha male in hominid evolution as a combination of Noam Chomsky and John Wayne: that got a laugh. At Burt's house in the Berkeley Hills they dined by the birdcage—a small, enclosed canyon, that housed the latest collection, and re-inspected the putative Burne-Jones's. Through the Berkeley graduate students he became involved with the hippie community. It was not a commune, but it was a community, held together by a young doctor who worked two days a week with rich patients so that he could serve the rest of the time as medical officer to the indigent hippies.

The hippies were good natured and eclectic, taking an innocent interest in things like old black-and-white British movies. They showed *Kind Hearts and Coronets,* and asked him to explain obscure references. The doctor's long-haired, very brown waif of a hippie wife, wandered naked through the house, through the grass and incense smoke, singing "Sad-Eyed Lady of the Lowlands," and the sad-eyed prophets and their ladies made love on mattresses in the corners, during the movie. (Why did curly-mop sing "Lay Lady Lay" to the female on the big brass bed? If "lay" was the imperative, and it seemed to be, then it should be "Lie lady lie." The hippies didn't know. Don't sweat it man, they advised. Have another joint) They recommended seeing *2001* while you were totally stoned; it was in fact the only way to see it. They thought the ape-men were cool. They said "PEACE" a lot. They believed in "doing their own thing" but what they did, and how they spoke and thought, was remarkably uniform. He liked the gentle hippies, especially the girls. In a way he agreed with them that modern societies had become too big, too complex, too removed from the eternal verities. But the answer was not to retreat into a kind of brain-deadening intellectual passivism. You needed a lot more than love, let's face it. Yes, they said, quoting someone called Leary, you need to turn on and drop out.

California was seductive. Ready at any minute to slide into the Pacific Ocean, and so living constantly on the edge, it was a kind of fantasyland that had been put together by shipwrecked Americans who tried to recreate what they remembered of their culture. Thus they remembered that "Waldorf" and "Ritz" were nice places to stay, but stuck the names on seedy motels. They came up with impossibilities like the "Robert E. Lee Delicatessen and Pizzeria" and tried to produce synthetic religions out of the bits and pieces of half-forgotten heresies, married to mystical imports from the East. Zen Albigensians jostled with Hindu Gnostics, and badly mispronounced Celtic witchcraft (supposed) competed with Pan-Indianism (syncretic.) The whole was suffused with noodle-vegetarian, pot-smoking, flower-worshipping, pseudo-Dionysiac, LSD-tripping nihilism. Even the suburban Republicans smoked joints (in designer roach holders) as a matter of course, and flocked to EST meetings to be insulted and deprived in search of self-fulfillment.

They had abolished ugliness and renounced sickness and death. Otherworldy gurus floated by in showy Rolls-Royces, their glassy-eyed followers seeing no contradiction. He was in a hotel near a main street with some Berkeley people, when outside the window he heard chanting which sounded like: "Hairy Christians! Hairy Christians!" It came from some faux-Hindu, orange-robed, shaven-headed young Americans, swaying and shuffling and tapping tiny finger cymbals like castanets. At that moment he knew he had to get back to the gritty, empiricist East Coast, before his synapses became totally elastic, and the line between dream and reality became psychedelically blurred. He would get away from this crazed Aldous version and back to the Julian reality of rational, logical persuasion, where solid fact and reasonable demonstration would change minds and the world in that order. That was the plan. The myriad gods of California only tittered a little.

10

The Book: Engaging the Living Fossils

"Tout être vivant est aussi un fossile," was one of the unforgettable sentences from the pen of the great geneticist Jacques Monod. Descartes had ruined the French for science with a combination of rationalism and dualism. *Cogito ergo sum* (or as they would prefer it in the language of ultimate reason: *je pense donc je suis*) had put clever thinking before honest fact. The French reveled in the freedom to exercise the autonomous *pensée*, or, as Lévi-Strauss put it in his delightful punning book title, *La pensée sauvage*: thoughts are as wild as the pansy L-S put on the book jacket. Thus they still feel it necessary to mount clever rationalizations of the obviously wrong Lamarck, just because he is French. But when they do get around to doing science, they do it very well indeed, and one of the best of them is Jacques Monod, as the Nobel Prize committee eventually decided.

The English edition of his popular book was called *Chance and Necessity*, and stressed the role of Lorenz's two "great constructors" in the evolutionary process: mutation and natural selection. But if the strictures of William James and Pragmatism were solid, the same processes worked for ideas. The chance workings of the human imagination gave them birth, but their staying power would be tested by the necessities of social usefulness: their pragmatic qualities. The very ideas of chance and necessity themselves had proved durable, even indispensable. There was an element of unpredictability in the origination of ideas, but useless ones fell by the wayside. Reality was a hard testing ground, but one idea of Monod's seemed utterly durable. Our duo had solemnly announced that the best evidence for the evolution of human behavior was human behavior, and Monod echoed this in his assertion: "Every living being is also a fossil."

The duo now had a publisher, an advance, and an editor, Steven Aronson. Steven was a rich kid who had never had to do much for himself. When he went out to work in the world, after prep school and Yale, for the first time on his own he bought a pair of shoes. After two weeks he took them back to the shop and complained. What was wrong with the shoes, the manager asked?

413

Steven pointed out that they were dirty; they shouldn't be dirty; shoes were never dirty. No sir; that was because someone cleaned them. The manager sent for a brush, a cloth and some shoe polish, and showed Steven what to do. Steven was amazed, thanked the manager, and took his little kit off to his apartment. He always had impeccable shoes after that. He also had, fortunately, equally impeccable taste in the use of English, and took their hurried chapters and patiently, line by line, put them into readable prose.

They never had any problem about writing together, something that people found mysterious. Lionel had a way with fancy prose, including a weakness for the creative oxymoron, like "opaque transparency" or "loquacious reticence." The child of Augustan simplicity could handle the crisp, economical, descriptive stuff. They both disliked the National Public Radio style of highly self-conscious essay composition, what Lionel called "Writing Writing"—or the "Look-Ma-I'm-Writing!" school of prose. It was probably something taught in "creative writing" courses, although our admirer of Mark Twain thought that it was the pervasive and pernicious influence of Ralph Waldo Emerson. "You need a punchy sentence at the beginning," said Lynn, "something to lead them in." Lionel found it: "We know ourselves surprisingly well." Perfect. That said it. They were not plumbing arcane mysteries beyond the ken of ordinary mortals; they were simply showing the scientific underpinnings of common sense. The social sciences would listen attentively; the public would respond warmly. The stern constructor necessity would do the rest. That was the plan.

They agreed always to write everything together: no taking home of chapters, no division of labor. They pooled all their notes and references in piles for each of the chapters, then took turns at the paragraphs, writing and rewriting each other's words until they became what they hoped was a seamless whole. There was no formal veto on anything. They would write until they sensed closure, then look at each other. If they both nodded, it was done. If either wrinkled a nose, or shrugged, or shook a doubtful head, it was back to the pounding of the keys. They preferred to work undisturbed and isolated. Home and office were too public, too fraught. Al and Margaret Ortiz loaned them their house during the day when they were out, and Judy Bergman, a Livingston administrator (who, because she wanted to be lawyer, and wore ruffled cravats, they called "Portia") prevailed on husband Richard to do the same. Hidden away, they worked away, consuming cigars and whiskey like old newspaper hands, and the pile of paper mounted.

The plan was relatively simple. They took an institutional area, like the economy, for example. They looked first at "the primate baseline" as evinced in comparative studies of monkeys and apes. What were the basic patterns of provisioning and exchange, and to what extent were these common to, say, all mammals (so very deep) or confined to the primates? Then they looked at hominid evolution, in particular the "hunting transition," to see how these patterns were modified or revolutionized over the long drag of the Paleolithic era: how did humans become peculiarly what they were? They then looked at what was established in the simplest of economies, before moving on to modern monetary and industrial economies, where they asked the question: how do these changed circumstances stack up against the basic needs that evolution has built into our economic behavior? Is the free market, the centralized socialist economy, or the welfare state most compatible with what we are and what we need? And so on. They could then tackle medicine and psychiatry, education (and its contrast with initiation), the family and marriage, courtship bonds versus parental bonds, male associations and politics, warfare and diplomacy, town planning, or any other "institutional complex."

And they were still Popper's children. Their theory must be able to produce refutable hypotheses. (Women's grades, on average, go down when their colleges become co-educational. Easy to test.) It must be vulnerable. (Children separated in infancy from their mothers will suffer well-defined pathologies in later life. Yes, but loving foster care and especially peer support can erase the deficit.) They must be doing science. (Children raised in physical proximity through childhood will not have strong sexual desires for each other. Only if they are together before age six—Shepher's finding in the kibbutz.) They could produce counter-intuitive propositions, but they must be refutable. (Concentration on the teacher rather than the task will inhibit learning in the students—after Chance, but it will get the task done faster: confirmed by the social psychologists.) They were happy to challenge accepted wisdom. (It was the quality of crowding rather than sheer density that raised levels of violence.) And they hoped sincerely that the Open Society they each cherished, albeit in a different way, would survive the intellectual carnage, but they vowed not to flinch at any outcome. (Bussing of school-children did not solve the problems caused by adult segregation.) Brave fellows!

Bob came over for the publication of *The Social Contract*, and our intrepid commentator reviewed it for the *New Republic*. The professionals were still snotty about Bob, so he tried to redress the balance, while at the same time evincing some criticism. Bob repeated his injunction about sticking together, but the ruffled reviewer countered that undiluted praise would be suspect, and in any case, he did think Bob had been wrong about race. But there could be no grudges between them ever, and Bob took the whole family to Sardis, and pleased the girls with his flattery, telling them, however, that Mr. Nicely was really a heavily disguised wolf, and they should be careful. They horrified Bob with their stories of what they were learning in school, such as that the goal of life was "to find yourself." "The goal is to develop a self worth finding," he told them, in a phrase worthy of Mr. Nicely himself. Kate agreed: "I *know* where I am," she insisted. Ellie said she wasn't sure, perhaps it might be a good idea to look. Anne wanted to know what they were looking *for.*

The girls were also getting lessons in the avoidance of "hypocrisy," which sounded good, but asked for examples, they produced the saying of "how nice of you to come" to friends of parents whom they in fact disliked. On the contrary, he told them, it is precisely *because* you dislike them that you *must* say this when they are visitors to your home. This is not hypocrisy, it is politeness; without it society would fall apart. But the events at Kent State shattered all their politeness. How could you explain this to children? To gun down students, however aggravating their protests and anger might have been. Who had sent these nervous boys with loaded guns onto an unarmed campus? Even the few uncommitted on campus were converted to the anti-war movement now. He found his poetic voice yet again as he contemplated the possibility of the girls, if they had been old enough, facing those same guns.

> some man's daughter died there
> and were his dreams less precious
> than my little dreams?

These had been dreams of gracious living in a west-of-Ireland house with "wolfhounds obedient/to your imperious little whims." But

> You
> cannot control the hounds
> and we wise dreamers fail
> to curb the wolf with dreams
> All I can give you now
> serious funny girls
> is question after question

They still did not have a title for the book. When still negotiating with Thomas Nelson, they had been persuaded by James Mitchell, their assigned editor, to think up something "less academic." Mitchell was a guilty agnostic who couldn't leave religion alone. He claimed that Billy Graham had made him "fall in love with him," and went on to edit a book called *The God I Want*. To please Mitchell, they adopted *The Amateur Animal*, which they quite liked at the time, but for some reason abandoned. They thought of "The Cultural Animal" but the term "Culture" still did not have, for the general public, its anthropological meaning, and tended to connote classical music, Russian ballet, and fine art. They were describing to a gathering of friends their efforts to redefine the social sciences. Wife said, "It all sounds very imperial, doesn't it?" It came as a flash, and without a really clear idea of what exactly it might mean: *The Imperial Animal*. Lionel had used the phrase "little empires of the mind"—why not? Other animals had territories; only man created empires. Empires were works of the imagination—peculiarly human. It wasn't obvious, but it was striking. They thanked wife and decided to use it as a working title anyway. Lynn thought it was terrific and told them to stay with it.

"The Cultural Animal" was to get its definitive outing at the promised Man and Beast conference in DC. Wilton Dillon of the Smithsonian Institution was determined to make this an occasion to remember. It was to be opened with a procession, two by two, in full academic dress, across the Mall, led by a Highland pipe major in full regalia. He had never acquired full academic dress, so he borrowed the Dean's doctoral hood and cap (Columbia, Physics.) The cap (a mortarboard complete with tassel) was couple of sizes too big, but what would that matter? They were to process from the Supreme Court, and those without gowns could borrow some of the spares from the Justice's robing room. The gown was equally too big, but he reckoned he could quickly grow to fit it. There wasn't much time for introductions, so he lined up with Margaret Mead, since they at least knew each other. All went well until they hit the open area of the Mall, where the day turned out to be blustery. The wind filled the gown and practically had him airborne. He fought to gather in the rebellious folds, at the same time grabbing the oversized cap, which began to spin round, whirling its tassel like a crazed propeller. Maggie could scarcely walk for laughing and was reduced to helpless giggles. Everyone was in some kind of sartorial trouble, and throughout it all the piper wailed solemnly on.

His was the first talk, because, Wilton said, it was the most general and inclusive and set the tone. He had a hard time concentrating because they had pointed out to him that Alice Roosevelt Longworth, Teddy's very individual daughter, had arrived with a bevy of nieces and granddaughters. They all wore white dresses and gloves, and Aunt Alice marshaled them in a row to sit quietly and learn something. It was an oddly moving sight. "I can't both run the country and manage Alice," Teddy had said in despair. But he would have been proud of her right then. What the girls made of the talk he didn't know, but they applauded politely like everyone else, as they did for Lionel, for Maggie, for Ed. Wilson, for Irv DeVore, for John Crook, for John Eisenberg, and for Bill Hamilton (who remembered well the chat among the pigeons, by the Albert Hall.) Dillon had shown prescience in bringing Bill over, since his work was still a bit obscure at the time, except to professional geneticists. On the bus, on the way from the hotel, the academic yenta introduced Bill to Ed.: "Bill Hamilton, this is Ed. Wilson." A true marriage, or at least engagement, of true minds. At such small moments the march of history seems to hesitate, ready to take a new direction.

They had "commentaries" on their talks, and a sociologist from Princeton (Marvin Bressler?) called him "the Hegel of New Brunswick" because of the "ambition and inclusiveness" of his, admittedly rather sweeping little opus. But the commentator had seen that he wanted to re-write the script of socio-

logical thinking, and, while not liking it altogether (too ambitious, too inclusive, too un-accepting of "the importance of small differences") had taken it
seriously, which was encouraging. In his reply he tried to explain that nothing much in the actual practice of the social sciences need change. All the
material gathered was valuable. Nothing he was doing on the Pueblos or Tory
would he do much differently. The difference would be in the interpretation
of the data of social science and history (and the humanities for that matter) at
a very general level. The boys were going to have to be tactful: there was
going to be a lot of turf protecting like this. But once the whole argument was
spelled out in the book, all would be clear. Everyone would see that we carry
around in our behavior the baggage of evolution. *Tout être vivant*... Need we
add that this was the plan?

People were generally taken by his notion that the social sciences were
suffering from "ethnographic dazzle." Remember his fascination, at Harvard,
doing linguistics, with "orthographic dazzle"—our inability to get behind
orthography to phonetics? Same thing with cultural differences: we were so
dazzled by the details of the differences, that we failed to see the underlying
constants. Some anthropologists, like Clifford Geertz (who had been appointed
to the plum job at the Princeton Institute for Advanced Study) were actually
arguing that there were no constants: the differences were the reality. Geertz
had written a paper that influenced him a lot: it argued that Culture—in the
form of tools and language—arose early enough in evolution to affect its
course. Dependence on Culture as an adaptation was itself a selection pressure. (This was, of course, Ashley's point about "reciprocal feedback interaction.") He eagerly seized on this: we were not only the producers of family,
kinship, beliefs, rules and taboos, we had been produced by them. So was it so
strange that we, the living-fossil residue, constantly reproduced that which
produced us? This view, he thought, made Culture a part of our evolved,
biological heritage, not something set apart from it.

But Geertz did not seem able to follow up on his own insight. We did not
learn Culture, Geertz was now arguing, we learned *a culture*. (Thus, we did
not learn Language, we learned *a language*.) Our innate capacity was to do
just that; so when we looked at a particular culture, we were looking at human
nature. Yes, was the counter argument, but the learning of a culture, like the
learning of a language, is not arbitrary: we learn a specifically *human* culture,
in a specifically human way: any new one we came across might have bizarre
particulars, but its general form would be totally recognizable. Its kinship
system might be unique, but it would have one, and we could analyze it in
terms of the general components he had established: it would revolve around
the mother-child bond and take one of the possible ways of attaching males
to this bond.

Chomsky's analogy with language learning seemed conclusive. In the end
the debate really turned on a matter of temperament. Geertz really had no

stomach for general theory (intellectual indigestion from Soc. Rel. probably), and preferred a kind of Baconian "thick description"—a kind of highly structured bucket induction. When Geertz examined a cockfight in Bali, he wanted to tease out all the threads of cultural meaning embedded in it, then stop there. When the Hegel of New Brunswick looked at a brawl on Tory Island, he wanted to link the cultural meanings to the ritualized fighting that was general among social animals. He wanted to know how the cultural local grammar derived from the universal species grammar. He wanted to lodge the particulars in the general. Some people didn't want to do that, so naturally they said it couldn't be done. Which idea would survive? Necessity would decide.

Senator Fulbright had asked them to give him and some colleagues a private seminar "on the hill." The senator, whose generosity of vision had enabled the callow graduand to travel to the U.S. all those years ago, listened and questioned and said he'd learned something. Joe Alsop invited him along with DeVore and Lionel, to dinner at his comfortable house in Georgetown, specifically to meet Daniel Patrick Moynihan, author of the controversial report on the black family, who had pronounced that the question of black advancement deserved a period of "benign neglect." Alice (Roosevelt) Longworth was also there. She had wanted to see them up close, she said. Robert McNamara's daughter completed the guest list. The dinner discussion (shad roe was in season) was about race—Joe was still exercised about it, and Moynihan wanted the latest word on the intelligence issue. It wasn't a success since the three of them were committed to the Montagu position that there were no such things as races, while the laymen thought it self-evident that there were. The other two deferred mostly to him, as the supposed expert, and he got bogged down in a definition of the breeding isolate. After dinner, the ladies retired and left the gentlemen to port and cigars: the first time this had ever happened to him. Then they watched the President on television explain why he had invaded Cambodia, or bombed Hanoi, or something. The youthful trio (and Miss McNamara) agreed that we should get out of this war; the Senator shook his head heavily; Aunt Alice said the young people should be listened to; Joe said they understood so little: the President had a plan.

John Robinson had arranged a reception at the National Zoo. The mammal house had large cages all around a central arena, and the crowd gathered there for its cocktails and chatter while the rhinoceroses and hippopotami looked on incuriously. The zoo had cleared two cages, one at each end, and in one they had a string quartet playing Mozart, and in another a mixed chorus singing madrigals. Asked to say a few words he volunteered that if we were to include the human mammal in an exhibit to show it off, we could do a lot worse than Mozart and Madrigals: this was the species at its undoubted best. Senator Fulbright made a little speech with good words for the dynamic duo, which was a surprise. But like everyone else, he was taken by the names. They were to prove a mixed asset, but at least they got attention. How could you blame the gang-of-two for thinking everything was rolling inexorably their way? Chance had had its day, now necessity would take over.

Roy was getting more and more disillusioned with California. He also had a yen to get home to New Jersey and be close to his family. What is more, he was willing to become department chairman, relieving the battle-scarred founder to get on with the book and the exploration of ideas that he felt he had neglected for empire building. At the same time Richard Lee was without a job. His Bushman work, following on his primate studies, had made him a perfect candidate. Colleagues rushed to "warn" that Lee would be a problem. His radical politics led him to extremism in behavior. But this was the wrong time for such warnings: radical politics, as long as it was "anti-war" was no handicap. We were all radicals then. Anyway, they had equally "warned" him about what difficult bastards Yehudi and Warren were, but so far they were just fine, good citizens. Yehudi's "reader" was in progress, he was arguing that C & P lost its way when it abandoned biology, and he wanted the *Zoological Perspective* paper for the first volume. He did tend to be a bit sharp with the Israeli students, but so far no real trouble. So warnings were set aside, and Lee was hired along with a research assistant he brought from Columbia.

Lee was a Marxist, cultural materialist—a close ally of Marvin Harris and Peter Vayda. They had all liked *Kinship and Marriage* because of its "materialist" insistence that there was an ecological basis to kinship systems; that they were adaptational responses to real-world problems. They didn't like Lévi-Strauss because the Frenchman's approach was "ideational." So be it. Our ecumenist could encompass both. A lot of kinship was about categories: it was in the head. If these category systems had a function in the real world, it must be because our ways of thinking had evolved to fit the real world. Anthropologists should not make a disjunction between category systems and the real world. The way we organized out categories was part of that reality.

In a flurry of chess moves, Jane Lancaster left a position and was also available. The glamorous Jane was, with Phyllis Jay, another Washburn protégé who was already famous in the primatalogical world, and who was interested in the origins of language. What is more, her husband Chet, an African ethnographer, came as part of the package. At one blow they could have a fully-grown program. The Dean wanted them to house a black lady musicologist "for a fixed period." Part of the push for "minority recruiting." This is the way deals were done, he was learning. You give us something; we'll give you something. The powers were struck by the obvious fact that here was a department that would easily eclipse its counterpart at Princeton. Eclipsing Princeton academically was not an easy thing, but it mattered almost as much as beating them at football. The incomers brought grants with them, and this made them even more precious to city hall. So special funds were co-opted and the quartet was appointed, applications for the graduate program tripled at the news. The progress was dizzying. What could go wrong?

The major complication was Helen Safa. He liked Helen a lot, but she did not fit the plans, and he had to stand firm on the agreement that limited her appointment. Fortunately he had this in writing, and although the Dean wriggled and tried out legalisms of one sort or another, the stubborn chairman was on firm ground. To get the appointments they wanted, Helen had to go. Again compromise: since she was an "urban anthropologist" Urban Planning was willing to have her. She asked if she could keep her anthropological title, and he was only too happy to give back something. She could go on teaching courses even for anthropology and be a full member of the Graduate Program. Poor Helen: how to foresee that in dark days ahead she would come like a knight to the rescue of an ailing operation. Fortunately, she too blamed the Dean (who was evidently paying off a debt to Stanley Diamond at the New School) and didn't bear a grudge. She was not a grudge-bearing person. At this point, however, he was refusing to talk to the Dean without a stenographer and a notary present. Yet he hated the whole business, and had fantasies of getting out from under it all. Roy's coming would help. He asked Roy what was the most important fact he had learned over the years. "Human relationships are impossibly difficult," said the wise one.

The major disaster at the time was on the home front. The drift apart had one inevitable consequence, but one he could not openly face. Anything that would take him from the children was unthinkable; whatever happened, that could not happen. But how did you face total rejection? When you were absolutely not wanted, how could you stay? In these circumstances, husbands did the moving; there was no other way. He could not face telling the girls, and when it happened, they reacted so badly it made him physically ill; his hands became total claws, and he had to drive using his wrists on the steering wheel. He lavished reassurance. He would never be far from them ever. That was a solemn and absolute promise. They cried and begged, but there was no way out. It was the worst thing ever, far worse than the physical pain.

He would have to set up another home for them nearby? How could he do that? He didn't have the time for one thing. The Dean and his ever-kind lady offered to put him up for a while. He was shaken by their generosity; it was just so very damned nice of them. The Dean didn't bear grudges; most of the time he didn't think he was doing anything wrong. He saw himself as a patient, rational man trying to survive the tantrums of prima donnas. Perhaps he was right. But Roy and Diane, who had moved their family nearby, stepped in and offered their attic. It was back to student living, with a garret and an army cot. He was over solicitous to Roy's children, probably out of guilt, but he genuinely liked them. Diane was sympathetic (she had never liked wife, unlike Roy) and to be with such a good family was something of a buffer. That was when Roy said things were not going all that well between them either. Was there no end?

At the Columbia seminar he had met, and fallen for, a Kentucky woman (she insisted "lady") of super-model beauty and considerable intelligence. Genie had lived for a while in Boston, married an MIT graduate, moved to LA, had a daughter, lost her husband in a car accident, done an anthropology degree at UCLA, then come east to do graduate work. He had known her for the best part of a year when the break-up came, and her apartment was a welcome place of refuge, grateful as he was for Roy's attic. With Roy now shouldering responsibility for the department, it was easy to slip away into the comfort of a welcoming, warm, familial embrace. They lived in an apartment over a pizza parlor that was a front for a Mafia family operation. He got to know the family rather well. They took care of the community: there was no petty theft or assault, since it was their mothers and sisters who were threatened. Petty criminals had a way of just disappearing. The smart kids went into the family's "legitimate" businesses; the not-so-smart went into the police force. One of the teenage sons asked him for advice: he didn't know whether to take up a career in medicine, go in with the Mafia, or try anthropology. Let the reply remain their secret.

It was a long ride from the town at the top of the Turnpike, to the campus, but he was still in New Jersey and could still see the children frequently, and had the prospect of another home to offer them. He also had the prospect of proving that he could be a success at marriage; he was not a congenitally bad husband. Given mutual love and respect a marriage could work. That was the plan. He shot up and down the Turnpike at well over the speed limit, in his second-hand black Buick convertible with the red leather seats, taking in, for the first time, the AM songs of the day. "Jeremiah was a Bullfrog," (was it "Joy to the World"?) jostled with "Jean" (you're young and alive,) while "Spinning Wheel" reminded him of his own carousel song, and he fought down the fear.

> What goes up, must come down,
> Spinning wheel turn around
> ...
>
> Ride a painted pony
> Let the spinning wheel spin.

He and Roy taught the introductory course for the graduate students, and decided to have them read together and try to understand, the first part of Levi-Strauss's *Elementary Structures*, which had come out in English translation. The *New Republic* again called on him as reviewer, and he had pointed out "the curious sniping" in the preface between the author and Rodney Needham, the editor and co-translator. (Rodney had explained to him that the original translation, by two Australians, was terrible, and, as editor, he had to do it all over again.) L-S, who now addressed him as "Dear Colleague" wrote him a long letter detailing the cause of this breach with Structuralism's strongest supporter in the Anglo-Saxon world. The Master was grateful to Rodney for taking up the cudgels on his behalf, but then became alarmed as the knight-defender took it on himself to speak for his liege lord's intentions and meanings, without consultation. L-S wrote because, he said, he thought the reviewer was owed an explanation. The reviewer didn't see that he was, but found the letter touching nevertheless. He had been deeply influenced by the French wizard, and not only in kinship. He wrestled with his notions of what was at the root of human nature, for he dearly wished it were compatible with what the evolutionary research was finding. If he could somehow figure out how they fit together, surely that would count for something? Mind and matter met in the living fossil that was the best evidence for the evolution of both. Archaic limbs and organs meshed with survivals of ancient emotions and categories: the result was… what we saw, if we could just step back and look afresh at the human fossil. Then we could rewrite Descartes correctly: Je suis, donc je pense.

The annual Anthropology meetings (up in another airplane) were in New Orleans, home of Jazz and the Blues and Oysters Rockefeller. How wonderful was this custom of annual corroborees in exotic places, with fine food, good music, and recreational sex. Lionel would know the discretely outrageous places to eat; the child of Dixieland, starved and deprived, would head for Preservation Hall. He wouldn't have to justify his enthusiasms here to anyone; they wouldn't be noticed. He had contracted to give a paper on "Lévi-Strauss and the Origins of Mind." He had spent the summer hammering this one out. It was as yet poorly formulated, but he took up L-S's insistence on the fundamental role of categorical thinking, the tendency to think in binary terms, and the use of natural kinds as metaphors for social groups—the basis of Totemism. He had to marry this to his "origins of language" ideas, which saw the evolving hominids developing cortical control of sex and aggression to facilitate the forming of social groups: and those groups would be kin groups, which formed alliances.

This basic evolutionary process would forge a specific primitive language, compounded initially of names and commands and possibly evaluative words. ("Crocodile-people mate emu-people; not mate kangaroo-folk; mate totem-woman bad.") The Japanese macaques were almost there with their ranked matrilines, which split into subgroups, and between which males moved. They were "only a naming system away" from human kinship systems: Iroquoian, with exogamous matrimoieties and matrilocal residence (for the record.) Humans had added "marriage"—parental liaisons for the rearing of children, something the macaques did not have. Some monkeys (and apes) did have such liaisons though, but then they didn't have the kinship groups. It was not easy and sometimes his brain ached with the effort of synthesis, and seemed as if it would spill out onto the Olivetti as he threw out page after frustrating page.

And he still had to incorporate the three L-S basic mental functions: the exigency of the rule as rule; the synthetic nature of the gift; the necessity of reciprocity. He used an analogy to translate it: if you made a perfect model of a rooster, and wound it up, what would it do? It would peck, cluck, preen, crow at dawn, fight other roosters... If you made a perfect model of a human being and wound it up, then what? It would define things into categories, start exchanging things so defined, according to rules it made up to govern the exchange, setting up a special relationship between giver and receiver. What it exchanged was typically, goods, information and women. The basis of exogamy was that we defined kin groups with a rule that we must marry out of them, which forced us to exchange wives with other groups and set up relationships of alliance with them.

"Feminists" were already "objecting" to this, not on the basis that it was wrong in fact, but that it was "demeaning to women" to talk about the "exchange of wives." But kin groups *do* exchange wives. That is what they do. They often divide the world up quite overtly into "wife givers" and "wife takers." "That's because men make these rules." That's right. You want to complain about this; I only want to describe it. If men did not try to control these systems they would be very different. Matrilineal systems only exist because property and status have to pass from male to male, even if descent is through females. You had to look first at what happened on the ground—who physically moved where; then you looked at what the natives said the rule was and how they applied it; then you looked at what explanatory model best fit these facts. One angry student said that her "feminist principles" would not allow her to accept this. Then what was he to do? He didn't make the rules, he just reported on them. Her principles, she said, prevented her from "accepting" it anyway. Perhaps you could have them removed, he suggested, but such answers no longer raised a laugh. With those afflicted by deep and sincere conviction, humor is the first thing to go. Such people are impervious to ridicule. God was the only one even smiling.

It was a matter of seizing the high moral ground. Liberals and such other "tender minded" thinkers (William James) were easily morally bullied. Claim that you were a victim of some kind of oppression, and they caved right in and became thoroughly ashamed of their part in the victimization. They then fell into the pattern of victimizing the victimizers: the old Puritan witch-hunt. There was nothing more unlovely, to paraphrase Macaulay, than the liberal public in one of its periodic fits of self-righteousness. In the process the guilty and outraged liberals began to define a new right: the right not to be offended. Thus he should not talk about "exchange of wives" because "feminists" with "strong feelings" would be offended. What about his strong feelings about messing with the truth? That was "different." Why? Were not defenders of the truth an oppressed minority? No cigar. It was the old horror he had had with the adults: state that you had strong feelings (or principles) about something, and that settled the matter; the very strength of the feeling established its truth. There could be no rational discussion.

> The virtues of the questing mind
> Are not as they are billed,
> For in the country of the blind
> The one-eyed man is killed.

Nixon and Kissinger pursued détente with the Soviet Union; Kissinger went to Peking (Beijing?) The U.S. and the Soviets were racing for Mars. A Rutgers graduate, Milton Friedman, wrote *A Theoretical Framework for Monetary Analysis*. Stanley Kubrick's next masterpiece, *A Clockwork Orange* (from Anthony Burgess's wicked pen) posed serious moral questions in a setting of social breakdown and violence. The People's Republic of China was admitted to the UN. *The Imperial Animal* hit the bookstores, with the sentence from Jacques Monod as its epigraph. It had not been easy. They had ditched the original publisher. They had been assigned a copy editor, a woman who's qualification was that she was a mistress of one of the senior editors, but who was incompetent, and knew it, and knew they knew it, and compensated with a bossy violation of the text. The editor would not, or could not, remove her (no names, no lawsuits) so Lynn did her job and negotiated a switch; they got Messrs. Holt, Rinehart and Winston, and the tough but superb Stephen, clean shoes and all.

The publishers expected great things, and arranged a "book tour"—another whisk through Wonderland. They did San Francisco and LA, Cleveland, some other mid-west places, and Boston, in a week. They did local TV and radio shows, press interviews, bookshop signings. Sign as many books as you can, Bob told them: if the book is signed the bookstore can't return it; they have to keep it and sell it. They got a great deal of coverage and very little sleep. They began the talk show rounds with Donahue and David Susskind. Donahue he thought very smart and a serious listener; Susskind very arrogant and yet cruelly insightful. I've seen all the great ones up close, he told them: they all sweat a lot and worry about their make-up and profile.

They appeared on New York TV with Susan Brownmiller who told them that women could play basketball successfully against men. A young actress called Cybill Shepherd, a tolerably pretty girl who struck attitudes and who was on the show because her agent wanted the "exposure," said she had always wanted to play basketball with the boys, and mentioned her forthcoming film a lot (*The Last Picture Show*?) They were given two pages in *Time*, which was a near disaster. The writer had started with "In direct opposition to Darwin's theory of natural selection, Tiger and..." Lynn had insisted on seeing the copy in advance. Just as well. They were slated for the cover of *Time*, but Krushchev died and for some reason this was deemed more important.

While staying in LA (was it at the Beverly Wilshire?) the oily bell captain, listing all the celebrities he had served in his time, put this to him, when explaining the policy on gratuities: "When Omar Sharif stays here, he lines all the staff up when he arrives, gives them each a hundred dollar bill, and says that he wants to hear no more about tipping for the duration of his stay." The crew was ready to line up, he added. So our tired traveler, a bit fed up by then with the whole business, had the unctuous little man line everyone up. He told the eager chorus line that he had worked out the ratio of Mr. Sharif's income to his own, and that he would tip in proportion. Did they think that was fair? They nodded suspiciously. He then handed them each a dollar bill, and told them he didn't want to hear any more about tipping for the rest of his stay.

They were invited to the *Today Show*, but our insomniac late riser finally drew the line. Who in God's name was watching television at that unholy hour? Certainly not people who buy books. The interviewer was a Barbara something. She had an aide call to say she had not had time to read the book, so what questions should she ask? He replied that they had done their job, now she should do hers. Lionel tactfully gave them some likely topics, and told him to set his alarm and miss the show at his peril. Mark his words, no one would be watching. The next day, everyone from the president of the university on down called to say they had seen him. He in turn was wholly consumed by chatting to the divine Joanne Woodward in the green room. They were slated to appear with Johnny Carson in what used to be Ashley's slot at the end of the Tonight Show. But as happened with Ashley so often (he told them) time ran out. Ashley added that all these publicity stunts were futile. Half the viewers missed the title of the book and the other half forgot the author, very few of them bought it. You would be better off, said Ashley, taking a handcart and a bell to all those places, and hawking copies in the street.

But they discovered a problem: the falling-between-two-two stools, or one-idea book problem. In aiming at their social science audience, they had stressed the complexity of issues. They assumed the sheer skill of their writing would convey the message to the public. But they discovered, on the shows and in the interviews, that what the public wanted, and what someone like Desmond could give them, was a one-idea book. "Man is an animal" was Desmond's idea: so lets treat him like an unknown animal and describe in him the behavior ethologists described in their animals. One idea, many striking illustrations; that was the successful formula. They didn't have it. They explained about the Nature/Culture dichotomy; they showed the evidence for the effects of the hunting transition; they outlined the physiological and clinical evidence for bonding mechanisms; they got polite indifference. The interviewers wanted tit-bits; they wanted the neat illustrations of how like animals we are; they wanted Desmond. They did not want earnest arguments about the reform of the social sciences. Perhaps the intelligent lay public of Lynn's imagination wanted these, and they were probably buying the book, but the public reached by the media was just not moved. This was the wrong audience. They should have been touring the college campuses, they said, but the publishers pointed out that students just don't buy books.

They adapted. "What have you found out about women?" they were asked. Their sense of smell increases 100,000 times at peak ovulation, they would come back. Faced with questions like, "Would you approve of a woman president?" he replied that he'd rather have a president who was pregnant some of the time than one who was impotent all of the time. The Ken and Barbie dolls that did the local TV shows were uneasy with the answer, but the crew chortled. It was always a good sign if you could make the crew laugh. Lionel, faced with a question about Kissinger's "shuttle diplomacy" peregrinations, called him "the shopkeeper of nations." They didn't get it, but his co-author fell off the stool laughing. Once back on the stool he fielded a question about the U.S. policy of supporting nasty dictators as long as they were pro-American: "Scoundrels are the last refuge of patriotism." While Lionel chewed on his handkerchief, the Ken-doll interviewer said that insight was very, very profound.

At an early morning call-in radio-show in Cleveland (or was it Detroit?)— "Howie Lund's Morning Watch"—callers asked for advice on their pets, having been told he was an animal expert. Howie Lund faced him at the end of the program: "Doctor, you are a man of science who has studied all his life the secrets of the universe. Do you believe there is a divine intelligence out there that orders everything?" Punch drunk and sleepy he rose to the bell: "Howie, I can honestly tell you, and your good listeners, that I believe there is... something." Howie was almost tearful. "Gee Doc, I thought you'd give me a straight 'no.'" There was no longer any such thing as a straight no.

The reviews cascaded in. Good agents and publishers could guarantee attention. The reviews were overwhelmingly favorable, in the press and the magazines. Anatole Broyard, in the *New York Times* (daily) was nice about it, but the Sunday review ominously ignored it. As a truly pleasant surprise, the *Saturday Review* had recruited Bernie Siegal of Stanford, whom he had last seen in the Pueblo of Picuris, with Roy. Bernie said they were: "True to the widest mandate of their discipline" and that the result was "one of the most creative contributions to the social science literature"—it was also "superlative writing." Nice. But a pattern of hostility from women reviewers, and the more "liberal/radical" males set in at the same time. With the women it was the same gripe: you are using "biology" to justify the oppression of women, as in the status quo. They weren't, of course, but women writers, and particularly the academic ones, were badly in need of academic targets, and the boys were two nice big fat ones.

They had come out in favor of female quotas where men were entrenched, on the grounds that established male-bonded groups would not voluntarily

photo by Burton Berinsky

admit females. It didn't help. Anthropological feminists (we should perhaps drop the scare quotes by now) had organized the Ruth Benedict Collective in New York. They passed two motions: first, there should be no Stalinism in the women's movement; second, Tiger and his co-author should be prevented, by any means, from speaking on any campus. Kate Millett had taught them about "sexual politics" and mantras like "the personal is political" were now part of the buzz.

The liberal academics were a bit slow off the mark but soon weighed in. Some, like Alexander Alland (in the *American Anthropologist*) were ambivalent, but suspicious that "Social Darwinism" was rearing its ugly head. There was nothing of course of Social Darwinism (wrongly named—it was Spencerism) in their book: they were strong communitarians and against unbridled individualism and laissez-faire. But their critics were not really looking to answer the arguments, but to level political accusations. There were no depths the good people would not stoop to. The journal *Natural History* published a sneering review with a cartoon showing a bandwagon holding Konrad Lorenz, Bob Ardrey, Desmond, and the two boys: accusing them of obvious meretricious intent. The boys were actually proud of the company, and really rather sad that their effort seemed to be puzzling rather than attracting readers. If you're going to be abused for money-grubbing, you might as well have the money. Their careful plan was probably attracting the "intelligent lay reader" as Lynn prophesied—there just obviously were not all that many of them. Not by best-seller standards that is, and this is what the publishers wanted. A good seller is not good enough. But the Book-of-the-Month Club asked for it as an "alternate selection." That cheered everyone up.

Out of the blue. His nemesis Max Gluckman surfaced again for the *New York Review of Books*, bible of the transatlantic liberal-intellectual caucus. Max did the standard number, accusing them of jumping on a "bandwagon load of monkeys" and similar high-class criticism. Someone had shown Max (he wouldn't have sought it out) Ed. Wilson's contribution to the Man and Beast symposium, where Ed. had mentioned that some gene frequencies could change very quickly—in as little as twelve-thousand years. Max used this, triumphantly, to argue that no "ancient" genes could still be operating. They wrote to the review pointing out that Ed. never meant that fundamental, structural genes affecting behavior could change in short order. They said that Max's argument, if true, would mean that there were indeed absolute and fundamental differences in ability between human races, which had had at least three times that period to evolve. They sent the latter to Max, who wrote back a bit abashed and said he was sorry he had got into this "gene thing" in the first place. He took bad advice, he said. Like Bishop Wilberforce from Richard Owen they thought.

But then they got their first inkling of the way the liberal-media mind worked. The editor of the review refused to publish their letter until, he said, he got an answer from Max to publish along with it. Fine, they said, relishing the climb down. Max had not only written to them, he had written to mutual friends in Israel and other places, boasting of his humbling of the infidels. But week after week the review refused to publish their letter, saying that Max was ill and couldn't write an answer: that it wouldn't be fair not to print his response simultaneously. Max is fine, they responded, he just doesn't want to reply, so you should publish the letter anyway. In the end, the review stopped returning phone calls from them, the publisher or the agent, and just retreated into hard-faced silence. He was with Mike Levitas and some journalists from the *Times* at Sardi's bar. He asked why the Sunday review had not tackled the book. It had a simple policy with "right wing books" they said, either get someone to do a hatchet job, or just ignore them. It isn't a right wing book, they protested. Maybe, said the guys: tell *them* that.

These are just examples. One could multiply them a hundred times. The boys had on their earnest endeavor to bring enlightenment to their discipline and the world, stepped into an intellectual minefield, and they were the targets. They should have known from the previous response to the others in the bandwagon that this would happen. But in their innocence they really thought that their careful, responsible, documented argument, demonstrating the inevitable interaction of Nature and Culture, indeed the fallacy of the distinction, would have to be treated with respect. They were not playwrights, or zoo men, or even German bird watchers; they were card-carrying social scientists with mainstream work to their credit, for goodness sake. Well, Mae West was wrong: goodness had everything to do with it.

To their critics what they proposed was, by definition, not just wrong; it was positively wicked. This issue had been alive for centuries; the battle had been fought on many fronts; rational argument and evidence would not settle the issue. The issue was, for the radical environmental determinists already settled: any kind of appeal to the innate, whether to innate ideas or innate emotions, or innate social bonding mechanisms, however carefully it avoided the simple-mindedness of the nature/nurture debate, would be vetoed as disreputable and even evil.

The notion that human nature had to be a tabula rasa for liberal/radical reform to be possible was at least as old as John Locke and John Stuart Mill. To the latter-day followers of these, the evils of Nazi Germany had showed once and for all the dangers of admitting any content to human nature. The Marxists had joined in: human nature was entirely shaped by society; good societies (i.e. communistic) would produce good people. The anthropologists added to the chorus: Culture, not Nature was the determinant of behavior. Human nature was both a blank slate, and also full of goodness (they could never sort that one out.) The feminists were sounding the same strident note: biology was not destiny; it was not anything. Any reversal of this doc-trine would undermine the liberal-reformist-progressive agenda. It would be back to original sin and superstition, eugenics, and the inevitable reactionary consequences. The boys were not correcting a few academic ideas; they were taking on the might of the Western progressive tradition.

The history of a soul is not the place to rehash this issue, O gentlest of readers, who has already been so sorely tried. Perhaps the soul reflecting on itself can be allowed to rethink the problem, at some later point. For the moment it is enough to see that the problem is there, and that our soul had stumbled, more or less by accident, and mainly from trying honestly to solve the incest problem, into the great debate. The duo was allocated a place in the argument that they didn't want: they were as much reformists as the good people; they just believed that reform was only possible if one understood what one was reforming. Lionel called their approach "Biological Fabianism" in an appeal to the spirit of the LSE. It was simply foolish to think that you could shape behavior in any way you wanted to. It bordered on the pathologi-cal, the delusional; it was metaphysics, not science. A just society might be possible, but it would have to take account of the givens and then figure out how to circumvent them; it couldn't just ignore them, wish them away, insist that they couldn't, on principle, exist. They called this the "Christian Sci-ence" attitude, which annoyed Ashley, who otherwise understood what they were doing, and, while differing about innate aggression (to be expected) saw their position clearly enough. The English edition of the book scored an almost unbelievable coup in carrying, on the dust jacket, two highly compli-mentary quotes, one from Ashley Montagu, the other from Robert Ardrey.

Life hurried on, regardless of the fate of the soul. They faced the first problem with male graduate students who needed to keep up a B grade aver-age to avoid the draft. Some were borderline cases; should their grades be inflated on moral grounds? Lee thought yes. The ex-draft dodger resisted. He certainly had done graduate studies to avoid the draft—in a way. But no one had handed him grades on a plate because of that. You could not compromise standards; they were all you had. It was the thin end of a potentially expan-sive wedge that would have grades inflated for all kinds of "moral" reasons. Students would just have to do better, or think of another solution: Canada perhaps. Lee said that all the other departments were doing it. So much the worse for them. But he couldn't stop Lee or anyone else doing it informally. And the grade-creep began. The system became essentially "pass/fail" with A as the passing grade, B the fail; C was unthinkable. It was happening at the undergraduate level too, ever since the silly business of student evaluations of faculty had been introduced. (Livingston had been forced back to letter grades by pressure from graduate schools.) Promotion depended partially on the outcome of these popularity contests, so untenured faculty began to pad their students' grades close to promotion time. Also, male students wanted desperately to get into highly selective graduate programs largely to dodge the draft, so they exerted pressure for higher grades. It was obvious, but no one knew what to do about it. The administrators were true to the first principle of their profession: no trouble on my watch.

The situation drifted down and down. Students came in from high school less and less well prepared, as their declining SAT scores showed, although their school grades continued to rise regardless. Once into college, their grades were inflated without regard to their true abilities; they then flooded the graduate schools (and many prepared to be teachers back in the high schools) where their grades were inflated yet again. Then, semi-educated but duly accredited, often with theses passed for correct ideology rather than serious scholarship, they poured into the faculty positions opening up to deal with the increasing numbers of students, who...

Things were getting ugly on the ideological front. He and Lionel were teaching The Evolution of Human Behavior jointly as an undergraduate course. A posse was sent over from the new "Women's Studies" department at Douglass College, to monitor the content and to see if there was a "hostile atmosphere" for women. They announced that they were there to see that "sexism" was not being taught at Rutgers, and to suppress it if it was. You can stay, they were told, if you behave properly as auditors and actually do the readings and take the tests. They were not prepared for this. They didn't need to take the tests, they said, they only needed to see if there was "gender bias" in the texts being assigned and in the lectures. You can't decide anything if you don't understand what you are reading, they were told, and you yourselves won't know that unless you take the tests to see if you have mastered the material. Most of them left, saying that this attitude was definite proof of gender bias and they would report it—to someone.

Two honest souls stayed and, for a while, read work on male-female differences and hormones and breast feeding (most of it done by women researchers.) They reluctantly decided that sexism "as such" was not being taught, but that to redress the "inherent gender bias in all science" the women in the class should go to "consciousness raising classes" in the Women's Studies department. They were followed by a group of radicals/activists who threatened to disrupt the lectures because of passages in the book that said adolescence was a time of raw emotions waiting to be filled with cultural content. This was, said the "morally committed" activists/radicals, a deliberate attempt to discredit the "youth movement." Which youth movement? he asked. The Hitler Youth? The Young Turks? The Children's Crusade? The Comsomol? The Young Englanders? The Labor Zionist League of Youth? The Boy Scouts? The Children of Mary? The Red Guards? The Young Republicans for Nixon? The Kamikazes? The Junior League? The ... ...??

Roy was becoming very disillusioned with the whole process. He foresaw anthropology descending into a mere ideological exercise, wrapped in "qualitative" fieldwork. But closer to home, he too couldn't handle the Dean. Then things began to unravel. Richard Lee could not resist pushing his radical points at any and every opportunity, regardless of the damage to the program. It was the moral bullying again; the sense of superiority that their self-righteousness gave them. Their agenda took automatic precedence because it was "politically correct"—a ghastly neologism that was gaining favor. Yehudi had his very personal agenda, which included blocking all promotions. Yehudi didn't think anyone should be promoted. Lionel was blocked. The Dean was sympathetic, but the "full professors" had to be unanimous. Then Warren and Yehudi began what was to become a life-long feud, involving bizarre accusations of Jewish anti-Semitism, and the intervention of the Bn'ai Brith Anti-Defamation League among other things.

In the end Roy decided to leave. Mel Spiro had started a department at La Jolla (U. of California at San Diego) and wanted him there. They made one last stab at a settlement. Roy presented his points to the provost: a major one being that the division of the university into "autonomous" undergraduate colleges was detrimental to the development of serious graduate and research programs. These would always have to bow to the primary needs of the undergraduate colleges. And since these colleges could make their own appointments, there could be no consistent plan to the development of disciplines. Rutgers College wanted to appoint three anthropologists, and while they paid lip service to "consultation" they clearly meant to hire the people they wanted for their own undergraduate needs. It was frustrating. Roy was right, and years later the university would be thrown into a violent upheaval while it reformed itself along the lines he originally suggested. For the moment the powers stood firm with the status quo. But the Provost, a smart man used to compromise, had a suggestion. The Graduate School had "lines" that were meant to bolster graduate programs. With Dean Torrey's cooperation, the boys could be transferred to lines in the Graduate School, and concentrate on the graduate program. Nothing much would change, except that they would no longer "report" to the Dean of Livingston. They would have a different boss. They would get out from under some of the mess they felt themselves mired in. The Graduate Dean (and Mason Gross) agreed. The plan was changed.

The Pentagon Papers were published by the *Times*; Ellsberg was threatened with prosecution. The U.S. went off the gold standard, and the Bretton Woods system collapsed. Roy left for California. It was very sad. Come out to La Jolla, he said, none of this nonsense there. Some other nonsense, though. It was still academia, wasn't it? Anyway, he had to stay near the girls. Genie decided to do ecological research in Ireland, even in Donegal, which meant if he went with her, at least over the summer, he had a shot at getting back to Tory. The girls could come too, and go to a horse farm in Galway for part of the time. They were going through the equine phase of female development, and this prospect raised their spirits no end. Anne would have to stay with her mother. Horse dander was almost fatal to her. The Bloomenfield house in Princeton had become vacant again, and he moved into it. It was near the children and had extra bedrooms where they could come and stay.

Things were working out. But Tory didn't. He tried twice, but the weather defeated him, and he had to be content with a reunion of friends and a long gaze through the rain and heaving seas to the misty distant rock in the Atlantic. He did get to see Séamus and Seán O hEochaidh again, and was touched at how they greeted him (in Irish of course) as an old friend (*"mo shean chara* !"*) They stayed with Derek Hill at Churchill. He had painted a portrait of John Sparrow, the master of All Souls, which had been much praised. Sparrow's only recent contribution to learning had been an article on *Lady Chatterley's Lover* explaining that "the Italian way" meant sodomy—with lots of learned quotes. They looked through some of Derek's scrapbooks with him; records of extraordinary passages through that ceremonious, unchanging, gracious house; the twilight of a gentle, privileged age.

He got the parents and the girls together, with some logistical difficulty, and it was as painful as ever to see them part. His father looked thin and aged. He hadn't been well. They thought it might be an ulcer, but the aging warrior quietly hated doctors and wouldn't take advice. The BBC flew him over to take part in a TV debate on the ridiculous proposal that "This house considers that women need a new deal." Who on earth could argue with that? It was no debating point. He was put on the stand to say his piece about the mother-child bond. The glamorous barrister arguing for the proposal, Nemone Lethbridge, asked him if he thought motherhood was all "women were fit for." Patience. He had said that the purpose of females in any sexually reproducing species was to bear the offspring: that is what they were for. It didn't mean that that was all they could do. "What do you propose to tell barren women?" If they want to be mothers they can adopt: but there are barren females in all species; that doesn't invalidate the proposition.

Then he had to hurry back because Al Ortiz was organizing a conference on the Pueblos in Santa Fe, and this meant he might at least be able to see Cochiti. The conference was on "New Perspectives on the Pueblos" and he did his thing, much updated, on the Rio Grande Pueblos. Fred Eggan said he was proposing a proto-system for the Keresans that was more complicated than its successors. He said no, he was proposing the simplest form of systematic kinship system that we knew, much as Eggan himself had done for the proto-Maya. Good discussion. And he did get back to the Pueblo, and saw Joe and Epifanio and Juanita and Juana, and all his clan relatives, and his baseball friends. They did a little work on clan membership and marriage preferences. But mostly he was shaken by the new Cochiti dam, which towered like a supernatural wall over the little neolithic village. The power of the Sun Father had been stolen at Los Alamos, now the sacred water that was the gift of the Cloud People, the ancestors, had been tamed to the insatiable needs of the Anglos.

The people were happy though. The lake the dam formed was on their land, and so they got to run all the concessions in this new, huge recreation area. The village was deserted as they all went up to run the boats and food stands. They come back for the Corn Dance, said Joe, but the medicine societies were now defunct. With the money they earned, however, the people could put in a modern clinic. Was he always to feel he was coming in on the last act of the social drama? He saw the last of the horse-drawn, steam-powered, smog-enshrouded cities of the industrial revolution; the last of the nineteenth-century farms of Hardy's Wessex; the last of the old Tory Island of the Gaelic crofters; the last of the Anglo-Irish aristocracy; the last of a new-stone-age Pueblo in New Mexico; the last of genteel rural Jane Austen England; even the last of the old Fabian LSE, and definitely the last of the all-male rah-rah American college campus.They would all persist in some form or other, but an essence was gone from them all.

> *Will the rest agree to die?*
> *Next Age or no? Shall its Sordello try*
> *Clue after clue, and catch at last the clue*
> *I miss?—that's underneath my finger too,*
> *Twice, thrice a day, perhaps,—some yearning traced*
> *Deeper, some petty consequence embraced*
> *Closer!*

In the fall, Rutgers opened its new Medical School, and things dramatically moved forward. The Department of Psychiatry hired Arthur Kling (again from California—everyone was coming east as the west became more conservative and hostile to the radical universities.) Kling brought with him NIMH and NSF grants, the brilliant Michael McGuire, and colonies of monkeys. Kling had done the basic work on the amygdala. It was a bit crude then—you just chopped it out, or took half of it away- but it was crucial to understanding that vital organ. (A lot of the brain studies were crude. They did pre-frontal lobotomies by inserting an ice pick up the eye socket and jiggling it about until enough tissue was damaged.) Kling wanted a research program, and so needed graduate students. He proposed a joint effort between his department, Biology and Anthropology. It would provide at least six scholarships a year. What a fantastic plan, they all agreed. And it was, and for a while it worked splendidly. Kling had contacts with primate research centers in Mexico, St. Kitts, and Bermuda (where C. R. Carpenter had kept his gibbons.) They had green vervets, stumptail and rhesus macaques, even chimpanzees, at command. Overnight, it seemed, they were a major primatological research center; student applications poured in. Meanwhile the undergraduate program struggled on. No one wanted to be chairman, so they hired Johnny Whiting's old collaborator, Margaret Bacon, to act as "Departmental Convenor" with few powers above the secretarial. She was a decent lady, and worked hard to make it work. It worked for a while.

But the dynamic duo still had an obligation to the book. They were heartened by a letter from Karl Popper, to whom they had sent a copy, who said, in response to their query, that he thought yes, they were doing science, and testable hypotheses could be derived from their theory. They should move in that direction. Then Noam Chomsky, who, despite his lily-white left-wing radical credentials, told them that he could see no other way to a "non-trivial social science." The foreign editions were coming out. First there was the British with its endorsement by the two old enemies. The Germans would be next, and they would go there if only to see Konrad Lorenz and the fabled geese at Seewiesen. But first to London, where the enterprising publisher, Tom Rosenthal, was so high on the book he produced a twenty page pamphlet with excerpts from the chapters to spark off bookshops and reviewers. Not since the early work of Freud and Jung, gushed the jacket, had such creative new work exploded onto the scene. A bit of oversell, they thought, but who would not be a little flattered? They arrived in the evening, threw their cases into the hotel, and rushed down to Ronnie Scott's in Soho, where Cleo Laine was singing with Johnny Dankworth (he was still "Johnny" then, before he got more formal.) She was singing Noel Coward, "Mad About the Boy," and did it in five different accents and characters. They hugged their overpriced drinks, and worshipped devoutly from the periphery.

David Attenborough recommended them to his channel for a program called *Controversy*. They found it hard to explain to the media wizards what was controversial about the whole thing. "Just get some feminists or Marxists in the audience and you'll see," said Lionel. They promised. The format had four interlocutors who rigorously questioned the proponents of the controversial views. Who should they get? Well, a feminist for sure, perhaps a sociologist. How about Max Gluckman? our man ventured, knowing Max would never accept. They didn't realize it was a joke, and Max did accept. The sociologist they co-opted was, of all people, Donald MacRae. Feminist Freudian Juliet Mitchell, and primatologist Gilbert Manley—a stickler for accuracy and the like, completed the foursome. The program was filmed in the lecture rooms of the Royal Society, and they were to stand behind Faraday's desk, with the audience looming over them in stacked semicircles. There was a pre-filmed opening with their statement, including film clips of Lionel watching a croquet game, and his companion singing in a barbershop quartet, and ended with an orchestra playing William Walton's *Crown Imperial*. Not many people got the reference.

The questioners were a flop. Max took up too much time making niggling ethnographic points, and no one could follow him. MacRae said he thought there was probably a very general biogrammar, but he thought the analogy with a computer was wrong. Computers were very fast, he said, but very stupid; humans were very slow, but very smart. Good point, but there wasn't much to say about it; it was just an analogy. The feminist waffled. She obviously wanted to be hostile, but was also unsure of herself: the feminism inspired anger, but this was tempered by the Freudiansim with its obvious relevance to their argument. When she wanted to attack them on the mother-child bond, Manley chastised her, then he, again, only quibbled about details. There were a bunch of Trotskyites in the audience who seemed largely to want to draw attention to the fact they were there. Then came the big event. A bunch of unidentified, eccentrically dressed ladies, sitting on one row, staged a noisy walk out. The cameras loved it, but no one knew who they were. It came out later that they were transvestites of some "activist" persuasion. What they were protesting against was again unclear. The BBC received some letters, which were passed on. One was from the wife of the Dean of Winchester Cathedral, who apologized to the "American visitors" and hoped they did not think these persons represented all English women. No, they did not.

While all this was going on, he heard that his father had been diagnosed with stomach cancer. In fact he heard just before the program, and went through in a daze, which was just as well. It was decided not to tell the failing man. Mother did not want that burden. Better just to be with him and nurse him, holding out hope that it was just a big ulcer. It was hard to agree to this deception, but she knew best what would work, so he went up and was shocked at the frailness and weakness of the old warrior. The tough old man complained that he had never missed a day's work in his life, and now, when he had retired and they had moved to a pretty cottage in Thornton, just down the hill from the Brontë birthplace, he couldn't enjoy it. He had joined the lawn bowling team and the Conservative club; they could have played together in the father-son tournament. He watched a lot of television now. He hadn't liked the program: no one seemed to know what they wanted to say, he grumbled, and those women... What was happening to the world? What indeed. He didn't say they were bloody fools. He hadn't the energy.

The English reviews showed the same mix: hostile feminists, turf-defending social scientists, snotty humanists and friendly laymen - and women for that matter. The bad one from Geoffrey Gorer was predictable (they were "appealing to conservatism"); but Gorer was not even acceptable to the professional anthropologists. The worst was from Maureen Duffy, in the left *New Statesman,* who compared the book to *Mein Kampf.* Tom Rosenthal insisted on calling in the lawyers, and they gave the review to an eminent barrister. The libel expert said it might be hard to make a case because the review was so incoherent it would be hard to prove motive. Duffy said she only meant that the English didn't take ideas seriously and this got them into trouble (as with Hitler's memoir.) But the analogy was still there. She had a good point though. It was clear that their worst sin, to the English, was the ambitious nature of their ideas, not so much the content. British Empiricism lived. No ideas wanted. Take them to France or especially Germany where they liked this kind of thing.

The worst review came from Edmund Leach, and this really shook him. He had always thought of Leach as a kind of ally, with him in his admiration of Lévi-Strauss, willing to include his heterodox notions in the Totemism book, admiring of his thesis diagrams, and his analysis of the family at the CIBA conference, sharing his uncompromising rationalism. But the review (in *New Society* of all places) was bitter, sarcastic, and, like the others, incoherent. It wasn't clear what was objected to, except a lot of quibbling details on the one hand, and the whole enterprise on the other, and, of course, the standard accusation of "courting notoriety." Why would Leach think this was any less of an honest effort than all his previous work? Did he think the impressionable lad had been seduced by mammon and the Yanks? Probably. There was a lot of sneering anti-Americanism at Oxbridge, and in the chattering classes generally. Anyway, Leach was running his own campaign to be the darling of the *New Left Review* and its coteries. So he was showing the flag to his reference group. The basis of his objection, though, was largely territorial.

The social anthropologists were secure in their cozy little enterprise; they weren't about to switch ideologies at a nod from the neo-Darwinists. They objected to any attempt to dislodge their Durkheimian assumptions about the "autonomy" of the social. But to the Malinowskian from the LSE, they were the deviants. He was just a simple Malinowskian social anthropologist trying to carry out the master's mandate. The old Pole would have understood the effort as a logical extension of his theory of needs: Malinowski had no Durkheimian delusions about the autonomy of the social. But, as they say, it was the tone of the review that was disturbing. It was not measured argument—they never ever got that, it was curt, offhand dismissal of their work as "propaganda"—propaganda for what? Our man saw himself as pretty good-natured. He was not one to bear grudges—he had more or less kissed and made up with the blustering, but unmalicious Max. But Sir Edmund Leach, Provost of King's College Cambridge, was the one person he never would forgive.

Before they left England, they got a surprise invitation from Ariana Stassinopoulos. She had written an anti-feminist tract to counter Germaine Greer's *The Female Eunuch*, and had called it *The Female Woman*. She was one of a growing number of independent-minded women who objected to the feminists arrogantly assuming they automatically spoke for all their sex (as it was still called in England then.) Ariana objected even more to the portrayal of women as eternal victims, who could only be saved by ideological education and social handouts. Stop whining and start working was her formula. Women could succeed by their individual efforts, because they were better than men. The feminists accused her of being a traitor to the sisterhood, of course. They couldn't get straight the argument as to whether women were no different from men, or whether they were inherently better. If the latter, then this was an admission of content to human (sexual) nature, which the former denied. It was the anthropologists' dilemma over goodness and the tabula rasa, revisited. Ariana was having a publishing party in the basement of a Greek restaurant in Soho, which she had taken over for the purpose. Lionel could not go, but bearing a signed copy as a gift, our eager man turned up. There was Greek food, wine, music, brandy, and piles of cheap crockery to smash.

The hostess, looking like a younger Callas, was a delightfully blatant collector, and seated herself at a table with all the best-looking young men, and the guest of honor who was Kingsley Amis. As the brandy disappeared, the men descended into maudlin camaraderie, the plates were mostly smashed, and the band started up the *Never on Sundays* music yet again, Kingsley decided enough was enough. He recruited his fellow Yorkshireman, demanding to know if he'd had enough of this foreign rubbish too, and tackled the startled Greek musicians. "Do you know 'Ilkley Moor Baht 'At'? (The Yorkshire national anthem.) They did not. They did not even understand what he was saying. He gave each of them a five-pound note and told them to go home, sat down at the piano, and with the willing assistance of his befuddled acolyte started on the marathon that is all the verses of Ilkley Moor. "Where 'as ta bin sin ah saw thee/On Ilkla Moor baht 'at?" The respondent explains: " Ah bin a-courtin' Mary Jane"—without said hat. From the warning that he'll catch his death of cold, he is given a preview of how, like Hamlet's beggar through the guts of the King, they will all end up eating him (having eaten the ducks that ate up the worms, etc.)

> Then we sal all 'ave e'en thee,
> > On Ilkla Moor baht 'at.
> Then we sal all 'ave e'en thee,
> Then we sal all 'ave e'en thee,
> > On Ilkla Moor baht 'at,
> > On Ilkla Moor baht 'at,
> > On Ilkla Moor baht 'at.

It is almost impossible to convey in words that, despite the admittedly rousing tune, and, it must be said, on this occasion, the bravura of the piano accompaniment, the total recital of the unfortunate protagonist's distressful alimentary adventures is a saga of unrelieved tedium such as would try the patience of a sunbather. The audience voted with its feet. Ariana could not shake the duet loose from its avowed and dedicated purpose. They were left to perpetrate their drastic warblings until the waiters threw them out. He has no recollection further than sitting on the pavement edge and swearing eternal friendship, before he awoke, horribly hung-over, in the National Liberal Club the next morning. He asked the ever-tolerant porters if they remembered his coming in the night before. "Oh yes sir. Your friend delivered you in a taxi," they said. "Gave us a fiver and told us to put you to bed." He would have pursued the eternal and undying friendship, but he had a sinking feeling that dear Kingsley would probably not remember him the next day. It was too much like an episode from *Lucky Jim* to be real, or transposed into the real world. Best to keep the memory, and let it go.

Life went on. In Ireland "Bloody Sunday" saw fourteen demonstrators shot by British troops in Derry. This was bound to happen at some point. The crowd provokes the troops, the IRA snipers, hidden behind the crowd, open fire, the people get caught in between. Thus the cause has its martyrs and an occasion to prod the conscience of the enemy in endless "inquiries." His former ex-con Gaelic-teacher/IRA-gunman turned up in the American press, pictures and all, as a "simple civil rights worker" trying to do his pacifist best in the face of British persecution. The fanatics were in control again, on both sides.

Fanaticism has its own agenda, independent of the cause to which it attaches itself. President Goheen of Princeton enlisted Mason Gross's help in forming a National Faculty for McGovern Committee. They had a press conference and Mason asked him and few other faculty to come along to lend support. He was not all that enthusiastic about McGovern, whom he saw as a one-issue candidate, but everyone was getting desperate to end the war. He made the gesture. Despite his plan to avoid political involvement, events took over and urgencies developed that defeated calculated indifference. In Afghanistan, the King—actually the son of the old usurper, one Zahir Shah, was in trouble, and his Prime Minister (a relative of course) was threatening to usurp him in turn and declare a republic. His father had laughed. Depend on it, the Russians would be back, said the old Pathan fighter; not that they had ever left. The Great Game would be played out to the end of history; history would probably end in Afghanistan.

There had been no published outcome of the Wenner-Gren conference, since the young man appointed editor had gone over to the alternative culture with his wife who thought "the system" so evil the only thing to do was to commit suicide. But Bernard Campbell was producing a volume to celebrate the centennial of Darwin's *The Descent of Man, and Selection in Relation to Sex*. Campbell assembled a stellar cast, Ernst Caspari, Loren Eisley, George Gaylord Simpson, Theodosius Dobzhansky, Ernst Mayer, John Crook, and a young biologist from Harvard, Robert Trivers. Trivers had been along with Wilson at the Harvard gathering, and had also seemed enthusiastic. The young genius (and it was agreed he was a theoretical genius—of the order of Hamilton) had said that a lot of work in evolutionary genetics was giving a new boost to Darwin's notions on sexual selection. Trivers had said that the stuff on the evolution of equilibration via competitive breeding was at the heart of it, but needed rethinking. How, would be clear when his own piece came out.

Campbell had got the message, and he and Trivers would appear shoulder to shoulder, the younger man announcing his dramatic new theory of Parental

Investment. This investment was the key to holding the human mating pair together, because otherwise male and female reproductive strategies were poles apart—accounting for a lot of male-female differences. But the helpless human infant needed "investment" from the parents, and the "father" had a genetic interest in providing it. So did the mother's brother, he told Trivers. Yes, but that was twenty-five percent as opposed to fifty. Trivers wanted to look comparatively at species with "High PI" and "Low PI" to find the underlying laws, which were quantifiable in that particular "qualitative math" used by evolutionary genetics. (Zuckerman used to say that when he came upon these equations, he hummed them.) It was in the Hamilton genre: he couldn't do it, but he found it admirable. To his own "soft" argument would be added the tough stuff from Bob, whose single-minded devotion to his work, dangerous indifference to mundane things, and passion for social justice, were already getting him called (fondly) "crazy Bob."

His own piece for Campbell tried to drive on with the argument about equilibration and brain evolution, bringing it into the most elementary of kinship systems (the Australian Aborigines) and how they worked. He worked out a basic scheme of three "blocks" of the primate social system. (He was thinking of building blocks, but editors kept changing it to "blocs" on the political model.) There was the block of males with their hierarchies, the block of females with their young, and the block of young males, who had left the female group and were bucking for membership in the male block. The secret of the transition to humanity lay in changes in the transactions between the blocks. The basic structure stayed the same, but instead, for example of mere equilibration determining the chances of young males getting into the hierarchy, initiation was added. Instead of all animals getting their own food, after the hunting transition the hominid males traded animal protein with the females for vegetable matter, thus giving rise to a cooperative division of labor. But above all, from his perspective, kinship ceased merely to *link* the three blocks together. Kinship became the basis for the *allocation* of women, as mates, among the men of the male block. This was exogamy: define groups of kin and marry out of them, making rules about the exchange of spouses with other such groups. Without the growth of the neo-cortex as a result of the polygamous breeding system, this could not have happened. But why did it happen in the evolving hominid line?

He took Freud's point about exogamy among the Australian Aborigines being an elaborate device to control the sexuality of the young. He re-wrote this as a device to control the *mating choices* of the young. (In this sense the device was part of the initiation process.) He showed how extreme this form of control was with the Australian Aborigines and their gerontocratic polygamy, where the old men cornered the young wives down to baby girls, and how it was built into the rules of marriage themselves. He had thoroughly accepted Warren's revision of his Murngin hypothesis, (this was science) and now set out to show the effects of exchanging sisters' daughters' daughters with men of the same moiety. (Or, more correctly, bestowing the sister's daughter as a mother-in-law on the appropriate moiety mate.) He produced diagrams of this that Roy thought were "beautiful." Campbell was alarmed. Biologists won't understand. Neither, countered the battle-scarred cynic, will anthropologists appreciate the sexual selection arguments. It is, he said, my fate to fall between these two stools. If there are two stools to fall between, fall I will. I can only put it out there for the record. Someone will get it, and maybe even find the missing link that synthesizes all the pieces. Perhaps Caspari will do the genetics of it. That was the plan, and Campbell went with it in the end. But the publisher made a crucial mistake with the first diagram, and then refused to print an erratum slip.

The Watergate scandal became the national pastime. How the peripherals love to see the dominant male fall, and how they then panic and want another right away to replace him. Why, in the late twentieth century, the century of science and technology and flights to the moon, were we still obsessed with this idea that we needed *one male* at the head of things? He could never get anyone to take the question seriously. A single President as "head of the executive" was not a fact of the man-made Constitution, it was fact of Nature. Why didn't they throw that idea out with the King? They voted George Washington powers that King George would have sacrificed his first-born to get. Then they let him appoint all his cronies to his personal "cabinet" leaving the elected officials to fume across the way. And what was the point of a second elected chamber to duplicate the first? Why not have a deliberative senate composed of the best minds available to us, rather than yet more politicians obsessed with being re-elected? And what was democratically representative about a second chamber where tiny states like Delaware and Rhode Island each sent two senators the same as California and Texas?

On and on he went, while listeners slipped away like players at the end of the Haydn symphony (where they blew the candles out.) What kind of system returns ninety-eight percent of incumbents? A one-party totalitarian regime, obviously? No. Our very own plutocracy. And what about the blatant juggling of electoral boundaries to produce "districts" that bore no relationship to any social or geographical units? When this was done in Northern Ireland by the Protestants it was violently condemned as "gerrymandering." When it was done here by the majorities in the State Senates, it was called "redistricting." What was representative about this system? The President's cronies who were making most of the decisions in this supposed democracy were not elected by the people at all.

This particular failing infuriated Virginia, who hated the unelected Kissinger with a passion, and who would have preferred to be in Canada were it not so far from New York. She had sent the Campbell piece to William Golding, initiating an irregular correspondence between the anthropologist and the fabulist, who was to provide epigraphs and insights for a lot of future work. In the meantime, Archibald Cox and the folksy Sam Ervin became the archetypal heroes, and Haldeman, Ehrlichman and Liddy, and the snitch John Dean, the appropriately sleazy villains in the national soap opera. Did the President know? Only the tapes would tell. The rest...

But what difference would it all make? He despaired of democracy and the corruption of politicians:

> The democratic roundabout
> Makes sure the people never win,
> For if they throw the rascals out
> They vote the other rascals in.

Obviously a benevolent despotism was the better solution, as long as you had a truly enlightened despot. But we know the problems with that, or with a class of enlightened guardians. Still, he was the child of Burke and Popper (and Oakeshott for that matter): you had to patch and mend the existing institutions; there was no formula for redoing the whole thing from scratch.

Even a department started from scratch soon became a set of compromises and jury-rigged contrivances, as the vicious egos thrashed around like piranhas in a tank. New agendas surfaced. Lee decided to make an issue of Kling's use of prisoners for psychiatric experiments. It was a good deal for the prisoners: they gave time doing some tests, and in return got free psychiatric care from Kling's team. But Richard needed an issue for his chronic activism to work on. His sidekick was in trouble for dumping a pot of paint on the statue of Teddy Roosevelt outside the Natural History Museum. Richard could not be upstaged by a junior, so did his number about the prisoners being "political prisoners" and Kling the tool of the capitalist-fascist exploiters etc. But the founding chairman was learning. Absolutely right, he announced at the college meeting: Dr. Lee is correct. This is a fascist state and all of us are tools of the system. There is no way we can continue to take the dirty money they pay us, and until they stop this exploitation, we must, as matter of grave principle, refuse to take our salaries from the fascists. He would propose a motion to that end, and expected Dr. Lee to second it. Dr. Lee had sudden second thoughts, and the motion was tabled for further discussion, which never came.

But Richard did take up the noble cause of the oppressed when the black lady musicologist's temporary appointment officially ended. This was, naturally, a "racist" arrangement, for "racist" had now come to mean not the attribution of genetic inferiority to racial groups, but rather anything that was not agreeable to black people (or more particularly the white activists.) Richard pushed the Dean to insist that "it would be politically impossible to fire a faculty member who was both a woman and black." You're not firing her; it was a temporary appointment. It was in the Dean's discretion to rehire her, but he compromised: he would put her in the music department. Fine. Kling knew of a first-class graduate student working on primate brains and behavior at Berkeley—Dieter Steklis. Dieter would fit perfectly what the NIMH program needed. The Graduate School offered a line. Margaret Bacon, who had been quietly efficient until then, suddenly emerged as a champion of "affirmative action" (the newest buzz-phrase to emerge) and insisted that the appointment should go to a woman. There was no woman even working in this area. That did not matter, she said when a "higher" principle was involved. The row was awful. They got their way because the line was in Dean Torrey's gift, and he was perhaps the last of the Dean's who thought an appointment should be of the best person for the job regardless of what was becoming called, erroneously, "gender." Richard announced that he was leaving along with his paint-throwing sidekick. No one wept.

He married Genie. It was not a wise thing to do, with hindsight; but what is wise with hindsight? When two people live passionately together for long enough, however glaring the incompatibilities, it seems the obvious thing. Tarn was the best man at the little ceremony at the Unitarian church. He gave them a self-illuminated manuscript of one of his poems (about sleeping with Miss America before she got married) to frame, as his present. The girls liked their stepmother and sister. They had a new house (it was the original Princeton hospital, which had been moved) and a new home, and a new stab at a settled life. They could make plans, which at this point had to include, except for poor Anne, a large dose of horses and horse fairs and competitions. This was the place for it. Great horse country, western New Jersey, ask the widow Kennedy. Things were on track again.

Out of the blue. Mason Gross had retired, and had been made President of the Harry Frank Guggenhiem Foundation in New York. Harry Guggenheim— of the mineral-rich Guggenheim Brothers, had been involved in all the Foundations that bear that name, but set up his own, without a clear idea of what he wanted. He consulted with Charles Lindbergh and General Jimmy Doolittle (Ten-Minutes-Over-Tokyo Doolittle), and decided it should devote itself to "Man's Relationship to Man" although it was not clear how. Nothing much happened under Harry's heir, Peter Lawson-Johnston (his mother was a Guggenheim), but Henry Allen Moe, who had been president of the American Philosophical Society was called in, and he had had talks with Bob Ardrey among others.

When Mason became president, Skinner's *Beyond Freedom and Dignity* had just come out, and Mason read it and didn't like it. He thought its view of human nature was bleak and quite wrong. Then he got his copy of *The Imperial Animal*. He saw it immediately as the creative counterweight to the dismal behaviorism of Skinner. What is more, it fit in with Harry's notion, supported by Moe, that any study of human behavior and society must recognize as basic "man's tendency to want to dominate other men." Harry was, as they were saying, "sensitized" to this dimension. One of the most typical Harry stories told of his refusing, during the depression, to drive a humble car to his Wall Street office (from Long Island) so as not to arouse antagonism. Harry was what he was, and wasn't about to be hypocritical about it. As his luxury vehicle arrived one day, a large crowd of unemployed gathered, shaking fists and shouting: "Capitalist! Capitalist!" Harry shook his umbrella and shouted back: "Flatterers! Flatterers!"

Mason called him on the phone: bring Lionel to the house in Rumsen, New Jersey. Bring swimsuits: they would go to the beach club for lunch. Mason's house at the shore was old and comfortable, with two grand pianos for him and his wife to play duets, and a large, baronial hallway lined with English rowing prints. Over burgers at the pool he asked them to come up with a program for the foundation. Were there enough people working in their field for a grant program to be feasible? Surely. And once a grant program was announced, there would be many more. Plenty of young people found it hard to get grants from the Foundations for this kind of innovative work. It was well known that NSF would only give grants for projects that had already been done before: the criterion of "replicability" effectively kept innovative work at arms length. They thought of Wilson and Trivers, of Chance and DeVore, of Jane Goodall and David Hamburg, of Desmond Morris and Nick Blurton Jones (now studying birth-spacing among the Bushmen), of their own Joseph Shepher and Ray Larsen, Kling and McGuire, and many others in the natural, social and behavioral sciences who needed support. Draw up the plans, said Mason. They hit the Olivetti and drew up the plans, and God saw that they were good, and God only smiled a little.

It was decided. The board liked it. They were, among others, Roger Strauss, the publisher, James Gavin, the general who took the bridge at Neijmhagen, the immortal Doolittle, William Baker, president of Bell Labs, James Edwards, ex-governor of North Carolina, and Ed. Pendray, who became their special friend, and who was one of those visionaries instrumental (with Goddard) in creating the US space program. They had a problem with the secretary, George Fountaine, an old-timer and long-time faithful retainer of the family, who could not grasp that the new "Research Directors" would work with relative autonomy and no day-to-day accountability. This was not how "business" operated. George was a Brooklynite who had come up the hard way. He told tales of the depression when he and his brothers used to play semi-pro basketball "to help put a little money on the family table." Kids didn't do that these days. When the new directors of research told him their own childhood tales of surviving the depression in less than easy circumstances, he warmed a little towards them.

An office was constructed from rooms in the basement of Lionel's town house. They had a policy that was deliberately counter to the prevailing practice in the foundations. They required from applicants only a brief statement of research plans and purposes, and two reference letters. If people sent them obvious, egregiously overdone national foundation applications, they sent them back and asked for a summary in English. They did not pay the forty-percent overheads that universities demanded to fund their overblown administrations. The appalled deans protested, but they never refused to let their employees take the money for research. They did not give "summer salaries"—those phony wage boosters, but only money dedicated directly to research. They preferred innovative, even risky, research to that which replicated previous work. They may have been the only foundation to tell an applicant he had not asked for enough money to do the job properly, and insist he take more.

They vetted each application personally and wrote a report and recommendation to the Board. Their ratio of expenses to grants was the lowest for any foundation on record; the Wenner-Gren people, castle, townhouse and all, couldn't believe it could be done. There was enough even so to hold a grand bash at the Guggenheim museum each year, and to enjoy seeing many semi-inebriated friends, allies and admirers, saunter dizzily round Frank Lloyd Wright's circular spiral widening-gyre extravaganza. George Fountaine took them afterwards as his guests to the Playboy Club, where Gloria Steinem was working undercover as a Bunny to expose the "exploitation" of her sister Bunnies. These same Bunnies never forgave her for what they saw as her perfidy. The boys often wondered if the one giving them their drinks with the bunny dip (and the cute little tail) was Gloria. It was hard to tell with the ears and all. They were all pretty.

After a couple of false starts the busy duo got a star secretary in the form of Karyl Roosevelt (ex-wife of William, son of Franklin) who sub-let Robert Altmann's apartment in The Village. She could touch type a dictated manuscript at prize-winning speed, while reading a novel and answering the speakerphone. She was from Colorado, and had been educated in Italy, where she married an aristocrat and had virtually to escape from the castle and claustration by the family, returning to Radcliffe. She had worked for Saul Bellow, in Chicago. He used to dictate his novels to her (she could type faster than even he could talk) while staring at her over the desk. He would watch for her reaction; if she didn't like it, he threw it out and started over. She wrote to Bellow about one of her new employers, saying that he knew Gilbert and Sullivan and great swaths of Swinburne and Browning by heart. Bellow replied, saying she should never have deserted him, and that her new employer sounded like a real jerk.

Steven-the-editor had moved to Harcourt, Brace, Jovanovitch; they moved around all the time in the publishing world. Steven wanted to follow up on the success, as he saw it, of the book, and bring out something else quickly. Strike while the iron... etc. How about a book of essays? I'm too young to have a "collected essays" protested our modest fellow; it's embarrassing. Not at all countered Steven: put them together in sections with little introductions, and write a general introduction and conclusion, and there you have another book. I don't have enough stuff. Don't you have some unpublished lectures? Yes, but they were not to be published since they were good lectures. They'll find a bigger audience in a book. The *Times* articles? Great as openers. Tougher stuff later. There was the CIBA paper on the family; a piece on kinship for a French encyclopedia that L-S had liked; the two *New Society* pieces on Tory and Cochiti; the lecture on "Marriage and Modern Literature" that perhaps should see print at last; ditto the one on Tory ritual fighting. There were the early articles from *Man;* the Pueblo baseball story that shouldn't remain hidden in an obscure journal; the long account of Amerindian religion... Perhaps it was not such a crazy idea. It will be a great "Introduction to Anthropology" without being a textbook, said Steven. The kids will love it; the public will love it. Start on the introduction: you can make your point about where Anthropology is stuck and where it should be going. It all had to be passed by Mr. Jovanovitch, who was never seen, but who ruled. (He probably had a first name, but he was always "Mr. Jovanovitch.") He liked the introduction ("very fine") but said (in a note) "Make it more personal. Write about how you became an anthropologist. After all, it isn't an obvious thing to do." More to the point, said Steven, write about why you stay an anthropologist, given your frustrating encounters. That gave them the title: *Encounter with Anthropology.*

Dieter Steklis came, and started on his brain, hormone and behavior research. They went with Kling to St. Kitts, where Frank Ervin (co-author of *Violence and the Brain*) was both catching vervet monkeys for sale to research labs, and helping to run a research compound where Dieter and Mike McGuire did their work. Our pale northern boy stayed out too long in the sun and was horribly afflicted. He lay in the shade swathed in iced towels, and watched the forest vervets nearby, who displayed the rank order of their males in an exact fashion by where they sat on the branches: top males, top branches. Mike explained that those below were subject to a constant drip: this was rain forest. There was a great initiative to rise in rank. Mike and his colleagues wrote a book on the St. Kitts vervet, and when Prince Charles visited the island republic, he was given a copy by the proud government. It perhaps reminded the student prince of his days in Anthropology at Cambridge. When the delirium was over, they took a native boat out to a promontory to see the vervets there. On the way back, at twilight, the old engine broke down. "De plugs is wet," explained the men, and took the damp plugs out to dry them. Kling panicked as they drifted out of sight of land: "We're going to die: we're all going to die!" But they sang calypsos, and talked of cricket, and drank rum and got merry, and eventually the men put the plugs in a can, poured gas

over them and lighted it. The flames terrified Arthur, but it did the job. Land ho, and back to goat curry and more rum and coke.

Rutgers College hired its three anthropologists. They were all good enough at what they did; one was a paleontologist, another a linguist. It was not so bad; they added to the graduate program. But they also tended to develop territorial urges, and thought of themselves as Rutgers College first and the program second, with potentially bad consequences. A coup was engendered, largely by Yehudi's initiative, when Pete Vayda, along with two colleagues, decided to leave a faltering Columbia department. Cook College (Agriculture and Environmental Sciences) was happy to have them as the nucleus of a Human Ecology Department. Fine, unless they too developed chronic territoriality. They did soon enough. It was all both energizing and depressing. You couldn't get people to work together. Selfish interests always took precedence in the end, whatever lip service might be paid to the greater good. The duo tended to withdraw more and more into the Foundation, especially when those more than generous people agreed to pay half their salaries in return for half-time off for research and Foundation work. Mason was a benevolent Magus, and Dean Torrey a kindly father figure. But his misery with the messiness of his colleagues' emotionality, and their enduring selfishness and willingness to put their fanatical agendas above the good of the general will, drove him away from them and into himself.

Like the return of the repressed, poetry re-surfaced and the muse took him for her own. He wrote a long poem for William Golding ("What the Hunter Saw.") The great fabulist always dealt with societies that were on the verge of some fatal change. So his fan described one in which a dying Paleolithic hunter comes upon a Neolithic farming town—a kind of Pueblo, and interrupts an animal sacrifice. He sees in the straight lines, the golden corn, the silver jewelry (like clinking ice), the structured priestly ceremony, and the pointless killing of an animal for something other than food, a disturbing vision of what is to come. The townspeople ("How can they be so slender, men and girls?") hear him singing his death-song ("nasal high sending/to hills sky plain herds all the listeners/beyond beneath) and they react:

> The graciles hear freeze
> horror surround horror hiss sacrilege
> surround
>   Feral one hill brute filthy thing
> surround close stab crawl stab roll stab
> Blood closes eyes laughter clinking ice
> How could they be so slender still give birth?
>
> They left him for the buzzards but at night
> the women came and took him to the hills

Nixon beat McGovern—humiliated him, which wasn't surprising. McGovern hadn't really tried. Like those arrogant English socialists, he thought his message so obviously superior that people would just flock to his standard. But the voters want to hear and see their candidates. McGovern was in New York, hobnobbing with poets and academics, when the faculty committee asked him to come to New Jersey and talk with the influential black leaders in Newark. No, said the lofty one, they know my position: if they agree with it they'll vote for me. He lost New Jersey. In fact McGovern lost everywhere but Massachusetts and the District of Columbia, which says something. But all was overwhelmed into insignificance when the message came that his father had not long to live. He dropped everything and went, but as he telephoned home from Heathrow, he heard it was too late. He cried a little in the telephone booth, largely from relief of tension, and left his raincoat there as he went off for the tube. It wasn't that he didn't have feelings. Yes, he was sorry, but somehow he thought he should be wracked to the depths of his being with the news, and he wasn't. He felt numb, helpless, puzzled and not a little guilty.

He had spent a lot of his life being taught to worship the warrior, and a lot more being taught to hate the man, for reasons that were never all that clear to him, except that he didn't live up to her expectations. (There had been "another woman" during the war, and the father had done the classic mix-up with the letters.) He didn't want to hate him, but he had nothing much in common with him except a love of sports. Even there his father was a devotee of soccer, which he didn't much like. They went together to the local games at Bradford City sometimes, but the father liked to stand with the crowd on the Spion Kop, while the son wanted to sit in the cheaper of the stands. Cricket they had shared, with his father umpiring games for the Erratics at Exeter, and they had been a good father-son lawn bowls team (father taking the brunt of the strategic decisions—("Left bias; go wide of him. Bloody hell!") But he never knew his father, and the man remained an enigma, a stranger almost. He loved him in the way we do a kind parent, whatever the circumstances. But the guilt was always there. Somehow he had failed, and it was too late to put it right.

People rallied round. His mother was brave and organized, although she had suffered a lot through the last nursing. "He got very tired. Wouldn't even try to get up. In the end he just turned his face to the wall and said, "I'm buggered." That was it. He'd only had a year of his retirement." All her past animosity was gone, evaporated, almost forgotten. (She would occasionally refer to "When we had that bit of trouble with your daddy.") They would cremate him and spread the ashes over the garden he had tended behind the cottage. The undertakers were genuinely decent and helpful people. They made up the corpse and invited them to see the handiwork. He went in alone, and knelt by the coffin, looked at the composed face, kissed the stone-hard cold, cold forehead, and said he was sorry. He went to see his old music master.

T. H. was approaching total blindness, but was as enthusiastic as ever about music, and life. "You were lucky," said Tojo, "you were a bit shaky for a while, but your mother pushed and your father didn't interfere. You were lucky." The vicar of Thornton would do the C. of E. ceremony. Father's religion had been formal, not theological—the social religion of the English, but he had never said he wasn't C. of E. even though he denied the idea of resurrection. "Six feet under. That's it." The Conservative Club flew the flag at half-mast; Sir Kenneth did the same at the mill; so did the school, in honor of a dead parent who had always served loyally on the Old Parents Committee. They informed the regiment, and got a nice letter and a promise there too to lower the flag, and play the last post. He was glad he didn't have to hear it. Then he would have wept seriously, for all the dead soldiers: the soldiers who had been his friends.

Relatives he knew turned up, including fateful cousin Mike who had left the theater, gone to the LSE and got his own degree, married and had children, and was now a teacher in Essex. Relatives he had never known turned up, including his cousin John, named after the father, a sign painter in Haworth. The words of the Anglican service brought back all the feelings of his childhood, miss-spent in graveyards on wet afternoons, with half-a-dozen black-clad, crying, pitiful people. "So when this corruptible shall have put on incorruption, and this mortal shall have put on immortality; then shall be brought to pass the saying that is written, Death is swallowed up in victory. O death where is they sting? O grave where is thy victory." His father had made fun of it, singing: "The bells of hell go ding-a-ling-a-ling for you and not for me/ O death where is thy sting-a-ling-a-ling, O grave thy victoree?" Now it was too late for the son, and he was guilty, and he was sorry, and he didn't know how he was supposed to feel, except that it ought to be more, and it wasn't.

He went to see the newfound cousin in Haworth as part of the usual pilgrimage. They discussed the aesthetics of sign painting: pub signs gave the most scope for the imagination. They drank together in the Black Bull and the Crossroads Inn and talked of Branwell, and old man Patrick, and Mrs. Gaskell's infamies, and the Worth Valley Railway with its rejuvenated steam trains, and other local things. They remembered the local sport the lads enjoyed of misdirecting southern tourists (Charlotte's "lisping cockneys") who asked the way to "Wethering Hates." The helpful lads would cheerfully send them off into some trackless bog and collapse laughing behind a dry-stone wall. It was raining and cold (of course) when he went into the parsonage. He was a life member of the Society and could have gone in free, but he always paid his two-shillings anyway; it was little enough. He looked out, from Emily's tiny room, at the churchyard, and remembered the poem Matthew Arnold wrote there about the three sisters. He thought he should write one for his father, but nothing came. Still, if the species was a fossil of itself, so was the person: whatever he was, the quiet man was in there somewhere, if he could ever find him. Somewhere, in the still eye of the subconscious storm, the dead warrior hovered, a memento mori, whispering in the soul's inner ear: "Don't be a bloody fool."

When he got back he decided that if there was a genetic predisposition to cancer, he ought not to help it along. Pipe smokers had thought themselves free from lung cancer, and their risk was lower than with cigarettes since they didn't inhale, but they did swallow the gunk, and stomach cancer could ensue. He gave his pipe racks and pipes to the chain-smoking Yehudi, his humidors and cigars to Lionel, and stopped the smoking dead. To be truthful, he enjoyed a cigar on his birthday and at Christmas and left it at that.

A strange package came from Derek Freeman, who had been quiet until then. He was, among other things, tracking Margaret Mead's earnings, and had calculated she had made "one hundred thousand dollars from her Samoan fantasies alone." She was a "penis-envying female" too busy courting popular success to get anything right. Included in the package was a multi-page document carefully listing hundreds of Samoan words in three columns: the English translation; the correct orthography of the Samoan; and Maggie's erroneous transcriptions. "She says we have obligations to the people we study. One of them is to record their language properly." Derek wanted to know who might publish his long list of corrections "to set the record straight." Just about nobody, he told the Messiah. Perhaps some obscure journal of Polynesiology might be interested, but don't try the regular journals; they surely have more important things to publish, and no one wants to offend Maggie anyway. She's the queen; you don't insult the queen. That seemed to be that. Why then did he think this was not the last we would hear of this anti-Maggie jihad?

There was a flurry of activity when Rodney Needham, in a fit of frustration with Oxford, and especially his miserable salary as a lecturer, decided he wanted to move to the States. His preference was the U. of Virginia, whose ambience, Rodney announced, was the closest in the USA to that of Oxford. But Virginia wasn't keen, for reasons never revealed: because on paper Rodney was certainly a catch. One Virginia faculty member let drop that they thought Rodney was "a bit uptight." Dave Schneider wrote gleefully that he would write Rodney a splendid reference for somewhere that needed to have a lesson taught: Harvard was high on the list. But our gallant little optimist decided that Rodney's personality problems were exaggerated; all he needed was the right place to be and some prestige and support. Rodney desperately wanted to be a professor, but he could scarcely step down from Oxford to accept a provincial university chair, even if one had been available. An American professorship, however, being outside the English system, could be seen as a step sideways rather than down.

Rodney too had wife problems. She was French and his complete opposite: a wispy, fey, distracted woman, who didn't seem able to cope with the world. On a visit to their humble college flat in Longwall Street, he was thrust into a scene out of Iris Murdoch, where *distrait* wife had been sent out to get chops to feed the boys, whom Rodney adored and overprotected. She forgot what she was out for, and came back, like king Leopold to the peasants, bearing lilies. She was upset with herself, but somehow unmoved by the practical problem of eating. Exasperated Rodney announced that he would leave them to each other while he went to supervise the boys' prep (they went to The Dragon School.) The decidedly awkward guest could only offer small talk, and help arrange the flowers. He was struck by the thought that she must have been very pretty as a young girl, back in her own country, in her real setting. He offered to go get some chops.

Rodney was interested in Princeton, and the gentlemen's school would have suited him, certainly, but no dice. Why not Rutgers? He could, like all the Rutgers profs who could afford it, live in Princeton, and the boys could go to Princeton Day School: not the Dragon, but not bad either. Wife would like the European colony in the town, at that point revolving around the elegant Stuart Hampshire, one of the Penguin philosophers doing his own brain-drain stint. ("He *is* Lord Peter Wimsey," said Dick Rorty.) Rodney looked up Rutgers in the encyclopedia, and when he found it was the eighth oldest college in the country, and saw the chapel and the imposing colonial Old Queens building, and had a jovial lunch with the powers in the faculty club, he warmed to the idea. Initially the department was enthusiastic. Chet Lancaster told the faculty meeting that Rodney was "a leading theorist"—Richard Lee liked the idea because Rodney was at odds with Lévi-Strauss. So the ever confident Rodney came to Livingston to present the ritual paper. It was on "Rethinking Kinship and Marriage"—the introduction to a book he was editing on that topic, and it was Rodney at his negative and destructive and hypercritical best/worst.

The result was disaster. Everyone was totally put off. The graduate students, who had not been at the paper, actually liked Rodney the man, who talked to them at a get-together in an easy and interested way about communes and their fragility, and drank beer and listened to Simon and Garfunkel LPs and eight-tracks of *Switched-On Bach,* which he liked, Moog Synthsizer and all. A definitely engaging, human side emerged, and it was obvious why his students could be very loyal to him, but it was too late. Lancaster and Lee took off against him, and the others (except for Warren) joined the nay vote. It didn't matter, since Rodney decided to stay at Oxford anyway. Evans-Pritchard was close to retirement, and there was only one possible internal successor.

The Association of Social Anthropologists made a truly nice gesture (evidently over Leach's objections) to invite him to organize a session on "Ethology and Social Anthropology" at the next (twenty-fifth anniversary?) meeting in Oxford. The sponsor was Edwin Ardener, someone he didn't know well and had always found decidedly odd. Edwin had some kind of fringe appointment at Oxford, having never taken a Ph.D. The latter was, unlike in the humanities in England, more or less *de rigueur* in anthropology, since it certified that you had done the necessary fieldwork. But somehow Edwin hung in there, and became one of the organizers and movers. Whatever his origins, Edwin had affected the mask of the Max Beerbohm ultimate-Oxford character: squeaky, too-precise voice, goatee, and all. Still, Edwin had pushed for this session, and the letters flew as the team was assembled: himself of course with his primate kinship ponderings, and Lionel naturally, who was now hot on "somatic states"—particularly hormones, and behavior. They must also have Nick Blurton Jones and his birth spacing and birth control, and a contact via Lorenz, Norbert Bischoff, who was working on animal dispersion and incest avoidance. The point of incest avoidance, thought Bischoff, was not so much the reduction of inbreeding dangers, as the sheer reduction of genetic variation it involved. Sexual reproduction evolved in the first place to foster such variation. Incest defeated the whole point of having sex in the first place.

Bill Hamilton had shown that you did get serious incest only in creatures like tree lice living in totally controlled conditions under the bark. Since there was no "environmental perturbation" they had no use for variation and so produced virtual clones of themselves through constant brother-sister matings: the exception proving the rule. Better then have Bill as well, even if he did tend to bemuse the anthropologists with his equations and wanderings through the paradoxes of the "prisoner's dilemma"—offshoot of that "game theory" our undergraduate learned from Hare and the moral philosophers, itself an offshoot of Princeton poker games. Round it out with Michael Chance and his latest on "attention structure" in primates, and there would be a pretty strong attention-getting presentation. It would be published. He would have to edit and introduce it. Perhaps this would make the academic critics a bit more respectful. Perhaps.

He was glad also to make a gesture to Michael Chance, who was stuck in relative obscurity with his pharmacists in Birmingham. There was no chair in Ethology there, and Michael would be a Reader for the rest of his days. These were still the days when it really mattered to be a Professor in Europe. It was, in the Germanic countries, like a title of nobility: *Herren* Professor Doctor... (The German title of their book was to be *Das Herrentier*: a nice pun since this was the word used in German for "primate" but which literally mean "the noble animal.") He had been to Upsaala where, at the inauguration of a professor, they had a public procession in full academic dress, led by the mayor and the town dignitaries, a service in the Cathedral, all the city bells ringing, and cannons sounding from the castle, with feasting until midnight. The professorial handle had meant something to him too, until he discovered that, unlike at the Harvard he knew, everyone in American academe used the blessed title. Even the lowliest assistant professor insisted on being called, and was called, "professor"—which took all the status out of the word, reducing it to the French "prof", a teacher of anything. (*"Professeur de Plonger"* for a diving teacher.) This passion for titles he thought unseemly in a nation that had officially abolished them.

But the hierarchical principle was ruthless, as Michael insisted. Every two-man car-sales company had its "president" and "vice-president"; the university had "vice presidents" for just about everything including garbage collection, and soon sprouted assistant and associate vice-presidents, and then of course senior vice-presidents, and even executive vice-presidents. Everyone in a publishing house was a "senior editor." Despite the official democratization, they loved titles; government officials were addressed by them in positively Scandinavian fashion: "Secretary Kissinger," "Ambassador Moynihan," "Director Hoover," "Speaker O'Neill," "Governor Cahill," "Chairman... Whomever." But the department could at least give Michael the opportunity to hear himself called "Professor Chance" and let him have a "visiting professorship" to put on his curriculum vitae. Michael struck up a rapport with Ray Larsen, dog, Leonard Cohen, and all, and they planned a book together on attention structure. Some things were just very good.

Leonard Cohen ran like a river through the valley of the shadow of their lives. His songs haunted them; stories of him amused them. The Montreal expatriates in Manhattan—all friends of Lionel's, included a successful actress and translator, Suzanne Grossman. Suzanne had been a huge success with an adaptation of Feydeau's perfect farce, *Un pouce à l'oreille—A Flea in His Ear*. She told wonderful Feydeau stories. The farceur was both a passionate devotee of beautiful women, and a very, very lazy man. He would settle himself in his favorite chair in his favorite bistro, and hold court, never wanting to move once settled. He was sitting thus with his back to the door, when his friends chorused in astonishment at a spectacular woman who had just come in. They insisted he look at her. He was paralyzed with indecision, then said with anguished finality: "Describe her to me!" Suzanne, who was herself quietly beautiful, was thought to be the inspiration for the Cohen song that Ray Larsen (in the version by Judy Collins) played all the time at parties:

> Suzanne takes you down
> To her place by the river
> You can hear the boats go by
> You can spend the night beside her...

The American Puritan censors struck again here, and the disc had to have the meaningless: "spend the night forever."

> And she brings you tea and oranges
> That come all the way from China...

And on in that vein. Suzanne was very annoyed by the song. She was a well brought up, Montreal bourgeois girl, of a strict and respectable Swiss-German family, and would never have dreamed of wearing rags and feathers from Salvation Army counters, and could speak very well for herself without needing to let the river answer (that you'd always been her lover.) She only got to go out with the troubadour, she insisted, because her German name allowed Leonard to pass her off to his mother as a nice Jewish girl. She was good, though, at adapting for television, and she liked our ex-historian's notion of a play for the upcoming bi-centennial celebrations, to be called *The Trial of George Washington.* Premise: Washington loses at Yorktown and is taken to London where he is tried for treason. Weave a nice plot about dirty politics (Ben Franklin and Charles James Fox the villains; Edmund Burke and Geoffrey Amherst the heroes) with the trial itself, which puts, naturally, the whole idea of revolution on trial. There would be appearances by Jefferson and Adams (for the defense) and Sir Benedict Arnold and Judge Jonathan Sewall, for the prosecution. George III (played by Peter Ustinov at his most sniffy) to get an appearance—brief. They tucked the idea away as something to work on nearer the time.

Life moved on. Raymond retired from the chair at the LSE, and there was a flurry of demand, largely from the grassroots, that he apply for the vacancy. He had called in there on the way back from the funeral, and seen his old friend Jeffrey, now a lecturer, who took him to the latest LSE review, a sad, amateur affair, where the students did a watered-down, un-costumed version of the Webb satire—"Two Sleepy People." Somehow the text had been preserved. None of the students knew where it came from. It had passed into the tradition as from time immemorial. So be it. "Have you come about the chair?" they all asked. No, he had not. Need he list all the reasons it was impossible? They gave it finally to a ho-hum Africanist. That kills that, he thought. Noel Annan (elevated to the Lords) had written from University College. They needed someone to succeed Daryll Forde, someone dedicated to anthropology as a holistic discipline, to hold together the physical and archaeological divisions with the social. He couldn't do it. He simply could not leave the children apart from anything else; and he had to give the Foundation a chance. He gave Lord Annan a reluctant no, for he would, ordinarily, have liked UCL as his Benthamite, rationalist home in London. A. J. Ayer had told them that he held the Grote chair in the Philosophy of Mind and Logic at UCL, on the condition that he had no religious convictions. Ayer now had a chair at Anglican Oxford—his lack of convictions being presumably overlooked. When the great philosopher was first introduced to the lady who became his second wife, she prattled on to him about rabbits in hats, disappearing doves, and the like. "No, no! I said *log*ician, not *mag*ician."

The old guard was passing. Sir Edward Evan Evans-Pritchard had retired as professor at Oxford, and to everyone's surprise, Maurice Freedman had been elected as the new incumbent. Freedman was probably a compromise candidate, since Rodney was the internal successor, but no one wanted him in charge. Even so, Freedman had an idea: take your sabbatical and come for a year to Oxford. They are trying to set up a "Human Sciences" tripos, and the anthropologists could use your input, he said. (Even the English were saying "input" now.) Why not? But he would not use up the sabbatical he was owed; he didn't want to fight that battle right now. He and Lionel struck a deal: rather than both being off half time, he could take the next year off, and Lionel would take the year after. He could fly back each term to deal with the grant applications for a week or so: there were cheap midweek fares then, and the Foundation would pay. So it was set.

He would not have done it except that Anne's asthma, even freed from the secondary smoke which must have done it no good, was getting so serious, maybe even fatal, that the doctors didn't think she should stay near the river with the damp and the pollution. But where to go? What about the English seaside? Pure, unpolluted air—bracing sea breezes, might not that work? The doctors could guarantee nothing—so what was new? But the maternal relatives could organize a rental house on the south coast near Brighton and Worthing—right on the beach. Anything was worth trying, and if he could be at Oxford it was only a train ride away (well, two train rides). The grandmothers would be delighted to be closer. At least it was doing something; it was "taking steps" rather than suffering the misery of not knowing what to do. It was settled.

The Oxford conference was certainly fun, although their session bombed—through no fault of their own. There had been much touting of a plan to have all the papers circulated in advance, so people could read them and so leave more time for discussion. Great plan. The people charged with it were some of Paul Stirling's group at Kent. The dutiful organizers of the Ethology session gathered the papers together, had them duplicated with a hundred copies each, and at great expense sent them air freight to Heathrow to meet the deadline, telegraphing Kent that they were there. And there they stayed. A week before the conference was due to start, they got a call from British Airways asking when someone was going to pick up the boxes. The evasive men of Kent said they had had "nobody to send" to get them. They didn't seem too concerned.

It was a bad omen. They said they would get them to Oxford and distribute them there. So when the sessions started it was assumed that everyone had read the papers. Not so. They had been "unavoidably delayed" but no one told the panel this. What is more, the sound system in the hall they were using was hopelessly distorted, and people at the back could hear very little. The sessions were moved to another hall the next day, too late. When he called for discussion, no one could discuss because they hadn't seen the papers. Les Hiatt, to whom he had sent an advance copy of his paper, bravely made some good comments. But it was only then that he learned of the fiasco. He reorganized things so that each panelist could give a brief presentation, but his paper was shot, and the others had not prepared a brief version for oral presentation. Michael got flustered and took up practically the whole time available. Bischoff's English was not intelligible—particularly without amplification. Bill gave a neat little summary—including a printout of his equations that formed a monkey face not unlike his own, to everyone's amusement. But no one could follow him without the matter in front of them (and how many even then?) Total unmitigated disaster. Still, there would be the published version. He had already got a title: he would use Yehudi's word: *Biosocial Anthropology.*

He took a brief time to renew an acquaintance with someone he had met in Dublin: the chaplain of St. Peter's Hall. They shared an interest in things Irish, and the chaplain had tried to persuade him to accept a fellowship, but of course he could not—for many reasons. Not least was the dominant clerical atmosphere of this small college, itself dominated by the Dickensian figure of the master, the Rev. J. Thornton-Duesberry, a stout advocate of Moral Rearmament. But the chaplain's lodgings, and the dozy conversation with the celibates at high table, were a nice (sort of Lewis Carroll) contrast with the frenetic intellectual energy at the conference.

He had never been close to any of the Oxford circle, unless you counted the decidedly odd case of Rodney. But at the inevitable garden party in a college quad (they were hard to tell apart without some experience) he was drawn in to the charmed circle of Evans-Pritchard and his court. The great man's research assistant was a tiny, very blonde, very vivacious feminist called, inappropriately, Juliet. It was love-hate at first argument. She dismissed all his theories as patriarchal rubbish, and affected to be annoyed by his comparing her eyes to the wings of captive hummingbirds used in Navaho rituals. (The singer held the birds by the legs and sprinkled corn meal over the frantically fluttering wings.) So he wrote her a poem apologizing for his remarks.

> Forget the hummingbirds I didn't mean
> to make you pretty speeches but your eyes
> demanded metaphors and I have seen
> the captive bird and all that it implies

It was a simply too-obvious piece of condescending male romanticism, she said. But she kept it anyway. She wanted to buy a house on the west side of Oxford (the unfashionable one), but couldn't make the payments without letting rooms to lodgers—fellow students, she supposed. How about a visiting scholar? She'd take his money, but she wouldn't wash or cook. Fine. There were launderettes now, run by Pakistanis, and he could cook.

They rounded the summer off with a trip to Germany at the invitation of the German publishers. They jumped at it because it meant they could go to Munich and see Konrad Lorenz in the magnificence of his natural surroundings, with the fabled geese at Seewiesen. They first had to pass the ordeal by journalists. The German editors were frankly disappointed that the book was not more left wing, even Marxist. That was the popular thing. The old public passion for Ethology had waned and leftism was back in fashion. They were sorry they could not oblige. Still, the publisher was glad that Lorenz had written a fine foreword to the book. This would go down well with the German public—except the left wing, of course, for whom Lorenz was a "crypto-fascist" etc. There had been threats to kill his geese (later carried out.) Lorenz had been in the German army medical corps in the war. Tinbergen was still in Holland then, and Lorenz tried to persuade him to leave for England while he still had a chance. But the feisty man refused to go unless his Jewish colleagues were allowed to leave also. Tinbergen had recently been to speak in Canada, where the student Left greeted him with demonstrations and banners saying: "Fascist Tinbergen Go Home."

There was a young woman journalist with a bevy of photographers who wanted them to pose in an "animal stance." She wanted them up in a tree, or peering out from behind bars. They resisted. Over large steins of strong lager in a beer garden they talked with her about the book. Lionel waxed eloquent, while his colleague got more and more incoherently drunk. Lionel ordered food in pretty good German, and the young lady was impressed. They explained that he had grown up speaking Yiddish, which explained his fluency. Her attitude changed to the stiff and businesslike. Let's get this over. Take the damn pictures. By the evening, the Englishman was too drunk to stand, and had to be left in his room to sleep (and vomit) it off, thus missing the dinner with Lorenz and Eibel-Eibesfeldt.

The next day, in a fog, he gave a paper to the seminar, which was his first formulation of the idea that the resistance to any doctrine of the innate was rooted in the liberal tradition starting with Bacon and Locke. They saw the doctrine of the *tabula rasa* as necessary to progress and reform through education and science. The point of the Enlightenment program was to teach new ways and overthrow the old. The doctrine of "innate ideas" was seen as in direct opposition to the empiricism necessary to the reformers' plans. Ideas had to come from the environment so that progress could take place. The latter day Lockeans saw the promotion of "instinct" as another version of the hated doctrine. As conceived by Lorenz and the other ethologists, of course, it was not. They proposed a view that stressed, in Eibel's words, "The Innate Basis of Learning." All ideas had to be learned, but there were innate mechanisms of learning that guided their acquisition. Lorenz had put this succinctly in his *Evolution and Modification of Behavior*: it was the Kantian counter to the empiricists; it was Chomsky's challenge to the behaviorists. But the whole Western tradition was against it. It was seen as threatening to the whole radical-progressive agenda. Anthropology saw it as a threat to the dominance of Culture, Sociology as a threat to the autonomy of the social.

Lorenz, looking as always like a cross between a Norse elder and George Bernard Shaw, with his white beard and knee-britches, was delighted with this analysis, even though it was delivered with painful effort and much sweat. He took them to see the geese, which honked unbearably loudly and followed him about enthusiastically. He knew every one by its facial markings. He told them of how people often said to him that he was very courageous as a young man to oppose the dominance of Behaviorism. He had to reply that he knew nothing of Behaviorism at the time; he was just pursuing the studies that Professor Heinroth set for him. Lorenz was never less than honest, but that was not going to save him from the wrath of the righteous. He had, in the thirties, accepted a scientific award from Hitler—then the legitimate Chancellor of Germany, and this would come to haunt him. The Dutch publishers refused to use his foreword in their translation, for fear of alienating the readership. The authors were for pulling the book, but evidently the contract gave this decision to the Dutch, and there was nothing they could do. These were, after all, the days when Joe Paterno, the football coach at Penn State, refused an invitation for his championship team to the Nixon White House. It was like that then.

A brief look at some of King Ludwig's fairy castles, then it was back to reality: the trip down the smelly New Jersey turnpike, the welcome sight of the Princeton towers. Yehudi announced that he and his—one had always assumed devoted—wife were "having difficulties." The perfectly matched Lionel and Virginia were having theirs too. It was something in the air. He had grown up in a world where divorce was unthinkable—as unthinkable as incest or insanity or leprosy. His parents had lived through marital hell, but had never even thought of divorce. Now it was becoming odd not to be divorced. When a couple proudly announced they'd been married for twenty years, the stock response was to ask "what's wrong with them?" But had things changed all that much? Until recently most people had not lived much beyond forty. Very few people would have remained married for twenty years, or even ten, because one partner would have died. Perhaps, life expectancy having almost doubled, divorce was just a way of reminding the couple that one of them should be dead? It was no comfort to the potential divorcee, however.

He could not face the possibility of failing again, but he had gradually to accept that he could not do this husband thing, whatever it was. He could do the father thing; he was even good at it; he could not imagine being without the children. But there he ran hard up against his own reasoning: women have the children; you couldn't get around it unless, as in Huxley's *Brave New*

World, you could grow children in bottles. The French translators of *Kinship and Marriage* had, in the course of a superb job, misunderstood his Huxley reference there, and for "bottles" had used *"biberons"*—meaning babies' drinking bottles. But breeding bottles there were not, and wives there were, and human relationships were impossibly difficult because humans had tangentially different *ideas* about life and how to live it. No animal would be so confused. Divorce is the price of consciousness, and he was about to pay it again. Chance had brought them together, and necessity would force them apart.

Oxford would at least give him a chance to get out from under it all, to have the girls to himself even, for a while. Perhaps for a while he could stop the dancing; perhaps the time had come to make the Woolworth ladies dance for him? Life at the ancient university would be very different, and at one time the rationalist LSE cynic in him would have laughed at the prospect. Now he thought of living with the ancient colleges, the medieval dining halls, the gothic chapels, the clerical fellows, the choirs, the cloisters, the bells, and he did not feel at all hostile. He had lost his old hostility to religion: at least to the benevolent Anglicanism of his youth. He still could not imagine how an intelligent, informed person could believe, as fact, those bizarre fairy tales, but he could see the pull of ceremony and certainty, and the undeniable beauty of the music and the language. Treat it as a benign tribal ritual system, he thought; accept it as you accepted the *kachinas* in the Pueblos or the *turus* on Tory. Treat it as group therapy. Take evensong as an aesthetic consolation for the soul; a soul still, like Sordello's, struggling with the corruption of this world. Remember what Charles Lamb taught us about grace before meat; apply the lesson. The content does not matter: the consecration is what matters. Let the words wash over you as they did when you were a child and felt so safe: "The peace of God which passes all understanding... keep us from the perils and dangers of this night." Sing the evening hymn again, perhaps: "Now the day is over/Night is drawing nigh/Shadows of the evening/Light across the sky." It was too soon for premonitions of death, too late to regret being born; it was time to regroup.

Part 2

Scenes from a Life

11

The Dances: Communing with Strange Gods

A very young man, in his early twenties, sat out on an adobe rooftop under the relentless Arizona sun, watching the masked dancers in the plaza below. He was thinking of how influenced he had been in his teens by D.H. Lawrence's interpretation of such dances—and how wrongheaded it now appeared to him in his few-months-old wisdom. But even if the interpretation was wrong, the evocation was uncannily right. And here he was, in Lawrence country; the country of *Mornings in Mexico*, of "sun, sand and alkali." The shattering heat of the noon sun, combined with the monotonous thud, thud, of the drum, was giving him a headache, despite his big hat and bottle of water. Old Joe, an Indian, but a visitor to this Pueblo, said quietly, "I can never wear a hat when I'm watching one of these dances." Old Joe was confusing his own Indian heritage with his Catholic sense of piety. You wouldn't wear a hat to church, ergo...And these masked *kachina* dances were secret in his Rio Grande Pueblos. The Hopi had no such sense of secrecy; Catholicism had never taken here. They were confident, in their isolated mesa tops, of little interference, and didn't mind if outsiders attended their sacred dances. Joe could never quite get over this: that same thing to him so sacred it must be totally hidden from the outside world, could be paraded for that world to see! But he took off his hat in Catholic reverence anyway.

The very young man had wanted to attend the famous Snake-Antelope dance and watch the dancers with live snakes in their mouths. But this was the wrong year. They had other dances all year round, of course, so there was always something to see. You just had to be prepared for long drives across the desert in punishing heat to get to them. Old Joe had relatives in this Hopi pueblo of Moenkopi—the result of the marriage of one of his nieces to a Hopi boy. So they had a place to stay—a rooftop to sleep on; a rooftop that gave them a close-up seat for the public dance that was the culmination of several days' secret ritual in the *kivas*. The Young Man hadn't slept much the night before—the drumming in the *kivas* and the various town noises had kept him awake. He was keenly aware of the smells: the sharp smell of the Indians on the rooftop around him; the acrid smell of dried urine from the alleys; the unmistakable smell of pinyon burning (it reminded him of the smell of peat-fires in Ireland); the pungent spicy odor of the green-chile stew; the warm smell of the tortillas coming from the outside clay ovens that had not yet cooled down from a day's baking; the smell of hot dirty dogs—the dogs that were everywhere.

No, he didn't sleep much. He was still remembering their visit to the Navaho 'squaw dance' on the way over. The wrongly named dance was, like this Hopi one, the public culmination of a private ritual: in the Navaho case, a curing ceremony, where the *yataalii*, the singer, would have made a sand painting for the patient to sit in. But the Navaho dance was a relaxing social affair, at which all those attending would be fed the inevitable mutton stew in large quantities. Then in the evening, they would all dance around a big bonfire. It was an odd affair. Couples danced backwards with a curious hop step, holding hands. The Navaho girls in their heavy velveteen dresses, dripping silver and turquoise jewelry, had to ask a male partner to dance, then, when finished had to be given a small coin—a dime or a nickel. The few white men there were popular choices because it was assumed they had endless supplies of coin. Several old men sang, and a young man beat a bedroll with a stick—all in the flickering firelight, with the huge emptiness of Navaho country lost in the blackness beyond the edge of the campground.

The night before the dance they had slept by the car next to the sheep pen, away from the eight-sided *hogan* where the patient and his carers were at work with the sand painting. They were awakened when the sun came up—hot from the first—by a group of three young Navaho girls in all their finery, chasing the sheep. It was a charming pastoral sight: the bright colors of the Spanish dresses hung about with silver and turquoise; the bright eyes and giggles and laughter of the girls; the bleating and baaing of the sheep as the girls tumbled around and among them. All with the background of the rising sun showing the mountains as sharp-edged silhouettes in the eastern distance. He smiled at the scene, propped on one elbow, while Old Joe blew on some still hot embers to start a fire for the morning coffee. He called to the girls—"*ya'eeh-te'h!*"—anxious to try out some Navaho he had learned in class, but not daring to go beyond a simple greeting. They looked away and giggled even more, hiding their faces behind their hands in the shy Navaho way. The girls finally shrieked with loud laughter as they rolled one of the sheep to the ground, and he laughed with them. Still laughing, two of them lay across the sheep while the biggest girl made a movement with her right hand. She cut the sheep's throat thoroughly and slowly, not stopping until she had hacked through the spine and severed the head. The sheep's eyes were still blinking, its blood gushing, its legs twitching. With yet more laughter the girls bore away the head and dragged the twitching carcass. It was the stew: the supper he would eat that evening.

The girls gathered sagebrush as they went. They would add it to the stew for flavor and to cut the fat. The world turned sharply from picturesque pastoral beauty to savage utilitarian reality. The sun was simply hard, brash and unrelenting as usual. The coffee was hot and bitter. Old Joe was non-committal. He was cautious of Navahos, but never offered judgments. The Young Man was trying desperately to remember all his lessons in cultural relativism. He burbled a few lines about the sheep not suffering much. "Oh", said Joe, "it suffered. It sure did suffer that old sheep." "I hope they cook it slowly for a good while," he added thoughtfully "or it will be tough to eat." Actually, it tasted pretty good. And that night each of the three girls asked him to dance, and he held their hands and hop-skipped backwards and gave them their coin as they looked away demurely—even the biggest one with the bright eyes and the big knife who had separated the head from the sheep in a couple of bloody minutes that morning.

Still remembering the sheep's head, and dizzy from lack of sleep and too much sun, he tried to concentrate on the dancers. He was here to learn after all. It was a "Navaho" *kachina* dance. The dancers, all men of course, were divided into two groups. One group wore a mask that was the usual inverted bucket shape with a beak and spruce ruff and crest of symbolic clouds. The other, smaller group were dressed as Navaho women and wore 'face masks' with bright-painted cheeks, Navaho women's hair styles, and little whistles for mouths. The male line of dancers danced on the spot with the usual Pueblo heavy tread, wearing the beautifully woven kilts that the Hopi men wove in the *kivas,* and moccasins and belts—gourd rattles in their right hands. They were arranged in a crescent, with the shorter female line tucked closely into the inside of the crescent, dancing the same step. The dancers sang—their song sounding muffled and eerie from inside the masks. A drummer with a big drum, made actually in Old Joe's Rio Grand Pueblo (he came sometimes to trade drums, he explained, for dance kilts. One did not *sell* these ceremonial objects—just exchanged them for others) pounded away the regular two-beat rhythm: ONE-two, ONE-two, ONE-two, ONE-two. But the singular feature of this dance was the 'shaman'. He was independent of the line dancers and wore a mask imitating a Navaho *Yeibichai*: one of their lesser gods—the "talking god" perhaps? (He must look it up once back at a library.) This mask had two ears of corn painted on the back. The Navaho had probably borrowed the idea of masked dancing gods from the Pueblos in the first place, and so the Hopi were here satirizing them: taking their borrowed god-mask and mocking it.

The *Yeibichai* caused much amusement and comment as he ran up and down the line making strange whistling and hooting noises. Joe smiled. "That's just how the Navaho do it," he said admiringly. The Young Man was puzzled. But what did it *mean*? This was a sacred dance? Certainly, said Joe, his hat off in misplaced reverence. But it's also poking fun at the Navahos?—"Oh yes," said Joe—"look, isn't that good? That's just how the *Yeibichai* whistle!" The

Young Man was about to pursue the issue when the proceedings were violently interrupted. Something that sounded like a pompous German hymn poured through the sky above them, sung by a huge, amplified, artificial-sounding massed choir of invisible, out-of-tune angels. It was accompanied by the pealing of church bells sounding incongruously across the adobe rooftops. The dancers in the plaza, and the watchers crowded together on the rooftops, paid no attention. "What the hell!" The Young Man burst out and stood up. "It's the missionaries," said Joe, "they do this every time." It was then he realized on the hill above the 'old village' was the breakaway 'new village' where Moravians had established a church and lured some dissident villagers to join their evangelical settlement. The missionaries, pursuing the intolerant work of their relentless and humorless god, had put up loudspeakers in the church tower and were broadcasting hymns at top volume to interrupt the pagan idolatry down the hill, near the fields and the mini-Grand Canyon of the Little Colorado river.

The Young Man was indignant. He wanted to get a box of dynamite and remove this disgusting reminder of European intolerance once and for all. Joe laughed. "We don't take no notice," he said. "Next year, you'll see, we'll have a 'missionary *kachina*' dance." The people around them laughed and nodded at Joe's words. There then was a pause in the action anyway as the dance stopped, and the *kachinas* began to walk up to the crowd, giving out presents: *kachina* dolls to the children; colored *piti* bread, thin and crisp, to the adults. These masked men were the representatives of the gods on earth while they danced. To the children they *were* the gods. The dolls all had their stories, and these educated the children in several hundred gods and their importance. ('Gods' is an alien and unsuitable word: 'incarnate spirits' might be better, but there is no simple translation. They had a Mickey Mouse *kachina* once.) For the Hopi boys, the turning point of their lives would come when they would be taken into the *kiva* and whipped with yucca rods by the *kachinas* who would then take off their masks and reveal themselves as men. The boys-on-the-edge-of-manhood knew that they themselves must now learn to take up the burden of incarnate divinity. The Young Man knew all this, and knew that the boys probably knew that it was their fathers and brothers out there. It was all "symbolic" wasn't it? But he was still in awe of the power the *kachinas* radiated; the dense, heavy, intense power of those huge heads nodding forward in unison to that driving pulse that was the heartbeat of the universe. Lawrence was still dancing in his head: white thin face, black short beard, intense eyes. They said he looked like the young Lawrence. Perhaps David Herbert was his personal *kachina*? Perhaps he had now to dance for D. H. To be D. H.

He shook himself out of his near trance. He was embarrassed. That was not objective science—it was *too* like D.H. Lawrence! He wasn't here to evoke and express and interpret—he was here to explain! This was a projective delusional system after all. Hadn't they taught him that at Harvard? These were collective representations, representations of the social. Had he learned nothing from Durkheim? Shouldn't he be looking for the "latent functions" of this event; for what it was *really* doing, utilitarian-wise; for the 'covert culture' as opposed to what he saw actually happening? Well, yes, he should. So whence this overpowering feeling of *being left out* that was so painful, so unbearable? He desperately felt the need to be part of this—to put on the mask himself and suffer and sing in the hammering heat. But this was not a religion you could join. This was tribal. You had to *be* a Hopi, and he could never be a Hopi. It was unfair and momentarily unbearable, and during this moment he was thankful for the Moravian cacophony since his anger at this drove out these other, unacceptable emotions.

It had been the same when as a boy his Protestant being had been shaken by the same power he felt when attending a Catholic Solemn High Mass—a sung mass, Benedictine. The exotic Latin, the arcana of the Gregorian chant, the sweet smell of incense, the color and swirl of the vestments. He asked his vicar about the feeling. It was, the vicar said, a good example of the vicious temptations that lay in the way of an honest Protestant lad. Popery was insidious in the way it played on the emotions like this—but one must resist. As a Protestant one stood alone before God; this was the great beauty of the faith. The vicar was fond of saying this, and the boy accepted it, but he still wanted to know why the feeling had been so much more *real* to him at the mass than anything he felt when bearing his pathetic little conscience to his Savior. He couldn't believe that God/Jesus *cared* about his insignificant wishes and misdemeanors. But he felt drawn by the ritual magnet of the mass, by a real power—a felt power, something the Protestants could only match with their greatest music: the Amen Chorus at the end of *Messiah* perhaps, which affected him similarly. Now these pagans were having a similar effect on his sun-drenched, tired brain. That must be the reason. A night's sleep and the unacceptable emotions would go away. But as he looked at the rapt faces around him as they accepted the presents from the gods, he knew sickeningly, that the *kachinas* made sense of the world to the Hopi in a way that nothing made sense to him. The unacceptable emotions surged again. Shake them off!

But they wouldn't go away. A group of students had passed the word that there was a summer *kachina* dance in Zuni, so he swung south on the way back to New Mexico and found himself at yet another ceremonial. Old Joe had a ride back with one of his nephews, so the Young Man was alone, not knowing what to expect, only knowing that Zuni was the Mecca of the Pueblos—the heart of spiritual power. Old Joe had sung him some Zuni songs to prepare him. One of them had a melody that echoed directly Debussy's *Girl with the Flaxen Hair.* It was, of course, based on an inversion of a chord of the major sixth (or a natural minor seventh?), and Debussy had no copyright on that. (But it could not be resolved as Debussy resolved it. For the Zuni there were no accidentals. The melody stayed in the simple Dorian mode: D as final.)

Wey hya   wey hya   weh hya   hyah   wey   ya   he   a-hey   yoh

It had sounded magical to European ears when they first heard it. Had Debussy been consciously messing with modes, or just doodling on the black keys? His father, who knew every popular song ever written, had pointed out that it was the tune of *Strawberry Moon*: "There's a Strawberry Moon in a Blueberry Sky" (In a garden high over Manhattan.) And here it was—a 'primitive chant' from a people who knew nothing of chords, or sixths, major or otherwise. There was perhaps a lesson in this rambling rumination, but he couldn't clear his head enough to figure it out. Better to let himself sink into the Zuni ritual.

He was surprised to find a blacktop road running up to the big Pueblo. His own little Rio Grande village was only approachable by dirt roads—often washed out after rains where they crossed the arroyos. The large ruined Catholic mission told its own story: the Catholics had made no more headway here than among the Hopi. On the Rio Grande, the proximity to Spanish settlements had meant the Indians had had to accept the missions. So they had done so, running the two religious systems side by side, sending only part of their indigenous animism underground (the *kachinas*). They even allowed some little overlap by having their summer 'green corn dance' on the official Saint's day and erecting a little bower to the statue of the Saint in the plaza. The Franciscan's were tolerant of what Friar Angelico Chavez had described to him as "natural religion"—simple people approaching God in their simple (pre-revelation) ways. As long as it was not obscene (the "sacred clowns" had to clean up their act) it was tolerated. The Indian religious leaders were equally tolerant, even indulgent, of the Catholic mission, and incorporated its governance into their own politico-ceremonial structure, by having one of the medicine societies oversee it, and providing the sacristan. But here, in the more isolated west, there were no such compromises. The Catholics had come, tried, failed and gone. The *kachinas* ruled.

He went up onto the rooftop over the plaza where the ceremony was already in progress. There was a spare place on the edge of a roof and he took it, looking down onto the relatively small plaza. There was something claustrophobic about the Zuni dance atmosphere. The plazas were relatively small and the houses high, so one looked down into this dense little rectangle of adobe and sand. The dancers seemed crowded into it—the watchers looming

over them, intent and silent. The silence was spooky. They had seen a heavy thundercloud moving over Black Mesa towards the village. If it would cross the village, and even more of it would open up and give them rain, it would be a most auspicious sign of the success of the ritual. The air was thick with anticipation and pre-storm electricity. Everyone seemed to be concentrating. The dancers were singing a low rumbling song like far-away thunder, to the beat of a stick on a bedroll to keep the time. No drums here. They were a sight out of an archetypal nightmare.

Usually the *kachinas* were identical—they all wore the same mask, but this summer "mixed" *kachina* dance had some forty different masks. These were only a small part of the total *kachina* repertoire, which ran between two and three hundred, but it was the most you ever saw at one time. Horns, beaks, crests, jaws, plumes—all fantastical nightmare heads; all nodding in that One two, One two, heavy stepping unison. And at the end of the line stood Zuni's most important priest: The Bow Priest of the North. He was naked except for a breechcloth, had very little body paint, and one parrot plume in his long black hair. In his right hand he held his small symbolic bow, and with his left, raised a basket of sacred cornmeal, the same cornmeal that he had used to trace a path to lead the *kachinas* into the plaza. This immobility was amazing. He simply stared straight ahead as he 'anchored' the line of dancers—they oriented to him, moving continually in the spot, but never approaching him, this immobility was essential. He was the stillpoint of the cosmos: he held everything in perfect balance as he held up the basket of cornmeal. With his bow he was the guarantor of protection; he was Apollo. If ever there were gods incarnate on this earth, thought our Young Man, then the Zuni Bow Priest was surely one.

Around him and the dancers the Mudhead clowns, the *koyemshi* circulated warily for the moment, subdued, swaying their distorted heads from side to side, rather than constantly forward like the *kachinas*. These legendary children of sibling incest, perhaps wrongly called clowns, were in fact a religious society of great power—the power to satirize any and everything. Their incestuous origin gave them their power; they were born of the breach of the ultimate taboo and lived to tell the tale. They pointed repeatedly to the cloud as it crossed the sun and put everything in shadow. The Young Man looked up and around and realized that the crowd had grown very large—the whole population was out watching it seemed. And he was the only white man there. A sudden flash from "The Woman Who Rode Away" came to him—the D.H. Lawrence story of a world-weary white woman who rode off to a Pueblo in the Mexican hills and became a willing victim of human sacrifice. But the sacrifice here was taking place below him.

No one paid him any attention. As the pregnant cloud finally broke its potent water over them, descending on crowd and dancers alike, soaking costumes, causing paint to run, the singers seemed to double their volume, and the Mudheads went crazy. They rolled in the mud, splashed into puddles, slid down ladders, ran in and out of the dance lines, roly polyed over each other like fat oversized puppies. One had pulled up his breechcloth to reveal his penis tied up behind so it disappeared, leaving him looking like a woman. The crowd howled and applauded. Another then pushed at him with a huge corncob stuck between his legs like an erect, yellow, reptilian penis. They chased, the "female" was caught, and the act consummated amidst even greater laughter and cheers. The children were laughing like white youngsters looking at cartoons. The Young Man was half-thinking "fertility, of course, fertility," and half fighting down panic at the thought that he really shouldn't be here—that at any moment they would seize him.

But he was invisible to them, and again the painful stab of rejection hit him. He was an outsider. He was nothing. And still the unblinking Bow Priest did not move. And still the dancers continued the rumbling, low-pitched, monotonous song that had brought this evidence of the nearness of the spirits so forcefully home. These Zunis were a piece of work. He understood why the other Indians held them in no little awe, and didn't seriously challenge their claim to be the center, the navel, of the universe. The Bow Priest alone would have been proof enough—that living statue with his rain-streaked paint.

In the Zuni store afterwards, he met up with an Indian trader—a small, cheerful white man dressed in Indian style, with long, unwashed hair, headband, turquoise earrings, moccasins and jeans that had seen better days. In later years such a figure would have passed unnoticed as just another hippie, but this was the fifties and he was definitely on the far side of eccentric. He was, he explained, bumming around the Pueblos looking for curios; old *kachina* dolls particularly. He had a beaten-up station wagon and a number of backpacks, and the unlikely name of Byron. But he was full of good tales, and as they were heading back to Santa Fé, they agreed to camp together along the way and visit the town together. That night, after drinking far too much rum, the Young Man woke up with a sweat-inducing nightmare, sobbing. He didn't remember what it was all about when he woke up—and threw up—the next morning. But Byron told him he had been pleading to be allowed to "dance with the Zuni." After extracting a promise that he could, he'd gone back to sleep at last.

With a splitting head and foul mouth he drove back to Santa Fé, following Byron's slow-paced, overloaded wagon. The radio was playing a top twenty (Ricky Nelson?):

> I used to play around the park,
> With carefree devil eyes...
>
> Poor little fool,
> I was a fool in love.

Well, he certainly felt like a poor little fool. The commercial interruption made him even thirstier:

> Tip it, and you will see it,
> Sip it, and you'll agree it's
> The real fruit that gives the fresh fruit flavor
> To a cool green bottle of Squirt.

Once in town, Byron gave him a bulky and torn pack to carry, and suggested they go into the town's finest establishment for a cold beer. He laughed a lot at this suggestion. The proposed hotel was a haunt of the rich and famous: at the very least a tie and jacket affair. They'd never, in their state, get past the door. But Byron insisted, and reluctantly he followed. As they passed through the door he waited for the bouncers to loom, and for angry men to pounce—but no. As if from nowhere, waiters, bellboys, maids and managers appeared, bowing and smiling and ushering them to a comfortable corner lounge settee of Byron's choosing, while cool beers in ice buckets sprang up on the coffee table. It appeared that Byron (or at least his family) owned the place, and many like it—inherited from a line of owners who pioneered hotels in the West. The trader thing *was* an eccentricity, as was the "Byron" thing—a substitute for the impossibly mundane "Fred." (He inconsistently kept the "III" though.) Byron was bored by the hotel business and fascinated by the Indians, about whom he was writing a book. That night they dined well on Mexican standards (chicken *mole* and chilies *rellenos*) and margaritas, and finished a bottle of tequila, worm and all. Byron proposed they go up to Taos for a dance the next day. Accepted—as was a decent bed and bath for the first time in a couple of weeks.

The next morning he went to the Palace of the Governors where Indians spread their wares for sale to the tourists. He knew some of his Indians would be there and would carry back a message. He didn't want old Joe and Juana and Juanita to think anything had happened to him. The ladies were his adoptive clan mothers, and took their responsibilities seriously. He hadn't known at first quite how seriously the little ceremony had been intended— just a courtesy perhaps, to a visitor? But no, Old Joe had said, they didn't do it for just anybody. They had to care, and to trust. He was amazed and touched. It was, Joe explained, as if he had married into the Pueblo and had no clan. This was an impossible situation. Any such person must be adopted into a clan, and the headwashing and naming ritual—with the inevitable sprinkling of cornmeal and ritual smoking, did mean membership with all its privileges (like healing) and its burdens (like exogamy.) But they were not strict about this with non-married-in adoptees, for whom the clan was a "little clan." He later learned that the dry green leaves that were always rolled into the native tobacco on these occasions were jimson weed—which perhaps accounted for his euphoric but hazy recollection of the events.

They had adopted him just before the Green Corn Dance so that Old Joe, as his 'ceremonial father' could take him into his *kiva* house (not the *kiva* itself of course—that was only for initiates, and initiation was beyond their power to offer a non-Indian.) There he could watch the painting of the big ceremonial drums, and listen to the rehearsal of the dance songs. There was much dispute that year, which, like most Pueblo disputes ran along "tradition-versus-progress" lines. The traditionalists wanted the songs to be the same as always—just the tunes could be different. The progressives wanted different words. To the traditionalists the words had a magical quality; it was dangerous to mess with the time-honored formulae. To the progressives, as long as the words were sincere, they could be changed. The results—largely engineered by Old Joe and his brother (head of the *Kwirena* society, and a powerful man) was the usual compromise. A few lines were changed; the body of the songs were left intact. The *Cacique* (the chief Priest) was asked, and he was of the opinion that the *shiwanna* (the cloud-dwelling spirits of the ancestors) would recognize that the lines were sincere and no disrespect was meant. Old Joe, who knew something of the world, explained that the *Cacique* was a not a priest like a Catholic priest, "more like a Rabbi."

The rehearsals continued to the accompaniment of a tiny practice drum, the men singing in a quiet falsetto until they mastered the tune and words. Even so, some of the other, more conservative moiety, affected to be shocked on the dance day when they heard the changes. The same thing had happened at Santo Domingo, thought to be the bastion of Rio Grande conservatism. Normally the men and their women partners never touched each other in the dance. The women danced their little shuffling steps behind the men, their eyes downcast as they waved their yucca wands gently from side to side. The man danced in front of his partner with a high-stepping, heavy tread, pounding the ground to make his ankle rattles and abalone shell necklaces jingle, and forcefully shaking his gourd rattle (sound of rain—'imitative magic,' the young man noted.) But the partners *never* touched. Each was concentrating in a solitary meditative way, while keeping perfect position in the line (down to the little children at the end.) They had been exhorted by the *Cacique*, and then by the *kiva* heads, to concentrate on the *shiwana*, on the crops, on rain, on health and welfare for the people. But that year in Santo Domingo they introduced a new step in which the man reached forward and put his left hand on the shoulder of the woman ahead of him. It shocked Old Joe and all the old timers. "I never thought I'd ever see this," Joe had said, shaking his head sadly. "They are doing it for the tourists, not for us." There was no sign of rain that day. Not even clouds. It was dry for weeks—and everyone knew why.

He found a group of his Indians putting out the pots and jewelry on their blankets. "*Kowatsina*," he greeted one of them politely, "*kowatsina yaya, tsi'ikushitiku.*" (Hello, mother, how are you?) For he recognized one of his Oak-clan mothers. "*Rawa'e, rawa'e, sa'uuti.*" (Fine, fine, my child) she replied softly. Yes, she would tell Old Joe when the boys took them home in the pick-up that night. He had thought to bring some fresh tortillas from the hotel, and he handed them round amid many smiles. No giggling Navaho shyness here. A Pueblo woman looked you straight in the eye and summed you up. They may let the men run the entire show, but as Old Joe had told him many times, the men would never deliberately offend the "old ladies"—the clan mothers. So great was the reverence of the maternal principle that the very male *Cacique* was always addressed as *yaya*—mother! He was the tribal nurturer after all. (It was, the Young Man reminded himself, going back to the impossibly different classroom, the *rôle* that was being emphasized, not the sex.) But his message was safe, he called "*patamak*" to the ladies, and the two lit out for Taos where, Byron intimated, great things were to be expected.

Taos. To him it was still Lawrence's Pueblo. Up there in the Sangre de Cristos mountains, near the fabulous blue lake. It was where, he supposed, The Woman had ridden away *to*! (Even if Lawrence did set it in Mexico proper.) And the farm where Lawrence stayed was still there, although now a kind of dude ranch 'creative writing center'—but it was still Taos, the Pueblo that didn't compromise—no electricity for example, lest TV pollute the sacred center. The Anglo town of Taos might be a tourist trap, but the Pueblo, multi-storied and post-card famous, was inviolate. The Taos tribe was also, as someone had said, "Plains Indians living in a Pueblo." They had no matrilineal clans, no *kachinas*, no moieties. And when there had been buffalo they had joined the Kiowa and Comanche in hunting them. They were different with their own kind of power, and alone among the Pueblos they had a chapter of the Peyote cult. Yes, they ate Father Peyote and followed the synecretic (he remembered that) Peyote Way. This meant that Peyote buttons were often floating around for those who wanted the experience without the ritual—always a reckless undertaking.

Anyway, once up there (almost 2,000 feet higher) and gathered around the inevitable bonfire outside the village, prices were negotiated and buttons bought. It was dangerous to start with too many, he was told, try two or three and see what happened. Patiently he chewed and took swallows of beer as the thirst grew and grew. Nothing at first, then nausea—some throwing up; swig more beer, chew again. He never knew when it happened—it was like slipping under gas at the dentist, but suddenly he was floating as in an out-of-body experience. The shock of this brought back to him the time as a child when he nearly died and had felt the same strange elevation. And this provoked a storm, like a whirlwind and a violent fireworks show of emotions in his head and body. He felt them smashing about in him and spilling out. He saw them in brilliant weird colors—and each emotion was a distorted Zuni *kachina* mask looming at him, disappearing to a pinpoint, then looming huge and booming in front of him.

He was conscious always of the Debussy tune coming through in distortions and inversions. He had a glimpse of the girl herself—a slender French girl walking through a mountain meadow up to her knees in wild flowers. He saw her from behind, and her hair *was* flaxen, and long and lifted gently by the wind. But the song was Indian: "Weh hya weh hya weh hya yah, weh yah he a-he yo" and the girl turned and she had a Navaho face and she suddenly held up a sheepshead dripping blood, and its lips were moving: "weh hya, weh hya, a-he yoh." And then the colors obscured his picture. They were dazzling and intense from a searing whiteness that was whiter than the most blinding light he'd ever experienced, to a red that was ruby and blood as from a vampire movie, and both dark and bright at the same time. And the colors and the feelings and the sounds were all strangely coming together—a huge tartan tapestry of sound, color and emotion like something from *Fantasia*.

It was starting to make a kind of sense. And then cascades of rainbow colors hit him from all sides and the whole *son et lumière* suddenly went totally black—a black that was sheer void, more like the total *absence* of any color. And it was endless and soundless except for a throbbing, drumming undertone—ONE, two, ONE, two, ONE two. He slowly realized that this was his own heartbeat. At that moment the sense of vastation, of total and absolute purposelessness that was never far from the surface, overwhelmed him like dense water, and just as he felt he would drown completely in the feeling, he found himself lying in the dirt by his car, in his own vomit. Someone was wiping his face with a damp cloth and offering sips of water and cold coffee. "Wow!" the distant voice said, "You were really gone there man!"

The Taos dances were not the masked, collective affairs of the other Pueblos. There were only a few dancers at a time, and they were not masked, although the deer dancers had antlers tied to their heads and held a stick in each hand. They used the sticks to do a delicate imitation of the elegant forelegs of the deer, as the deer maidens coaxed them to their deaths. Two girls danced a dance of enticement to two men wearing buffalo heads—playing out the myth of the buffalo husband. The songs were higher, more nasal, somehow more urgent and anxious than the more controlled and heavy songs of the other Pueblos. It was the Plains style—or was it the thin air of the Rockies and the after effects of the Peyote? He felt he was drifting above them, not sitting groggily on the rooftop. At last, floating into a consciousness that had no clear grip in time and space, came the eagle dancers, with these swaying, looping encircling movements, imitating the flight of the sacred bird—their arms covered with perfect eagle wings, and yellow beaks with hard cold eyes covering their heads.

For a moment, as he saw the wings striking the sand, he slipped through a crack in time and saw a little boy on the Yorkshire moors watching a plover as it trailed its seemingly broken wing across the heather. The little boy was sorry for the injured bird, but a large, laughing adult was explaining that it was all a ruse to distract them from the nest, to lure him away from the eggs, to lure him to follow where every wise myth said you should not go with a fairy hand in hand, for you would never come back, and if you did come back you would be changed beyond recognition. But he knew he had to get back—that he had almost gone too far. He shook his head and tried and tried to make the plover become an eagle again, in desperation he looked up to the mountains, to that cold blue place where even the air did not go, and birds avoided, and men could never trespass. The thin, sad cry of the plover lingered, and his mind trailed off into its own silence.

12

The Man: Outwitting the British

A young man—in his late twenties—sat in the hot sun at the edge of a dizzyingly high cliff on an island in the Atlantic, wondering for a moment, what he was doing there. Perhaps it was just vertigo, plain and simple. Perhaps, though, it was one of those unexplained moments of free-floating panic he sometimes felt—when life seemed suddenly void of meaning and purpose. He had been staring for an hour at the sun-bright ocean, listening to the gunshot pounding of waves on the rocks, hearing the banshee scream of the gulls and cormorants. He was trying to keep his attention on the rope, and on the Playboy, his best friend among the young men of the island, at the other end of the rope, crawling and edging across the cliff toward a nest of frightened puffins some fifty or more feet below.

The young man called his friend the Playboy after Synge's Christy Mahon, although there was nothing boastful or patricidal about this playboy, and the girls adored him. But he did have a gaiety and recklessness about him, and he enjoyed escapades—the more dangerous the better. He had wanted a baby puffin to have as a pet. He was sure it could be done—but first catch your puffin. They were undoubtedly attractive little birds with their multicolored toucan-like beaks, but the young man doubted they could be kept in cages successfully. They were uncompromisingly wild creatures, massing in great colonies on the cliff face. They screamed at the Playboy's intrusion, and lined up in rows to peer at him, but did nothing to prevent him when he seized a youngster and signaled that he was ready to climb back up. The rope was secured round a solid outcrop; all the young watcher had to do was keep shaking it out so it didn't tangle with the jagged edges of the cliff, and reel it in as the Playboy climbed. The snatcher had stuffed the puffin in his jacket, and its forlorn little face peered out awkwardly as he finally made it to the cliff top. He laughed and shook his curly black hair. *"Char bhris é"* he said, referring to the young man's fear that the old hemp rope would break. *"Char bhris, go cinnte."* (It didn't break, for sure). The Playboy, from his more than six feet, stared at him, at the puffin, at the sea, the sun and the cliff and laughed his easy laugh again. He looked down and indicated his daring climb. *"Bhí sé ionntach, nach raibh?"* (That was wonderful, was it not?) It was, said the young man, and meant it. But he was still overwhelmed with that feeling of doubt about what he was doing there in the first place.

Officially he was "learning the language," and he was, the Playboy being a tolerant and amused informant, among others. But it was the "why bother?" feeling that was uppermost. He dismissed it and they walked down the long slope of the cliff through the remains of the old Iron Age fort, over the successive ramparts and down to the little village—the smaller of the two on the island. The Playboy had an uncle there and they stopped by to celebrate the puffin escapade—soon to be elaborated into a saga for telling and re-telling with details added, songs composed, and heroism embellished. The uncle brought out from under the cottage floorboards some liquid treasure. No, not unfortunately poteen; the islanders had stopped making it when the turf bogs were exhausted, and the marginal land, once rich with barley, reverted to moorland and common pasture. But this was a fine substitute the uncle said. It was beet wine. They made it by adding stout to beet juice and then a little more sugar and yeast for the fermentation. The vintage about to be opened was a classic of its kind. The aspiring language learner would have much preferred the usual cup of milk—and even some cold porridge with salt and cream as a snack—but there was no refusing. This was an occasion. The cups were filled and raised *"Sláinte!"* *"Sláinte mhór!!"* It was the foulest tasting stuff ever to pass as a beverage. He was reminded of the Great Professor telling of how he first drank *kava* in the South Pacific; or his student's story of a kind of yam soup made partly with human spittle (to ferment it again) and mixed with the ashes of ancestors, that she had swallowed down in an Amazonian Indian village. There was a downside to this participant observation business, and it was usually the food and drink.

The constantly growing crowd (word passed quickly among the houses) was having the very devil of a good time by now, and the inevitable singing began. The furniture, such as it was, was pushed back. A fiddler appeared from nowhere. Fiddlers were like that (For I am the fiddler of Dooney/And dance like the waves of the sea): opportunists all. He talked to the fiddler, who had read in a newspaper about "orgies" (pronounced with a hard "g") in America. What exactly was an "orgy" then? Well, he had explained, mostly a bunch of people took off all their clothes and did wicked things with each other. The response was immediate: "Would they have need a fiddler at all?" They might, he pondered. It might add quite a touch to the proceedings. The fiddler smiled with the few teeth he had left and struck up a tune. It was "Port Láige" (Waterford) and the young man was called on to sing because the words were from the south and the Islanders were uncertain of some of them. (Nor did they know that Beethoven and Haydn had set versions of the song). But the words were appropriate to the occasion, and he was pleased to be able to contribute rather than just be the passive observer.

Bhí mé an lá a Port Láige
   fol di fol dee foddle de dol do
Bhí fín is punt ar clára
   fol di foldee foddle de dol do
Bhí cailiní deas óg liom
   fol di foldee fol do fol diddle
Agus mé ag ól ár sláinte
   fol di fol dee foddle dee do dum

Not a sophisticated song: wine and pints of porter on the table in Waterford, pretty young girls with me and me a-drinking-of their health - and all that. *Clára*—the classic Gaelic for table, would have been *tábla*—a loan word—on the island. But they liked to hear the old words! It was a grand time all the same. The fiddler excelled himself and the uncle did the daddy of all step dances. More songs, more dances, more stories. The younger men insisted on singing rebel songs, although they were out of keeping with the spirit of easy levity. But no *ceilidh* would have been complete without the death of Kevin Barry or the doings of Seán South of Garryowen. For the old men, many of whom had actually fought in the rebellion and the war of independence and the civil war, these songs were not so important. They had come back to the island and all but forgotten these things, preferring the songs of unrequited love, emigration, death at sea, and mourning for things gone. But for the younger men the rebel songs and the republican spirit were more of a religion than their perfunctory, if sincere, Catholicism. So they celebrated Father Murphy and the Foggy Dew and more lightheartedly, Dr. Johnson's motor car—commandeered right here in Donegal. The songs were always sung in English and no one seemed to think this strange. Why abuse the English in a language they didn't understand? But it was always a relief to him to get back to the old Gaelic songs and their playfulness or mournful complaints. The Gaelic of the island was so close to Scottish Gaelic that they liked him to sing songs in that dialect, of which he knew a few, out of curiosity. (They often listened to the BBC Scottish program on their battery radios, when it had its weekly Gaelic half-hour.) They finished the evening on a chorus of the Hebridean "Bhéir mé óró bhean ó" and with much backslapping and blessings departed for their own houses, some still singing, high on the beetroot wine.

The two young men had to walk the two miles back to the other village in the dark, and the Playboy insisted on a visit to his house first, which was accepted. These invitations were never refused. The father was asleep, but his mother—one of the more literate of the islanders who often wrote out the words of songs for the young man—was waiting up. "*Beannacht Dé agat,*" said the young man, guiltily giving her God's blessing. "*Cupán té,*" said the Playboy brusquely, and the mother, intelligent woman that she was, but who seemed to become dowdy and inconspicuous when the men were around,

scuttled off to get the brew from the pot that was kept constantly warm on the hob of the turf fire. There was a tricolor on one wall, and a huge print depicting the scene in the Dublin post office at Easter 1916, on the other. Pádraig Pierce was loftily and with godlike dignity, giving orders to the noble O'Rahilly and everyone looked like heroes from the Iliad. The Playboy clutched the cup of dark brown liquid and took a big gulp. It was then he broke the news— the news the young man had dreaded hearing. The Playboy was also clearly deeply uneasy about it. It was at the same moment they noticed that the little puffin had died. The frustrated bird snatcher threw it on the fire, disgusted. *"Bhi sé marbh nuir a dtimigh sé a' nead,"* he commented, and it probably had died not long after being taken from the nest. They drank the rest of their hearty tea.

The next day was too stormy to leave the island. In fact, it was so stormy that the islanders decided to winch one of the larger herring boats to the top of the slip for safety. The young man never quite found out how this collective enterprise was organized, if at all. Several men would appear by the big winch and attach the cable to the boat and next thing there were forty men in sea boots there helping—some on the winch taking turns, the others lending their backs to supporting the boat as it inched up the slipway while the gale-force winds and rising seas lashed at them. No one was invited; everyone came. Should any able-bodied man (or boy) not help it would be cause for serious notice and censorious gossip. Boats were the lifeline of the island. Their safety was everyone's concern.

When he dried out he decided to go see the King. The King was not often a lot of help, since his main occupation was self-boosterism and it was hard to get a word in. But sometimes he could be persuaded to listen and proffered advice of sorts. The young man walked to the other end of the village, to the King's house, and knocked hopefully. *"Bhuil sé fein anseo?"* Himself was indeed in, but unfortunately *An Rí* was holding his *cuirt,* to which the guest was, however, enthusiastically welcomed. This day the little monarch was anxious to display his erudition to the visitor and after the traditional greetings with family and courtiers and the inevitable cup of tea and slice of soda bread, the King produced two large books from the secret store up in his bedroom.

"Now what do you think of those?" he asked with a huge tight-lipped smile that made him look like Punch.

The guest thought they were fine looking books, to be sure.

"Indeed," said the King, "but see this." And he turned over the books, which had been lying face down on the table.

"See this one" he indicated. It was *The Queen's English Dictionary*, published since her current Majesty's coronation; the other was a battered copy of an old *King's English Dictionary.*

"Well?" Asked the King. The guest was at a loss. The King pounced:

"Do you not see the difference in size? The second dictionary—*her* dictionary—is only half the size of the old King's dictionary. Why, clearly she has only half the vocabulary he had." The latter was flung out to the assembly with imperious scorn.

"The business of making dictionaries should be left to men, should it not? She is not the scholar the King her father was, at all."

They all agreed—even the women: especially the women, who would have no truck at all with this dictionary-making business. Why would you want a great big book of words you were never going to use at all? Or for those you did use, why would you want a dictionary in the first place? The King, however, prided himself on his English. It was a major part of his claim to the title, otherwise dubious. He wrote letters for the Islanders in English with his prized fountain pen. (If you wanted to get in his good graces, give him a new fountain pen.) He wrote to TD's and Ministers and county officials and cardinals. He also put false advertisements for marine engines in boat magazines and pocketed the deposits. Eventually the law caught up with him, and the government had to send one of its two corvettes to the island with the *gardaí* to arrest him, for no one would ship them over otherwise.

The King was put in Portloighse prison, and from there he wrote asking the young man to pay a visit, on his way to the island from London. The young man obliged, and took the slow train from Dublin after an unpleasant crossing on the night ferry from Liverpool. It was raining, of course, and there were no taxis from the station to the prison. But miserable and wet as he was he was more miserable to see the pale little sovereign in his drab convict uniform. They sat opposite each other across a table in a bare room. The visitor showed the incarcerated King some pictures of his family. The guard who was present said loudly:

"Don't be passing him anything now! And speak English!"

The visitor was angry. He demanded to see the prison governor. He lectured the startled little fat man on the constitutional rights of every Irishman (which he was not, but who knew?) to speak in his native tongue, convicted felons not excepted. The governor was cautious.

"Are you a lawyer then?" he asked.

"What do you think?" replied the visitor, pleased at being an enigma.

"Well," said the governor, a reasonable but now puzzled man, "What should we do? We can't have you planning escapes in Irish can we?"

This seemed reasonable too, and flattered the young man's imagination.

"Why not find a guard who speaks Gaelic?" suggested the visitor.

"Bejasus! What a grand idea," shouted the governor. "O'Sullivan, who of the guards speaks Irish?"

"Well" replied the baffled O'Sullivan, "all of them. Did we not have to pass an exam in it to get the job?"

The governor was exasperated.

"Passing an *exam* in Irish O'Sullivan is one thing, *speaking* the damn language is another thing entirely! Now who *speaks* Irish?"

O'Sullivan finally found an Irish-speaking guard. "From a *gaeltacht* himself he is." But the pale, freckled-faced fellow was from Munster, and they could not understand his almost falsetto, singsong Irish. Reciprocally, the Munsterman had no idea what the great conspirators were planning in their barbaric northern tongue, as they looked at the pictures and reminisced about the island. But the form was preserved. The King never forgot. He was able to dine out on that story, with chocolate from the other prisoners, for the rest of his short sentence. Before he left, the King asked him if *he* would be writing a book. Answer affirmative.

"Will it be a big book?"

"Pretty big."

The King was pleased, and smiled his Punchinello smile. He dismissed him from the presence, laughing: "*Bí ina' shiúil leat!*" Our man was indeed on his way: back first to Dublin, and then the North.

If that little encounter was one for the books, his brief interview with the head of the Valuation Office, while passing again through the capital, was one for the ages. The trouble with writing about Ireland is not the danger of falling into stage Irish. The trouble is that any honest and accurate account soon begins to sound like stage Irish anyway. You have, if anything, to tone it down a lot, as the greatest observer of Irish customs and mores, Honor Tracy, herself observed. He needed very much to see records at the Valuation Office, records of early nineteenth-century rating valuations, with their careful maps of all land ownership in Ireland. He was directed to the very top floor of the Office in a charming Georgian town house in one of those too-perfect Dublin squares. The Commissioner's room was cluttered and cosy, with a peat fire smoldering away in an ash-ridden black grate. The man himself, small and thin this time, with a look of cunning watchfulness, was throwing lumps of turf onto the fire from behind his desk, on which he had a bottle of stout and a half-empty glass.

"Will you be having a glass? Or a drop of Powers?"

He declined the whiskey, but accepted the stout.

"A pint of plain is yer only man!" declared the high official emphatically.

Was he quoting *At Swim-Two-Birds*? Or was Flann O'Brien himself quoting a Dublinism? But agreement was in order: It was indeed; indeed it was. Salutations over (and no question but that English would be used) our earnest scholar described his needs, and between throws and gulps, the man-in-charge explained:

"For all that kind of business, you have to see Duffin. For maps and all that stuff, Duffin is yer man. I can't do more for you than ring down to the basement, where the maps are kept, for Duffin. That I will gladly do, for yours is a serious purpose and one I can only applaud. But you're wasting yer breath on me young feller, for d'ye see, I'm what they call a 'political appointment'—I have this job from the party—God bless the cause—and I don't know the divil of a thing about what goes on down there."

The conversation should have stopped right then. Duffin should have been summoned. But there is sometimes no rational control over these things, so the fatal question was asked:

"Then what do you do all day, up here, on your own, sir?"

And answered:

"Well now, I sign things. There's a whole heap of things to be signed. Duffin sends them up; I sign them. But mostly I work on my special project, for like yourself it is a scholar I am, and some day will be known for my work on the names of the Wild Geese. Do you know of the Wild Geese?"

"To be sure: the Irish and Scottish soldiers of fortune who scattered over Europe and ran its armies. They melded into its populations, killing people they did not hate, serving people they did not love."

"Holy Mother! An apt quotation; a subtle reference! Willie Yeats is yer only man! But yes, the Wild Geese disappeared into their adopted countries, and their names were often lost. But they are still there if you look. Who was Judas Maccabeus?"

This asked with that cunning, foxy, sideways look, always quizzical, like Sweeney in his tree, peering down while feeding on watercress.

"Jewish hero. Saved Jerusalem or something. Handel opera about him."

"Right. But who was he? I'll tell you: Maccabeus was the Latin version; he was Judah Maccabee, which is properly Yudah Maccabee, and that was Aoidh MacÁb—'the son of the Abbott.' He was Hughdie MacAbe; a Wild Goose; a soldier hero of good Irish stock."

"You can't be serious?"

"Oh indeed I am, indeed, indeed. What about the good Archbishop Makarios?"

"The Greek?"

"The Cypriot. That name was originally MacArius—the son of Arius; he of the heresy, perhaps, but it was a common name. The son of the Aryan; the son of Erin."

"Oh my God." Trapped with the Commissioner of Valuation, and him losing his sodding mind.

"And in Northern Italy, where the Wild Geese lived in the valleys of Lombardy. There was the great one: Machiavelli. Perhaps Scottish this one: Mac 'ich a' Bhaile—'the son of the town—of the burgher, the townsman.' And a fine Celtic mind he had too."

"Is there no end?"

"Many more. What of Onassis?"

"As in Aristotle?"

"As in. That one is: O Naoise—'the grandson of Noah.' The original Aristotle Onassis was Harry O'Neesey—or Nesse, or Nassis, or however they transliterated it. But they couldn't hide it. Not from me at least. And is it coincidence that the descendants of Noah should make their fortunes in shipping, and in very large ships at that?"

The tiny eyes were gleaming now with a kind of mad triumph; there was no escape. Like a crazed dentist the Political Appointee drilled on.

"What is the Mafia code of silence called?"

"You mean Omertà? Oh no... no..."

"I mean just that."

"Oh Lord. You don't mean to say... I mean it means 'silence' doesn't it?"

"That's what they'd have you believe. But who invented the code? I'll tell you, and then we'll ring for Duffin. It was the most powerful and least known of the Wild Geese, it was the first of the Mafia boys—and Mafia is of course Mór Fear: the Big Man. It was an O Muircheartaigh—Murtagh - O'Murty to them."

"Muirchearteach? It was a *Murdock*?! Jaysus! Ring for Duffin."

"Duffin it is. If its maps yer after..."

"I know: Duffin's yer man."

He jerked his mind back to the present, where the King was finally finishing his disquisition on the defects of royal scholarship, and dismissing the courtiers. Alone with his majesty, the young man poured out his dilemma. But on this day the King was no help. "You should stay away from those boyos," was all he would volunteer. The young man knew that. But markers were being called in. He had people he couldn't disappoint. So the next fine day, The Playboy appeared, looking a bit sheepish. *"Tá an fhairrige cúin marbh,"* he announced—and the sea was indeed suspiciously 'dead calm.' They took a boat to the mainland, to where the car was stored, and set off for the border town to collect The Man. The intermediary was to be an old-time Republican rendered mostly deaf from playing with too many explosives at too close quarters. He had been given some kind of sinecure (selling fishing licenses?) by the current Republican government, but it was barely a living wage. Like all Westerners, of course, he collected the dole as well. It was nothing for an employer to give a man the afternoon off to collect his unemployment money. Island wives begged their husbands not to make any employment too obvious and so "lose the dole"—the only secure and steady income.

The license man (we'll call him that) lived in a big damp house by the border town. He kept pigs loose behind the house, and had a child a year. The young man could not count them (pigs or children). The house stank of unwashed diapers, and there was a constant wail of unattended youngsters. The license man would only speak Gaelic as a matter of principle, but his deafness meant you had to shout it slowly at him, and he did the same back.

Since the young man's Irish was adequate, but rudimentary, this worked fine, and the license man was impressed. "Would to God," he yelled in Irish "that the lazy devils out there having a good time could hear you! They would be shamed to hear such fine Gaelic from the lips of an Englishman!"

He was convinced that the young man, rather than being a deeply unwilling and coerced participant in this venture, was in fact some reincarnation of Roger Casement or even Charles Stewart Parnell, come to save the Republican cause. The main issue, it seemed, was how the hero should be properly introduced to The Man.

"I shall call you *an t-Ollamh*," said the license man.

"But I am not a professor" said the young man with becoming modestly, "you may call me *an dochtúr.*"

"Ah no—they'll think you're a medical man and plague you with questions about their livers," was the reply. So *an t-Ollamh* it was.

The plan was this: he and three others would take the car and cross the border into Northern Ireland close to the town. There would be no problem, especially since the car had English plates and registration and he was English and had an English license etc. An Englishman and three friends going over for a bit of shopping and a few jars. Once over they would meet The Man in a local Catholic pub, he would change coats and hats with one of the passengers. Once they got word that the soldiers at the crossing point were the same as had let them through, they would sail back with merry smiles and waves and be let through without any detailed inspection. The Man would be on the back seat, pretending to be asleep, with the cap over his face—one jar too many. Timing was all. The young man had insisted on two conditions: he wanted to know nothing about The Man, and they were to be absolutely *no guns*. The conditions were agreed to.

On the way there the journey was made miserable by the license man who yelled at them his disgust at the local paper for printing the names of local lads suspected of being involved in a raid on a Northern police station. He broke down, raging in English:

"Suspected! Suspected! How can they print that? Don't they think of the families? Don't they?" Evidently they didn't.

"For God's sake shut up now," said the third man.

"*Go dti an diabhal!*" said the aggrieved license man, disgusted—sending them to the devil in his preferred tongue.

The crossing went smoothly. The bored young soldiers, seeing the English license, waved them through, the contact was made, the formal introduction performed impeccably, and a few jars of porter downed. The Man seemed innocuous enough, small and rather shy. He changed clothes as planned. On the return it was the license man who actually fell asleep, to their relief. The Man propped him on his shoulder as he snored. The indifferent English soldiers scarcely gave them a second glance—but no smiles. They were waved through. Once they got back to the license man's damp and baby-ridden house, the young man ran around to the pig trough and threw up in it. The pigs ate on regardless. The Man came to find him, to thank him properly. As he wiped his mouth he nodded in response, and when The Man bent down to scratch the pigs there was, clearly, in the back pocket of his tight pants, the outline of a small flat pistol. The Man stood up and saw him staring. He put on a light smile and said gently, "Aw sure now, *a chara*, 'tis not loaded."

Weeks later, on the Island again, he pieced together from the always-late newspapers, and from rather obvious clues, who The Man was and what he had done. He was numb. He felt no emotion one way or the other. All he felt was a deep conviction that fighting for a cause—any cause - was stupid, and dying for it, deeply stupid. The sense of purposelessness that was always waiting to surface had another field day with him. It was his own fault—his own vanity, his love of the sense of danger, of power even. It was one way to combat the vastations. But this had gone too far, and the temptation to meddle had to be resisted. He told the Playboy, and, decent fellow that he was, he fully understood. "The lads will never forget what you did," he said. Nor will I, thought the young man.

But from then on he strictly avoided the political and buried himself in the domestic. He meticulously collected the names of all the fields, every rock, every inlet and cliff and odd formation. He took detailed genealogies stretching over seven generations. He correlated them with the names in the faded, copperplate, handwriting he had found and copied from the documents of the Valuation Office. The Playboy went through every change in landholding with him, and they were able to connect back to the late eighteenth century, thanks to the conscientious help of the subterranean Duffin. The King had the old *sloinnteoraí* recite the generations of the *clanna* for him, prompting and commenting as they recited. He set himself to learn a hundred Gaelic songs by heart—a great way of mastering the language. He did a complete census of the households. He buried himself in the trivia of domestic concerns over land and boats. He sang at the weekly *ceilidh* (on the island this was *damhsa*— a dance) his newly-learned Irish songs, and an occasional John McCormack ballad, for these were well liked. He only meddled in quarrels when invited as a mediator—and strictly domestic quarrels at that. It was like a penance, an expiation, a purging of his silly pride. He learned all the set dances and never missed one, even the complicated "Waves of Tory." He even tried a few step dances, modeled on those of the Playboy's uncle, which were greeted with indulgent applause. This was better.

To appease his friend he was still willing to do risky things as long as they were purely risky to himself—no outside involvements. The Playboy liked to fish on the north side, at the foot of the great cliff (*Tór Mór*), which they had climbed for the puffin. Here the Atlantic surged into the gorges and sucked out again with a power that would have smashed even a large boat. The two

Playboys of the Western World would scramble down the cliffs and on to the rocks—for they were convinced that in this mackerel-crowded sea, the variety of fish was greatest here. It was foolhardy of course. Neither of them could swim and one slight slip could mean inevitable death, but it harmed no one except themselves, and they were both high on the danger. And the fishing was good. They landed some glasan, mackerel, pollock, salmon and a red fish whose name they didn't know: enough for a good stew, island style. While they sat and chewed dried seaweed, the mother put the cleaned fish whole—heads and tails intact, with whole potatoes (as always in their jackets) and onions, into the big iron pot. She let them simmer for a couple of hours over the turf fire. She put in two cans of soup "for flavor" and when it was done they each took a whole fish and a potato, picked the flesh off and drank the broth. Then she boiled carigeen moss (itself a seaweed) in milk, to make an island blancmange. Nothing had ever tasted so good. They laughed and sang into the night, and embroidered the saga of The Climb for the Puffin 'til it shamed the deeds of Finn. The Man was forgotten. The borders of pointlessness receded from this little center of pure human warmth.

13

The Hetaerae: Surviving Sex in the Seventies

"What are you reading?"

"*Memoirs of Hecate County*. Edmund Wilson"

"Doesn't that have a whole bunch in French? I seem to remember it from Wellesley: Contemporary Lit. class."

"Not much. It's easy French."

"Isn't that an odd book to be reading in a hotel bar at an anthropology conference?"

"No odder than to be asked that question out the blue. Not that I mind, given the questioner."

"Why sir, you make me blush."

"Somehow, I don't think so. I'm sure they taught you how to handle these things at Wellesley."

"You overestimate Wellesley. But you are making my friend blush."

"And very pretty she looks with it."

"You're English?"

"Thank you. Most people say British."

"Is that wrong?"

"Just imprecise."

"How precise does one have to be?"

"Let's see. You're a dark-haired, fair-skinned, fine-featured, perhaps mid-western but Ivy-league-educated WASP. Your friend is fair-haired, warm-complexioned, and Jewish. You must be from New York."

"Not bad. How did you get the Jewish, and New York?"

"I looked at your name tags."

"And saw our affiliations?"

"Of course. I cheated... a bit. But all's fair in war and flirtation at conferences, isn't it?"

"Have you been to many conferences in the USA?"

"Enough to know the rules."

"What rules?"

"Basically the scoring scale used, if only by implication, by the hetaerae."

"The what?"

"The female graduate students."

"Tell us, do. We *are* graduate students, although we both teach."

"The most dangerous kind! Well let's see. I think it's roughly zero points for a same-year graduate student; 5 for an ABD; 10 for a recent PhD; 15 for one with a job offer; 20 for an assistant professor; 30 for an associate with tenure; 50 for a full professor; add 5 for each article in a refereed journal and 20 for each book; and 100-plus in bonuses for a departmental chairman who knows Margaret Mead personally. Something like that."

"So where do you rank?"

"Triple figures. But only technically: pretty nominal department so far."

"We know Margaret Mead."

"Did you do an interview with her for the *New York Times Magazine*?"

"Did you? Why haven't we seen it?"

"They didn't publish it. But at least I was long in the presence. That seems to count with the better class of candidate."

"Which is?"

"Those from New York City."

"So we are especially prime candidates. Why New York?"

"Well. Manhattan. It's the glamour. You have little apartments in picturesque neighborhoods, and live those very Manhattan lives: intimate foreign restaurants; exclusive parties of witty intellectuals and émigrés; chic concerts of mediaeval music in city churches; walks in Central Park in winter; dinner for two with candles in the tiny dining nook."

"You make it sound more attractive than it is. The apartments have plumbing problems, the churches are cold, the restaurants are expensive, the food often dubious. Central Park isn't safe. But the candlelight dinner is usually OK."

"If she can cook."

"We've never had complaints."

"What you do is very simple dear."

"I'm a simple fellow."

"Nonsense, dear. You have a wild imagination. You should apply it to sex."

"Was that all right, dear?"

"What do you mean? It was great."

"I mean, perhaps I should have thrashed about more, and perhaps moaned a bit. The others all said I should. Do you like thrashing, dear?"

"You thrashed just fine. The moaning could use some work."

"The others all liked moaning. But Stanley liked the thrashing best. He wanted more thrashing. And the words. But I didn't like shouting the words. What if the neighbors heard? I used to whisper them in his ear. But I did feel an obligation. He was flying in every weekend, poor dear. Practically became a charter member of United Airlines. Of course, Stanley was Jewish, and Jewish men are so very *attentive*."

"We should get Stanley in for a consultation."

"That is a disgusting suggestion, dear."

"Dear, we can't just hide in my apartment and fuck. We have to go out sometime."

"It's bloody cold out there. The wind nearly cut my head off when I tried to pass Grant's tomb. Why don't they clean that up, by the way? The wind from the river is worse than the wind from the lake in Chicago, and that was hellish. The only civilized thing to do in this weather is stay in and fuck. Where would we go?"

"I want to see *The Graduate*. Everyone is talking about it. Then there is *The Play of Daniel* in that pretty church. They have such cute little lions, and countertenors."

"The churches are cold. Remember. And I can do countertenor. Mediaeval if you like. Listen…"

"That was very nice dear. What was it?"

"The Athanasian Creed by John Merbeck. One of the first pieces of written English music."

"How nice. What about *The Graduate*?"

* * *

"Good evening Dr. Mead. Are you OK down there?"

"Oh, hello. It's the honorable journalist, no?"

"Indeed it is Dr. Mead. Although our interview, never published, scarcely counts."

"We said such interesting things. What on earth did they want? Call me Margaret. Not Maggie. I hate Maggie."

"Margaret it is, Dr. Mead. Gossip and scandal, they wanted, Margaret: the low-down on unsuccessful marriages, and all that."

"What bad luck for them. All my marriages were a great success."

"Indeed they were, Dr. Mead. Will I be filling that martini glass you're about to drop on the floor?"

"You sound Irish."

"Only when I'm drunk. The maternal genes take over."

"Fill the glass. Then lie down where I can see you. I'm hurting my neck looking up. I suppose these graduate students are all over you? Is it like this at all conferences?"

"The hetaerae? They are plentiful here in the land of the free-and-easy, Dr. Mead. In England's green-and-pleasant it was cold mutton—that's Oscar Wilde, the darlin' man. But the world is changing, even that damp little world."

"But I thought English girls were easy? Didn't we discuss this in the interview? The GIs thought so. In England the boys are supposed to restrain themselves—not the girls as it is here."

"And as I told you in the interview, old dear, not this boyo. Barreled away to no effect for many miserable teenage years. Tight as a drum, those virgins of Albion."

"You *must* be Irish. In any case, they'll like you here; you're exotic."

"Exotic! Holy Jaysus! Me mother would be gobsmacked. I can't be exotic, madam: I'm British!"

"You're the stranger come into town. Aren't you supposed to know about incest and out-breeding? You're exotic; so learn to like it."

"Will I fill up your glass again Dr. Mead, dear."

"I'm leaving. Help me up."

"Will I be getting your forked stick for you?"

"It's a thumb stick. Go be exotic somewhere else."

"Right you are then, Dr. Mead."

* * *

"Why are we waiting? Why don't we just do it? We do want to, don't we?"

"I want you to absolutely *insist*!"

"Against your will? I thought you were willing?"

"But I want you to *insist*! Tell me I have no option. Tell me I'm helpless."

"You mean like rape?"

"It would only be rape if I didn't want to."

"So if you want to, then why not just do it?"

"Oh for Christ's sake just *insist*!"

"I insist! I insist!"

* * *

"Just before I come, pull my hair a bit."

"How will I know you are coming?"

"Can't you tell? I get excited."

"Too vague. We should have an attack word. "Pull" – or something."

"OK. I'm close. Pull so I feel it, but don't hurt me."

"That's a fine line to walk. Keep saying "pull" until it's too hard, then stop."

"I'll say "stop" – but that's just for the pulling."

"Understood. Over and out."

"Pull !!"

* * *

"I'm glad we got away from those people. It's always the same thing at conferences. They all get drunk and excited and talk shop. But they don't mean it. It's all foreplay; everyone sizing each other up."

"Well, it worked for us."

"Oh, well, yes, but you're an obvious pick, aren't you?"

"You mean my charm, my wit, my looks, my obvious sensuality?"

"Oh no. You're not particularly handsome. Too effeminate. And English-men are not usually sexy. You talk a lot, if that's charm."

"So why am I obvious?"

"Because you are arrogant and sarcastic, and a male-chauvinist pig."

"I'll take the male. The rest is an insult to inoffensive porkers. But why is anything so repulsive attractive to a self-confessed feminist?"

"I don't know. Sleeping with the enemy? It means you probably hate women enough to treat them badly in bed."

"You *want* to be treated badly?"

"For a so-called ethologist, you don't seem to observe behavior very well. Dominance and aggression are exciting—in sex anyway."

"I don't think I can do dominance and aggression on demand."

"I'll talk you through it."

* * *

"OK. Holding me down and biting my tits was good in its limited way. Now use the hairbrush."

"For what? Your hair looks OK. Bit twisted, true."

"Spank me with it, asshole. Quick or I'll lose it."

"Shouldn't I turn you over to spank you?"

"I'll hold my ankles. OK?"

"Shall I use the smooth side or the bristles?"

"Just *spank* for fuck's sake!"

* * *

"Sometimes they have a wife, and they lead you on, you know, then when you're all ready, you know, they dump you and go off to wifey. I hate that. I made my mind up tonight to make a big fuss and a scene, you know, like cry and carry on and make you come back to my room. My friends wouldn't care, but they'd want to join in. No harm in that, you know, like it's better than being dumped in a corridor. Only professors would do that, I mean, they're not fuckin' human, are they? I mean, you're OK, but you're British, you know, you have manners. You wouldn't, like, dump a girl in a corridor when she was all excited, would you?"

"Never!"

* * *

"Good wine and elegant conversation. I like a man who can provide both."

"What else do you like in a man?"

"Certainly not all this sensitivity shit. I like a man who's in control; even a bit hard. Do you understand?"

"I'm beginning to."

"If a woman is successful herself, she doesn't want – need – that sensitivity and understanding stuff. She can take care of herself. So she is into men who can take care of her—not domestically, she can do that. She wants a man who can take her or leave her, who's a challenge. That's exciting."

"Do you have a litmus test for such a man?"

"You said the wine had body, and the body was like a woman. Very neat. If it *were* a woman, what would you do with it?"

"Betray it."

"Let's take it up with us."

* * *

"They say 'How long did it take you to grow your legs?'—and think that is real wit."

"They are very long legs, and very slender. And your hair is indeed very long—you can sit on it. So I guess it's a pretty obvious pick-up line."

"Better than, 'Hey babe, let's get it on' —which is all about they seem to manage."

"If the babes are so willing to get it on, why waste words? In my day— God, am I really saying that?—you were expected to make a bit of verbal effort at least—to say nothing of dinner and a show."

"Dinner and a show! That'll be the day. One guy did take me to see *Oh Calcutta*! But that was just his turn on. He was amazed they didn't all get erections."

"Well, it's a bit arse-ends-forward, but would you like to see *Jesus Christ Superstar*? It's on across from the hotel. We could skip the annual meeting."

"I never go to those. Full of people with lists of complaints, wanting to condemn this and that. I'd rather stay here and try stuff. OK?"

"Not hair brushes?"

"For spanking? OK. I prefer a riding crop, but I don't have it with me. You have a leather belt? OK If that's what you're into. You can't hang me up here, but you could tie me to the headboard with that silk tie. Nice."

"It was just a question."

"But you're into it. I can tell. It's what's different about you. You have a Victorian imagination. You're into Swinburne and Jack the Ripper. OK? The pain thing; the Kraft-Ebbing. Do you think I'm weird?"

"You're just an old-fashioned girl."

"OK. But I like the long slow stuff better. If I do the belt thing, then can we do the marathon thing, OK?"

"It's on the menu."

"Then let's start. There's a lot of the night left. OK?"

"OK it is. If we ever do fall asleep, how should we wake up? Doing what?"

"I'll take care of that. I'm always awake early. You'll find me down there when you wake up. OK? Then something for me."

"Fire away."

"Do you find me too submissive? I mean I like being underneath. I like you to do whatever you want to. OK? You will do whatever you want?"

"As long as you tell me what it is."

"OK. I'm very anal."

"Retentive?"

"The long slow thing."

"We'd better get started."

* * *

"What did you think of *Hair*?"

"I liked the bit about Margaret Mead. Did I ever tell you… "

"No, no. Not that. The nude scene."

"Oh. Once I would have been shocked I suppose – no, I know I would. But we've been satiated by now. One sees so many naked bodies; a few on stage aren't a novelty."

"So did you see me?"

"See you?"

"I was in the chorus. Hair long and blonde then. Flowers in the hair. No clothes."

"Describes them all. No. Didn't see you in particular."

"It was all the ones with big boobs. You were looking at them."

"I was really looking at the men."

"Tell me."

"I was wondering why they didn't get erections."

"Not when they're *working*, idiot. They got them afterwards, I can tell you."

"All of them? You can vouch for that?"

"Oh yes. Like a yacht marina it was. All those different pricks up and ready to go. You just picked a likely one and sat on it."

"Sounds like a bee hive."

"No. Only one queen bee there. More like a kangaroo orgy: hopping from one erection to the next."

"Interesting image. You know kangaroos…"

"Yes. Every anthropologist has read the article. They have a bifurcate penis. Two barrels for the price of one. So bloody male. I wouldn't trust them."

"Quite right. 'Kangaroo fuck with forked dong.'"

"Oh very clever. Is that supposed to impress?"

"Don't be so tetchy. You've been seeing male chauvinists under the bed."

"Better than in it."

"Some women like it. Especially the libbers. They like a touch of the old SS treatment."

"Some of the sisters are totally unreconstructed. Have they not been to consciousness raising sessions?"

"They're more interested in raising something else."

"Poor desperate things. Poor darlings. Why can't they take it or leave it? Fuck 'em and get rid of 'em—simplest way."

"But you enjoy it, no?"

"Of course. But it's no big thing. Not something to make a life of. Take it, enjoy it, get on with it. If it makes a friend happy, fine."

"A sort of charitable duty?"

"No duty. None of that shit. But I never think of sex as being particularly for me. They all want it so much it just seems best to let them have it. If you don't they get angry or miserable. Better to have a satisfied angry man than a frustrated one. And anything is preferable to male misery."

"I'm angry, and I'm miserable."

"Very funny. You want it, let's do it. Only afterwards…"

"Yes?"

"Can we cuddle a bit? OK?"

*   *   *

"I have this really, *really* good marriage. I mean *really* good. I wouldn't do anything to spoil it. I never meant to do this. It was the bullfight. I was so scared and you were so nice. And, well, Mexico City is so *damned* romantic. I never do this usually —not at all, you understand. I really love Stanley. He's gentle and sensitive and he trusts me. Of course he's off every weekend to New York on this consulting job. He comes back so tired, but he works so hard. I have to try to understand. I feel bad, *really* bad, about this. It's only this one time. I'd *die* if Stanley ever found out. We have such a fine relationship, so close. We're best friends as well as lovers. It is such a *good* marriage. I have to call him now to let him know I'll be taking a later flight back. Will you do something for me?"

"Sure, what?"

"Come inside me while I talk to him."

*   *   *

"I know I take a long time, but I'm well within the normal curve of expectations."

"Well now—would that be a Gaussian distribution? I think the curve might be quite skewed: some come right off, some take a long time to come, but most come reasonably easily."

"Oh yes—you're so *experienced*, aren't you?" Studies—*objective* studies —show that orgasm is *not* vaginal, and that *most* women require considerable manual or oral stimulation of the clitoris to achieve it. *You* are the one with the skewed sample."

"Objective studies?"

"Kinsey. He studied masturbation to orgasm. He used a sample of female nursing students. He paid them of course."

"So they couldn't be accused of not raising a finger in aid of their own education."

"Joke all you want. Women are entitled to have as many orgasms as their male partners. A considerate partner will vary oral and manual manipulation with intercourse to ensure climax."

"For those who need it."

"Studies show *all* women need it."

"Like hell. Some little bunnies hop on command. Others, like you, seem to need an army of moles digging down there to get a result."

"Simultaneous orgasm is a myth. I've had a miserable sex life because of that myth. There's no going back for women now. We can demand satisfaction, or we have the means to ensure multiple orgasms without male assistance."

"OK, OK. All engines firing. We have blast off."

"It isn't funny."

"You are so right."

* * *

"You pile cushions at the side of the bed, about half way up. Then I lie on my back with my head over the edge, touching the cushions, with my hair hanging over them. I put my arms along the edge of the bed, helpless. You come close, kneeling on the cushions, and grip my head, upside down in between your thighs, and go deep into my mouth. You lean forward and I pull my knees back and out so you can get a good mouthful of me, then you reach back and gather my hair and pull it over my head so I am all enclosed down there. I'll be tonguing like mad, so then you should be ready to come, but hold it—you're good at that I hope, then climb over me carefully and lie on your back. I'll swarm over you and go down. When you come, and you will then, I'll keep it in my mouth and come up and get on you to keep you erect. You open your mouth and I'll give you half the stuff, then I'll go down again, then come back on you, and keep doing that. When you are ready to come again, grab my hair and we'll kiss open mouthed, exchanging the stuff, then when you come, twist my hair hard, viciously, and I'll scratch you as hard as I can and we'll swallow together. OK. Let's go."

"Could you run that by me one more time...?"

* * *

"So Wilson had water poured over his head. Big deal. Spoonful of water and he calls a press conference. It was clean water. Women in Africa have to drink filth and their children die of dysentery."

"That's scarcely Ed's fault."

"But what does he *do* about it?"

"What do you do about it? Pawn those gold earrings and send the money to Africa. Then we'll talk about doing."

"That's irrelevant. Wilson is part of the white male establishment that has the power. All he does is make biological excuses for white male oppression."

"In Africa it's black male oppression."

"Yes it is. Males are males."

"But the black males suffer from white male oppression."

"A good thing too if it stops their victimization of their downtrodden women. A glass of water. It wasn't even half a glass; it was few drops in the bottom of a glass—I'm told. Consider it a purification ritual. Big fucking deal. I suppose he has a biological explanation for cliterectomy."

"It's clitoridectomy. And no, he doesn't."

"He will. The thing is not to explain it, but to *stop* it."

"It's the local custom. Doesn't it have to be seen in its local context? The women favor it. When the black male authorities ban it, they do it in secret."

"Yes. They are the dupes of the dominant male ideologies. They haven't had their consciousness raised. We're working on it."

"But don't you oppose the imposition on indigenous peoples of universal values manufactured by white Western outsiders?"

"Of course."

"But isn't that what you are doing?"

"Of course not. The moral autonomy of the Other is only to be respected when it does not involve the hegemonic patriarchal oppression of women. We must stand together to empower our sisters."

"Even if they don't want your help?"

"They will once they fully understand the nature of their situation"

"When they understand it as well as you do?"

"Yes, of course."

"Could we get on with the sex please?"

* * *

"You are a typical example of Western, rational, logical thinking."

"Coming from one who looks so dazzling in her turquoise sari, I take that as a compliment."

"It isn't meant to be. It represents everything that is wrong with the world."

"It also represents everything that is right with the world. That is perhaps the world's paradox."

"How so?"

"That what is best about the world produces what is worst."

"If it produces the worst, how it can it be good?"

"Ah, there you are. Women are Utilitarians, men are Kantians."

"Please explain yourself."

"A man asks of an action 'Is it right?' and judges accordingly. A woman asks 'What harm does it do?' and judges likewise."

"Typical Western rationalism. All harm could be avoided if we learned to pursue enlightenment."

"When I say 'enlightenment' I mean 'Enlightenment—capital E: the eighteenth-century pursuit of universal truths and values."

"Yes, the source of our current world misery."

"Hold on. You mean there was and is no misery in the non-Western world?"

"There is local and personal misery. But there is no misery that threatens our very existence, which is the product of Western rationalism. Your logic and reason compound the misery. You block the path to enlightenment with your reason."

"But what other way is there to deal with the real world? Oh sorry. I guess 'real' opens a can of metaphysical worms."

"You answer yourself. Reality and truth are not the slaves of reason and logic. There is a truth that is beyond reason."

"But then how do we know it?"

"We experience it."

How do I know your experiences are the same as mine? At least with language, logic, reason and science, we can agree on some objective procedures for arriving at shared knowledge. Karl Popper..."

"Useless. Language is another trap. It impedes true thought which is beyond language."

"But your philosophers and gurus and mandala-wallahs use language quite freely, and often elegantly and precisely."

"How little you understand. It is only secondary, for education. The ultimate truths of the spirit are beyond language."

"But you still *talk* about them. I'm with Wittgenstein: 'Of that whereof thou can'st not speak, thereof thou should'st remain silent.' "

"Clever Wittgenstein. But even he saw that language was a trap."

"He also saw the way out."

"Did he ever have Tantric sex?"

"I doubt it. What has that do with it?"

"The way out is through action that releases us from the tyranny of the self."

"Where does sex come in? Isn't it pretty selfish?"

"Not if it is done properly."

"Are you going to talk about it, or just let it happen?"

"The talk is necessary for the uninitiated. Once you know, there will be no need for words."

"Know what?"

"The secret of Tantric sex."

"Intercourse without ejaculation?"

"Yes. Quite good. More precisely: orgasm without ejaculation. Ejaculation is simply the desire to reproduce oneself. To refrain from it, while achieving oneness with the partner, is to transcend the crude ego-self. It is a step towards the renunciation of self."

"It sabotages it in a vital spot."

"One way of putting it."

"So doesn't this require the female partner to be very passive? Women today often like to be ritually submissive, but not usually passive."

"The female partner, at least in this case, is anything but passive. Do not confuse quietness with passivity. I am not a mechanism for controlled masturbation; I am fully participating in my own control. You don't have to thrash about and moan to participate."

"No hairbrushes?"

"What?"

"Never mind. So slow and easy wins the race. How long do we need?"

"We should meditate first to achieve tranquility. There should be no excitement. Erection will come with concentration."

"You sure about that?"

"Quite sure. You will contemplate my Yoni and be quite erect."

"I imagine so. Still, Western rational logic means I must make plans. I had meant to join some people this evening to watch a football game. So how long?"

"How long do we have?"

"Let's see the program. Today is all about rhetoric, post-modernism and deconstruction. I'd say we have all afternoon at least."

"We'll need it. Please undress."

* * *

"Vous êtes Américain. Dîtes-moi: qu'est-ce-qu'elles veulent ces féministes? Je vous demande au nom de toutes les Françaises."

"Je suis Anglais. Je pense qu'elles veulent un monde différent. Un monde ou il n'existe pas de difference entre les hommes et les femmes."

"Quel horreur! Pourquoi?"

"Liberté, égalité, sororité … "

"Mais moi, je voudrais l'égalité entre les deux sexes. Donc, je suis féministe, n'est-ce-pas?"

"Vous n'êtes pas féministe. Jamais."

"Bien. Je suis…?"

"Vous êtes une jeune femme avec des fleurs dans les cheveux."

"Et vous?"

"Moi, je suis un homme qui recueillis celles-là."

"Bon: à la cueillette!"

* * *

14

The Bulls: Managing a Magus in Colombia

On a hot afternoon in southern Colombia, a middle-aged man, who should know better, is about to enter the bullring. He should know better because he is not properly prepared for the coming encounter with 350 pounds of young but angry beef. The lack of preparation is partly his own fault and partly Mario's. Mario is a Magus: he enjoys playing games with people's lives. This sometimes has spectacular results. When, being disgusted with the state universities in Columbia, he decided to found a new private one, he went to Princeton and asked Einstein to sit on its board of trustees. Einstein, who knew something of Colombian politics, asked him how he was going to deal with the two political parties who would want to be in on it. "Why," said Mario, "I'll put six Conservatives and six Liberals on the board." Einstein laughed and quoted a proverb: "The fly who does not wish to be swatted, sits on the handle of the fly swatter." He joined the board.

Mario the Magus had a simple enough system for extracting excitement out of other people's lives: he never quite gave them all the information they would need to survive the situation he put them in. He always left something to chance and their ingenuity. So it was with the middle-aged man about to step into the arena. It was Mario's own ring on his own ranch in the department of Tolíma. The young bulls were Mario's, who bred fighting bulls. They were the two-year-olds not destined for the professional ring, hence suitable material for amateurs and beginners: *novilleros*. A professional had been engaged for the killing of the bulls, for that was not allowed to the beginners. Mario had wanted the middle-aged man—who was respectably well known in his academic field—to lecture at the university, which had grown and become quite famous in its own right. So a deal had been struck. It seems the academic gentleman was a devotee of the *corrida* and knew Mario had a ring and bulls on hand. A series of lectures in return for a chance in the ring? Mario readily agreed.

The lectures were successfully delivered, and the party decamped from Bogotá to Altamira where a fiesta was arranged. That morning most of the party had gone out on horseback to watch or help in rounding up the young bulls; they must not meet a man on foot before the *corrida*. Mario had used the time to give a few words and demonstrations of instruction, playing the part of the bull himself. He taught the basic *verónica*. He made it seem even rather easy—the making of a simple pass. And how to remember to pivot quickly as the bull turned to charge—short distance—from behind, after the pass was made. Then he poured the sherry and told of how the Great Matador (Dominguín? Girón?) had stayed in this very ranch the night before he appeared in the ring. At dawn Mario heard a noise and came downstairs and there in the great living room with its long carved and painted *vegas* and large stone fireplace, with all the furniture pushed back to the walls, the Great Matador was practicing simple passes. Mario stood for a moment drinking in the privilege of watching this grace and perfection in his own house at such close quarters. Then the Great Matador noticed him and they conversed a little.

"Tell me" said Mario, "why do you, one of Spain's greatest *toreros*—a man who has killed over five hundred bulls, why do you, for a simple little provincial South American *corrida* with animals that cannot match the *Miuras* of Spain that you have mastered, why do you get up at dawn to practice these elementary passes?"

"Ah, Don Mario," said his gracious guest, sipping the *café chocoláte* he had made for himself to get the proportions exactly right, "no matter how often you fight, how experienced you become, there will come that time in the arena when, in a careless moment, you will make a small, elementary error. It will be your last. Few great matadors have died because some complicated pass turned sour on them. They died because a foot was not planted correctly, because a move was made a fraction of a second too soon. That is why, before any fight, with any bulls anywhere, I get up at dawn and practice the elements, over and over and over."

"And that" said Mario the Magus," is why you are indeed the greatest of them all."

He told the story beautifully, and the middle-aged academic from the ever over-confident USA, listened delightedly, knowing he too had mastered the elements in that same, hallowed place. And so, fortified with sherry, and strong Argentine wine, and slivers of raw beef sliced with sharp knives from a whole skinned calf for lunch, and a little *aguardiente* to settle the stomach after, he stood behind the barrier to see the first animal loosed into the ring. It was understood that the professional and Mario—no mean player of bulls himself, would do the major work. Once the bull was tired, he might then make a few passes as his debut. The crowd—Mario's ranch hands, their relatives and friends, Mario's relatives, neighbors and friends, and friends of relatives and relatives of friends, knew the situation and was delighted with it. Another foolish *gringo* was about to play the hero with the bulls. And this one wore white jeans—so they had a name for him at once: *"El Gringo*

Blanco." And they called it, and chanted it, and passed down to him Coke cans filled with *aguardiente* for hefty swigs, and screws of paper with *coca* for him to chew, which, in his excited and confused state, he did. It was only polite.

When the first angry animal was loosed he sobered up quickly. This was a very angry beast. It charged his *barrera* and he felt the force that rattled that solid palisade like a battering ram. Mario and one of his peons who fancied himself with the cape, played the bull, dragging their capes along the ground to infuriate it further. Then the *torero*, the professional, stepped out to place the *banderillas* (these small bulls were not subjected to the *pica*—which meant, in fact that they could keep up their heads and hence be, if anything, more dangerous.) The first disaster struck. The *torero* slipped and the bull pounced, slamming into his back. The *torero* managed to get up, but he was pinned against the fence and a horn went several inches into his right thigh. Mario and several of the hands rushed out with capes to distract the bull and the *torero* dragged himself behind a barrier where a tourniquet was applied and hard excuses exchanged. The bull was left angry as ever, and holding the ring as his own. Mario looked at this friend, shrugged, declared that it would be wise to abandon the *banderillas* and proceed to try the first cape work himself. This he did, gracefully and even elegantly, for two minutes, until disaster struck again. The bull caught his cape on one horn, ripped it from his hands, stood on it and proceeded to shred it to pieces in a growing fury with his tormentors. Mario, limping, made it back behind the barrier and handed the middle-aged hero a cape. It felt incredibly heavy. "You're on" he said. "But" began the hero—"But nothing," said Mario, "the bull is angry, the crowd is getting restless, and you're all we have."

To (sarcastic?) cries of "*Viva el Gringo Blanco!*" He edged out waving his cape and weakly calling "Hey, *toro, toro.*" The bull pawed the sand and didn't move, didn't seem to notice him. Then he remembered the advice of Mario the Magus: the bull always marked out for himself a circle that was his territory, the *querencia*. To get his attention you must break that circle. The expert knew exactly how and where to do this; our hero, just stalked in, like, he thought cockily to himself, Achilles careless of the Trojans, confident of victory. To the crowd, now in a frenzy of good-humored blood lust, he seemed to be wandering about aimlessly and they screamed at the bull to come for him. It obeyed. Suddenly and without warning it charged. There was very little time to remember the brief instructions "Remember," Mario had said, "the bull will always follow the cape, so make darn sure you are *never* behind the cape, when the bull gets to you." But that was the art of it: you kept the cape loose in front of you until the bull was almost on you, then, at the very last moment (the later you could leave it the greater the art) you put the left foot slightly forward and swept the cape outwards at arms length. The ideal was a smooth swish of the cape, leading the tips of the horns.

And by God it worked. As he swept the cape sideways (too near the sand he was told later, by the armchair matadors and critics, who didn't realize that the cape was a dead weight in his numb hands) the bull, as if directed by remote control, swerved and followed: close, but passing safely to his left. It was intoxicating to smell the bull-scent, to feel the power of moving this wild killer at will where he wanted it to go. He remembered in time to pivot ("Pivot, young man! Pivot!") and meet the return charge, change feet and sweep it to his right. Despite the horns, the blood on the sand, the shredded cape, the sheer brutal savage purposeful force of the animal, he was exhilarated. It had been faced; he had followed the rules, intellect was triumphing over brute force, culture over nature, man over beast. A piece of cloth and a human brain and you could bend the terrors of nature to your will. You were not stronger, you were just smarter, and that was enough. He was on what turn now? He lost count. But he was getting slower, he only knew the one pass, and the bull did not seem to be tiring. The cape felt now like a sheet of lead. Sweat was blinding his eyes. Then it struck him. "I have no idea how to stop this sequence; Mario never told me how to *stop it!*"

He kept blindly turning, helpless to end the dangerous dance. The bull's horns tangled with the cape, it knocked him off his feet, but luckily it seemed pre-occupied with the cape, and left him alone. This feisty little bull seemed to have a thing for capes; it started to shred this one. They rushed out from behind the barriers to distract it. The middle-aged academic from the USA hobbled back behind his barrier, disappointed, but not knowing quite what else he might have done. The crowd was generous; called him *mucho macho* and handed down more alcoholic Coke cans. Some of the hands who fancied their chances played the bull for a while. The professional was taken off to hospital. The bull was not killed. Some more volunteers were found and a fresh heifer brought on. Our hero did a few passes but only after having arranged to have the hands rush out on his signal so he could sprint for the barrier. A big and angry heifer was as dangerous as any bull, but Spanish culture, being what it was, heifers were only for practice. The male bull was the real thing. Mario and his daughter, herself accomplished in the ring did a neat pass together, and then "*la fiesta esta terminada!*"

The next day they went riding—but of course Mario did not tell them that the horses were only half-broken. One of them took a spectacular spill and *el gringo* decided to go after the loose horse. This spooked his own and he was bucked across several miles of *pampas* before Mario, expert with *laso* and *bolas* came to the rescue. When the battered *gringo* tried to complain about the horses, Mario's comment: "Fully broken horses are too predictable to be an interesting ride." They saw many other sights and wonders, including a tame ocelot for sale in the market at Calí. It licked his hand, and in his delirious state he wanted to buy it. They restrained him. But he always remembers the supple beauty of that sleek enormous cat, how it seemed to call out to him, drawing him into its amber eyes, calling him: "We belong together. In another life I was a beautiful woman and was chosen as a sacrifice for the gods. Take me and love me." Delirious? The raw beef et al. had smitten his bowels and Mario had given him the basic local cure of heavy doses of laudanum. The rest of the journey was a dream, or rather that Coleridgean state of not clearly distinguishing dream from waking that is the stuff of the Latin American novel. How many of those authors ate too much raw beef and took the laudanum cure, (to say nothing of chewing coca) he wondered?

He remembered dreamlike episodes watching painfully beautiful girls like exotic butterflies with soft brown bodies doing an elaborate dance with candles in a darkened club in the old city of Bogotá that specialized in folk dances for the tourists. That was the dream part. These creatures could not be real. But later (Mario knew the owner, so they stayed later) he saw them leave in street clothes, laughing, smoking and cursing among themselves. They were available, evidently, for a price, but he was too befuddled to have had the chance to mate with a butterfly had he wanted to, or had he, in his state, been able to take advantage of the opportunity. He remembered having his pocket expertly picked in the streets of Bogotá—about $100—by a duo who used the 'bump and excuse me' trick to perfection. He was so taken by the speed and skill of the thing that he couldn't concentrate on the loss.

Then there were strange discussions at gatherings of politicians. The arguments were not the usual kind he was used to among politicians. First, there was the language difficulty. His Spanish was OK for general purposes, but for intellectual discussion it fell short. But Colombian politicians were a cosmopolitan crowd, and most of those he met (Mario was a Conservative in politics) had been educated in Europe (the liberals were largely educated in the USA). So he found himself arguing in French, German and English more than Spanish. One animated conversation concerned utopia. The issue that was exercising the company was the right of the left to claim utopianism as its own. He was appealed to: was not the first great utopia written by an English Catholic nobleman, Sir Thomas More? "Mais certainment" he agreed—More was a knight of the realm, not a nobleman (not *de la noblesse*) but that was too fine a point to disagree on. In fact he became quite indignant along with his newfound conservative friends with their fine French brandy and Chilean Cabernets fifty years old. He told them of Tomás de Campanella and *The City of the Sun*, and they were dazzled. "L'utopie n'est pas une monopolie de la Gauche!" he roundly assured them, and was applauded and congratulated.

Mario was cynically amused. "Enjoy your fame," he said. That night, as mortar shells fell with loud pops into the grounds of the presidential palace just down the hill, he lay wide-eyed and sleepless, and wondered again and again how a country so wretchedly violent and criminal in its heart could produce such almost oriental, decadent beauty and such erudite politicians, who actually *cared* about who owned utopia? Well, it produced Mario and he was one of the seven wonders.

"How do you really think I did at the *corrida*?" he asked Mario.

"That you did it at all was amazing" said his host, "but you will never be a great *torero*."

"Some special reason?"

"Yes, you are lacking in fear. A great *torero* is always in fear of his life."

They saw many more marvels and had more strange encounters before leaving for the *costa* and the Sierra Madre de Santa Marta where strange Indians lived who had been untouched since before Cortez. Mario had a *ranchito* there with some cattle and his usual feudal following of *paisanos* not altogether in his pay yet somehow in his service—and, of course, their numerous relatives. Mario had problems with squatters so he went to the town of Santa Marta to see his lawyer who could not be disturbed because he was with his mistress. Mario gave his usual shrug, seemed to think this a perfectly valid excuse, and went off on some mysterious errand of his own, while the others went to buy supplies—mostly rice, some dried fish, salt, tins of things. The little party had been joined by Mario's son, Juan-Mario, who had returned from school in Paris (the Lycée Henri IV). He (the son) was contemplating military school in the USA. "I have been a soldier for God," he said (referring to his Jesuit teachers) "and now I shall be a solider for the state." He said this in French, since he knew only a very little schoolboy English, so French became the language of common discourse. He was given to asking intense questions about things English on which he considered our man an expert—his having been born there. "Que-est-ce que c'est la rôle de la Reine dans la constitution Anglaise?" he would pose—and expect a serious and lengthy answer. His response was always the same. "Mais c'est absurde, ça! Incroyable! Ils sont fous ces Anglais."

They sipped their lime juice, swigged the laudanum, and stashed rice in the jeep. As they passed into the *costa*, Mario explained that the lean and healthy peasants they saw in the fields along the pitted road were that way because they largely lived on rice and fish, and avoided vegetables. He followed the same regimen and to that, and always wearing a hat, (the flat tweed English style) he attributed his own perfect health which never required the laudanum. Keep your head warm and avoid vegetables. The early middle-aged Americanized academic had learned to shrug, and take a swig of the little brown bottle at the slightest twinge. The problem with the squatters was that, despite having an eviction order for them from the city magistrates, the local sheriff would not move them because "they had families and little children." One couldn't argue with *los niños*. So the party moved into the *ranchito* which turned out to be a half-built, half-ruined concrete maze of something that had been intended for a house but never made it. A wide tract of pure tropical jungle cut it off from the mountains. At the other side was the sea. There was coal in the mountains and the Colombian politicians had been quarreling about which U.S. company should be licensed to mine it. "Why don't you mine it yourselves?" produced hysterical laughter. "Might as well ask us to send a rocket to the moon" they said (in French, Spanish, German or English, or some mixture of them all).

On Sunday morning the Colombians left to trek through the jungle on mules to go to Mass. "How can you be so sophisticated and still buy into all that superstitious rubbish?" Big shrugs. "We like the ritual. We prefer to argue things out within the bosom of mother church." While they were gone he lay in a hammock. It had been a bad night with swarms of mosquitoes and God knows what other crawling, biting things—and the only salve was to soak oneself in *aguardiente* (a crate of which materialized from the jeep). The opium and liquor were having those postmodern, surrealistic-novel effects again. He was watching the little daughter of the lady (statuesque, beautiful, dignified, ethereal etc) who cooked the rice and fish. The little girl was trying unsuccessfully to herd the goats (their milk was the best thing so far) and stumbling in and around the flock. She seemed to be (in the novels we would never hear 'she seemed to be'—the author would simply imply it happened) — she seemed to be changing imperceptibly back and forth from goat to girl to goat-girl to kid, to girl to goat, on and bemusedly on. A goat in a ragged dress would giggle and laugh aloud, while a girl with hooves and hair would bleat and skip about, and all combinations thereof. A poem occurred to him—"Caterina among the goats"—he tried to scribble it on a pad. It sounded like a bad imitation of D.H. Lawrence at *his* worst.

When they came back from church Mario suggested a swim, but only the two of them went. There at the river estuary was a tempting sandbar not too far out. Mario was a strong swimmer; the visitor could scarcely swim at all. Even thoughts of swimming made him panic and gave him nightmares. But Mario found a piece of dead tree and they clung to this for rests and paddled hard to reach the sandbar. They lay there watching the churning water. It was, Mario explained, where the fresh water from the river met the salt water from the sea. It created a rare oxygenated mix which attracted huge schools of fish, he said; that was why the sharks gathered there in such numbers. At that he dove back in and swam strongly to the shore. Bereft of opium, the guest paddled back in slow terror and staggered, shaking, back to the rambling ruin of a hacienda where rice was boiling, the fish on the grill. He started to try to expostulate about the sharks. Mario shrugged. "Ils ne mangent pas les hommes," he said. "Pourquoi n'existe-t-il pas une partie Communiste en Angletère?" Juan-Mario had successfully changed the subject. Our guest reached for the little brown bottle. That night he discovered chiggers and fleas added to his epidermal torments, and he slept in a bath of alcohol, soaking his underwear repeatedly to get relief.

The ever-efficient Juan-Mario reminded him early, early the next morning (he'll like military school) that he was to fly back from Baranquilla (or was it Cartagena) that afternoon. In the night there had been a torrential downpour. The jungle was flooded. They would have to ride out on mules. Cancel the plane?

"Pas de téléphone!"

"Oh Christ!"

"Mais oui, maintenant on appelle à notre seigneur! Ha!"

So through the jungle it was. Mario went along: the cycle had to be completed by the Magus. Two *paisano* guides with huge machetes hanging from their saddles and Zapata mustaches from their upper lips, led the mules, including those to which the suitcases were tied. But for half the journey they were up to their waists in aromatic mud and sludge. The itching was now totally unbearable, but he had long ago stopped trying to beat off the vicious marauding gringo-loving insects. His skin was a mottled, pestilent mess. When they got to the bus, no one would sit near them, until it go so crowded there was no option, but there was much muttering in a Spanish beyond comprehension. The bus, loaded with ornaments and religious statues, shot around the winding cliff road, horn blowing all the time, and at certain hair-raising corners the driver called out numbers—*"Vente! Tres! Cinco!."* These were the number of traffic deaths on each corner this year to date, it turned out. The passengers dutifully crossed themselves at each number.

The little brown bottle was almost empty. The itching had achieved the intensity of a steady scream of the flesh. As they descended towards town they were stopped by soldiers at a roadblock. The *capitano* passed his hat to the driver who passed it among the passengers and they stoically dropped in the requisite number of *pesos*. *El gringo blanco* made to protest, but Mario explained: "Everyone on this bus has some reason to be examined—you for your passport for example—and if the soldiers in fact did their job, we'd be here for hours and you'd miss your plane. This way we just pay up and roll on." "These guys don't get paid very often," Mario continued, indicating the defeated and bedraggled soldiery who looked as if they would surrender at the sound of a firecracker, "at least this means some money will go directly to their families." *Los niños* strike again. El gringo was about to comment, probably about the evils of a military not wholly responsible to the civil government or some such blather, but was cut off with a: "Think of it as a tourist tax." They made the plane with five minutes to spare. They knew who Mario was, so they held the plane, and our hero, whimpering at the empty bottle, which they gently removed from him, was led aboard by kind but obviously appalled flight attendants. "Take care of him," said the Magus "he is the world's expert on utopias."

His seat companion didn't seem to mind the smell—the combination of unwashed body, alcohol-soaked underwear, jungle mud, human and male sweat, and discreet overtones of dried urine and dead fish. She was terrified at having to fill in some forms. He helped her in his slurred and hesitant Spanish—it was a relief not to be speaking French. She helped him with her grateful smile. Some kind of emotional decompression chamber was in action. Normality was being restored. Only the deterioration of his stinking, itching flesh remained to underline the reality of his unreal experience.

At JFK, despite his condition (and his having flown in from a notorious drug-smuggling port)—or perhaps even because of it—he was ushered straight through customs. He dashed, dragging the mud-covered suitcases, into the airport pharmacy, and bought two cans of Solarcaine and a clean T-shirt and some shorts. He staggered to the men's room, found an empty stall, undressed completely, sprayed himself from head to foot until both cans were empty, dumped the foul garments in a litter box, then went to find a taxi. A smartly dressed young woman used an elbow and umbrella to beat him to the lone vehicle waiting. The spell of the Magus was broken. He was home.

15

The Meals: Eating Well While Thinking Big

A man who probably looked younger than his actual middle years, sat by an outdoor table in the hot afternoon sun at a café in a square on the Left Bank. The restaurant was tucked away—not like on the boulevards, and the main view was the church in the center of the square. It was close to the Elysée Palace; bureaucrats, ministers and the like favored it. He used to meet Clément there because they both liked the mushrooms—shipped in fresh from the country, dozens of different types—*morels, chanterelles, cèpes*. They served them just lightly grilled, and with a nice Chablis or a Muscadet they were the perfect lunch, or even dinner—on the light side. Dining in Paris, he discovered, was a serious business, however light the conversation became—and it could really leave the ground sometimes. With Clément it was usually a mixture of social science shop talk and high level gossip, and made for a good two hours of entertainment. Clément was remarkable. For a start he was not a Parisian but Viennese. Then—so many of his Parisian friends were not even French: Argentinean, Canadian, South African, American, Italian, Austrian. But Clément had established himself at the center of the Paris social-science network and ran a Foundation that was always mysteriously well funded and generous, and survived the rapid changes in political regime with an adroitness that would have astonished Talleyrand.

Clément arrived. He always bustled in, overflowing with greetings in several languages. He had brought visitors to sample the fabled mushrooms—a Famous Biologist and his daughter-in-law. The Famous Biologist was reasonably well known to our man, but the daughter-in-law was a surprising, startling novelty. Such extraordinary airs. Such an air of careless elegance. Hair loosely piled up, escaping its pins and brooches; casual sweater doubling as a short dress. And an air of intense curiosity combined with arrogant aloofness that was irresistible. They had all been reading Feyarabend—Clément also published avant-garde social science and was free with complimentary copies. So once the mushrooms were ordered he was anxious to hear comments. Our man was called upon. This was not a seminar, but more of a salon (outdoors—but a salon nonetheless.) One was expected to *étonne* the company. Our man was at a loss until he remembered a remark his friend (who was supposed to join them) had made about a review in the *New York Times* and he shamelessly appropriated it. "Feyarabend is like a tight rope walker," he said, "who is doing a very skillful job maneuvering on the tight-rope, except that it is lying on the living-room carpet." The men laughed heartily. She was not amused, she knew male showing-off when she saw it. She wasn't impressed. He changed the subject to language, and the Great Biologist was of the opinion that the rules of universal grammar (Chomsky was much in the air at the time) could be, as he put it, "Tucked away in a small corner of the genome—no problem with that."

Massimo joined the party. Massimo, the enigmatic Florentine aristocrat who was some how connected with Clément and floated around the interstices of the social science world, organized congresses, edited volumes, watched and listened, and occasionally proffered advice. He saw our man's interest in the daughter-in-law and volunteered in a whisper—"Be careful— dangerous ground." Our man, pleased with the success of his earlier plagiarized witticism, responded slickly, "What a delightful invitation, *mon ami.*" "Come into my parlor —" said Massimo, who wanted to talk about the latest exhibition by Léonor Fini at the Galérie Altmann Carpentier. Everyone had been. Even the aloof daughter-in-law had been impressed. This was a good sign. You had to be a little *vicieuse* to get a kick from Fini. She had, after all, done the illustrated *Story of O*. Her painting of the ultimately humiliated (and hence ultimately satisfied?) O, in the owl costume at the party, was discussed, as was our man's stubborn devotion to Boris Vian—something of a joke with the company, although Vian was enjoying a revival of sorts. "*L'écume des jours* is one of the least appreciated novels of the century," he volunteered— just to start an argument. She thought Vian was "irrelevant."

"What is relevant?"

"Whatever improves the lot of women."

"Are you a feminist?"

"I am a woman."

"I can see that—but what kind of woman?"

"One who likes to chart her own course."

"Does she take on passengers?"

"As long as they are aware of the dangers of the voyage."

The flirtation was proceeding apace and he felt he was holding his own, but Clément spoiled it unwittingly by demanding that he tell of his recent disastrous arrival in Paris and how it had come about. "He was coming from Israel," said Clément, "on the day after the Arab terrorists had shot a rocket at an El-Al plane at Orly." They all remembered the incident. Everyone had been jumpy. The airports had been swarming with armed police and troops. "It was not a good time to arrive from Israel without a passport."—Clément laughed again.

Well, that wasn't quite right. He had detoured from Israel to Rome to see Bob and Berdine, and from there to Briançon next to see the children. The story became very involved. He had been in Israel for a congress—perhaps even one Massimo had helped float, and had used the spare time on either side to study for a while on a kibbutz with some friendly *sabras* who taught at Haifa University. They took him to see the fortifications of Acre, some crusader castles, the Golan Heights, and Bethlehem. He wanted to see the castles partly in memory of his boyhood hero-worship of T.E. Lawrence. The Arabs were happy to show them, and to point out the moral: the Crusaders, like the Jews, thought they were here to stay forever. The congress concluded in Jerusalem where he spent hours wandering in the Old City, eating decent Arab food as a relief from Israeli boiled chicken. He visited the Wailing Wall with a young Israeli woman somehow attached to the organizers and detached from her husband doing national service. It was one of the few real perks of the academic life—otherwise underpaid and tedious—that one got to go to exotic places at other people's expense to give relatively brief papers and otherwise see something of the world.

Once on the conference merry-go-round it was easy to keep moving and the basic law (this being the seventies and quantitative sex being the rule) that there were willing—and often interesting—women at every conference, had held good to date. The Israeli meeting had been a bit heavy: moral and contentious, and spoiled by fanatic Zionists who wanted references to Judaism in every "declaration." He had enjoyed the company of the famous: Berlin, Bell, Hampshire, and the like. They had organized a public debate on the promising subject: "Is Mankind Doomed?" There was no one willing to propose the motion, so with careless bravado he volunteered and went to ask Bell if he would second it. The reply was a marvelous New York Jewish shrug on hearing the proposition, and an expressive: "Why not?" They actually won the debate hands down; by the time they had finished cataloguing mankind's faults like a couple of latter-day Jeremiahs, the opposition was in tatters. He finished with a flourish, giving the human race at best 200 years and at worst fifty. A little man rushed up to him after: "I bought fifty-year Israeli bonds," he wailed, "what shall I do? My wife will kill me?" But the audience voted against them. They were, as Berlin explained, essentially sacrificial lambs—no Israeli audience was going to vote for the demise of mankind. Hampshire delighted the audience and astonished the conferees by agreeing that the Israelis had the moral right to use nuclear weapons in their own defense. Again, our duo invoked: "Why not?"

At the Arab restaurant afterwards, he put the question of the debate to some charming English-speaking Arab neighbors with whom they had struck up acquaintance. "If it is the will of Allah," they said. How nice, this Islamic stoicism. The Jews were grimly set to defy fate; the Arabs to accept it. Or something like that. He drank a little too much that night as usual, and carried on at Berlin about nationalism and how everyone had thought it would go away, but it was back as virulent as ever and was going to get worse. Berlin said he would scrap his speech for the morrow (he was introducing a session) and talk about just that. He did. Several years later he published his thoughts. He never mentioned our man's input. So be it. Ideas that were spilled out over *arak* on warm nights on Mount Carmel, to Isaiah of all people, are not copyright. He would do his own version later and politely footnote the great man. The academic world has its own way of dealing with these things.

He bought a Bedouin rug from an Arab merchant in the Old Town ("I have six hungry children—make it ten Israeli pounds *sayyíd* for the love of God, for the little children.") I have three children myself, he thought. They are trying to overcome the dreadful handicap of asthma in the French Alps—the only place they seem able to breathe freely. The pain of the separation—his almost unbearable fear that something might happen and he *might not be there* was almost too much. He gave the man more than he asked and was showered with thanks. "*Shukran! Shukran jidan sayyíd!*" It echoed through the superstitious corridors and alleys.

It was Christmas Eve. The conferees had gone to Bethlehem, but he'd been, and he didn't want to do the tourist number. He went with her to the Wall. They separated while he went to the men's section, putting on a yarmulka from a box provided at the gate. He stood among the nodding and mumbling Jews feeling slightly ridiculous, but awed by the immensity of the Wall. Then he decided he wanted to plug into something of his own cultural Christmas past. They found a Franciscan church in the Arab quarter where midnight mass was in progress. *Adeste Fideles* was being badly sung by the monks, and it sounded odd. The sacristan handed them a hymn sheet. It was in Arabic. This was post–Vatican II, and the vernacular ruled. He had wanted the Latin mass. No. But the lessons would be read in English and Hebrew. They left. Better, he thought, to celebrate the rites of Aphrodite (Ishtar/Astarte)—not that far from her old shrine of Magdala. And the girl's name was Mariam, after all. The great thing about being a Westerner was that we had such a rich variety of cultural excuses available for doing the most obvious of things. It kept the mind busy, the vastations at bay.

The next day he took two psychologists to dinner at an internationally famous restaurant in the district just outside the Old City known as Mishkenot Sha'anim. It was a writers' and artists' colony that had been tastefully restored by Sir Moses Montefiore. He was surprised to find that it was a kosher restaurant; he perhaps shouldn't have been surprised, but he was. The wild duck with wild berry sauce was excellent, and the cabernet from one of the old and reliable vineyards in Lebanon, was even superb. He had wanted to loosen the tongues of these clever experimenters, to get them to tell him what they thought their studies in human reasoning—or the lack of it—told us about the human condition. Halfway through the second bottle, one of them (a future Nobel Prize winner) burst out: "In evolutionary terms we are an imperfect creature. We have an unfinished mind." So there it was. We did not reason very well or for very long at a time. We easily abandoned reason for intuition under stress, even defying rational premises we had rationally agreed on. It made sense, even if it was not very encouraging. The next day he set off on the quest for hopeless rationality once more.

"So he was coming back from Israel with a big rolled-up Bedouin Rug..." —Clément was filling in the background. Not quite. He had gone to Rome first to see Bob and Berdine in the apartment they rented from the famous film producer in the Trastevere. Bob liked it because it was a short walk from the best restaurants in the city, in his opinion, where they did the deep-fried *mozzarella* and the *tripa à la Romana*, and a *vitello parmagiana* with a *risotto formagia* to die for. Our man wanted to see his old friends to cement the arrangement to meet in Paris. Of course, it was great to be in their warm and gracious company again, and to join Bob at the grand in choruses of "Button Up Your Overcoat" and "Sweet Georgia Brown." Berdine was as beautiful and eloquent as ever—but pining for South Africa. Rome grated on her, but she bore it for Bob's sake. They had chosen it because it was kind of mid-way between New York, London, Paris and Cape Town. Easy flights. But our man's ulterior motive had to do with Berdine's sister, the Countess of H. He had only seen her Vogue photographs, (she held the record for cover appearances) but it was love at first portrait. They had corresponded. He even sent her a poem. (In French. He called it *Image de la Comtesse.*) He was invited. Paris beckoned. It was arranged. After Briançon. After the girls.

That really *is* too long a story. "I went to Briançon, first you see," he explained to Clément and the company (now augmented by the Famous Psychologist and his girlfriend) "by train from Rome to Milan, then to Turin, then I was picked up and driven over the border into France." The border at this point was a perfunctory affair of a bored gendarme and a bored caribinieri playing chess and drinking red wine. Unless there was a pretty girl in the car they might chat up, they waved you through without checking. This part of the world had changed hands so many times that the locals were not quite sure whether they were French or Italian, spoke both languages, accepted both currencies and cooked in both cuisines. The border actually ran right through a little town: it was Mont Genèvre on one side and Monte Genevro on the other. No one in the town was quite sure where the border was. He liked these liminal places. His children spoke French in school and Italian in the streets. But the absolutely wild joy of that reunion is not the point of the story.

"When I was due to return to Paris, the nearest airport was in fact Turin in Italy. So my ex-wife drove me over the border and down to the airport. She had put our passports on the dashboard in the unlikely event that the border guards would ask for them (they didn't), and when we arrived at the airport she was in a hurry to get back, and so turned straight around and left for the mountains. It was only as she pulled away that I realized my passport was still on the dashboard. Too late. What to do? That evening I was to go to an elaborate and evidently very grand dinner party given by Bernard Malle (Louis Malle's brother—the bibliophile) and there, among other things, I could meet the Countess. I was *not* going to miss this. I reasoned that had I taken the train (too slow), the passport issue would not have arisen. The French authorities, being logical and reasonable people, would understand this."

At this point Clément, Massimo and the psychologist (Argentina) burst into peals and cackles of laughter. The Famous Biologist and his aloof daughter-in-law didn't see what was so funny. Our man ploughed on. "I first had to get out of Italy without a passport. That was the easy bit. In my bad tourist Italian I waved at the plane and mumbled that my passport, by mistake, was already aboard—*in mio valliso*. The official rolled his eyes to heaven and waved me in. I was full of confidence. So far so good. On arrival at de Gaulle I was a bit surprised to see the armed police and troops. Nonplused and clutching my Bedouin rug rolled up like a bedroll and tied with string, I approached one of the airport police and asked to whom I should speak concerning my temporary lack of a passport. In seconds, it seems, I was surrounded, my rug seized and searched, and I was hustled off to a closed room somewhere in what novelists, I'm sure, would call the bowels of the building (possibly because of the smell?) Here I was interrogated, good-cop bad-cop style, by two of the airport *flics* with a crowd of interested hangers-on nervously fingering their triggers. No, I did not come from the Middle East (I hadn't shaved and was considerably sun tanned), I came from Briançon in the French Alps. No, I was not French, I was British but lived in the USA. Yes, I did buy the rug in Israel, but that was weeks ago. No, I was not leaving the country immediately, I had to get my passport back from my ex-wife—they could call her in Briançon. Yes, I did have other identification—I had an international driver's license with my picture (it made me look like a Mafia boss) but it was *dans ma valise*. How had I got out of Italy without a passport? (What should I do? Lie again? Why not? It had worked once. In for a penny.) The airport was busy, there was a big crowd. No one asked me for the thing. *'O! Ces Italiens! Quel désordre! Inefficase!'* Cluck Cluck. Finally, having called *mon ex-femme* in Briançon and verified the story, and having retrieved my license, they decided to let me go. But I must report to X police station with my passport when it arrived, and I must give the names of three *personages d'importance* who would vouch for me. I figured the French were suckers for a little rank (particularly low rankers like these), so I remembered the guests at the dinner party. How about the brother of the Minister of Justice, I said, naming the Prince in question (Poniatowski?) And a Countess? And remembering the distinguished friend I was to visit, I added with a flourish the name and titles of a member of the *Académie Française*. It would perhaps have had more effect had I been sans rug, clean-shaven and less totally disheveled, but it was enough. I got loose. I got to my hotel, nearly in tears, cleaned up and made it to the dinner—a bit late but with a great story to tell. My hostess said I had missed my calling, I should be in espionage."

"You are in a kind of espionage," said Massimo, and the non-anthropological gathering laughed gaily, high now on the mushrooms and Muscadet. He did not tell them of how, at the dinner, and at the mercy of the hostess who rang a small silver bell to call the maids, he was not seated next to the Countess (however smiles and courtesies and eye contact had been exchanged.) Because of his recent visit to Israel, they put him next to a young scion of the Rothschild family who wished to talk about their experiments with the wine industry there. The talk went well enough, and the meal was memorable—jugged hare (cooked in its own blood with bitter chocolate) hunted on the Malle estates, and wine made ditto. The young Rothschild asked in eagerness and all innocence what our man thought of their Mount Carmel Red—the latest attempt at a popular kosher wine in Israel. He had seen the label—it had words in Hebrew on it. They told him it was to assure the drinkers of its kosher status, but he was convinced it was some ancient biblical curse against grapes. But what was he to say? This was a Rothschild after all. My God: they *owned* Chateau Lafitte and he was on the verge of an invitation. Flattery was called for. On the other hand, they knew wines like no one knew wines, and could not be hoodwinked. He opted for the brutal truth: "*Inbuvable!*" And in truth the Mount Carmel red *was* undrinkable—although (for the record) they did make a halfway decent Cabernet. The young Rothschild hesitated, bit his lip, and then cried out in anguish, "Oh mon Dieu, vous avez raison! C'est vrai! C'est vrai! Quelle chute!! Mon dieu! Mon Dieu!" Several glasses of really good Armangnac (Malle's own) later, the young nobleman was restored to good spirits and the party continued. Later his hostess looked severely at our man and asked, "What *did* you do to young M. de Rothschild?" He answered that M. de R. had been overwhelmed by evidence of courage and honesty, in an age sadly lacking in both qualities. But he did not get the invitation to Lafitte. The Countess was another matter.

He had daydreamed into this one, and lost the drift of the conversation. The great biologist and the daughter-in-law were leaving.

"Shall we meet again?"

"Perhaps. I'm in the book."

The table fell to gossiping. There was something between the Great Biologist and the daughter-in-law. The son was estranged from both father and wife now, and no one was too sure who was the father of the child. But all were insistent that when she came from the country she was wild "*comme un chat.*" Now, she had class—but the wildness was not gone. She got what she wanted, who she wanted. (She did.) Well this *was* Paris. These were extraordinary people, why should they live ordinary lives? "As for living, our servants can do that for us." (Who did not know his *Axel*?) "As for lying, our savants can do that for us." He was in his worst punning form, and they were all weary enough to be amused. It was a good afternoon.

He usually met Bob for lunch when they were back in Paris. There were only two places they went, both within easy walking distance of the Hotel St. Simon (in the Rue St. Simon, of course) where they were staying. They loved the tiny hotel, which was a veritable antique fair with bougainvillea, little rooftop dining places, and ancient bathrooms. And what social scientist could resist the association with St. Simon? They went either to Au Bougnat de la Chambre (The Coal Scuttle in the Bedroom?) which had the delicious *pâté de grève,* or the-other-restaurant-round-the-corner which did the daring sole in *red* wine sauce. Bob loved to bash the academy and extol the independent author's life.

"You have your tenure," he said, "I have three million loyal readers. Take your pick."

"I'm too lazy. Tenure suits my temperament better. What if your readers desert you?

What if you get a string of lousy reviews?"

"Never matters," said Bob." My first book got nothing but lousy reviews. I only took off with the second. Now can you tell me the name of any of the lousy reviewers?"

He couldn't.

"Nor can anyone I ask" said Bob. "So much for the power of reviewers."

One day they decided they were in a rut and should try another place. Do something daring: cross St. Germaine, go up Raspail. They got to the corner—a bit like Laurel and Hardy, the gawky thin one, the shorter tubby one and found the wind blowing strongly against them. He took Bob's arm and they made a couple of attempts. It didn't work. "The hell with it," said Bob, and they went back to the coal scuttle in the bedroom.

Settled with the *pâté* and Côte-du-Rhône and with the braised wild boar ordered, Bob asked about the Friend. . Well, he was overdue, but definitely coming. They were to go to a meeting together in Stockholm. He'd forgotten what the meeting was about—'modernization' or something such—but he'd never been to Stockholm. The Friend was somehow in charge of the arrangements by the grace of some Foundations that were footing the bill. So he would see Scandinavia for the first time. In the meantime, the two older girls were coming up to spend a few days. They had wonderful adventures, which demand their own telling, but the inevitable time of parting came. The train leaving the station seemed to drag the breath out of him as it pulled ever more rapidly away. He told himself he must get on with making the world better for them, then there would be time enough for all that father-daughter stuff. But he knew this for his usual shallow attempt at self-deception. He would try harder, though. The hurt was too much.

He fought down the pain and found what solace he could with the Countess's schemes for an Indian theme party with sitar players, authentic Punjabi food, etc. The crowd was, as usual, amusing, except for the famous film director (Bernard's brother) who somehow always got our man's goat with his arrogant opinions on all topics. The Countess said they didn't get along because they were too alike. He was making the usual surrealistic, sort of Alice-in-Wonderland, sort-of-film at the time, and had a little cockney actress—a total unknown—playing the Alice part. "I'm the one all the 'orrible things 'appen to," she explained. His exquisite Canadian wife (shortly to be estranged) was in it too—"Mostly nude, I'm afraid. It's essential to the plot, evidently. I'm working on the total body tan." She had tiny breasts, but was lip-biting beautiful. To hear the sitar players under ideal conditions the Countess had arranged to have the grand salon filled with mattresses and pillows where everyone could sit, Indian style, or lie, as they pleased. He moved to the back of room where the beautiful wife was lying, eyes closed, listening to the ragas. He lay down beside her and took her hand, and they lay there quite still, eyes closed, holding hands through the long piece. "That was nice," she said, "we should do it again." The smile killed him; he knew in a flash why Menelaus had forgiven Helen without question. The Countess, who had noticed, was not pleased. "It was harmless," he said. "Tcha! It was the most erotic thing I've seen in years—in public at least!" She never stayed angry for long. She was never in any particular mood for more than a few minutes. Her mind ran, Bob said affectionately, on silver roller skates. She would have been perfect with Fred Astaire.

The Friend arrived and they left for Stockholm. The King of Sweden had loaned them a palace for the gathering, but the meeting was a long yawn, and when he couldn't sleep he sat up and wrote a satire on the event in the form of a debate among battery hens about their terrible conditions. The Swedes were intriguing. It was like being surrounded by bunches of twittering albinos. He wasn't able to cultivate many friendships, but they did get invited to the home of an old cavalry officer who poured out his misery at the "moral destruction" of his nation for not fighting in WWII. As he got drunker, the old warrior insisted in showing them all his sword drills with his ceremonial sword. It was both sad and dangerous—somewhat Japanese. But the main point of the expedition, as far as the Friend was concerned, was to dine at The Opera House Restaurant. It had been recommended as one of the best in Europe. "Why not?" The Friend, as well as being a colleague and co-author and all that, and one of the smartest people he'd ever known, was also the consummate winer and diner and cultivator of those-who-knew-where-to-dine-out. That is why they were deep into incredibly delicious pecan game hens at Caroline Dunbar's in New Orleans, when the rest of the conferees were chewing away on indifferent Oysters Rockefeller mass-produced for the tourists at Antoine's. Repeat that experience conference city by conference city about a hundred times. Maybe the best was Charlie Trotter's in Chicago: eight courses, eight wines. It amounted to a short encyclopaedia of the best eating on the academic conference circuit. The Friend was later to write definitive books on the cooking of China and Japan. He knew whereof he wrote. And his Feast à l'Opèra was to be one of the great ones. Could we afford it? The Foundations (including the infinitely wealthy Nobel) were footing the food bill—all would be well. They took along the Famous Architect, because he was always good value at such an event—not only as a good dinner companion, but because his elegant presence seemed automatically to command the attention of waiters. If he only slightly raised his gold-cufflinked, French-cuffed wrist, they materialized at his elbow like Jeeves at the beckoning of Bertie Wooster. The Friend was in an expansive mood. There was great slack in the budget. They would eat well.

With the wisdom of dining-out experience, and after the subtle hint that money was no object (flashes of gold cufflinks), they left it to the headwaiter to suggest what specialties of the day were the most appropriate. Menus were never furnished; such vulgarities as prices were never discussed. They took in at their leisure the extraordinary frescoes of the Opera House Restaurant, with the very Swedish theme of black centaurs pursuing blonde nymphs. A bottle of the finest chilled aquavit was brought to cleanse their pallets instantly. The headwaiter suggested as an appetizer (not on the menu) a heap of fresh crayfish, gently boiled and served cold with huge sprigs of wild dill to accompany them. A second bottle of aquavit was produced to wash down the crayfish. They didn't talk much while attending to the serious business of crunching, snacking, chewing and drinking that this serious opener required. Communication was limited to grunts, eye gestures, occasional hand waving and exclamations of gustatory ecstasy. But between courses, each volunteered some story or anecdote to ease the passage into the next bout, while sorbets were toyed with (to cleanse the pallet again). The Famous Architect began—responding to the Friend's complaint that architects were arrogant and concerned only with the externals of design and not the real lives of the human who must inhabit their fantasy structures. He cited a building by a Very Famous Architect at Princeton, which looked exquisite, but where all the offices were on the top floor and all the washrooms in the basement, with not much but open space in between, and no lifts. The Famous Architect responded.

"Granted, we err. There is no question. But we are learning to learn. Let me give you an example. We recently designed a small college as a series of quadrangles. No better principle for the design of a college has been discovered since cloisters were converted to schoolrooms in the Middle Ages—inspired, as so many other things, by the Muslim example. But, the usual annoyance of architects you so rightly criticize, would have laid out strict and elegant geometrical paths in the quads. The very geometrical structure of the quad more or less demands it on the grounds of pure design. What we had noticed, of course, is that no one keeps to the paths; they cut corners, go around, meander across. So we decided to do this 'bottom up' rather than 'top down.' We simply seeded the quads and left them as lawns for the first year, inviting the users to walk where they pleased. At the end of the year we looked at the patterns of wear on the grass—the paths the users had made for themselves. Then we laid down paths in tile, with gardens around them, exactly where the users had made them. The interesting thing was that the asymmetrical result (for people *do* cut corners) was aesthetically strangely pleasing—not clumsy, or random or merely utilitarian. It actually *looked* good. So you see, we learn, we observe, we act."

The *aquavit* (it could be they were on a third bottle by now) was making our man argumentative; and he was prepared to argue. But on the Friend it was having the opposite effect. He was turning benign as a smiling Buddha and refused to let any intellectual belligerence ruin the expansive harmony of the occasion. The next course was the order of business; the architect's vision and human compassion were lauded. The headwaiter materialized as from a bottle at the flash of the cufflinks and suggested (not on the menu) the greatest delicacy the day could offer: a huge *sklar* had been obtained—just the one, fresh from the fishing boat. It would be slit down the sides, and each slit packed with fresh chopped herbs; then it would be gently spit roasted whole to crisp the skin, brought to the table on the spit, and served directly with side dishes of exotic pickles and rare, fresh-picked wild greens. The Friend was ecstatic. Let the games begin! And only a truly noble wine should accompany such a truly noble fish: a Corton-Charlemagne. He named the vintage (no wine list, of course)—and bring two bottles; they would undoubtedly be needed.

Our man had his first twinges of alarm. The price of one bottle of that vintage would set them back the cost of an average fine meal for four. But his cautions were gracefully turned aside by the Buddha, now so composed as to be in almost in a trance. It was all taken care of. Be at Peace! In the interval he would talk about his experiences of dining in China.

"You can tell much about a people by their dining habits. See us, here, in a typical Northern European dining setting. We sit separately. Our places are spaced and well defined, with mats, glasses, cutlery etc. We each have our own implements and plates—something we take so much for granted it seems odd to mention it. We are served separately and, of course, eat from separate plates and dishes. The tables are all separated, and each party has its own space. Tables are reserved and occupied by one party at a time. I see your eyebrows raised as of to ask, how else it could be? At one of Beijing's finest restaurants—one not aping the Western fashion but serving in the Traditional Chinese style, there is no such separation. There are communal tables and communal dishes. Each person has a rice bowl, but otherwise the diners dip into the communal dishes and heap food on their rice. There are no reservations. Those who are waiting for places look to see who is close to finishing, then crowd behind them and urge them on. No one finds this odd and annoying. The way things are done, even in a small café here, would seem like rude unsociability to the Chinese, just as to us, their system would appear chaotic and equally anti-social."

"But tell us" almost chorused his companions, "which do you *really* prefer?"

"I'm a child of my culture," said the Buddha, his smile now expanding to fill the universe. He went on to tell of the Japanese, having been asked how their eating habits reflect their culture's ethos.

"When I was there they were overwhelmed by the plenitude of beef at the newly opened McDonald's. Traditionally they did not eat much meat and it was very expensive. There is not a lot of space for cattle raising on that tight little island. But they would take a few choice cattle, feed them on beer and rice, and massage them intensively every day to spread the fat deep into the meat thus producing incredibly well-marbled steaks. Of course, only the very rich could afford it—and only small amounts even then. Mostly they ate fish, of course, but even here there were extremes. There is a particular blowfish that has an extremely toxic poison sac; a tiny amount of the poison is fatal. If the fish is eaten raw (as it is) the chef has to be extremely skillful to avoid contaminating the flesh. It is a kind of macho thing among Japanese men to eat this fish. There are seven or eight deaths a year. But as we know, the Japanese attitude towards the death of an individual is different from ours. Freshness is everything—one reason the freshest fish is eaten raw. There is a skilled art known as 'The Cuisine of Cruelty'. The chef takes a live fish and rapidly fillets it, slices up the fillets, and replaces them on the skeleton, which is then placed immediately in front of the customer. The aim is to do this so quickly that the fish is still flapping although completely filleted. This is the ultimate in freshness."

"And cruelty."

The Buddha deepened his smile and added an expansive but distinctly non-Buddhist shrug.

"And could we," the F.A. mused, "have predicted Auschwitz from the German diet?" "Hitler was a vegetarian," ventured the Friend.

"To rob an omnivorous metabolism entirely of animal protein is both pointless and even dangerous." our man contributed, portentously, and not a little unsteadily by now.

But the point was rendered moot for by now the giant *sklar* had been wheeled in, and our diners suspended talk to tend to business. The carving was eloquent; not a syllable was wasted. The noble fish fell before the delicate onslaught and choice morsels from the head were carefully partitioned among the trio. The sharp white burgundy helped both the thirst and the appreciation of the delicate flesh. Sighing and replete, the diners were about to consider refraining from dessert, but the headwaiter would hear none of it.

"The theme, gentlemen, all evening has been one of wild things, fresh, natural things, tamed and presented but not tampered with too much."

Our man could not resist: "Culture intruding but gently into Nature—enhancing her rather than trying to transform the natural. Perfect!"

"Yes indeed, sir" said the appreciative headwaiter, "and we would like to continue the theme. We have obtained a most extraordinary array of fresh berries—twelve different kinds that you will recognize as blue berries, raspberries, blackberries, myrtle berries and others that, coming from Finland, perhaps have no English equivalents, but which grow on the wild heather."

"Bilberries," said our man, remembering childhood expeditions to the moors, "we call them bilberries, I think."

They were to be presented fresh, with just a little fresh cream and some *crème fraiche*, and a certain rare goat cheese that had been aged in caves. Well—a little fruit to round off the meal? Why not? But by now the Buddha-Friend-of-all-The-World was getting glassy-eyed and his eye had a fanatic gleam. This delicate dessert must be accompanied by a delicate dessert wine. Dessert wines were so under appreciated these days in the vulgar rush to buy 'dry white'– usually for the wrong reasons. We owed it to—something or other—to keep up the traditions that were dead before we were born, and honor such a great meal with a great finish. Nothing but a fine Sauterne could do this, and of the Sauternes, only a Chateau Y'Quem could do the sentiment (the meal) justice. Again a year was named; again two bottles were commanded; and again our man blanched at the thought of the soaring bill. He was calmed by the now beatific Friend who assured him it was all taken care of—the money was there; relax and enjoy; living well was still the best revenge. The Friend, in fact was by now on another dimension: he had an epiphany.

"I have just received an answer to Freud's most famous question!"

"You mean: 'What does a woman want?' "

"Exactly."

"And the answer?"

"More!"

They broke into undignified giggles over the sherbet, and in anticipation of the berries asked our man to contribute his set piece to the evening. He was urged to tell "one of his wine stories"—but not, the Friend insisted, the one about his encounter with the younger Rothschild; that had been done to death. Our man was mildly hurt, but had ideas up his sleeve. He collected wine stories to help enliven wine tastings he conducted at the College—not because he was any kind of expert, but he liked wine and the culture of wine, and had a sound "I know what I like" approach that made for convivial wine tastings. His last one had been on Chianti Classico; the Friend had not been there, so he had a story he could recycle for this occasion.

"This was told to me by Maria Teresa, a great-great-niece of Byron's last mistress in Italy, Teresa Guiccioli. At their house, north of Florence, they have copies of Petrach with Byron's notes in the margins and fly leaves. Scholars don't even know about them. My informant won my private prize for decadent aristocratic remark of the year: when she asked me to come and stay, I said I would have the three girls with me and they wouldn't have room for all of us. On the contrary, she said, the ballroom was collapsing, so they'd converted it into bedrooms. The family was delighted at having outmaneuvered the Communist Town Council by supporting their move to take over the majority of the estate garden as a 'park for the people.' Now the town must pay for its upkeep, while the townspeople rarely used it. Thus the revolutionaries had been tricked into maintaining the status quo.

"Anyway, such is my source, and she told the story of a grand old Marquesa of the Antinori's who lived alone with her servants in the old family villa during World War II. As the Germans were retreating northwards they decided that the villa, on a hill above the river, was too strategic a location for the advancing allies, and must be blown up. They sent a young *Oberleutnunt* with trucks and crew to accomplish the task. The young man drove his column up to the sweeping steps, politely rang the bell and asked to speak to the Marquesa. He explained to her that they had orders to blow up the villa. He apologized for the inconvenience, but would have to ask her to leave quickly. She nodded gravely and asked only one favor: there were several cases of very rare and fine vintages of Chianti Classico in the cellar, would there be time to get them out? And perhaps a few pieces of her personal furniture? Of course, said the young officer, and he ordered some of his men to go, under the direction of the butler, to get these things. He offered to place one of his trucks at her disposal to take them to the other side of the river, to a safe distance. She accepted, and had her chauffeur bring around her ancient Rolls to take them across also. The wine and furniture were loaded, and the little procession went across the bridge and up the hill on the other side. She had asked the *Oberleutnunt* to accompany her, and he agreed, leaving it to his sergeant to set the dynamite and the fuses. On the little elevation across the river, she had the men set up a small table and two chairs, and ordered the butler to open one of the best bottles and produce two fine crystal glasses. She sat, holding onto her cane, and looking across at the beautiful house. It had been her home since she was a girl, she told the soldier, inviting him to sit with her. King Umberto had stayed there, the Duke D'Aosta (who should have been King)— many artists and musicians. It was a house always full of life and gaiety. The solider started to stammer an apology, to explain his position. "Oh young man," she said, "my father was a soldier, my husband and my sons are all soldiers. You do not need to explain to me about obeying orders. I fully understand about obeying orders." She had the butler pour, and she and the soldier drank a last toast to the beautiful house that was her home. And as they drank the order was given and with a huge roar the house exploded into dust and fragments. The old Marquesa remained impassive, sipping her Antinori

Gran Riserva; the young soldier put down his glass, held his head on his hands, and wept without ceasing."

This had been overheard by a German waiter, who was so overcome he burst out:

"Ah! Mein Hertz war mit dem jungen Soldaten!"

He hurried away, dabbing his eyes with his serviette. He was cloned immediately, and the level of service diminished not one iota. During the consumption of the berries they asked him about his source.

"Ah yes—she gave the best informal dinner parties in New York. Her best friend had married the Prince de Liège, who, in the absence of heirs, would inherit the Belgian throne. The Prince was enthusiastic about evolution, and fascinated to hear of the small Belgian school of ethologists that had flourished just after World War I, and then fizzled out. The Princess was not impressed. She was a Catholic; she didn't believe in evolution, she said. How do they know? The Prince expostulated, "On a des crains ! On a des crains!" But she was not convinced. It was with Maria Teresa that I learned to appreciate the best of Chianti Classico. People don't realize it is both a mixed wine (Sangiovese grapes and a little white Trebbiano to give it its characteristic fizz) and a deliberately invented one. The Barone Ricasoli —Independent Italy's second Prime Minister—invented it in the 1850s. Well, it was a custom at the informal dinners for guests to bring a bottle, and one evening, I found two bottles of Ricasoli's own *Castello di Brolio* of a vintage no longer easily obtainable, and, I thought, long since totally consumed. Who brought them? A charming Italian lady was pointed out. I went over and asked her how on earth she had managed to find them. "Oh," she said, "they were just lying around the house." I asked my source who she was that she would have such treasures lying around her house. "Well," she told me, as the lady in question left in a flurry of *ciaos* and waves, "that was the Baronessa Ricasoli." She had come amongst us, and I knew her not!"

The berries were gone, too, by now, and the liquid gold of the sauternes had joined them. The diners were ready to call it a day (well, perhaps a little *digestif* to round it off?) when the headwaiter intervened again. He was, he said, so delighted—the restaurant was so delighted—to have such discerning clients, that it intended to extend to them an extraordinary privilege, one that was usually reserved for season box holders at the Opera who dined there. A golden key was produced, which was the key to the deepest wine cellars, wherein was entombed a small and exclusive bar among the bottles and the barrels. Only the most special and choice of liqueurs were kept there. Would they come to take advantage? Our man, seeing only further huge expense, was about to decline, but the Friend, who was now floating several feet off the ground, overruled and graciously accepted on their behalf.

"There can't possibly be enough, even in these rich coffers, to cover this," he protested.

"Peace" said the floating Buddha, "there is."

So down they went and it was charming, and how could you, sitting there as privileged guests of the Opera, amidst the candlelit barrels and bottles, have anything other than a bottle of Napoleon brandy to round it off? Anything less would have been an insult to the occasion. It was ordered.

Halfway through the bottle, the Famous Architect excused himself, since he had to give a paper the next day and must get *some* sleep. He would surely sleep elegantly and well. (Did his pajamas have gold cufflinks?) It was after he left that our man casually asked what the Friend had arranged by way of a banquet for the twenty-five conferees the next evening.

The Buddha crashed to earth. The smile shrank to a twitch. He gulped the unbelievably expensive brandy and choked. "Oh my God—the banquet. I'd forgotten!" And there it was. The money that should have gone on the banquet for twenty-five, had been lavished on the confident threesome—and a little more to boot. Disaster loomed. The pall was cast. The evening, so bright and brilliant so far, looked like ending in tragedy (on at least excruciating embarrassment). But these circumstances asked for all their cunning, and having rallied the Friend with the rest of the brandy, paid the mind-numbing bill and its necessary lavish tip with palpitations approaching heart failure, they hit the hotel and the calculator. There was a little left—and something could be juggled from another column to swell it a little more.

At this point the Famous Architect, unable to sleep, came down into the hotel lobby to polish his paper a little more. He found our hapless twosome groaning over the pitiful sum remaining. He calmed them down.

"The point is," he said, "that while our eminent colleagues are great scholars and scientists, they are not bon vivants. What they want is a good time and a jolly occasion; they won't pay all that much attention to the food and drink. Stockholm, like other European capitals, is very cosmopolitan and has many ethnic bistros that are cheap but lively. There is, for example, a wonderful Polish café with a gypsy band, and accordionists playing polkas, and waitresses in peasant costume, and not half bad, robust cooking—and above all very, very cheap."

So it was arranged. The owner was delighted and set up a long table to accommodate his distinguished clientele, and promised the works as far as entertainment went. The dinner would be pork chops and dumplings, and the house wine, in giant carafes, was a Hungarian Egri Bikaver (Bull's Blood) and more than tolerable, if a little over sugared. The price for all twenty-five would be slightly less than the cost of one course at the previous evening's blowout. The party was a huge success. The conferees loved the music, ate heartily of the chops and dumplings, and quaffed the plentiful Hungarian plonk like seasoned topers. The evening was dominated by the Mayor of

Budapest. His name was Bognar, and his manner so regal that he was dubbed Bognar Regis. He was also the President of his nation's Academy of Sciences. He told hearty tales of his feuds with the General Secretary of the Communist Party, ending with what was obviously his favorite joke, or riddle: "Q: What are the three most useless things in the world? A: A man's tits; the Pope's prick; and the General Secretary of the Communist Party." Encouraged by the general applause he told the story of the visiting Russian commissar: He-Who-Must-Be-Impressed. They put on a special production of a stage version of *Anna Karenina* for him. He was not pleased. "But tell us, comrade commissar, what was wrong?" "You made the aristocrats look too stupid," he told them. "If the aristocrats were really that stupid, the revolution would have been too easy. "

They promised to up the I.Q. of the aristocrats next time. The moral was, it seemed, that there was no pleasing some people. But the Mayor, having been deputed to give a toast of thanks to the organizers, insisted that he and his colleagues had been indeed well pleased beyond measure (violins shrieked, accordions wailed, tambourines rattled) and thanked the organizers—our twosome—for their noble and valiant efforts. Cheers! Hear Hear! The Friend had to respond, and with becoming modesty disclaimed the credit, thanking the Foundations for their generosity, and the King for lending them a palace. He said that, yes, it had been a time-consuming and arduous task, but that they would be prepared to go through it all again for such a splendid result. No one seemed to notice, above the polkas and gypsy din, that our man, having caught a broad wink from the Famous Architect, had laughed himself into a crying fit at the other end of the table.

Part 3

Reflections on a Life

16

The Point: Connecting with the Teenage Murderer

William Golding always knew how to present the counter-intuitive situation in a story, to grab our attention and make a point. In *The Scorpion God* he has Pretty Flower, the king's daughter in some pre-pharoanic Nile kingdom, shock the chief priest to the core by refusing to have sex with her brother, and denying her "lawful desire" for her father. She confesses to being titillated by the tales of The Liar, a non-relative and so not a lawful object of lust. No wonder, says the horrified priest, that the very elements of nature are against us. In *Clunk-clunk*, the unlikely hero is a flute-playing cripple boy, in an early hunting and gathering band, who is despised by the hunters (the Leopard Men), but adored by the Bee women, who invite him to their secret rites so they may get pregnant by him. The Leopard Men are useless at getting food, being only interested in hunting leopards for prestige. The women tolerate the men, whom they need for breeding purposes, and keep them fed with the vegetables and fruit they gather, while sarcastically pretending to admire them. ("O great Leopard men!") In *Pincher Martin*, the shipwrecked Pincher, hopelessly stranded on a bare rock in the Atlantic, devises a survival strategy: he names every natural feature of his rock—"I will tie it down with names." Safety Rock, Food Cliff, Prospect Cliff, Oxford Circus, Piccadilly, Leicester Square. "If this rock tries to adapt me to its way I will refuse and adapt it to mine."

These examples show how the fabulist can go straight to the heart of the matter, including anticipating the evolutionary principle of "selection for a handicap"—which might explain the peacock's tail. But it is in *Free Fall* that Golding scores a point dear to our Sordellian purpose. His middle-aged protagonist contemplates how he would feel if he were suddenly arrested for a murder he committed when he was fifteen. He would feel shocked and indignant. What had anything that odd young boy did then to do with him now? That was a different person, a different place and time; it was unconnected with anything to do with him today; he could not be responsible for something that little stranger did. There was simply *no connection*.

Tell that to the judge. For the law there is a physical continuity, and that is enough. For us, however, the continuity of selfhood is harder to establish; the development of the self, of the soul, is fraught with freakish accidents that bounce the physical person around and send him off in unintended directions. Like someone in an old Irish legend, he is fish one day, fowl the next.

> Among herds of boars I was,
> Though today I am among bird-flocks;
> I know what will come of it:
> I shall still be in another shape!

How close he felt to Tuan Mac Cairill, the shape-changer, the magician, the trickster, or to the mad Sweeney living in the trees on watercress. What, he thought, did they think was the point of such an existence? The point was to keep changing in order to keep alive, nothing much more. They had no choice in the matter. This is what life was; this is what you did. They didn't worry about sense of self or continuity; this was not the point. He worried about it, and felt less and less any sense of continuity with his old lives or any confidence in those to come. He had a vague sense of direction, but no strong convictions about it.

His strongest convictions were largely negative: the greatest enemy of man was fanaticism. If we could only learn to avoid fanaticism, we might just survive. He would have to think about that. Why did we seem unable to live without attributing blame to someone, without fanatical attachments? They did not have to be foaming at the mouth fanaticisms: they could be of the "quiet devotion to..." type he saw in the religious English. It was the grip that mattered: you were in the grip of the idea. He had broken the grip of many ideas, and was now living among them again. Sweeney in the treetops. He was repeatedly hit with mini-vastations as he tried to feel at ease among the dreaming spires. What was the point of it all, except perhaps to ask this very question?

If he felt any sense of continuity with the elusive former selves, it was at the level of fear as it manifested itself in dreams: those soap operas of the diabolical unconscious. There was the performance anxiety dream in all its guises: the lines not learned, the solo cello part not rehearsed, the exam not studied for. This dream saw life as merely an elaborate vehicle for self-humiliation. Then there were the dreams of the living dead, whole cities and countries of them: soulless, ash-white, black-eyed zombies crowding in on him, and him naked as Sweeney in the treetops, frozen and unable to escape. But most of all there were the dreams of the house of the soul, often stuffed with furniture and possessions and people, with many rooms complexly joined and surprising, including always a rotting ballroom for the dead to dance in.

Whatever went on in the soul's dwelling, one thing was constant: there was an attic that let in the rain, and it was always raining. Rain poured down the attic walls, destroying the rafters and the floor and threatening to invade the over-furnished rooms below. He always panicked in the dream and called out that they must sell the house, just before he woke.

The discontinuity of things struck him immediately in Oxford. He asked where the undergraduates were. The last time he had been there he had seen them swarming about in their short gowns going to lectures, tutorials and, in white bow ties, to exams. Now, he complained, the town seemed full of longhaired builders' laborers in pea jackets and jeans. These *were* the under-graduates, Rodney told him. What could you do? They had simply aban-doned the gowns, and you couldn't gate the whole undergraduate body. Some of the men's colleges were admitting women, and there were regular sit-ins and street demonstrations against those that hadn't moved fast enough to please the pea-jacketed reformers. "Let women into Merton," proclaimed the banners. The joke went that Oxford, being at root conservative and gradual-ist, had only demanded: "Let heterosexuals into All Souls."

Each college had its "junior common room," which organized student affairs. Now the self-proclaimed "activists" were demonstrating for a univer-sity-wide "students union" so that they would be just like all the provincial universities. The student politicians were no doubt frustrated because with-out such a union they did not get all the perks of travel abroad to student conferences and the chance to wield direct power in Labour politics. What-ever their motives, it was easy in those days to get up a protest and a "demo"— if you were activists you had to be active about something. The CND movement had been a fertile training ground for organized indignation. The local foxhunts were already feeling the effect of this routinized passion. There was to be no escape from it even among the gleaming spires, it seemed.

He had tried to ease this transition by traveling on what proved to be the last journey of the *SS France*. This allowed him to bring more baggage— winter clothes mostly—than the plane. It also allowed him to indulge his interrupted penchant for ballroom dancing. There was always a dance compe-tition, so he watched carefully and spotted a first class partner who seemed unattached. She was a mother of two on her way to join a soldier husband in Germany. He was better with the shyness now, and asked her to dance, and then be his partner in the competition. They won a bottle of champagne for the slow waltz. She was perfect in her execution of the fishtail and the whisk. Those hours with the chair as a partner, and the pivot, pivot, pivot, had not been wasted after all.

It was a gentle transition, but his arrival coincided with the death of Evans-Pritchard, his alcohol-rich body discovered in the bath. He had to comfort a distraught Juliet, who had been sincerely fond of the old eccentric, whom she had taken to the ancestral castle in Scotland, where he enjoyed taking tweedy walks with the dogs and having the locals touch their caps and call him "Sir Edward." This was something lacking in the post-deferential society that was now Oxford. There was a memorial service for him in All Souls' Chapel—the professor of anthropology was automatically a fellow All Souls. The visitor had to separate himself from the student friends of Juliet and join the senior faculty for the service, conducted by John Sparrow, looking very like his Derek Hill portrait. There were readings and prayers and some music, but no eulogy. After, on the carpet-smooth lawn, in the main quadrangle, with the men all in black, and the women looking funereally elegant, he got his first mix-and-mingle with the anthropologists. It was a sad, but perhaps appropriate *entré* to his place of retreat.

The little row house Juliet had painted entirely white. It was in the oddly named "Jeune Street"—which the locals pronounced "June." He installed a small fridge (he now needed ice in his drinks—a sign of something) and joined the local wine club, which gave discounts to faculty. He made an expansive desk out of a flush door nailed across the two halves of a second-hand dressing table sawn down the middle—all painted white. This gave lots of surface area, and several useful drawers. The Olivetti was in place and he was ready to start. But he felt he needed something other than unrelieved brightness around him. A local frame shop was selling a new version of solid laminated prints: large and inexpensive. He bought his favorite pre-Raphaelites: *The Lady of Shalott, The Death of Ophelia, King Cophetua and the Beggar Maid,* and *The Enchantment of Merlin.* With his dying women and frustrated males safely about him, he was ready. It kept him busy; it kept him from the nagging surges of doubt; it established a point, at least for the near future.

Get down to the business of writing his contribution to *Biosocial Anthropology,* including a short introduction, and most important, editing the other contributions. Norbert Bischoff's was based on an article, which had useful illustrative diagrams. But Norbert had left these out of the conference version. So the unhappy editor had to go through and put them all back in, and at the same time revise the translation into English, on the basis of his not too secure German. It worked out in the end. He had to ask Bill Hamilton to write an appendix explaining the Prisoner's Dilemma, since without this he doubted if any but the initiated would understand the article. Bill good-naturedly complied, and sent a three-dimensional diagram to help clarify the whole business. Perhaps it did. But before he could go any further, he had to go see how the girls were doing in their seaside house at Ferring on the Surrey coast. Particularly worrisome was the state of the schools. They would have to go to the local schools, whatever they were.

Kate was *not happy* with her school. She described it as not knowing whether it was a grammar school or a comprehensive (it was in fact a merger) and coming from the relatively free-and-easy atmosphere of a Princeton private school, she found the teachers dowdy, the students sullen, and the rules ridiculous. "They treat us like schoolchildren," she complained. She brought home a report card with great marks in the subjects, but a poor mark on the section oddly called "behaviour." She was evidently guilty of excessive fidgeting. What's that, Kate? "Anything above breathing." Ellie and Anne went to the local Church of England primary school. He had agnostic qualms, but in its way such a school had saved him, and he gave the benefit of the doubt to this one. It was perfect. They did *Peter and the Wolf* for the school show, and Ellie was a super a Peter with her beret and red scarf. "I want to be an actress Daddy," she said in her rapidly acquired home-counties accent. "Of course." But it couldn't last. Anne was no better—well, a bit. Freedom from pollution might have helped, but the cold channel winds and a house which turned out to have been once full of cats, offset any advantages. Where could one go? What could one do? She couldn't miss school and ride about on Ellie's back forever.

Once, in the earlier incarnation in England, they had gone to France to a little village in the Massif Central, and remembered she had been better there, in the higher, drier, warmer altitude. Could that be the answer? Desperation. Her little face so piqued. He thought of Ireland: a clean and unpolluted country, and compared with New Jersey not humid in the summer, or cold in the winter. Kate had survived there, but more by act of will than purity of ozone. Her attacks could be as bad as Anne's, but they were less frequent. They did not persist all the time, day and night; nor did they require the prop-up-on-a-kitchen-chair-back-and-read-for-two-hours-at-a-time that Anne required, unable as she was to sustain unaided the weight of her inflamed lungs.

Kate and Ellie, with their stepsister, had gone for a few weeks of a summer to a horse farm near Galway, in the shadow of Croagh Patrick. This despite the usually terrible effects horse dander had on fragile bronchial tubes. Kate of the indomitable will. Kate of the I-will-succeed-at-whatever-I-choose oldest-child personality. He flew with them to Dublin and took them across to the west, to the rough and ready, scruffy but friendly horse farm, with its few nags, one good pony, and the inevitable charming and friendly family. "We all muck in here," they said, "one big happy family." Right enough.

The girls were in heaven. They put him on the naggiest nag (he stayed one night in the local—damp and noisy—hostelry) which pulled furiously to the right and turned that way into any open gate or hole in the wall. He only got any kind of ride by getting it into the biggest field and making it gallop clockwise, such that its dextral proclivities could be turned into an asset. Of course, it rained the whole time, and he was glad to flee the place and leave it to the horse maidens. To get them to clean up their rooms was impossible, but they would spend hours cleaning shit-impregnated straw out of horseboxes—for fun, they said.

Business took him to Paris, then back to London where the telephone call came, to the National Liberal Club, still his home away from home. Kate was in a bad way—very, very bad attacks; doctor said she must be got away from the horses and the continual rain. Kate on the phone, wheezing, coughing and choking: "Give me 'til the end of the week, *please* Daddy! I'll beat this thing, I will—please, three days then call back. I'll be fine." This last through a giant wheeze and hacking cough. The lady of the house agreed to three days—but then it was off and away. Ellie was fine; poor Ellie was always fine, always shoved aside while the sick ones were attended to.

"Let her stay, Daddy," she said, "she'll beat it."

"It's not a matter of will power, Ellie."

"With Katie it is."

And on the third day she rose again from the bed and ascended onto horseback, and sitteth on the right-hand-turning horse, and canters clockwise round the green, green fields of that rain-drenched bit of heaven across the Irish sea. There were minor episodes, but she survived and enjoyed.

So perhaps Ireland, perhaps France, perhaps...In the meantime he had to plough on. He was not much involved in college life, since he had no official college affiliation. He dined in hall often enough, a few times with Rodney at Merton, where they chatted with Harvard's Willard van Orman Quine about natural selection and the social origin of categories early in linguistic evolution, and found the philosopher quite sympathetic, much to Rodney's surprise. Natural selection had obviously honed our mentalities to expect causality, said Quine: the origin of categorical thinking was clearly adaptational. Hume had understood this. Quine told them his name was Manx, and was a form of Quinn, who was a giant in Manx legend.

At the same table was the marine biologist Alister Hardy, who had created a stir and a small industry with his theory that man evolved in the sea. This came about, said the scientist with a hint of mischief, through a challenge from a colleague. Hardy was complaining about all the attention the behavioral biologists like Tinbergen and Morris got, while marine biologists were ignored. Well, the colleague said, marine biology has no attention grabbing theories about humans. "I could write you now six reasons why man evolved in the sea," replied Hardy, adding that this was right off the top of his head. Do that, suggested the colleague, and you'll have instant fame. So Hardy scrapped an already prepared after-dinner talk and, in the train on the way to the event, wrote down his list on a scrap of paper and gave that as his address to the rather startled audience. The publisher of *New Scientist* was there, and the rest is history. But now, said a somewhat wistful Hardy, it had perhaps got out of hand. They were organizing symposia in the States, and a woman with a Welsh name (Morgan?) was pestering him for more details because she wanted to write a "feminist" book about the "aquatic theory." But Hardy was defensive. He'd come to like his theory, he said. It was as good as any of the other just-so stories circulating; they were all equally probable or improbable. Let it ride. Anyway, he was enjoying the attention.

He had lunch at All Souls with Freedman, and admired the photos of T. E. Lawrence and Radcliffe-Brown. Dinner there had him in an awkward moment with A. L. Rowse. For a start he had to fend of Rowse's not-too-serious advances, but then he had the temerity to bring up the subject of the authorship of Shakespeare. He even worse had to mention Enoch Powell's quite passionate espousal of the cause of the Earl of Oxford. He knew Rowse had written a "biography" of the Bard—full of suppositions rather than facts, since there were so few facts, and those contradictory. He did not know quite how passionate a bardolator Rowse was in turn. "Idiotic stuff!" spluttered the indignant one. "De Vere, de Vere! My God! Earls don't write plays. What Earl ever wrote a play? Clever grammar school boys write plays!" Despite sounding like an exaggerated version of Ashley Montagu at his most exaggerated, Rowse was a tin miner's son from Cornwall, and a clever grammar school boy himself. As a card-carrying member of the clever-grammar-school-boys' club, our boy granted the man his point in general, but said in a loud aside that it proved nothing about the case in question. Freedman was much amused, being himself, like Ashley, a product of the poor Jewish East End of London who had polished up his diction: yet another of the clever-grammar-school Mafia.

Oxford exhibited all the English contradictions over class that so dragged the country down and were such a damnable bore. The genius of social class as a system of domination is its elevation of difference into worth: the placing of a vowel or a fork; the timing of a comment or a meal; the done and the not done; the U and the non-U. These were not the obsessions of the aristocracy, whom he rather liked with their tolerant, un-fanatical manner, but the fabrications of the threatened middle classes, who retreated into Freud's "narcissism of small differences." He was horrified to see the cruel lengths the socially mobile would go to over-adapt to the milieu, while at the same time, with stunning reverse snobbery, boasting about their own humble origins.

He was asked to help with the new Human Sciences degree course (tripos?) that was being introduced. This was intended as a fusion of social science and biology, but no one seemed clear how to do that, except to have students dabble across the board. There had been talk of having some "integrative seminars" and this is where he was supposed to come in. But then it was decided to "let integration occur in the natural course of the classes and lectures." No one, including the writers, knew what that meant. So he was assigned to help out Godfrey Lienhardt with the social anthropology class for the new Human Sciences students, and to help ensure that integration occurred in the natural course... etc etc.

Godfrey, who had written a wonderful youthful study of Dinka religion, and then nothing else, was another grammar school product of a northern industrial town, but you would never have known it. Like Edwin Ardener, he had worked assiduously at the total Oxford mask, voice, manner, dress, the lot. And like all of these assimilators, he seemed to be wildly overcompensating. The buttonhole, the monocle, the silver cigarette box, the cane: the gestures and the too, too careful, over careful, enunciation. But our ex-Edwardian of the beard and snuffboxes remembered his own masks and was sympathetic to a point. Except that he had used them, and lost them, and moved on. Godfrey, like the others, was totally trapped. Could they have survived anywhere else but Oxbridge? Doubtful.

But Godfrey also liked his drink. After a seminar or lecture, the anthropologists would retire to the local pub (what was its name? The Lamb and Flag? The Eagle and Child? There were so many.) Godfrey would maintain his over-cultivated, excessively polite manner, until a few pints in, when inevitably he would break down and start insulting people. It got so raucous at one point that they had been thrown out of the regular pub and were meeting on neutral territory. Be warned, they told him, Godfrey will turn on you in his cups. And he did. But our fellow Yorkshireman, practicing a kind of hypnosis by inebriation, was always able to turn Godfrey's insults against Godfrey himself, by reminding him of his origins in Dewsbury. It would then all come out. The family had been outcasts in two world wars because of the name. They had a small wool mill, with the name "Lienhardt" in large brass letters down the mill chimney. They had added, in smaller but conspicuous letters, "Swiss" to try to deflect some of the bigotry. Godfrey's mother was locked in a constant status struggle with the lady over the back-garden wall. When Mrs. Lienhardt announced in triumph that son Godfrey had won a scholarship to Oxford, the neighbor thought for a moment then shot back, "Aye well. You can educate 'em till they're daft, can't you?" "Oh God," said Godfrey, "how glad I was to get away from it all!" And get away he did.

The classes in effect were just straightforward seminars in social anthropology, and that was fine. Godfrey was really a very good teacher, under it all, and it was fun to do all the old classics of the ethnographer's trade. They concentrated on Africa, and he drew on his resources from his days with Schap and Barnes and Lucy Mair. The students were dutiful, but dull compared with the LSE; they were super-literate compared with Rutgers. It was not burdensome, and it was voluntary. He could concentrate on the editing and his chapter. He had amassed a file of primate material and he had to sort it out. He was ambitiously trying to look for the most general features of primate systems and match them with the same of human systems, to try to see how the one may have arisen from the other. He boiled down the human to two features: descent and alliance. Humans divide kin into groups, and then assign mates on the basis of group membership. Now he had already found that both these features existed in primate societies, (his "Baboon I" and "Baboon II") but never in the same system. Thus there were, broadly, "multi-male" systems (macaques, common baboons, chimpanzees) in which there were kinship groups (descent), and "one-male" systems (geladas, hamadryas, gorillas) in which there were enduring pair bonds (usually a polygamous system), but no kinship groups (no descent.) Somehow, in the course of human evolution, these two different systems had been fused into one. He reckoned his theory of the growth of inhibition, which covered the incest taboo, would help with explaining this related development: without the growing cortical control of sex and aggression, such an outcome would be impossible.

He showed how this improved on Lévi-Strauss, because the Master had assumed things to be cultural impositions that were already there in nature: culture simply "amplified" them; it gave them names and articulated rules in language. But it did not invent them. What he did not anticipate was that, after the French translation came out, the extreme right-wing press would use this to show that L-S was wrong about human nature in general, and hence in his deductions about politics. They were after the Master's blood because of his support of radical causes, particularly over Algeria, and were glad of anything that discredited him. It was the nightmare of strange bedfellows.

The ever-indignant knight-errant offered to write a rebuttal—political decisions like these did not follow logically from any position on human nature, but L-S advised him not to bother. These things were ephemeral, said the older and wiser one; next week it would be something else. It was the old question of learning to pick your battles, a question he had never success-fully answered. He wavered between the old indignant desire to smite the unrighteous, and the equally old sense of futility: what was the point?

He asked the contributors for suggestions about a dedicatee, or perhaps two. There was remarkable agreement. Since they were trying to marry An-thropology and Ethology (broadly conceived) they decided on Sherry Washburn and Niko Tinbergen. All of them had been touched and influenced by both and Bill Hamilton said they should put "respectfully and affection-ately" in the dedication. So it was done. The nice thing about his contributors was their seriousness in trying to make this marriage. Their number was grow-ing. Hilary Callan, right here at Oxford, had written a thesis, published as *Ethology and Society*, outlining these pioneering efforts. But the entrenched interests were strong, and often bitter and hostile. He had realized by now, and laid it out for the Lorenz seminar, that they were taking on not just academic inertia and turf protection, but the Western progressivist tradition and its doctrine of human perfectibility. The *tabula rasa* was as essential an article of faith to this tradition as the incarnation was to Christianity, or reincarnation to Hinduism. It seemed that no amount of rational argument and demonstra-tion was going to make much of a dent in this religious rigidity. The "blank-slate" orthodoxy may have been unnecessary to any real, and above all practical, progressive agenda, but this did not matter: the liberal-humane majority were deeply afraid to give it up, and deeply suspicious of anything that suggested the reality of original sin.

He had made an effort to point out that there had always been the contrary tradition, although it was hard to give it a name. "Idealist" was the philosophical term, but this had an irritatingly wrong connotation in normal usage. The others were not much better: "nativist" was equally imprecise, and "intuitionist" equally unfortunate. Nevertheless, from Leibnitz and Bolingbroke through Kant and the Moral Sense school (including Jefferson), through Schopenhauer to Bradley and Bergson, to McDougall and Freud, Lorenz and Monod, there was an opposition to the tyranny of the *tabula rasa*. There was an insistence that the organism brought something to the situation and did not just take from it. To try to make it clearer, he redefined instinct as: "The organism's demand for an appropriate environment." He kept hearing the accusation of "genetic determinism." Genetic determinism didn't bother him. The genes had got us here and made a pretty good job of it; it was not the genes we had to fear, it was cultural determinism that was scary. He hoped there would always be something in the genes that would rebel against the tyranny of culture, and had been intrigued to see the great humanist Lionel Trilling arguing much the same thing in his appropriately titled *Beyond Culture*.

As he plugged away at his self-appointed task of rescuing the nativist tradition from the stranglehold of Locke and empiricism, *Encounter with Anthropology* came out in the States. He had formed a trust to use any income from it for the girls' education, so the copyright went to the "Katelian Trust." (From Kate-Ellie-Anne.) Lionel gallantly volunteered to be the trustee, and his adroit management, with the help of Sony and McDonald's, took care of quite a chunk of their expenses, although in those days it was hard to keep abreast of inflation. An Arab oil embargo, in the wake of the Yom Kippur war, threatened to drive rising prices still higher. The world would not go away, but Oxford cushioned the blow. It was a place very much unto itself, and since it was the epicenter of civilization, all other events circled round it like planets round a distant sun. His favorite Oxford story happened during World War I, when young women were going around handing out the white feathers of cowardice to able-bodied men not in the army. They came across a young don, capped and gowned, walking in the quiet of the quad and studiously reading Virgil. They handed him the feather and demanded to know why he was not out trying to save civilization. "Ladies," he answered, "I *am* the civilization they are out there trying to save."

The Oxfordians were much concerned with the super-smooth grass of their college lawns, where weeds and other blemishes were banished by full-time eliminators, always on their knees with little pointed trowels. Freedman told how, when he was first a Fellow of All Souls, he had tentatively asked a porter if he could walk on the grass. "It's your grass, sir," said the porter, eyelid unbatted. Yes, the Fellows owned the college. To boost local morale in the face of obvious American economic superiority, they told the story of the visiting rich Texan (was there any other kind?) who demanded to know how he could get a similar lawn, no expense spared. It's really very simple and inexpensive they told him. You prepare the ground, rake it carefully, seed it with good grass, then water it, roll it and mow it. "Is that all I have to do?" asked the Texan. "Yes, but you have to do it for eight hundred years."

Rodney liked *Encounter*. He enjoyed its "rebelliousness" even if he didn't share its specific sentiments. He was in charge of graduate examinations, and was always happy to get hold of something that might provide useful exam questions. Bernard Shaw had said you knew you were finished as an intellect once you began to appear as an exam question. Rodney especially liked the claim that anthropology, as taught, was not difficult, and attracted a few first-rate minds and many third-class intellects. There was no doubt where Rodney ranked himself. But the Oxfordian cynic was not impressed by his pleas for a "species-centered ethic." It offended against some Wittgensteinian canon or other to which Rodney was devoted. But it would make a good exam question: Rodney's students would know how to tear it apart. Rodney also enjoyed putting the visitor on thesis committees, and using him as external examiner, since he was conveniently on the spot. Freedman was delighted also: the Institute was being run on a shoestring, and this saved wonderfully on expenses.

He gave a seminar paper on Tory Island marriage and household. One of Rodney's students was now studying Tory, but she was elusive and refused to discuss it with him. She didn't come to the talk, because, Rodney reported, she didn't want to "contaminate" her own impressions. She refused his offer to let her see his unpublished field notes. She was working on "canons of truth" on Tory. Good luck to her. He wondered what she'd make of the King. There was no getting back there; between his writing and his ongoing duties there was no time. And the vacations were for the children. He managed a couple of visits to his mother. She refused to be lonely, and had even joined an organization that arranged for holiday stays in Spain, where she picked up rudimentary Spanish and even became adopted by a Catalan family, and espoused Catalan nationalism. "They should be able to have their own language. It isn't right!" Her indignation needed some focus. He felt sorry for Franco.

There was to be a referendum on joining the EEC, and to his surprise she intended to vote yes. The yes vote eventually won out two to one, and analysts suggested that the breakdown in insularity consequent on foreign holidays, was a major factor. She had thought that to vote no would have been insulting to her new friends. This was a huge step from the days when the *Times* would run as a headline: "Fog in Channel: Continent Isolated." On one visit home (which already felt like a strange, almost alien place) they went together to the St. George's Hall in Bradford to hear a concert: Beethoven *Emperor* concerto, Elgar *Sea Pictures*. There was, despite the strangeness, still a lingering sense of connection to this strange gray-green, damp, cloudy northern land—to the deep love of music there that had seen him through the worst of childhood and youth. He was growing so rapidly away from it all that it was warming to the soul to feel at home, briefly.

The thing that struck him was the audience. These were ordinary people—men in stiff-collared shirts and Sunday suits, ladies in modest hats, with big handbags and best winter coats. But their attention was rapt, their silence absolute. Coughs were stifled immediately; no handbags were clicked; no bangles were rattled; no sweets unwrapped. Applause was vigorous, but contained. He thought of the contrast with New York, where audiences seemed to think they were watching television and anything was allowed, and where applause was overdone and ridiculous, with the exhibitionists yelling their "bravo!" and even "brava!" (to show how really knowledgeable they were) and giving wild standing ovations to any and all merely passable performances. Those were audiences out to make their precious selves felt; this was an audience out simply to enjoy the music. He clung to these little things, because there was not a lot in the England he had come back to that inspired confidence. This was the "winter of discontent," and had the English at their fractious worst.

Labour and Wilson were back in office, having ousted the hapless Heath, but with a decided minority of the popular vote. The Liberals were as usual in receipt of a lot of votes, but very few seats. But whoever was in office, the unions were in the saddle. The issues were the usual unrestricted wage increases versus hesitant "wage restraint." But the real issue was who ruled the country. The unions were at the height of their arrogance, and a battle was as usual raging inside Labour between the moderates and the hard left—with Benn leading the faithful fundamentalists, demanding the nationalization of the twenty-five leading corporations. After the battle between the unions and Heath, and the "four-day week," no one grumbled much when Wilson decided to buy off the miners and other unions with huge wage increases, even if this could clearly only be a short-term expedient. Perhaps, our suspicious returnee thought to himself, Wilson really has a plan: he will just let wages spiral out of hand until the hard facts of inflation bite, and the unions cry uncle. Who knows?

But the lunacies of Socialism, the greed of Unionism, and the futility of Conservatism (and the continuing impotence of the Liberals) were alive and well. The usual dismal suspects were back at their game: Wilson, Callaghan, Foot, Castle, Healey, Crosland, Jenkins, Benn. In the midst of the sheik-induced slump they had no answers except to hang on until the North Sea oil flowed; the unions had no plan but to grab ever more of the dwindling GNP. The Tories and Liberals were engaged in the endless wrangling about economic micro-management that seemed to be all that politics was about. It was depressing. But the world was depressing. The CIA helped overthrow a democratic regime in Chile, putting a bullyboy general in charge. Peron came back to power in Argentina. The coup in Afghanistan had finally taken place, and the king was packed off for Italy and exile. What a pity the old man was not still there to remind us that they were all bloody fools.

But the world was put on hold while he went down to the shore to see what was happening with Anne. Kate and Ellie had come up for a week and they had had a high old time, doing the colleges and concerts, punting (badly) on the river, visiting country pubs, and partying. Kate decided she *never* wanted to go back to America ("at least not until they've finished it"); she wanted to stay here and come to Oxford. Ellie was not sure; it depended where everyone else was. But they reported that the sea air was not helping Anne who was just as wheezy and in pain as in the humid, polluted, mold-rotten, sea level of New Jersey, where she had been a little captive in an oxygen tent, struggling for every breath. She had been shot up with insulin against the terrible asthma; Kate was only marginally better. Only Ellie seemed immune: lovely, lively, blonde Ellie. She had cheerfully carried her little sister around on her back for a year when the pain was too great for her to walk.

It was a terrible thing to face—that one's own children were sick unto death, that the medical profession had thrown up its hands, and that there seemed to be nothing that could be done. How can a parent face such a thing? The doctors had said—and stupidly in her hearing—that they couldn't guarantee Anne would live through another New Jersey winter. The cold and the pollution, and in summer the heat and humidity, would kill her, they said. A less humid, less cold, less polluted climate might help. But they still insisted the causes were probably emotional. They usually looked over their glasses and stared hard at this point, knowing about the divorce. He struggled not to yell at them that these kids had two loving parents, never less. But they were the same ones who faced his own physical symptoms with, "Is there any stress in your life?" What miraculous trouble-free world did they live in, for God's sake? Life *was* stress.

He wished for a moment he did believe in God. He would have someone to hate and vent his anger and frustration on. But mostly he fought his own feelings of terror and helplessness. Karl Marx had said the worst thing in life was to know your children are sick and dying and to be helpless in the face of it. Poor Karl, who was as deep then in his own projects to interpret/change the world as our ambitious, scared young man.

Poor, brave Anne. He remembered how if she came within fifty meters of a horse she swelled up, choked, and had to be rushed to hospital for insulin shots. The otherwise much-loved rodeos were out, and there was no farm school, petting zoo, or riding lessons for her. And through it all her amazing bravery and sweetness. She broke his heart with her bravery—he called her Braveheart. In the clinic where all the other children, mostly older boys, were bawling and hollering during the painful skin tests, she bore it stoically. After the last of the thirty odd pricks, one small tear (*una furtiva lagrima*) trickled down her nose. He was devastated. No kid should need to be that brave, that cheerful, that uncomplaining. He raged silently. But what was to be done? For a brief holiday they had once gone to the Massif Central, and all reports had Anne better there in the high dry air. So he packed Anne and her mother into the mini, and said: "Go south—find somewhere." The brave pair were waved off on the ferry at Dover, heading for the warm, high, dry south.

With the help of some local cousins, he survived a week or so, caring for the two girls left in his charge, cooking in the big Aga cooker—whole chickens in a big pot surrounded with vegetables, simmered all day in the mild, coke-fired oven. But in the end he asked his mother to come down and help. He was falling behind with the editing; there were deadlines to meet. Godfrey and Rodney kindly carried his burdens at Oxford. She came down and, as always, rescued them. He was attacked by the wracking pains again—hands, feet, hips. And they waited for news. The brave pair returned with their own wild tale of adventures with mountains, sorceresses and acupuncture. But eventually they heard of Shangri-la—the place where all those so afflicted tried to go, children and adults. So they ended up on the magic mountain, in the Hautes-Alpes, in the ancient province of the Dauphinée, in the medieval town of Briançon, with the seventeenth-century fortifications (by the amazing Vaubon) on the Italian border; the town that was a *stage* in the Tour de France.

There were good schools (French *lycée* style) there—so Kate and Ellie could join them. It was a lively ski resort in the winter, a tourist spot in the summer. A rambling apartment in the old town had been secured. It was straight out of *La Bohème*. They would be supplied with huge snow boots to be in fashion, and big fur hats. They knew a little French from a colleague who was a passionate missionary of the language and gave them lessons in Princeton. So off they went. A language teacher was hired for evenings and weekends, and they were thrown into the deep end at school.

Now here was stress—big time, one would suppose. Emotions should have been *boulversé*. But Anne thrived. It was not instant, but quite quickly the very worst was over, and after a few weeks she was ice skating, playing on the *Ecole des Enfants* mixed soccer team, and practicing with the junior ice-hockey crowd. Skis were next—they were as important as footwear here. She still had the puffer handy and had exercises to expand her lungs, but she was miraculously better. It was a matter of meters: as she went up the mountains you could see the effects. The weight of the air was lifted from her lungs, color came into her cheeks, the smile passed from brave to natural. She actually took her first deep breaths without pain. Cross the five-hundred-meter mark and she was a changed child. At one thousand meters she became stable: the higher the better. Here her punished lungs could be reprieved and heal—perhaps her heart too.

Young Teddy Roosevelt, to judge by the accounts, suffered one of the worst cases of childhood asthma ever recorded. His biographer, keen to be up with the medical times, put it down to his deep subconscious fears of separation from his father. With clinical thoroughness the dates and time of the attacks were correlated with separation events, and it mostly worked. What was missed was that on those exceptional occasions when little Teddy should have been smitten mightily, but was, strangely, unaffected, the lad was hiking healthily in the Alps (Swiss). Daddy or no, at over one thousand meters he was fine.

Encouraged, enheartened, he could return to Oxford and finish the term, then go to France at Christmas. He gave a few lectures on the evolutionary perspective, and endured the mix of sarcasm and condescension that passed for serious discussion in Oxford. You cannot, he told them, pretend that history began only a few thousand years ago, and relegate what came before to "pre-history." Evolution is simply history over a long enough period of time for genetic changes to occur. We must revise our notions of history to include the whole of human experience, and its consequences. What we called history was merely a blip on the end of the trajectory. It was an experiment that might very well not succeed. What was at issue in this debate, he urged, was not just a theoretical matter for the behavioral sciences, it did not just involve a shift in practice for psychology and anthropology; it involved mankind taking a fresh look at itself before it was too late.

But this did him no good with the sneeringly superior ones. It was even worse to set yourself up as some kind of prophet, as they saw it; it was so very, well… un-English. He had been corrupted by the Teutonic romanticism of the Yanks, and now wanted to save the world. Freedman gave him a resounding vote of confidence for the Tory paper. That is what you are good at; that is what you should stick to. Leave all this evolution stuff alone. I can do both, he retorted stubbornly. It was important, he persisted, to do both. If I can show my peers that I can do what they do just as well as they do it, then perhaps they will listen more respectfully to what else I have to say. Don't count on it, said Freedman.

But he plugged away as was his wont. He hit the psychologists with his argument about the "normal." He went back to Chance's argument that the pharmacists did not know what the normal behavior of their animals was, so how could they measure deviations from it? We had whole industries of psychological, social and political analysis of and healing for "social pathologies." But how did we know that these things were pathologies if we did not know what the normal state of society and of people in it was? The whole frantic rate of increase in numbers and complexity over the past few thousand years was seen as "progress." But was it not really a massive deviation from the Paleolithic norm: that state of nature in which our emotions and behavior and thinking had been molded over three or more million years? The political philosophers made up the "state of nature" to suit their own theories: nasty, brutish and short, or noble savagery. Now we had the chance to define it objectively: it was the state and time that was responsible for our own evolution as a distinct species.

He used the metaphor of Leviathan. Society the Great Leviathan—the stranded beast thrashing and heaving in a desperate attempt to live, as it becomes massively bloated, poisoned and tormented. Bad as its condition is, there is resilience; there is an endogenous healing power; there are social antibodies and a cultural immune system. Leviathan struggles to heal itself; it struggles to restore the basic healthy condition it knew before its ambition brought about its near collapse. The healing process itself is painful, and the beast suffers much. Now the problem is this: the diagnosticians of the wounded state have mistaken this state for normality. So they see the pains and sufferings of the healing process as pathologies. (Such as the "epidemics" of illiteracy, teenage pregnancy, divorce, juvenile delinquency, city gangs, drug taking, terrorism, nationalism, even perhaps feminism.) In their rush to cure the pathologies, perhaps the diagnosticians are in fact hampering the healing process? Some vaguely recognize that Leviathan is wounded, but they say we must accept the wounds and "adapt" to them, because we have no alternative. Modern, industrial, global economies have come too far. We cannot put the clock back. No. But we can learn to tell the time better.

His schoolboy French was rusty, and his knowledge purely literary (they never really *spoke* the damn language at school) so he bought the Berlitz tapes to brush up, and to amass those colloquial phrases so necessary to buying stamps, ordering meals and asking the way. He bought ferry and train tickets—to Calais and Paris first, where he stayed the night near the Gare du Nord. His French was tested the next day, when a young woman asked him directions. "Je ne connais pas, mademoiselle," he struggled, "je suis étrange." The young lady brightened up, "Moi aussi! Moi aussi, monsieur!" She started to say more but was dragged away, protesting, by a horrified companion. He almost got into a fight with some Algerians over a taxi, but finally made it to the train for Lyon and Briançon, and found himself on the sleeper going up into the Alps.

When he woke there and peered out of the *wagon lit* window, the shock was as sudden as the sight of the Rockies had been. You slept through the long central plain, then woke up amid precipices and peaks, and the whiteness and vastness. For the first time he understood the Romantics and their Alpine fascination. The girls had already assimilated and become native, pouting, shrugging and punctuating every sentence with "*bouf!*" or "*chouette!*" They spoke English only at home and in English classes. They learned Latin and Spanish and Italian "through French." The Latin sounded odd to the Anglophone dad:

"What is the genitive plural of *rosa*, Daddy?"

"*Rosarum?*"

"*Non, non, non! Rhozaghrhooooom!*"

They had made friends with the local magistrate, M. Rabbi, and his wife. He was an amazing man, if only for being the only Jew in the canton, and the magistrate at that. He was much respected in the town, even though he was autocratic and not above interfering in the morals of those under his jurisdiction. He would never grant divorces on mere evidence. He would lecture the parties and order them to go back and try to work things out for a while then come back to him if they failed. In the war, when the Germans were rounding up Jews, the Rabbis were hidden on a distant farm in the hills, and successfully passed off as simple-minded relatives of the farmer. Everyone knew, even those whom Rabbi had sentenced without fear or favor, yet throughout the whole occupation no one told.

M. Rabbi's daughter, the dark Jewish daughter, was at the Sorbonne studying Hebrew. She was much into the Jewish thing, and wrote poetry about it, and had changed her name back to Rabbinovitch from her father's shortening. She had spent time in the States and been a nanny for some Kennedy children. She was translating a book of California psychobabble, and having trouble with sentences like, "I don't know where my kid's head is." He tried to help: "Je ne sais pas ou se trouve la tête de mon gosse," was literal, but peculiar, while "Je ne comprend pas la condition psychologique de mon enfant," somehow missed the punch of the colloquialism. He left her to it. Rabbi read English, but was shy about speaking it. He was not shy about asking questions in French. So the struggling Englishman had to deal with rapid-fire stuff about Lévi-Strauss and *l'origine de l'exogamie* in his Berlitz-enhanced school French. Back in Oxford he told Freedman about the judge, and the mentor went to his shelves and took down a French journal of Jewish studies, and there was an article by M. Rabbi. It warned liberal French Jews not to allow their hatred of Arabs to cloud their judgment on Algeria, where it was clear that their sympathies should lie with the abused natives.

Oxford was drab and grim in the winter. But the celebrations had their usual English cheeriness, especially the concert by the King's Singers, starting with medieval Polish madrigals and ending with calypsos ("If you want to be happy, and live a good life/Never make a pretty woman your wife.") They were an all-male group, from the King's College choir in Cambridge originally, and they used two counter tenors for the soprano parts—one of them with an almost treble purity of tone. Hearing them he had a sudden flash of pain somewhere in himself that he couldn't place. It brought back those uncontrollable floods of memory for things, places, people, and above all music, which were incoherent but powerful. It was as though something was being wrenched out of him and immediately replaced by parts that were too new to work properly. He was a mental and emotional cyborg, but the new parts were effectively displacing the old. How long before there would be no old parts, except in some anguished memory that could only struggle through the metallic newness with anxiety and pain? Items could be remembered; they were stored neatly in the memory boxes. But the emotions that should have gone with them seemed not to be there any more; the appropriate emotions could not be remembered. What was the motive of the teenage murderer? The adult didn't know.

Perhaps the self has periodically to reconstitute and redefine itself. Mostly this is a case of minor nudges at predictable points in the life cycle, and societies mark these changes with appropriate rituals to help in the redefinition. But sometimes, when the points of change are not predictable, the self's equilibrium gets pushed out of whack into a state of near chaos, and the outcome is either self-destruction or a creative re-integration at a different level of selfhood that in turn becomes itself a creative force. That's what he told himself as he tried to come to terms with his sense of loss. But he thought it more likely that the self meandered back and forth between states, never coming to rest, always uncertain where it belonged.

A Christian group, via his chaplain friend, asked him to give them a "sermon" on violence. Remembering his Unitarians fondly, he agreed. He called it "The Problem of Violence" and tried to make it as sermon-like as he could. Its point was that there was no "problem of violence" as an intellectual problem, only a practical problem. Violence had its normal place in the process of natural selection, as normal as eating or sex; it was often closely linked to them in fact. It only became a problem for a creature that wanted there to be no violence. This could only happen with a conscious animal, and man was the only conscious animal. We could imagine that things that were different, and we could act on our imagination. But this was a double-edged weapon: we could also put our conscious imagination to the service of violence. Raw violence, as in nature, took care of itself. Violence between conspecifics could be ritualized, as Lorenz had shown, thus taking the sting out of it. But this was on the small natural scale. The real problem of violence for humans was not the violence itself, but the imaginative use of violence: its creative/destructive orchestration in large-scale wars.

At the small-scale level again, ritualization was both possible and common (remember the Tory "fighting"), but this was not possible with mass populations and weapons of mass destruction. It is, he perorated, our violent imaginations that are our are problem, not our natural violence. Is there no hope they asked him? Yes, he said. The basic tendency to ritualization meant that men loved the treaties as much as the wars—even loved them better. War, he suggested, was diplomacy's way of creating more diplomacy. The time spent on diplomacy outstripped that spent on war. We should keep talking. The Christians liked that, and thanked him for the words of hope.

But he didn't have much hope. The rapid growth of population and social complexity over the period of "history" had made us think we could do anything, fix anything. But the size and complexity were defeating us, grafted as they were onto a stone-age creature with the emotional equipment of a chimpanzee. He saw only the power hunger of the few, the gullibility of the many, and the xenophobia of all. The goodness and altruism of individuals was soon swamped by hatred and the need to blame: to find scapegoats when things went wrong. The fanatics bubbled just below the surface, waiting to boil over once they defined their object of blame. The shadow of the bomb still hung over all thinking about the future, and made it hard to be optimistic. But even without the bomb, he thought gloomily as he trudged over Magdalen Bridge in the slush and sleet, we would fall back on the savage ways and ideological battles that were native to us. "They" were the other tribe, the not-people, the enemies of God. Their ideas were not our ideas, their totems not our totems; they must go.

He remembered reading an odd book produced in the early twenties, called *The Origin of Man and His Superstitions,* by one Carveth Read. The "superstitions" part had seemed out of date, and a second edition had left it out and truncated the title. He had pursued a copy of the original in the British Museum Library. Read had coined the lovely term *Lycopithecus* (wolf-ape) for the human ancestor that forsook the forests and the vegetarian way of life and went hunting on the savanna. This was for Read a hypothetical creature, and although he was a contemporary of Raymond Dart, he knew nothing of *Australopithecus* and his stone cutting-tools. But in the rejected second part, Read had asked the basic question: what survival value did "superstitions" have for this wolf-ape? For superstitions read ideas, or ideologies, or magic, or religion, or philosophy or science; these were not differentiated anyway for early man. What price, in other words, consciousness? You don't *need* consciousness to be a successful savanna hunter. It must have had some value to this precarious amateur carnivore. What, asked Read, was the value of illusion to the early hunter, struggling to emerge from his apeness? On the surface he should have been better off without it; it conveys false information after all, by definition. Animals will not in fact come to be killed if you chant songs and dance in the firelight, or paint on cave walls. But perhaps the future would have been too hard to face without illusion. There was too much chance; you needed the illusion of necessity.

But this meant that men came to operate not in terms of raw nature, but in terms of their ideas and illusions about nature. And these ideas rapidly became part of the property of the hunting band, and later the tribe—its most precious possessions, to be guarded jealously and passed on to the young through the rituals of initiation as part of their identity, their selves. We became utter slaves to our ideas, no matter how wrong. It didn't matter; our ideas were what defined us. We acted in terms of our ideas about the world, and we saw as dangerous those with different ideas. They threatened our very world; they must be watched, and if necessary disposed of. This didn't matter very much when we were spread out across the earth in small bands and tribes; there was no possibility of annihilation. But now we had the means of annihilation, and we continued to think like the idea-dominated, illusion- riddled, tribal creatures we were.

There was no way out. This is the way human consciousness works. The brain itself was the great organ of illusion: it gave us not accurate information about the world, but information we would be confident to act on. Consciousness was a design failure as great as the size of the dinosaurs. It could only lead to disaster in our changed conditions. We were the victims of consciousness, yet we thought it was our crowning glory. It was a peacock's tail of an adaptation: spectacular but disastrous. We could not operate without illusion, but it would be the death of us, operating outside its Paleolithic context of adaptation. We took a huge gamble when we left the Old Stone Age. Too much, too far, too fast. Yet we went on doing more, more, more, and ever faster and ever bigger. What was the point? That we could. We were like adolescents in a fast car: it may be meant to cruise at sixty, but if it could do one hundred twenty, then that's what we would do: foot to the pedal and damn the consequences.

In the meantime, life was interesting enough. He had to go to Cambridge to give a paper. Jack Goody invited him: big-bearded, big-hearted Jack, who never finished a sentence, but who was the most erudite of the Anthropologists, and a nice man to boot. It meant, however, a possible run-in with Edmund, and he really, really didn't want that. The break had been too painful: so no salt in the wound. But Jack was persuasive. So he went, and gave his "Human Kin and Primate Kinship" paper in the detail it had now achieved, with his complete survey of all primate species, and an armful of diagrams so lovingly worked on with a pencil compass and perspex ruler, finished in Indian ink. It was the standard Oxbridge audience, out not to understand or learn but to show how clever *it* was by showing what an idiot the *speaker* must be. Edmund showed them a good example by not criticizing the paper at all, but throwing the diagrams on the table and dismissing it as "nothing more than gynecology."

Jack had suggested that if Edmund did something like this—and everyone expected him to, that it should just be ignored, and he (Jack) would move right on to another comment or question. It worked. Edmund sat and fumed. Roy Rappoport, who was visiting from Michigan, actually asked a real question about evolution and ecology. But the youngsters there were almost embarrassingly anxious to show their party colors by sneering. Some years later one of them wrote to him, full of obviously sincere apologies for this behavior, which was remembered in clear detail. The apologist announced a full conversion to the reformed point of view. At the time, our harassed presenter was consoled by a few physical anthropologists, and some Primatology students of Robert Hinde's, who took him for a drink, including a strikingly blonde Danish girl who was off to study chimpanzees with Jane Goodall at Gombe.

troglodytes genus *Pan*
peering with suspicion on
wilful woman reckless man
sapiential semblance gone

How easily affronts to dignity can be erased. Some affirmations are more important than the condescending and uncertain praise of peers. Even so, Jack said, come and spend a year at Cambridge and campaign for your ideas. Nice Jack. He would tuck that one away. Edmund was not all of Cambridge, even if he behaved as though he were.

He went to London to give yet another paper, and took in the Cattaneos. He always tried to get in a visit, usually for a night or two before flying out. Rita or Tony would drive him to the airport, Heathrow being close to Twickenham—just beyond the England Rugby stadium. Emma and Pete were growing as fast as the girls. Plans were made for them all to visit and stay for a while in the Alps in the summer. The girls adored Emma, who lectured them on how they had to suffer for the sake of beauty, and spent hours working on her Twiggy-like fringe. Fragile, delicate, utterly beautiful Emma, the fairy child who didn't want to grow up, and who made sure it never happened. But that was in the future, and for now he had to sympathize with Pete, taciturn Pete: (Where have you been Pete? "Out." What did you do? "Not much.") The poor boy, when all the girls were together, felt just overwhelmed by "all the girl stuff." There was nowhere to get away from it. The girls got together and learned the opening paragraphs of *Gone with the Wind,* and chanted them out loud. Then they ganged up and recited the witches' speech in *Macbeth* in exaggerated Yorkshire accents: "Double, double, toil and trouble/Fire burn and cauldron bubble." And they draped girl things on every spare rod and hook in the bathroom. "They should have their own bathroom, and we could have another one." Right, young Pete, in an ideal world, right.

There were strange affairs that the times spawned. Harrods opened a roof garden, all done by a performance artist in gigantic papier maché flowers. Lit up at night, the gilded ones sat under gigantic mushrooms and sunflowers and ate canapés and sipped champagne. The artist, a languid young man, (what was his name?) announced that his next project was The Lake District. He felt it was the business of art to improve on nature. The Lakes were pretty boring as they stood. Then there was the London ball where the men were ordered to appear in dinner jackets, and all the women had to wear white. Juliet never wore anything else. With the aid of trick lighting, the men were obliterated (except for cuffs and shirtfronts) and the white-clad ladies appeared a ghostly-pale, whitish blue. Oxford was more staid. The staple was the wine and cheese reception (sherry always on hand), with cultivated chatter, usually centering on the celebrity du jour wheeled in for that purpose.

Maurice Bowra was always good as entertainment. He enthralled everyone with a disquisition on the origins of music and dance: quite wrong-headed, but delightfully presented. There had been some debate between Bowra and the Fellows of the college where he was Master (Wadham?) Finally they called for a vote. Bowra was for the motion; all the Fellows were against it. "Oh dear, gentlemen," he said, "we have an impasse." Christopher Hill and he had a great talk about polygamous cults in the seventeenth century. These were more numerous than was generally appreciated. Hill thought it a good point that monogamy was something imposed rather than a natural expression of human preference. "Perhaps that is what makes it so interesting," he observed. Isaiah Berlin was always good value. He was writing some piece about the basic questions of Philosophy, and intended to insist on the distinction between analytic and synthetic propositions as the root of it. What about the Greek, "What can we know; what should we do?" Those, said Berlin, are the basic questions of life. Philosophy has not much to do with life. Iris Murdoch disagreed. This cutting itself off from life was precisely what was wrong with modern Philosophy. She agreed—contra Rousseau, that people were not born good; it was something they had to achieve. "They work hard at it all the time," she said. This is what Philosophy should pay attention to. And (he thought) what her exquisite novels were all about. He tried to put his point that being good was not as important as being human, which included good and bad in proportion. Iris said she thought she agreed, but they didn't have time to pursue it. In another time and place he would have been madly in love with the elusive Iris. But then, all the men were.

There was a very Oxford episode, with a nighttime performance in a ruined abbey by candlelight, of Sheridan Le Fanu's vampire play Carmilla. (A vampire can change its name, but must use only the letters of the original: thus "Mircalla"—an important clue in the proceedings.) The audience sat on rugs with picnics—wine was obligatory. An Anthropology student played the governess with a suitable foreign accent. She was a friend of theirs, one Tamara, a Georgian princess whose family claimed to be descended from Cleopatra. Her brother, the prince Peter, was aide de camp to the recently exiled King Constantine of Greece: ousted in a dramatic coup. The royal entourage was out of work and out of funds. (He was reminded of that Greek royal cousin, that other prince Peter, of polyandry and penury fame at the old LSE. Where was he now? No one seemed to know, or care very much.) Big efforts were made to find the King something suitable in PR or advertising; something that was not incompatible with royal dignity, and within royal competency.

Tamara had to keep going down to London to play *pricipessa* with her brother at receptions, and borrowed freely from Juliet's wardrobe, since she too was not in funds. But she did get back to Georgia, with difficulty, from time to time. She told of how they were translating *Kinship and Marriage* into Georgian (illegally—Penguin knew nothing of this.) This was anathema to Moscow, because the book said disparaging things about L. H. Morgan, who had been elevated to the Marxist pantheon (via Engels), but mostly because the Georgian language was prohibited to students who were expected to use Russian. In demonstrations against this imposition, the students brandished copies of the transcript and shouted slogans. What on earth did they shout? No matter. This was a *cause*, if not very *célèbre*.

Some reviews of *Encounter with Anthropology* came in, with a predictable pattern. The academic reviews were carping; the popular reviews enthusiastic. Of all things, the *New Yorker* fell over itself to praise the book: witty, elegant, sympathetic, understanding. Goodness. But an anthropologist, rejoicing in the appropriate name of Crapanzano, declared it, in the *Village Voice*, to be "mediocre." Takes one to know one, was his uncharitable first thought. He had no idea who this was, except that he had heard Clifford Geertz responding to the name with obvious distaste. Cliff wouldn't say why. But it was typical of what he had come to think of as punk reviewing. Lord knows, he had reviewed enough books himself, and had not always been fair to them. In a fit of temper, when reviewing Desmond Morris's *The Human Zoo*, he had lapsed into the punk mode. Desmond had said that only people who could not handle their own pair bonds would claim that humans were promiscuous or polygamous by nature. This seemed a low kind of ad hominem attack, and he had responded that perhaps only people with an overdeveloped maternal dependency neurosis would make such a fuss about pair bonds. Fair enough, but he had started the review (in the *New Republic*) with "In his previous work of science fiction..." (referring to *The Naked Ape*)—and on in that vein. Once he saw it in print he regretted the impulse, deeply. Desmond might have been wrong, but this was not an appropriate response.

A reviewer's personal opinion of a book was, he thought, of little consequence. What kind of colossal arrogance did it take to assume that your judgment on a book was of any importance or interest to thousands of readers? You were just one opinion. What the business of the reviewer entailed, was to tell the reader what was in the book, first and foremost. But the punk reviewer (like the Oxbridge seminar student) saw only an opportunity to show off his cleverness: to enhance his own ego at the expense of the author. Editors should automatically turn down reviews that were such exercises in self-aggrandizement, and that failed to give a balanced account of the book's argument and content. But then, what did one do about the punk editors? He finally decided he would simply opt out of the whole business. It was too corrupt, too ideological, too fundamentally rotten. He gave up reviewing *d'un seul coup*, as he had given up tobacco, and he felt cleaner and healthier for it.

He had to fly back at Easter to help Lionel with the latest batch of grant applications. He had a great surge of warmth at the sight and feel of New York. He had to realize that he was in his sixth year in the States (not counting two at Harvard/New Mexico) and that, despite the temporary retreat to England, this is where his life was now. It was too much to expect a sense of "home" perhaps; there would never be that, he thought, anywhere. Protean man has no home, only a current environment to which he must adapt. But he couldn't deny the feeling that it was good to be "back." When he returned he would get a small flat in the Village, he decided. Near to Lionel, near to Balducci's, near to the Path station that would whisk him to Newark and an easy connection for New Brunswick. It would have to be a small and cheap apartment, because most of his money was going on the French venture. But no matter; it would be a base for his hunting expeditions. He could go to the New York State Opera every week (there was no affording the Met), and the Village was the home of jazz. The airport was close, and France really only a few hours away. It was a good plan.

People asked him if he missed England, if he didn't still feel English and find the adaptation to American culture difficult. He didn't feel that at all. He had worked through the initial strangeness at Harvard, and once over that he began to enjoy assimilating. His accent didn't change much, but his usage did. He said "I guess" and "I reckon" and suchlike often enough for his mother to complain that he talked like a Yank. When people asked him if he was English (they always did), he took to replying: "Not for a long time." He was English though, and in some sense always would be, but this past had no absolute grip on him. He was a child of the meritocratic ideal, an ideal that embraced not just material advantage, but *being*. He was what he achieved, not what he was born as. His original position did not define him; his accomplishments did. There had been so many changes, and he had incorporated them all into his ever-changing self. He saw others, like Stuart Hampshire, who came over and never for a second emerged from behind the mask of Englishness. They could not; it was the essential part of their being; they always went back for good at some point. He would be asked about a possible "cultural identity crisis." But to have any kind of identity crisis you must first have an identity. His identity was constantly in creation; it was as unfinished as his ideas. He was a stranger wherever he went, not least in the country of his birth.

He only had a week or two for the grant work, and there was a pile of excellent applications. The duo thought of themselves as like the original Royal Society before it became a formal institution: an "Invisible College." They didn't have an Institute, like Geertz in Princeton, to which people could come. Rather they went out to the people—drew them into the web, put them in touch with each other, gave them support. An enterprise was underway. George Fountaine and Mason kept saying, why not use the resources to found a new learned society (an Association for Biosocial Anthropology perhaps? Or a Society for the Evolutionary Study of Human Behavior?) They could have a journal, meetings, factions, scandal, gossip, just like all the others. But they resisted this idea. They were both wary of guruhood; disciples meant trouble and bother. They had established a principle at Rutgers, which lasted:

that they would not hire their own graduates. Dispersal was the name of the game. Seed the virgin environments. This was at one with their idea that they were not founding a new discipline, or even a sub-discipline; they were trying to return their own discipline to its true mandate. There was no need for a new discipline so long as Anthropology would regain its evolutionary roots. The other behavioral sciences would follow. That was the plan.

So they plugged away with the grants. Some old friends: Blurton Jones, Michael Chance, Irven DeVore, Roger Larsen (now graduated), Sherry Washburn, Frank Ervin from St. Kitts with his vervet monkeys. Lionel was working with Joseph Shepher (their first graduate from the program) on what was to become *Women in the Kibbutz*, which documented the revolt of the Kibbutz women against collective child rearing. He thought back to Joseph's incest research, which had established such a crucial point. There were some sixteen exceptions to his "no marriage between *sabras*" finding. Look closely at these exceptions, he told Joseph; what do they have in common? It was there: these *sabras* had only come to live together *after the age of six*, Joseph found. Was this then a discovery of a human "critical period" for the learning of incest avoidance? If so it was an amazing breakthrough. It also cast doubt on his Johnny-derived "negative reinforcement" theory, suggesting rather a "negative imprinting" period. Great. The hypothesis had been vulnerable. They were doing science. There were also some new faces: Norman Alcock from Canada on civil war; Napoleon Chagnon on his fierce Yanomamo in the Amazon; Robert J. Lifton from Yale on death imagery and violence.

An unusual but welcome one was Alexander Marshack who had discovered what looked like symbolic markings on the artifacts of early *Homo sapiens*: they tracked the phases of the moon. Mike McGuire from Rutgers had a proposal comparing the St. Kitts vervets with their West African relatives, and then there was Bob Trivers, who continued his saga of genius and would stay with them for several years, working on an extension of the theory of altruism, to include non-relatives. Tony Forge, from Canberra, came up with a plan to look at violence and its control in Bali, and Desmond Morris (along with Collett and Marsh from Oxford) had a proposal for the future on human gestures: to be both a book and a BBC TV program. Desmond was a thoroughly decent fellow, and they had kissed and made up.

He tried to persuade Bill Hamilton to apply: anything you do is relevant to the understanding of violence and dominance, they told Bill. Your theories about inclusive fitness will revolutionize the study of kinship, they urged. But Bill was too honest and too modest. I don't really do "research" he told them. I just think about things. Look into a young zoologist from Oxford, Bill told them, called Richard Dawkins: he was to be the coming man in evolutionary genetics. Our man eventually met him for lunch at Brown's, which was where everyone met for lunch sooner or later. Richard, who looked schoolboy young (a trait they shared), told him about his work on wasps, their evolution from solitary to social, the role of aggression in that evolution, and the genetics thereof. Genes, he said were basically selfish: they were concerned with nothing but their own replication. Thus Bill's altruistic genes were basically self-serving: they were protecting replicas of themselves. Great, but wasn't there the same problem in calling genes "selfish" as there had been with calling them "altruistic"? These were metaphors that suggested intention, motivation. Wouldn't this confuse people? Only idiots, said the delightfully forthright Richard, for only an idiot would think that little snippets of DNA had intentions.

One could not help liking such a total rationalist, at the same time as fearing for the consequences of his metaphor. The idiots were swarming like wasps, and were just as aggressive. The Foundation would find some money for the research though, even if it was sometimes hard to persuade the Board of the need for fundamental research. The Board was, like the rest of the ever-anxious world, demanding "relevance." There was plenty of that fortunately. There were plenty of applicants now, happily from the social sciences and psychology, who wanted in on the action. It looked good. It felt good. Surely it *was* good. They would penetrate all fields, and reform would spread from within. The Invisible College was busily at work.

He had been invited, via Joseph Shepher, to the fiftieth anniversary celebration of the Israel Institute of Technology at Haifa. They were to have a symposium on "Ethics in an age of Technology." Berlin was enthusiastic about it, and was to be a leading speaker. So he downed tools on Tory marriage and land inheritance, and tried to work out the implications of the evolutionary view for ethics and rights. He was back to where he had more or less started: he even revived his old title of "Rational Ethics and Human Nature." He rehearsed his ideas about man having replaced "needs" with "wants" to the point where he could no longer figure out what the needs were, and had to resurrect them as "rights." As though we had to plead for the cock's "right" to crow. He must work in his old conviction that goodness what not the end of human action: goodness was always relative. The whole aim was to discern what was truly "human"—again not a catalogue of invented rights, but a true inventory of human qualities. It may not be altogether pretty, a lot of it would not be "good" as we understood that abused concept, but we had to try to regain the human scale of things. The new context otherwise could only overwhelm us.

He thought he had worked this out for violence, and for kinship. The Invisible College would plug away at the rest. But he was not sanguine. We still thought—and the social sciences aided and abetted us in this, that we could do anything we chose to do: create any kind of human we chose to create. We would not accept any doctrine of limitations on imperial humanity. We were free to create our own destruction. Perhaps there was some point in trying to run against the tide. Perhaps.

Papers for the Haifa conference began to come in, and he was struck by one on the weaknesses of human logic, by two psychologists, Daniel Kahneman and Amos Tversky. They found, with clever experiments, that people would agree to some obvious statements about the logic of probability, but when it came to making judgments they ditched the logic in favor of stereotypes. The psychologists (at least Kahnemen) thought this was evidence of an "unfinished mind" in humans: an evolutionary failure. But he was not so sure. He remembered Quine saying that our minds had evolved to assume causation, because otherwise we would not have survived. If we had spent our time calculating probabilities, we would not have survived either. Operating by stereotypes ("prejudice") was a way of playing the odds. We would be right enough of the time for that kind of thinking to become fixed. He remembered Karl Pribram putting the question to him: "Is the mind one thing, or is it many?" His own prejudices and experience meant he preferred to see the mind as a patched together *bricolage* of bits and pieces doing their various adaptive jobs: like the brain itself, the house of mind, cobbled together in evolution, in turn like the body itself. He must work this into his "Evolution of Mind" paper, which, like so many others, he did not publish since it made such a good lecture. But he would take the two psychologists to dinner once he met them. They must be brought into the fold, their work supported. He had a hunch of real importance here.

The preceptors of The Invisible College were anxious to get the entomologist from Harvard, E. O. Wilson, aboard, and eventually they did. But for the moment he was writing a big tome and wanted to get it finished. He was writing a final chapter on the evolution of human behavior. He asked our man if he could send it to him for comment, since it contained a lot of reference to his work. Of course, send it. It went to Rutgers, then to his Princeton address, then to Oxford, but to the Institute who sat on it. Finally it caught up with him in France in the summer, far too late for his comments to be useful. In any case, he suggested it be left out. He was too aware of the reception this kind of thinking had already received. It was clear that Ed. had written a fantastic compilation, taking his own theories, and the work of Hamilton and Trivers, and marrying it to the empirical findings of Ethology. It made a convincing, overwhelming case that there were laws of evolutionary genetics that applied to all species. Of course this must include our own, but was this book the place to make that case?

Darwin understood, and merely hinted at the implications for man at the end of *The Origin of Species.* The knee jerk reaction of the ideologically pure, seeing such a discussion, however convincing, at the end of this book, would ignore the solidity of the case and howl their distaste and disapproval with the standard clichés in the standard places. And Ed., being wholly a natural scientist, did not seem to understand that the social scientists would not thank him for throwing such light on human social behavior. They would go into their territorial, turf-defending mode immediately. The left wing would strike at him for his "social Darwinism" and his "biologization of history" and their standard catalogue of complaints. God only knows what the feminists would do. He and Lionel, and the others of the bandwagon, had suffered it all already; it was inevitable, and would detract from the reception of the basic science.

Why not establish the general case, have it accepted, then later deal with the implications for human behavior in a separate book? Ed. figured his massive demonstration would overwhelm such politically motivated opposition. It would, as he put it, "stake the vampires once and for all." Oh well. Our battle-bruised skeptic was not convinced. But the whole thing was in press anyway. Ed. had a good title: *Sociobiology: The New Synthesis* (echoing Julian Huxley's *The Modern Synthesis*?) It would come out, with hype and fanfare from Harvard University Press, next year, quite eclipsing his little *Biosocial Anthropology*. But that was fine. The more the merrier, even if that title would terrify the sociologists. The biosociologists, of whatever stripe and derivation, were all on the same side of Bob Ardrey's great line drawn in the sand. They were all part of the Invisible College.

Lionel and Virginia had produced young Sebastian, destined to be another wonder child. Virginia announced that her child would be both seen and heard, and he was. He was a prototype for the advocates of independence training. The parents revolved in planetary deference around this bright, precocious son. With the sage experience of three small daughters behind him, our indulgent father banged the small kid on his shoulder to cure his colic, persuading the distraught parents not to call the paramedics. When Sebastian was older, he got to baby sit the hyperactive youngster, and found that the only way to curb his exuberance (he had bitten Karyl Roosevelt on the leg when she attempted it) was to dump him in an armchair and sit on him. "It's not fair!" yelled Sebastian. "Right you are! You are learning a valuable lesson about life." For Sebastian's birthday the girls, and their step-sister, arranged a puppet show for him which they called *The Dragon that Wasn't Quite,* about a timid dragon who only wanted to sing Christmas carols—a good excuse to have the party audience join in some. Sebastian thanked them very gravely. He was going to be a terrific young man.

Back on the home front there was a stab at reconciliation, but it clearly was not going to work. They were simply too different; they had totally diverse agendas. His mind was wholly on the girls and their new situation. He didn't see how he could reconcile all the demands. He had dreams (or were they fantasies?) in which he took all the women in his life, all making their claims and demands at the tops of their voices, and locked them in the hall of a castle with a stout oak door. He told them he would let them out when they had decided among themselves how to divide him up. In the meantime he threw away the key. Sometimes the depression felt like a vice gripping his head that he couldn't shake off. The demands were too many, but they had to be met. When the Woolworth ladies said dance, you said "how fast?" She was so much of the opposite temperament: if a demand was made, it was automatically resisted. He ducked and ran and felt like a coward, but what was there to do? Something had to give. The vastations returned with the grip of the vice, and the pain shrieked through his joints. Is that all there is, Peggy? You struggle and strive, you dance and skate, there are a few pleasant sensations here and there, and then you die? He was always looking at the difference and likeness between us and the chimps. The chimps just got on with it. They fought and fed, made little chimp replicas, and died. They were spared the problem of accounting for and rationalizing it all. This was perhaps all we had really added to a primitive chimp-like existence: we were chimps with existential questions:

> And did some sly   malicious god
> when an ape first stood and faced the sky
> prepare a two-edged gift   a rod
> it thought to cure this hubris by
> It did and so the creature choked
> then straining through its tears it croaked
> the first   pathetic   "why?"

He shook off the attack of self-pity and returned to London, where he looked up the glamorous barrister who had grilled him at the BBC mock trial. She had been married to one of the oddest men in London. He was a cockney ex-con, a bank robber, who must have made history by using a horse and cart as the getaway vehicle. Now divorced, and banned from practicing as a barrister because she married a convicted felon, Nemone was writing courtroom dramas for the BBC. She was angry because the BBC had pulled the latest under pressure from the Greek shipping tycoon who was the subject—thinly disguised. This left her broke with two children and an expensive rented house decorated by homosexuals, with whole-mirrored walls in the bedrooms and satyrs and nymphs cavorting round the dining room. She was friendly with the crowd at *Private Eye*, and had kept a copy that showed he and Lionel had made "Pseud's Corner." This was a column reserved for taking shots at the pompous, and the editors neatly found an out-of-context quote that did sound painfully sententious. Still: no such thing as bad publicity.

He left reluctantly for Oxford, for he was anxious to leave now, to get back to France and the children. The city looked dirty, bleak and washed out, not romantic or glamorous. The spires were dripping rather than gleaming. He had never had the time to do much wandering in Oxford: down the High, with a side trip to the Bodleian, or Blackwell's—not Foyle's, but not bad, or to the Union to see the Pre-Raphaelite murals, faded but moving. Sometimes he walked down Banbury Road from the Institute to see his psychologist friends in South Parks Road. He would drop in to the redbrick horror of Keble College ("Don't think of this as a college," announced some graffiti, "think of it as a Fair Isle sweater.") It was Pusey's monument to the Oxford Movement and High Church Anglicanism, but its chapel housed Holman Hunt's *The Light of the World*. A brief moment of contemplation, then down past St. John's, by the memorial to the Protestant Martyrs, through Cornmarket, and left to Christ Church. He would sometimes slip into the Cathedral when there was sung evensong, and sit at the back, listening to the perfect choir in quiet, agnostic reverence. Then he would walk along the river, through Christ Church meadows to the Botanical Gardens before going over Magdalen Bridge to the little white house, and the Pre-Raphaelite ladies.

His discussions with Juliet and her energetic female friends about Feminism and feminist Anthropology never really got anywhere. He was fascinated by the movement, but persisted in asking "why Feminism?" Why was there this periodic upsurge in female protest against the status quo? It happened at some times and not others; there must be some reason, some demographic or social cause? But for the committed Juliet such a question was like asking "why Mariansim?" to a convinced Catholic. While all other social movements are open to analysis, your own movement is exempt. It has no causes other than its own obvious grasp of the truth. And it was hard to pin down what the movement was. Most American feminist demands, emanating from NOW and *Ms* magazine, Juliet scornfully dismissed as mere "careerist Feminism." Her version was more concerned with a root-and-branch change of society in line with feminist egalitarian ideals. Thus feminists in general never seemed to know what to do about the rise of Margaret Thatcher. She should have been some kind of idol, but she offended against the radical and "activist" canons of the egalitarians, and the careerists were uneasy that she became the longest-serving prime minister, in a thoroughly male world, without the help of quotas and affirmative action.

He wanted to pursue Ashley's point and find those areas in which women were naturally superior to men as a result of differing patterns of adaptation in evolution. They were better at detail, personal relationships, multi tasking, language, diplomacy, and nurturing, among other things. But while Juliet was willing to accept the superiority, she, like the others, balked at attributing it to biology. This would mean that "biology was destiny" and that was unacceptable. It would also mean accepting that men might be biologically superior in some things. Yes. This too was unacceptable. Then where did female superiority come from? Female experience.

On May Day morning the choir of Magdalen sang carols from the tower. A big crowd of undergraduates gathered on the bridge and in punts on the river. They made so much noise you could scarcely hear the carols, but they were cheerfully drunk on champagne and eventually a good number jumped in the river. Shades of *Zuleika Dobson*: this was the Oxbridge we loved to hate. The

Morris Dancers did their number with sticks and handkerchiefs and an accordionist playing the theme from Beethoven's Ninth. A Jack-in-the-Green figure bobbed along with the dancers, under a framework all covered in ivy and leaves. In the old days he was supposed to entice girls to come in under the greenery, and he "laid eggs" as he went along. This modern version called out "Get your fertility here!" and laid empty Guinness bottles. Frazer was alive and well and moving with the times.

He helped Rodney and Godfrey with the exams at the end of the year, thanked Freedman for his enduring kindness and hospitality, and prepared to leave the sanctuary and return, like Sordello, to the veritable business of mankind. That business was taking a new turn. The world of the Woolworth ladies was good and gone, although in Oxford a bit of it lingered. Even here, though, it was clear that the deferential, stable world of the War generations had been trampled by the march of the baby boomers: the pig in the python. A civilization has to initiate its young successfully, or it will fall away from the inside. The pill had freed this generation from effective adult control; they were in charge of their own sexuality for the first time ever, since they could easily avoid the consequences of untrammeled sex, and the shock waves of this revolution were being felt throughout the system. Millions of years of evolution were being challenged here, not just the manners of the adults. The last American soldiers had left Vietnam, but the war there had corrupted their societies, leading them to despise their adults and their institutions, and to have an overweening faith in their own efforts to change the world for the better. They were absolutely certain that they knew best how to do it. They had, unlike his uncertain generation, a monopoly on virtue.

They were, at their best, an idealistic and energetic generation; at their worst they were selfish and fanatical. They were not hypocrites—they saw themselves as the enemies of the hypocrisy of the older generations. This virtue could, however, easily become a vice. With hypocrites there is always the possibility of negotiation: the virtuous are implacable. With their combination of piety and radicalism they were flooding into the universities, especially Anthropology and the social sciences. They would probably cause the subject to drift deeper into cultural relativism and the rejection of the innate. It did not bode well for the movement. He was not sure he was going to like them, or live easily with them. But the girls were a part of it; they were baby boomers; they were not immune from the influences. Kate was certainly showing the effects already. What was the use of preaching limitations to these determined youngsters? Clarion calls to moderation do not get people to the barricades. They would only see this as part of the adult plot against the youth movement. But at least he was in on one of the greatest social experiments ever. Sit back, observe, comment and teach. Perhaps he had found a final shape? Perhaps he would be released from the toils of constant change? Perhaps he would find some continuity? Perhaps.

In the meantime he must get on with the Haifa paper. He would be delivering this in embattled Israel, in the insanity of the Middle East: a kind of paradigm of the tyranny of the idea, a cockpit of fanaticism run riot. He would spend his fortieth birthday in Jerusalem perhaps. He could always try slouching towards Bethlehem to be reborn. He gave up and put a record on the old wheezy gramophone that came with the house. It was the divine, if oddly named, Baden Powell, playing that marvelous Brazilian music (*The Girl from Ipanema?*) that must have been derived from the Chopin Prelude in E minor, with its descending chromatic whole chords, made for the guitar frets. Sometimes you could lose yourself in the music, as in those old days so long lost and so unreal. He must look after the children. The rest—well it was in the end the world's problem, was it not? What imbecility to assume you could do anything to sway the frenetic movement of mankind; it was hell bent on its own improvement. There was no stopping, as they often said, the march of progress, even if illusion-riddled humanity was only crawling to another place on the flypaper of history. Prophets bearing bad news were not welcomed, especially by the social sciences whose creed was the inevitable improvement of our lot. We are improving ourselves to death. But yes, it was their problem.

> Pity to disconcert one versed as you
> In fate's ill nature! But its full extent
> Eludes Sordello, even: the veil rent,
> Read the black writing—that collective man
> Outstrips the individual.

* * *

A man still young at heart but old enough to have three pre-teen daughters bouncing around him, was sitting on the terrace of a dingy resort bar in the French Alps, sipping a cold beer against the heat. The large crowd was pressed against the police-erected barriers at the roadside, and was zinging with tense anticipation.

"*Ça-y-est! Ça-y-est!*"—someone began the cry and they all took it up, pressing harder. The large car park of the second-rate resort had been converted to a finish area for this *stage* of the Tour de France: the cruel mountain-climb stage of the Alpine leg of the world's premier cycle race. This was the stage only the toughest would win, and then don the *maillot jaune* of daily victory for the next stage. There was one sure favorite, the Spaniard Aja and his Pyrrenes-trained Spanish team. They were the best in the mountains; they were the children of the mountains; they were Spanish Basques.

They were true to form. Aja stormed through well in the lead, and his countrymen were close behind, mixed with French and Italian riders. The champagne was popped and the pretty girls were popped up on cue to kiss the winner, and hand him flowers and the coveted yellow jersey.

As the crowd began to drift away, the support cars and vans, loaded with technicians and spare bikes, poured in. The camp followers in team colors swarmed out and around and began the frantic business of fixing bikes and riders before darkness and dinner. Since, on the Tour, you did not have the normal two hours for lunch, it had to be made up for at the evening meal. The resort and the local ski hotels—freed up in the summer—were ablaze with effort in their kitchens. The high hot sun was ready itself to pack it in behind the white peaks, now edged with streaks of red and pink (sand blown over from Africa, they said.) It was a perfect Alpine evening.

They were all to pile into the mini and, sunburned and happy, go back the short distance to Briançon for dinner themselves. The three girls were all in love with the biker heroes—the dashing Spaniards, and ecstatic at the prospect of a brief visit with Aja and his mercurial men. This was made possible by Lilianne, and Lilianne needs her own explanation. No job description fit her exactly. The girls' mother—the youngish man's ex-wife—was off on a two-week break. She and her boy friend had gone to Italy, leaving the father to spend his best time of the year with the girls all to himself. So he had come from the USA to England, thence to Paris, and finally by the slow train to Lyon and the even slower one that crawled up through the gorges and valleys to the highest town in the Alps, Vaubon's frontier fortress of Briançon.

Lilianne was collecting the girls from the car park where they formed a giggling fan club of three. He looked across from the crowd and the cars, and the colored bikes stacked around the white vans, and saw their merriment and felt a wave of relief. Then he saw Ellie break from the others; he reached for a spare paper napkin and took out his pen.

My daughter with the golden hair
so worldly wise and so aware
now in her twelfth engrossing year
had left me to the freezing beer
I sipped because the day was hot
And sauntered through the parking lot
I watched her from the noisy bar
reach out and touch a rakish car
Alfa-Roméo fresh from Rome
A gigolo in red and chrome

How could sisters be so unlike? Yet they had been from birth. Kate the fierce introvert; Ellie the gentle extrovert; and Anne fitting into that odd third-child niche which had to carve it's own way, little being left to it after the first two had grabbed the major roles. So Anne the tomboy, the practical, the curious, stubborn and sweet by turns. He recognized himself in the first and the last, but Ellie was always a bit of a mystery.

> Sensations hit me with a rush
> to see her girlish fingers brush
> this object so caressingly
> for almost simultaneously
> my thoughts in an electral whirl
> went spinning to my other girl
> (the dreamy one with nut brown tress)
> to when I saw the long caress
> she planted once and then again
> upon her favorite horse's mane
> and fiercely told me "Oh papa
> j'adore mon cheri Mustaphá"
> (for being Arab then his name
> appropriately was the same)

He had long since stopped punctuating poems; he didn't see the point. Poetry he thought of as essentially oral; the punctuation simply indicated where to breathe. You could do this with a double space. It was why he couldn't stomach free verse. If you read it out, it sounded like prose with peculiar and inexplicable hitches, rather than like poetry. It was a pure product of the typographer's art; it would not survive in an oral culture, which was the natural environment of verse. He jogged the lines along, thinking of *The Death of Dr. Swift.*

> It was I thought by some mischance
> an odd result of school in France
> but no it was true love and she
> shared love between the horse and me
> with tenderness for me of course
> but passion lavished on the horse.

He had started things off when he arrived with, at the mother's request, the first of a series of annual lectures on how they must not turn into awful French children and make their poor mother miserable (it never worked.). He then tried to establish order in the house by making a list of House Rules, and putting them up in strategic places like the bathroom, sink and laundry room. Over the washing machine he printed: "Do not mix whites with colors." "Racist!" they scrawled across it. Kate had picked up all the political attitudes of her new companions. He told her he thought Giscard was perhaps the best person, on balance, to be president of France. "Mon Dieu papa!" she shot back, "tu es *centriste*!! C'est pas normal, ça!" Then she rushed off to the riding stables, to her favorite horse, for consolation. He thought he would call his poem "Memo to Dr. Oedipus."

> I tell you grave psychologist
> there is a phase that you have missed
> From father (Alpha) they must go
> not straight to pimply Rómeo

but to a horse or to a car
or anything that stops the jar
they feel when hormones activate
that heady pre-pubescent state
of shy uncertain womanhood

He was working of course—he was always working, but he had a nice studio looking out onto a fine view of the mountains, and Anne came over and helped him with the tedious business of calculating the age-at-marriage of his Irish subjects from the death, birth and wedding records. He was already poking about the records here, and thinking, as he chatted with local peasants over *coups de rouge* in the local tavern, how he could do a comparative study of land tenure and inheritance. He was fascinated, as the snow melted on the ski slopes under the chair lifts, to see that the land was divided into horizontal strips: peasant fields in the summer; fields of sport for the wealthy in the winter. A whole theme here. Stop! Attend to the girls. While he was off doing peasantology, he had forgotten that Anne was coming "for tea." She brought him some little cakes he liked from the patisserie. She left a note. He was, as usual, pierced and distressed, and rushed off to get her the homemade ice cream with fresh peaches that she liked, and to take it to the flat. But that meant an encounter with Lilianne.

Lillianne had seemed like a good idea at the time: a nanny/housekeeper for two weeks while mother was away. She was Colombian, confident, brown, energetic. She spoke Spanish, French and English, and was reported to have been the mistress—or whatever in his case was the equivalent—of Salvador Dali. She turned up in the local hippie community where the girls spent weeks making mandalas out of old quilts and bits of colored cloth. The boys played bluegrass, or its latest version as "new-grass." They asked him to translate things like "Momma's got a brand new bag..." which came out badly as "Maman a trouvé un chic métier nouveau..."

Lilianne came highly recommended in the community for her nurturing skills since she had her own *niño*—the demand-fed, un-toilet-trained, still-on-the-bottle, dribbling, whining, roughly two-year-old Jetti. He could indeed have been some child of a surrealist nightmare, but Lilianne was tight-lipped on the paternity issue. His nose perpetually running, Jetti wandered, weeping, through adult legs, clutching his *biberon* and sucking his dummy. But she was cheerful and forceful and said that while the children could call her Lillianne, they must not *tutoyer* her: they must use the respectful *vous*. This impressed with its promise of correctness and she was hired.

How does one gauge success? With Jetti bawling and balanced on one hip, she had the girls eating artichoke leaves to the rhythm of "pull-dip-eat-throw" while she sang the anvil chorus from *Il Trovatore*. The spent leaves ended up in a large bowl in the middle of the table. Any girl missing the bowl or breaking the one-TWO-one-TWO rhythm was condemned to Jetti-minding for five minutes, while Lillianne enjoyed her share of the artichoke. It was, as his mother would say, an experience. The girls sailed into later life able to deal with just about anyone. He put this down to his wisdom in exposing them early to the likes of Lilianne.

But as they prepared to leave the parking lot to find Aja and the Spanish team, he was less confident. Lilianne had evidently left Spain and Dali in a hurry, and no one was clear why. And just what was her thing with the Basque cyclists? No matter. The issue was made moot when the deux-cheveaux (which had replaced the mini) stuttered to a halt outside the Spaniards' hotel. Not to worry, insisted Lilianne, in her mixture of the three languages, *le méchanique de l'équippe,* would assist them, and *pronto*, or at least *poco tiempo*. The place was awash with mechanics and she knew them all. One was produced and fiddled with the choke, adjusted a screw and started the engine, to girlish cheers. The team was tired, but turned out to greet Lilianne; the great man gave kisses and autographs and smiled gallantly and everyone was happy. They sat for a while among the busy chaos of bikes, cars and oil-stained, grimy, but constantly charming men, then the light went altogether and it was time to go home for more musical vegetables.

As they pulled out to the main road their way was blocked by two cars with colored lights flashing, and disgorging uniformed *flics*—the national, military kind, not the amiable Alpine locals. A plainclothes officer interrogated while the uniforms looked nervous and fingered their guns. Identification, address, profession, purpose of visit to the hotel. What were an English professor resident in America and a Colombian national late of Spain doing at this hour, at the hotel of the Spanish? Asthma, nannies, everyone was at the Tour, for Christ's sake! Take care how you address the men with guns, *monsieur*!! Bring passports to the *gendarmerie* the next morning, if you have passports. Of course we have passports! Lilianne said nothing. They were tailed all the way back to town.

Briançon had seemed such a haven; the ultimate refuge; the place of good health and a chance of an ordinary life. Well, he thought, perhaps the fact that they seemed incapable of leading an ordinary life meant they were extraordinary people. Cold comfort as Lilianne clammed up and they remained under military surveillance. The little one was the least unafraid of them all, and he regretted all over again that he didn't see enough of her. They had snatched a brief idyllic interlude in Paris. They stayed in a neat little hotel in the *Rue Cambon,* near the garden door of the Ritz, where they went for cocktails and Shirley Temples. She had to teach the bartender to make them ("Je connais bien l'actrice, mais pas le boisson!")

They went to the ballet in the courtyard of the Louvre and saw Baryshnikov in *Parade*. She liked the Satie so much that he persuaded a pianist at the *Closerie des Lilas* to play a *Gymnopédie* during their early dinner, when there were not too many foreign patrons who might object and demand show-tunes. They went to Versailles, where the English guide was unintelligible so they followed the French, and Anne was delighted with her aphorism and repeated it over and over in English: "Louis XIV built it; Louis XV lived in it; Louis XVI paid for it!" She had taken up the classical guitar, and needed a case for hers. They had been recommended a shop near the Pompidou center, and her first sudden view of it stopped her dead. "Why have they put the plumbing pipes on the outside? And why is it *colored*?"

Back at the little hotel, in the afternoon, they were exhausted and decided to lie down for a while. They fell asleep. When he woke it was twilight and they were lying opposite each other. Her hand was in his, and her face was relaxed and without pain or worry pinching her eyes. He thought of those Victorian "children poems" that were condemned as "sentimental." But sometimes you had to risk sentiment; it was the only true response. He was flooded with it, and began to snivel and woke her:

"Are you alright, Daddy?"

"Fine. Just a bad dream woke me. Let's go get a Shirley Temple."

The times in Paris were very special to him. The two older girls had come up by train from Briançon to stay in Paris for a few days. His friend Bob, the writer, was delighted. He remembered them well from New York and Sardis. Bob had once had a couple of Broadway successes—Noel Coward was a great admirer—and was still well liked in the theatre district. He once commandeered a large round table in Sardis and entertained various people including the girls. He had introduced them to handsome young actors and they had been suitably shy and charming, and the whole evening glowed with his warmth and overflowing love of life. The girls had loved it. But this time, unfortunately, Bob and his actress wife Berdine, had to return to Rome and their paths would only cross briefly. The newly acquired Countess, however, would figure out how to entertain them. Entertaining was her vocation.

The girls adored the St. Simon hotel, where they had their own room that gave on to a little crenellated rooftop with iron tables and chairs, where they could order *brioches* and *chocolat* for breakfast while he slept in a little. The day they were to go up the Eiffel tower, he was stricken with a *crise de foie*. He shivered and shook through the whole vertiginous episode, including a long conversation in very precise and elegant Parisian French with the grandfather of the little friend they met at the Tower. It covered the military careers of the grandfather and his own father, and was full of an old-world courtesy that he'd begun to forget still existed. It helped relieve the intensities of the *crise* and prompted a visit to the *Musée Militaire* where the gallery of magnificent stuffed horses and riders in Napoleonic uniforms prompted Ellie to ask:

"Why did they dress so beautifully when they were going to war, perhaps to be killed?"

"They don't anymore."

But Ellie was in love with the beautiful, sad soldiers, destined for death. Kate thought it was simply unbearable that they killed the horses. They pretended disdain at the Parisian boys who whistled at them, but they cast surreptitious glances.

> They hear the whisper in the blood
> but still cling to the father's hand
> because they do not understand
> that jolting elemental force

He forgot to go to American Express in the Rue Scribe to cash travelers' checks, and the next day was Sunday. So he announced they must eat somewhere that took credit cards. In St. Germain they found an Algerian restaurant open, had their first *couscous*, and discovered that not all Algerian wines are only fit for mass consumption as "Bordeaux-type." But the Countess enlisted the Young Lawyer, who was handsome and charming, and had the prettiest and most delicate of girlfriends who always used the subjunctive to perfection ("Il faut que j'aille a là banque.") They all went off to an Alsatian Restaurant on the Ile de la Cité in the shadow of Notre Dame. It was famous for its parking problem, which is to say there was no legal parking on the Ile. So people parked anyway, and a waiter stood at the window with a gong. If the *flics* appeared he banged it loudly over the hubbub, and all the drivers dashed out and drove their cars around the block a few times until the law disappeared. Meanwhile, waiters rushed to keep the food—mostly sausages and sauerkraut—warm, in the special ovens kept heated for that purpose. He found another plain paper napkin:

> They touch a car or kiss a horse
> and stroke each young mammalian thing
> yet wander even while they cling
> to that paternal certainty
> which will without condition be
> there to indulge the horse   the car
> there to adore however far
> they must so soon decide to go
> when magnetized by Rómeo

The girls loved the excitement, and once sated on sausages, the young lawyer showed them all how to sneak into the forbidden after-dark grounds of Notre Dame where he hid in the bushes and rushed out doing an imitation of a hunchback shouting "Quasimodo! Quasimodo! Donnez-moi de l'eau pour l'amour de Dieu!" The girls shrieked and were suitably terrified and the whole heap of them collapsed in laughter. They drove fast down the boulevards in the two sports cars and sang together the girls' version of an old folk song:

A là claire fontaine,
Ou je me promenais,
J'ai trouvé l'eau si belle,
Mais c'était poluée.

It was hard when the girls had to go back. He would join them later, but any parting was always impossible. The pain was beyond being described as unbearable—and he desperately missed seeing the little one. They would have their time, but for now she was at least safe in the mountain retreat where she lived like a tiny heroine of a Thomas Mann novel.

He jerked out of the reverie and found himself heading home in the car, to Briançon, with Anne huddled in the back along with her sisters. She was quite energized with curiosity about the whole police business:

"Are we going to be arrested?"

"Don't be *silly*," said Kate, "they *can't* arrest us, we're not *French*."

The suspicious gendarmes broke off the pursuit and everyone felt more or less safe back in the new apartment in the new town. Later that evening he went down in the dim light of the parking-lot lamps, to get the car and go off to his studio at the other end of town, near the army barracks. Two squat men in black overcoats and black homburgs were poking around the car. They didn't look like car thieves, more like overweight businessmen. "Ça va, messieurs?" he called out for want of something better. They looked up startled, and hurried off, saying something in French but with decidedly Spanish accents. The next evening, the TV news opened with a flash: in a hotel car park, at the end of the next *stage* in the Tour de France, the vans and cars and bikes of the Spanish team had been shattered by a large bomb. The team was off at dinner; no one was hurt.

The next morning, Lilianne announced defensively that she had lost her passport and had to go to Paris immediately to get a new one at the Colombian embassy. There would, she added, surely be a generous bonus, in addition to her wages—to cover the fare? She got on the train—sitting the whole way to Paris—with Jetti still bawling, sucking and oozing. He stood with the three girls in a pathetic row at the station, waving weakly as the train pulled out to begin its steep, slow descent to Lyon and the real world. Lilianne didn't respond.

It was a sad little party that went back through the new town to the apartment, but it was also something of a relief for them to be alone together again. He made them their favorite roast chicken stuffed with forty cloves of garlic, and added a second one stuffed with paté for good measure. Rhythmic artichokes were forgotten, work was forgotten, all life outside the enchanted circle was forgotten. They had a new cheese to try—goat wrapped in vine leaves, and a new cheese always pleased them more than a new dessert. As they giggled and laughed, and drank their watered wine, all sense of futility evaporated; the vastations were banished. There was no longer a mystery. This was the one thing with which he could feel an absolute connection. *This was the point.*

> What fortune thus to rationalize
> to be so calm urbane and wise
> So then dear doctor tell me why
> despite the beer my throat is dry
> despite the heat my skin is cold
> and why I suddenly feel old

FIN

Recessional

"Nothing corrupts a man more deeply than writing a book," said Rex Stout's Nero Wolfe. And perhaps no book is so corrupting as an autobiography. But by leaving it unfinished, perhaps, as with witchcraft from the imperfect Cochiti pot, some of the corruption evaporates. Still, you will ask, "What about the rest?" The rest is footnotes—and they are in the record. By all means read them; preferably buy the books. But there is an air of unreality about this afterlife, for by the fortieth year all had been set in place, as with Sordello (who had the good grace to exit on this hopeful note.) What is left is a playing out of the necessary consequences of these chance events. The prism had been carved; its facets were aligned. Like Sordello he had made his fateful choice; the refraction more or less took care of itself. For an assessment you here at least have some of the facts—facts loosely based on fiction, it is true. The judgment is your own. Was Sordello a failure, as history records, or was he in some ways a kind of imperfect exemplar, as Browning saw him? Chesterton thought that Browning's obsession with human imperfection was basically optimistic, because the imperfect demands a conception of the perfect to be itself understood. God too was, in Browning's scheme, imperfect, which was all that made sense of the incarnation: if God had not endured and overcome suffering, He would have been less perfect than His creation. But the creative imperfections of *Sordello* have been too much for most impatient readers. Harriet Martineau was so baffled on trying to read the poem that she thought she must be gravely ill. The reviews, of course, were all wary or just plain bad, but Browning knew that bad reviews matter, in Iris Murdoch's lovely words, like whether it's raining in Patagonia. He saw that people found him cryptic and obscure, and that they would misunderstand him. But he was generous. "I blame no one," he announced, "least of all myself." Thomas Carlyle said his wife couldn't figure out if Sordello was a man, a city, or a book. The great and good (and mellifluous) Tennyson, who was devoid by nature of any sense of the grotesque, said he only understood two lines of the poem - the first and the last, and both were lies.

"Who would has heard Sordello's story told."